D0876009

ATLA BIBLIOGRAPHY SERIES
edited by Dr. Kenneth E. Rowe

1. *A Guide to the Study of the Holiness Movement,* by Charles Edwin Jones. 1974.
2. *Thomas Merton: A Bibliography,* by Marquita E. Breit. 1974.
3. *The Sermon on the Mount: A History of Interpretation and Bibliography,* by Warren S. Kissinger. 1975.
4. *The Parables of Jesus: A History of Interpretation and Bibliography,* by Warren S. Kissinger. 1979.
5. *Homosexuality and the Judeo-Christian Tradition: An Annotated Bibliography,* by Thom Horner. 1981.
6. *A Guide to the Study of the Pentecostal Movement,* by Charles Edwin Jones. 1983.
7. *The Genesis of Modern Process Thought: A Historical Outline with Bibliography,* by George R. Lucas, Jr. 1983.
8. *A Presbyterian Bibliography,* by Harold B. Prince. 1983.
9. *Paul Tillich: A Comprehensive Bibliography . . .,* by Richard C. Crossman. 1983.
10. *A Bibliography of the Samaritans,* by Alan David Crown. 1984.
11. *An Annotated and Classified Bibliography of English Literature Pertaining to the Ethiopian Orthodox Church,* by Jon Bonk. 1984.
12. *International Meditation Bibliography, 1950 to 1982,* by Howard R. Jarrell. 1984.
13. *Rabindranath Tagore: A Bibliography,* by Katherine Henn. 1985.
14. *Research in Ritual Studies: A Programmatic Essay and Bibliography,* by Ronald L. Grimes, 1985.
15. *Protestant Theological Education in America,* by Heather F. Day. 1985.
16. *Unconscious: A Guide to Sources,* by Natalino Caputi. 1985.
17. *The New Testament Apocrypha and Pseudepigrapha,* by James H. Charlesworth. 1987.
18. *Black Holiness,* by Charles Edwin Jones. 1987.
19. *A Bibliography on Ancient Ephesus,* by Richard Oster. 1987.
20. *Jerusalem, the Holy City: A Bibliography,* by James D. Purvis. 1988.
21. *An Index to English Periodical Literature on the Old Testament and Ancient Near Eastern Studies,* by William G. Hupper. Vol. I, 1987; Vol. II, 1988.
22. *John and Charles Wesley: A Bibliography,* by Betty M. Jarboe. 1987.
23. *A Scholar's Guide to Academic Journals in Religion,* by James Dawsey. 1988.
24. *The Oxford Movement and Its Leaders: A Bibliography of Secondary and Lesser Primary Sources,* by Lawrence N. Crumb. 1988.
25. *A Bibliography of Christian Worship,* by Bard Thompson. 1989.

A BIBLIOGRAPHY OF CHRISTIAN WORSHIP

by

Bard Thompson

ATLA Bibliography Series, No. 25

The American Theological Library
Association and The Scarecrow Press, Inc.
Metuchen, N.J., & London
1989

The border decoration used on the title page is taken from the first English edition of The Book of Common Prayer, 1549.

British Library Cataloguing-in-Publication data available

Library of Congress Cataloging-in-Publication Data

A Bibliography of Christian worship / by Bard Thompson, general
    editor ; in cooperation with the Liturgical Faculty of New Jersey
    and New York.
        p.   cm. -- (ATLA bibliography series ; no. 25)
    Includes index.
    ISBN 0-8108-2154-0
    1. Liturgics--Bibliography. 2. Public worship--Bibliography.
I. Thompson, Bard, 1925- . II. Series.
Z7813.B5   1989
[BV176]
016.264--dc19   88-38650

Manufactured in the United States of America

Printed on acid-free paper

CONTENTS

PART ONE: REFERENCE WORKS AND GENERAL WORKS

PART THREE: WORD AND SACRAMENTS--THEOLOGY,
             LITURGY, AND SPIRITUALITY

xix

PART FOUR: THE DAILY OFFICE AND
THE CHURCH YEAR

xxiv

EDITOR'S FOREWORD

In Memory of Bard Thompson
1925-1987

Bard Thompson died of a massive heart attack August 12, 1987.
An alumnus of Mercersburg (Pa.) Academy, Haverford College (Phi
Beta Kappa), Union Theological Seminary and Columbia University,
Thompson joined the faculty of Drew University in 1965 after teaching stints at Emory University's Candler School of Theology, Van-
derbilt Divinity School and Lancaster Theological Seminary. A professor of church history, he became the dean of Drew's Graduate
School in 1969, and at the time of his death was still active as an
emeritus professor of history and a member of the Center of Theological Inquiry at Princeton.

Bard Thompson was my teacher. When I joined Drew's faculty
he became a personal friend and wise adviser. His subject was
Renaissance-Reformation and Liturgy. His object was the rebirth
of intellectual insight that could reform our modern identity.

Surpassing scholar and a leader with a steady hand to match
his vision, Bard Thompson leaves us a bibliography as well as a
book on liturgy upon which we shall continue to rely. His <u>Liturgies
of the Western Church</u>, first published in 1962, is now in its 10th
printing. At Drew he leaves us a program in Liturgical Studies ten
years old and thriving, and the sustaining memory of a faithful
friend.

We are pleased to publish this guide to the study of liturgy
as number twenty-five in the American Theological Library Association Bibliography Series.

Kenneth E. Rowe
Series Editor

Drew University Library
Madison, NJ 07940

PREFACE: A CALL FOR RESPONSES

"The ideally successful book could, we should guess,
at best be a magnificent failure."--W. K. Lowther
Clarke

"Magnificent failure" may be the most apt description which can be
given to this bibliography. It has no predecessors; to that extent
it can claim to be the beginning of something useful. But isn't it
preposterous that a handful of people, however painstaking and
well intended, could comprehend all of the literature of Christian
worship?

This bibliography, if substantial, is also provisional. It comes
to you with a call for responses and a promise of improvement. If
those whose traditions we have slighted or misunderstood will teach
us our mistakes, we will gladly amend them in a second edition.
The main task we faced was the completion of citations, some twenty
percent of which lacked some kind of information. It gradually became clear that we could not supply the information in all cases without immediate indefinite postponement of publication. We decided to
proceed with publication and made the editorial decision not to re-
duce all citations to a lowest common denominator but to present as
much bibliographic information as we could find in a reasonable
amount of time in each case. Therefore this bibliography has a
slightly higher number of unidentified publishers (n.p.'s) and dates
(n.d.'s). This is more noticeable in the case of series, for which
we were often able to find the dates of single volumes but not the
full range of dates, and in which we sometimes found evidence of
changes of publisher over long periods of time.

As it stands, A Bibliography of Christian Worship purports to
contain books and periodical literature through 1982.

The structure of the bibliography is historical, with final sections given over to topics--Word and Sacraments; Ministry to the
Sick; etc.--which are also likely to have an historical organization.

A Bibliography of Christian Worship should be received as the cooperative effort of those scholars who have constituted a liturgical faculty in New Jersey and New York--professors Gabriel M. Coless, O.J.B., Horton Davies, Charles W. Gusmer, Howard G. Hageman, James H. Pain, Erik Routley, and Bard Thompson. In the ten years we have been together, we have been many things--professors, presidents, deans, writers, Benedictines, diocesan priests; one of us has died: Erik Routley, requiescat in pace. To each other, we have been a precious association of learned and pacific people who have bent what time and energy we could afford to the important ecumenical, theological, and pastoral considerations of Christian worship.

Dean John Meyendorff, Professor Charles L. Rice, and Professor Thomas J. Talley have lately joined this society of liturgical scholars. I include their names, although they did not contribute to the production of the bibliography and should not be held accountable for errors in it.

The bibliography could not have been produced without the help and determination of several candidates for the Ph.D. in the Graduate School of Drew University where the Ph.D. in Liturgical Studies has its academic locus. Donald M. Vorp, now of the Speer Library of Princeton Theological Seminary, was the first to urge its production and oversaw its beginning. Larry Nyberg contributed more to the production than any other person and gave it much of its present character. Many other Drew graduate students, including in particular Harvey Nelson, Jill Fritz-Piggott, and Marian Adell, contributed in one way or another to the preparation of the manuscript.

Please send amendments to: Theological Librarian, Drew University Library, Madison, NJ 07940.

Bard Thompson
Drew University
June 1987

LIST OF ABBREVIATIONS

AA	Archivio Ambrosiano
AAAbo	Acta academiae Abo
AB	Analecta Bollandiana. Subsidia Hagiographica
ABib	Analecta Biblica
ACC	Alcuin Club Collections
ACh	Arts of the Church
ACM	Alcuin Club Manuals
ACP	Alcuin Club Prayer Book Revision Pamphlets
ACT	Alcuin Club Tracts
ACW	Ancient Christian Writers
AG	Analecta Gregoriana
AGP	Arbeiten zur Geschichte des Pietismus
AGTL	Arbeiten zur Geschichte und Theologie des Luthertums
AHAWP	Abhandlungen der Heidelberger Akademie der Wissenschaften. Philosophisch-Historische Klasse.
AK	Arbeiten zur Kirchengeschichte
AKML	Abhandlungen zur Kunst-, Musik-, und Literaturwissenschaft
AL	Ardens et lucens
AMN	Analecta mediaevalia Namurcensia
AMT	Aspekte moderner Theologie
AOC	Archives de l'Orient chrétien
AP	Arbeiten zur Pastoraltheologie
APL	Alba Patristic Library
ASNU	Acta Seminarii Neotestamentici Upsaliensis
ASP	Albury Society Publications
AT	Arbeiten zur Theologie
ATANT	Abhandlungen zur Theologie des Alten und Neuen Testaments
AUS	Acta Universitatis Stockholmiensia
AUU	Acta Universitatis Upsaliensis. Studia historico-ecclesiastica Upsaliensia
AWR	Aus der Welt der Religion, Religionswissenschaftliche Reihe
BAC	Biblioteca de autores cristianos

BAK	Beiträge zur altbayerischen Kirchengeschichte
BAP	Bibliotheca analectorum praemonstratensium
BAR	Bonner akademische Reden
BBA	Berliner byzantinische Arbeiten
BBB	Bibliotheca bizantina bruxellensis
BCA	Bibliothèque des cahiers archéologiques
BCSR	Bibliothèque catholique des sciences religieuses
BE	Biblical Encounters
BEFAR	Bibliothèque des Ecoles françaises d'Athenes et de Rome
BEL	Bibliotheca Ephemerides Liturgicae
BET	Beiträge zur evangelische Theologie
BFCT	Beiträge zur Förderung christlicher Theologie
BGL	Bibliothek der griechischen Literatur
BGLRK	Beiträge zur Geschichte und Lehre der reformierten Kirche
BGNR	Die Botschaft Gottes. Neutestamentliche Reihe
BGPMA	Beiträge zur Geschichte der Philosophie und Theologie des Mittelalters, Texte und Untersuchungen
BGQM	Beiträge zur Geschichte und Quellenkunde des Mittelalters
BHF	Bonner historische Forschungen
BhistR	Bibliothèque d'histoire religieuse
BHR	Bibliotheca humanistica et reformatorica
BHT	Beiträge zur historischen Theologie
BK	Bibliothek der Kirchenväter
BL	Bibliothèque liturgique
BM	Bibliothèque du Muséon
BMGKK	Beihefte zur Monatsschrift für Gottesdienst und kirchliche Kunst
BOR	Beihefte zur Okumenische Rundschau
BOS	Bonner orientalistische Studien
BPT	Beiträge zur praktischen Theologie
BRHE	Bibliothèque de la Revue d'histoire ecclésiastique
BS	Benedictine Studies
BSHT	Breslauer Studien zur historische Theologie
BSM	Biblioteca degli studi medievali
BT	Bibliothèque de théologie
BTG	Biblioteca teológica granadina
BTN	Biblioteca teológica napoletana
BTP	Bibliotheca theologiae practicae
BTS	Biblisch-theologische Studien
BZNW	Beihefte, Zeitschrift für die neutestamentlichen Wissenschaft
CAD	Collection l'Art et Dieu
CALS	Canadian Anglican Liturgical Studies
CambPT	Cambridge Patristic Texts
CBL	Collectanea biblica latina
CC	Corpus Christianorum

CCath	Corpus Catholicorum
CF	Collectanea Friburgensia
CFV	Cahiers de "Foi et Vérité"
CHLS	Cambridge Handbooks of Liturgical Study
CHS	Church Historical Society
CI	Collection Irénikon
CISSM	Centro italiano di studi sull'alto medioevo, settimane di studio
CLO	Collana liturgia orientali
CLRC	Courtenay Library of Religious Knowledge
CLRK	Catholic Library of Religious Knowledge
CLS	Canon Law Studies (Catholic University of America)
CPL	Collection de pastorale liturgie
CPT	Collection parole et tradition
CRHPR	Cahiers de la Revue d'histoire et de philosophie religieuse
CROP	The Christian Religion, Its Origin and Progress
CS	Cistercian Studies
CSCO	Corpus Scriptorum Christianorum Orientalium
CSEL	Corpus Scriptorum Ecclesiasticorum Latinorum
CSEMH	Cambridge Studies in Early Modern History
CSRT	Courtenay Studies in Reformation Theology
CST	Contemporary Studies in Theology
CTAP	Cahiers théologiques de l'actualité protestante
CTM	Calwer theologische Monographien
CTR	Collectio theologica romana
CTT	Chrétiens de tous les temps
CUSECL	Columbia University Studies in English and Comparative Literature
CUSM	Columbia University Studies in Musicology
CW	Contemporary Worship
EB	Etudes bibliques
EECM	Early English Church Music. Supplementary Volume
EET	Einführung in die evangelische Theologie
EETS	Early English Text Society
EH	Existenz heute
EHPRC	Etudes d'histoire et de la philosophie religieuse. Cahiers
EHT	Europäische Hochschulschriften; Reih 23: Theologie
ELG	Erneuerung des lutherischen Gottesdienstes
ENT	English Non-conformist Texts
EO	Ecclesia Orans: zur Einführung in den Geist der Liturgie
ES	Evangelischer Schriftendienst
ESH	Ecumenical Studies in History
EsL	L'Esprit liturgique
ESML	Erganzungsheft zu den "Stimmen aus Maria Laach"
ESW	Ecumenical Studies in Worship
ETHS	Etudes de théologie et d'histoire de la spiritualité
ETS	Etudes de théologie sacramentaire

FCLD	Forschungen zur christlichen Literatur und Dogmen-geschichte
FCT	Foundations of Catholic Theology
FDTSC	Folger Documents of Tudor and Stuart Civilization
FGIL	Forschungen zur Geschichte des innerkirchlichen Lebens
FGLP	Forschungen zur Geschichte und Lehre des Protestantismus
FGTIL	Forschungen zur Geschichte der Theologie und des innerkirchlichen Lebens
FIPT	Franciscan Institute Publications, Theology Series
FKCA	Forschungen zur Kunstgeschichte und christlichen archäologie
FKD	Forschungen zur Kirchen- und Dogmengeschichte
FKRK	Forschungen zur kirchlichen Rechtsgeschichte und zum Kirchenrecht
FOC	Fathers of the Church
FP	Florilegium Patristicum
FRLANT	Forschungen zur Religion und Literatur des Alten und Neuen Testaments
FTS	Freiburger theologische Studien
FV	Foi vivante
GBMW	Grove Booklets on Ministry and Worship
GCP	Graecitas christianorum primaeva
GF	Glaube und Forschung
GLS	Grove Liturgical Studies
GTP	Grenzfragen zwischen Theologie und Philosophie
HBS	Henry Bradshaw Society. Publications
HCW	Handbücherei des Christen in der Welt
HD	Herders Handbuch der Dogmengeschichte
HF	Das Heilige und die Form
HTS	Hamburger theologische Studien
ICL	International Catholic Library
ILSOP	Institute of Liturgical Studies Occasional Papers
IR	Iconology of Religion
ITS	Innsbrücker theologische Studien
JAC	Jahrbuch für Antike und Christentum, Ergänzungsband
JSJC	Je sais, je crois: encyclopédie du catholique au XXe siècle
KBM	Kölner Beiträge zur Musikforschung
KKS	Konfessionskundliche und kontroverstheologische Studien
KLKZG	Katholisches Leben und Kämpfen im Zeitalter der Glaubensspaltung

KSNAK	Kerkhistorische studien behorende bij het Nederlands Archief voor Kerkgeschiedenis
KSWS	Kirchlich-theologische Sozietät in Württemburg. Schriftenreihe
KT	Kleine Texte für theologische und philologische Vorlesungen und übungen
LACT	Library of Anglo-Catholic Theology
LatM	Latimer Monographs
LC	Lettres chrétiennes
LCL	Loeb Classical Library
LCP	Latinitas christianorum primaeva
LD	Lectio divina
LF	Liturgiegeschichtliche Forschungen
LG	Lebendiger Gottesdienst
LH	Laacher Hefte
LLE	Library of Liturgiology and Ecclesiology
LM	Liturgie und Mönchtum; Laacher Hefte
LO	Lex Orandi
LOS	London Oriental Studies
LPSU	Laurentius Petri Sällskapets Urkundsserie
LPT	Library of Protestant Theology
LQ	Liturgiegeschichtliche Quellen
LQF	Liturgiewissenschaftliche Quellen und Forschungen (originally Liturgiegeschichtliche Quellen und Forschungen)
LS	Liturgical Studies
LSMT	Lancaster Series on the Mercersburg Theology
LTS	Luzerner theologische Studien
LUA	Lunds Universitets Arsskrift
MAAP	Medieval Academy of America. Publications
MAC	Monumenta di antichità cristiana
MB	Monumenta Bergomensia
MBM	Miscellanea Byzantina monacensis
MBT	Münsterische Beiträge zur Theologie
MCTS	Le Mystère chrétien, théologie sacramentaire
MEL	Monumenta ecclesiae liturgica
MHS	Monumenta Hispaniae Sacra. Serie litúrgica
MLB	Museum Lessianum, section biblique
MLEA	Monumenta Liturgica Ecclesiae Augustanae
MMB	Monumenta Musicae Byzantinae
MMS	Münstersche Mittelalter-Schriften
MPT	Manuels et précis de théologie
MS	Message of the Sacraments
MSHT	Münchener Studien zur historischen Theologie
MTS	Münchener theologische Studien
MTU	Münchener Texte und Untersuchungen zur deutschen Litteratur des Mittelalters
MU	Münchener Universitätsreden

NA	Neutestamentliche Abhandlungen
NBMA	Nouvelle bibliothèque du moyen âge
NCTC	Nuovo Corso di teologia cattolica
NLCK	New Library of Catholic Knowledge
NPMS	NPM Studies in Church Music and Liturgy
NSGTK	Neue Studien zur Geschichte der Theologie und der Kirche
NTF	Neutestamentliche Forschungen

OBL	Orientalia et biblica lovaniensia
OBT	Overtures to Biblical Theology
OC	Orientalia Christiana
OCA	Orientalia Christiana Analecta
OF	Okumenische Forschungen
OHEL	Oxford History of English Literature
OLPT	Oxford Library of Practical Theology
OS	Oecumenismus spiritualis
OstC	Das östliche Christentum
OT	Okumenische Theologie
OTHE	Opuscula et Textus historiam ecclesiae eiusque vitam atque doctrinam illustrantia, Ser. liturgica
OW	Orthodox Worship

PAM	Publikationen älterer Musik
PBGALT	Paradosis: Beiträge zur Geschichte der altchristlichen Literatur und Theologie
PBS	Prayer Book Studies
PH	Pastorale Handreichungen
PHSA	Papers of the Hymn Society of America
PIOL	Publications de l'Institut orientaliste de Louvain
PL	Paroisse et Liturgie: Collection de pastorale liturgique
PLL	Popular Liturgical Library
PM	Philosophes médiévaux
PMMS	Plainsong and Medieval Music Society
PO	Patrologia Orientalis
POTTS	Pittsburgh Original Texts and Translations Serices
PR	Philosophia religionis, bibliothek van geschriften over de godsdienst wijsbegeerte
PS	Parker Society. Publications
PSQ	Philologische Studien und Quellen
PT	Le Pointe théologique
PTH	Praktisch theologische handboekjes
PTS	Patristische Texte und Studien

QAMK	Quellen und Abhandlungen zur mittelrheinischen Kirchengeschichte
QD	Questiones Disputatae
QFR	Quellen und Forschungen zur Reformationsgeschichte

QGT	Quellen zur Geschichte der Täufer
QRL	Quaderni di Revista liturgica
QUKO	Quellen und Untersuchungen zur Konfessionkunde der Orthodoxie

RAT	Recherches africaines de théologie
RBSS	Regulae Benedicti Studia. Supplementa
RC	Records of Civilization, Sources and Studies
RED	Rerum Ecclesiasticarum Documenta
RIC	Repertoire bibliographique des institutiones chrétiennes
RILOB	Recherches de l'Institut de lettres orientales de Beyrouth
RM	Die Religionen der Menschenheit
RQS	Römische Quartalschrift für christliche Altertumskunde und für Kirchengeschichte. Supplement-Hefte
RS	Rites et symboles
RSSH	Recherches et synthèses. Section d'histoire
RST	Reformationsgeschichtliche Studien und Texte
RVDCG	Religionsgeschichtliche Völksbücher für die deutsche christliche Gegenwart

SA	Studia Anselmiana
SAC	Studi di antichità cristiana
SAEK	Schriftenreihe des Arbeitskreises für evangelische Kirchenmusik
SAMH	Studies in Anabaptist and Mennonite History
SANT	Studien zum Alten und Neuen Testaments
SAPT	Studia Anselmiana philosphica theologica
SB	Stuttgarter Bibelstudien
SBK	Schriftenreihe der bekennenden Kirche
SBLD	Society of Biblical Literature Dissertation Series
SBT	Studies in Biblical Theology
SC	Sources chrétiennes
SCA	Studies in Christian Antiquity
SCT	Sources of Christian Theology
SCW	Studies in Christian Worship
SDCU	Studia doctrinae christianae Upsaliensia
SDF	Studia et Documenta Franciscana
SDST	Studien zur Dogmengeschichte und systematischen Theologie
SECM	Studies in English Church Music
SEFP	Studies in Eucharistic Faith and Practice
SEH	Studies in European History
SF	Spicilegium Friburgense
SFTM	Scripta Facultatis Theologicae Marianum
SGKA	Studien zur Geschichte und Kultur des Altertums
SGR	Studien zu den Grundlagen der Reformation
SGTK	Studien zur Geschichte der Theologie und der Kirche
SGVS	Sammlung gemeinverständlicher Vorträge und Scriften

	aus dem Gebiet der Theologie und Relgionsgeschichte
SHCT	Studies in the History of Christian Thought
SHEPL	Studies in History, Economics and Public Law
SJCA	Studies in Judaism and Christianity in Antiquity
SK	Sakrale Kunst
SL	Schriftenreihe der Luthergesellschaft
SLH	Scriptores Latini Hiberniae
SLPT	Sammlung von Lehrbüchern der praktischen Theologie in gedrängter Darstellung
SLR	Supplemental Liturgical Resources
SLS	Studia Latina Stockholmiensia
SLW	Schriftenreihe Lebendige Wissenschaft
SMB	Série monographique de "Benedictina," Section biblico-oecumenique
SMKS	Studien und Mitteilungen aus der Kirchengeschichtliche Seminar in Wien
SMRT	Studies in Medieval and Reformation Thought
SMV	Studi di musica veneta
SMW	Studies in Ministry and Worship
SNRSM	Supplementa--Nouvelle revue de science missionnaire
SNT	Studien zum Neuen Testament
SNTSM	Society for New Testament Studies. Monograph Series
SNVA	Skrifter utgitt av det Norske videnskapsakademi i Oslo
SPIB	Scripta Pontificii Instituti Biblici
SPL	Studia Patristica et Liturgica
SPM	Studia patristica mediolanensia
SR	Symbolik der Religionen
SRR	Studies in the Reformed Rites of the Catholic Church
SRV	Studien zur religiösen Volkskunde
SSKQD	Schöninghs Sammlung kirchengeschichtlicher Quellen und Darstellungen
SSL	Spicilegium Sacrum Lovaniense, études et documents
SSP	Surtees Society. Publications
SSS	Semitic Study Series
SSSKH	Sammlinger och studier till Svenska Kyrkans historia
SST	Studies in Sacred Theology
ST	Studi e Testi
STex	Studies and Texts
StF	Studia Friburgensia
STL	Studia theologica Lundensia
STS	Strassburger theologische Studien
SUNT	Studien zur Umwelt des Neuen Testaments
SWR	Supplemental Worship Resources
TaS	Texts and Studies
TB	Theologische Berichte
TBib	Theologische Bibliothek
TBT	Theologische Bibliothek Töpelmann
TBuch	Theologische Bucherei
TC	Traditio Christiana

TCEC	Twentieth Century Encyclopedia of Catholicism
TCL	Translations of Christian Literature
TCO	Theologie des christlichen Ostens
TEH	Theologische Existenz heute
TEL	Textes et études liturgiques
TET	Textes et études théologiques
TFH	Theologische Fragen heute
TFS	Texts for Students
TH	Théologie historique
ThA	Theologische Arbeiten
THS	Textes pour l'histoire sacrée
TICP	Travaux de l'Institut catholique de Paris
TPL	Textus patristici et liturgici
TPS	Théologie, pastorale et spiritualité: recherches et syntheses
TS	Theologische Studien
TSL	Theologische Studien der Leo-gesellschaft
TTS	Trierer theologische Studien
TuA	Texte und Arbeiten. 1er Abt.: Beiträge zur Ergrundung des älteren lateinischen christlichen Schriftums und Gottesdienstes
TUGAL	Texte und Untersuchungen zur Geschichte der altchristlichen Literatur
UC	Unio und Confessio
UCLD	Universitas catholica Lovaniensis. Dissertationes
UPT	Untersuchungen zur praktischen Theologie
US	Unam Sanctam
VABKO	Veröffentlichungen der Arbeitsgemeinschaft Begegnung mit den Kirchen des Ostens
VAKTB	Veröffentlichungen der Arbeitsgemeinschaft katholisch-theologischer Bibliotheken
VEGL	Veröffentlichungen der Evangelischen Gesellschaft für Liturgieforschung
VGI	Veröffentlichungen des Grabmann-Instituts zur Erforschung der mittelalterlichen Theologie und Philosophie
VIEG	Veröffentlichungen des Instituts für Europäische Geschichte, Mainz
VIO	Veröffentlichungen der Institut für Orientforschung, Deutsche Akademie der Wissenschaften zu Berlin
VIRS	Veröffentlichungen des Instituts für Romanische Sprachwissenschaft, Deutsche Akademie der Wissenschaften zu Berlin
VKSM	Veröffentlichungen aus dem Kirchenhistorisches Seminar München
VT	Vivante tradition

WBS	Wiener byzantinische Studien
WBT	Wiener Beiträge zur Theologie
WF	Wege der Forschung
WS	Woodbrooke Studies
WSB	Westminster Source Books
YHP	Yale Historical Publications
ZBR	Zürcher Beiträge zur Reformationsgeschichte

OTHER ABBREVIATIONS

n.F.	Neue Folge
N.S.	New Series

PART ONE:

REFERENCE WORKS AND GENERAL WORKS

I. GENERAL BIBLIOGRAPHIES

Bibliography: The Mystery of Faith. Washington: Federation of Diocesan Liturgical Commissions, 1983.

CABROL, Fernand. Introduction aux études liturgiques. Paris: Bloud & Cie, 1907.

COLESS, Gabriel. "Recent Liturgical Study." American Benedictine Review, 22 (1971): 387-427.

COURATIN, A. H. "Liturgiology 1939-1960." Theology, 63 (1960): 451-458.

HATCHETT, Marion J. "An Updated Annotated Bibliography in Liturgics." St. Luke's Journal of Theology, 15, 3 (1972): 54-72.

INSTITUT BIBLIOGRAPHIE DE LITURGIE. Fichier bibliographique de liturgie. Leuven: Abbaye du Mont César, 19--.

JAGGER, Peter J., ed. The Alcuin Club and Its Publications: An Annotated Bibliography, 1897-1974. London: Alcuin Club, 1975.

JANERAS, Sebastiá. Bibliografia sull liturgie orientali (1961-1967). Rome: Pontificium Institutum Liturgicum Anselmianum, 1969.

JASPER, R. C. D. The Search for an Apostolic Liturgy: A Brief Survey of the Work of British Scholars on the Origins of the Eucharistic Liturgy. ACP, 18. London: Mowbray, 1963.

MISTRORIGO, Antonio. La liturgia. Rome: A. Armando, 1968.

1

RASMUSSEN, Niels Krogh. "Some Bibliographies of Liturgists."
Archiv für Liturgiewissenschaft, 11 (1969):   214-218; "Supplement." 15 (1973):   168-171.

SAUGET, Joseph M. Bibliographie des liturgies orientales (1900–
1960). Rome: Pontificium Institutum Orientalium Studiorum,
1962.

VISMANS, Thomas A., and BRINKHOFF, Lucas. Kritische Bibliographie der Liturgie. Nijmegen: Bestelcentrale der V.S.K.B.,
1959; Critical Bibliography of Liturgical Literature. Translated
by Ramund W. Fitzpatrick and Clifford Howell. Bibliogrpahia
ad usum seminariorum, E.1. Nijmegen: Bestelcentrale der
V.S.K.B., 1961.

ZACCARIA, Francesco Antonio. Bibliotheca ritualis, concinnatum
opus. 2 vols. in 3. Rome: Octavii Puccinella, 1776-1781; reprint ed., New York: Burt Franklin, 1964.

II. DICTIONARIES AND ENCYCLOPEDIAS

ADAM, Adolf, and BERGER, Rupert. Pastoralliturgisches Handlexikon. Freiburg: Herder, 1980.

AIGRAIN, R., ed. Liturgia: encyclopédie populaire des connais-
sances liturgiques. Paris: Bloud & Gay, 1935.

BERGER, Rupert. Kleines liturgisches Wörterbuch. Freiburg:
Herder, 1969.

BRAUN, J. Liturgisches Handlexikon. 2. Aufl. Regensburg:
Kösel & Pustet, 1924.

BRINKHOFF, Lucas. Liturgisch Woordenboek. Roermond: Romen
& Zonen, 1962.

CABROL, Fernand, and LECLERCQ, Henri, eds. Dictionnaire
d'archéologie chrétienne et de liturgie. 15 vols. in 30. Paris:
Letouzey, 1907-1953.

DAVIES, John G., ed. A Dictionary of Liturgy and Worship. London: SCM Press, 1972; American ed. published as The Westminster Dictionary of Worship. Philadelphia: Westminster Press,
1979.

_____. A Select Liturgical Lexikon. ESW, 14. Richmond:
John Knox Press, 1965.

HOLLAARDT, A. Liturgisch Woordenboek. Supplement: Liturgische orientatie na Vaticanum II. Roermond: Romen & Zonen,
1970. [Supplement to BRINKHOFF, above]

JUNG, Wolfgang. Liturgisches Wörterbuch. Berlin: Verlag Merseburger, 1964.

LERCARO, Giacomo. Piccolo Dizionario Liturgico. 2d ed. Genoa:
Bevilacqua & Solari, 1950; A Small Liturgical Dictionary. Edited
by J. B. O'Connell. Collegeville: Liturgical Press, 1959.

LESAGE, Robert, ed. Dictionnaire pratique de liturgie romaine.
Paris: Bonne Presse, 1952.

MISTRORIGO, Antonio. Dizionario liturgico-pastorale: dai documenti de Concilio Vaticano II e dagli altri documenti ufficiali fino
al 1977. Padova: Messaggero, 1977.

NITSCHKE, Horst. Wörterbuch des gottesdienstlichen Lebens:
Liturgie, christliche Kunst, Kirchenmusik. Evangelische Enzyklopädie, 10. Gütersloh: Gütersloher Verlagshaus, 1966.

PODHRADSKY, Gerhard. Lexikon der Liturgie. Innsbruck: Tyrolia Verlag, 1962; New Dictionary of the Liturgy. Preface by
Josef Jungmann. Foreword by Clifford Howell. English ed.
edited by Ronald Walls and Michael Barry. Staten Island:
Alba House, 1966.

III. PERIODICALS

Accent on Liturgy. Liturgical Conference, Washington. 1, 1980+.

Ambrosius: Bollettino liturgico ambrosiano. Milano. 1, 1925+.

Archiv für christliche Kunst. Ravensburg. 1-44, 1883-1929.

Archiv für Liturgiewissenschaft. Abt-Herwegen-Institut für liturgische und monastische Forschung, Abtei Maria Laach, Regensburg. 1, 1950+. [Supersedes Jahrbuch für Liturgiewissen-
schaft]

Ars sacra. Zürich. 1-22, 1927-1952/53.

Art chrétien. Paris, 1, 1965+.

L'Art d'Eglise. Monastère Saint-André-lez-Bruges, Bruges. 1,
1927+. [Suspended 1941-1945. 1927-1940 as Artisan liturgique;
1946-1949 as Artisan et les arts liturgiques]

Arte cristiana. Milano. 1-32, 1913-1944. 33, 1946+. [Supplement:
    Amico dell'arte cristiana. Milano, 1, 1929+]

Bibel und Liturgie. Klosterneuberg b. Wien. 1-15, 1926-1940/41;
    16, 1949+.

Boletin de Pastoral Liturgica. Centro de pastoral liturgica de
    Barcelona, Barcelona. 1, 1961+.

Bulletin of the Hymn Society of Great Britain and Ireland. Edin-
    burgh. 1, 1937+.

Church Music. River Forest, IL. 1966+.

Collana bibbia e liturgia. Brescia.

Communautés et liturgies. Monastère Saint-André, Ottignies, Bel-
    gium. 1975+. [Supersedes Paroisse et liturgie]

Dienst am Wort. Freiburg im Breisgau. 1, 1966+.

Ephemerides liturgicae. Rome. 1-50, 1887-1936; 62, 1948+. 51-61,
    1937-1947, published in two parts: Analecta historisco-ascetica
    and Lus et praxis liturgica.

Etudes liturgiques. Paris. 1, 1952+.

Eucharistisch tijdschrift. Tongerloo. 1-19, 1922-1940 (?).

Faith and Form: Journal of the Interfaith Forum on Religion, Art
    and Architecture. Washington, D.C. 1, 1968+.

Folk Mass and Modern Liturgy. Resource Publications, Saratoga,
    CA. 1, 1973-3/5, 1976. [Continued by Modern Liturgy]

Das Heilige und die Form. Marburg. 1, 1926+. [Supplement to
    Monatsschrift für Gottesdienst und kirchliche Kunst]

Historia Salutis. Serie liturgica. M. D'Auria Editore Pontificio,
    Naples. 1, 1967+.

The Hymn. Hymn Society of America, New York. 1, 1949+.

Jaarboek voor de Eredienst. (Nederlandse Hervormde Kerk),
    Boekencentrum, The Hague. 1, 1959+.

Jahrbuch für Liturgiewissenschaft. Münster. 1-14, 1921-1935; 15,
    1941. [Superseded by Archiv für Liturgiewissenschaft, 1950]

Jahrbuch für Liturgik und Hymnologie. Kassel. 1, 1955+.

Journal of Church Music. Philadelphia. 1, 1959+.

Kirchenkunst. Wien. 1-9, 1929-1938.

Kirchenmusik. Langensalza. 1-15, 1920-1934?

Kirchenmusikalisches Jahrbuch. Regensburg, New York. 1-10,
   1876-1885 [published as Caecilienkalendar]. N.S. 1, 1886+.

Kunst und Kirche. Verein für religiöse Kunst in der Evangelischen
   Kirche, Berlin. 1, 1924+.

Liturgia. Silos.

Liturgia: Dottrina, legislazione, arte, apostolate: Rivista mensile.
   Torino. 1, 1933+.

Liturgia: Revista Benedictina. Burgos. 1, 1945+. [Supersedes
   Liturgia: Revista Mensual de Orientación Liturgica.]

Liturgia: Revista Mensual de Orientación Liturgica. Toledo. 1-2,
   1944-1945. [Superseded by Liturgia: Revista Benedictina]

Liturgia e Vida. Instituto Pio X de Rio de Janeiro. 1, 1954+.
   [Title varies: 1-10? as Revista Gregoriana]

Liturgica. Abadia de Montserrat, Barcelona. 1, 1956+. [Issued in
   Scripta et Documenta]

Liturgica. Centro de Azione Liturgica, Rome. 1, 1961+.

Liturgical Arts: A Quarterly devoted to the Arts of the Catholic
   Church. Liturgical Arts Society, Concord, NH; New York. 1,
   1939+.

Liturgical Music.

Liturgical Review. Scottish Academic Press, Edinburgh. 2, 1973+.
   [Continues Liturgical Studies, Edinburgh]

Liturgical Studies. Church Service Society. Scottish Academic
   Press, Edinburgh. 1, 1971. [Supersedes Church Service Society Annual; continued in Liturgical Review]

Liturgical Studies. University of Notre Dame, Notre Dame, IN. 1,
   1953+.

Liturgie et vie chrétienne. Chanoines Reguliers de l'Immaculée Conception, Brigham. 1956+.

Liturgie und Mönchtum. Verein der Förderer und Freunde des Abt-
   Herwegen Instituts, Freiburg im Breisgau. 1, 1948+.

Liturgisch Tijdschrift. Leuven (Louvain). 1-5, 1910-1919.
[Superseded by Tijdschrift voor liturgie]

Liturgische Zeitschrift. Regensburg. 1-5, 1929-1932/33. [Super-
seded by Liturgisches Leben]

Liturgisches Jahrbuch. Münster. 1, 1951+.

Liturgisches Journal. Halle. 1-9, 1802-1809?

Liturgisches Leben. Berlin. 1-6, 1934-1939. [Supersedes Liturgische Zeitschrift]

Liturgy. Liturgical Commission, London. 1, 1976+.

Liturgy. Bulletin of the Liturgical Conference, Elsberry, MO. 1,
1956+.

Liturgy. Journal of the Liturgical Conference, Washington, DC.
1, 1956-1980. N.S., 1, 1980+.

Living Worship. Liturgical Conference, Washington, DC. 1, 1967-
1980. [Superseded by Accent on Liturgy]

La Maison-Dieu. Centre de pastorale liturgique, Paris. 1, 1945+.

Modern Liturgy. Resource Publications, Saratoga, CA. 3/6, 1976+.
[Continues Folk Mass and Modern Liturgy]

Monatsschrift für Gottesdienst und kirchliche Kunst. Göttingen.
1, 1896+.

Music and Liturgy. Official organ of the Society of St. Gregory,
Hinckley. 1-12, 1929-1940.

Musica Divina: Kirchenmusikalische Werke für Praxis und Forschung.
Regensburg. 1, 1950+.

Musica Divina: Monatsschrift für Kirchenmusik. Schola Austriaca,
Vienna. 1-26, 1913-1938.

Musica Sacra. Allgemeiner Cäcilienverein für Deutschland, Öster-
reich und die Schweiz, Cologne. 1, 1866-1910 as Fliegende
Blätter für katholische Kirchenmusik; 1911-1949 as Cäcilien-
vereinsorgan; 1950-1955 as Zeitschrift für Kirchenmusik. [Ab-
sorbed Musica Sacra, Regensburg, in 1929]

Musica Sacra: Monatsschrift zur Förderung der katholischen Kirch-
enmusik. Regensburg. 1-21, 1866-1888. N.S. 1-58, 1889-1928.
[Merged into Cäcilien-vereinsorgan in 1929--see Musica Sacra,
Cologne]

Musica sacro-hispana: revista mensual liturgico-musical. Organo de los Congresos españoles de musica sagrada, Bilboa. 1-16, 1908-1923.

Musik und Altar. Freiburg im Breisgau. 1, 1948+.

Musik und Gottesdienst. Zürich. 1, 1947+.

Musik und Kirche. Kassel. 1, 1929+. [Continued as Zeitschrift für evangelische Kirchenmusik]

Musique et liturgie. Centre de pastorale liturgique, Paris. 1, 1948+.

National Bulletin on Liturgy. Publication Service, Canadian Conference of Catholic Bishops, Ottawa. 1, 1967+. [Also published in French as Bulletin nationale de liturgie]

National Liturgical Week. Liturgical Conference. 1-16, 1940-1955. [Continued by North American Liturgical Week]

North American Liturgical Week. Liturgical Conference, Washington, DC. 17-28, 1956-1967.

Notes de pastorale liturgique. Centre national de pastoral liturgique, Paris. 1, 1955+.

Notitiae. Sacra congregatio pro culto divino, Città del Vaticano. 1, 1965+.

Opus Dei: Revista liturgica mensual. Braga. 1-10, 1926-1936.

Ora et Labora: Revista liturgica benedictina. Negrelos, Port. 1, 1954+.

Orate Fratres: A Liturgical Review. Collegeville, MN. 1-25, 1926/27-1951. [Continued by Worship]

L'Ouvroir liturgique. Luphem-les-Bruges, Belg. 1, 1923/33+. [1923-1933 as supplement to Bulletin paroissial liturgique; 1934-1937 suspended; 1938+ as supplement to Artisan liturgique]

Paroisse et liturgie. Abbaye de Saint-André, Bruges. 1, 1919-1974. [Superseded by Communautés et liturgies]

Periodica de re morali, cononica, liturgica. Pontificia Universita Gregoriana, Rome. 1, 1907+.

Questions liturgiques. Abbaye du Mont César, Louvain. 1, 1910/11+. [1929-1969 as Questions liturgiques et paroissiales]

Reformed Liturgics. Church Service Society of America. Philadelphia, PA. 1-6/1, 1963-1969. [Supersedes Sanctus; continued
as Reformed Liturgy and Music]

Reformed Liturgy and Music. Church Service Society of America, Philadelphia, PA. 6/2, 1971/1972+. [Continues Reformed Liturgics]

Research Bulletin of the Institute for the Study of Worship and Religious Architecture, University of Birmingham. Birmingham,
Eng. 1971+.

Response--in Worship, Music, the Arts. Lutheran Society for Worship, Music and the Arts, St. Paul, MN. 1, 1959+.

Revista liturgica Argentina: publicatión periódica de liturgia y
ciencias auxillares. Buenos Aires. 1, 1942?+.

Revue du chant grégorien. Grenoble. 1, August 1892+.

Revue liturgique et monastique. Abbaye de Maredsous, Belg. 1-12,
1899-1910 as Messager de Saint Benoît. 2e Serie, 1-4, 1911-1915 as
Revue liturgique et bénédictine. Resumed with vol. 5, 1919.

Rivista di liturgia. ?

Rivista liturgica. Padua. 1, 1914/15+.

Ruch biblijny i liturgiczny. Polskie Towarzystwo Teologiczne, Krak-
ow. 1, 1948+.

Sacred Music. Church Music Association of America, St. Paul, MN.
92, 1965+. [Formed by union of Catholic Choirmaster and Caecilia]

Sacris Erudiri: jaarboek voor godsdienstwetenschappen. St. Piet-
ersabkij, Steenbrigge, Belg. 1, 1948+.

Studia Liturgica. Rotterdam. 1, 1962+.

Svenskt Gudstjänstliv: Arsbok för Liturgi, Kyrkokonst, Kyrkomusik och Homiletik. Laurentius Petri Sällskapet, Lund. 1,
1926+. [1926-1941 as Tidskrift för Kyrkomusik och svenskt
Gudstjänstliv]

Tijdschrift voor liturgie. Hekelgem. 1, 1919+. [Supersedes Liturgisch tijdschrift, Leuven]

La Vie et les arts liturgiques. Paris. 1-12, 1913-1926.

Worship. Collegeville, MN. 26, 1952+. [Continues Orate Fratres]

Yearbook of Liturgical Studies. Notre Dame, IN. 1-8, 1960-1967.

Zeitschrift für evangelische Kirchenmusik. 1, 1929+. [1929-1933
    as Musik und Kirche]

IV. SERIES

Alcuin Club Collections. London: S.P.C.K., 1, 1899+.

Alcuin Club Leaflets. London: Mowbray, 1, 1937+.

Alcuin Club Papers. London: Mowbray, 1946-.

Alcuin Club Prayer Book Revision Pamphlets. London: Mowbray,
    1-15, 1912-57.

Alcuin Club Tracts. London: Mowbray, 1, 1898+.

Analecta hymnica Medii Aevi. Leipzig: n.p., 1-55, 1886-1922.
    [New York: Johnson Reprint Corp., 1961].

The Arts of the Church. London: n.p., n.d.

Bibliotheca "Ephemerides liturgicae." Rome: n.p.
    --Sectio historica. n.d.
    --Sectio practica. 1, 1947+.
    --Sectio pastoralis. n.d.

Bibliotheca Liturgica Danica. Egtved, Denmark: Edition Egtved.
    --Series latina. 1, 1970+.

Bibliothèque liturgique. Paris: A. Picard et Fils, 1893+.

Beihefte zur Monatsschrift für Gottesdienst und kirchliche Kunst.
    Göttingen: n.p., 1895-1941.

Cambridge Handbooks of Liturgical Study. Cambridge: n.p.,
    1910+.

Canadian Anglican Liturgical Series. Toronto, Ont.: Anglican Book
    Centre, 1, 1974.

Christ in der Welt. Eine Enzyklopädie. Aschaffenburg: Pattloch.
    n.d.
    -- 9. Ser. Die Liturgie der Kirche. n.d.
    --12. Ser. Bau und Gefüge der Kirche. n.d.
    --15. Ser. Die christliche Kunst. n.d.

Church Music Pamphlet Series.
    --Hymnology. St. Louis, MO: Concordia Publishing House, 1,
    1946+.

Collection de pastorale liturgique (see Paroisse et liturgie).

Contemporary Worship. [Inter-Lutheran Commission on Worship].
    Minneapolis, MN: Augsburg Publishing House, 1969+.

Un Corpus des Liturgies chrétiennes sur Microfiches. Paris:
    Cipol, 1973+.

Documenta liturgiae polychoralis sanctae ecclesiae Romanae. Rome:
    n.p., 1, 1957+.

Documenta maiora liturgiae polychoralis sanctae ecclesiae Romanae.
    Societas Universalis Sanctae Ceciliae, Trent, Italy: n.p., 1,
    1958+.

Documenta majora polyphoniae liturgicae sanctae ecclesiae Romanae.
    Societas Universalis Sanctae Ceciliae, Trent, Italy: n.p., 1,
    1964+.

Documentation liturgique. Montreal: n.p., 1, 1958+.

Early English Church Music. Supplements. London: Stainer and
    Bell [for British Academy], 1972+.

Ecclesia Orans: zur Einführung in den Geist der Liturgie. Frei-
    burg im Breisgau: Herder, 1-22, 1918 [1920?]-1939.

Ecumenical Studies in Worship. Richmond, VA: n.p., 1, 1958+.

Erneuerung der lutherischen Gottesdienstes. n.p., n.d.

L'Esprit liturgique. Paris: Editions du Cerf, n.d.

Etudes de théologie sacramentaire. Louvain: Nauwelaerts, n.d.

Etudes liturgiques. Louvain: Centre de documentation et d'informa-
    tion liturgiques, Abbaye du Mont César [issued by Centre de
    pastorale liturgique], 1, 1952+.

Grove Booklets on Ministry and Worship. Bramcote, Nottingham-
    shire: Grove Books, n.d.

Grove Liturgical Studies. Bramcote, Nottinghamshire: Grove Books,
    1, 1975+.

Henry Bradshaw Society. Publications. London: The Society, 1,
    1891+.

Historia salutis. Serie liturgica. Naples: M. D'Auria Editore
    Pontificio, 1967+.

Institute of Liturgical Studies Occasional Papers. [Valparaiso Univ.]. Valparaiso, IN: n.p., 1, 1949+.

Lebendiger Gottesdienst. Münster: Verlag Regensberg, 1, 1961+.

Lex Orandi. [Collection du Centre de pastorale liturgique]. Paris: n.p., 1, 1944+.

Library of Liturgiology and Ecclesiology for English Readers. London: n.p., 1-9, 1902-1911.

Life and Worship. [Society of Saint Gregory]. London: n.p., 39, 1970+.

Liturgia: Eine Einführung in die Liturgie durch Einzeldarstellungen. Mainz: n.p.
--1. Gruppe. Abhandlungen über die Liturgie im allgemeinen. 1-7, 1924-1931.

Liturgical Studies. Notre Dame, IN: University of Notre Dame Press, 1, 1955+.

Liturgie und Mönchtum: Laacher Hefte. Maria Laach: Verlag Ars Liturgica, 1-43, 1948-1968.

Liturgiegeschichtliche Forschungen. Münster: Aschendorff, 1-10, 1918-1927.

Liturgiegeschichtliche Quellen. Münster: Aschendorff, 1-22, 1918-1927.

Liturgiegeschichtliche Quellen und Forschungen. Münster: Aschendorff, 23-31, 1928-1939.

Liturgiewissenschaftliche Quellen und Forschungen. Münster: Aschendorff, 32, 1957+.

The Message of the Sacraments. Wilmington, DE: Glazier, n.d.

Monumenta Ecclesiae liturgica. Paris: n.p., 1-6, 1890-1912.

Monumenta Hispaniae Sacra. Serie litúrgica. Madrid: Consejo superior de investigaciones cientificas, 1, 1946+.

Monumenta Liturgica Ecclesiae Augustanae. Aoste: n.p., n.d.

Monumenta liturgiae polychoralis sanctae ecclesiae Romanae. [Societas Universalis Sanctae Ceciliae]. Rome: n.p.
--Ordinarium missae cum duobus choris. 1, 1957+.
--Ordinarium missae cum quatuor choris. 1, 1950+.
--Ordinarium missae cum tribus choris. 1, 1958+.

--Proprium de sanctis. 1, 1960+.
--Proprium de tempore. 1, 1960+.
--Psalmodia cum duobus choris. 1, 1953+.
--Psalmodia cum quatuor choris. 1, 1950+.
--Psalmodia cum sex choris. 1, 1950+.
--Psalmodia cum tribus choris concertata. 1, 1955+.

Monumenta Musicae Byzantinae. [International Union of Academies].
Copenhagen: n.p.
--Subsidia. 1, 1935+.
--Transcripta. 1, 1936+.
--Lectionaria. 1, 1939+.
--American Series. 1, 1947.

Monumenta musicae sacrae. Mâcon: n.p., 1, 1952+.

Monumenta polyphoniae liturgicae Sanctae Ecclesiae Romanae. Rome:
n.p.
--1. Ser. 1, 1948+.
--2. Ser. 1, 1947+.

NPM Studies in Church Music and Liturgy. Washington, DC: National Association of Pastoral Musicians, n.d.

Orthodox Worship. Crestwood, NY: St. Vladimir's Seminary Press, n.d.

Papers of the Hymn Society of America. [New York?]: n.p.   1, 1930+.

Paroisse et liturgie: Collection de pastorale liturgique. Bruges: n.p.n.d.

Pietas liturgica. Erzabtei Sankt Ottilien: EOS Verlag, 1, 1983+.

Popular Liturgical Library. Collegeville, MN: Liturgical Press, n.d.

Prayer Book Studies. [Issued by the Standing Liturgical Commission of the Protestant Episcopal Church in the United States of America] New York: n.p., 1-29, 1950-1976.

Quaderni di Revista liturgica. Torino: Elle Di Ci, n.d.

Rites et symboles. Paris: Editions du Cerf, n.d.

Sakrale Kunst. [Schweizerische St. Lukasgesellschaft]. Zürich: n.p., 1, 1954+.

Schriftenreihe des Arbeitskreises für evangelische Kirchenmusik. Zürich: Zwingli Verlag, 3, 1966+.

Studia Patristica et Liturgica. Regensburg: Friedrich Pustet, 1,
    1967+.

Studies in Christian Worship. London: Faith Press, 1, 1964+.

Studies in English Church Music. London: Barrie and Jenkins, n.d.

Studies in Eucharistic Faith and Practice. London; n.p., 1, 1957+.

Studies in Ministry and Worship. London: S.C.M. Press 1, 1957+.

Studies in the Reformed Rites of the Catholic Church. New York:
    Pueblo Publishing Co., n.d.

Study Texts. Washington, DC: n.p., 1, 1973+.

Supplemental Liturgical Resources. [Prepared by the Joint Office
    of Worship for the Presbyterian Church (U.S.A.) and the
    Cumberland Presbyterian Church] Philadelphia, PA: West-
    minster Press, 1, 1984+.

Supplemental Worship Resources. Nashville, TN: Abingdon, 1976-1984

Sussidi Liturgici. Milano: n.p., 1, 1969+.

Textes et études liturgiques. Louvain: n.p., [1932-1935?]

Textus Patristici et Liturgici. Regensburg: Friedrich Pastet, 1,
    1964+.

Veröffentlichungen der evangelischen Gesellschaft für Liturgie-
    forschung. Göttingen: 1, 1947+.

V. GENERAL WORKS

A. ANTHROPOLOGICAL BACKGROUND:
    RITUAL, MYTH AND SYMBOL

BOUYER, Louis. Le rite et l'homme: sacralité naturelle et liturgie.
    LO, 32. Paris: Cerf, 1962; Rite and Man: Natural Sacred-
    ness and Christian Liturgy. Translated by M. Joseph Costelloe.
    LS, 7. Notre Dame, IN: University of Notre Dame Press, 1963.

CAZENEUVE, Jean. Les rites et la condition humaine, d'après des
    documents ethnographiques. Paris: Presses universitaires de
    France, 1958.

CHENU, M. D. "Anthropologie et liturgie." La Maison-Dieu, 12
   (1947): 53-65.

CIRLOT, Juan Eduardo. Diccionario de simbolos tradicionales.
   Barcelona: Miracle, 1958; A Dictionary of Symbols. Translated by Jack Sage. New York: Philosophical Library, 1962.

COLLINS, Mary. "Ritual Symbols and Ritual Process." Worship,
   50 (1976): 336-346.

COPE, Gilbert F. Symbolism in the Bible and the Church. London:
   SCM Press; New York: Philosophical Library, 1959.

CRICHTON, J. D. "Signs, Symbols, and Mysteries." Worship, 39
   (1965): 469-479.

DILLISTONE, Frederick W. Christianity and Symbolism. London:
   Collins; Philadelphia, PA: Westminster Press, 1955.

DOUGLAS, Mary. Natural Symbols: Explorations in Cosmology.
   2d ed. New York: Vintage Books; London: Barrie & Jenkins,
   1973.

ELIADE, Mircea. Images et symboles: essai sur le symbolisme
   magico-religieux. Les Essais, 60. Paris: Gallimard, 1952;
   Images and Symbols: Studies in Religious Symbolism. Translated by Philip Mairet. New York: Sheed & Ward, 1961.

_____. Myth and Reality. Translated by Willard R. Trask.
   New York: Harper & Row, 1963; reprint ed., New York:
   Harper Torchbooks, 1968.

_____. Le mythe de l'éternel retour: archétypes et répétition.
   Paris: Gallimard, 1949; The Myth of the Eternal Return:
   Cosmos and History. Translated by Willard R. Trask. Bollin-
   gen Series, 46. Princeton, NJ: Princeton University Press,
   1954; reprinted as Cosmos and History. New York: Harper
   Torchbooks, 1959.

_____. The Sacred and the Profane: The Nature of Religion.
   Translated by Willard R. Trask. New York: Harcourt, Brace
   & World, 1959.

GELINEAU, J. "The Nature and Role of Signs in the Economy of
   the Covenant." Worship, 39 (1965): 530-550.

HAHN, Alois et al. Anthropologie des Kults. Freiburg: Herder,
   1977.

HOOKE, S. H., ed. Myth and Ritual: Essays on the Myth and
   Ritual of the Hebrews in Relation to the Culture Pattern of the
   Ancient East. London: Oxford University Press, 1933.

JAMES, E. O. Christian Myth and Ritual: A Historical Study.
London: J. Murray, 1933; reprint eds., Cleveland, OH:
Meridian Books, 1965; Gloucester, MA: Peter Smith, 1973.

_____. Origins of Sacrifice. 2d ed. London: J. Murray, 1937.

JASPERS, Karl. Von der Wahrheit. München: Piper, 1947; Truth
and Symbol. Translated with an introduction by Jean T. Wilde,
William Kluback, and William Kimmel. New York: Twayne,
1959.

JETTER, Werner. Symbol und Ritual: anthropologischen Elemente
in Gottesdienst. Göttingen: Vandenhoeck & Ruprecht, 1978.

LE BRAS, G. "Liturgie et sociologie." In Mélanges en l'honneur
de Mgr Michel Andrieu, pp. 291-304. Strasbourg: Palais universitaire, 1956.

MacGREGOR, Geddes. Rhythm of God: A Philosophy of Worship.
New York: Seabury Press, 1974.

MALDONADO, Luis, and POWER, David, eds. Symbol and Art in
Worship. Concilium, 132. New York: Seabury Press, 1980.

MASURE, Eugène. Le signe: le passage du visible à l'invisible.
Psychologie, histoire, mystère: le geste, l'outil, le langage,
le rite, le miracle. Paris: Bloud & Gay, 1954.

MITCHELL, Leonel Lake. The Meaning of Ritual. New York:
Paulist Press, 1977.

MOWINCKEL, Sigmund. Religion og Kultus. Oslo: Land og
Kirche, 1950; reprinted 1971; Religion and Cult. Translated
by John F. X. Sheehan. Milwaukee, WI: Marquette University,
1981.

OTTO, Rudolf. Das Heilige. 9. Aufl. Breslau: Trewendt &
Granier, 1922; The Idea of the Holy. Translated by John W.
Harvey. 2d ed. London: Oxford University Press, 1950.

PANNIKAR, Raymond. Worship and Secular Man: An Essay on the
Liturgical Nature of Man, considering Secularization as a Major
Phenomenon of Our Time and Worship as an Apparent Fact of
All Times. Maryknoll, NY: Orbis Books, 1973.

PARRINDER, Geoffrey. Worship in the World's Religions. 2d ed.
London: Sheldon Press, 1974; reprint ed., Totowa, NJ: Little-
field, Adams, 1976.

PIEPER, Josef. Zustimmung zur Welt: eine Theorie des Festes.
München: Kösel, 1963; In Tune with the World: A Theory of

Festivity. Translated by Richard and Clara Winston. New York: Harcourt, Brace & World, 1965; new ed., Chicago: Franciscan Herald Press, 1973.

SHAUGHNESSY, James D., ed. The Roots of Ritual. Grand Rapids, MI: Eerdmans, 1973.

SMART, Ninian. The Concept of Worship. New York: St. Martin's Press, 1972.

SOHNGEN, Gottlieb. Symbol und Wirklichkeit im Kultmysterium. 2. Aufl. GTP, 4. Bonn: Hanstein, 1940.

TILLICH, Paul. "The Religious Symbol." In Symbolism in Religion and Literature, pp. 75-97. Edited by Rollo May. New York: George Braziller, 1960.

TURNER, Victor. The Forest of Symbols: Aspects of Ndembu Ritual. Ithaca, NY: Cornell University Press, 1967.

_____. The Ritual Process: Structure and Anti-Structure. Chicago: Aldine; London: Routledge & Kegan Paul, 1969.

WILL, Robert. Le culte: étude d'histoire et de philosophie religieuses. 3 vols. EHPRC, 10, 21, & 29. Paris: Librairie Istra, 1925-1935.

B.   GENERAL HISTORIES AND INTRODUCTIONS

ABBA, Raymond. Principles of Christian Worship: With Special Reference to the Free Churches. New York: Oxford University Press, 1957.

ALLMEN, Jean-Jacques von. Célébrer le salut: doctrine et pratique du culte chrétien. Paris: Cerf; Genève: Editions Labor et Fides, 1984.

_____. Worship: Its Theology and Practice. London: Oxford University Press, 1965.

ALSTON, A. E., and TURTON, Zouch H. Origines Eucharisticae: A Study of the Liturgy under the Light of Recently Published Documents. London: Wells, Gardner, Darton, 1908?

BAUMSTARK, Anton. Liturgie comparée: principes et méthodes pour l'étude historique des liturgies chrétiennes. 3. éd., revue par Bernard Botte. Chevetogne: Editions de Chevetogne, 1953; Comparative Liturgy. English ed. by F. L. Cross. Westminster, MD: Newman Press; London: Mowbray, 1958.

_____ . Vom geschichtlichen Werden der Liturgie. EO, 10.
Freiburg: Herder, 1923; reprint ed., Darmstadt: Wissenschaftliche Buchgesellschaft, 1971.

BOTTE, Bernard et al. Eucharisties d'orient et d'occident. 2 vols.
LO, 46-47. Paris: Cerf, 1970.

BRENNER, Scott F. The Way of Worship. New York: Macmillan,
1944.

BRILIOTH, Yngve T. Nattvarden i evangeliskt gudstjänstliv.
Stockholm: Svenska Kyrkans Diakonistyrelses Bokförlag, 1926;
Eucharistic Faith & Practice: Evangelical and Catholic. Translated by A. G. Hebert. New York: Macmillan, 1930; revised
and shortened ed., London: SPCK, 1965.

BURKITT, Francis C. Christian Worship. CROP, 3. Cambridge:
Cambridge University Press, 1930.

CARSON, Herbert M. Hallelujah! Christian Worship. Welwyn,
Hertfordshire: Evangelical Press, 1980.

CATTANEO, Enrico. Il culto cristiano in occidente. 3d ed. BEL,
13. Rome: Edizioni Liturgiche, 1978.

CLARK, Neville. Call to Worship. SMW, 15. London: SCM Press,
1960.

COFFIN, Henry S. The Public Worship of God. WSB. Philadelphia, PA: Westminster Press, 1946; reprint ed., Freeport,
NY: Books for Libraries Press, 1972.

COMPER, John. A Popular Handbook of the Origin, History, and
Structure of Liturgies. 2 vols. in 1. Edinburgh: R. Grant,
1891-1898.

COURATIN, A. H. "Liturgy." In The Pelican Guide to Modern
Theology, vol. 2: Historical Theology, pp. 131-240. Edited
by J. Daniélou, A. H. Couratin and John Kent. Harmonds-
worth Middlesex: Penguin Books, 1969.

CRICHTON, J. D. Christian Celebration: The Prayer of the
Church. London: Geoffrey Chapman, 1976.

DAVIES, Horton. Christian Worship: Its Making and Meaning.
Rev. ed. Wallingford, Surrey: Religious Education Press,
1957.

DAVIES, Horton. Worship and Theology in England. 5 vols.
Princeton, NJ: Princeton University Press, 1961-1975.
1. From Cranmer to Hooker, 1534-1603. 1970.

2. From Andrewes to Baxter and Fox, 1603-1690. 1975.
3. From Watts and Wesley to Maurice, 1690-1850. 1961.
4. From Newman to Martineau, 1850-1900. 1962.
5. The Ecumenical Century, 1900-1965. 1965.

DAVIES, John G. "The Study of Worship." In Preface to Christian Studies, pp. 239-258. Edited by F. G. Healey. London:
Lutterworth Press, 1971.

DEARMER, Percy. The Church at Prayer and the World Outside.
Boston: Pilgrim Press, 1923.

DIX, Gregory. The Shape of the Liturgy. 2d ed. Westminster,
MD: Dacre Press, 1945; reprint eds., London: A. & C. Black,
1975; New York: Seabury Press, 1982.

DUNSTAN, Alan. Interpreting Worship. London: Mowbray, 1984.

FORRESTER, Duncan, McDONALD, James I. H., and TELLINI,
Gian, eds. Encounter with God. Edinburgh: T. & T. Clark,
1983.

GALLEN, John, ed. Christians at Prayer. LS. Notre Dame, IN:
University of Notre Dame Press, 1977.

GAMBER, Klaus. Liturgie Übermorgen: Gedanken über die Geschichte und Zukunft des Gottesdienstes. Freiburg: Herder,
1966.

GARRETT, T. S. Christian Worship: An Introductory Outline.
2d ed. New York: Oxford University Press, 1963.

GOLTERMAN, Willem Frederik. Liturgiek. Haarlem: Erven F.
Bohn, 1951.

GRAU, F. C. SODEN, W. von, KASEMANN, E., KRETSCHMAR, G.
"Liturgie." Die Religion in Geschichte und Gegenwart.

HARRIS, Thomas Leonard. Christian Public Worship: Its History,
Development and Ritual for Today. Garden City, NY: Doubleday, Doran, 1928.

HATCHETT, Marion J. Sanctifying Life, Time and Space: An Introduction to Liturgical Study. New York: Seabury Press,
1976.

HEDLEY, George P. Christian Worship: Some Meanings and Means.
New York: Macmillan, 1953.

HEILER, Friedrich. Das Gebet: eine religionsgeschichtliche und
religionspsychologische Untersuchung. München: Reinhardt,

1923; Prayer: A Study in the History and Psychology of Religion. Translated by Samuel McComb and J. Edgar Park. London: Oxford University Press, 1932; reprinted 1958.

_____. Katholischer und evangelischer Gottesdienst. 2. Aufl.
München: Reinhardt, 1925; The Spirit of Worship: Its Forms
and Manifestations in the Christian Churches. Translated by
W. Montgomery. Foreword by G. K. A. Bell. London: Hodder & Stoughton, 1926.

HERING, Hermann. Hülfsbuch zur Einführung in das liturgische
Studium. Wittenberg: R. Herrosé, 1888.

HISLOP, David H. Our Heritage in Public Worship. New York:
Scribner, 1935.

JONES, Cheslyn, WAINWRIGHT, Geoffrey, and YARNOLD, Edward,
eds. The Study of Liturgy. London: SPCK; New York:
Oxford University Press, 1978.

JOSUTTIS, M. "Gottesdienst." In Praktisch-theologisches Handbuch, pp. 219-240. Herausgegeben von Gert Otto. Hamburg:
Furche-Verlag, 1970.

KIRCHGASSNER, Alfons. Die mächtigen Zeichen: Ursprünge, Formen und Gesetze des Kultus. Basel, Freiburg, Wien: Herder,
1959.

KLAUSER, Theodor. Kleine abendländische Liturgiegeschichte.
Bonn: Hanstein, 1965; A Short History of the Western Liturgy.
Translated by John Halliburton. 2d ed. New York: Oxford
University Press, 1979.

LEEUW, Gerardus van der. Liturgiek, Nijkerk: Callenbach, 1946.

MARTIMORT, A. G., ed. L'Eglise en prière. 3. éd. Paris:
Desclée, 1965; partial adaptations in The Church at Prayer:
Introduction to the Liturgy. Translated by Robert Fisher et
al. English ed. edited by Austin Flannery and Vincent Ryan.
New York: Desclée, 1968; and The Church at Prayer, Vol. 2:
The Eucharist. Edited by Austin Flannery and Vincent Ryan.
New York: Herder & Herder, 1973.

MAXWELL, William Delbert. Concerning Worship. London: Oxford
University Press, 1949.

_____. An Outline of Christian Worship. London: Oxford Uni-
versity Press, 1936; reprint ed., A History of Christian Worship: An Outline of Its Development and Forms. Foreword by
Robert G. Rayburn. Grand Rapids, MI: Baker, 1982.

MICKLEM, Nathaniel, ed. Christian Worship: Studies in Its History and Meaning. Oxford: Clarendon Press, 1936.

MICKS, Marianne H. The Future Present: The Phenomenon of Christian Worship. New York: Seabury Press, 1970.

_____. The Joy of Worship. Library of Living Faith, 10. Philadelphia: Westminster, 1982.

MILLER, John H. Fundamentals of the Liturgy. Notre Dame, IN: Fides, 1964.

MOHLBERG, Cunibert. Ziele und Aufgaben der liturgiegeschichtlichen Forschung. LF, 1. Münster: Aschendorff, 1919.

NAGEL, William. Geschichte des christlichen Gottesdienstes. 2. Aufl. Berlin: De Gruyter, 1970.

NEUNHEUSER, Burkhard. Storia della liturgia attraverso le epoche culturali. BEL, 11. Rome: Edizioni Liturgiche, 1977.

OPPENHEIM, Philippus. Introductio historica in literas liturgicas. Institutiones systematico historicae in sacram liturgiam. Series I: De scientia liturgica, 1. Ed. alteras. Taurini: Marietti, 1945.

RATCLIFF, E. C. "Christian Worship and Liturgy." In The Study of Theology, pp. 409-476. Edited by Kenneth E. Kirk. New York: Harper, 1939.

RATTENBURY, John E. Vital Elements of Public Worship. 3d ed. London: Epworth Press, 1954.

REIFENBERG, Hermann. Fundamentalliturgie: Grundelemente des christliches Gottesdienstes. 2 Bde. Klosterneuburg: Osterreich. Katholisches Bibelwerk, 1978.

RIGHETTI, Mario. Manuale di storia liturgia. 3. ed. 4 vols. Milan: Ancora, 1959-1969.

SCHMEMANN, Alexander. Vvedenie v liturgiceskoe bogoslovie. Paris: YMCA-Press, 1961; Introduction to Liturgical Theology. London: Faith Press, 1966.

SHEPHERD, Massey H., Jr. The Liturgy and the Christian Faith. Greenwich, CT: Seabury Press, 1957.

_____, ed. Worship in Scripture and Tradition. New York: Oxford University Press, 1963.

SPERRY, Willard L. Reality in Worship: A Study of Public Worship and Private Religion. New York: Macmillan, 1925.

SPIELMAN, Richard M. History of Christian Worship. New York: Seabury Press, 1966.

STAHLIN, Rudolf. "Die Geschichte des christlichen Gottesdienstes von der Urkirche bis zur Gegenwart." In Leiturgia: Handbuch des evangelischen Gottesdienstes, Bd. 1, pp. 1-81. Herausgegeben von K. F. Müller und Walter Blankenburg. Kassel: Stauda, 1954.

STEUART, Benedict. The Development of Christian Worship: An Outline of Liturgical History. Foreword by J. B. O'Connell. London: Longmans, 1953.

UNDERHILL, Evelyn. Worship. New York: Harper, 1936; reprint ed., New York: Continuum Books, 1982.

WEBBER, Robert E. Worship, Old and New. Grand Rapids, MI: Zondervan, 1982.

WHITE, James F. Introduction to Christian Worship. Nashville, TN: Abingdon Press, 1980.

WILLIMON, William H. Word, Water, Wine and Bread: How Worship Has Changed Over the Years. Valley Forge, PA: Judson Press, 1980.

C. THEOLOGIES AND THEORIES OF WORSHIP

1. General and Miscellaneous Studies

ALLMEN, Jean-Jacques von. "The Theological Meaning of Common Prayer." Studia Liturgica, 10 (1974): 125-136.

ANDRONIKOF, Constantin. "The Meaning of Rite." St. Vladimir's Theological Quarterly, 20 (1976): 3-8.

BARTLETT, Gene E. "Worship: The Ordered Proclamation of the Gospel." Review and Expositor, 62 (1965): 275-292.

BECKMANN, Joachim. "Die Aufgabe einer Theologie des Gottesdienstes." Theologische Literaturzeitung, 79, 9 (September 1954): 519-526; "The Function of a Theology of Worship." Lutheran Quarterly, 7 (1955): 259-267.

BIERITZ, Karl-Heinrich. "Ansätze zu einer Theorie des Gottesdienstes." Theologische Literaturzeitung, 100 (1975): 721-737.

BOTTE, Bernard. "On Liturgical Theology." St. Vladimir's Seminary Quarterly, 12 (1968): 170-173.

BRODDE, O. "Liturgie." Evangelisches Kirchenlexikon, 2:1132-1139.

BRUNNER, Peter. "Theologie des Gottesdienstes." Kerygma und Dogma, 22 (1976): 96-121.

_____. "Zur Lehre vom Gottesdienst der im Namen Jesu versammelten Gemeinde." In Leiturgia: Handbuch des evangelischen Gottesdienstes, vol. 1, pp. 83-364. Edited by K. F. Müller and W. Blankenburg. Kassel: Stauda, 1952.

BRUNNER, Peter. Zur Lehre vom Gottesdienst der im Namen Jesu. Kassel: Stauda, 1954; Worship in the Name of Jesus. Translated by M. H. Bertram. St. Louis, MO: Concordia, 1968.

BURGHARDT, Walter. "A Theologian's Challenge to Liturgy." Theological Studies, 35 (1974): 233-248.

COLLINS, Mary. "Critical Questions for Liturgical Theology." Worship, 53 (1979): 312-317.

CORNEHL, Peter. "Offentlicher Gottesdienst: zum Strukturwandel der Liturgie." In Gottesdienst und Offentlichkeit: zur Theorie und Didaktik neuer Kommunikation, pp. 118-196. Herausgegeben von Peter Cornehl und Hans-Eckhard Bahr. Hamburg: Furche-Verlag, 1970.

_____. "Theorie des Gottesdienstes--ein Prospekt." Theologische Quartalschrift, 159 (1979): 178-195.

CRANFIELD, C. E. B. "Divine and Human Action: The Biblical Concept of Worship." Interpretation, 12 (1958): 387-398.

CRICHTON, J. D. "A Theology of Worship." In The Study of Liturgy, pp. 3-29. Edited by Cheslyn Jones, Geoffrey Wainwright and Edward Yarnold. New York: Oxford University Press, 1978.

DALMAIS, I. H. "La liturgie comme lieu théologique." La Maison-Dieu, 78 (1964): 97-105.

DAVIES, Horton. "The Integrity of Worship: The Marriage of Word and Sacrament, Worship and Service." Theology and Life, 7 (1964): 219-229.

EHRENFEUCHTER, Friedrich. Theorie des christlichen Cultus. Hamburg: F. & A. Perthes, 1840.

EHRENSPERGER, Alfred. Die Theorie des Gottesdienstes in der späten deutschen Aufklärung (1770-1815). Zürich: Theologischer Verlag, 1971.

FEDERER, Karl. Liturgie und Glaube: eine theologiegeschichtliche Untersuchung. PBGALT, 4. Freiburg (Schweiz): Paulus-Verlag, 1950.

FEINER, Johannes, and LOHRER, Magnus. Mysterium Salutis: Grundriss heilsgeschichtlicher Dogmatik, vol. 4, part 2: Das Heilsgeschehen in der Gemeinde. Einsiedeln: Benziger, 1973.

FINK, Peter E. "Towards a Liturgical Theology." Worship, 47 (1973): 601-609.

FISCHER, B. "Liturgie." Lexikon für Theologie und Kirche, 6:1085-1095.

GALLEN, John. "American Liturgy: A Theological Locus." Theological Studies, 35 (1974): 302-311.

GEORGE, A. Raymond. "The Theology of Worship." London Quarterly and Holborn Review, 186 (1961): 127-138.

GOTTWALD, Norman K. "The Biblical Basis of Worship." The Harvard Divinity Bulletin, 25, 1 (October 1960): 1-6.

GRIESE, Erhard. "Perspektiven einer liturgischen Theologie." Una Sancta, 24 (1969): 102-113.

HAUSSLING, A. "Die kritische Funktion der Liturgiewissenschaft." In Liturgie und Gesellschaft, pp. 103-130. Edited by H. B. Meyer. Innsbruck: Tyrolia, 1970.

HARDY, Daniel W., and FORD, David F. Jubilate: Theology in Praise. London: Darton, Longman & Todd, 1984.

HOLMER, Paul L. "About Liturgy and Its Logic." Worship, 50 (1976): 18-28.

JUNGMANN, Josef Andreas. "Liturgy I." Sacramentum Mundi, 3:320-331.

KAVANAGH, Aidan. On Liturgical Theology. New York: Pueblo, 1984.

KAY, J. Alan. The Nature of Christian Worship. London: Epworth Press, 1953.

KLAPPER, G., ed. Zur Theologie des Gottesdienstes. Hamburg: Luther Verlagshaus, 1976.

KNAUS, Earl T. "In Search of a Theology of Worship." Lutheran Quarterly, 10 (1958): 291-314.

KRETSCHMAR, Georg. "Die Eucharistie in liturgischen Vollzug
und in der kirchlichen Lehre." In Die Eucharistie, pp. 75-119.
Herausgegeben vom Kirchlichen Aussenamt der Evangelischen
Kirche in Deutschland. Bielefeld: Luther-Verlag, 1974.

KUHN, Ulrich. "Theologie als Gottesdienst." Theologische Literaturzeitung, 89 (1964):   117-126.

LANDGRAF, Artur Michael. "Liturgie und Dogma." In his Dogmengeschichte der Frühscholastik, Bd. 2, 1, pp. 31-55.
Regensburg: Pustet, 1953.

LEKKERKERKER, Arie Frederik Nelis. "Liturgiek." In Inleiding
tot de theologische studie, pp. 222-231. Groningen: Wolters,
1965.

LENGELING, Emil Joseph. "Kult." Handbuch theologischer Grundbegriffe, 1:865-880.

LENGELING, Emil Joseph. "Liturgie." Handbuch theologischer
Grundbegriffe, 2:75-97.

_____. Liturgie, Dialogue zwischen Gott und Mensch. Heraus-
gegeben und bearbeitet von Klemens Richter. Freiburg:
Herder, 1981.

LUBIENSKA DE LENVAL, Hélène. La liturgie du geste. Tournai:
Casterman, 1956; The Whole Man at Worship: The Actions of
Man before God. Translated by Rachel Attwater. New York:
Desclée; London: Chapman, 1961.

LUKKEN, G. "De liturgie als onvervangbare vindplaats voor di
theologie." In Tussentijds: Theologische Faculteit te Tilburg:
Bundel Opstellen bij Gelegenheid van haar Erkenning, pp. 317-
332. Onder redaktie van H. H. Berger. Tilburg: Hart van
Brabant, 1974?

_____. "La liturgie comme lieu théologique irremplacable."
Questions liturgiques, 56 (1975):   97-112.

MOLONEY, Raymond. "The Theology of Worship in the Works of
Oscar Cullmann." Dissertation, Pontificia Universitas Gregoriana, 1968.

MULLER, K. F. "Liturgiewissenschaft." Evangelisches Kirchenlexikon, 2:1140-1143.

NICHOLLS, William. Jacob's Ladder: The Meaning of Worship.
ESW, 4. London: Lutterworth Press; Richmond, VA: John
Knox Press, 1958.

PAQUIER, Richard. Traité de liturgique. MPT, 25. Neuchâtel:
Delachaux & Niestlé, 1954; Dynamics of Worship. Translated by
Donald Macleod. Philadelphia, PA: Fortress Press, 1967.

PERRY, Michael Charles. The Paradox of Worship. London:
SPCK, 1977.

PINTO, Manuel. O valor teologico da liturgia: ensaio de um tra-
tado. Braga: Livraria Cruz, 1952.

POWER, David. "Two Expressions of Faith: Worship and Theology." In Liturgical Experience of Faith, pp. 95-103. Concilium, 82. Edited by Herman Schmidt and David Power. New
York: Herder & Herder, 1973.

_____. "Unripe Grapes: The Critical Function of Liturgical
Theology." Worship, 52 (1978): 386-399.

PRENTER, Regin. "Liturgie et Dogme." Revue d'histoire et de
philosophie religieuses, 38 (1958): 115-128.

RAHNER, Karl. "Zur Theologie des Gottesdienst." Theologische
Quartalschrift, 159 (1979): 162-169.

RATZINGER, Joseph. Das Fest des Glaubens: Versuche zur The-
ologie des Gottesdienstes. Einsiedeln: Johannes-Verlag, 1981;
The Feast of Faith: Approaches to a Theology of the Liturgy.
Translated by Graham Harrison. San Francisco: Ignatius
Press, 1986.

SCHMEMANN, Alexander. For the Life of the World: Sacraments
and Orthodoxy. Crestwood, NY: St. Vladimir's Seminary
Press, 1973; also published as The World as Sacrament. London: Darton, Longman & Todd, 1966.

SCHMEMANN, Alexander. "Liturgy and Theology." The Greek
Orthodox Theological Review, 17 (1972): 86-100.

STENDAHL, Krister. "The How and Why: Theology and Liturgy."
The Harvard Divinity Bulletin, 25, 3-4 (April-July 1961): 1-7.

STENZEL, A. "Cultus Publicus: ein Beitrag zum Begriff und
ekklesiologischen Ort der Liturgie." Zeitschrift für katholischen
Theologie, 75 (1953): 174-214.

STRATHMANN, H., and MEYER, R. "Leitourgeo." Theologisches
Wörterbuch zum Neuen Testament, 4:221-238: "Leitourgeo."
Theological Dictionary of the New Testament, 4:215-231.

VAGÁGGINI, Cipriano. Caro salutis est cardo: corporetà, eucaristia e liturgia. Rome: Desclée, 1965; The Flesh, Instrument

of Salvation: A Theology of the Human Body. Translated by
Charles Underhill Quinn. Staten Island, NY: Alba House,
1969.

_____. Il senso teologico della liturgia. 4. ed.
Rome: Edizioni Paoline, 1965; Theological Dimensions of the Liturgy: A General
Treatise on the Theology of the Liturgy. Translated by Leonard
J. Doyle and W. A. Jurgens. Collegeville, MN: Liturgical
Press, 1976.

VAJTA, Vilmos. "Gottesdienst als Glaubensexperiment." In Gott
und Gottesdienst, pp. 9-20. Frankfurt: Lembeck, 1973.

VAJTA, Vilmos. "The Theological Basis and Nature of the Liturgy."
Lutheran World, 6, 3 (December 1959): 234-246.

VAN HOOYDONK, P., and WEGMAN, H. Zij breken hetzelfde
brood: een kritische wegwijzer bij de viering van de Eucharistie op basis van een liturgie-historische en -sociologische
analyse. Amersfoort: (Horstink), Pastoraal Instituut van de
Nederlandse Kerkprovince, 1972.

VERHEUL, Ambrosius. Inleiding tot de liturgie. Roermond: Romen,
1962; Einführung in die Liturgie: zur Theologie des Gottesdienstes. Auf Grund der 2. erweiterten Aufl. aus dem Nieder-
landischen übertragen von Mathilde Lehne. Wien: Herder,
1964; Introduction to the Liturgy: Towards a Theology of Worship. Translated from the German by Margaret Clarke. London: Burns & Oates; Collegeville, MN: Liturgical Press, 1968;
reprint ed., Wheathampstead, Eng.: Anthony Clarke Books,
1972.

VOS, Wiebe, ed. Worship and the Acts of God. Nieuwendam:
Studia Liturgica Press, 1963.

WAINWRIGHT, Geoffrey. Doxology: The Praise of God in Worship,
Doctrine, and Life: A Systematic Theology. New York: Oxford University Press, 1980.

WARE, K. "The Theology of Worship." Sobornost, 5 (1969): 729-
735.

2. Dom Odo Casel and Mystery-Theory

CASEL, Odo. Das christliche Festmysterium. Paderborn: Bonifacius-Druckerei, 1941.

_____. Das christliche Kultmysterium. 4. Aufl. hrsg. von
Burkhard Neunheuser. Regensburg: Pustet, 1960; The Mystery of Christian Worship and Other Writings. Edited by

Burkhard Neunheuser. Preface by Charles Dairs. Westminster, MD: Newman Press, 1962.

_____. Das christliche Opfermysterium: zur Morphologie und Theologie des eucharistischen Hochgebetes. Herausgegeben von Viktor Warnach. Graz: Styria, 1968.

_____. Die Liturgie als Mysterienfeier. EO, 9. Freiburg: Herder, 1918.

_____. "Die logike thusia der antiken Mystik in christlichliturgischer Umdeutung." Jahrbuch für Liturgiewissenschaft, 4 (1924): 37-47.

_____. "Das Mysteriengedächtnis der Messliturgie im Lichte der Tradition." Jahrbuch für Liturgiewissenschaft, 6 (1926): 113-204.

_____. "Neue Zeugnisse für das Kultmysterium." Jahrbuch für Liturgiewissenschaft, 13 (1933): 99-171.

_____. Vom christlichen Mysterium: Gesammelte Arbeiten zum Gedächtnis. Herausgegeben von Anton Mayer, Johannes Quasten und Burkhard Neunheuser. Düsseldorf: Patmos-Verlag, 1951.

FILTHAUT, Theodore. Die Kontroverse über die Mysterienlehre. Warendorf: J. Schnell, 1947; La théologie des mystères: exposé de la controverse. Traduit par J.-C. Didier et A. Liefoognie. Paris: Desclée, 1954.

FITTKAU, Gerhard. Der Begriff des Mysteriums bei Johannes Chrysostomus: eine Auseinandersetzung mit dem Begriff des "Kultmysteriums" in der Lehre Odo Casels. Theophaneia, 9. Bonn: Hanstein, 1953.

SANTAGADA, Osvaldo D. "Dom Odo Casel." Archiv für Liturgiewissenschaft, 10 (1967): 7-77.

SCHILSON, Arno. Theologie als Sakramententheologie: die Mysterienlehre Odo Casels. TTS, 18. Mainz: Matthias-Grünewald Verlag, 1982.

D. THE BIBLE IN THE LITURGY

BARROIS, Georges. Scripture Readings in Orthodox Worship. Crestwood, NY: St. Vladimir's Seminary Press, 1977.

BERTHIER, René. "Comment l'église annonce la Parole de Dieu." La Maison-Dieu, 80 (1964): 201-216.

DALMAIS, Irénée-Henri. "La Bible vivant dans l'Eglise." La
    Maison-Dieu, 126 (1976):   7-23.

DANIELOU, Jean. Bible et liturgie. LO, 11. Paris: Cerf, 1951;
    The Bible and the Liturgy. LS, 3. Notre Dame, IN: Univer-
    sity of Notre Dame Press, 1956; reprint ed., Ann Arbor, MI:
    Servant Books, 1979.

_____. Bible et liturgie. 2. éd. LO, 11. Paris: Cerf, 1958.

DAVIES, J. G. "Bible, Use of in Worship." Dictionary of Liturgy
    and Worship, pp. 75-76.

GANTOY, Robert. "Intégrer les fonctions de la parole dans la
    célébration." Paroisse et liturgie, 54 (1972):   195-204.

HERWEGEN, Ildephonse. "L'Ecriture sainte dans la liturgie." La
    Maison-Dieu, 5 (1946):   7-20.

HILL, Edmund. "The Word of God in the Liturgy." Liturgy (Eng-
    land), 33, 4 (1964):   81-86.

KEIR, Thomas H. The Word in Worship: Preaching and Its Setting
    in Common Worship. London: Oxford University Press, 1962.

KUNZE, Gerhard. Die gottesdienstliche Schriftlesung. VEGL, 1.
    Göttingen: Vandenhoeck & Ruprecht, 1947.

LAMB, John A. "The Place of the Bible in the Liturgy." In The
    Cambridge History of the Bible, vol. 1:   From the Beginnings
    to Jerome, pp. 563-586. Edited by P. R. Ackroyd and C. F.
    Evans. Cambridge: Cambridge University Press, 1970.

_____. The Psalms in Christian Worship. London: Faith Press,
    1962.

LATHROP, Gordon. "Scripture in the Assembly: The Ancient and
    Lively Tension." Liturgy, 2, 3 (Summer 1982):   21-23.

LEE, Charlotte I. Oral Reading of the Scriptures. Boston, MA:
    Houghton Mifflin, 1974.

MARTIMORT, A. G. et al. Parole de Dieu et liturgie. LO, 25.
    Paris: Cerf, 1958; The Liturgy and the Word of God. College-
    ville, MN: Liturgical Press, 1959.

McELENEY, John J. "The Bible and the Liturgy." Bible Today,
    25 (October 1966):   1742-1748.

La Parole dans la liturgie. Semaine liturgique de l'Institut Saint-
    Serge. LO, 48. Paris: Cerf, 1970.

ROSE, André. "La parole vivante de Dieu dans la Bible et dans la liturgie." La Maison-Dieu, 82 (1965): 43–58.

SHEPHERD, Massey H., Jr. The Psalms in Christian Worship: A Practical Guide. Minneapolis, MN: Augsburg, 1976.

VAN DIJK, S. J. P. "The Bible in Liturgical Use." In The Cambridge History of the Bible, vol. 2: The West from the Fathers to the Reformation, pp. 220–252. Edited by G. W. H. Lampe. Cambridge: Cambridge University Press, 1969.

WILLIMON, William H. The Bible: A Sustaining Presence in Worship. Valley Forge, PA: Judson Press, 1981.

E. MISCELLANEOUS METHODOLOGICAL, THEOLOGICAL AND HISTORICAL STUDIES

ALLMEN, J. J. von. "The Theological Meaning of Common Prayer." Studia Liturgica, 10 (1974): 125–136.

_____. "Worship and the Holy Spirit." Studia Liturgica, 2 (1963): 124–135.

BAUMSTARK, Anton. "Das Gesetz der Erhaltung des Alten in liturgisch hochwertiger Zeit." Jahrbuch für Liturgiewissenschaft, 7 (1927): 1–23.

BOUYER, Louis. "Principes historiques de l'evolution liturgique." La Maison-Dieu, 10 (1947): 47–85.

CHUPUNGCO, Anscar J. The Cosmic Elements of Christian Passover. SA, 72. Analecta liturgica 3. Rome: Editrice Anselmiana, 1977.

COLLINS, Mary. "Liturgical Methodology and the Cultural Evolution of Worship in the United States." Worship, 49 (1975): 85–102.

CRICHTON, J. D. "Phases in Liturgical History." In Studia Patristica, vol. 8, pp. 189–208. Edited by F. L. Cross. TUGAL, 93. Berlin: Akademie-Verlag, 1966.

DALMAIS, I. H. "La liturgie, acte de l'Eglise." La Maison-Dieu, 19 (1947): 7–25.

_____. "Signification de la diversité des rites au regard de l'unité chrétienne." Istina, 7 (1960): 301–318.

L'Eglise dans la liturgie. Conférences Saint-Serge 1979. BEL, 18. Rome: Edizioni Liturgiche, 1980.

FISCHER, Balthasar. "Wissenschaft vom christlichen Gottesdienst:
zum Verhältnis der Liturgiewissenschaft zu ihren Nachbardis-
ziplinen." Trierer theologische Zeitschrift, 83 (1974): 246-251.

FULLER, Reginald H. "Worship, Sacraments and the Unity of the
Church." Anglican Theological Review, 52 (1970): 214-227.

GRISBROOKE, W. Jardine, and SCHMEMANN, Alexander. "Debate
on the Liturgy." St. Vladimir's Theological Quarterly, 13
(1969): 212-224.

JUNGMANN, Josef. "Wirkende Kräfte im liturgischen Werden." In
Gott in Welt: Festgabe für Karl Rahner, Bd. 2, pp. 229-245.
Herausgegeben von J. B. Metz, W. Kern, A. Darlapp, H.
Vorgrimler. Freiburg: Herder, 1964.

LANGEVIN, Ernst. "The Word of God and the Eucharist." Canadian Journal of Theology, 8 (1962): 244-248.

Ministères et célébration de l'eucharistie. SAPT, 61- . Rome:
Anselmiana, 1973- .

MOHLBERG, C. "Antwort, die auf Beachtung hoffen: ein Beitrag
zur Förderung liturgiewissenschaftlichen Studiums." In
Mélanges en l'honneur de Mgr Michel Andrieu, pp. 339-349.
Strasbourg: Palais universitaire, 1956.

PETERSON, Erik. Das Buch von den Engeln: Stellung und Beden-
tung der heiligen Engel im Kultus. 2. Aufl. München: Kösel,
1955; The Angels and the Liturgy: The Status and Significance of the Holy Angels in Worship. Translated by Ronald
Walls. London: Darton, Longman & Todd; New York: Herder
& Herder, 1964.

PISTOIA, A., ed. Le Saint-Esprit dans la liturgie. Conférences
Saint-Serge, 1969. Rome: Edizioni Liturgiche, 1977.

RISSI, Matthias. "Gottesdienst und Gotteshaus." Theologische
Zeitschrift, 12 (1956): 305-319.

RUPKE, Ursula Irene. Liturgische Zeitschriften und Reihen des
deutschen Sprachgebiets im 20. Jahrhundert. VAKTB, 2.
Paderborn: Arbeitsgemeinschaft katholischtheologischer Biblio-
theken, 1974.

SCHANZE, Wolfgang. "Die Stimme der Jahrtausende in der Kirche
der Gegenwart: Bemerkungen zur Problem der Liturgie." In
Evangelium und mündige Welt, pp. 176-183. Herausgegeben
von Helmut Ristow und Helmuth Burgert. Berlin: Evangelische
Verlagsanstalt, 1962.

STEVENSON, Kenneth, ed. Authority and Freedom in Liturgy.
GLS, 17. Bramcote, Eng.: Grove Books, 1979.

STEVENSON, Kenneth W. "Dom Gregory Dix: A Silver Jubilee."
Studia Liturgica, 12 (1977): 207-216.

TAFT, Robert F. "The Structural Analysis of Liturgical Units:
An Essay in Methodology." Worship, 52 (1978): 314-329.

TORRANCE, Thomas F. "The Mind of Christ in Worship: The
Problem of Apollinarianism in the Liturgy." In his Theology
in Reconciliation, pp. 139-214. Grand Rapids, MI: Eerdmans,
1975.

TRIACCA, A. M., and PISTOIA, A., eds. L'Economie du salut
dans la liturgie. Conférences Saint-Serge, 1970. BEL, 25.
Rome: Edizioni Liturgiche, 1982.

VOLP, Rainer. "Perspektiven der Liturgiewissenschaft." Jahrbuch
für Liturgik und Hymnologie, 18 (1973-1974): 1-35.

WAINWRIGHT, Geoffrey. "The Praise of God in the Theological
Reflection of the Church." Interpretation, 39 (1985): 34-45.

WINKLER, Gabriele. "Considerations on a New Study of Liturgy."
Worship, 53 (1979): 242-249.

F. COLLECTED ESSAYS ON LITURGICAL HISTORY

BOOTY, John E., ed. The Divine Drama in History and Liturgy:
Essays Presented to Horton Davies on his Retirement from
Princeton University. Pittsburgh Theological Monographs,
N.S., 10. Allison Park, PA: Pickwick Publications, 1984.

BUCHHOLZ, Friedrich. Liturgie und Gemeinde: Gesammelte Aufsätze. Herausgegeben von Joachim Melhausen. TBuch, 45.
Munich: Kaiser, 1971.

BURSON, Malcolm C., ed. Worship Points the Way: A Celebration
of the Life and Work of Massey Hamilton Shepherd, Jr. New
York: Seabury Press, 1981.

CABANISS, Allen. Liturgy and Literature: Selected Essays. University, AL: University of Alabama Press, 1970.

CAPELLE, Bernard. Travaux liturgiques de doctrine et d'histoire.
3 vols. Louvain: Centre liturgique, Abbaye du Mont César,
1955-1967.

1. Doctrine. 1955.
2. Histoire: La Messe. 1962.
3. Histoire: Varia, L'Assomption. 1967.

CLARKE, William K. L., and HARRIS, Charles, eds. Liturgy and Worship: A Companion to the Prayer Book of the Anglican Communion. London: SPCK, 1932; reprinted 1954.

Eulogia: miscellanea liturgica in onore di P. Burkhard Neunheuser O.S.B., preside del Pontificio instituto liturgico. SA, 68. Rome: Editrice Anselmiana, 1979.

FISCHER, Balthasar, and MEYER, Hans Bernhard, eds. J. A. Jungmann, ein Leben für Liturgie und Kerygma. Innsbruck: Tyrolia, 1975.

KLAUSER, Theodor. Gesammelte Arbeiten zur Liturgiegeschichte, Kirchengeschichte, und christliche Archäologie. JAC, 3. Münster: Aschendorff, 1974.

LEGG, J. Wickham. Ecclesiological Essays. LLE, 7. London: A. Moring, 1905.

_____. Essays, Liturgical and Historical. London: SPCK, 1917.

MAYER, Anton L. Die Liturgie in der europäischen Geistesge-schichte: Gesammelte Aufsätze. Darmstadt: Wissenschaftliche Buchgesellschaft, 1971.

Mélanges liturgiques offerts au R. P. Dom Bernard Botte. Louvain: Abbaye du Mont César, 1972.

Miscellanea liturgica in honorem L. Cuniberti Mohlberg. 2 vols. Rome: Edizioni Liturgiche, 1948-1949.

Miscellanea liturgica in onore di Sua Eminenza Cardinale Giacomo Lercaro. 2 vols. Rome: Desclée, 1966-1967.

NEALE, John Mason. Essays on Liturgiology and Church History. With an appendix on liturgical quotations from the isapostolic Fathers, by Gerard Moultrie. 2d ed., with preface by R. F. Littledale. London: Saunders, Otley, 1867; reprint of 1st ed. (1863), New York: AMS Press, 1976.

RATCLIFF, E. C. Liturgical Studies of E. C. Ratcliff. Edited by A. H. Couratin and D. J. Tripp. London: SPCK, 1976.

SPINKS, Bryan D., ed. The Sacrifice of Praise: Studies on the Themes of Thanksgiving and Redemption in the Central Prayers of the Eucharistic and Baptismal Liturgies, in honour of Arthur Herbert Couratin. BEL, 19. Rome: Edizioni Liturgiche, 1981.

STALEY, Vernon. Liturgical Studies. London: Longmans, Green, 1907.

STEVENSON, Kenneth J., ed. The Liturgy Reshaped: Festschrift for Geoffrey Cuming. London: SPCK, 1982.

TAFT, Robert. Beyond East and West: Problems in Liturgical Understanding. NPMS. Washington, DC: Pastoral Press, 1984.

G. ASSEMBLY

ADAMS, William S. "The Eucharistic Assembly: Who Presides?" Anglican Theological Review, 64 (1982): 311-321.

L'assemblée liturgique et les différents rôles dans l'assemblée. Conférences Saint-Serge, XXIIIe Semaine d'études liturgiques, Paris, 28 Juin-1 Juillet, 1976. Rome: Edizioni Liturgiche, 1977; Roles in the Liturgical Assembly: The Twenty-Third Liturgical Conference Saint-Serge. Translated by Matthew J. O'Connell. New York: Pueblo, 1981.

The Assembly: A People Gathered in Your Name. Milwaukee, WI: Office of Worship, 1981.

Bishops' Committee on the Liturgy. "The Assembly in Christian Worship." Newsletter, 13 (September 1977): 81-82.

CNEUDE, Paul. "L'assemblée." La Maison-Dieu, 100 (1969): 89-103.

CONGAR, Yves. "L'ecclesia ou communauté chrétienne, sujet intégral de l'action liturgique." In La liturgie après Vatican II, pp. 241-282. Edité par J. P. Jossua and Yves Congar. Paris: Cerf, 1967.

_____. "Reflexions et recherches actuelles sur l'assemblées liturgiques." La Maison-Dieu, 115 (1973): 7-29; abridged translation in "Reflections on the Liturgical Assembly." Theology Digest, 22, 2 (Summer 1974): 150-153.

CRICHTON, J. D. "The Worshipping Community." In his Christian Celebration: The Mass, pp. 31-44. London: Geoffrey Chapman, 1971.

CROSS, F. L. "Synaxis." Oxford Dictionary of the Christian Church, p. 1314.

DANEELS, Godfried. "L'assemblée. Foi et experience." Questions liturgiques et paroissiales, 58 (1977): 12-26.

DAVIS, Charles. "The Mass as the Assembly of Believers." In Theology for Today, pp. 232-247. New York: Sheed & Ward, 1962.

DeROSA, Peter. "The Sense of Community and Liturgical Prayer." Worship, 38 (1964): 246-253.

DIEKMANN, Godfrey. "The Church as a Community of Prayer." Pastoral Music, 3, 5 (June-July 1979): 16-21.

EMPEREUR, James L'. "The Meaning of Liturgical Community." Folk Mass and Modern Liturgy, 3, 3 (March 1976): 11-13.

FLORISTAN, Casiano. "The Assembly and Its Pastoral Implications." In The Church Worships, pp. 33-44. Concilium, 12. New York: Paulist Press, 1966.

_____. The Parish Eucharistic Community. Notre Dame, IN: Fides, 1964.

GANTOY, Robert. "Pas de célébration possible sans communauté préalable?" Pariosse et liturgie, 56 (1974): 399-415.

GURRIERI, John A. "The Praising Assembly: Reassessing the Term 'Faithful' in the Light of Today's Eucharist." In The Assembly: A People Gathered in Your Name, pp. 12-15. Milwaukee, WI: Office of Worship, 1981.

HARVEY, Anthony Ernest. Priest or President? London: SPCK, 1975.

HENDERSON, J. Frank. "Worship of the Entire Assembly." National Bulletin on Liturgy, 14, 81 (November-December 1981): 206-210.

HEUSCHEN, Louis. "L'église locale, communauté de prière." Paroisse et liturgie, 49 (1967): 338-345.

HOFFMAN, Lawrence A. "Assembling in Worship." Worship, 56 (1982): 98-112.

HOVDA, Robert. "The Primacy of the Ministry of the Assembly." In The Assembly: A People Gathered in Your Name, pp. 16-17. Milwaukee, WI: Office of Worship, 1981.

_____. "The Symbol of the Living Person." Liturgy, 21, 9 (November 1976): 260-262.

LAHAISE, L. "La liturgie est 'l'église en prière.'" Cours et conférences des semaines liturgiques, 14 (1937): 47-62.

LECHNER, Robert.   "The People of God in Assembly."   Worship,
39 (1965):   259-264.

LECLERCQ, Jean.   "L'assemblée locale dans la communion de l'église
universelle."   La Maison-Dieu, 79 (1964):   81-105.

LECUYER, Joseph.   "The Liturgical Assembly: Biblical and Patristic Foundations."   In The Church and the Liturgy, pp. 3-11.
Concilium, 2.   Glen Rock, NJ: Paulist Press, 1965.

LEGRAND, Hervé-Marie.   "The Presidency of the Eucharist according
to the Ancient Tradition."   Worship, 53 (1979):   413-438.

LLOYD, Trevor, ed.   Lay Presidency at the Eucharist?   GLS, 9.
Bramcote, Eng.:   Grove Books, 1977.

MAERTENS, Thierry.   "La liturgie de l'assemblée face aux problèmes d'aujourd'hui."   Paroisse et liturgie, 51 (1969):   106-120.

_____.   L'assemblée chrétienne: de la théologie biblique à la
pastorale du XXe siècle.   CPL, 64.   Bruges: Publications de
Saint-André, 1954.

MARTIMORT, Aimé-Georges.   "L'assemblée liturgique."   La Maison-
Dieu, 20 (1949):   153-175.

_____.   "L'assemblée liturgique, mystère du Christ."   La Maison-
Dieu, 40 (1954):   5-29.

_____.   "Précisions sur l'assemblée."   La Maison-Dieu, 60 (1959):
7-34.

_____, ed.   The Church at Prayer: Introduction to the Liturgy,
pp. 77-106.   Edited and translated by Austin Flannery and Vincent Ryan.   New York: Desclée, 1968.

McNAMARA, Martin.   "The Liturgical Assemblies and Religious Worship of the Early Christians."   In The Crisis of Liturgical Reform, pp. 20-36.   Concilium, 42.   New York: Paulist Press,
1969.

MEMERCIER, Henri.   "A propos des assemblées chrétiennes: regard
et essai de perspective."   Paroisse et liturgie, 51 (1969):   3-8.

MINCHIN, Basil.   Every Man in His Ministry.   Worship in the Body
of Christ.   London: Darton, Longman & Todd, 1960.

MORTIMER, R. C.   The Celebrant and Ministers of the Eucharist.
SEFP.   Alcuin Club ed.   London: Mowbray, 1957.

NORRIS, Frank S.   "A Theology of Liturgical Assembly."   Modern
Liturgy, 8, 8 (November 1981):   4-5.

PANFOEDER, C. Die Kirche als liturgische Gemeinschaft. Liturgia,
2. Mainz, 1924.

PERNOT, P. "La notion de communauté dans les actes de Vatican
II." La Maison-Dieu, 91 (1967): 65-75.

POTVIN, Raymond. "The Liturgy and Community: A Sociological
Appraisal." Liturgical Week Proceedings, 28 (1967): 87-93.

QUITSLUND, Sonya A. "Priests and People in Biblical Perspective:
Called to Be a Worshipping People." Liturgy, 1, 4 (1981):
11-17.

REMY, J. "Communauté et assemblée liturgique dans une vie sociale en voi d'urbanisation." La Maison-Dieu, 91 (1967): 76-104.

SCHMIDT, Herman, ed. Prayer and Community. Concilium, 52.
New York: Herder & Herder, 1970.

STAHLIN, W. "'Koinonia' and Worship." Studia Liturgica, 1
(1962): 220-227.

TERRIER, L. "De l'assemblée chrétienne à la communauté des
hommes." La Maison-Dieu, 40 (1954): 108-117.

WALLE, Ambros-Remi van de. "How We Meet Christ in the Liturgical Community." In The Church Worships, pp. 19-32. Concilium, 12. New York: Paulist Press, 1966.

WHITE, James F. "Coming Together in Christ's Name: Where
Church Begins." Liturgy, 1, 4 (1981): 7-10.

WINSTONE, H. E. "The Mass and the Worshipping Community."
In The Liturgy and the Future, pp. 26-38. Edited by J. D.
Crichton. Techny, IL: Divine Word Publications, 1966.

ZIZIOULAS, J. D. "La communauté eucharistique et la catholicité
de l'église." Istina, 14 (1969): 67-88.

H. LITURGICAL LANGUAGE

BOGLER, Theodor, ed. Sakrale Sprache und kultischer Gesang:
Gesammelte Aufsätze. LM, 37. Maria Laach: Ars Liturgica,
1965.

BROOK, Stella. The Language of the Book of Common Prayer.
New York: Oxford University Press, 1965.

BROOKS, Cleanth. "Prayer Book Revision: Literary Style."
Anglican Theological Review, 44 (1962): 18-33.

BRUNNER, Peter. "Die Sprache der Liturgie: eine theologische
Uberlegung zu ihrer geistlichen Bedeutung." In Martyria,
Leiturgia, Diakonia, pp. 320-339. Herausgegeben von Otto
Semmelroth. Mainz: Grünewald, 1968.

CHAPMAN, Raymond. "Linguistics and Liturgy." Theology, 76
(1973): 594-599.

CUNLIFFE, C. R. A., ed. English in the Liturgy: A Symposium.
London: Burns & Oates; Springfield, IL: Templegate, 1956.

DE MARCO, Angelus A. The Church of Rome and the Problem of
the Vernacular versus the Liturgical Language. SST, 2d ser.,
123 A. Washington, DC: Catholic University of America Press,
1960.

_____. Rome and the Vernacular. Westminster, MD: Newman
Press, 1961.

DUFFIELD, G. E. "The Language of Worship." In Towards a Modern Prayer Book, pp. 68-73. Edited by R. T. Beckwith. Appleford, Eng.: Marcham Manor Press, 1966.

EMSWILER, Sharon Neufer, and EMSWILER, Thomas Neufer. Women
and Worship: A Guide to Non-Sexist Hymns, Prayers, and Liturgies. New York: Harper & Row, 1974.

FROST, David L. The Language of Series 3: An Essay on Modern
Liturgical Language, with an account of the Debate on Series 3
Communion Service, and an Analysis of the Language of the
Congregational Text. GBMW, 12. Bramcote, Eng.: Grove
Books, 1973.

_____. "Liturgical Language from Cranmer to Series 3." In The
Eucharist Today: Studies on Series 3, pp. 142-167. Edited by
R. C. D. Jasper. London: SPCK, 1974.

GARRETT, Paul D. "The Problem of Liturgical Translation: A
Preliminary Study." St. Vladimir's Theological Quarterly, 22
(1978): 83-113.

GILKEY, Langdon. "Addressing God in Faith." In Liturgical Experience of Faith, pp. 62-72. Edited by Herman Schmidt and
David Power. Concilium, 82. New York: Herder & Herder,
1973.

GRAINGER, Roger. The Language of the Rite. London: Darton,
Longman and Todd, 1974.

KASCH, Elisabeth. Das liturgische Vokabular der frühen lateinischen
Mönchsregeln. RBSS, 1. Hildesheim: Gerstenberg, 1974.

KLAUSER, Theodor. "Der Ubergang der römischen Kirche von der griechischen zur lateinischen Liturgiesprache." In Miscellanea Giovanni Mercati, vol. 1, pp. 467-482. Vatican City: Biblioteca Apostolica Vaticana, 1946.

KOROLEVSKY, Cyril. Liturgie en langue vivante: orient et occident. LO, 18. Paris: Cerf, 1955; Living Languages in Catholic Worship: An Historical Inquiry. Translated by Donald Attwater. Westminster, MD: Newman Press, 1957.

LADRIERE, Jean. "The Performativity of Liturgical Language." In Liturgical Experience of Faith, pp. 50-61. Edited by Herman Schmidt and David Power. Concilium, 82. New York: Herder & Herder, 1973.

LENTNER, Leopold. Volkssprache und Sakralsprache: Geschichte einer Lebensfrage bis zum Ende des Konzils von Triente. WBT, 5. Wien: Herder, 1964.

LEWIS, C. S. English Literature in the Sixteenth Century Excluding Drama, pp. 215-221. OHEL. Oxford: Clarendon Press, 1954.

LIVER, Ricarda. Die Nachwirkung der antiken Sakralsprache im christlichen Gebet des lateinischen und italienischen Mittelalters: Untersuchungen zu den syntaktischen und stilistischen Formen dichterisch gestalteter Gebete von den Anfängen der lateinischen Literatur bis zu Dante. Romanica Helvetica, 89. Bern: Francke, 1979.

LUKKEN, Gerard. "The Unique Expression of Faith in the Liturgy." In Liturgical Experience of Faith, pp. 11-21. Edited by Herman Schmidt and David Power. Concilium, 82. New York: Herder & Herder, 1973.

MANIGNE, Jean-Pierre. "The Poetics of Faith in the Liturgy." In Liturgical Experience of Faith, pp. 40-49. Edited by Herman Schmidt and David Power. Concilium, 82. New York: Herder and Herder, 1973.

MOHRMANN, Christine. Etudes sur le latin des chrétiens. 3 vols. Storia e letteratura, 65, 87, ? Rome: Edizioni di storia e letteratura, 1958-1965.
1. Le latin des chrétiens. 1958; 2d ed., 1961.
2. Latin chrétien et médiéval.
3. Latin chrétien et liturgique. 1965.

_____. Liturgical Latin: Its Origins and Character. London: Burns & Oates, 1959.

_____. "Les origines de la latinité chrétienne à Rome." Vigiliae Christianae, 3 (1949): 67-106, 163-183; reprinted in her Etudes sur le latin des chrétiens, vol. 3, pp. 67-126. Rome: Edizioni di storia e letteratura, 1965.

"Le problème des langues en liturgie." La Maison-Dieu, 53 (1958). [Special issue]

ROBINSON, Ian. "Religious English." In his The Survival of English, pp. 22-65. Cambridge: Cambridge University Press, 1973.

ROUTLEY, Erik. "The Gender of God: A Contribution to the Conversation." Worship, 56 (1982): 231-239.

_____. "Sexist Language: A View from a Distance." Worship, 53 (1979): 2-11.

SALIERS, Don E. "On the 'Crisis' of Liturgical Language." Worship, 44 (1970): 399-411.

SCHANZE, Wolfgang. "Die Sprache der Liturgie." Jahrbuch für Liturgik und Hymnologie, 7 (1962): 40-51.

SCHMIDT, Gail Ramshaw. "De Divinis Nominibus: The Gender of God." Worship, 56 (1982): 117-131.

SCHMIDT, Herman. "Language and Its Function in Christian Worship." Studia Liturgica, 8 (1971-1972): 1-25.

_____. Liturgie et langue vulgaire: le problème de la langue liturgique chez les premiers Réformateurs et au Concile de Trente. AG, 53. Rome: Universitatis Gregorianae, 1950.

SPEAIGHT, Robert. "Liturgy and Language." Theology, 74 (1971): 444-456.

STEVICK, Daniel B. Language in Worship: Reflections on a Crisis. New York: Seabury Press, 1970.

THISELTON, Anthony Charles. Language, Liturgy and Meaning. GLS, 2. Bramcote, Eng.: Grove Books, 1975.

TOPOROSKI, Richard. "Language of Worship." Communio, 4 (1977): 226-260.

VOLP, Rainer, ed. Zeichen: Semiotik in Theologie und Gottesdienst. In Verbindung mit Rudi Fleischer. München: Kaiser; Mainz: Grünewald, 1982.

WAINWRIGHT, Geoffrey. "The Language of Worship." In The Study of Liturgy, pp. 465-473. Edited by Cheslyn Jones, Geoffrey Wainwright, and Edward Yarnold. New York: Oxford University Press, 1978.

WARE, James H., Jr. Not with Words of Wisdom: Performative Language and Liturgy. Washington, DC: University Press of America, 1981.

WATKINS, Keith. Faithful and Fair: Transcending Sexist Language in Worship. Nashville, TN: Abingdon Press, 1981.

WESTLAKE, John H. J. "The Liturgical Use of Modern Translations of the Bible." Studia Liturgica, 8 (1971-1972): 98-118.

_____. "The Problems of Modern Vernacular Liturgy." Studia
   Liturgica, 6 (1969): 147-157.

WINNINGER, Paul. Langues vivantes et liturgie. Rencontres, 59.
   Paris: Cerf, 1961.

I. WORSHIP, ETHICS, AND MISSION

AVILA, Rafael. Apuntes sobre las implicaciones socio-políticas de
   la Eucaristia. Bogotá: Policrom Artes Gráficas, 1977; Worship
   and Politics. Translated by Alan Neely. Maryknoll, NY:
   Orbis Books, 1981.

BALASURIYA, Tissa. The Eucharist and Human Liberation. Maryknoll, NY: Orbis Books, 1979.

DAVIES, John G. Worship and Mission. London: SCM Press,
   1966; New York: Association Press, 1967.

GODSEY, John D. "The Life of the Church and Its Duty in the
   World: Ethical Implications of Word and Sacrament." Encounter,
   20 (1959): 436-445.

HAGEMAN, Howard G. "Liturgy and Mission." Theology Today,
   19 (1962): 169-170.

HEBERT, Arthur G. Liturgy and Society: The Function of the
   Church in the Modern World. London: Faber & Faber, 1939;
   reprinted 1969.

HELLWIG, Monika K. The Eucharist and the Hunger of the World.
   New York: Paulist Press, 1976.

HOFINGER, J., and KELLNER, J., eds. Liturgische Erneuerung in
   der Weltmission. Innsbruck: Tyrolia Verlag, 1957; Worship:
   The Life of the Missions. Translated by M. Perkins Ryan. LS,
   4. Notre Dame, IN: University of Notre Dame Press, 1958.

HOFINGER, Johannes, ed. Mission und Liturgie: der Kongress
   vom Nimwegen 1959. Mainz: Grünewald, 1960; Liturgy and the
   Missions: The Nijmegen Papers. New York: Kenedy, 1960.

KIRK, P. T. R., ed. Worship: Its Social Significance. London:
   Centenary Press, 1939.

NIEBUHR, Reinhold. "Worship and the Social Conscience." Radical
    Religion, 3, 1 (Winter 1937): 5-7; reprinted in his Essays in
    Applied Christianity, pp. 48-51. Edited by D. B. Robertson.
    New York: Meridian Books, 1959.

RAMSEY, Paul. "Liturgy and Ethics." Journal of Religious Ethics,
    7 (1979): 139-171.

SALIERS, Don E. "Liturgy and Ethics: Some New Beginnings."
    Journal of Religious Ethics, 7 (1979): 173-189.

SCHMIDT, Herman, and POWER, David, eds. Politics and Liturgy.
    Concilium, 92. New York: Herder & Herder, 1974.

SEARLE, Mark, ed. Liturgy and Social Justice. Collegeville, MN:
    Liturgical Press, 1980.

SHEPHERD, Massey H., Jr. Liturgy and Education. New York:
    Seabury Press, 1965.

WESTERHOFF, John H., and WILLIMON, William H. Liturgy and
    Learning through the Life Cycle. New York: Seabury Press,
    1980.

J. GENERAL CEREMONIAL

ATCHLEY, E. G. C. F., BISHOP, Edmund, DEARMER, Percy, and
    LEGG, J. W. Essays on Ceremonial. LLE, 4. London: De
    La More Press, 1904.

BERESFORD-COOKE, Ernest. The Sign of the Cross in the Western
    Liturgies. ACT, 7. London: Longmans, Green 1907.

BRENNER, Scott Francis. The Art of Worship: A Guide in Cor-
    porate Worship Techniques. New York: Macmillan, 1961.

DUNLOP, Colin. Processions: A Dissertation together with Practi-
    cal Suggestions. ACT, 20. London: Mowbray; London: Ox-
    ford University Press, 1932.

FRERE, Walter Howard. The Principles of Religious Ceremonial.
    2d ed. OLPT. London: Mowbray, 1928.

JORDAHL, Leigh D. "Liturgy and Ceremony: Catholic-Protestant
    Cross Currents." Worship, 44 (1970): 171-181.

K. OTHER PRACTICAL AND CRITICAL STUDIES
    IN CONTEMPORARY WORSHIP

AUDET, Jean-Paul. "The Future of Liturgy." Worship, 43 (1969):
   449-464.

CARTER, H. A. The Prayer Tradition of Black People. Valley
   Forge, PA: Judson Press, 1976.

The Church and the Liturgy. Concilium, 2. Glen Rock, NJ:
   Paulist Press, 1965.

The Church Worships. Concilium, 12. New York: Paulist Press,
   1966.

CONE, James H. "Sanctification, Liberation, and Black Worship."
   Theology Today, 35 (1978-1979): 139-152.

"Créativité et liturgie." La Maison-Dieu, 111 (1972). [Special
   issue]

The Crisis of Liturgical Reform. Concilium, 42. New York: Paulist Press, 1969.

DAVIES, John G. Every Day God: Encountering the Holy in World
   and Worship. London: SCM Press, 1973.

_____. New Perspectives on Worship Today. London: SCM
   Press, 1978.

DEARMER, Percy. The Art of Public Worship. 2d ed. London:
   Mowbray; Milwaukee, WI: Morehouse, 1920.

FISCHER, Balthasar. Kult in der säkularisierten Welt. Regensburg: Pustet, 1974.

HAHN, Wilhelm T. Die Mitte der Gemeinde: zur Frage des Gottes-
   dienstes und des Gemeindeaufbaus. Gütersloh: Mohn, 1958;
   Worship and Congregation. Translated by Geoffrey Buswell.
   ESW, 12. Richmond, VA: John Knox Press, 1963.

_____. "Prolegomena to the Ecumenical Discussion on the Litur-
   gy." Studia Liturgica, 2 (1963): 2-7; also published as Worship and the Acts of God, pp. 2-7. Edited by Wiebe Vos.
   Nieuwendam: Studia Liturgica Press, 1963.

HOENDERDAAL, G. F. Riskant Spel: Liturgie in een gesecular-
   iseerde wereld. PTH, 42. 's-Gravenhage: Boekencentrum,
   1977.

HOON, Paul Waitman. The Integrity of Worship: Ecumenical and
    Pastoral Studies in Liturgical Theology. Nashville, TN:
    Abingdon Press, 1971.

KRIKKE, S. Veranderd levensbesef en liturgie. PR, 18. Assen:
    Van Gorcum, 1976.

LANGE, Ernst. Chancen des Alltags: Uberlegungen zur Funktion
    des christlichen Gottesdienstes in der Gegenwart. HCW, 8.
    Stuttgart: Verlagsgemeinschaft Burckhardthausund Kreuz-
    Verlag, 1965.

LEEUW, Gerardus van der, NOORDMANS, O., and POL, W. H. van
    de. Liturgie in de crisis. Nijkerk: Callenbach, 1939?

Liturgie de l'Eglise particulière et liturgie de l'Eglise universelle.
    Conférences Saint-Serge: XXIIe Semaine d'études liturgiques,
    Paris, 30 Juin-3 Juillet 1975. Rome: Edizioni Liturgiche, 1976.

MALDONADO ARENAS, Luis. Secularización de la liturgia. Mad-
    rid: Ediciones Marova, 1970.

MARTIN, Ralph P. The Worship of God: Some Theological, Pas-
    toral and Practical Reflections. Grand Rapids, MI: Eerdmans,
    1982.

MULLER, Karl Ferdinand. "Theologische und liturgische Aspekte
    zu den Gottesdiensten in neuer Gestalt." Jahrbuch für Litur-
    gik und Hymnologie, 13 (1968): 54-77.

NAGEL, William. "Die theologische und praktische Bedeutung der
    Liturgiegeschichte für die gegenwärtige kirchliche Situation."
    Theologische Literaturzeitung, 92 (1967): 341-344.

NIEBUHR, Reinhold. "The Weakness of Common Worship in Amer-
    ican Protestantism." Christianity and Crisis, 11 (1951): 68-
    70; reprinted in his Essays in Applied Christianity, pp. 57-63.
    Edited by D. B. Robertson. New York: Meridian Books,
    1959.

PAPANDREOU, Damaskinos. "Das Okumenismus-Problem von der
    Liturgie her gesehen." Liturgie und Mönchtum, 40 (1967):
    32-36.

POWER, David, and MALDONADO, Luis, eds. Liturgy and Human
    Passage. Concilium, 112. New York: Seabury Press, 1979.

RENNINGS, Heinrich. "What is the Liturgy Supposed to Do?" In
    The Crisis of Liturgical Reform, pp. 120-137. Concilium, 42.
    New York: Paulist Press, 1969.

RIVERS, C. J. Soulfull Worship. Washington, DC: National Office for Black Catholics, 1974.

RYAN, John Barry. The Eucharistic Prayer: A Study in Contemporary Liturgy. New York: Paulist Press, 1974.

SCHILLEBEECKX, Edward. "Secular Worship and Church Liturgy." In his God the Future of Man, pp. 91-116. Translated by N. D. Smith. New York: Sheed & Ward, 1968.

SCHMEMANN, Alexander. "Prayer, Liturgy, and Renewal." The Greek Orthodox Theological Review, 14 (1969): 7-16.

_____. "Worship in a Secular Age." St. Vladimir's Theological Quarterly, 16 (1972): 1-16; reprinted in his For the Life of the World: Sacraments and Orthodoxy, pp. 117-134. Crestwood, NY: St. Vladimir's Seminary Press, 1973.

SCHMIDT, Herman, ed. Liturgy: Self-Expression of the Church. Concilium, 72. New York: Herder & Herder, 1972.

_____, ed. Prayer and Community. Concilium, 52. New York: Herder & Herder, 1970.

SCHMIDT, Herman, and POWER, David, eds. Liturgical Experience of Faith. Concilium, 82. New York: Herder & Herder, 1973.

_____, eds. Liturgy and Cultural Religious Traditions. Concilium, 102. New York: Seabury Press, 1977.

SCHNIJDER, Augustinus C. J. M. "Cosmopolitanizaiton of Mankind and Adaptation of the Liturgy." Studia Liturgica, 8 (1971-1972): 169-184.

SEIDENSPINNER, Clarence. Form and Freedom in Worship. Chicago: Willett, Clark, 1941.

SEILS, Martin. "Der Gott der Welt und die Welt des Gottesdienstes." In Gott und Gottesdienst, pp. 21-49. Mit Beiträgen von Vilmos Vajta. Frankfurt am Main: Lembeck, 1973.

SIMPSON, R. S. Ideas in Corporate Worship. Edinburgh: T. & T. Clark, 1927.

STAHLIN, W. "'Koinonia' and Worship." Studia Liturgica, 1 (1962): 220-227.

THURIAN, Max. "Creativité et spontaneité dans la liturgie." Notitiae, 14 (1978): 169-175.

TRAUTWEIN, Dieter. "Gottesdienst als Feld ökumenischer

Realisierung: Okumenische Impulse für die Arbeit am Gottesdienst nach 1945." Wissenschaft und Praxis in Kirche und
Gesellschaft, 4 (1974): 161-174.

VOGT, Von Ogden. Modern Worship. New Haven, CT: Yale University Press, 1927.

VOS, Wiebe, ed. "Worship and Secularization." Preface by Lukas
Vischer. Studia Liturgica, 7 (1970).

WAINWRIGHT, Geoffrey. "Christian Worship and Western Culture."
Studia Liturgica, 12 (1977): 20-33.

WEBBER, Robert E. Worship Is a Verb. Waco, TX: Word Books,
1985.

WHITE, James F. New Forms of Worship. Nashville, TN: Abingdon Press, 1971.

_____. The Worldliness of Worship. New York: Oxford Univer-
sity Press, 1967.

_____. "Worship and Culture: Mirror or Beacon?" Theological
Studies, 35 (1974): 288-301.

WICKER, Brian. Culture and Liturgy. New York: Sheed & Ward,
1963.

WILLIMON, William H. Worship as Pastoral Care. Nashville, TN:
Abingdon Press, 1979.

WILLIMON, William H., and WILSON, Robert L. Preaching and Worship in the Small Church. Nashville, TN: Abingdon Press,
1982.

WINSTONE, Harold, ed. Pastoral Liturgy: A Symposium. London:
Collins, 1975.

World Council of Churches. Commission on Faith and Order.
Gottesdienst in einem säkularistierten Zeitalter. Eine Konsulta-
tion der Kommission für Glauben und Kirchenverfassung des
Okumenischen Rates des Kirchen. In deutscher Sprache mit
eine Vorwort von Lukas Vischer und ein Konsultationsbericht
herausgegeben von Karl Ferdinand Müller. Kassel: Stauda;
Trier: Paulinus-Verlag, 1971.

Worship in the City of Man. Twenty-seventh North American Liturgical Week, Houston, Texas, August 22-25, 1966. Washington,
DC: Liturgical Conference, 1966.

ZIZIOULAS, J. D. "La Communauté eucharistique et la catholicité
de l'Eglise." Istina, 14 (1969): 67-88.

L. GENERAL COLLECTIONS OF LITURGICAL TEXTS

BECKMANN, Joachim. Quellen zur Geschichte des christlichen Gottesdienstes. Gütersloh: Bertelsmann, 1956.

DANIEL, Hermann Adalbert, ed. Codex liturgicus ecclesiae universae in epitomen redactus. 4 vols. Lipsiae: Weigel, 1847-1853;
reprint ed., Hildesheim; Olms, 1966.
1. Codex liturgicus ecclesiae romano-catholicae. 1847.
2. Codex liturgicus ecclesiae lutheranae. 1848.
3. Codex liturgicus ecclesiae reformatae atque anglicanae.
1851.
4. Codex liturgicus ecclesiae orientali. 1853.

FRANCIS, Leslie, and SLEE, Nicola M., eds. A Feast of Words:
An Anthology for Exploring Christian Worship. London: Collins, 1983.

JASPER, R. C. D., and CUMING, G. J., eds. Prayers of the
Eucharist: Early and Reformed. 2d ed. New York: Oxford
University Press, 1980.

LINTON, Arthur, ed. Twenty-Five Consecration Prayers. TCL,
Ser. 3. London: SPCK; New York: Macmillan, 1921.

LODI, Enzo, ed. Enchiridion euchologicum fontium liturgicorum.
BEL, 15. Rome: Edizioni Liturgiche, 1979.

_____. Enchridion euchologicum fontium liturgicorum: clavis
methodologica, cum commentariis selectis. Bononiae: n.p.,
1979. [Companion volume]

Prayers We Have in Common: Agreed Liturgical Texts. Prepared
by the International Consultation on English Texts. 2d revised
ed. Philadelphia, PA: Fortress Press, 1975.

THOMPSON, Bard. Liturgies of the Western Church. Cleveland:
World, 1961; reprint ed., Philadelphia, PA: Fortress Press,
1981.

THURIAN, Max, and WAINWRIGHT, Geoffrey, eds. Baptism and
Eucharist: Ecumenical Convergence in Celebration. Geneva:
World Council of Churches; Grand Rapids, MI: Eerdmans, 1983.

VI. THE LITURGICAL REVIVAL

ALLMEN, J.-J. von. "Theological Frame of a Liturgical Renewal."
Church Quarterly, 2 (1969): 8-23.

ANDREN, C. G. "Tradition och förnyelse: två principer i liturgiskt reformarbete." Svensk Teologisk Kvartalskrift, 45 (1969): 160-167.

ARIES, Philippe, et al. Religion populaire et réforme liturgique. Paris: Cerf, 1975.

The Assisi Papers: Proceedings of the First International Congress of Pastoral Liturgie, Assisi-Rome, Sept. 18-22, 1956. Collegeville, MN: Liturgical Press, 1957.

"Avenir et risques du renouveau liturgique." La Maison-Dieu, 25 (1951). [Special issue]

BEAUDUIN, Lambert. Mélanges liturgiques recueillis parmi les oeuvres de Dom Lambert Beauduin O.S.B. à l'occasion de ses 80 ans (1873-1953). Louvain: Centre liturgique, Abbaye du Mont César, 1954.

_____. La piété de l'église: principes et faits. Louvain: Abbaye du Mont César, 1914; Liturgy: The Life of the Church. 2d ed. Translated by Virgil Michel. PLL, Ser. 1, 1. Collegeville, MN: Liturgical Press, 1929.

BENOIT, Jean D. Liturgical Renewal: Studies in Catholic and Protestant Developments on the Continent. Translated by Edwin Hudson. SMW, 5. London: SCM Press, 1968.

BIERITZ, K. H. "Gottesdienst und Gemeinschaft." Theologische Literaturzeitung, 90 (1965): 739-746.

BIRNBAUM, Walter. Das Kultusproblem und die liturgischen Bewegungen des 20 Jahrhunderts. 2 Bde. Tübingen: Katzmann, 1966-1970.
--1. Die deutsche katholische liturgische Bewegung. 1966.
--2. Die deutsche evangelische liturgische Bewegung. 1970.

BOGLER, Theodor, ed. Liturgische Bewegung nach 50 Jahren: Gesammelte Aufsätze. LH, 24. Maria Laach: Ars Liturgica, 1959.

_____, ed. Liturgische Erneuerung in aller Welt. Maria Laach: Ars Liturgica, 1950.

BOTTE, Bernard. Le mouvement liturgique: témoignage et souvenirs. Paris: Desclée, 1973.

BRAND, Eugene L. "Reflections on the Ecumenical Aspects of the Liturgical Movement." Worship, 51 (1977): 49-55.

BRINER, L. A. "Some Remaining Problems in Liturgical Renewal." McCormick Quarterly, 21 (1968): 325-331.

BROWN, L. W. Relevant Liturgy. London: SPCK; New York:
Oxford University Press, 1965.

BUGNINI, Annibale, ed. Documenta pontificia ad instaurationem
liturgicam spectantia. 2 vols. BEL, sectio practica, 6 & 9.
Rome: Edizioni Liturgiche, 1953-1959.
--1. 1903-1953. 1953.
--2. 1954-1959. 1959.

CAPELLE, Bernard. "Le Saint-Siège et la mouvement liturgique."
Questions liturgiques et paroissiales, 21 (1936): 125-147.

CARLTON, J. W. "New Emphasis on Worship and Liturgy." Review and Expositor, 64 (1967): 309-321.

CLARK, Neville. Call to Worship. SMW, 15. London: SCM
Press, 1960.

CRICHTON, J. D. The Once and Future Liturgy. Dublin: Veritas; New York: Paulist Press, 1977.

DALMAIS, I. H. "Le renouveau liturgique dans le Protestantisme
d'expression française." La Maison-Dieu, 19 (1949): 48-53.

DANIELOU, Jean. "Die liturgische Bewegung seit dem Konzil."
Internationale katholische Zeitschrift, 1 (1974): 1-7.

DAVIES, Horton. "The Art of Adoration: The Modern Liturgical
Movement in Europe." Moravian Theological Seminary Bulletin,
(1963): 1-13.

_____. "The Contemporary Liturgical Movement: Non-Episcopal
Protestantism in England." Encounter, 20 (1959): 257-268.

_____. "The Continental Liturgical Movement in the Roman
Catholic Church." Canadian Journal of Theology, 10 (1964):
148-165.

_____. "Orthodox, Anglican, and Free Church Contributions to
the Liturgical Movement." Canadian Journal of Theology, 10
(1964): 223-236.

DAVIS, Charles. Liturgy and Doctrine: The Doctrinal Basis of
the Liturgical Movement. London: Sheed & Ward, 1960.

DELAMARE, R. La Renaissance liturgique dans les diocèses de
Normandie, 1824-1934: étude historique, essai bibliographique,
revision des propres diocésains. Paris: Picard, 1935.

DIEKMANN, Godfrey. "Is there a Distinct American Contribution to
the Liturgical Renewal?" Worship, 45 (1971): 578-587.

DURIG, Walter. Die Zukunft der liturgischen Erneuerung. Mainz: Grünewald, 1962.

EDWALL, Pehr, HAYMAN, Eric, and MAXWELL, William D., eds. Ways of Worship: The Report of a Theological Commission of Faith and Order. New York: Harper, 1951.

FESTUGIERE, Maurice. La liturgie catholique: essai de synthèse, suivi de quelques développements. Maredsous: Abbaye de Maredsous, 1913.

FISCHER, Henry. Eucharistiekatechese und liturgische Erneuerung: Rückblick und Wegweisung. Düsseldorf: Patmos, 1959.

FISHER, P. "Present-Day Liturgical Renewal: Some Guidelines." Studia Liturgica, 8 (1971-1972): 42-51.

FLANNERY, Austin, ed. The Liturgy: Renewal and Adaptation: Liturgical Reform in the Roman Catholic Church. 7th ed. Dublin: Scepter Books, 1968.

FRERE, Walter Howard. Some Principles of Liturgical Reform. 2d ed. London: John Murray, 1914.

FRERE, Walter Howard. Walter Howard Frere: His Correspondence on Liturgical Revision and Construction. Edited by R. C. D. Jasper. ACC, 39. London: SPCK, 1954.

GAMBER, Klaus. Ritus Modernus: Gesammelte Aufsätze zur Liturgiereform. SPL, 4. Regensburg: Pustet, 1972.

GRANSKOU, D. M. "Historical Critical Exegesis and the Renewal of the Liturgy." Lutheran Quarterly, 19 (1967): 74-86.

GRISBROOKE, W. J. "Liturgical Theology and Liturgical Reform: Some Questions." St. Vladimir's Theological Quarterly, 13 (1969): 212-217.

HAGEMAN, Howard G. "The Coming-of-Age of the Liturgical Movement: Report on Section IV of the Montreal Conference." Studia Liturgica, 2 (1963): 256-265.

_____. "The Liturgical Revival." Theology Today, 6 (1950): 490-505.

HAMMAN, Adalbert. Liturgie et apostolat. EsL, 24. Paris: Cerf, 1964; The Grace to Act Now: Liturgy and the Apostolate in the Light of the Early Christian Centuries. Translated by Malachy Carroll. Chicago: Franciscan Herald Press, 1966.

HAQUIN, André. Dom Lambert Beauduin et le renouveau liturgique. RSSH, 1. Gembloux: Duculot, 1970.

HEILER, Friedrich, ed. "Liturgische Erneuerung der abendländisch-
    en Kirchen." Eine heilige Kirche, Heft II (1955-1956).

HOFER, Albert. Modelle einer pastoralen Liturgie: Vorschlage zur
    Reform. Graz: Styria, 1969.

JAGGER, Peter J. A History of the Parish and People Movement.
    Leighton Buzzard: Faith Press, 1978.

JASPER, R. C. D., ed. The Renewal of Worship: Essays by Mem-
    bers of the Joint Liturgical Group. New York: Oxford Univer-
    sity Press, 1965.

JUNGMANN, Josef A. Liturgische Erneuerung: Rückblick und
    Ausblick. Kevelaer: Butzon & Bercker, 1962; Liturgical Re-
    newal in Retrospect and Prospect. London: Challoner, 1965.

KOENKER, Ernest B. The Liturgical Renaissance in the Roman
    Catholic Church. Chicago: University of Chicago Press, 1954;
    2d ed., St. Louis, MO: Concordia, 1966.

LANGE, Ernst. Chancen des Alltags: Uberlegungen zur Funktion
    des christlichen Gottesdienstes in der Gegenwart. HCW, 8.
    Stuttgart: Verlagsgemeinschaft Burckhardthausund Kreuz-
    Verlag, 1965.

LENGELING, E. J. "Der gegenwärtige Stand der liturgischen Er-
    neuerung im deutschen Protestantismus." Münchener theolo-
    gische Zeitschrift, 10 (1959): 83-101, 200-225.

LESCRAUWAET, J. F. De liturgische beweging onder de Neder-
    landse Hervormden in oecumenisch perspectief: een fenomeno-
    logische en kritische studie. Bussum: Paul Brand, 1957.

McMANUS, Frederick R., ed. The Revival of the Liturgy. New
    York: Herder & Herder, 1963.

MARX, Paul B. Virgil Michel and the Liturgical Movement. Col-
    legeville, MN: Liturgical Press, 1957.

MELAND, Bernard Eugene. Modern Man's Worship: A Search for
    Reality in Religion. New York: Harper, 1934.

MENSCHING, Gustav. Die liturgische Bewegung in der evangelischen
    Kirche. Tübingen: Mohr, 1925.

MITCHELL, Leonel Lake. Liturgical Change: How Much Do We
    Need? New York: Seabury Press, 1975.

MURPHY, John L. The Mass and the Liturgical Reform. Milwaukee,
    WI: Bruce, 1957.

NEUHAUS, R. J. "Has the Liturgical Movement Failed?" Una
   Sancta, 24 (1967): 49-58.

NEUNHEUSER, Burkhard. "Der Beitrag der Liturgie zur theologischen Erneuerung." Gregorianum, 50 (1969): 589-614.

_____. "Die klassische liturgische Bewegung (1909-1963) und
   die nachkonziliare Liturgiereform." In Mélanges liturgiques
   offerts au R. P. Dom Bernard Botte, O.S.B., pp. 401-416.
   Louvain: Abbaye du Mont César, 1972.

NOORDMANS, Oepke. Liturgie. Amsterdam: Uitgeversmaatschappij
   Holland, 1939.

OLSON, O. K. "Contemporary Trends in Liturgy viewed from the
   Perspective of Classical Lutheran Theology." Lutheran Quarterly, 26 (1974): 110-157.

PARSCH, Pius. Volksliturgie: ihr Sinn und Umfang. 2. Aufl.
   Klosterneuberg: Volksliturgisches Apostolat, 1952.

PHIFER, Kenneth G. A Protestant Case for Liturgical Renewal.
   Philadelphia, PA: Westminster Press, 1965.

READ, David H. C. "The Reformation of Worship." Scottish Journal of Theology, 7 (1954): 393-407; 8 (1955): 64-79, 272-287.

RICHARDS, Michael. The Liturgy in England. London: Geoffrey
   Chapman, 1966.

ROBINSON, John A. T. Liturgy Coming to Life. 2d ed. London:
   Mowbray, 1963; Philadelphia, PA: Westminster Press, 1964.

ROUSSEAU, Olivier. Histoire de mouvement liturgique: esquisse
   historique depuis la début du XIXe siècle jusqu'au pontificat de
   Pie X. LO, 3. Paris: Cerf, 1945; The Progress of the Liturgy: An Historical Sketch from the Beginning of the Nineteenth
   Century to the Pontificate of Pius X. Translated by the Benedictines of Westminster Priory, Vancouver, B.C. Westminster,
   MD: Newman Press, 1951.

The Sacerdotal Communities of Saint-Séverin of Paris and Saint-
   Joseph of Nice. Le renouveau liturgique. Paris: Fayard,
   1960; The Liturgical Movement. Translated by Lancelot Sheppard. TCEC, 115. New York: Hawthorn Books, 1964.

SCHMEMANN, Alexander. "Liturgical Theology, Theology of Liturgy, and Liturgical Reform." St. Vladimir's Theological Quarterly, 13 (1969): 217-224.

SCHMIDT, Herman, ed. Liturgy in Transition. Concilium, 62.
   New York: Herder & Herder, 1971.

SEASOLTZ, R. Kevin, ed. The New Liturgy: A Documentation,
    1903-1965. New York: Herder & Herder, 1971.

SHANDS, Alfred R. The Liturgical Movement and the Local Church.
    Rev. ed. London: SCM Press, 1965.

SHEPHERD, Massey H., Jr., ed. The Eucharist and Liturgical
    Renewal. 2d National Liturgical Conference, 1959. New York:
    Oxford University Press, 1960.

_____, ed. The Liturgical Renewal of the Church. 1st National
    Liturgical Conference, 1958. New York: Oxford University
    Press, 1960.

_____, ed. The Liturgical Revival. New York: Oxford Univer-
    sity Press, 1960.

_____. The Reform of Liturgical Worship. New York: Oxford
    University Press, 1961.

SHEPPARD, Lancelot, ed. The People Worship: A History of the
    Liturgical Movement. New York: Hawthorn Books, 1967, c1965.

SKOGLUND, John E. Worship in the Free Churches. Valley Forge,
    PA: Judson Press, 1965.

SRAWLEY, James H. The Liturgical Movement, Its Origin and
    Growth. ACT, 27. London: Mowbray, 1954.

TAYLOR, Michael J., ed. Liturgical renewal in the Christian
    Churches. Baltimore, MD: Helicon, 1967.

_____. The Protestant Liturgical Renewal: A Catholic View-
    point. Westminster, MD: Newman Press, 1963.

THURIAN, Max. "The Present Aims of the Liturgical Movement."
    Studia Liturgica, 3 (1964): 107-114.

TILIANDER, B. F. "Uppgifter och problem för den liturgiska
    förnyelsen i Sydindien." Svensk Missionstidskrift, 55 (1967):
    243-261.

TIMIADIS, E. "Renewal of Orthodox Worship." Studia Liturgica,
    6 (1969): 95-115.

TRAPP, Waldemar. Vorgeschichte und Ursprung der liturgischen
    Bewegung, vorwiegend in Hinsicht auf das deutsche Sprach-
    gebiet. Regensburg: Pustet, 1940.

WAGNER, J. "Le mouvement liturgique en Allemagne (1918-1950)."
    La Maison-Dieu, 24 (1950): 75-82.

WAINWRIGHT, Geoffrey. "Risks and Possibilities of Liturgical Reform." Studia Liturgica, 8 (1971-1972): 65-80.

WINWARD, Stephen F. The Reformation of Our Worship. London:
Carey Kingsgate Press, 1964; Richmond, VA: John Knox
Press, 1965.

"Worship and the Oneness of Christ's Church: Report on Section
IV of the Montreal Conference." Studia Liturgica, 2 (1963):
243-255.

PART TWO:

WORSHIP AND THE LITURGY IN THE
CHRISTIAN TRADITIONS

VII. THE EARLY CHURCH

A. COLLECTED TEXTS

ADAM, Alfred, ed. Zur Geschichte der orientalischen Taufe und
Messe im II. und IV. Jahrhundert. Auf Grund der Auswahl
von Hans Lietzmann neubearbeitet und erweitert von Alfred
Adam. 3. Aufl. Liturgische Texte, 1. KT, 5. Berlin: De
Gruyter, 1960.

BORGIA, Nilo. Frammenti eucaristici antichissimi. Grottaferrata:
Scuola tipografica italo-orientale S. Nilo, 1932.

BRIGHTMAN, F. E., ed. Liturgies Eastern and Western. Vol. 1:
Eastern. Oxford: Clarendon Press, 1896; reprinted 1965.

CABROL, Fernand, and LECLERCQ, Henri, eds. Reliquiae liturgicae vetustissimae ... ab aevo apostolico ad pacem ecclesiae.
2 vols. MEL, 1-2. Paris: Firmin-Didot, 1900-1912.

DEISS, Lucien, ed. Aux sources de la liturgie: textes choisis et
traduits. VT, 3. Paris: Fleurus, 1963; Early Sources of the
Liturgy. Translated by Benet Weatherhead. London: Geoffrey
Chapman; Staten Island, NY: Alba House, 1967.

_____. Hymnes et prières des premiers siècles. VT, 2. Paris:
Fleurus, 1963.

DEISS, Lucien, ed. Printemps de la liturgie: Textes liturgiques
des 4 premiers siècles. Paris: Levain, 1979; Springtime of
the Liturgy: Liturgical Texts of the First Four Centuries.

Translated by Matthew J. O'Connell. Collegeville, MN: Liturgical Press, 1979.

GRANDE, Carlo del. Liturgiae preces, hymni christianorum. Naples: Loffredo, 1934.

HAMMAN, Adalbert, ed. La messe: liturgies anciennes et textes patristiques. LC, 9. Paris: Grasset, 1964; The Mass: Ancient Liturgies and Patristic Texts. English editorial Supervisor: Thomas Holton. APL, 1. Staten Island, NY: Alba House, 1967.

_____, ed. Prières des premiers chrétiens. THS, 6. Paris: Fayard, 1952; Early Christian Prayers. Translated by Walter Mitchell. Chicago: Regnery, 1961.

_____, ed. Prières des premiers chrétiens. Paris: Desclée de Brouwer, 1981.

HANGGI, Anton, and PAHL, Irmgard, eds. Prex eucharistica. Textus e variis liturgiis antiquioribus selecti. SF, 12. Fribourg: Editions universitaires, 1968.

HATCHETT, Marion J. "Seven Pre-Reformation Eucharistic Liturgies: Historic Rites arranged for Contemporary Celebration. A Pre-Nicene Liturgy." St. Luke's Journal of Theology, 16, 3 (1973): 17-26.

Liturgies and Other Documents of the Ante-Nicene Period. Ante-Nicene Christian Library, vol. 24. Edinburgh: T. & T. Clark, 1872.

NEALE, John Mason. The Liturgies of S. Mark, S. James, S. Clement, S. Chrysostom, and the Church of Malabar. Translated with Introduction and Appendices by J. M. Neale. London: J. T. Hayes, 1859; reprint ed., New York: AMS Press, 1969.

_____, ed. The Liturgies of S. Mark, S. James, S. Clement, S. Chrysostom, S. Basil; or according to the Use of the Churches of Alexandria, Jerusalem and Constantinople and the Formula of the Apostolic Constitutions. 4th ed. London: Richard Dickinson, 1896.

NEALE, John M., and LITTLEDALE, R. F., eds. Liturgies of SS. Mark, James, Clement, Chrysostom and Basil and the Church of Malabar. 4th ed. London: J. T. Hayes, 1883.

QUASTEN, Johannes, ed. Monumenta eucharistica et liturgica vetustissima. Collegit, notis et prolegomenis instruit J. Quasten. 7 vols. FP, 7, pars 1-7. Bonn: Hanstein, 1935-1937.

SCHERMANN, Theodor, ed. Die algemeine Kirchenordnung, frühchristliche Liturgien und kirchliche überlieferung. 3 vols.
SGKA, 3. Paderborn: Schöningh, 1914-1916; reprint ed.,
3 vols. New York: Johnson Reprint, 1968.

SOLANO, Jesus. Textos eucaristicos primitivos. 2 vols. 2d ed.
BAC, 88. Madrid: Editorial Catolica, 1978- .

B. GENERAL STUDIES

ADAM, Alfred. Lehrbuch der Dogmengeschichte, vol. 1: Die Zeit
der alten Kirche. Gütersloh: Mohn, 1965.

_____. "Ein vergessener Aspekt des frühchristlichen Herren-
mahles." Theologische Literaturzeitung, 88 (1963): 9-20; reprinted in his Sprache und Dogma, pp. 9-23. Herausgegeben
von Gerhard Ruhbach. Gütersloh: Mohn, 1969.

ALT, Heinrich. Der christliche Cultus nach seinen verschiedenen
Entwicklungsformen und seinen einzelnen Theilen historisch
dargestellt. 2 Bde. 2. Aufl. Berlin: Müller, 1851-1860.

ANDRESEN, Carl. Die Kirchen der alten Christenheit. RM, 29/1-2.
Stuttgart: Kohlhammer, 1971.

ASTORI, Alfredo. L'eucaristia ne primi tre secoli della Chiesa.
Milano: Unione tipografica editrice milanese, 1935.

AUDET, Jean-Paul. "Genre littéraire et formes culturelles de
l'eucharistie 'Nova et Vetera.'" Ephemerides liturgicae, 80
(1966): 353-385.

AUNE, D. E. "The Presence of God in the Community: The Eucharist in its Early Christian Cultic Context." Scottish Journal
of Theology, 29 (1976): 451-459.

BACCHIOCCHI, Samuele. From Sabbath to Sunday: A Historical
Investigation of the Rise of Sunday Observance in Early Christianity. Rome: Pontifical Gregorian University, 1977.

BAUR, Ferdinand Christian. "Die Lehre vom Abendmahl (nach Dr.
L. J. Rückert, Das Abendmahl: Sein Wesen und seine Ge-
schichte in der alten Kirche, 1856)." Theologische Jahrbücher
(Tübingen), 16 (1857): 533-576.

BAUS, Karl. "Die eucharistische Glaubensverkündigung der alten
Kirche in ihren Grundzügen." In Die Messe in der Glaubensverkündigung, pp. 55-70. Herausgegeben von F. X. Arnold
und B. Fischer. 2. Aufl. Freiburg: Herder, 1953.

BETZ, Johannes. "Eucharistie." Handbuch theologischer Gründ-
    begriffe, 1:336-355.

_____. "Eucharistie." Lexikon für Theologie und Kirche (2.
    Aufl.), 3:1142-1147.

_____. Eucharistie: In der Schrift und Patristik. HD, 4/4a.
    Freiburg: Herder, 1979.

BOUR, R. S. "Eucharistie." Dictionnaire de théologie catholique,
    5: 1183-1210.

BOUYER, Louis. "L'improvisation liturgique dans l'église anci-
    enne." La Maison-Dieu, 111 (1972): 7-19.

BRADSHAW, Paul F. "Authority and Freedom in the Early Litur-
    gy." In Authority and Freedom in Liturgy. Edited by Ken-
    neth Stevenson. GLS, 17. Bramcote, Eng.: Grove Books,
    1979.

CIRLOT, Felix L. The Early Eucharist. London: SPCK, 1939.

COKE, Paul T. Mountain and Wilderness: Prayer and Worship in
    the Biblical World and Early Church. New York: Seabury
    Press, 1978.

COPPENS, J. "La célébration eucharistique: ses origines et son
    adaptation." Ephemerides theologicae lovanienses, 50 (1974):
    263-269.

_____. "L'évolution des rites eucharistiques du Nouveau Testa-
    ment au IVe siècle." Ephemerides theologicae lovanienses, 50
    (1974): 269-272.

COTTON, Paul. From Sabbath to Sunday: A Study in Early
    Christianity. Bethlehem, PA: Times Publishing Co., 1933.

DANIELOU, Jean. Message évangélique et culture hellénistique aux
    IIe et IIIe siècle. Histoire des doctrines chrétiennes avant
    Nicée, 2. BT. Paris: Desclée, 1961; Gospel Message and
    Hellenistic Culture. History of Early Christian Doctrine before
    the Council of Nicaea, 2. Translated by James A. Baker.
    Philadelphia, PA: Westminster, 1973.

_____. Théologie du Judéo-Christianisme. Histoire des doctrines
    chrétiennes avant Nicée, 1. BT. Paris: Desclée, 1958; The
    Theology of Jewish Christianity. History of Early Christian
    Doctrine before the Council of Nicaea, 1. Translated by John
    A. Baker. London: Darton, Longman & Todd; Philadelphia,
    PA: Westminster Press, 1964.

DOLGER, Franz Josef. Sol salutis: Gebet und Gesang in christlichen Altertum, mit besonderer Rücksicht auf die Ostung in Gebet und Liturgie. 3. Aufl. LQF, 16-17. Münster: Aschendorff, 1972.

DROWER, Ethel Stefana. Water into Wine: A Study of Ritual Idiom in the Middle East. London: Murray, 1956.

DUGMORE, Clifford W. "The Study of the Origins of the Eucharist: Retrospect and Revaluation." In Studies in Church History, vol. 2, pp. 1-18. Edited by J. G. Cuming. London: Nelson, 1965.

DU TOIT, Andreas B. Der Aspekt der Freude im urchristlichen Abendmahl. Winterthur: Keller, 1965.

ELERT, Werner. Abendmahl und Kirchengemeinschaft in der alten Kirche hauptsächlich des Ostens. Berlin: Lutherisches Verlagshaus, 1954; Eucharist and Church Fellowship in the First Four Centuries. Translated by N. E. Nagel. St. Louis, MO: Concordia, 1966.

FISCHER, Balthasar. "The Common Prayer of Congregation and Family in the Ancient Church." Studia Liturgica, 10 (1974): 106-124.

FUCHS, Ernst. Das urchristliche Sakramentsverständnis: Vorlesungen. KSWS, 8. Bad Canstadt: Müllerschön, 1958?

FULLER, Reginald H. "The Double Origin of the Eucharist." Biblical Research, 8 (1963): 60-72.

GAMBER, Klaus. Sacrificium Missae: zum Opferverständnis und zur Liturgie der Frühkirche. SPL, 9. Regensburg: Pustet, 1980.

GELINEAU, Joseph. "Tradition--Invention--Culture." In Liturgy: A Creative Tradition, pp. 10-18. Edited by Mary Collins and David Power. Concilium, 162. New York: Seabury Press, 1983.

GOGUEL, Maurice. L'eucharistie des origines à Justin Martyr. Paris: Fischbacher, 1910; The Eucharist from the Beginning to the Time of Justin Martyr. Translated by Charles Porter Coffin. Evanston, IL, 1933.

GOLTZ, Eduard Alexander. Tischgebete und Abendmahlsgebete in der altchristlichen und der griechischen Kirche. TUGAL, 29 (n.F. 14), 2b. Leipzig: Hinrichs, 1905.

GOOSENS, Werner. Les origines de l'eucharistie sacrement et sacrifice. Paris: Beauchesne, 1931.

GRASS, Hans. "Abendmahl II: Dogmengeschichte." Die Religion in Geschichte und Gegenwart (3. Aufl.), 1:21-34.

HAHN, Ferdinand. "Abendmahl." Praktisch theologisches Handbuch, pp. 25-26, 26-34.

_____. "Die alttestamentliche Motive in der urchristlichen Abendmahlsüberlieferung." Evangelische Theologie, 27 (1967): 337-374.

_____. Der urchristliche Gottesdienst. SB, 41. Stuttgart: Verlag Katholisches Bibelwerk, 1970; The Worship of the Early Church. Translated by David Green. Edited with Introduction by John Reumann. Philadelphia, PA: Fortress Press, 1973.

_____. "Zum Stand der Erforschung des urchristlichen Herrenmahls." Evangelische Theologie, 35 (1975): 553-563.

HAHN, Wilhelm Traugott. Gottesdienst und Opfer Christi. VEGL, 5. Berlin: Evangelische Verlagsanstalt, 1951.

HAMMAN, Adalbert. "De la célébration eucharistique à la vie quotidienne dans l'antiquité chrétienne." Parole et pain, 8 (1971): 296-302.

_____. "Liturgie, prière et famille dans les trois premiers siècle chrétiens." Questions liturgiques, 57 (1976): 81-98.

HANSON, R. P. C. "Eucharistic Offering in the Early Church." Proceedings of the Royal Irish Academy, 76 (1976): 75-95.

_____. "The Liberty of the Bishop to Improvise Prayer in the Eucharist." Vigiliae Christianae, 15 (1961): 173-176.

HARNACK, Theodosius. Der christliche Gemeindegottesdienst im apostolischen und altkatholischen Zeitalter. Erlangen: Bläsing, 1854; reprint ed., Amsterdam: Rodopi, 1969.

HARRELSON, Walter J. From Fertility Cult to Worship. Garden City, NY: Doubleday, 1969.

HEITMULLER, Wilhelm. Taufe und Abendmahl im Urchristentum. RVDCG, 22-23. Tübingen: Mohr (P. Siebeck), 1911.

JONES, Bayard H. "The Quest for the Origins of the Christian Liturgies." Anglican Theological Review, 46 (1964): 5-21.

JUNGMANN, Josef Andreas. The Early Liturgy to the Time of Gregory the Great. Translated by Francis A. Brunner. LS,6. Notre Dame, IN: University of Notre Dame Press, 1959.

KAHLEFELD, Heinrich. Das Abschiedsmahl Jesu und die Eucharistie der Kirche. Frankfurt am Main: Knecht, 1980.

KILMARTIN, Edward J. The Eucharist in the Primitive Church.
Englewood Cliffs, NJ: Prentice-Hall, 1965.

KLAUCK, Hans-Josef. Hausgemeinde und Hauskirche im frühen
Christentum. SBS, 103. Stuttgart: Verlag katholisches Bibelwerk, 1981.

KNELLER, C. "Sacramentum unitatis." Zeitschrift für katholische
Theologie, 40 (1916): 676-703.

KOTTJE, Raymond. "Das Aufkommen der täglichen Eucharistiefeier
in der Weltkirche und die Zölibatsforderung." Zeitschrift für
Kirchengeschichte, 82 (1971): 218-228.

KRETSCHMAR, Georg. "Die Bedeutung der Liturgiegeschichte für
die Frage nach der Kontinuität des Judenchristentums in nacha-
postolischer Zeit." In Aspects du Judéo-christianisme, Colloque
de Strasbourg, 23-25 avril 1964, pp. 113-137. Paris: Presses
universitaires de France, 1965.

_____. Studien zur frühchristlichen Trinitätstheologie. BHT,
21. Tübingen: Mohr, 1956.

LAMPE, G. W. H. "The Eucharist in the Thought of the Early
Church." In Eucharistic Theology Then and Now, pp. 34-58.
London: SPCK, 1968.

LEIPOLDT, Johannes. Der Gottesdienst der ältesten Kirche. Leipzig: Dorffling & Franke, 1937.

LENGELING, Emil-Josef. "Ordnung und Freiheit in der Liturgie der
frühen Kirche." In Einheit in Vielfalt, pp. 52-74. Herausgegeben von Wilhelm Ernst und Konrad Feiereis. Leipzig: St.
Benno-Verlag, 1974.

LIETZMANN, Hans. "Der altchristliche Gottesdienst." In his
Kleine Schriften, Bd. 3, pp. 28-42. Herausgegeben von der
Kommission für spätantike Religionsgeschichte. Berlin:
Akademie-Verlag, 1962.

_____. "Die Entstehung der christlichen Liturgie nach den ältes-
ten Quellen." In his Kleine Schriften, Bd. 3, pp. 3-27. Herausgegeben von der Kommission für spätantike Religionsgeschichte. Berlin: Akademie-Verlag, 1962.

_____. Messe und Herrenmahl. AK, 8. Bonn: Marcus &
Weber, 1926; Mass and Lord's Supper. Translated by Dorothea
H. G. Reeve. Issued in 7 fascicles. Leiden: Brill, 1953;

reprint ed., with introduction and further inquiry by Robert
Douglas Richardson. Leiden: Brill, 1979.

_____. Messe und Herrenmahl. 3. Aufl. AK, 8. Berlin: De
Gruyter, 1955.

LIGIER, Louis. "De la cêne de Jésus à l'anaphore de l'Eglise."
La Maison-Dieu, 87 (1966): 7-51; "From the Last Supper to the
Eucharist." In The New Liturgy, pp. 113-150. Edited by
Lancelot Sheppard. London: Darton, Longman & Todd, 1970.

_____. Péché d'Adam et péché du monde: Bible, Kippour, Eu-
charistie. 2 vols. Théologie, 43. Paris: Aubier, 1960-1961.

LOHMEYER, Ernst. "Das Abendmahl in der Urgemeinde." Journal
of Biblical Literature, 56 (1937): 217-253.

_____. "Vom christlichen Abendmahl." Theologische Rundschau,
n.F. 9 (1937): 168-227, 237-312; 10 (1938): 81-99.

MacDONALD, Alexander B. Christian Worship in the Primitive
Church. Edinburgh: T. & T. Clark, 1934.

MacGREGOR, George H. C. Eucharistic Origins. Glasgow: J.
Clarke, 1929.

MOLONEY, R. "The Early Eucharist: An Hypothesis of Development." Irish Theological Quarterly, 45 (1978): 167-176.

MOSNA, Corrado S. Storia della domenica dalle origini fino agli
inizi de V secolo. AG, 1970. Rome: Libreria editrice dell'
Universita gregoriana, 1969.

PERROT, Charles. "Worship in the Primitive Church." In Liturgy:
A Creative Tradition, pp. 3-9. Edited by Mary Collins and
David Power. Concilium, 162. New York: Seabury Press,
1983.

PETERSON, Erik. Frühkirche, Judentum und Gnosis: Studien und
Untersuchungen. Rome: Herder, 1959.

PROBST, Ferdinand. Lehre und Gebet in den drei ersten christlichen Jahrhunderten. Tübingen: Laupp, 1871.

_____. Liturgie der drei ersten christlichen Jahrhunderts.
Tübingen: Laupp, 1870; reprint ed., Darmstadt: Wissenschaftliche Buchgesellschaft, 1968.

_____. Liturgie des vierten Jahrhunderts und deren Reform.
Münster: Aschendorff, 1893.

RAUSCHEN, Gerhard. Eucharistie und Busssakrament in den ersten sechs Jahrhunderten der Kirche. 2. Aufl. Freiburg:
Herder, 1910; Eucharist and Penance in the First Six Centuries
of the Church. Authorized translation. St. Louis, MO: B.
Herder, 1913.

REICKE, Bo. Diakonie, Festfreude und Zelos, in Verbindung mit
der altchristlichen Agapenfeier. UUA, 5. Uppsala: Lund-
quistska bokhandeln, 1951.

RICHARDSON, R. D. "Eastern and Western Liturgies: The Primitive Basis of their Later Differences." Harvard Theological Review, 42 (1949): 125-148.

RORDORF, Willy. Der Sonntag: Geschichte des Ruhe- und Gottesdiensttages im ältesten Christentum. ATANT, 43. Zürich:
Zwingli Verlag, 1962; Sunday: The History of the Day of Rest
and Worship in the Earliest Centuries of the Christian Church.
Translated by A. A. K. Graham. Philadelphia, PA: Westminster Press; London: SCM Press, 1968.

RUCKERT, Leopold Immanuel. Das Abendmahl: sein Wesen und
seine Geschichte in der alten Kirche. Lepzig: Brockhaus,
1856.

SCHERER, Pedro F. "Creative Improvisation, Oral and Written, in
the First Centuries of the Church." In Liturgy: A Creative
Tradition, pp. 29-37. Edited by Mary Collins and David Power.
Concilium, 162. New York: Seabury Press, 1983.

SCHOUSBOE, J. "La messe la plus ancienne: recherches sur les
origines du christianisme." Revue d'histoire des religions, 96
(1927): 193-256.

SCHURMANN, H. "Abendmahl." Lexikon für Theologie und Kirche
(2. Aufl.) 1:26-31.

SCHUERMANS, Marie Philippe. Parole de Dieu et rite sacramentel:
étude critique des antiennes de communion néotestamentaires.
Brussels: Lumen Vitae, 1963.

SHEPHERD, Massey H., Jr. "The Origin of the Church's Liturgy."
Studia Liturgica, 1 (1962): 83-100.

SRAWLEY, James H. The Early History of the Liturgy. 2d ed.
CHLS. Cambridge: Cambridge University Press, 1947.

_____. "Eucharist--To the End of the Middle Ages." Encyclo-
pedia of Religion and Ethics, 5:540-634.

VOLKER, Karl. Mysterium und Agape: die gemeinsamen Mahlzeiten
in der alten Kirche. Gotha: L. Klotz, 1927.

WARREN, F. E. The Liturgy and Ritual of the Ante-Nicene
    Church. 2d rev. ed. London: SPCK, 1912; reprint ed.,
    New York: AMS Press, 1973.

WERNER, Eric. The Sacred Bridge: The Interdependence of Lit-
    urgy and Music in the Synagogue and Church during the First
    Millenium. New York: Columbia University Press, 1959; re-
    print ed., New York: Da Capo Press, 1979; abridged ed.,
    New York: Schocken Books, 1970.

WETTER, Gillis P. Altchristliche Liturgien. 2 Bde. FRLANT, 30
    & 34 (n.F. 13 & 17). Göttingen: Vandenhoeck & Ruprecht,
    1921-1922.
    1. Das christliche Mysterium. 1921.
    2. Das christliche Opfer. 1922.

WIEFEL, Wolfgang. "Erwägungen zur soziologischen Hermeneutik
    urchristlichen Gottesdienstformen." Kairos, 14 (1972): 36-51.

WOOLEY, Reginald M. The Liturgy of the Primitive Church. Cam-
    bridge: Cambridge University Press, 1910.

C. STUDIES OF EARLY LITURGICAL ELEMENTS

1. Liturgy of the Word

ASTING, Ragnar Kristian. Der Verkündigung des Wortes im Ur-
    christentum. Stuttgart: Kohlhammer, 1939.

BAUER, Walter. Der Wortgottesdienst der ältesten Christen.
    SGVS, 148. Tübingen: Mohr, 1930.

SCHLIER, Heinrich. "Die Verkündigung im Gottesdienst der
    Kirche." In his Die Zeit der Kirche: Exegetische Aufsätze
    und Vorträge, pp. 244-265. 5. Aufl. Freiburg: Herder,
    1972.

URNER, Hans. Die ausserbiblische Lesung im christlichen Gottes-
    dienst: ihre Vorgeschichte und Geschichte bis zur Zeit Augus-
    tins. VEGL, 6. Göttingen: Vandenhoeck & Ruprecht, 1952.

2. Eucharistic Prayers

BOULEY, Allan. From Freedom to Formula: The Evolution of the
    Eucharistic Prayer from Oral Improvisation to Written Texts.
    SCA, 21. Washington, DC: Catholic University of America
    Press, 1980.

BOUYER, Louis. "The Different Forms of Eucharistic Prayer and

Their Genealogy." In Studia Patristica, vol. 8, pp. 156-170.
Edited by F. L. Cross. TUGAL, 93. Berlin: Akademie-
Verlag, 1966.

CLERCK, Paul de. La "Prière universelle" dans les liturgies latines
anciennes: témoignages patristiques et textes liturgiques.
LQF, 62. Münster: Aschendorff, 1977.

DAHL, Nils A. "Anamnesis: mémoire et commémoration dans le
christianisme primitif." Studia Theologica (Lund), 1 (1948):
69-95.

DIX, Gregory. "The Origins of the Epiclesis." Theology, 28
(1936): 125-137, 187-202.

_____. "Primitivie Consecration Prayers." Theology, 37 (1938):
261-283.

FRERE, Walter H. The Anaphora; or Great Eucharistic Prayer.
CHS. London: SPCK; New York: Macmillan, 1938.

GAMBER, Klaus. Sacrificium laudis: zur Geschichte des frühchristlichen Eucharistiegebet. SPL, 5. Regensburg: Pustet,
1980.

_____. "Zur Geschichte des frühchristlichen Eucharistiegebetes."
Heiliger Dienst, 26 (1972): 149-163.

KILMARTIN, Edward J. "Sacrificium laudis: Content and Function
of Early Eucharistic Prayers." Theological Studies, 35 (1974):
268-287.

LIGIER, Louis. Magnae orationis eucharisticae seu anaphorae origo
et significatio. (Ad usum privatum.) Rome, 1964.

_____. "Les origines de la prière eucharistique de la cêne du
Seigneur à l'eucharistie." Questions liturgiques, 53 (1972):
181-201; "The Origins of the Eucharistic Prayer: From the
Last Supper to the Eucharist." Studia Liturgica, 9 (1973):
161-185.

McKENNA, J. H. Eucharist and Holy Spirit: The Eucharistic Epi-
clesis in Twentieth Century Theology (1900-1966). ACC, 57.
Great Wakering, Eng.: Published for the Alcuin Club by
Mayhew-McCrimmon, 1975.

MICHELL, Gilbert Arthur. Eucharistic Consecration in the Primitive
Church. London: SPCK, 1948.

NEWNS, Brian. "The Origins of the Eucharistic Prayer." The
Clergy Review, 54 (1969): 373-379.

N. L. K. "De evolutione precis eucharisticae conspectus historicus." Notitiae, 84 (June 1973): 214-220.

RATCLIFF, E. C. "The Sanctus and the Pattern of the Early Anaphora." Journal of Ecclesiastical History, 1 (1950): 29-36,
125-134; reprinted in his Liturgical Studies of E. C. Ratcliff,
pp. 18-40. Edited by A. H. Couratin and D. J. Tripp. London: SPCK, 1976.

TALLEY, Thomas J. "The Eucharistic Prayer of the Ancient Church
according to Recent Research: Results and Reflections."
Studia Liturgica, 11 (1976): 138-158.

WERNER, Eric. "The Genesis of the Liturgical Sanctus." In Essays Presented to Egon Wellesz, pp. 19-32. Edited by J.
Westrup. Oxford: Clarendon Press, 1966.

3. Creeds

CULLMANN, Oscar. Les premières confessions de foi chrétiennes.
2. éd. CRHPR, 30. Paris: Presses universitaires de France,
1948; The Earliest Christian Confessions. Translated by
J. K. S. Reid. London: Lutterworth Press, 1949.

KELLY, J. N. D. Early Christian Creeds. 3d ed. London: Longmans; New York: McKay, 1972.

RORDORF, Willy. "La confession de foi et son 'Sitz im Leben' dans
l'Eglise ancienne." Novum Testamentum, 9 (1967): 225-238.

4. Hymns

DEICHGRABER, Reinhard. Gotteshymnus und Christushymnus in
der frühen Christenheit. SUNT, 5. Göttingen: Vandenhoeck
& Ruprecht, 1967.

JORNS, Klaus-Peter. Das hymnische Evangelium: Untersuchungen
zu Aufbau, Funktion und Herkunft der hymnischen Stücke in
der Johannesoffenbarung. SNT, 5. Gütersloh: Mohn, 1971.

KROLL, Josef. Die christliche Hymnodik bis zu Klemens von Alex-
andreia. Konigsberg: Hartungsche Buchdruckerei, 1921; reprint ed., Darmstadt: Wissenschaftliche Buchgesellschaft, 1968.

LIGIER, Louis. "L'hymne christologique de Philippiens 2, 6-11, la
liturgie eucharistique et la bénédiction synagogale 'Nishmat kol
hay.'" Analecta biblica, 18 (1963): 161-185.

MARTIN, Ralph P. Carmen Christi: Philippians 2:5-11 in Recent

Interpretation and in the Setting of Early Christian Worship.
SNTSM, 4. London: Cambridge University Press, 1967.

SANDERS, Jack T. The New Testament Christological Hymns.
Cambridge: Cambridge University Press, 1971.

SCHILLE, Gottfried. Frühchristliche Hymnen. Berlin: Evangelische Verlagsanstalt, 1965.

STANLEY, David M. "Carmenque Christo quasi Deo Dicere."
Catholic Biblical Quarterly, 20 (1958): 173-191.

THOMPSON, Leonard. "Hymns in Early Christian Worship." Anglican Theological Review, 55 (1973): 458-472.

WENGST, Klaus. Christologische Formeln und Lieder des Urchrist-
entums. SNT, 7. Gütersloh: Gütersloher Verlagshaus, 1972.

5. Other Liturgical Texts

CAPELLE, Bernard. "Le texte du Gloria in excelsis." Revue d'histoire ecclésiastique, 44 (1949): 439-457.

LEBRETON, J. "La forme primitive du Gloria in excelsis, prière au
Christ, ou prière à Dieu le Père?" Recherches de science religieuse, 13 (1923): 322-329.

RORDORF, Willy. "The Lord's Prayer in the Light of Its Liturgical
Use in the Early Church." Studia Liturgica, 14 (1980): 1-19.

UNNIK, W. C. van. "Dominus Vobiscum: The Background of a
Liturgical Formula." In New Testament Essays: Studies in
Memory of Thomas Walter Manson, pp. 270-305. Edited by
A. J. B. Higgins. Manchester: Manchester University Press,
1959.

D. JEWISH BACKGROUND AND INFLUENCE

ANDREASEN, Niels Erik A. The Old Testament Sabbath: A Tradi-
tion-Historical Investigation. SBLD, 7. Missoula, MT: Society
of Biblical Literature, 1972.

ARON, Robert. "Les origines juives du Pater." La Maison-Dieu,
85 (1966): 36-40.

ASHKENASY, Y. "La Pâque juive." Questions liturgiques et
paroissiales, 52 (1971): 141-153.

AUDET, Jean-Paul. "Esquisse historique du genre littéraire de la
  'bénédiction' juive et de l' 'eucharistie' chrétienne." Revue
  biblique, 65 (1958): 371-399.

BAIER, W. "Liturgie und Kult in der frühjüdischen und frühchristlichen Welt und Umwelt (etwa 200 v.--200 n. Chr.)."
  Archiv für Liturgiewissenschaft, 13 (1971): 282-295; 14 (1972):
  218-252; 16 (1974): 206-244.

BARROSSE, Thomas. "The Passover and the Paschal Meal." In
  The Breaking of Bread, pp. 23-24. Concilium, 40. New York:
  Paulist Press, 1969.

BAUMSTARK, Anton. "Trishagion und Qeduscha." Jahrbuch für
  Liturgiewissenschaft, 3 (1923): 18-32.

BICKELL, Gustav. Messe und Pascha: der apostolische Ursprung
  der Messliturgie und ihr geneuer Anschluss an die Einsetzungs-
  feier der heilige Eucharistie durch Christus aus dem Pascharitual
  nachgewiesen. Mainz, 1872; The Lord's Supper and the Passover Ritual. Translated by W. F. Skene. Edinburgh: T. &
  T. Clark, 1891.

BOER, Pieter Arie Hendrik de. Gedenken und Gedächtnis in der
  Welt des Alten Testaments. Stuttgart: Kohlhammer, 1962.

BOX, G. H. "The Jewish Antecedents of the Eucharist." Journal
  of Theological Studies, 3 (1902): 357-369.

BROCKE, Michael, and PETUCHOWSKI, Jakob L., eds. The Lord's
  Prayer and Jewish Liturgy. New York: Seabury Press, 1978.

CAZELLES, H. "Eucharistie, bénédiciton et sacrifice dans l'Ancien
  Testament." La Maison-Dieu, 123 (1975): 7-28.

CROSS, F. L. "Berakah." Oxford Dictionary of the Christian
  Church, p. 158.

DANIELOU, Jean. "Les répas de la Bible et leur signification."
  La Maison-Dieu, 18 (1948): 7-33.

DREYFUS, Robert. "Liturgie domestique juive." Questions liturgiques et paroissiales, 52 (1971): 111-119.

DUGMORE, Clifford W. The Influence of the Synagogue upon the
  Divine Office. London: Oxford University Press, 1944; reprint ed., Westminster, MD: Faith Press, 1964.

EATON, J. H. Vision in Worship: The Relation of Prophecy and
  Liturgy in the Old Testament. London: SPCK, 1981.

ELBOGEN, Ismar. Der jüdische Gottesdienst in seiner geschichtlichen Entwicklung. Leipzig: Fock, 1913; reprint ed., 4.
Aufl. Hildesheim: Olms, 1962.

FINKELSTEIN, Louis. "The birkat ha-mazon." Jewish Quarterly
Review, 19 (1928-1929): 211-262.

GAMBER, Klaus. "Anklänge an das Eucharistiegebet bei Paulus und
das jüdische Kiddusch." Ostkirchliche Studien, 9 (1960): 254-
264.

GAVIN, Frank S. B. Jewish Antecedents of the Christian Sacraments. New York: Macmillan, 1928; reprint ed., New York:
Ktav Publishing House, 1969.

GESE, Hartmut. "Ps 22 und das Neue Testament: Der älteste
Bericht vom Tode Jesu und die Entstehung des Herrenmahles."
Zeitschrift für Theologie und Kirche, 65 (1968): 1-22; re-
printed in his Vom Sinai zum Zion, pp. 180-201. BET, 64.
München: Kaiser, 1974.

GIRAUDO, Cesare. La struttura letteraria della preghiera eucaristica: saggio sulla genesi letteraria di una forma: Toda vetero-
testamentario, Beraka giudaica, Anafora cristiana. ABib, 92.
Rome: Biblical Institute Press, 1981.

GRANT, Frederick C. "Modern Studies of the Jewish Liturgy."
Zeitschrift für alttestamentliche Wissenschaft, 65 (n.F. 24)
(1953): 59-77.

GRELOT, P. "Du sabbat juif au dimanche chrétien." La Maison-
Dieu, 123 (1975): 79-107; 124 (1975): 14-54.

_____. "God's Presence and Man's Communion with Him in the
Old Testament." In The Breaking of Bread, pp. 7-22. Edited
by P. Benoit, R. Murphy and B. van Iersel. Concilium, 40.
New York: Paulist Press, 1969.

GUILDING, Aileen. The Fourth Gospel and Jewish Worship. Oxford: Clarendon Press, 1960.

HEDEGARD, David, ed. Seder R. Amram Gaon, Part I: Hebrew
Text with Critical Apparatus, Translation with Notes and Introduction. Lund: Lindstedts Universitets-Bokhandel, Gleerup,
1951. (See also KRONHOLM below.)

HELLWIG, Monika K. "The Christian Eucharist in Relation to Jewish Worship." Journal of Ecumenical Studies, 13 (1976): 322-
328.

HENGEL, Martin. "Proseuche und Synagoge: Jüdische Gemeinde,

Gotteshaus und Gottesdienst in der Diaspora und in Palästina."
In Tradition und Glaube: Festgabe für K. G. Kuhn, pp. 157-
184. Herausgegeben von G. Jeremias, H.-W. Kuhn and H.
Stegemann. Göttingen: Vandenhoeck & Ruprecht, 1971.

HENRIX, Hans Hermann, ed. Jüdische Liturgie: Geschichte,
Struktur, Wesen. QD, 86. Freiburg: Herder, 1979.

HOFFMAN, Lawrence A. The Canonization of the Synagogue Service. SJCA, 4. Notre Dame, IN: University of Notre Dame
Press, 1979.

HRUBY, K. "La 'Birkat ha-mazon'--la prière de grâce après le
repas." In Mélanges liturgiques offerts au R. P. Dom Bernard
Botte, pp. 205-222. Louvain: Abbaye du Mont César, 1972.

_____. "La notion de 'berakah' dans la tradition et son caractère
anamnétique." Questions liturgiques, 52 (1971): 155-170.

JENNI, Ernst. Die theologische Begründung des Sabbatgebots im
Alten Testament. TS, 46. Zollikon-Zürich: Evangelischer
Verlag, 1956.

JOUASSARD, G. "Aperçu sur l'importance de l'Ancien Testament
dans la vie liturgique des premiers siècles chrétiens." Revue
des études byzantines, 16 (1958): 104-115.

KRAUS, Hans Joachim. "Gottesdienst im alten und im neuen Bund."
Evangelische Theologie, 25 (1965): 171-206.

_____. Gottesdienst in Israel. 2. Aufl. BET, 19. Munich:
Kaiser, 1962; Worship in Israel. Translated by Geoffrey Buswell. Richmond, VA: John Knox Press, 1966.

KRETSCHMAR, Georg. "Die Bedeutung der Liturgiegeschichte für
die Frage nach der Kontinuität des Judenchristentums in nacha-
postolischer Zeit." In Aspects du judéo-christianisme, pp. 113-
136. Paris: Presses universitaires de France, 1965.

KRONHOLM, Tryggve, ed. Sedar R. Amram Gaon, Part II: The
Order of Sabbath Prayer. Lund: Lindstedts Universitets-
Bokhandel, Gleerup, 1974.

KUHN, Karl Georg. Achtzehngebet und Vaterunser und der Reim.
WUNT, 1. Tübingen: Mohr, 1950.

LE DEAUT, Robert. Liturgie juive et Nouveau Testament, le
témoignage des versions araméenes. SPIB, 115. Rome: Institut Biblique Pontifical, 1965.

LERLE, Ernst. "Liturgische Reformen des Synagogengottesdienstes

als Antwort auf die judenchristliche Mission des ersten Jahrhunderts." Novum Testamentum, 10 (1968): 31-42.

LEVY, Isaac. The Synagogue: Its History and Function. London:
Valentine, Mitchell, 1963.

LIGIER, Louis. "Le bénédiction hebraica seu 'berakah' et anaphora
christiana." Notitiae, 84 (1973): 221-224.

MILLER, Patrick D., Jr. "Enthroned on the Praises of Israel: The
Praise of God in Old Testament Theology." Interpretation, 39
(1985): 5-19.

MILLGRAM, Abraham K. Jewish Worship. 2d ed. Philadelphia,
PA: Jewish Publication Society of America, 1975.

NAKARAI, T. W. "Worship in the Old Testament." Encounter, 34
(1973): 282-286.

OESTERLEY, William O. E. The Jewish Background of the Christian
Liturgy. Oxford: Clarendon Press, 1925.

_____, and BOX, George H. The Religion and Worship of the
Synagogue. New York: Scribner, 1907.

OTTO, Eckart, and SCHRAMM, Tim. Fest und Freude. Stuttgart:
Kohlhammer, 1977; Festival and Joy: Sources and Forms of Joy
in Judaism and Early Christianity. Translated by James L.
Blevins. BE. Nashville, TN: Abingdon Press, 1980.

PETERSON, Erik. "Die geschichtliche Bedeutung der jüdischen
Gebetsrichtung." Theologische Zeitung, 3 (1947): 1-15; re-
printed in his Frühkirche, Judentum und Gnosis, pp. 1-14.
Rome: Herder, 1959.

PRICE, C. P. "Jewish Morning Prayers and Early Christian Anaphoras." Anglican Theological Review, 43 (1961): 153-168.

RANKIN, O. S. "The Extent of the Influence of the Synagogue
upon Christian Worship." Journal of Jewish Studies, 1 (1948-
1949): 27-32.

RICHARDSON, R. D. "Berakah and Eucharistia." Church Quarterly Review, 148 (1949): 194-220.

ROGERS, V. M. "Some Reflections on Worship in the Old Testament." Reformed Review, 30 (1977): 190-197.

ROUILLARD, Philippe. "La lecture de l'Ecriture dans la liturgie
juive et les traditions occidentales." Paroisse et liturgie, 51
(1969): 483-497.

ROWLEY, H. H. Worship in Ancient Israel: Its Forms and Meaning. London: SPCK; Philadelphia, PA: Fortress Press, 1967.

SEGAL, Judah Benzion. The Hebrew Passover from the Earliest Times to A.D. 70. LOS, 12. London: Oxford University Press, 1963.

STAERK, W., ed. Altjüdische liturgische Gebete. 2. Aufl. KT, 58. Berlin: De Gruyter, 1930.

TALLEY, Thomas J. "From Berakah to Eucharistia: A Reopening Question." Worship, 50 (1976): 115-137.

TESTA, E. "Influssi giudeo-cristiani nella liturgia eucaristica della Chiesa primitiva." In Studia Hierosolymitana, in onore di P. Bellarmino Bagatti, vol. 2, pp. 192-225. Jerusalem: Franciscan Printing Press, 1976.

VOS, Clarence J. Woman in Old Testament Worship. Delft: Judels & Brinkman, 1968?

E. NEW TESTAMENT

(See also VII. A-D above.)

AALEN, Sverre. "Das Abendmahl als Opfermahl im Neuen Testament." Novum Testamentum, 6 (1963): 128-152.

ALLMEN, Jean-Jacques van. "Some Notes on the Lord's Supper." Study Encounter, 2 (1966): 54-56.

ARNOLD, August. Der Ursprung des christlichen Abendmahls. 2. Aufl. FTS, 45. Freiburg: Herder, 1939.

AUDET, J. P. "Literary Forms and Content of a Normal eucharistia in the First Century." In Studia Evangelica, pp. 643-662. Edited by Kurt Aland, F. L. Cross, Jean Daniélou, Harald Riesenfeld, and W. C. van Unnik. Berlin: Akademie-Verlag, 1959.

BACIOCCHI, J. de. "Le mystère eucharistique dans les perspectives de la Bible." Nouvelle revue théologique, 77 (1955): 561-580.

BAIRD, William. "The Problem of Worship." In his The Corinthian Church: A Biblical Approach to Urban Culture, pp. 119-158. New York: Abingdon Press, 1964.

BEHM, Johannes. "Klao, etc." Theologische Wörterbuch des Neuen

Testament, 3:726-743; "Klao, etc." Theological Dictionary of
the New Testament, 3:726-743.

BENOIT, Pierre. "Le récit de la cène dans Lc. xxii, 15-20." Revue biblique, 48 (1939): 357-393.

BENOIT, Pierre, MURPHY, Roland E., and IERSEL, Bastiaan van,
eds. The Breaking of Bread. Concilium, 40. New York:
Paulist Press, 1969.

BERNAS, C. "Eucharist (Biblical Data)." New Catholic Encyclopedia, 5:594-599.

_____. "Last Supper." New Catholic Encyclopedia, 8:991.

BETZ, Johannes. "Der Abendmahlskelch im Judenchristentum." In
Abhandlungen über Theologie und Kirche: Festschrift für Karl
Adam, pp. 109-137. Herausgegeben von Marcel Reding. Düs-
seldorf: Patmos-Verlag, 1952.

BILLERBECK, Paul. "Ein Synagogengottesdienst in Jesu Tagen."
Zeitschrift für die neutestamentliche Wissenschaft, 55 (1964):
143-161.

_____. "Ein Tempelgottesdienst in Jesu Tagen." Zeitschrift
für die neutestamentliche Wissenschaft, 55 (1964): 1-17.

BORNKAMM, Gunther. "Herrenmahl und Kirche bei Paulus." In
his Studien zu Antike und Urchristentum, pp. 138-176. Munich:
Kaiser, 1959; "Lord's Supper and Church in Paul." In his
Early Christian Experience, pp. 123-160. London: SCM Press,
1969.

BROCKHAUS, Ulrich. Charisma und Amt: Die paulinische Charis-
menlehre auf dem Hintergrund der frühchristlichen Gemeinde-
funktionen. Wuppertal: Theologischer Verlag Rolf Brockhaus,
1972.

BUCHANAN, George Wesley. "Worship, Feasts and Ceremonies in
the Early Jewish-Christian Church." New Testament Studies,
26 (1979-1980): 279-297.

CARSON, D. A., ed. From Sabbath to Lord's Day: A Biblical,
Historical and Theological Investigation. Grand Rapids, MI:
Eerdmans, 1982.

COGGAN, F. D. The Prayers of the New Testament. New York:
Harper & Row, 1967; Washington, DC: Corpus Books, 1968.

CONZELMANN, Hans. "Christus im Gottesdienst der neutestamentlichen Zeit." In Bild und Verkundigung: Festgabe für Hanna

Jursch zum 60. Geburtstag, pp. 21-30. Berlin: Evangelische
Verlagsanstalt, 1962.

COOKE, Bernard. "Synoptic Presentation of the Eucharist as a
Covenant Sacrifice." Theological Studies, 21 (1960): 1-44.

COPPENS, J. "L'eucharistie des temps apostoliques." Ephemerides
theologicae Lovanienses, 53 (1977): 192-201.

COURATIN, A. H. "The Sacrifice of Praise: The Church's Thanksgiving in New Testament Times." Theology, 58 (1955): 285-
291.

CROSS, F. L. I Peter: A Paschal Liturgy. London: Mowbray,
1954.

CULLMANN, Oscar. "La signification de la Saint-Cène dans le
christianisme primitif." Revue d'histoire et de philosophie
réligieuses, 16 (1936): 1-22; "The Meaning of the Lord's Supper in Primitive Christianity." In Essays on the Lord's Supper,
pp. 5-23. By Oscar Cullmann and F. J. Leenhardt. Translated by J. G. Davies. ESW, 1. Richmond, VA: John Knox
Press, 1958.
--German version: "Die Bedeutung des Abendmahls im Urchristentum." In his Vorträge und Aufsätze, 1925-1962, pp.
503-523. Herausgegeben von Karlfried Fröhlich. Tübingen:
Mohr; Zürich: Zwingli Verlag, 1966.

_____. Urchristentum und Gottesdienst. Basel: H. Majer, 1944;
partial translation in Le culte dans l'église primitive. Translated by J.-J. von Allmen. 3e éd. Neuchâtel: Delachaux et
Niestlé, 1948.

_____. Urchristentum und Gottesdienst. 2. Aufl. Zürich:
Zwingli Verlag, 1950; and Les sacrements dans l'évangile johan-
nique. Paris: Presses universitaires de France, 1951; published together in English as Early Christian Worship. Translated by A. Stewart Todd and James B. Torrance. Chicago:
Regnery; London: SCM Press, 1953; reprint ed., Philadelphia,
PA: Westminster Press, 1978.

_____. Urchristentum und Gottesdienst. 4. Aufl. Zürich:
Zwingli Verlag, 1962.

CUMING, Geoffrey J. "The New Testament Foundation for Common
Prayer." Studia Liturgica, 10 (1974): 88-105.

_____. "Service Endings in the Epistles." New Testament
Studies, 22 (1975-1976): 110-113.

DELLING, Gerhard. Gottesdienst im Neuen Testament. Göttingen:

Vandenhoeck & Ruprecht, 1952; Worship in the New Testament.
Translated by Percy Scott. Philadelphia, PA: Westminster
Press, 1962.

_____. "Zum gottesdienstlichen Stil der Johannes-Apokalypse."
Novum Testamentum, 3 (1959): 107-137.

DELORME, J., et al. The Eucharist in the New Testament: A Symposium. Translated by E. M. Stewart. Baltimore, MD: Helicon, 1964.

EMERTON, John Adney. "The Aramaic Underlying to aima mou tes
diathekesin Mk. xiv.24." Journal of Theological Studies, N.S.
6 (1955): 238-240.

_____. "To aima mou tes diathekes: The Evidence of the Syriac
Versions." Journal of Theological Studies, N.S. 13 (1962):
111-117.

EVANS, C. F. "Romans 12.1-2: The True Worship." In Dimensions de la vie chrétienne (Rm 12-13), pp. 7-49. SMB, 4.
Rome: Abbaye de S. Paul, 1979.

FARRER, A. M. "Eucharist and Church in the New Testament."
In The Parish Communion, pp. 75-94. Edited by A. G. Hebert.
London: SPCK, 1937.

_____. "The Eucharist in I Corinthians." In Eucharistic Theol-
ogy Then and Now. London: SPCK, 1968.

FEELEY-HARNICK, Gillian. The Lord's Table: Eucharist and
Passover in Early Christianity. Philadelphia, PA: University
of Pennsylvania Press, 1981.

GARDNER, Percy. The Origin of the Lord's Supper. London,
New York: Macmillan, 1893.

GAUGLER, Ernst. Das Abendmahl im Neuen Testament. ATANT,
2. Basel: Majer, 1943.

GODART, Jules. "Aux origines de la célébration eucharistique."
Questions liturgiques et paroissiales, 51 (1970): 89-112.

GOPPELT, L. "Der eucharistische Gottesdienst nach dem Neuen
Testament." Erbe und Auftrag, 49 (1973): 435-447.

_____. "Pino, etc." Theologische Wörterbuch des Neuen Testa-
ments, 6:135-158 (esp. 141-144, 146-148, 153-158); "Pino, etc."
Theological Dictionary of the New Testament, 6:135-158 (esp.
141-144, 146-148, 153-158).

_____. Typos: die typologische Deutung des Alten Testaments im Neuen. BFCT, 2. Reihe, 43. Götersloh: Bertelsmann, 1939; reprint ed., Darmstadt: Wissenschaftliche Buchgesellschaft, 1969; Typos: The Typological Interpretation of the Old Testament in the New. Translated by Donald H. Madvig. Grand Rapids, MI: Eerdmans, 1982.

GOTTLIEB, Hans. "To aima mou tes diathekes." Studia Theologica (Lund), 14 (1960): 115-118.

GREEVEN, Heinrich. Gebet und Eschatologie im Neuen Testament. NTF, 3/1. Gütersloh: Bertelsmann, 1931.

GUZIE, Tad W. Jesus and the Eucharist. New York: Paulist Press, 1974.

HAHN, Ferdinand. "Charisma und Amt." Zeitschrift für Theologie und Kirche, 76 (1979): 419-449.

HAMM, Fritz. Die liturgischen Einsetzungsberichte im Sinne vergleichender Liturgieforschung untersucht. LQF, 23. Münster: Aschendorff, 1928.

HAMMAN, Adalbert, ed. La prière. Thèmes bibliques, 7. Paris: Apostolat des Editions, 1971; Prayer: The New Testament. Chicago: Franciscan Herald Press, 1971.

HEITMULLER, Wilhelm. Taufe und Abendmahl bei Paulus. Göttingen: Vandenhoeck & Ruprecht, 1903.

HIGGINS, Angus John Brockhurst. The Lord's Supper in the New Testament. SBT, 6. Chicago: Regnery, 1952.

HOOK, Norman. The Eucharist in the New Testament. London: Epworth Press, 1964.

HORST, Johannes. Proskynein: Zur Anbetung im Urchristentum nach ihrer religionsgeschichtlichen Eigenart. NTF, 3/2. Gütersloh: Bertelsmann, 1932.

IRWIN, Kevin. "The Supper Text in the Gospel of Saint Matthew." Dunwoodie Review, 11 (1971): 170-184.

JEREMIAS, Joachim. Die Abendmahlsworte Jesu. 3. Aufl. Göttingen: Vandenhoeck & Ruprecht, 1960; The Eucharistic Words of Jesus. Translated by Norman Perrin. New York: Scribner, 1966.

_____. Die Abendmahlsworte Jesu. 4. Aufl. Göttingen: Vandenhoeck & Ruprecht, 1967.

KASEMANN, Ernst. "Anliegen und Eigenart der paulinischen Abend-
mahlslehre." In his Exegetische Versuche und Besinnungen,
Bd. 1, pp. 11-34. 2. Aufl. Göttingen: Vandenhoeck &
Ruprecht, 1960; "The Pauline Doctrine of the Lord's Supper."
In his Essays on New Testament Themes, pp. 108-135. Trans-
lated by W. J. Montague. London: SCM Press; Naperville,
IL: Allenson, 1964.

_____. "Gottesdienst im Alltag der Welt: zu Römer 12." In
his Exegetische Versuche und Besinnungen, 2. Bd., pp. 198-
204; "Worship in Everyday Life: A Note on Romans 12." In
his New Testament Questions of Today, pp. 188-195. Translated by W. J. Montague. London: SCM Press; Philadelphia,
PA: Fortress Press, 1969.

KILMARTIN, Edward. The Eucharist in the Primitive Church.
Englewood Cliffs, NJ: Prentice-Hall, 1965.

_____. "The Last Supper and the Earliest Eucharists of the
Church." In The Breaking of Bread, pp. 35-47. Edited by
P. Benoit, R. Murphy, and B. van Iersel. Concilium, 40.
New York: Paulist Press, 1969.

KILPATRICK, G. D. "Eucharist as Sacrifice and Sacrament in the
New Testament." In Neues Testament und Kirche: für Rudolf
Schnackenberg, pp. 429-433. Herausgegeben von Joachim
Gnilka. Freiburg: Herder, 1974.

_____. "L'eucharistie dans le Nouveau Testament." Revue de
théologie et de philosophie, 14 (1964): 193-204.

KLINZING, Georg. Die Umdeutung des Kultus in der Qumrange-
meinde und im Neuen Testament. SUNT, 7. Göttingen: Vandenhoeck & Ruprecht, 1971.

KNOCH, Otto. "'In der Gemeinde von Antiochia gab es Propheten
und Lehrer' (Apg 13,1): Was sagt das Neuen Testament über
Wortgottesdienste und deren Leiter?" Liturgisches Jahrbuch,
32 (1982): 133-150.

KOOLE, Jan Leunis. Liturgie en Ambt in de apostolische Kerk.
Kampen: Kok, 1949.

KUHN, Karl Georg. "The Lord's Supper and the Communal Meal at
Qumran." In The Scrolls and the New Testament, pp. 65-93.
Edited by Krister Stendahl. New York: Harper, 1957.

LAMBERT, John C. The Sacraments in the New Testament. Edinburgh: T. & T. Clark, 1903.

LEBEAU, Paul. Le vin nouveau du royaume: étude exégétique et

patristique sur la parole eschatalogique de Jésus à la Cène.
MLB, 5. Paris: Desclée, 1966.

LEENHARDT, Franz J. Ceci est mon corps: explication de ces
paroles de Jesus-Christ. CTAP, 37. Neuchâtel: Delachaux
et Niestlé, 1955; "This is My Body." In Essays on the Lord's
Supper, pp. 24-85. By Oscar Cullmann and F. J. Leenhardt.
Translated by J. G. Davies. ESW, 1. Richmond, VA: John
Knox Press, 1958.

_____. "La structure du chapitre 6 de l'évangile de Jean."
Revue d'histoire philosophique et religieuse, 39 (1959): 1-13.

LEON-DUFOUR, X. "Das letzte Abendmahl: Stiftung und kultische
Aktualisierung." Bibel und Liturgie, 46 (1973): 167-173.

LESSIG, Hans. "Die Abendmahlsprobleme im Lichte der neutestamentlichen Forschung seit 1900." Dissertation, Bonn, 1954.

LOHFINK, Gerhard. "Gab es im Gottesdienst der neutestamentlichen
Gemeinden eine Anbetung Christi?" Biblische Zeitschrift, n.F.
18 (1974): 161-179.

LOHSE, Eduard. "Hosanna." Theologische Wörterbuch des Neues
Testamentes, 9:682-684; "Hosanna." Theological Dictionary of
the New Testament, 9:682-684.

McCORMICK, Scott. The Lord's Supper: A Biblical Interpretation.
Philadelphia: Westminster Press, 1966.

MARSHALL, I. Howard. Last Supper and Lord's Supper. London:
Paternoster Press, 1980; Grand Rapids: Eerdmans, 1981, c1980.

MARTIN, Ralph P. "Aspects of Worship in the New Testament
Church." In Vox Evangelica II, pp. 6-32. London: Epworth
Press, 1963.

_____. The Spirit and the Congregation: Studies in 1 Corinthi-
ans 12 to 15. Grand Rapids, MI: Eerdmans, 1984.

_____. Worship in the Early Church. Revised ed. Grand
Rapids, MI: Eerdmans, 1974.

MARXSEN, Willi. "The History of Eucharistic Tradition in the New
Testament." In Word and Sacrament, pp. 64-73. Edited by
R. R. Williams. London: SPCK, 1968.

MOE, Olaf. "Das Abendmahl im Hebräerbrief." Studia Theologica
(Lund), 4 (1951-1952): 102-108.

MOULE, C. F. D. Worship in the New Testament. ESW, 9. Richmond, VA: John Knox Press, 1961.

NEUENZEIT, Paul. Das Herrenmahl: Studien zur paulinischen
Eucharistieauffassung. SANT, 1. Munich: Kösel, 1960.

NIELEN, Josef M. Gebet und Gottesdienst im Neuen Testament.
Freiburg: Herder, 1937; The Earliest Christian Liturgy.
Translated by Patrick Cummins. St. Louis, MO: Herder, 1941.

_____. Gebet und Gottesdienst im Neuen Testament. 2. Aufl.
Freiburg: Herder, 1963.

OLD, Hughes Oliphant. "The Psalms of Praise in the Worship of
the New Testament Church." Interpretation, 39 (1985): 20-33.

PATSCH, Hermann. Abendmahl und historische Jesus. CTM, 1.
Stuttgart: Calwer Verlag, 1972.

_____. "Abendmahlsterminologie ausserhalb der Einsetzungs-
berichte." Zeitschrift für die neutestamentliche Wissenschaft,
62 (1971): 210-231.

PETERSON, Erik. "MERIS: Hostien Partikel und Opferanteil."
Ephemerides liturgicae, 61 (1947): 3-12; reprinted in his
Frühkirche, Judentum und Gnosis, pp. 97-106. Rome: Herder,
1959.

PRIGENT, R. "Une trace de liturgie judéo-chrétienne dans le chapitre XXI de l'Apocalypse de Jean." Recherches de science religieuse, 60 (1972): 165-172.

PUSTOUTOV, Iosif. "Die Eucharistie nach dem Neuen Testament."
In Die Eucharistie, pp. 42-74. Herausgegeben vom Kirchlichen
Aussenamt der Evangelischen Kirche in Deutschland. Bielefeld:
Luther-Verlag, 1974.

REICKE, Bo. "Some Reflections on Worship in the New Testament."
In New Testament Essays: Studies in Memory of Thomas Walter
Manson, pp. 194-209. Edited by A. J. B. Higgins. Manchester:
Manchester University Press, 1959.

ROBINSON, John A. T. "Traces of a Liturgical Sequence in I.
Cor. 16:20-24." Journal of Theological Studies, N.S. 4 (1953):
38-41.

ROLOFF, Jürgen. "Anfänge der soteriologischen Deutung des Todes
Jesu (Mk. x.45 und Lk. xxii.27)." New Testament Studies, 19
(1972-1973): 38-64 (esp. 50-64).

_____. "Der frühchristliche Gottesdienst als Thema der neutesta-
mentlichen Theologie." Jahrbuch für Liturgik und Hymnologie,
17 (1972): 92-99.

RORDORF, Willy. L'eucharistie des premiers chrétiens. PT, 17. Paris: Beauchesne, 1976; The Eucharist of the Early Christians. Translated by Matthew J. O'Connell. New York: Pueblo, 1978.

_____. "Sonntagnachtgottesdienste der christlichen Frühzeit?" Zeitschrift für die neutestamentliche Wissenschaft, 68 (1977): 138-141.

RUCKSTUHL, Eugen. "Literarkritik am Johannesevangelium und eucharistische Rede (Joh 6, 51c-58)." Divus Thomas, 33 (1945): 153-190, 301-333.

SANDVIK, Bjorn. Das Kommen des Herrn beim Abendmahl im Neuen Testament. ATANT, 58. Zürich: Zwingli Verlag, 1970.

SCHERMANN, Theodor. "Das 'Brotbrechen' im Urchristentum." Biblische Zeitschrift, 8 (1910): 33-52, 162-183.

SCHILLE, Gottfried. "Zur Frage urchristlichen Kultätiologien." Jahrbuch für Liturgik und Hymnologie, 10 (1965): 35-54.

SCHLIER, Heinrich. "Das Herrenmahl bei Paulus." In his Das Ende der Zeit: Exegetische Aufsätze und Vorträge 3, pp. 201-215. Freiburg: Herder, 1971.

SCHURMANN, Heinz. "Das apostolische Interesse am eucharistischen Kelch." Münchener theologische Zeitschrift, 4 (1953): 223-231.

_____. "Die Eucharistie als Repräsentation und Applikation des Heilsgeschehens nach Joh 6, 53-58." Trierer theologische Zeitung, 68 (1959): 30-45, 108-118.

_____. "Die Gestalt der ursprünglichen Eucharistiefeier." Münchener theologische Zeitschrift, 6 (1955): 107-131.

_____. "Jesu Abendmahlshandlung als Zeichen für die Welt." In his Jesu ureigener Tod, pp. 66-96. Freiburg: Herder, 1975.

_____. Eine quellenkritischen Untersuchung des lukanischen Abendmahlsberichtes, Lk 22. 7-38. 3 vols. Münster: Aschendorff, 1953-1957.
1. Das Paschamahlbericht, Lk 22, (7-14) 15-18. NA, 19/5. 1953; 2. Aufl., 1968.
2. Die Einsetzungsbericht, Lk 22, 19-20. 1955.
3. Jesu Abschiedsrede, Lk 22, 21-38. 1957.

SCHURMANN, Heinz. Der Abendmahlsbericht Lukas 22, 7-38 als Gottesdienstordnung, Gemeindeordnung, Lebensordnung. 4. Aufl. BGNR, 1. Leipzig: St. Benno-Verlag, 1967.

SCHWEIZER, Eduard. "Abendmahl, I. In NT." In Religion in
Geschichte und Gegenwart, Bd. 1, cols. 10-21. 3. Aufl.
Tübingen: Mohr, 1957; The Lord's Supper According to the
New Testament. Translated by James M. Davis. Philadelphia,
PA: Fortress Press, 1967.

_____. "Gottesdienst im Neuen Testament und heute." In his
Beiträge zur Theologie des Neuen Testaments, pp. 263-282.
Zürich: Zwingli Verlag, 1970.

_____. "Gottesdienst im Neuen Testament und Kirchenbau heute."
In his Beiträge zur Theologie des Neuen Testaments, pp. 249-
261. Zürich: Zwingli Verlag, 1970.

_____. "Das Herrenmahl im Neuen Testament." Theologische
Literaturzeitung, 79 (1954): 577-592; reprinted in his Neo-
testamentica, pp. 344-370. Zürich: Zwingli Verlag, 1963.

_____. "The Service of Worship: An Exposition of I Corinthians
14." Interpretation, 13 (1959): 400-408.

SEIDENSTICKER, Philipp. Lebendiges Opfer (Röm 12, 1): Ein
Beitrag zur Theologie des Apostels Paulus. NA, 20/1-3. Münster: Aschendorff, 1954.

SHEPHERD, Massey H., Jr. The Paschal Liturgy and the Apocalypse. ESW, 6. London: Lutterworth Press; Richmond, VA:
John Knox Press, 1960.

SIMPSON, R. L. The Interpretation of Prayer in the Early Church.
Philadelphia, PA: Westminster Press, 1965.

STAATS, Reinhart. "Die Sonntagnachtgottesdienste der christlichen
Frühzeit." Zeitschrift für die neutestamentliche Wissenschaft,
66 (1975): 242-263.

THUSING, Wilhelm. "'Lasst uns hinzutreten ...' (Hebr 10,22):
Zur Frage nach dem Sinn der Kulttheologie im Hebräerbrief."
Biblische Zeitschrift, n.F. 9 (1965): 1-17.

WILCKENS, Ulrich. "Der eucharistische Abschnitt der johanneischen
Rede vom Lebensbrot (Joh 6, 51c-58)." In Neues Testament
und Kirche: Festschrift für Rudolf Schnackenburg, pp. 220-
248. Herausgegeben von Joachim Gnilka. Freiburg: Herder,
1974.

WILLIAMSON, R. "The Eucharist and the Epistle to the Hebrews."
New Testament Studies, 21 (1975): 300-312.

F. GNOSTICISM AND THE MYSTERY RELIGIONS

1. General Studies

DODD, Charles Harold. The Bible and the Greeks. London: Hodder & Stoughton, 1935.

DODDS, Eric Robertson. The Greeks and the Irrational. Berkeley: University of California Press, 1951.

NILSSON, Martin P. Grekisk religiositet. Stockholm: Geber, 1946; A History of Greek Religion. 2d ed. Translated by F. J. Fielden. Oxford: Clarendon Press, 1949.

NOCK, A. D. "Hellenistic Mysteries and Christian Sacraments." Mnemosyne, 5, 4 (1952): 177-213.

REITZENSTEIN, Richard. Die hellenistischen Mysterienreligionen, ihre Grudgedanken und Wirkungen. Leipzig: Teubner, 1909, 1910; 3. Aufl., 1927.

2. New Testament Apocrypha and Gnostic Writings

a. Texts

FESTUGIERE, André Marie Jean. La révélation d'Hermès Trismégiste. 4 vols. Etudes bibliques. Paris: Lecoffre, 1944-1954; 2. éd., Paris: Lecoffre, gabalda, 1949-1954.

HENNECKE, Edgar, and SCHNEEMELCHER, Wilhelm, eds. Neutestamentliche Apokryphen. 2. Bde. Tübingen: Mohr, 1959-1964; New Testament Apocrypha. 2 vols. Translated and edited by R. McL. Wilson. Philadelphia, PA: Westminster Press, 1963-1965.

JANSMA, T., ed. A Selection from the Acts of Judas Thomas. SSS, 1. Leiden: Brill, 1952.

KLIJN, A. F. J., ed. The Acts of Thomas: Introduction, Text, Commentary. NTS, 5. Leiden: Brill, 1962.

LIPSIUS, Richard Adelbert, and BONNET, Maximilian, eds. Acta Apostolorum Apocrypha. 2 pts. in 3 vols. Leipzig: H. Mendelssohn, 1891-1903; reprint ed., Hildesheim: Olms, 1959. --"Acta Thomae," in pars 2, vol. 2.

TILL, Walter C., ed. Das Evangelium nach Philippos. PTS, 2. Berlin: De Gruyter, 1963.

WILSON, Robert McLachan, ed. The Gospel of Philip. London:
Mowbray; New York: Harper & Row, 1962.

b. Studies

GAFFRON, H. G. "Studien zum koptischen Philippusevangelium
unter besondere Berücksichtigungen der Sakramente." Dissertation, Bonn, 1969.

GRANT, R. M. "The Mystery of Marriage in the Gospel of Philip."
Vigiliae Christianae, 15 (1961): 129-140.

SEGELBERG, Eric. "The Coptic-Gnostic Gospel according to Philip
and Its Sacramental System." Numen, 7 (1960): 189-200.

UNNIK, Wilhelm Cornelius van. "Three Notes on the 'Gospel of
Philip.'" New Testament Studies, 10 (1963-1964): 465-469.

G. THE CHURCH FATHERS AND CONTEMPORARIES

1. Collected Patristic Texts

Ancient Christian Writers. Westminster, MD: Newman Press.
1, 1946- .

Bibliothek der Kirchenväter. Kempten. 1, 1869--80, 1888.
2. Aufl. 1, 1911--62/63, 1931.
2. Reihe. 1, 1932--20, 1938.

Cambridge Patristic Texts. Cambridge: Cambridge University
Press. 1, 1899- .

Corpus Christianorum. Turnholt: Brepols.
Serie Latina. 1, 1953-- .
Continuatio mediaevalis. 4, 1966-- . 1, 1971.

Corpus scriptorum Christianorum orientalium. Roma.
Scriptores Aethiopici. 1, 1903-- .
Scriptores Arabici. 1, 1903-- .
Scriptores Armeniaci. 1, 1953-- .
Scriptores Coptici. 1, 1906-- .
Scriptores Iberici. 1, 1950-- .
Scriptores Syri. 1, 1903-- .
Subsidia. 1, 1950-- .

Fathers of the Church. Washington, DC: Fathers of the Church.
1947- .

Die griechischen christlichen Schriftsteller der ersten drei

Jahrhunderts. Herausgegeben von der Kirchenväter-Commission der königl. preussischen Akademie der Wissenschaften. Vols. 1-40, Leipzig: Hinrichs, 1897-1936; vols. 41 +, Berlin: Akademie Verlag, 1953- .

HEILMANN, Alfons, ed. Texte der Kirchenväter: eine Auswahl, nach Themen geordnet. 5 vols. München: Kösel-Verlag, 1963-1966.

MIGNE, Jacques Paul, ed. Patrologiae cursus completus. Paris.
Series Graeca. 1, 1857--167, 1866; Reg. 1, 1928--2, 1936.
Series Latina. 1. Ser. -- 1, 1841--79, 1849.
2. Ser. -- 80, 1850--217, 1855.
Ind. 1-4 -- 218, 1862--221, 1864.
Suppl. 1, 1958--5, 1970.
Series Graeca et orientalis. Patrologiae Graecae Latine tantum editiae. 1, 1856--81, 1867.

Patrologia Orientalis. Paris. 1, 1907- .

Patrologia Syriaca. Paris. 1, 1897--3, 1926.

ROBERTS, Alexander, and DONALDSON, James, eds. Ante-Nicene Christian Library. 24 vols. Edinburgh: T. & T. Clark, 1867-1872.

ROBERTS, Alexander, DONALDSON, James, and COXE, Cleveland, eds. The Ante-Nicene Fathers. 10 vols. American reprint of the Edinburgh edition revised by Cleveland Coxe. Buffalo: Christian Literature Co., 1885-1896; New York: Scribner, 1899-1900; reprint ed., Grand Rapids, MI: Eerdmans, 1951-1956.

SCHAFF, Philip, and WACE, Henry, eds. A Select Library of Nicene and Post-Nicene Fathers. 1st and 2d Series. 28 vols. New York: Christian Literature Co., 1886-1900; reprint ed., Grand Rapids, MI: Eerdmans, 1952-1956.

Sources chrétiennes. Paris: Cerf. 1, 1941-- .

STRUCKMANN, Adolf, ed. Eucharistische Texte griechischer Väter aus der Zeit vor dem Konzil von Nicäa. SSKQD, 21. Paderborn: Schöningh, 1927.

_____, ed. Eucharistische Texte lateinischer Väter aus der Zeit vor dem Konzil von Nicäa. SSKQD, 22. Paderborn: Schöningh, 1927.

2. General Studies

ASHWORTH, H.   "The Relation between Liturgical Formularies and
Patristic Texts."   In Studia Patristica, vol. 8, pp. 149-155.
Edited by F. L. Cross. TUGAL, 93. Berlin: Akademie-
Verlag, 1966.

BAREILLE, G.   "Eucharistie d'après les Pères." Dictionnaire de
théologie catholique, 5:1122-1183.

BETZ, Johannes. Die Eucharistie in der Zeit der griechischen
Väter. 2. Aufl. Freiburg: Herder, 1964.

_____. "Die Prosphora in der patristischen Theologie." In Op-
fer Christi und Opfer der Kirche, pp. 99-116. Herausgegeben
von B. Neunheuser. Düsseldorf: Patmos-Verlag, 1960.

BRAKMANN, H. G.   "Die angeblichen eucharistischen Mahlzeiten des
4. und 5. Jahrhunderts." Römische Quartalschrift für christliche Altertumskunde, 65 (1970): 82-97.

CAMELOT, Th.   "L'eucharistie dans l'école d'Alexandrie." Divinitas,
1, 1 (1957): 71-92.

CAPELLE, Bernard.   "Autorité de la liturgie chez les Pères." Recherches de théologie ancienne et médiévale, 21 (1954): 5-22.

CHADWICK, Henry.   "Eucharist and Christology in the Nestorian
Controversy." Journal of Theological Studies, N.S. 2 (1951):
145-164.

Convivium dominicum: studi sull' eucaristia nei padri della chiesa
antica e miscellanea patristica. Catania: Centro di studi sull'
antico cristianesimo, Universita di Catania, 1959.

DOLLAR, George W.   "The Lord's Supper in the Second Century."
Bibliotheca Sacra, 117 (1960): 144-154.

_____. "The Lord's Supper in the Third Century." Bibliotheca
Sacra, 117 (1960): 249-257.

_____. "Views of the Lord's Supper in the Fourth and Fifth
Centuries." Bibliotheca Sacra, 117 (1960): 342-349.

DUGMORE, C. W.   "Sacrament and Sacrifice in the Early Fathers."
Journal of Ecclesiastical History, 2 (1951): 24-37.

GEISELMANN, Josef Rupert. Die Eucharistielehre der Vorscholastik.
FCLD, 15/1-3. Paderborn: Schöningh, 1926.

HAMMAN, Adalbert.   "La messe et sa catéchèse chez les Pères de l'Eglise." In Miscelanea Patristica: Homenaje al P. Angel C. Vega, pp. 37-48. Real Monasterio de El Escorial: Biblioteca La Ciudad de Dios, 1968.

HAMMERICH, Holger. "Der tägliche Empfang der Eucharistie im 3. Jahrhundert." Zeitschrift für Kirchengeschichte, 84 (1973): 93-95.

HANSON, R. P. C. "Eucharistic Offering in the Pre-Nicene Fathers." Proceedings of the Royal Irish Academy, 76 (1976): 75-95.

HARTMANN, Edward Joseph. "Koinonia-Communio in Orthodox Christian Literature from A.D. 200 to 325: A Theological-Philological Study." Ph.D. dissertation, Marquette University, 1968.

HOFFLING, Johann Wilhelm Friedrich. Die Lehre der ältesten Kirche vom Opfer im Leben und Cultus der Christen. Erlangen: Palm, 1851. [On Apsotolic Fathers, Justin, Irenaeus]

LEBEAU, P. "La coupe eucharistique après les Pères." In Studia Patristica, vol. 10, pp. 366-373. Edited by F. L. Cross. TUGAL, 107. Berlin: Akademie-Verlag, 1970.

LECUYER, Joseph. "Théologie de l'anaphore selon les Pères de l'école d'Antioche." Orient syrien, 6 (1961): 385-412.

MOLLAND, Einar. The Conception of the Gospel in the Alexandrian Theology. SNVA, 2/2. Oslo: Dybwad, 1938.

QUASTEN, Johannes. "Mysterium tremendum: Eucharistische Frömmigkeitsauffassungen des 4. Jahrhunderts." In Vom christlichen Mysterium, pp. 66-75. Herausgegeben von A. Mayer, J. Quasten, and B. Neunheuser. Düsseldorf: Patmos Verlag, 1951.

TORRANCE, Thomas F. "The Mind of Christ in Worship: The Problem of Apollinarianism in the Liturgy." In his Theology in Reconciliation, pp. 139-214. Grand Rapids, MI: Eerdmans, 1975.

WIELAND, Franz. Der vorirenäische Opferbegriff. VKSM, 3/6. München: J. J. Lentner, 1909.

3. Ambrose

a. Texts

BOTTE, Bernard, ed. Ambroise de Milan: Des Sacraments, des Mystères. SC, 25bis. Paris: Cerf, 1961.

CHADWICK, Henry, ed. Saint Ambrose on the Sacraments. SEFP,
   5. London: Mowbray, 1960; Chicago: Loyola University
   Press, 1961.

DEFERRARI, Roy J., ed. "The Mysteries" and "The Sacraments."
   In Saint Ambrose: Theological and Dogmatic Works, pp. 3-28
   and 265-328. FOC, 44. Washington, DC: Catholic University
   of America Press, 1963.

FALLER, Otto, ed. "De sacramentis" and "De mysteriis." In
   Sancti Ambrosii Opera, Pars 7, pp. 13-116. CSEL, 73. Vin-
   dobonae: Hoelder-Pichler-Tempsky, 1955.

SRAWLEY, J. H., ed. Saint Ambrose on the Sacraments and on
   the Mysteries. Rev. ed. Translated by T. Thompson. London: SPCK, 1950.

b. Studies

JOHANNY, Raymond. L'eucharistie, centre de l'histoire du salut,
   chez saint Ambroise de Milan. TH, 9. Paris: Beauchesne,
   1968.

LISIECKI, Stanislaus. Quid sanctus Ambrosius de sanctissima eucharistia docuerit. Inaugural dissertation, Breslau, 1910.

QUASTEN, Johannes. "Sobria ebrietas in Anbrosius, De Sacramentis." In Miscellanea liturgica in honorem L. Cuniberti Mohlberg, vol. 1, pp. 117-125. BEL, 22. Rome: Edizioni Liturgiche, 1948.

YARNOLD, E. J. "Did St. Ambrose Know the Mystagogic Catecheses
   of St. Cyril of Jerusalem?" In Studia Patristica, vol. 12, pp.
   184-189. Edited by Elizabeth A. Livingstone. TUGAL, 115.
   Berlin: Akademie-Verlag, 1975.

4. Apollinaris

BATES, W. H. "The Background of Apollinaris's Eucharistic Teaching." Journal of Ecclesiastical History, 12 (1961): 139-154.

5. The Apostolic Fathers

a. Texts

GLIMM, Francis X., ed. The Apostolic Fathers. FOC, 1. New
   York: Christian Heritage, 1947.

GOODSPEED, Edgar J., ed. The Apostolic Fathers: An American
   Translation. New York: Harper, 1950.

KLEIST, James A., ed. The Didache, Barnabas, Polycarp, Papias, Diognetus. ACW, 6. Westminster, MD: Newman Press, 1948.

LAKE, Kirsop, ed. The Apostolic Fathers. 2 vols. LCL. London: Heinemann; New York: Putnam, 1912.

LIGHTFOOT, J. B. The Apostolic Fathers. Edited and completed by J. R. Harmer. London: Macmillan, 1891; reprint ed., Grand Rapids, MI: Baker, 1956.

RICHARDSON, Cyril C., ed. Early Christian Fathers. LCC, 1. Philadelphia, PA: Westminster Press, 1953; reprint ed., New York: Macmillan, 1970.

STANIFORTH, Maxwell, ed. Early Christian Writings: The Apostolic Fathers. Baltimore, MD: Penguin Books, 1968.

b. Studies

BIEDER, Werner. "Das Abendmahl im christlichen Lebenszusammenhang bei Ignatius von Antiochia." Evangelische Theologie, 16 (1956): 75-97.

GAMBER, Klaus. "Das Papyrusfragment zur Markusliturgie und das Eucharistiegebet im Clemensbrief." Ostkirchliche Studien, 8 (1959): 31-45.

KRAFT, Robert Alan. The Epistle of Barnabas: Its Quotations and Their Sources. Ph.D. dissertation, Harvard University, 1961.

UNNIK, Wilhelm Cornelius van. "1. Clemens 34 and the 'Sanctus.'" Vigiliae Christianae, 5 (1951): 204-248.

6. Augustine

ADAM, Karl. Die Eucharistielehre des heiligen Augustin. FCLD, 8/1. Paderborn: Schöningh, 1908.

_____. "Zur Eucharistielehre des hl. Augustinus." Theologische Quartalschrift, 112 (1931): 490-536; reprinted in his Gesammelte Aufsätze zur Dogmengeschichte und Theologie der Gegenwart, pp. 237-267. Herausgegeben von Fritz Hoffmann. Augsburg: P. Haas, 1936.

CAMELOT, Th. "Réalisme et symbolisme dans la doctrine eucharistique de saint Augustin." Revue des sciences philosophiques et théologiques, 31 (1947): 294-410.

DEKKERS, Eligius. "La codification des prières liturgiques: le rôle de saint Augustin." In Forma futuri: studi in onore del Cardinale Michele Pellegrino, pp. 845-855. Torino: Bottega d'Erasmo, 1975.

DONEGAN, Augustine Francis. St. Augustine and the Real Presence. SST, 2d ser., 72. Washington, DC: Catholic University Press, 1952.

FRANCOVICH, Lawrence F. "Augustine's Theory of Eucharistic Sacrifice." Ph.D. dissertation, Marquette University, 1976.

GESSEL, Wilhelm. Eucharistische Gemeinschaft bei Augustinus. Cassiciacum, 21. Würzburg: Augustinus-Verlag, 1966.

LECORDIER, Gaston. La doctrina de l'eucharistie chez saint Augustin. Paris: Gabalda, 1930.

MARINI, A. "La partecipazione dei fedeli alla Messa negli scritti di s. Agostino." Ephemerides liturgicae, 93 (1979): 3-37.

MEER, Frederik van der. Augustinus de Zielzorger: een studie over de praktijk van een kerkvader. Utrecht: Spectrum, 1947; Augustine the Bishop: The Life and Work of a Father of the Church. Translated by Brian Battershaw and G. R. Lamb. New York: Sheed & Ward, 1961.

MURPHY, Joseph M. "The Contra Hilarum of Augustine, Its Liturgical and Musical Implications." Augustinian Studies, 10 (1979): 133-143.

RATZINGER, Joseph. Volk und Haus Gottes in Augustins Lehre von der Kirche. MTS, 2/7. München: Zink, 1954.

ROETZER, Wunibald. Des heiligen Augustinus Schriften als liturgiegeschichtliche Quelle: eine liturgiegeschichtliche Studie. München: Hueber, 1930.

VOLPI, Italo. Communione e salvezza in S. Agostino: una controversia durante il Concilio di Trento e la rinascita scolastica. Mysterium, 1. Roma: Officium Libri Catholici, 1954.

WILLIS, G. G. Saint Augustine and the Donatist Controversy. London: SPCK, 1950.

7. Caesarius of Arles

CAESARIUS OF ARLES. [Sancti Caesarii Arelatensis] Sermones. 2 vols. Edited by G. Morin. 2d ed. CC, 103-104. Turnhout: Brepols, 1953.
--esp. Sermon 227: On the Consecration of the Altar.

_____. Sermons. 2 vols. Translated by Mary Magdaleine
Mueller. FOC, 31 & 47. Washington, DC: Catholic University
Press, 1956-1964.

8. The Cappadocians

a. Texts

BARBEL, Joseph, ed. Gregor von Nyssa: Die grosse katechetische
Rede. BGL, 1. Stuttgart: Hiersemann, 1971.

b. Studies

ALTHAUS, Heinz. Die Heilslehre des heiligen Gregor von Nazianz.
MBT, 34. Münster: Aschendorff, 1972.

BALAS, David L. METOUSIA THEOU: Man's Participation in God's
Perfections According to Saint Gregory of Nyssa. SA, 55.
Roma: "I.B.C." Libreria Herder, 1966.

DANIELOU, Jean. L'être et le temps chez Grégoire de Nysse.
Leiden: Brill, 1970.

MAIER, Johannes. "Die Eucharistielehre der drei grossen Kappa-
dozier." Dissertation, Breslau, 1915.

SCAZZOSO, Piero. Introduzione alla ecclesiologia di San Basilio.
SPM, 4. Milano: Vita e pensiero, 1975.

9. Peter Chrysologus

a. Texts

PETER CHRYSOLOGUS. Selected Sermons. Translated by George
E. Ganss. FOC, 17. Washington, DC: Catholic University of
America Press, 1953.

b. Studies

OLIVAR, Alejandro. "La eucaristica en la predicacion de san Pedro
Crisologo." Ciencia tomista, 86 (1959): 605-628.

_____. Los sermones de San Pedro Crisologo: estudio critico.
Scripta e documenta, 13. Abadia de Montserrat, 1962.

10. John Chrysostom

a. Texts

HARKINS, Paul W., ed. St. John Chrysostom: Baptismal Instructions. ACW, 31. Westminster, MD: Newman Press, 1963.

PAPADOPOULOS-KERAMEUS, Athanasios, ed. Varia Graeca Sacra.
St. Petersburg, 1909.

WENGER, Antoine, ed. Jean Chrysostome: Huit catéchèses baptis-
males inédites. SC, 50 & 50 bis. Paris: Cerf, 1957, 1970.

b. Studies

FITTKAU, Gerhard. Der Begriff des Mysteriums bei Johannes
Chrysostomus: eine Auseinandersetzung mit dem Begriff des
"Kultmysteriums" in der Lehre Odo Casels. Theophaneia, 9.
Bonn: Hanstein, 1953.

KACZYNSKI, Reiner. Das Wort Gottes in Liturgie und Alltag der
Gemeinden des Johannes Chrysostomus. FTS, 94. Freiburg:
Herder, 1974.

LAMPEN, W. "Doctrina S. Joannis Chrysostomi de Christo se of-
ferentes." Antonianum, 18 (1943): 3-16.

NAEGLE, August. Die Eucharistielehre des hl. Johannes Chrysostomus, des Doctor Eucharistiae. STS, 3/4-5. Freiburg, St.
Louis, MO: Herder, 1900.

PAVERD, Franz van de. Zur Geschichte der Messliturgie in Antio-
cheia und Konstantinopel gegen Ende des vierten Jahrhunderts:
Analyse der Quellen bei Johannes Chrysostomos. OCA, 187.
Rome: Pontificium Institutum Orientalium Studiorum, 1970.

STOCKER, C. "Eucharistische Gemeinschaft bei Chrysostomus."
In Studia Patristica, vol. 2, pp. 309-316. Edited by Kurt Aland
and F. L. Cross. TUGAL, 64. Berlin: Akademie-Verlag, 1957.

11. Clement of Alexandria

MARSH, H. G. "The Use of Mysterion in the Writings of Clement of
Alexandria with Special Reference to his Sacramental Doctrine."
Journal of Theological Studies, 37 (1936): 64-80.

VAN EIJK, A. H. C. "The Gospel of Philip and Clement of Alexandria: Gnostic and Ecclesiastical Theology on the Resurrection
and the Eucharist." Vigiliae Christianae, 25 (1971): 94-120.

12. Cyril of Alexandria

DU MANOIR DE JUAYE, Hubert. Dogme et spiritualité chez saint Cyrille d'Alexandrie. ETHS, 2. Paris: J. Vrin, 1944.

GEBREMEDHIN, Ezra. Life-Giving Blessing: An Inquiry into the Eucharistic Doctrine of Cyril of Alexandria. SDCU, 17. Uppsala: Almqvist & Wiksell, 1977.

MAHE, Joseph. "L'eucharistie d'après saint Cyrille d'Alexandrie." Revue d'histoire ecclésiastique, 8 (1907): 677-696.

STRUCKMANN, Adolf. Die Eucharistielehre des heiligen Cyrill von Alexandrien. Paderborn: Schöningh, 1910.

13. Cyril of Jerusalem

a. Texts

CROSS, F. L., ed. St. Cyril of Jerusalem's Lectures on the Christian Sacraments: The Procatechesis and the Five Mystagogical Catecheses. London: SPCK, 1951.

McCAULEY, Leo P., and STEPHENSON, Anthony A., eds. The Works of St. Cyril of Jerusalem. 2 vols. FOC, 61 & 64. Washington, DC: Catholic University of America Press, 1969-1970.

PIEDAGNAL, Auguste, ed. Cyrille de Jérusalem: Catéchèses Mystagogiques. Traduciton de Pierre Paris. SC, 126. Paris: Cerf, 1966.

RIESCHL, Wilhelm, and RUPP, Joseph, eds. Tou en hagiois patros hemon kyrillou Hierosolymon archiepiskopou ta sozomena. S. Patris nostri Cyrilli Hierosolymorum archiepiscopi opera quae supersunt omnia. 2 vols. München: Lentner, 1848-1860.

TELFER, William, ed. Cyril of Jerusalem and Nemesius of Emesa. LCC, 4. Philadelphia, PA: Westminster Press, 1955.

b. Studies

CUTRONE, Emmanuel J. "Cyril's Mystagogical Catecheses and the Evolution of the Jerusalem Anaphora." Orientalia Christiana Periodica, 44 (1978): 52-64.

RENOUX, Athanase. "Les catéchèses mystagogiques dans l'organisation liturgique hiérosolymitaine du IVe et du Ve siècle." Muséon, 78 (1965): 335-355.

SWAANS, W. J. "A propos des 'Catéchèses mystagogiques' attri-
buées à saint Cyrille de Jérusalem." Muséon, 55 (1942): 1-43.

14. Ephraem Syrus and Aphrahat

a. Texts

EPHRAEM SYRUS. S. Ephrem et la saint eucharistie. Choix de
47 textes de ce saint docteur touchant la présence réelle, la
transsubstantiation, les fruits de la communion. Texte syriac
avec traductions arabe, français, anglaise, et latine. Beyrouth: Imprimerie Catholique, 1926.

_____. Sancti Ephrem syri hymni et sermones. Edited by
Thomas J. Lamy. 4 vols. Mechliniae: H. Dessain, 1882-1902.

b. Studies

AALST, P. van den. "De h. Eucharistie bij de h. Ephrem." Het
christelijk Oosten en hereniging, 10 (1957-1958): 219-230.

BECK, Edmund. "Die Eucharistie bei Ephräm." Oriens Christianus,
38 (1954): 41-67.

_____. "Symbolum--Mysterium bei Aphraat und Ephräm." Oriens
Christianus, 42 (1958): 19-40.

JONG, J. P. de. "La connexion entre le rite de la consignation et
l'épiclèse dans saint Ephrem." In Studia Patristica, vol. 2,
pp. 29-37. Edited by Kurt Aland and F. L. Cross. TUGAL,
64. Berlin: Akademie-Verlag, 1957.

VOOBUS, Arthur. History of the School of Nisibus. CSCO, 266,
sub. 26. Louvain: CSCO, 1965.

15. Eusebius

SHEPHERD, Massey H., Jr. "Eusebius and the Liturgy of St.
James." Yearbook of Liturgical Studies, 4 (1963): 109-125.

WALLACE-HADRILL, D. S. "Eusebius and the Institution Narrative
in the Eastern Liturgies." Journal of Theological Studies, 4
(1953): 41-42.

16. Firmilian

MICHELL, G. A. "Firmilian and Eucharistic Consecration." Journal
of Theological Studies, N.S. 5 (1954): 215-220.

17.   Hilary of Poitiers

a.   Texts

BRISSON, Jean-Paul, ed.   Traité des mystères.   SC, 19.   Paris:
Cerf, 1947.

b.   Studies

GAMBER, Klaus.   "Der Liber Mysteriorum des Hilarius von Poitiers."
In Studia Patristica, vol. 5, pp. 40-49.   Edited by F. L. Cross.
TUGAL, 80.   Berlin: Akademie-Verlag, 1962.

18.   Irenaeus

ALES, A. d'.   "La doctrine eucharistique de saint Irénée."   Recherches de science religieuse, 13 (1923):   24-46.

EYNDE, D. van den.   "Eucharistia ex duabus rebus constans: St.
Irénée, Adv. Haer. 4, 18, 5."   Antonianum, 15 (1940):   13-28.

JONG, J. P. de.   "Der ursprungliche Sinn von Epiklese und Mischungsritus nach der Eucharistielehre des heiligen Irenäus."
Archiv für Liturgiewissenschaft, 9 (1965):   28-47.

PALACHKOVSKY, V.   "La théologie eucharistique de s. Irénée,
évêque de Lyon."   In Studia Patristica, vol. 2, pp. 277-281.
Edited by Kurt Aland and F. L. Cross.   TUGAL, 64.   Berlin:
Akademie-Verlag, 1957.

WINGREN, Gustaf.   Människan och Inkarnationen enligt Irenaeus.
Lund: Gleerup, 1947; Man and the Incarnation: A Study in
the Biblical Theology of Irenaeus.   Translated by Ross Mackenzie.   Edinburgh, London: Oliver & Boyd; Philadelphia, PA:
Muhlenberg Press, 1959.

ZIEGLER, A. W.   "Das Brot von unseren Feldern: ein Beitrag zur
Eucharistielehre des heiligen Irenäus."   In Pro Mundi Vita:
Festschrift zum Eucharistischen Weltcongress, 1960, pp. 21-43.
München: Hueber, 1960.

19.   John of Damascus

JOHN OF DAMASCUS.   "Epistola de hymno Trisagio."   In Die
Schriften de Johannes von Damaskos, Bd. 4, pp. 289-332.
Edited by Bonifatius Kotter.   PTS, 22.   Berlin: De Gruyter,
1981.

_____.   "The Orthodox Faith," Book 3.   In his Writings.

Translated by Frederic H. Chase, Jr.   FOC, 37.   Washington:
Catholic University of America Press, 1958.
--3, 9:   "On Faith and Baptism," pp. 343-348.
--3, 12:   "On Worshipping to the East," pp. 352-354.
--3, 13:   "On the Holy and Undefiled Sacrament of the Lord,"
   pp. 354-361.
--3, 15:   "On the Honor Due to the Saints and their Relics,"
   pp. 367-370.
--3, 16:   "On Images," pp. 370-373.

20.   Justin Martyr

a.   Texts

BLUNT, A. W. F., ed.   The Apologies of Justin Martyr.   Cambridge:
Cambridge University Press, 1911.

FALLS, Thomas B., ed.   Saint Justin Martyr: The First Apology,
the Second Apology, Dialogue with Trypho, Exhortation to the
Greeks, Discourse to the Greeks, The Monarchy; or, The Rule
of God.   FOC, 6.   Washington, DC: Catholic University of
America Press, 1948.

THOMPSON, Bard.   "The First Apology of Justin Martyr."   In his
Liturgies of the Western Church, pp. 1-10.   Cleveland, OH:
World, 1961; reprint ed., Philadelphia, PA: Fortress Press,
1981.

b.   Studies

BERNARD, Leslie William.   Justin Martyr: His Life and Thought.
Cambridge: Cambridge University Press, 1967.

FUNK, Franz Xaver von.   "Die Abehdmahlselemente bei Justin."
In his Kirchengeschichtlichen Abhandlungen und Untersuchungen, Bd. 1, pp. 278-292.   Paderborn: Schöningh, 1897.

HAMMAN, Adalbert.   "Valeur et signification des renseignements
liturgiques de Justin."   In Studia Patristica, vol. 13, pp. 364-
374.   Edited by Elizabeth A. Livingstone.   TUGAL, 116.   Berlin: Akademie-Verlag, 1975.

HARNACK, Adolf von.   Brot und Wasser, die eucharistischen Elemente bei Justin.   Leipzig: Hinrichs, 1891.

JALLAND, T. G.   "Justin Martyr and the President of the Eucharist."   In Studia Patristica, vol. 5, pp. 83-85.   Edited by F. L.
Cross.   TUGAL, 80.   Berlin: Akademie-Verlag, 1962.

NIGNO JESUS, Otilio del.   "Doctrina eucharistica de san Justino, filosofo y martiri." Revista española de teologia, 4 (1944): 3-58.

PERLER, O. "Logos und Eucharistie nach Justinus 1 Apol. c. 66." Divus Thomas, 18 (1940): 296-316.

PORTER, H. Boone. "The Eucharistic Piety of Justin Martyr." Anglican Theological Review, 39 (1957): 24-33.

RATCLIFF, E. C. "The Eucharistic Institution Narrative of Justin Martyr's First Apology." Journal of Ecclesiastical History, 22 (1971): 97-102; reprinted in his Liturgical Studies of E. C. Ratcliff, pp. 41-48. Edited by A. H. Couratin and D. J. Tripp. London: SPCK, 1976.

21. Lactantius

LACTANTIUS. The Divine Institutes, Book 4: "On True Worship," pp. 391-469. Translated by Mary Francis McDonald. FOC, 49. Washington, DC: Catholic University of America Press, 1964.

WLOSOCK, Antonie. Laktanz und die philosophische Gnosis: Untersuchungen zu Geschichte und Terminologie der gnostischen Erlösungsvorstellung. AHAWP, 1960/2. Heidelberg: C. Winter, 1960.

22. Marcellus of Ancyra

TETZ, Martin. "Zur Theologie des Markell von Ankyra, I." Zeitschrift für Kirchengeschichte, 75 (1964): 217-270.

23. Maximus the Confessor

a. Texts

Maximus the Confessor. The Church, the Liturgy, and the Soul of Man: The Mystagogia of St. Maximus the Confessor. Translated by Julian Stead. Still River, MA: St. Bede's Publications, 1982.

b. Studies

BALTHASAR, Hans Urs von. Kosmische Liturgie: Das Weltbild Maximus' der Bekenner. 2. Aufl. Einsiedeln: Johannes-Verlag, 1961.

DALMAIS, Irénée-Henri. "Place de la Mystagogie de s. Maxime le

Confesseur dans la théologie liturgique byzantine." In Studia
Patristica, vol. 5, pp. 277-283. Edited by F. L. Cross.
TUGAL, 80. Berlin: Akademie-Verlag, 1962.

_____. "Théologie de l'Eglise et mystère liturgique dans la Mys-
tagogie de S. Maxime le Confesseur." In Studia Patristica, vol.
13, pp. 145-153. Edited by Elizabeth A. Livingstone. TUGAL,
116. Berlin: Akademie-Verlag, 1975.

24. Niceta of Remesiana

NICETA OF REMESIANA. "An Explanation of the Creed" and "Liturgical Singing." In his Writings, pp. 43-53, 65-76. Translated by Gerald G. Walsh. FOC, 7. Washington, DC: Catholic
University of America Press, 1949.

25. Origen

a. Texts

GOGLER, Rolf, ed. Origenes: Das Evangelium nach Johannes.
MKZU, n.F. 4. Einsiedeln: Benziger, 1959.

b. Studies

CROUZEL, Henry. "Origène et la structure du sacrement." Bulletin de littérature ecclésiastique, 63 (1962): 81-104.

DANIELOU, Jean. Origène. Paris: La table ronde, 1948; Origen.
Translated by Walter Mitchell. New York: Sheed & Ward, 1955.

GREGG, J. A. F. "The Commentary of Origen upon the Epistle to
the Ephesians." Journal of Theological Studies, 3 (1902): 233-
244, 398-420, 554-576.

HANSON, R. P. C. Allegory and Event: A Study of the Sources
and Significance of Origen's Interpretation of Scripture. London: SCM Press; Richmond, VA: John Knox Press, 1959.

JENKINS, Claude. "Origen on I Corinthians." Journal of Theological Studies, 9 (1908): 231-247, 353-372, 500-514; 10 (1909):
29-51.

LIES, Lothar. Wort und Eucharistie bei Origines: zur Spiritual-
isierungstendenz des Eucharistieverständnisses. ITS, 1. Innsbruck: Tyrolia Verlag, 1978.

26. Philo of Alexandria

LAPORTE, Jean. La Doctrine eucharistique chez Philon d'Alexandrie. TH, 16. Paris: Beauchesne, 1972.

27. The Pliny Correspondence

LIETZMANN, Hans. "Die liturgischen Angaben des Plinius." In his Kleine Schriften, Bd. 3, pp. 48-53. Herausgegeben von der Kommission für spätantike Religionsgeschichte. Berlin: Akademie-Verlag, 1962.

MARTIN, Ralph P. "A Footnote to Pliny's Account of Christian Worship." In Vox Evangelica III, pp. 51-57. Edited by Ralph P. Martin. London: Epworth Press, 1964.

28. Proclus of Constantinople

LEROY, F. J. L'homiletique de Proclus de Constantinople: tradition manuscrite, inédits, études connexes. ST, 247. Città del Vaticano: Biblioteca Apostolica Vaticana, 1967.

29. Prudentius

PRUDENTIUS. "Hymns for Every Day." In The Poems of Prudentius, pp. 3-92. Translated by Sr. M. Clement Eagan. FOC, 43. Washington, DC: Catholic University of America Press, 1962.

30. Pseudo-Dionysius the Areopagite

a. Texts

PARKER, John, ed. The Celestial and Ecclesiastical Hierarchy of Dionysius the Areopagite. London: Skeffington, 1894.

b. Studies

BEBIS, George S. "'The Ecclesiastical Hierarchy' of Dionysios the Areopagite: A Liturgical Interpretation." Greek Orthodox Theological Review, 19 (1974): 159-175.

BOULARAND, E. "L'eucharistie d'après le pseudo-Denys l'Aréopagite." Bulletin de littérature ecclésiastique, 58 (1957): 193-217; 59 (1958): 129-169.

COLET, John. Two Treatises on the Hierarchies of Dionysius.

Edited and translated by J. H. Lupton. London: Bell & Daldy,
1869; reprint ed., Ridgewood, NJ: Gregg Press, 1966.

RUTLEDGE, Denys. Cosmic Theology: The Ecclesiastical Hierarchy
of Pseudo-Denys: An Introduction. London: Routledge &
Kegan Paul; Staten Island, NY: Alba House, 1964.

31. Tertullian

a. Texts

EVANS, Ernest, ed. Tertullian's Homily on Baptism. London:
SPCK, 1964.

LE SAINT, William P., ed. Tertullian: Treatises on Penance.
ACW, 28. Westminster, MD: Newman Press; London: Longmans, Green, 1959.

REFOULE, R. F., ed. Tertullian: Traité du baptême. Traduction
en collaboration avec M. Drouzy. SC, 25. Paris: Cerf, 1952.

b. Studies

BERAN, J. "De ordine missae secundum Tertulliani Apologeticum."
In Miscellanea liturgica in honorem L. Cuniberti Mohlberg, vol.
2, pp. 7-32. BEL, 23. Rome: Edizioni Liturgiche, 1948.

CAMELOT, Th. "Un texte de Tertullien sur l'amen de la communion." La Maison-Dieu, 79 (1964): 108-113.

DANIELOU, Jean. "Le traité De centesima, sexagesima, tricesima
et le judéo-christianisme avant Tertullian." Vigiliae Christianae,
25 (1971): 171-181.

DEKKERS, Eligius. Tertullianus en de geschiedenis der liturgie.
Catholica: VI. Liturgie, 2. Bruxelles: De Kinkhoren, 1947.

KOLPING, A. Sacramentum Tertullianum. Münster: Regensburg,
1948.

MICHAELIDES, Dimitri. Sacramentum chez Tertullian. Paris:
Etudes Augustiniennes, 1970.

32. Theodore of Mopsuestia

a. Texts

MINGANA, Alphonse, ed. Commentary of Theodore of Mopsuestia
on the Lord's Prayer and on the Sacraments of Baptism and the
Eucharist. WS, 6. Cambridge: Heffer, 1933.

RUCKER, Adolf, ed. Ritus baptismi et missae, quem descripsit
Theodorus ep. Mopsuestenus in sermonibus catecheticis e ver-
sione syriaca ab A. Mingana nuper reperta in linguam latinam.
OTHE, ser. liturgica, 2. Münster: Aschendorff, 1933.

TONNEAU, Raymond, and DEVREESSE, Robert, eds. Les homélies
catéchétiques de Théodore de Mopsueste. ST, 145. Città del
Vaticano: Biblioteca Apostolica Vaticana, 1949.

b. Studies

ABRAMOWSKI, Luise. "Zur Theologie Theodors von Mopsuestia."
Zeitschrift für Kirchengeschichte, 72 (1961): 263-293.

BRIGHTMAN, F. E. "The Anaphora of Theodore." Journal of
Theological Studies, 31 (1930): 160-164.

LIETZMANN, Hans. "Die Liturgie des Theodor von Mopsuestia."
In his Kleine Schriften, Bd. 3, pp. 71-97. Herausgegeben von
der Kommission für spätantike Religionsgeschichte. Berlin:
Akademie-Verlag, 1962.

QUASTEN, Johannes. "The Liturgical Mysticism of Theodore of
Mopsuestia." Theological Studies, 15 (1954): 431-439.

REINE, Francis J. The Eucharistic Doctrine and Liturgy of the
Mystagogical Catecheses of Theodore of Mopsuestia. SCA, 2.
Washington, DC: Catholic University of America Press, 1942.

H. THE DIDACHE

1. Texts

AUDET, Jean Paul. La Didachè. Paris: Gabalda, 1958.

GLIMM, Francis X., ed. "The Didache or Teaching of the Twelve
Apostles." In The Apostolic Fathers, pp. 167-184. FOC, 1.
New York: Christian Heritage, 1947.

GOODSPEED, Edgar J., ed. "The Teaching of the Twelve Apostles
--the Didache." In his The Apostolic Fathers: An American
Translation, pp. 9-18. New York: Harper, 1950.

KLEIST, James A., ed. "Didache." In The Didache, Barnabas,
Polycarp, Papias, Diognetus, pp. 1-25. ACW, 6. Westminster,
MD: Newman Press, 1948.

KRAFT, Robert A., ed. The Apostolic Fathers: A New Translation and Commentary, vol. 3: Barnabas and the Didache. General Editor: Robert M. Grant. New York: Nelson, 1965.

LAKE, Kirsopp, ed. "Didache." In The Apostolic Fathers, vol. 1, pp. 303-333. LCL. London: Heinemann; New York: Putnam, 1912.

LIETZMANN, Hans, ed. Die Didache. 6. Aufl. KT, 6. Berlin: De Gruyter, 1962.

LIGHTFOOT, J. B. "The Didache, or Teaching of the Apostles." In The Apostolic Fathers, pp. 121-129. Edited and completed by J. R. Harmer. London: Macmillan, 1891; reprint ed., Grand Rapids, MI: Baker, 1956.

RICHARDSON, Cyril C., ed. "The Teaching of the Twelve Apostles, commonly called the Didache." In Early Christian Fathers, pp. 161-179. LCC, 1. Philadelphia, PA: Westminster Press, 1953; reprint ed., New York: Macmillan, 1970.

STANIFORTH, Maxwell, ed. "The Didache." In Early Christian Writings: The Apostolic Fathers, pp. 225-237. Baltimore, MD: Penguin Books, 1968.

2. Studies

BETZ, Johannes. "Die Eucharistie in der Didache." Archiv für Liturgiewissenschaft, 11 (1969): 10-39.

CLERICI, Luigi. Einsammlung der Zerstreuten: Liturgiegeschichtliche Untersuchungen zur Vor- und Nachgeschichte der Fürbitte für die Kirche in Didache 9,4 und 10,5. LQF, 44. Münster: Aschendorff, 1966.

DANIELOU, Jean. "La Didachè et les origines liturgiques." La Maison-Dieu, 56 (1958): 157-160.

DECROOS, M. "De eucharistische liturgie van Didache IX en X." Bijdragen, 28 (1967): 376-398.

DIBELIUS, M. "Die Mahlgebete der Didache." Zeitschrift für die neutestamentliche Wissenschaft, 37 (1938): 32-41; reprinted in his Botschaft und Geschichte, Bd. 2, pp. 117-127. Herausgegeben von Günther Bornkamm. Tübingen: Mohr, 1956.

GIBBINS, H. G. "The Problem of the Liturgical Section of the Didache." Journal of Theological Studies, 36 (1935): 373-386.

MAZZA, E. "Didache IX-X: Elementi per una interpretazione eucaristica." Ephemerides liturgicae, 92 (1978): 393-419.

MIDDLETON, R. D. "The Eucharistic Prayers of the Didache." Journal of Theological Studies, 36 (1935): 259-267.

PETERSON, Erik. "Didache cap. 9 e 10." Ephemerides liturgicae,
   58 (1944): 3-13.

_____. "Uber einige Probleme der Didache-Uberlieferung."
   Rivista di archeologia cristiana, 27 (1951): 37-68; reprinted in
   his Frühkirche, Judentum und Gnosis, pp. 146-182. Rome:
   Herder, 1959.

VOOBUS, Arthur. Liturgical Traditions in the Didache. Stockholm:
   ETSE, 1968.

_____. "Regarding the Background of the Liturgical Traditions
   in the Didache." Vigiliae Christianae, 23 (1969): 81-87.

VOKES, Frederick E. "The Didache Still Debated." Church Quarterly, 3 (1970): 57-62.

_____. The Riddle of the Didache. CHS. London: SPCK,
   1938.

I. HIPPOLYTUS

1. Texts

BOTTE, Bernard, ed. La tradition apostolique de saint Hippolyte.
   Introduction, traduction et notes par Bernard Botte. 4. Aufl.
   SC, 11 bis. Münster: Aschendorff, 1972.

COQUIN, René-Georges, ed. Les Canons d'Hippolyte. Edité de la
   version arabe. PO, 31/2. Paris: Firmin Didot, 1966.

CUMING, G. J., ed. Hippolytus: A Text for Students. GLS, 8.
   Bramcote, Eng.: Grove Books, 1976.

DIX, Gregory, ed. The Apostolic Tradition of St. Hippolytus. 2d
   ed. Re-issued with corrections, preface and bibliography by
   Henry Chadwick. CHS. London: SPCK, 1968.

DUENSING, Hugo, ed. Der aethiopische Text der Kirchenordnung
   des Hippolytus. Göttingen: Vanderhoeck & Ruprecht, 1946.

HANSSENS, Jean Michel, ed. La liturgie d'Hippolyte. Rome:
   Libreria editrice dell' Universita gregoriana, 1970.

THOMPSON, Bard. "The Apostolic Tradition of Hippolytus." In
   his Liturgies of the Western Church, pp. 11-24. Cleveland:
   World, 1961; reprint ed., Philadelphia, PA: Fortress Press,
   1981.

TILL, Walter, and LEIPOLDT, Johannes, eds. Der koptische Text
der Kirchenordnung Hippolyts. TUGAL, 58. Berlin: Akademie-
Verlag, 1954.

2. Studies

BOTTE, Bernard. "A propos de la 'Tradition apostolique.'" Recherches de théologie ancienne et médiévale, 33 (1966): 177-
186.

_____. "L'authenticité de la Tradition apostolique de s. Hippo-
lyte." Recherches de théologie ancienne et médiévale, 16
(1949): 177-185.

_____. "L'épiclèse de l'anaphore d'Hippolyte." Recherches de
théologie ancienne et médiévale, 14 (1947): 241-251.

_____. "Note historique sur la concélébration dans l'Eglise anci-
enne." La Maison-Dieu, 35 (1953): 9-23.

_____. "L'origine des canons d'Hippolyte." In Mélanges en
l'honneur de Mgr Michel Andrieu, pp. 53-63. Strasbourg:
Palais universitaire, 1956.

_____. "Un passage difficile de la 'Tradition apostolique' sur le
signe de la croix." Recherches de théologie ancienne et médiévale, 27 (1960): 5-19.

CAPELLE, Bernard. "A propos d'Hippolyte de Rome." Recherches
de théologie ancienne et médiévale, 19 (1952): 193-202; reprinted in his Travaux liturgiques, vol. 2, pp. 61-70. Louvain:
Centre liturgique, Abbaye du Mont César, 1962.

_____. "Hippolyte de Rome." Recherches de théologie ancienne
et médiévale, 17 (1950): 145-174; reprinted in his Travaux
liturgiques, vol. 2, pp. 31-60. Louvain: Centre liturgique,
Abbaye du Mont César, 1962.

CONNOLLY, Richard H. "The Eucharistic Prayer of Hippolytus."
Journal of Theological Studies, 39 (1938): 350-369.

CONNOLLY, Richard H. The So-Called Egyptian Church Order and
Derived Documents. TaS, 8/4. Cambridge: Cambridge University Press, 1916; reprint ed., Nendeln: Kraus, 1967.

ELFERS, Heinrich. "Neue Untersuchungen über die Kirchenordnung
Hippolyts von Rom." In Abhandlungen über Theologie und
Kirche: Festschrift für Karl Adam, pp. 169-211. Herausgege-
ben von Marcel Reding. Düsseldorf: Patmos, 1952.

HANSSENS, J. M. La liturgie d'Hippolyte: ses documents, son titulaire, ses origines et son charactère. 2. éd. OCA, 155. Rome: Pontificium Institutum Orientalium Studiorum, 1965.

————. "La sacrifice de louange: lecture de la liturgie euchar-istique d'Hippolyte de Rome." Foi et Vie, 70 (1971): 180-195.

LORENTZ, Rudolf. De Egyptische kerkordening en Hippolytus van Rome. Haarlem: Enschede, 1929.

MAGNE, Jean. "La prétendue Tradition apostolique d'Hippolyte de Rome s'appelait-elle AI DIATAXEIS HAGION APOSTOLON, Les statuts des saint apôtres?" Ostkirchliche Studien, 14 (1965): 35-67.

RICHARDSON, Cyril C. "A Note on the Epiclesis in Hippolytus and the Testamentum Domini." Recherches de théologie ancienne et médiévale, 15 (1948): 357-359.

————. "The So-Called Epiclesis in Hippolytus." Harvard Theo-logical Review, 40 (1947): 101-108.

SALLES, A. "La 'Tradition apostolique' est-elle un témoin de la liturgie romaine?" Revue d'histoire religieuse, 148 (1955): 181-213.

SCHWARTZ, Eduard. Uber die pseudoapostolischen Kirchenordnun-gen. Strassburg: Trübner, 1910.

J. APOSTOLIC CONSTITUTIONS, DIDASCALIA,
    AND RELATED DOCUMENTS

1. Texts

CONNOLLY, Richard H., ed. Didascalia apostolorum: The Syriac Version Translated and Accompanied by the Verona Fragments. Oxford: Clarendon Press, 1929; reprinted 1969.

COOPER, James, and MacLEAN, Arthur J. Testament of Our Lord. Translated from the Syriac, with introduction and notes. Edin-burgh: T. & T. Clark, 1902.

CRESSWELL, Richard H., ed. The Liturgy of the Eighth Book of "The Apostolic Constitutions," Commonly Called the Clementine Liturgy. London: SPCK; New York: E. & J. B. Young, 1900.

CURETON, William, ed. "Doctrina Apostolorum." In Ancient Syriac Documents relative to the Earliest Establishment of Christianity

in Edessa and the Neighbouring Countries, from the Year after
our Lord's Ascension to the beginning of the Fourth Century,
pp. 24-35. Amsterdam: Oriental Press, 1967.

FUNK, F. X., ed. Didascalia et Constitutiones Apostolorum. 2
vols. Paderborn: Schöningh, 1905.

HARDEN, J. M., ed. The Ethiopic Didascalia. TCL, Ser. 4.
London: SPCK; New York: Macmillan, 1920.

LAGARDE, Paul de, ed. Didascalia apostolorum syriace. Göttingen:
Dieterich, 1911.

LAGARDE, Paul de, ed. [Doctrina Apostolorum.] In Reliquiae iuris
ecclesiastici antiquissimae syriace primus, pp. 32-44, 89-95.
Leipzig: Teubner, 1856; London: Williams & Norgate, 1865.

LIETZMANN, Hans, ed. Die klementinische Liturgie aus den Constitutiones apostolorum VIII. Liturgische Texte, VI. KT, 61.
Bonn: Marcus & Weber, 1910.

PLATT, Thomas Pell, ed. The Ethiopic Didascalia; or the Ethiopic
Version of the Apostolic Constitutions. London: Oriental Translation Fund by R. Bentley, 1834.

RAHMANI, Ignatius Ephraem II, ed. Testamentum Domini nostri
Jesu Christ. Mainz: Kirchheim, 1899.

TIDNER, Erik, ed. Didascaliae apostolorum, Canonum ecclesiasticorum, Traditionis apostolicae versiones latinae, TUGAL, 75.
Berlin: Akademie-Verlag, 1963.

2. Studies

BATES, W. H. "The Composition of the Anaphora of Apostolic
Constitutions VIII." In Studia Patristica, vol. 13, pp. 343-355.
Edited by Elizabeth A. Livingstone. TUGAL, 116. Berlin:
Akademie-Verlag, 1975.

BOUSSET, Wilhelm. "Eine jüdische Gebetssammlung im siebenten
Buch der Apostolischen Konstitution." Nachrichten der Akademie der Wissenschaften in Göttingen, (1945): 435-489.

BURKITT, F. C. "The Didascalia." Journal of Theological Studies,
31 (1930): 258-265.

DREWS, Paul Gottfried. Untersuchungen über die sogenante clem-
entinische Liturgie im VIII. Buch der apostolischen Konstitution-
en. 2 vols. (His) Studien zur Geschichte des Gottesdienstes
und des gottesdienstliche Lebens, 2-3. Tübingen: Mohr, 1906.

FUNK, Franz Xaver. Das Testament unseres Herrn und die verwandten Schriften. FCLD, 2/1-2. Mainz: Kirchheim, 1901.

KAUFHOLD, Hubert. "Die 'Lehre des Apostels Addai' ('Lehre der Apostel')." In Paul de Lagarde und die syrischen Kirchengeschichte, pp. 102-128. Herausgegeben von Göttinger Arbeitskreis für syrische Kirchengeschichte. Göttingen: Lagarde-Haus, 1968.

MAZZA, E. "La 'Gratiarum Actio Mystica' del Libro VII delle Constituzioni Apostoliche: Una tappa nella storia della anafora eucaristica." Ephemerides liturgicae, 93 (1979): 123-137.

PITT, William E. "The Anamnesis and Institution Narrative in the Liturgy of Apostolic Constitutions Book VIII." Journal of Ecclesiastical History, 7 (1958): 1-7.

RICHARDSON, Cyril C. "A Note on the Epiclesis in Hippolytus and the Testamentum Domini." Recherches de théologie ancienne et médiévale, 15 (1948): 357-359.

TURNER, C. H. "Notes on the Apostolic Constitutions." Journal of Theological Studies, 31 (1929-1930): 128-141.

_____. "A Primitive Edition of the Apostolic Constitutions and Canons: An Early List of Apostles and Disciples." Journal of Theological Studies, 15 (1914): 53-65; 16 (1915): 54-61, 523-538.

K. EGERIA

1. Texts

BLUDAU, Augustin. Die Pilgerreise der Aetheria. SGKA, 15/1-2. Paderborn: Schöningh, 1927; reprint ed., New York: Johnson Reprints, 1968.

FRANCHESCHINI, Ezio, and WEBER, Robert, eds. Itinerarium Egeriae. Editio critica cura et studio. CC, 1. Turnholt: Brepols, 1958.

GINGRAS, George E., ed. Egeria: Diary of a Pilgrim. ACW, 38. New York: Newman Press, 1970.

PETRE, Hélène, ed. Journal de voyage. Texte latin, introd. et trad. de Hélène Pétré. SC, 21. Paris: Cerf, 1948.

WILKINSON, John, ed. Egeria's Travels. Newly translated with supporting documents and notes. London: SPCK, 1971;

revised ed., Jerusalem: Ariel; Warminster, Eng.:   Aris &
Phillips, 1981.

2. Studies

BASTIAENSEN, A. A. R.   Observations sur le vocabulaire liturgique dans l'Itinéraire d'Egérie.   LCP, 17.   Nijmegen: Dekker
& Van de Vegt, 1962.

CABROL, Fernand.   Les Eglises de Jerusalem, la discipline et la
liturgie au IVe siècle: étude sur la peregrinatio Sylviae.
Paris: Librairie religieuse H. Oudin, 1895.

FEROTIN, M., and LECLERCQ, H.   "Etheria."   Dictionnaire d'archéologie chrétienne et de liturgie, 5:552-584.

L. SERAPION

1. Texts

BRIGHTMAN, F. E.   "The Sacramentary of Serapion of Thmuis."
Journal of Theological Studies, 1 (1899-1900):   88-113, 247-277.

WOBBERMIN, Georg, ed.   Altchristliche liturgische Stücke aus der
Kirche Agyptens.   TUGAL, 17 (n.F. 2)/3b1.   Leipzig: Hinrichs, 1898.

WORDSWORTH, J., ed.   Bishop Serapion's Prayer Book.   2d ed.
TCL, Ser. 3.   London: SPCK, 1923; reprint ed., Hamden,
CT: Archon Books, 1964.

2. Studies

BOTTE, Bernard.   "L'eucologe de Sérapion est-il authentique?"
Oriens Christianus, 48 (1964):   50-56.

CAPELLE, Bernard.   "L'anaphore de Serapion: essai d'exégèse."
Le Muséon, 59 (1946):   424-443; reprinted in his Travaux litur-
giques, vol. 2, pp. 344-358.   Louvain: Centre liturgique,
Abbaye du Mont César, 1962.

RODOPOULOS, Archimandrite P.   "Doctrinal Teaching in the Sacramentary of Serapion of Thmuis."   Greek Orthodox Theological
Review, 9 (1963-1964):   201-214.

M. THE AGAPE MEAL

BAKER, Frank. "Love Feast." Dictionary of Liturgy and Worship, pp. 247-250.

DRESCHER, Johann G. F. De veterum Christianorum agapis. Giessen: Schroeder, 1824.

FUNK, Franz Xaver. "Die Agape." In his Kirchengeschichtliche Abhandlungen und Untersuchungen, Bd. 1, pp. 1-41. Paderborn: Schöningh, 1907.

GAMBER, Klaus. "Das Eucharistiegebet im Papyrus von Dêr-Balizeh und die Samstagabend-Agapen in Agypten." Ostkirchliche Studien, 7 (1958): 48-65.

KOCH, Hugo. "Zur Agapen-Frage." Zeitschrift für die neutestamentliche Wissenschaft, 16 (1915): 139-146.

LECLERCQ, Henri. "Agape." Dictionnaire d'archéologie chrétienne et de liturgie, 1:775-848.

LEIPOLDT, Johannes. "Agapen." Die Religion in Geschichte und Gegenwart (3. Aufl.), 1:169-170.

RIEHM, Heinrich. "Zur Wiederentdeckung der Agape." Jahrbuch für Liturgik und Hymnologie, 20 (1976): 144-148.

N. THE EARLY NORTH AFRICAN LITURGY

BISHOP, W. C. "The African Rite." Journal of Theological Studies, 13 (1911-1912): 250-277.

CASATI, G. "La liturgia della messa al tempo di S. Agostino." Augustinianum, 9 (1969): 484-514.

GAMBER, Klaus. "Ordo Missae Africanae. Der nordafrikanische Messritus zur Zeit des hl. Augustinus." Römische Quartalschrift, 64 (1969): 139-153.

SCHWEITZER, Erich. "Fragen der Liturgie in Nordafrika zur Zeit Cyprians." Archiv für Liturgiewissenschaft, 12 (1970): 69-84.

O. MISCELLANEOUS STUDIES

"Aberkios." Reallexikon für Antike und Christentum, 1:12-17. [On early inscriptions.]

BAUMSTARK, Anton. "Das Gesetz der Erhaltung des Alten in
    liturgischer hochwertiger Zeit." Jahrbuch für Liturgiewissen-
    schaft, 7 (1927): 1-23.

BORNKAMM, Gunther. "Das Anathema in der urchristlichen Abend-
    mahlsliturgie." Theologische Literaturzeitung, 75 (1950): 227-
    230.

BROWE, Peter. "Die Sterbekommunion im Altertum und Mittelalter."
    Zeitschrift für katholischen Theologie, 60 (1936): 1-54, 211-249.

CASEL, Odo. "Die logike thusia der antiken Mystik in christlich-
    liturgischer Umdeutung." Jahrbuch für Liturgiewissenschaft, 4
    (1924): 37-47.

DAVIES, John G. "The Introduction of the Numinous into the Lit-
    urgy: An Historical Note." Studia Liturgica, 8 (1971-1972):
    216-223.

DOLGER, Franz Joseph. "Die Eucharistie als Reiseschutz." Antike
    und Christentum, 5 (1936): 232-247.

_____. ICHTHUS: Das Fisch symbol in frühchristlicher Zeit.
    5 vols. Münster: Aschendorff, 1922-1943.
    1. Religionsgeschichtliche und epigraphische Untersuchungen.
        2. Aufl. 1928.
    2-3. Der heilige Fisch in den antiken Religionen und im Christ-
        entum. Textband und Tafeln. 1922.
    4-5. Die Fischdenkmäler in der frühchristlichen Plastik, Malerei
        und Kleinkunst. Textband und Tafeln. 1927, 1943.

_____. "Sacramentum infanticidii." Antike und Christentum, 4
    (1934): 188-228.

ENGBERDING, H. "Das angeblicke Dokument römischer Liturgie aus
    dem Beginn des dritten Jahrhunderts." In Miscellanea liturgica
    in honorem L. Cuniberti Mohlberg, vol. 1, pp. 47-71. Rome:
    Edizioni Liturgiche, 1948.

ENGEMANN, J. "Fisch." Reallexikon für Antike und Christentum,
    7:959-1097.

FRANKE, Peter. "Zur Fragen frühchristlichen liturgischer Mahl-
    zeiten in Aquileia." Archiv für Liturgiewissenschaft, 14 (1972):
    139-155.

HAMMAN, Adalbert. Vie liturgique et vie sociale, repas des pauvres,
    diaconie et diaconat, agape et repas de charité, offrandre dans
    l'antiquité chrétienne. Paris: Desclée, 1968.

HIERS, H. H. "The Bread and Fish Eucharist in the Gospels and

Early Christian Art." Perspectives in Religious Studies, 3
(1976): 20-47.

KILMARTIN, Edward J. "The Eucharistic Cup in the Primitive Liturgy." Catholic Biblical Quarterly, 24 (1962): 32-43.

KOTTJE, Raymond. "Das Aufkommen der täglichen Eucharistiefeier
in der Westkirche und die Zölibatsforderung." Zeitschrift für
Kirchengeschichte, 82 (1971) 218-228.

KRETSCHMAR, Georg. "Ein Beitrag zur Frage nach dem Ursprung
frühchristlichen Askese." Zeitschrift für Theologie und Kirche,
61 (1964): 27-67; reprinted in his Askese und Mönchtum in der
alten Kirche, pp. 129-180. Herausgegeben von K. Suso Frank.
WF, 409. Darmstadt: Wissenschaftliche Buchgesellschaft, 1975.

LEBRETON, J. "Le désaccord de la foi populaire et de la théologie
savante dans l'Eglise chrétienne du IIIe siècle." Revue d'histoire ecclésiastique, 19 (1923): 481-506; 20 (1924): 5-37.

LEGRAND, Hervé-Marie. "The Presidency of the Eucharist According to the Ancient Tradition." Worship, 53 (1979): 413-438.

MARTINEZ-FAZIO, Luis M. "Eucaristia, Banquete y Sacrificio en
la Iconografia Paleocristiana." Gregorianum, 57 (1976): 459-
521.

MILBURN, Robert L. P. "Symbolism and Realism in Post-Nicene
Representations of the Eucharist." Journal of Ecclesiastical
History, 8 (1957): 1-16.

MULLER-BARDORFF, Johannes. "Nächtlicher Gottesdienst im apostolischen Zeitalter." Theologische Literaturzeitung, 81 (1956):
347-352.

ROBINSON, J. M. "Die Hodajot-Formel in Gebet und Hymnus des
Frühchristentums." In Apophoreta: Festschrift für Ernst
Haenchen zu seinem siebzigsten Geburtstag am 10.1964, pp.
194-236. Herausgegeben von W. Eltester und F. H. Kettler.
Berlin: Töpelmann, 1964.

SAXER, Victor. Vie liturgique et quotidienne à Carthage vers le
milieu du IIIe siècle. SAC, 29. Rome: Pontificio Instituto di
Archeologia Cristiania, 1969.

SCHINDLER, Alfred. "Gott als Vater in Theologie und Liturgie der
christlichen Antike." In Das Vaterbild im Abendland, Bd. 1,
pp. 55-69. Herausgegeben bon Hubertus Tellenbach. Stuttgart: Kohlhammer, 1978.

SIMPSON, R. L. The Interpretation of Prayer in the Early Church.
Philadelphia, PA: Westminster Press, 1965.

STUIBER, Alfred. "Apophoreton." Jahrbuch für Antike und
    Christentum, 3 (1960): 155-159.

TANGHE, A. "L'eucharistie pour le rémission des péchés."
    Irénikon, 34 (1961): 165-181.

VEILLEUX, Armand. La liturgie dans le cenobitisme pachômien au
    quatrième siècle. SA, 57. Rome: Herder, 1968.

VOLKL, L. "Apophoretum, Eulogie und Fermentum als Ausdrucks-
    former der frühchristlichen Communio." In Miscellanea G. Bel-
    vederi, pp. 391-414. Vatican City, 1954.

VOGEL, Cyrille. "Le repas sacré au poisson chez les chrétiens."
    Revue des sciences religieuses, 46 (1966): 1-26.

WAINWRIGHT, Geoffrey. "Baptismal Eucharist before Nicaea: An
    Essay in Liturgical History." Studia Liturgica, 4 (1965): 9-36.

WATTEVILLE, Jean François Noel de. Le sacrifice dans les textes
    eucharistiques des premiers siècles. BT. Neuchâtel: Dela-
    chaux et Niestlé, 1966.

WERNER, Eric. "The Eucharist in Hebrew Literature during the
    Apostolic And Post-Apostolic Epoch." Journal of Ecumenical
    Studies, 13 (1976): 316-320.

WINSLOW, Bede. "Liturgy and Reunion: II. Some Leading Ideas
    in the Primitive Liturgies." Eastern Churches Quarterly, 4
    (1940-1941): 47-53.

VIII.   THE EASTERN CHURCHES

A.   COLLECTED TEXTS

Anaphorae Syricae. Rome: Pontificium Institutum Orientlaium
    Studiorum, 1939- .

ASSEMANI, G. L., ed. Codex liturgicus ecclesiae universae in quo
    continentur libri rituales, missales, pontificales, officia, dypticha,
    etc. ecclesiarum Occidentis et Orientis. 13 vols. Rome: Kom-
    arek, 1749-1766; reprint eds., Paris: Huberti Welter, 1902;
    Farnborough, Eng.: Gregg, 1968.

ATTWATER, Donald. Eastern Catholic Worship. New York: Devin-
    Adair, 1945.

BRIGHTMAN, F. E., ed. Liturgies Eastern and Western. Vol. 1:
Eastern. Oxford: Clarendon Press, 1896; reprinted 1965.

DANIEL, Hermann Adalbert, ed. Codex liturgicus ecclesiae universae in epitome redactus, vol. 4: Codex liturgicus ecclesiae
orientali. Lipsiae: Weigel, 1853; reprint ed., Hildesheim:
Olms, 1966.

DAY, Peter D., ed. Eastern Christian Liturgies: The Armenian,
Coptic, Ethiopian, and Syrian Rites. Shannon: Irish University Press, 1972.

DENZIGER, Heinrich Josef Domenik. Ritus Orientalium Coptorum,
Syrorum et Armenorum. 2 vols. in 1. Würzburg: Stahel,
1863-1864; reprint ed., Graz: Akademische Druck- und Verlagsanstalt, 1961.

HANGGI, Anton, and PAHL, Irmgard, eds. Prex eucharistica.
Textus e variis liturgiis antiquioribus selecti. SF, 12. Fribourg: Editions universitaires, 1968.

Liturgies and Other Documents of the Ante-Nicene Period. Ante-
Nicene Christian Library, vol. 24. Edinburgh: T. & T. Clark,
1872.

NEALE, John Mason. The Liturgies of S. Mark, S. James, S.
Clement, S. Chrysostom, and the Church of Malabar. Translated with Introduction and Appendices by J. M. Neale. London: J. T. Hayes, 1859; reprint ed., New York: AMS Press,
1969.

_____, ed. The Liturgies of S. Mark, S. James, S. Clement, S.
Chrysostom, S. Basil; or according to the Use of the Churches
of Alexandria, Jerusalem and Constantinople and the Formula of
the Apostolic Constitutions. 4th ed. London: Richard Dickinson, 1896.

NEALE, John M., and LITTLEDALE, R. F., eds. Liturgies of SS.
Mark, James, Clement, Chrysostom and Basil and the Church of
Malabar. 4th ed. London: J. T. Hayes, 1883.

QUASTEN, Johannes, ed. Monumenta eucharistica et liturgica vetustissima. Collegit, notis et prolegomenis instruit J. Quasten.
7 vols. FP, 7, pars 1-7. Bonn: Hanstein, 1935-1937.

RENAUDOT, Eusèbe. Liturgiarum orientalium collectio. 2 vols.
Paris: J. B. Coignard, 1716; ed. 2a correctio, Francofurti
a.M.: Baer, 1847.

SWAINSON, Charles Anthony, ed. The Greek Liturgies. Cambridge: Cambridge University Press, 1884.

B. GENERAL STUDIES

ATTWATER, Donald. The Christian Churches of the East. Rev.
ed. 2 vols. Lancashire, Eng.: Thomas More Books; London:
Geoffrey Chapman; Milwaukee, WI: Bruce, 1961.

_____. A List of Books in English about the Eastern Churches.
Foreword by Leo M. McMahon. Newport, RI: St. Leo Shop, 1960.

BAUMSTARK, Anton. Die Messe im Morgenland. Sammlung Kösel,
8. Kempten: Kösel, 1906.

CHAVASSE, Antoine. "L'épiclèse eucharistique dans les anciennes
liturgies orientales: une hypothèse d'interprétation." Mélanges
de science religieuse, 2 (1946): 197-206.

CLUGNET, Léon. Dictionnaire grec-français des noms liturgiques
en usage dans l'église grecque. Paris: Picard, 1895.

CONNOLLY, R. H., ed. Anonymi auctoris expositio officiorum ecclesiae Georgio Arbelensi vulgo adscripta. 4 vols. CSCO, 64,
71, 72, 76. Paris: Typographeo Reipublicae, 1911-1954; reprint ed., Louvain: Secretariat du Corpus SCO, 1960-1961.

DALMAIS, Irénée-Henri. "The Expression of Faith in the Eastern
Liturgies." In Liturgical Experience of Faith, pp. 77-85.
Edited by Herman Schmidt and David Power. Concilium, 82.
New York: Herder & Herder, 1973.

_____. Les liturgies d'Orient. Paris: Fayard, 1959; Eastern
Liturgies. Translated by Donald Attwater. TCEC, 112. New
York: Hawthorn Books, 1960.

_____. Les liturgies d'Orient. RS, 10. Paris: Cerf, 1980.

EDELBY, Neophytos, and DICK, Ignace. Les églises orientales
catholiques: Decret Orientalium Ecclesiarum. Texte latin et
traduction française. Commentaire par N. Edelby et I. Dick.
US, 76. Paris: Cerf, 1970.

ENGBERDING, Hieronymus. "Zur Geschichte der Liturgie der
vorgeweihten Gaben." Ostkirchliche Studien, 13 (1964): 310-
314.

FINN, Edward E. These are My Rites: A Brief History of the
Eastern Rites of Christianity. Collegeville, MN: Liturgical
Press, 1980.

FORTESCUE, Adrian K. The Lesser Eastern Churches. London:
Catholic Truth Society, 1913; reprint ed., New York: AMS
Press, 1972.

_____. The Orthodox Eastern Church. London: Sands, 1907; reprint ed., New York: Burt Franklin, 1969.

_____. The Orthodox Eastern Church. 3d ed. London: Catholic Truth Society, 1929.

_____. The Uniate Eastern Churches. Edited by George D. Smith. London: Burns, Oates & Washbourne; New York: Benziger, 1923; reprint ed., New York: Ungar, 1957.

GODART, J. "Traditions anciennes de la grand prière eucharistique." Questions liturgiques et paroissiales, 47 (1966): 258-278; 48 (1967): 9-36, 198-218.

HAMMERSCHMIDT, Ernst. "Das Liturgische Formkriterium: ein Prinzip in der Erforschung der orientalischen Liturgien." In Studia Patristica, vol. 5, pp. 50-68. Edited by F. L. Cross. TUGAL, 80. Berlin: Akademie-Verlag, 1962.

_____. "Probleme der orientalischen Liturgiewissenschaft." Ostkirchliche Studien, 10 (1961): 28-47.

HANSSENS, Jean Michel. Institutiones liturgicae de rebus orientalibus. 2 vols. and appendix. Rome: Universitas Gregoriana, 1930-1932.

HEILER, Friedrich, and HARTOG, Hans. Die Ostkirchen. Herausgegeben von Anne Marie Heiler. München: Reinhardt, 1971.

HOPPE, Ludwig Augustin. Die Epiklesis der griechischen und orientalischen Liturgien und der römische Consekrationskanon. Schaffhausen: Hurtersche Buchhandlung, 1864.

JANIN, Raymond. Les églises orientales et les rites orientaux. 4e éd. Paris: Letouzey & Ané, 1955.

KING, Archdale A. The Rites of Eastern Christendom. 2 vols. Rome: Catholic Book Agency, 1947-1948; reprint ed., New York: AMS Press, 1972.

LECLERCQ, Henri. "Messe, XLI: La Messe des présanctifiés." Dictionnaire d'archéologie chrétienne et de liturgie, 11:770-771.

LIESEL, Nikolaus. Die Liturgien der Ostkirche: die Eucharistiefeier der orientalischen Katholiken. Fulda: Familienverlag, 1956; The Eastern Catholic Liturgies: A Study in Words and Pictures. Photographs by T. Makula. Westminster, MD: Newman Press, 1960.

_____. Die Liturgien der Ostkirche. Freiburg: Herder, 1960; The Eucharistic Liturgies of the Eastern Churches. Translated

by David Heimann.   Photographs by T. Makula.   PLL.   Collegeville, MN: Liturgical Press, 1963.

LIGIER, Louis.   "Autour du sacrifice eucharistique: anaphores
orientales et anamnèse juive de Kippour."   Nouvelle revue théologique, 82 (1960):   44-55.

Liturgical Arts Society, New York.   The Eastern Branches of the
Catholic Church: Six Studies in the Oriental Rites.   Introduction by Donald Attwater.   New York: Longmans, Green, 1938.

MADEY, Johannes.   Lasst uns danksagen: Gebete aus den Eucharistiefeiern der Kirchen des Ostens.   Freiburg: Herder, 1965.

MAX, Prince of Saxony.   Praelectiones de liturgiis orientlaibus.   2
vols.   Freiburg: Herder, 1908-1913.

MOREAU, F. J.   Les liturgies eucharistiques: notes sur leur origine et leur développement.   Bruxelles: Vromant, 1924.

PRADO, G.   "Los sacramentos en los ritos orientales."   Liturgia,
15 (1960):   288-293.

RAES, Alphonse.   "La concélébration eucharistique dans les rites
orientaux."   La Maison-Dieu, 35 (1953):   24-47.

_____.   Introductio in liturgiam orientalem.   Rome: Pontificium
Institutum Studiorum Orientalium, 1947.

RAHMANI, Ignace Ephrem II.   Les liturgies orientales et occidentales.   Mont Liban, 1924.

SALAVILLE, Sévérien.   "La consécration eucharistique d'après quelques auteurs grecs et syriens."   Echos d'Orient, 13 (1910):
321-324.

_____.   Liturgies orientales.   3 vols.   Paris: Bloud & Gay,
1932-1942.

_____.   Liturgies orientales: notions générales, éléments prin-
cipaux.   BCSR, 47.   Paris: Bloud & Gay, 1932; An Introduction to the Study of Eastern Liturgies.   Adapted from the French
with a preface and some additional notes by John M. T. Barton.
London: Sands, 1938.

_____.   Studia orientalia liturgico-theologica.   Rome: Ephemerides
Liturgicae, 1940.

SALAVILLE, Sévérien, and NORWACK, G.   Le rôle du diacre dans
la liturgie orientale: étude d'histoire et de liturgie.   AOC, 3.
Paris: Institut Français d'Etudes Byzantines, 1962.

SCHMIDT, H. J. "De liturgische taal in de oosterse ritus." Sacris
Erudiri, 1 (1948): 323-349.

SCHNEIDER, Carl. "Studien zum Ursprung liturgischer Einzelheiten
östlicher Liturgien." Kyrios, 3 (1938): 149-190, 293-311.

TAFT, Robert F. Eastern-Rite Catholicism: Its Heritage and Vocation. Glen Rock, NJ: Paulist Press, 1963.

_____. "The Spirit of Eastern Christian Worship." Diakonia, 12
(1977): 103-120.

USPENSKY, Nikolai D. "Liturgy of the Presanctified: Its Origins."
Journal of the Moscow Patriarchate, 2 (1976): 69-80.

VERGHESE, Paul. The Joy of Freedom: Eastern Worship and Modern Man. ESW, 17. Richmond, VA: John Knox Press, 1967.

WEGMAN, H. A. J. Geschiedenis van de christelijke eredienst in
het Oosten: een wegwijzer. Hilversum: Gooi en Sticht, 1976.

WINKLER, Gabriele. "Der geschichtliche Hintergrund der Praesank-
tifikatenvesper." Oriens Christianus, 56 (1972): 184-206.

ZIADE, I. "Présanctifiés (Messe de)." Dictionnaire de théologie
catholique, 13:77-111.

C. EAST SYRIAN CHURCHES (CHALDEAN RITE)

1. Texts

a. Historical

BADGER, G. P. The Nestorians and Their Rituals. 2 vols. London: J. Masters, 1852; reprint ed., Farnborough, Eng.:
Gregg, 1969.

DAHANE, D. Liturgie de la sainte messe selon le rite chaldéen.
Paris: Enault, 1937; Liturgy of the Holy Mass according to the
Chaldean Rite. Translated by Mary Loyola Hayde. Techny,
IL: Mission Press, 1939.

ENGBERDING, Hieronymus. "Die syrischen Anaphora der zwölf
Apostel und ihre Paralleltexte einander gegenübergestellt und
mit neuen Untersuchungen zur Urgeschichte der Chrysostomusliturgie begleitet." Oriens Christianus, 34 (1937): 213-247.

Liturgia sanctorum apostolorum Adaei et Maris: Cui accedunt duae
aliae in quibusdam festis et feriis dicendae, necnon ordo

baptismi. Urmiae: Typis Missionis Archiepiscopi Cantuariensis,
1890.

La messa caldea detta degli Apostoli. CLO, 2. Rome: Pontificium
Institutum Studiorum Orientalium, 1948.

MACOMBER, William F. "The Oldest Known Text of the Anaphora
of the Apostles Addai and Mari." Orientalia Christiana Periodica,
32 (1966): 335-371.

SPINKS, Bryan D., ed. Addai and Mari: The Anaphora of the
Apostles: A Text for Students. GLS, 24. Bramcote, Eng.:
Grove Books, 1980.

    b. Contemporary

Church of the East and the Assyrians. The Liturgy of the Holy
Apostolic and Catholic Church of the East. Translated by Eshai
Shimun XXIII. Chicago: The Patriarchate of the East, 1949.

2. Other Historical Sources

CYRUS OF EDESSA. Six Explanations of the Liturgical Feasts by
Cyrus of Edessa, an East Syrian Theologian of the Mid Sixth
Century. Edited by William F. Macomber. 2 vols. CSCO,
355-356. Louvain: Corpus SCO, 1974.

ISHO'YABH IV. Nestorian Questions on the Administration of the
Eucharist: A Contribution to the History of the Eucharist in
the Eastern Church. Edited by W. C. van Unnik. Haarlem:
Enschedé, 1937; reprint ed., Amsterdam: Grüner, 1970.

[NARSAI.] CONNOLLY, R. H., ed. The Liturgical Homilies of
Narsai. Translated with an introduction by R. H. Connolly.
TaS, 8/1. Cambridge: Cambridge University Press, 1909;
reprint ed., Nendeln: Kraus, 1967.

_____. MINGANA, Alphonse, ed. Narsai: Homiliae et carmina.
Mausilii: Typis Fratrum Praedicatorum, 1905.

3. Studies

BOTTE, Bernard. "L'anaphore chaldéene des apôtres." Orientalia
Christiana Periodica, 15 (1949): 259-276.

_____. "L'épiclèse dans les liturgies syriennes orientales."
Sacris Erudiri, 6 (1954): 48-72.

_____. "Problème de l'anaphore syrienne des apôtres Addai et
Mari." L'Orient Syrien, 10 (1965): 89-106.

CODRINGTON, Humphrey W. Studies of the Syrian Liturgies.
London: G. E. J. Coldwell, 1952.

CUTRONE, Emmanuel J. "The Anaphora of the Apostles: Implications of the Mar Esa 'Ya Text." Theological Studies, 34 (1973):
624-642.

DALMAIS, Irénée-Henri. "L'Esprit Saint et le mystère du salut
dans les épiclèses eucharistiques syriennes." Istina, 18 (1973):
147-154.

DELLY, E. K. "L'édition du Missel chaldéen de 1901." Orientalia
Christiana Periodica, 23 (1957): 159-170.

ENGBERDING, Hieronymus. "Der Kirche als Braut in der ostsyrischen Liturgie." Orientalia Christiana Periodica, 3 (1937):
5-45.

_____. "Zum anaphorischen Fürbittgebet des ostsyrischen Litur-
gie Addaj und Mar(j)." Oriens Christianus, 41 (1957): 102-
124.

_____. "Zum Papyrus 465 der John Rylands Library zu Manches-
ter." Oriens Christianus, 42 (1958): 68-76.

GALVIN, R. J. "Addai and Mari Revisited: The State of the Question." Dunwoodie Review, 10 (1970): 3-31.

GODART, J. "Traditions anciennes de la grand prière eucharistique, II: la tradition syrienne orientale." Questions liturgiques et paroissiales, 48 (1967): 9-36.

JAMMO, Sarhad Y. Hermiz. "Gabriel Qatraya et son commentaire
sur la liturgie chaldéene." Orientalia Christiana Periodica, 32
(1966): 39-52.

_____. La structure de la messe chaldéene: du début jusqu'à
l'anaphore: étude historique. OCA, 207. Rome: Pontificium
Institutum Studiorum Orientalium, 1979.

JONES, Bayard H. "The Formation of the Nestorian Liturgy."
Anglican Theological Review, 48 (1966): 276-306.

_____. "The History of the Nestorian Liturgies." Anglican
Theological Review, 46 (1964): 155-176.

_____. "The Liturgy of Nestorius: The Structural Pattern."
Anglican Theological Review, 48 (1966): 397-411.

_____. "The Sources of the Nestorian Liturgy." Anglican
Theological Review, 46 (1964): 414-425.

LASSUS, Jean. "Liturgies nestoriennes médiévales et l'églises syri-
    ennes antiques." Revue de l'histoire des religions, 137 (1950):
    236-252.

MACOMBER, William F. "A History of the Chaldean Mass." Wor-
    ship, 51 (1977): 107-120.

_____. "The Liturgy of the Word according to the Commentators
    of the Chaldean Mass." In The Word in the World: Essays in
    Honor of Frederick L. Moriarty, pp. 179-190. Edited by R. J.
    Clifford and G. MacRae. Cambridge, MA: Weston College
    Press, 1973.

_____. "The Maronite and Chaldean Versions of the Anaphora of
    the Apostles." Orientalia Christiana Periodica, 37 (1971): 55-
    84.

_____. "The Sources for a Study of the Chaldean Mass." Wor-
    ship, 51 (1977): 523-536.

_____. "A Theory on the Origins of the Syrian, Maronite, and
    Chaldean Rites." Orientalia Christiana Periodica, 39 (1973):
    235-242.

RAES, Alphonse. "The Enigma of the Chaldean and Malabar Ana-
    phora of Apostles." In The Malabar Church, pp. 1-8. Edited
    by Jacob Vellian. Rome: Pontificium Institutum Studiorum
    Orientalium, 1970.

_____. "L'étude de la liturgie syrienne: son état actuel." In
    Miscellanea liturgica in honorem L. Cuniberti Mohlberg, vol. 1,
    pp. 333-346. Rome: Edizioni Liturgiche, 1948.

_____. "La paix pascale dans le rite chaldéen." L'Orient syrien,
    6 (1961): 179-212.

_____. "Les paroles de la consécration dans les anaphores syri-
    ennes." Orientalia Christiana Periodica, 3 (1937): 486-504.

RAES, Alphonse. "Le récit de l'institution eucharistique dans l'ana-
    phore chaldéene et malabare des Apôtres." Orientalia Christiana
    Periodica, 10 (1944): 216-226.

RATCLIFF, E. C. "A Note on the Anaphoras described in the Lit-
    urgical Homilies of Narsai." In Biblical and Patristic Studies in
    Memory of Robert Pierce Casey, pp. 235-249. Edited by J. N.
    Birdsall and R. W. Thompson. Freiburg: Herder, 1963; re-
    printed in his Liturgical Studies of E. C. Ratcliff, pp. 66-79.
    Edited by A. H. Couratin and D. J. Tripp. London: SPCK,
    1976.

_____. "The Original Form of the Anaphora of Addai and Mari:
A Suggestion." Journal of Theological Studies, 30 (1928): 23-
32; reprinted in his Liturgical Studies of E. C. Ratcliff, pp.
80-90. Edited by A. H. Couratin and D. J. Tripp. London:
SPCK, 1976.

SPINKS, Bryan D. "The Original Form of the Anaphora of the Apostles." Ephemerides liturgicae, 91 (1977): 146-161.

TAFT, Robert F. "On the Use of the Bema in the East-Syrian Liturgy." Eastern Churches Review, 3 (Spring 1970): 30-39.

_____. "Some Notes on the Bema in the East and West Syrian
Traditions." Orientalia Christiana Periodica, 34 (1968): 326-359.

VELLIAN, Jacob. "The Anaphoral Structure of Addai and Mari compared to the Berakoth preceding the Shema in the Synagogue
Morning Service." Le Muséon, 85 (1972): 201-223.

_____. "The Church as Bride in the East Syrian Liturgy." In
Studia Patristica, vol. 11, pp. 59-64. Edited by F. L. Cross.
TUGAL, 108. Berlin: Akademie-Verlag, 1976.

WEBB, Douglas. "La liturgie nestorienne des apôtres Addai et Mari
dans la tradition manuscrite." In Eucharisties d'orient et d'occident, vol. 2, pp. 25-50. Paris: Cerf, 1970.

_____. "Variations dans les versions manuscrites de la liturgie
nestorienne d'Addai et de Mari." Sacris Erudiri, 18 (1967):
478-523.

WEGMAN, H. A. J. "Pleidooi voor een tekst. De Anaphora van
de apostolen Addai en Mari." Bijdragen, 40 (1979): 15-43.

D. WEST SYRIAN CHURCHES (ANTIOCHENE RITE)

1. Texts

a. Historical

CODRINGTON, H. W. "The Syrian Liturgy of the Presanctified."
Journal of Theological Studies, 4 (1903): 69-81; 5 (1904):
369-377, 535-545.

FUCHS, Hermann, ed. Die Anaphora des monophysitischen Patri-
archen Jôhannan I. Herausgegeben und im Zusammenhang der
gesamten jakobitischen Anaphorenliturgien untersucht von H.
Fuchs. LQ, 9. Münster: Aschendorff, 1926.

KHOURI-SARKIS, G. "L'anaphore syriaque de Saint Jacques: Introduction, traduction." L'Orient Syrien, 4 (1959): 385-448.

MERCIER, B.-Ch., ed. La liturgie de saint Jacques: édition critique du texte grec avec traduction latine. PO, 26/2. Paris: Firmin-Didot, 1946; reprint ed., Turnhout: Brepols, 1974.

Missale iuxta ritum Ecclesiae apostolicae antiochenae syrorum auctoritate recognitum. Monte Libano: Typis patriarchalibus in Seminario Sciarfensi, 1922.

RUCKER, Adolf, ed. Die syrische Jacobusanaphora nach der Rezension des Ja'qob(h) von Edessa mit dem griechischen Paralleltext. LQ, 4. Münster: Aschendorff, 1923.

TROLLOPE, W., ed. He tou hagiou Iakobou leitourgia: The Greek Liturgy of St. James. Edited with an English Introduction and Notes; together with a Latin Version of the Syriac Copy, and the Greek Text restored to its Original Purity and accompanied by a literal English translation. Edinburgh: T. & T. Clark, 1848.

    b. Contemporary

GRIFFITHS, Bede, ed. The Book of Common Prayer of the Antiochean Syrian Church. Translated by Bede Griffiths. Syrian Churches Series, 3. New York: John XXIII Center, Fordham University, 197?.

HAPGOOD, Isabel F., ed. The Service Book of the Holy Orthodox Catholic Apostolic Church. 5th ed. Englewood, NJ: Syrian Antiochian Orthodox Archdiocese of New York and All North America, 1975.

SAMUEL, Athanasius Yeshue, ed. Anaphora: The Divine Liturgy of St. James, the First Bishop of Jerusalem, according to the Rite of the Syrian Orthodox Church of Antioch. Hackensack, NJ: Athanasius Yeshue Samuel, 1967.

    2. Other Historical Sources

BARHEBRAEUS, Gregorius. Jakobitische Sakramententheologie im 13. Jahrhundert: der Liturgiekommentar des Gregorius Barhebraeus. Herausgegeben von Radbert Kohlhaas. LQF, 36. Münster: Aschendorff, 1959.

CONNOLLY, Richard H., and CODRINGTON, H. W., eds. Two Commentaries on the Jacobite Liturgy, by George, Bishop of the Arab Tribes, and Moses Bar Kepha. London: Williams & Norgate, 1913; reprint ed., Farnborough, Eng.: Gregg, 1969.

DIONYSIUS BAR SALIBI. Expositio liturgicae. Editit et interpretatus est Hieronymus Labourt. CSCO, 13-14; Scriptores Syriaci, 2/93. Paris: Typographeo reipublicae, 1903; reprint ed., Louvain: Durbecq, 1955.

RAHMANI, Ignatius Ephraem II. "Vetusta documenta liturgica." In his Studia Syriaca; seu, Collectio documentorum hactonus ineditorum ex codicibus Syriacis, fasc. 4. Monte Libano: In Seminario Scharfensi, 1909.

3. Studies

BARSOUM, Severius Ephrem. The Golden Key to Divine Worship, with Commentary on the Ritual of the Syriac Church. Translated by James E. Kinnear. West New York, NJ: [Syrian Orthodox Church of Antioch in the United States and Canada], 1951.

CODY, Aelred. "L'eucharistie et les heurs canoniales chez les Syriens Jacobites: une description des cérémonies." L'Orient Syrien, 12 (1967): 55-82, 151-186.

DANIEL, K. N. A Critical Study of Primitive Liturgies, especially that of St. James. 2d ed. Tiruvalla, India: T. A. M. Press, 1949.

ENGBERDING, Hieronymus. "Urgestalt, Eigenart und Entwicklung eines altantiochenischen eucharistischen Hochgebetes." Oriens Christianus, 29 (1932): 32-48.

GODART, J. "Traditions anciennes de la grand prière eucharistique, I. La tradition syrienne occidentale." Questions liturgiques et paroissiales, 47 (1966): 258-278.

HEIMING, Odilo. "Palimpsestbruchstücke der syrischen Version der Jakobusanaphora aus dem 8. Jahrhundert in der Handschrift add. 14615 des British Museum." Orientalia Christiana Periodica, 16 (1950): 190-200.

IWAS, Severius Zaka. "The Doctrine of One Nature in the Syrian Rites." The Greek Orthodox Theological Review, 13 (1968): 309-315.

KAWERAU, Peter. Die jakobitische Kirche im Zeitalter der syrischen Renaissance. BBA, 3. Berlin: Akademie-Verlag, 1955.

KHOURI-SARKIS, G. "Notes sur l'anaphore syriaque de S. Jacques." L'Orient Syrien, 5 (1960): 3-32.

LASSUS, Jean. "La liturgie antique de la Syrie du Nord." In Neue Beiträge zur Kunstgeschichte des 1. Jahrtausends, vol.

1: Spätantike und Byzanz, pp. 45-52. FKCA, 1. Baden-Baden: Verlag für Kunst und Wissenschaft, 1952.

LECUYER, Joseph. "Théologie de l'anaphore chez les Pères de l'église d'Antioch." L'Orient Syrien, 6 (1961): 389-412.

MADEY, Johannes. "Der von dir, Vater, ausgeht und von deinem Sohne nimmt": der Heilige Geist im Beten der Syro-Antiochenischen Kirche. OS, 3. Paderborn: Verlag Bonifacius, 1980.

MOUNAYER, J. "Die Struktur der syrisch-antiochenischen eucharistischen Liturgie." Kyrios, 12 (1972): 185-198.

SHEPHERD, Massey H., Jr. "Eusebius and the Liturgy of St. James." Yearbook of Liturgical Studies, 4 (1963): 109-125.

_____. "The Formation and Influence of the Antiochene Liturgy." In Dumbarton Oaks Papers, vol. 15, pp. 23-44. Washington, DC: Trustees for Harvard University, The Dumbarton Oaks Research Library and Collection, 1961.

SIMAN, Emmanuel Pataq. "La dimension pneumatique de l'eucharistie d'après la tradition syrienne de l'Antioche." In L'expérience de l'esprit: Mélanges E. Schillebeeckx, pp. 97-114. Paris: Beauchesne, 1976.

_____. L'expérience de l'Esprit par l'Eglise d'après la tradition syrienne d'Antioche. TH, 15. Paris: Beauchesne, 1971.

SPINKS, Bryan D. "The Consecratory Epiclesis in the Anaphora of St. James." Studia Liturgica, 11 (1976): 19-38.

VERGHESE, Paul. "Relation between Baptism, 'Confirmation' and the Eucharist in the Syrian Orthodox Church." Studia Liturgica, 4 (1965): 81-93.

4. The Jerusalem Liturgy

(See also VII. K. Egeria.)

CUMING, G. J. "Egyptian Elements in the Jerusalem Liturgy." Journal of Theological Studies, N.S. 25 (1974): 117-124.

CUTRONE, Emmanuel J. "Cyril's Mystagogical Catecheses and the Evolution of the Jerusalem Anaphora." Orientalia Christiana Periodica, 44 (1978): 52-64.

KRETSCHMAR, Georg. "Die frühe Geschichte der Jerusalemer Liturgie." Jahrbuch für Liturgik und Hymnologie, 2 (1956): 22-46.

TARBY, André.   La prière eucharistique de l'église de Jerusalem.
   TH, 17.   Paris: Beauchesne, 1972.

5.   The Maronite Church

a.   Texts

EID, Joseph, ed.   The Maronite Catholic Mass.   Fall River, MA,
   1962.

HAYEK, Michel.   Liturgie Maronite: Histoire et textes eucharistiques.   Tours: Mame, 1964.

KHALIL, Louis, ed.   The Maronite Mass and Devotions.   Boston,
   MA: St. Paul Editions, 1957.

Officium feriale iuxta ritum ecclesiae syrorum Maronitarum.   Roma:
   S. Congregationis de Propaganda fides, 1853 (etc.); Beryti:
   Typis Soc. Jesu, 1904.

SFEIR, Peter F., ed.   The Syriac-Maronite Mass in English, Explanation of the Ceremonies, the Mass, Responses of the Server
   and Hymns of the Choir.   2d ed.   Buffalo, NY: The author,
   1953.

b.   Studies

DIB, Pierre.   Etude sur la liturgie maronite.   Paris: P. Lethielleux, 1919.

_____.   Histoire de l'église maronite.   Mélanges et documents,
   1.   Beirut: Editions La Sagesse, 1962; History of the Maronite
   Church.   Detroit, MI: Maronite Apostolic Exarchate, 1971.

GEMAYEL, P. E.   Avant-messe maronite: histoire et structure.
   OCA, 174.   Rome: Pontificium Institutum Orientalium Studiorum,
   1965.

E.   BYZANTINE CHURCHES

1.   General Works (Greek and Slavic Churches)

a.   Historical Texts

ARRANZ, Miguel, ed.   Le Typicon du Monastère du Saint-Sauveur
   à Messine: Codex Messinensis Gr 115, A.D. 1131.   OCA, 185.
   Rome: Pontificium Institutum Studiorum Orientalium, 1969.

BAUMSTARK, Anton, ed. Die konstantinoplitanische Messliturgie
vor dem 9. Jahrhundert. Liturgische Texte, III. KT, 35.
Bonn: Marcus & Weber, 1909.

BRIGHTMAN, F. E., ed. The Divine Liturgy of Saint John Chrysostom. London: Faith Press, 1922.

CODRINGTON, H. W. The Liturgy of St. Peter. Preface and Introduction by Placid de Meester. LQF, 30. Münster: Aschendorff, 1936.

Euchologium sinaiticum: starocerkvenoslovanski glagolski spomenik.
Izdajo priredil Rajko Nahtigal. 2 vols. Akademija znanosti in
umetnosti v Ljubljani, Filozofsko-filoloskohistoricni razred, 1-2.
Ljubljana, 1941-1942.

FRCEK, Jean, ed. Euchologium Sinaiticum, texte slave avec
sources grecques et traduction française. 2 vols. PO, 24/5
& 25/3. Paris: Firmin-Didot, 1933-1939; reprint ed., Turnhout: Brepols, 1974.

GOAR, Jacques. Euchologion, sive Rituale Graecorum. Editio 2a.
Venice: B. Javarin, 1730; reprint ed., Graz: Akademische
Druck- und Verlagsanstalt, 1960.

HABERTI, Isaac, ed. Archieratikon: Liber pontificalis ecclesiae
graecae. Paris: P. Blasius, 1643; reprint ed., Farnborough,
Eng.: Gregg, 1970.

MALTZEW, Alexios von, ed. Andachtsbuch der orthodox-katholisch-
en Kirche des Morgenlandes. Deutsch und Slavisch unter
Berücksichtigung des griechischen Urtextes. Berlin: Siegismund, 1895.

_____, ed. Begräbniss-ritus und einige specielle und alterthüm-
liche Gottesdienste der orthodox-katholischen Kirche des Morgenlandes. Deutsch und slavisch unter Berücksichtigung des
griechischen Urtextes. Berlin: Siegismund, 1898.

_____, ed. Bitt-, Dank-, und Weihegottesdienste der orthodox-
katholischen Kirche des Morgenlandes. Deutsch und slavisch
unter Berücksichtigung des griechischen Urtextes. Berlin:
Siegismund, 1897.

_____, ed. Fasten- und Blumen-triodion nebst den Sonntags-
liedern des Oktoichos der orthodox-katholischen Kirche des
Morgenlandes. Deutsch und slavisch unter Berücksichtigung
des griechischen Urtextes. Belrin: Siegismund, 1899.

MALTZEW, Alexios von, ed. Die göttlichen Liturgien unserer Väter
unter den Heiligen, Joannes Chrysostomos, Basilios des Grossen

und Gregorios Dialogos. Deutsch und slavisch unter Berücksichtigung des griechischen Urtextes. Berlin: Siegismund, 1890; reprint ed., Darmstadt: Wissenschaftliche Buchgesellschaft, 1967.

_____, ed. Die göttlichen Liturgien unserer Väter unter den Heiligen, Joannes Chrysostomos, Basilios des Grossen und Gregorios Dialogos. 4. Aufl. Berlin: Verlag des St. Wladimir-wohlthätigkeits-vereins "Bratswo," 1911.

_____, ed. Liturgikon: Die Liturgien der orthodox-katholischen Kirche des Morgenlandes. Unter Berücksichtigung des bischöflichen Ritus, nebst einer historischvergleichenden Betrachtung der hauptsächlichsten Liturgien des Orients und Occidents. Berlin: Siegismund, 1902.

_____, ed. Die Nachtwache: oder, Abend- und Morgengottesdienst der orthodox-katholischen Kirche des Morgenlandes. Deutsch und slavisch unter Berücksichtigung des griechischen Urtextes. Berlin: Siegismund, 1892.

_____, ed. Die Sakramente der orthodox-katholischen Kirche des Morgenlandes. Deutsch und slavisch unter Berücksichtigung des griechischen Urtextes. Berlin: Siegismund, 1898.

MATEOS, Juan, ed. Le Typicon de la grand église. 2 vols. OCA, 165-166. Rome: Pontificium Institutum Studiorum Orientalium, 1962-1963.

MEESTER, Placide de, ed. La divine liturgie de notre père S. Jean Chrysostome. Texte grec et traduction française avec introduction et notes par Placide de Meester. 3. éd. Rome: Typographie Polyglotte Vaticane, 1925; The Divine Liturgy of our Father among the Saints. Greek text with introduction and notes by Dom Placid de Meester. Translated by the Benedictines of Stanbrook. London: Burns, Oates & Washbourne, 1926.

MERCENIER, F., and PARIS, François, eds. La prière des églises de rite byzantin. 2. éd. CI. Chevetogne: Monastère de Chevetogne, 1948- .

La prière des églises de rite byzantin. Chevetogne: Editions de Chevetogne, 1975- .

MORAITES, Demetrios N., ed. He leitourgia ton proegiasmenon. Thessalonike: Aristoteleion Panepistemion Thessalonikes, 1955.

NOLI, Fan Stylian, ed. Three Liturgies of the Eastern Orthodox Church. Boston: Albanian Orthodox Church in America, 1955. [From Mega Euchologion, Athens, 1902.]

PATRINACOS, Nicon D. The Orthodox Liturgy: The Greek Text
    with a completely new Translation followed by notes on the
    Text, the Sunday Gospel and Apostolic Readings, together with
    tracing the development of the Orthodox Liturgy from the 2nd
    Century to this Day. Foreword by Archbishop Iakovos. Gar-
    wood, NJ: Graphic Arts Press, 1974.

PATRINACOS, Nicon D., ed. The Orthodox Liturgy: The Greek
    Text of the Ecumenical Patriarchate with a Translation into
    English by the Liturgical Commission of the Greek Orthodox
    Archdiocese of North and South America, together with a
    Study of the Development of the Orthodox Liturgy from the
    2nd Century to this Day. Garwood, NJ: Graphic Arts Press,
    1976.

ROBERTSON, J. N. W. B., ed. The Divine and Sacred Liturgies
    of our Fathers among the Saints John Chrysostom and Basil the
    Great. With an English translation. London: D. Nutt, 1886.

STORF, Remigius. Griechische Liturgien. BK, 5. Kempton:
    Kösel, 1912.

TREMPELAS, Panagiotes N., ed. Hai treis leitourgiai. Athens:
    Verlag der Byzantinischneugriechischen Jahrbücher, 1935; The
    Orthodox Liturgy. London: SPCK, 1935.

WALTER, Wolfhard, ed. Die göttliche Liturgie unseres heiligen
    Vaters Johannes Chrysostomus. Sophia, 15. Leipzig: St.
    Benno Verlag, 1976.

         b. Typical Editions of the Greek Liturgies (Rome)

[Evangelistarion.] Theion kai hieron Evangelion ex aristou ekdoseou
    tes neas diathekes akribos diorthothen. Rome, 1880.

[Horologion.] Horologion periechou ten hemeronyktion akolouthi
    meta ton synethon prosthekon. 2. ed. Rome: Typois tes
    Hieras kai Enagous Mones Kryptopherras, 1937.

[Leitourgikon.] Hagiasmatarion. Rome, 1954.

_____. Hieratikon. Rome, 1950.

_____. [Excerpt] Akolouthiai to Hesperinon kai tou Orthrou.
    Rome, 1950.

[Menaion.] Menaia tou holou eniautou. 6 vols. Rome, 1888-1901.

[Mikron euchologion.] Mikron euchologion syn Theoi hagioi. Rome:
    Polyglottou typographias, 1872.

[Oktoechos.] Oktoechos tou en hagiois patros hemon Ioannou to
Damaskenou. Rome, 1886.

_____. Parakletike; etoi, Oktoechos he megale. Rome, 1885.

[Pentekostarion.] Pentekostarion, charmosynon teu apo tou Pascha
mechri tes ton agion pantou kyriakes anekousan auto akolou-
thion, Rome, 1883.

[Triodion.] Triodion katanyktikon. Rome, 1879.

c. Contemporary Texts

HAPGOOD, Isabel F., ed. Service Book of the Holy Orthodox
Catholic Apostolic Church. Boston: Houghton Mifflin, 1906.

_____, ed. _____. Rev. ed., with endorsement by Patriarch
Tikhon. New York: Association Press, 1922.

_____, ed. Service Book of the Holy Orthodox Catholic Apos-
tolic Church. 5th ed. New York: Syrian Antiochian Orthodox
Archdiocese of New York and All North America, 1975.

HATCHETT, Marion J. "Seven Pre-Reformation Eucharistic Litur-
gies: Historic Rites arranged for Contemporary Celebration.
A Post-Constantinian Eastern Liturgy." St. Luke's Journal of
Theology, 16, 3 (1973): 27-42.

MASTRANTONIS, George, ed. Divine Liturgy of St. John Chrysostom of the Eastern Orthodox Church. New York: Greek
Orthodox Archdiocese of North and South America, 1966.

RAYA, Joseph, and VINCK, José de. Byzantine Daily Worship.
Allendale, NJ: Alleluia Press, 1969.

_____. Byzantine Missal: For Sundays and Feast Days, with
Rites of Sacraments, and Various Offices and Prayers. Birmingham, AL: St. George's R. C. Byzantine Church, 1958.

d. General Studies

ANTONIADIS, Sophie. Place de la liturgie dans la tradition des
lettres grecques. Leiden: Sijthoff, 1939.

BARROIS, Georges. Scripture Readings in Orthodox Worship.
Crestwood, NY: St. Vladimir's Seminary Press, 1977.

BASDEKIS, A. "Grundfragen orthodoxen Gottesdienstverständ-
nisse." Okumenische Rundschau, 28 (1979): 259-276.

BEBIS, George S. "The Influence of Jewish Worship on Orthodox

Christian Worship." The Greek Orthodox Theological Review, 22 (1977): 136-142.

_____. "Worship in the Orthodox Church." The Greek Orthodox Theological Review, 22 (1977): 429-443.

BORNERT, René. "Die Symbolgestalt der byzantinischen Liturgie." Archiv für Liturgiewissenschaft, 12 (1970): 54-68.

BOROS, Ladislaus. "Meditationen über die Eucharistie." Orientierung, 27 (1963): 117-119, 134-136.

BOUWEN, Frans. "For a Liturgical Renewal in the Byzantine Liturgy." Diakonia, 4 (1969): 314-325.

BRAKMANN, H. "Zum Gemeinschaftlichen Eucharistiegebet byzantinischer Konzelebranten." Orientalia Christiana Periodica, 42 (1976): 319-367.

BRANISTE, E. "Liturgiereform in der orthodoxen Kirche: ihre Notwendigkeit, ihre Grenzen und ihre Aussichten auf Verwirklichung." Ostkirchliche Studien, 27 (1978): 128-142.

CLEMENT, O. "Brève introduction à la liturgie byzantine." Etudes théologiques et religieuses, 37 (1962): 49-93.

CONSTANTELOS, Demetrios J. "The Holy Scriptures in Greek Orthodox Worship." The Greek Orthodox Theological Review, 12 (1966): 7-83.

EDELBY, Néophytos. Liturgikon: Messbuch der byzantinischen Kirche. Recklinghausen: Bongers, 1967.

ENGDAHL, Richard, ed. Beiträge zur Kenntniss der byzantinischen Liturgie: Texte und Studien. NSGTK, 5. Berlin: Trowitzsch & Sohn, 1908; reprint ed., Aalen: Scientia-Verlag, 1973.

ENGBERDING, Hieronymus. "Das anaphorische Fürbittgebet der Basiliusliturgie." Oriens Christianus, 47 (1963): 16-52; 49 (1965): 18-37.

_____. "Das anaphorische Fürbittgebet der byzantinischen Chrysostomusliturgie." Oriens Christianus, 45 (1961): 20-29; 46 (1962): 33-60.

_____. "Die Angleichung der byzantinischen Chrysostomusliturgie an die byzantinischen Basiliusliturgie." Ostkirchliche Studien, 13 (1964): 310-314.

_____. Das eucharistische Hochgebet der Basileiosliturgie. TCO, 1. Münster: Aschendorff, 1931.

_____. "Die 'EUCHE TES PROSKOMIDES' der byzantinischen Basiliusliturgie und ihre Geschichte." Muséon, 79 (1966): 287-313.

ENGBERDING, Hieronymus. "Die Kunstprosa des eucharistischen Hochgebetes der griechischen Gregoriusliturgie." In Mullus: Festschrift Theodor Klauser, pp. 100-110. JAC, 1. Münster: Aschendorff, 1964.

FENWICK, John. The Eastern Orthodox Liturgy. GBMW, 56. Bramcote, Eng.: Grove Books, 1978.

FLOROVSKY, Georges. "The Worshipping Church." In The Festal Menaion. Edited by Mother Mary and Kallistos Ware. London: Faber, 1969.

FRENCH, Reginald M. The Eastern Orthodox Church. London: Hutchinson's University Library, 1951.

GAVIN, Frank. Some Aspects of Contemporary Greek Orthodox Thought. Milwaukee, WI: Morehouse, 1923.

GONZALEZ, Arthur E. John, and CHAPMAN, Matthew G. "The Lex Orandi of the Eastern Church: Critical Addenda to Professor Davies' Assessment of Orthodox Worship." The Greek Orthodox Theological Review, 23 (1978): 53-68.

GOUILLARD, Jean, ed. Le Synodikon de l'Orthodoxie: édition et commentaire. Paris: Centre français d'études byzantines, 1967.

GUNSTONE, John Thomas Arthur. The Feast of Pentecost: The Great Fifty Days in the Liturgy. SCW, 8. London: Faith Press, 1967.

HARAKAS, Stanley S. "The Orthodox Priest as Leader in the Divine Liturgy." The Greek Orthodox Theological Review, 21 (1976): 163-176.

HOLLOWAY, Henry A. A Study of the Byzantine Liturgy. London: Mitre, 1933.

HOPKO, Thomas. The Orthodox Faith: Worship. New York: Department of Religious Education, The Orthodox Church in America, 1973.

IVANOV, N. "Der Kelch der Gemeinschaft." Stimme der Orthodoxie, (September 1964): 41-44.

_____. "Der Kelch des Lebens." Stimme der Orthodoxie, (Mai 1963): 54-58; (Juni 1963): 45-48.

KATZEKOSTAS, Leontios. "He Theia Eucharistia kata ton Ious-
tinon." Gregorios ho Palamas, 40 (1957): 144-151.

KUCHAREK, Casimir A. The Sacramental Mysteries: A Byzantine
Approach. Allendale, PA: Alleluia Press, 1976.

LEDOGAR, Robert J. Acknowledgement: Praise Verbs in the Early
Greek Anaphora. Rome: Herder, 1968.

MEESTER, Placide de. Studi sui sacramenti, amministrati secondo
il rito bizantino. AL, 7. Rome: Edizioni Liturgiche, 1947.

MIRKOVIC, Lazar. Pravoslavna liturgika ili nauka o bogosluzenju
pravoslavne istocne crkve. 2 vols. in 1. Sremski Karlovci:
Srpska Manastirska Stamparija, 1918-1926.

OAKLEY, Austin. The Orthodox Liturgy. London: Mowbray,
1958.

ONASCH, Konrad. "Der Funktionalismus der orthodoxen Liturgie:
Grundzüge einer Kritik." Jahrbuch für Liturgik und Hymnologie, 6 (1961): 1-48.

POKORNY, L. "Liturgie peje siovansky." In Solunsti bratri, 1100
let od prichodu sv. Cyrila e Metodeje na Moravu, pp. 158-191.
Prague: Ceska katolicka charita, 1963.

PULLAN, Leighton. A Guide to the Holy Liturgy of St. John
Chrysostom. London: SPCK, 1921.

RAHLFS, Alfred. Die alttestamentlichen Lektionen der griechischen
Kirche. Berlin: Weidmannsche Buchhandlung, 1915.

RILEY, Athelstan. A Guide to the Divine Liturgy in the East.
London: Mowbray, 1922.

SCHMEMANN, Alexander. For the Life of the World. New York:
National Student Christian Federation, 1963.

_____. Sacraments and Orthodoxy. New York: Herder &
Herder, 1965; British ed., The World as Sacrament. London:
Darton, Longman & Todd, 1966.

_____. For the Life of the World: Sacraments and Orthodoxy.
Crestwood, NY: St. Vladimir's Seminary Press, 1973.

SCHULZ, Hans-Joachim. Die byzantinische Liturgie: vom Werden
ihrer Symbolgestalt. Sophia, 5. Freiburg: Lambertus-Verlag,
1964.

_____. Die byzantinische Liturgie: Glaubenszeugnis und Sym-
bolgestalt. 2. Aufl. Trier: Paulinus Verlag, 1980.

SIOTES, Markos. "Das Abendmahl nach der griechisch-orthodoxen Exegese." Eine heilige Kirche, 27, 2 (1953-1954): 1-15.

_____. "Theia Eucharistia: Hai peri tes theias eucharistias plerophoriai tes Kainos Diathekes hupo to phos tes ekklesiastikes hermeneias." Epistemonike epeteris tes theologikes scholes tou panepistemiou Thessalonikes, 2 (1957): 153-223.

SPASSKIJ, T. "L'office liturgique slave de la Sagesse de Dieu." Irénikon, 30 (1957): 164-188.

TARCHNISVILI, Michael. Die byzantinische Liturgie als Verwirklichung der Einheit und Gemeinschaft in Dogma. Wurtzbourg: Rita-Verlag, 1939.

TKADLCIK, V. "Byzantinischer und römischer Ritus in der slavischen Liturgie." In Wegzeichen: Festgabe zum 60. Geburtstag von Prof. Dr. Hermenegild M. Biedermann, pp. 313-332. Herausgegeben von E. Chr. Suttner und C. Patock. Würzburg: Augustinus-Verlag, 1971.

TREMPELAS, Panagiotes Nikolaou. "Der orthodoxe christliche Gottesdienst." In Die Orthodoxe Kirche in griechischer Sicht, Bd. 1, pp. 157-168. Edited by Panagiotis Bratsiotis. Stuttgart: Evangelisches Verlagswerk, 1959.

TZOGA, Charilaos E. "Ho trishagios humnos." In Theologikon Symposion: [Festschrift] Panagiotes K. Chrestou, pp. 275-287. Thessaloniki, 1967.

VASICA, J. "Slovanska liturgie sv. Petra." Byzantinoslavica, 8 (1939-1940): 1-54.

WALTER, Christopher. Art and Ritual of the Byzantine Church. Birmingham Byzantine Series, 1. London: Variorum, 1982.

WARE, Kallistos. "Church and Eucharist, Communion and Intercommunion." Sobornost, 7 (1978): 550-567.

WAWRYK, Michael. Initiatio monastica in liturgia byzantina. OCA, 180. Rome: Pontificium Institutum Orientalium Studiorum, 1968.

ZERNOV, Nicolas. "The Worship of the Orthodox Church and Its Message." In The Orthodox Ethos: Essays in Honour of the Centenary of the Greek Orthodox Archdiocese of North and South America, pp. 115-121. Edited by A. J. Philippou. Oxford: Holywell Press, 1964.

e. Historical Studies

CUMING, G. J. [Untitled Review of G. Wagner, Der Ursprung der
Chrysostomusliturgie.] Eastern Churches Review, 7 (1975):
95-97.

GERO, Stephen. "The Eucharistic Doctrine of the Byzantine
Iconoclasts and Its Sources." Byzantinische Zeitschrift, 68
(1975): 4-22.

HANNICK, Christian. Studien zu den griechischen und slavischen
liturgischen Handschriften der Osterreichischen Nationalbiblio-
thek. Byzantina Vindobonensia, 6. Vienna: Böhlau, 1972.

JACOB, A. "La traduction de la liturgie de Saint Jean Chrysostome par Léo Toscan." Orientalia Christiana Periodica, 32
(1966): 111-162.

KHOURI-SARKIS, G. "L'origine syrienne de l'anaphore byzantine
de Saint Jean Chrysostome." L'Orient syrien, 7 (1962):3-68.

KUCHAREK, Casimir A. The Byzantine-Slav Liturgy of St. John
Chrysostom: Its Origin and Evolution. Allendale, PA: Alleluia Press, 1972.

MATEOS, Juan. Le célébration de la parole dans la liturgie byzantine: étude historique. OCA, 191. Rome: Pontificium
Institutum Orientalium Studiorum, 1971.

_____. "Evolution historique de la liturgie de Saint Jean Chry-
sostome." Proche Orient Chrétien, 15 (1965): 333-351; 16
(1966): 3-18, 133-161; 17 (1967): 141-176; 305-325; 20
(1970): 97-122.

MATEOS, Juan. "The Evolution of the Byzantine Liturgy." In
John XXIII Lectures, vol. 1: Byzantine Christian Heritage,
pp. 76-112. New York: John XXIII Center for Eastern Christian Studies, Fordham University, 1966.

MEESTER, Placide de. Liturgica bizantino: studi di rito bizantino
alla luce della teologica, del diritto ecclesiastico della storia,
dell' arte et dell archeologia. Rome: Tipografia Leonina, 1930.

_____. "Les origines et les developpements du texte grec de
la liturgie de St. Jean Chrysostome." In Krisostomika: studi
e ricerche intorno a S. Giovanni Crisostomo, pp. 245-357.
Rome: Pustet, 1908.

OPELT, I. "Die Essener 'Missa Graeca' der liturgischen Handschrift Düsseldorf D2." Jahrbuch der österreichischen Byzantinistik, 23 (1974): 77-88.

PAVERD, Franz van de. Zur Geschichte der Messliturgie in Anti-
ocheia und Konstantinopel gegen Ende des vierten Jahrhunderts: Analyse der Quellen bei Johannes Chrysostomos.
OCA, 187. Rome: Pontificium Institutum Orientalium Studiorum, 1970.

PITT, W. E. "The Origin of the Anaphora of the Liturgy of St.
Basil." Journal of Ecclesiastical History, 12 (1961): 1-13.

RAES, Alphonse. "L'authenticité de la liturgie byzantine de saint
Basile." Revue des études byzantines, 16 (1958): 158-161.

_____. "L'authenticité de la liturgie byzantine de saint Jean
Chrysostome." Orientalia Christiana Periodica, 24 (1958):
5-16.

_____. "Un nouveau document de la liturgie de S. Basile."
Orientalia Christiana Periodica, 26 (1960): 401-411.

RYCAUT, Paul. The Present State of the Greek and Armenian
Churches. London: Printed for John Starkey, 1679.

SIDARUS, Adel. "La divine liturgie d'après les sources chrysos-
tomiennes: note bibliographique." Proche Orient Chrétien,
22 (1972): 305-322.

SOLOVEY, Meletius Michael. Bozhestvenna liturhiia. Rome, 1964;
The Byzantine Divine Liturgy: History and Commentary.
Translated by Demetrius Emil Wysochansky. Washington, DC:
Catholic University Press, 1970.

_____ [SOLOWIJ, Meletij M.]. De reformatione liturgica Heraclii
Lisowskyj archiepiscopi Polocensis (1784-1809). 2 ed. Analecta OSBM, Ser. 2, 2. Rome: PP. Basilianorum, 1950.

STRITTMATTER, A. "Missa Graecorum, Missa Sancti Johannis
Chrysostomi, the oldest Latin Version known of the Byzantine
Liturgies of St. Basil and St. John Chrysostom." Ephemerides
liturgicae, 55 (1941): 2-73.

TAFT, Robert F. "Evolution historique de la liturgie de saint
Jean Chrysostome." Proche Orient Chrétien, 22 (1972): 241-
287; 24 (1974): 3-33, 105-138; 25 (1975): 16-45, 274-299.

TAFT, Robert F. The Great Entrance: A History of the Transfer
of Gifts and Other Preanaphoral Rites of the Liturgy of St.
John Chrysostom. OCA, 200. Rome: Pontificium Institutum
Studiorum Orientalium, 1975.

_____. "How Liturgies Grow: The Evolution of the Byzantine
'Divine Liturgy.'" Orientalia Christiana Periodica, 43 (1977):
355-378.

_____ . "Towards the Origins of the Offertory Procession in the
Syro-Byzantine East." Orientalia Christiana Periodica, 36
(1970): 73-107.

TREMPELAS, Panagiotes Nikolaou. Leitourgikoi typoi Aigyptou kai
Anatoles, symbolai eis ten historian tes Christianikes latreias.
Athens: Ekdosis tes Apostolikes Diakonias tes Ekklesias tes
Hellados, 1961.

WAGNER, Georg. Der Ursprung der Chrysostomusliturgie. LQF,
59. Münster: Aschendorff, 1973.

WINKLER, Gabriele. "Die Interzessionen der Chrysostomusanaphora
in ihrer geschichtlichen Entwicklung." Orientalia Christiana
Periodica, 36 (1970): 301-336; 37 (1971): 333-383.

     f. Early Commentaries (esp. Nicolas Cabasilas)

     (1). Texts

CABASILAS, Nicholas. Explication de la divine liturgie. Traduction et notes de Sévérien Salaville. SC, 4. Paris: Cerf,
1943; A Commentary on the Divine Liturgy. Translated by
J. M. Hussey and P. A. McNulty. London: SPCK, 1960;
reprint ed., Crestwood, NY: St. Vladimir's Seminary Press,
1977.

_____ . Explication de la divine liturgie. 2e éd., munie du
texte grec, revue et augmentée par René Bornert, Jean
Gouillard et Pierre Périchon. SC, 4 bis. Paris: Cerf, 1967.

_____ . The Life in Christ. Translated by Carmino J. de Catanzaro. Introduction by Boris Bobrinskoy. Crestwood, NY:
St. Vladimir's Seminary Press, 1974; reprinted, 1982.

GERMANUS I, Patriarch of Constantinople. Il commentario liturgico
di S. Germano patriarca Constantinopolitano e la versione latina
di Anastasio bibliotecario. Nuova edizione con aggiunte di Nilo
Borgia. Grottaferrata: Tip. italo-orientale S. Nilo, 1912.

_____ . "Rerum ecclesiasticarum contemplatio." Edited by Nilo
Borgia. Rome e l'oriente, 2 (1911): 144-156, 219-228, 286-
296, 346-354.

_____ . "Rerum ecclesiasticarum contemplatio (historia mystagogica)." Edited by F. E. Brightman. Journal of Theological
Studies, 9 (1908): 257-267, 387-397.

     (2). Studies

BORNERT, René. Les commentaires byzantins de la divine liturgie du VIIe au XVe siècle. AOC, 9. Paris: Institut français d'Etudes Byzantines, 1966.

BRIGHTMAN, F. E. "The Historia Mystagogica and Other Greek Commentaries on the Byzantine Liturgy." Journal of Theological Studies, 9 (1908): 248-267, 387-397.

CRAIG, R. N. S. "Nicolas Cabasilas: An Exposition of the Divine Liturgy." In Studia patristica, vol. 2, pp. 21-28. Edited by Kurt Aland and F. L. Cross. TUGAL, 64. Berlin: Akademie-Verlag, 1957.

LECUYER, J. "L'eucharistie et le don de l'Esprit selon Nicolas Cabasilas." In Ecclesia a Spiritu Sancto edocta, pp. 213-232. Gembloux: Duculot, 1970.

TSIRPANLIS, Constantine N. The Liturgical and Mystical Theology of Nicolas Cabasilas. New York, 1979.

VOLKER, W. Die Sakramentsmystik des Nikolaus Kabasilas. Wiesbaden: Steiner, 1977.

2. Russian Use

a. Texts

The Divine Liturgies of Our Holy Fathers John Chrysostom and Basil the Great. With the authorization of the most holy governing synod of Russia. New York: Dutton, 1873.

The Divine Liturgy of the Holy Orthodox Catholic Apostolic Graeco-Russian Church. Translated by P. Kuvochinsky. London: Cope & Fenwick, 1909.

ENGLERT, Clement C., ed. The Byzantine Liturgy. New York: Fordham Russian Center, 1956.

[Euchologion.] An Abridged Euchologion. Edited by David F. Abramtsov. Philadelphia, PA: Orthodox Catholic Literature Association, 1954.

[Euchologion.] A Manual of Eastern Orthodox Prayers. London: SPCK for the Fellowship of SS. Alban and Sergius; New York: Macmillan, 1945.

HEITZ, Sergius, ed. Der Orthodox Gottesdienst. Mainz: Matthias-Grünewald-Verlag, 1965- .

[Horologion.] Chasoslov. Moskva: Moskovskaia Patriarkhiia, 1961.

[Horologion.] Chasoslov. Paris: YMCA Press, 1949.

Horologion: A Primer for Elementary Village Schools. Translated
    from the Slavonian ed. of 1894, St. Petersburg, by N. Orloff.
    London: J. Davy, 1897; reprint ed., New York: AMS Press,
    1969.

LITTLEDALE, Richard Frederick, ed. Offices from the Service-
    Books of the Holy Eastern Church. London: Williams & Nor-
    gate, 1863; reprint ed., New York: AMS Press, 1970.

[Menaion.] The Ferial Menaion; or, The Book of Services for the
    Twelve Great Festivals and the New Year's Day. Translated
    by N. Orloff. London: J. Parry, 1900; reprint ed., New
    York: AMS Press, 1969.

[Menaion.] The Festal Menaion. Translated by Mother Mary and
    Kallistos Ware. Introduction by Georges Florovsky. London:
    Faber & Faber, 1977.

[Menaion.] The General Menaion; or, The Book of Services Com-
    mon to the Festivals of Our Lord Jesus Christ, of the Holy
    Virgin and of the Different Orders of Saints. Translated from
    the Slavonian ed. of 1862, Moscow, by N. Orloff. London:
    J. Davy, 1899; reprint ed., New York: AMS Press, 1969.

[Molitvoslov.] Euchology, a Manual of Prayers of the Holy Ortho-
    dox Church. Edited by G. V. Shann. Kidderminster, Eng.:
    n.p. 1891; reprint ed., New York: AMS Press, 1969.

Ochtoechos; or, The Book of Eight Tones, a Primer containing the
    Sunday Service in Eight Tones. Translated from the Slavonian
    1st ed. of 1891, St. Petersburg, by N. Orloff. London: J.
    Davy, 1898; reprint ed., New York: AMS Press, 1969.

Orthodox Eastern Church in America. The Divine Liturgy. Trans-
    lated by David Drillock, John H. Erickson, Helen Breslich
    Erickson. Crestwood, NY: St. Vladimir's Seminary Press,
    1982.

Prayer Book. Jordanville, NY: Holy Trinity Monastery, 1960.

SOKOLOV, Dmitri P. A Manual of the Orthodox Church's Divine
    Services. Jordanville, NY: Holy Trinity Monastery, 1962.

THOMPSON, Patrick, ed. The Orthodox Liturgy, Being the Divine
    Liturgy of S. John Chrysostom and S. Basil the Great, accord-
    ing to the Use of the Church of Russia. London: SPCK for
    the Fellowship of Ss. Alban and Sergius, 1939; reprinted, 1960.

[Trebnik.] Book of Needs of the Holy Orthodox Church, with an

Appendix containing Offices for the Laying on of Hands.
Edited by G. V. Shann. London: D. Nutt, 1894; reprint ed.,
New York: AMS Press, 1969. [From Trebnik. Moscow, 1882.]

[Triodion.] The Lenten Triodion. Translated by Mother Mary and
Kallistos Ware. London: Faber & Faber, 1978.

b. Studies

AFANASSIEV, Nikolai. Trapeza Gospodnya. Pravoslavnie v sovre-
mennost, 2-3. Paris, 1952.

BULGARKOV, Sergei Vasilevich. Nastolnaia kniga dlia sviash-
chenno-tserkovno-sluzhitelei. Kharkov: Tip. Gub. pravleniia,
1900; reprint ed., Graz: Akademische Druck- und Verlagsanstalt, 1965.

DMITRIEVSKII, Aleksei. Opisanie liturgicheskikh rukopisei khrani-
aschikhsia v bibliotekakh pravoslavnogo Vostoka. 3 vols.
Kiev, 1895-1917; reprint ed., Hildesheim: Olms, 1965- .

EVDOKIMOFF, Paul. La prière de l'église d'orient: la liturgie de
saint Jean Chrysostome. Paris: Casterman, 1966.

GOGOL, N. V. The Divine Liturgy of the Eastern Orthodox Church.
Translated by Rosemary Edmonds. London: Darton, Longman
& Todd, 1960.

[KERN], Archimandrite Kiprian. Evkharistiia: iz chtenii v pravo-
slavnom bogoslobskom institutie v Parizhie. Paris: YMCA
Press, 1947; reprint ed., 1974.

_____. Liturgika: gimnografiia i eortologiia. Paris: Voda
Zivaia, 1964.

KING, John Glen. The Rites and Ceremonies of the Greek Church
in Russia: Containing an Account of Its Doctrine, Worship,
and Discipline. London: W. Owen, 1772; reprint ed., New
York: AMS Press, 1970.

NIKOLSKII, Konstantin. Posobie k izucheniiu ustava bogosluzh-
eniia pravoslavnoi tserkvi. 5. ed. St. Petersburg, 1894.

Pisania Sv. Otsov i uchiteley Tserkvi otnosyachchikhsya k istol-
kovaniu pravoslavnago bogosluzheniya. 2 vols. St. Petersburg, 1855-1856.

ROMANOFF, H. C. Sketches of the Greco-Russian Church: The
Divine Liturgy of St. John Chrysostom. London, 1871.

SCHYLTZE, Bernhard. "Eucharistie und Kirche in der russischen

Theologie der Gegenwart." Zeitschrift für Kirche und Theologie, 77 (1955): 257-300.

SKABALLANOVICH, Mikhail. Tolkovyi Tipikon. Kiev, 1910-1915.

ZVEGINTZOV, Catherine. Our Mother Church: Her Worship and
Offices, compiled from Standard Russian Textbooks. New York:
Russian Orthodox Church of America, 1968.

3. Ruthenian (Ukrainian) Use

a. Texts

Byzantine Book of Prayer. Compiled by the Inter-Diocesan Liturgical Commission of the Byzantine-Ruthenian Metropolitan Province. Pittsburgh, PA: Byzantine Seminary Press; Allendale,
PA: Alleluia Press, 1976.

Byzantine Seraphic Typicon: The Order of Divine Services according to the Usage of the Custody of St. Mary of the Angels.
New Canaan, CT: Franciscan Friars, 1963- .

The Divine Liturgy. New Canaan, CT: Byzantine Franciscans,
1965.

GRIGASSY, Julius, ed. Liturgikon sir'ic' Sluzebnik dl'a greko-
kath. mirjan staro-slavjanskaho obrjada. Braddock, PA:
n.p., 1945.

_____, ed. Main Services of Holy Week and Glorious Resurrec-
tion in the Greek Rite (Byzantine-Slavonic) Catholic Church.
Braddock, PA: n.p., 1950.

Ordo celebrandis vesperarum, matutini et divinae liturgiae iuxta
recensionem Ruthenorum. Editio altera. Roma: Tipografia
Pio X, 1953; The Order for the Celebration of Vespers, Matins,
and the Divine Liturgy, according to the Ruthenian Recension.
Translated by Matthew A. Berko. Washington, DC: n.p.,
1958 [1957?].

SEMBRATOVICH, Leo I., ed. Let Us Pray to the Lord: A Manual
of Prayers for the Ukrainian Catholics of the Greek Rite.
Philadelphia, PA: Orphanage Bookstore, 1941.

SENYSHYN, Ambrose, ed. Christ With Us: Divine Liturgy of St.
John Chrysostom. Stamford, CT: Ambrose Senyshyn, 1954.

SHEREGHY, Basil, ed. The Liturgy of St. John Chrysostom,
Ruthenian Form. Historical background, introduction and
commentary by Basil Shereghy. Collegeville, MN: Liturgical
Press, 1961.

Ukrainian Orthodox Church. Sluzhebnyk. Bound Brook, NJ:
   Ukrainian Orthodox Church of the U.S.A., 1963.

Ukrainian Orthodox Church. Trebnyk: The Book of Administration of Sacraments and Other Rites and Ceremonies according
   to the Ukrainian Orthodox Church of U.S.A. New York:
   Ukrainian Orthodox Church of U.S.A., 1954- .

   b. Studies

CHUBATY, Nicholas. "Development of the Kiev-Ruthenian Rite."
   Diakonia, 4 (1969): 247-258; 5 (1970): 42-54.

RAES, Alphonse. "Le Liturgicon ruthène depuis l'Union de Brest."
   Orientalia Christiana Periodica, 8 (1942): 95-143.

_____. "Le Rituel ruthène depuis l'Union de Brest." Orientalia
   Christiana Periodica, 1 (1935): 361-392.

SHEREGHY, Basil. The Divine Liturgy of St. John Chrysostom.
   Pittsburgh, PA: Byzantine Seminary Press, 1970.

VASICA, J. "Slovanska liturgie nove osvetlena Kijevskymi listy."
   Slovo a Slovesnost, 6 (1940): 65-77.

4. Carpatho-Ruthenian (Rusin) and Hungarian Ruthenian Uses

   a. Texts

The Divine Liturgy of Saint John Chrysostom. Lisle, IL: The
   Monks of St. Procopius Abbey, 1942.

GRIGASSY, Julius, ed. Prayer Book for Greek Catholic Rusins
   in America. Braddock, PA: n.p., 1940.

_____. Prayer Book for Greek Catholic Hungarians of America.
   Braddock, PA: n.p., 1940.

HANULYA, Joseph P. The Eastern Ritual. Cleveland, OH: n.p.,
   1942.

   b. Studies

ADRIANYI, G. "Die Bestrebungen der ungarischen Katholiken des
   byzantinischen Ritus um einige Liturgie und Kirchenorganisation
   um 1900." Ostkirchliche Studien, 21 (1972): 116-131.

5. Other Eastern European Uses

[Euchologion.] Sluzebnik. Belgrade: [Holy Episcopal Synod of
the Serbian Orthodox Church], 1962; The Serbian-Orthodox
Service Book in English. Trial ed. Richfield, OH: Library
of the Path of Orthodoxy, 1973.

NOLI, Fan Stylian, ed. Liturgy and Catechism of the Eastern
Orthodox Church in Albanian and English. Boston: Albanian
Orthodox Church in America, 1955.

Trebnik. Sophia: Sv. Sinod na Bulgarskata Tserkva, 1949.

6. Georgian Rite

Dve drevnie redaktsii gruzinskogo Irmologiia (po rukopisiam X-XI
vekov). Red. Al. Gamgrelidze. Tbilisi: Metsniereba, 1971.

TARCHNISVILI, Michael, ed. Liturgiae Ibericae antiquiores.
CSCO, 122-123. Louvain: Durbecq, 1950.

7. The Melkites

a. Texts

BLACK, Matthew, ed. Rituale Melchitarum: A Christian Palestinian
Euchologion. BOS, 22. Stuttgart: Kohlhammer, 1938.

NASSAR, Seraphim, ed. Book of Divine Prayers and Services of
the Catholic Orthodox Church of Christ. New York: Black-
shaw Press, 1938.

b. Studies

COUTURIER, Abel. Cours de liturgie grecque-melkite. 3 vols.
Jerusalem: Franciscains de Terre Sainte, 1912-1930.

HUSMANN, H. "Eine alte orientalische christliche Liturgie: alt-
syrisch-melkitisch." Orientalia Christiana Periodica, 42 (1976):
156-196.

MADEY, Johannes. "Liturgical Reform in the Melkite Catholic
Church." Eastern Churches Review, 3 (1971): 307-309.

_____. "Die Reform der eucharistischen Liturgie in der grie-
chisch melkitischen katholischen Kirche." Kyrios, 12 (1972):
1-9.

8. Western Rite Orthodox

MENSBRUGGHE, Alexis van der. La liturgie orthodoxe, de rit
occidental: essai de restauration. Paris: Editions Setor,
1948.

SCHNEIRLA, William S. "The Western Rite in the Orthodox
Church." St. Vladimir's Seminary Quarterly, 2, 2 (Spring
1958): 20-46.

9. Theological and Miscellaneous Studies

BOBRINSKOY, Boris. "Ascension et liturgie." Contacts, 11
(1959): 166-184; "Ascension and Liturgy: The Ascension and
High Priesthood of Christ in Relation to Worship." St. Vladimir's Seminary Quarterly, 3, 4 (Fall 1959): 11-28.

_____. "Liturgie et ecclésiologie trinitaire de S. Basile." Ver-
bum Caro, 23 (1969): 1-32.

_____. "La Saint-Esprit dans la liturgie." Studia liturgica, 1
(1962): 47-60.

BOETZKES, E. "The Fear of God in the Byzantine Liturgy."
Diakonia, 13 (1978): 197-213.

BULGAKOV, Sergius. "Das eucharistische Dogma." Kyrios, n.
F. 3 (1963): 32-57, 78-96.

CHIROVSKY, A. "Revelation and Liturgy: The Epiphanic Functions of the Human Body in Byzantine Worship." Diakonia, 13
(1978): 111-119.

JUNGCLAUSSEN, E. "Maria im liturgischen Kult der orthodoxen
Kirche." Una Sancta, 30 (1975): 127-145.

KARMIRIS, John. "The Christological Dogma in Orthodox Worship."
The Greek Orthodox Theological Review, 13 (1968): 241-257.

LEDIT, Joseph. Marie dans la liturgie de Byzance. TH, 39.
Paris: Beauchesne, 1976.

MADEY, Johannes. "Die Rolle des Heiligen Geistes in der Eucharistiefeier im Anschluss an die göttliche Liturgie des hl.
Johannes Chrysostomus." Catholica, 28, 3 (1974): 227-243.

PAPANDREOU, Damaskinos. "Gottesdienst-geschlossene Gesellschaft? Solidarität mit der Welt." Okumenische Rundschau,
22 (1973): 319-334.

ROMANIDES, John S. "Man and His True Life according to the
    Greek Orthodox Service Book." The Greek Orthodox Theologi-
    cal Review, 1 (1954): 63-83.

SABODAN, Vladimir. "Der eucharistische Gottesdienst und der
    Mensch des 20. Jahrhunderts." In Die Eucharistie, pp. 160-
    171. Herausgegeben vom Kirchlichen Aussenamt der Evangel-
    ischen Kirche in Deutschland. Bielefeld: Luther-Verlag,
    1974.

SALAVILLE, Sévérien. Christus im orientalium pietate. BEL, 20.
    Rome: Edizioni Liturgiche, 194?.

SCHMEMANN, Alexander. "Liturgy and Theology." The Greek
    Orthodox Theological Review, 17 (1972): 86-100.

SOLOVEY, Meletius Michael. Eastern Liturgical Theology. Weston,
    Ont.: Ukrainian Catholic Religion and Culture Society, 1970.

TYCIAK, Julius. Gegenwart des Heils in den östlichen Liturgien.
    Sophia, 9. Trier: Paulinus-Verlag, 1968.

_____. Das Herrenmysterium im byzantinischen Kirchenjahr.
    2. Aufl. Sophia, 1. Trier: Paulinus-Verlag, 1976.

_____. Die Liturgie als Quelle östlicher Frömmigkeit. Freiburg:
    Herder, 1937.

F. EGYPTIAN CHURCHES (ALEXANDRIAN RITE)

1. Texts

BURMESTER, O. H. E., ed. The Egyptian or Coptic Church: A
    Detailed Description of her Liturgical Services and the Rites
    and Ceremonies observed in the Administration of the Sacra-
    ments. Cairo: Publications de la Société d'archéologie copte,
    1967.

_____, ed. The Horologion of the Egyptian Church: Coptic and
    Arabic Text from a Medieval Manuscript. Translated by
    O. H. E. Burmester. Studia orientalia christiana, Aegyptica.
    Cairo: Edizioni del Centro Francescano di Studi Orientalia
    Cristiani, 1973.

The Coptic Liturgy. Authorized by H. H. Abba Kyrillos VI.
    Cairo: Coptic Orthodox Patriarchate, 1963.

DORESSE, Jean, and LANNE, Emmanuel. Un Témoin archaique de
    la liturgie copte de S. Basile. BM, 47. Louvain: Publications
    universitaires et Institut Orientaliste, 1960.

JOHN, Marquis of Bute [John Patrick Crichton-Stuart], ed. The
Coptic Morning Service for the Lord's Day. London: Cope &
Fenwick, 1908; reprint ed., New York: AMS Press, 1973.

LANNE, Emmanuel, ed. Le Grand Euchologe du Monastère Blanc.
PO, 28/2. Paris: Firmin-Didot, 1958.

MACOMBER, William F. "The Anaphora of Saint Mark according to
the Kacmarcik Codex." Orientalia Christiana Periodica, 45
(1979): 75-98.

_____. "The Greek Text of the Coptic Mass and of the Ana-
phoras of Basil and Gregory according to the Kacmarcik Codex."
Orientalia Christiana Periodica, 43 (1977): 308-334.

MALAN, Solomon Caesar, ed. Original Documents of the Coptic
Church. 6 vols. London: D. Nutt, 1872-1876.
1. The Divine Liturgy of Saint Mark the Evangelist. 1872.
2. The Calendar of the Coptic Church. 1873.
4. The Holy Gospel and Versicles for Every Sunday and Other
Feast Day in the Year, as used in the Coptic Church.
1874.
5-6. The Divine Euchologion, and the Divine Liturgy of S.
Gregory the Theologian. 1875.

ROBERTS, C. H., and CAPELLE, B., eds. An Early Euchologium:
The Dêr-Balizeh Papyrus. BM, 23. Louvain: Bureaux du
Muséon, 1949.

2. Studies

ABD AL-MASIH, Y. "Doxologies in the Coptic Church." Bulletin
de la Société d'Archéologie Copte, 5 (1939): 175-192.

AMIN, Hakim. "The Orthodox Faith in the Liturgies and Prayers
of the Coptic Church." The Greek Orthodox Theological Review, 13 (1968): 226-239.

ANDRIEU, M., and COLLOMP, P. "Fragments sur papyrus de
l'anaphore de saint Marc." Revue des sciences religieuses, 8
(1928): 489-515.

BRAKMANN, H. G. "Zur Geschichte der eucharistischen Nüchtern-
heit in Agypten." Muséon, 89 (1971): 197-211.

BURMESTER, O. H. E. "The Greek Kirugmata, Versicles and Responses and Hymnus in the Coptic Liturgy." Orientalia Christiana Periodica, 2 (1936): 363-394.

_____. "Rites and Ceremonies of the Coptic Church." The

Eastern Churches Quarterly, 7 (1947-1948): 373-403; 8 (1949-
1950); 1-39, 291-317; 9 (1951-1952): 1-27, 245-260, 306-319;
10 (1953-1954): 9-27, 217-229, 325-337; 11 (1955-1956): 3?-
45, 179-190, 282-288, 321-335.

_____. "Vesting Prayers and Ceremonies of the Coptic Church."
Orientalia Christiana Periodica, 1 (1935): 305-314.

CODRINGTON, H. W. "The Heavenly Altar and the Epiclesis in
Egypt." Journal of Theological Studies, 39 (1938): 141-150.

COQUIN, R. G. "L'anaphore alexandrine de saint Marc." Le
Muséon, 82 (1969): 307-356.

_____. "Vestiges de concélébration eucharistique chez les mel-
kites égyptiens, les coptes et les éthiopiens." Le Muséon, 80
(1967): 37-46.

CRAMER, Maria. Koptische Liturgien: eine Auswahl. Sophia, 11.
Trier: Paulinus Verlag, 1973.

CUMING, G. J. "The Anaphora of St. Mark: A Study in Development." Le Muséon, 95 (1982): 115-129.

DALMAIS, Irénée-Henri. "Les structures de la célébration comme
expression de la communion ecclésiale dans l'Eglise copte." In
L'assemblée liturgique et les différents rôles dans l'assemblée,
pp. 167-182. Rome: Edizioni Liturgiche, 1977.

ENGBERDING, Hieronymus. "Das anaphorische Fürbittgebet der
griechischen Markusliturgie." Orientalia Christiana Periodica,
30 (1964): 398-446.

_____. "Eucharisterion in ägyptischen liturgischen Texten."
Byzantinischen Forschungen, 2 (1967): 148-161.

_____. "Neues Licht über die Geschichte des Textes der ägypt-
ischen Markusliturgie." Oriens Christianus, 40 (1956): 40-68.

_____. "Untersuchungen zu den jüngst veröffentlichen Bruch-
stücken sa'idischen Liturgie." Oriens Christianus, 43 (1959):
59-75.

_____. "Das Verhältnis der syrischen Timotheusanaphora zur
koptischen Cyrillusliturgie." Oriens Christianus, 42 (1958):
55-67.

GAMBER, Klaus. "Das Eucharistiegebet im Papyrus von Dêr-
Balizeh und die Samstagabend-Agapen in Agypten."
Ostkirchliche Studien, 7 (1958): 48-65.

_____. "Der griechische Urtext des Eucharistiegebetes in der
Ägyptischen Kirchenordnungen." Ostkirchliche Studien, 17
(1968): 44-47.

_____. "Das koptische Ostraka London B. M. Nr 32 799 & 33
050 und seine liturgiegeschichtliche Bedeutung." Ostkirchliche Studien, 21 (1972): 298-308.

_____. "Der liturgische Papyrus von Deir el-Bala'izah in Ober-
ägypten (6./7. Jh.)." Le Muséon, 82 (1969): 61-83.

GODART, J. "Traditions anciennes de la grand prière eucharistique. III. La tradition d'Alexandrie." Questions liturgiques
et paroissiales, 48 (1967): 198-218.

HAMMERSCHMIDT, Ernst. Die koptische Gregoriosanaphora: Syrische und griechische Einflüsse auf eine ägyptische Liturgie.
BBA, 8. Berlin: Akademie-Verlag, 1957.

HOUSSIAU, A. "The Alexandrine Anaphora of St Basil." In The
New Liturgy, pp. 228-243. Edited by Lancelot Sheppard.
London: Darton, Longman & Todd, 1970.

KOPP, Clemens. Glaube und Sakramente der koptischen Kirche.
OC, 75. Rome: Pontificium Institutum Studiorum Orientalium,
1932.

KRETSCHMAR, Georg. "Beiträge zur Geschichte der Liturgie,
insbesonders der Taufliturgie in Agypten." Jahrbuch für
Liturgik und Hymnologie, 8 (1963): 1-54.

LANNE, E. "Liturgie alexandrine et liturgie romaine: l'onction
des Martyrs et la Bénédiction de l'huile." Irénikon, 31 (1958):
138-155.

LEFORT, L. Th. "Coptica lovanensia." Le Muséon, 53 (1940):
1-66.

MACOMBER, William F. "The Kacmarcik Codex: A 14th Century
Greek-Arabic Manuscript of the Coptic Mass." Le Muséon, 88
(1975): 391-395.

MALAK, Hanna. "Die Rolle der eucharistischen göttlichen Liturgie
im Leben der koptischen Kirche gestern und heute." Kyrios,
12 (1972): 159-184; "Le rôle de la divine liturgie eucharistique
dans la vie de l'Eglise copte hier et aujourd'hui." Proche-
Orient Chrétien, 23 (1973): 266-283.

MEINARDUS, Otto. Christian Egypt: Faith and Life. Cairo:
American University in CAiro Press, 1970.

MITCHELL, Leonel L. "The Alexandrian Anaphora of St. Basil of Caesarea: Ancient Source of 'A Common Eucharistic Prayer.'" Anglican Theological Review, 58 (1976): 194-206.

QUECKE, H. "Ein saidischer Zeuge der Markusliturgie (Brit. Mus. 54.036)." Orientalia Christiana Periodica, 37 (1971): 40-54.

SCHERMANN, Theodor. Agyptische Abendmahlsliturgien des ersten Jahrtausends, in ihrer Uberlieferung dargestellt. SGKA, 6/1-2. Paderborn: Schöningh, 1912; reprint ed., New York: Johnson Reprint, 1967.

VIAUD, Gérard. La liturgie des coptes d'Egypte. Paris: Librairie d'Amerique et d'Orient maisonneuve, 1978.

G. ETHIOPIAN CHURCHES

1. Texts

EURINGER, Sebastian, ed. Die äthiopische Anaphora des heiligen Basilius. OCA, 98. Rome: Pontificium Institutum Orientalium Studiorum, 1934.

_____, ed. Die äthiopischen Anaphoren des heiligen evangelisten Johannes des Donnersohnes und des heiligen Jacobus von Sarug. OCA, 90 Rome: Pontificium Institutum Orientalium Studiorum, 1934.

HAMMERSCHMIDT, Ernst. Athiopische liturgische Texte der Bodleian Library in Oxford. VIO, 38. Berlin: Akademie-Verlag, 1960.

HARDEN, John Mason. The Anaphoras of the Ethiopic Liturgy. TCL, Series 3. London: SPCK; New York: Macmillan, 1928.

The Liturgy of the Ethiopian Church. Translated by Marcus Daoud and revised by H. E. Blatta Marsie Hazen. Cairo: Egyptian Book Press, 1959.

Missale aethiopicum, continens ordinem communem et varias anaphoras in ritu alexandrino-aethiopico usurpatas. Rome, n.p., 1945.

SEMHARAY SELAM, T. M. "Textus aethiopicus anaphorae sancti Marci." Ephemerides liturgicae, 42 (1928): 507-531.

2. Studies

BURMESTER, O. H. E. "A Comparative Study of the Form of the Words of Institution and the Epiclesis in the Anaphorae of the Ethiopic Church." The Eastern Churches Quarterly, 13 (1959): 13-42.

HAMMERSCHMIDT, Ernst. Stellung und Bedeutung des Sabbats in Athiopien. Studia Delitzschiana, 7. Stuttgart: Kohlhammer, 1963.

_____. Studies in the Ethiopic Anaphoras. BBA, 25. Berlin: Akademie-Verlag, 1960.

MERCER, S. A. B. "The Epiclesis in the Ethiopic Liturgy." In Oriental Studies dedicated to Paul Haupt, pp. 446-453. Baltimore, MD: The Johns Hopkins Press, 1926.

_____. The Ethiopic Liturgy: Its Sources, Development, and Present Form. London: Mowbray, 1915; reprint ed., New York: AMS Press, 1970.

Revisione e ristampa del missale etiopico. Rome: Oriental Congregation, 1938.

H. THE ARMENIAN CHURCH

1. Texts

Armenian Apostolic Church in America. Sacraments and Prayers of the Armenian Church. n.p.: Diocese of the Armenian Church, 1956.

CONYBEARE, F. C., ed. Rituale Armenorum. Oxford: Clarendon Press, 1905.

Divine Liturgy of the Armenian Apostolic Orthodox Church. New York: Delphic Press, 1950.

The Divine Liturgy of the Holy Apostolic Church of Armenia. Translated by two Armenian priests. London: Cope & Fenwick, 1908.

ISSAVERDENZ, James, ed. The Armenian Liturgy. Translated into English by James Issaverdenz. Venice: Armenian Monastery of St. Lazaro, 1862. 2d ed., 1873.

_____, ed. The Divine Ordinances according to the Armenian Ritual. Translated and notes by James Issaverdenz. Venice: Armenian Monastery of St. Lazaro, 1867.

KOGY, Lorenz, ed. Sunday Missal of the Armenian Rite. Vienna:
    n.p., 1947.

RENOUX, Athanase. Le Codex arménien Jerusalem 121. 2 vols.
    PO, 35/1 & 36/2. Turnhout: Brepols: 1969-1971.

                            2. Studies

ENGBERDING, Hieronymus. "Das anaphorische Fürbittgebet der
    älteren armenischen Basiliusliturgie." Oriens CHristianus, 51
    (1967): 29-50.

GARITTE, G. "Un opuscule grec traduit de l'arménien sur l'addi-
    tion d'eau au vin eucharistique." Le Muséon, 73 (1960): 297-
    310.

ISSAVERDENZ, Jacques (James). Rites et cérémonies de l'église
    arménienne. Venise: Imprimerie Arménienne de Saint-Lazare,
    1876; Sacred Rites and Ceremonies of the Armenian Church.
    Venice: Armenian Monastery of St. Lazzaro, 1876.

KRIKORIAN, M. K. "Christology in the Liturgical Tradition of the
    Armenian Church." The Greek Orthodox Theological Review,
    13 (1968): 212-223.

LAGES, M. F. "The Hierosolumitain Origin of the Catechetical
    Rites in the Armenian Liturgy." Didaskalia, 1 (1971): 233-
    250.

_____. "The Most Ancient Penitential Text of the Armenian Lit-
    urgy." Didaskalia, 1 (1971): 43-64.

ORMANIAN, Malachia. L'Eglise arménienne, son histoire, sa doc-
    trine, son régime, sa discipline, sa liturgie, sa littérature, son
    présent. 2. éd. Antélias, Liban: Catholicossat Arménien de
    Cilicie, 1954; The Church of Armenia, her History, Doctrine,
    Rule, Discipline, Liturgy, Literature, and Existing Condition.
    2d (rev.) English ed. Translated by G. Marcar Gregory.
    Edited by Terenig Poladian. London: Mowbray, 1955.

RENOUX, Athanase. "Eucharistie et rémission des péchés dans les
    Anaphores arméniennes." Didaskalia, 3 (1973): 201-214.

RYCAUT, Paul. The Present State of the Greek and Armenian
    Churches. London: Printed for John Starkey, 1679.

SALAVILLE, Séverien. "L'explication de la messe de l'arménian
    Chosrov (950), théologie et liturgie." Echos d'Orient, (July
    1940-December 1942): 349-382.

SHRIKIAN, Gorun. Rules and Procedures of the Armenian Apostolic Church for Celebrant, Deacons, Acolytes, and Fan Bearers during Divine Liturgy. New York: Armenian Apostolic Church of America, 1980.

WINKLER, Gabriele. "Zur Geschichte des armenischen Gottesdienstes im Hinblick auf den in mehreren Wellen erfolgten griechischen Einfluss." Oriens Christianus, 58 (1974): 154-172.

I. THE EASTERN CHURCHES OF INDIA

1. Background Studies

BROWN, Leslie. The Indian Christians of St Thomas: An Account of the Ancient Syrian Church of Malabar. Revised ed. Cambridge: Cambridge University Press, 1982.

HAMBYE, Edouard R., and MADEY, Johannes. 1900 Jahre Thomas-Christen in Indien. VABKO, 2. Freiburg: Kanisius-Verlag, 1972.

MATHEW, C. P., and THOMAS, M. M. The Indian Christians of St. Thomas. Delhi: ISPCK, 1967.

MENACHERY, George, ed. The St. Thomas Christian Encyclopedia of India. Vol. 2: Apostle Thomas, Kerala, Malabar Christianity. Trichur: St. Thomas Christian Encyclopedia of India, 1973.

PHILIPOS, Edavalikel. The Syrian Christians of Malabar, otherwise called the Christians of S. Thomas. Edited by G. B. Howard. Oxford: J. Parker, 1869.

POTHAN, S. G. The Syrian Christians of Kerala. Bombay: Asia Publishing House, 1963.

TISSERANT, Eugène. "Syro-Malabar (Eglise)." In Dictionnaire de théologie catholique, 14/2; Eastern Christianity in India: A History of the Syro-Malabar Church from the Earliest Time to the Present Day. Authorized adaptation from the French by E. R. Hambye. London: Longmans; Westminster, MD: Newman Press, 1957.

VELLIAN, Jacob, ed. The Malabar Church. OCA, 186. Rome: Pontificium Institutum Orientalium Studiorum, 1970.

2. The Malabar Church (Chaldean Rite)

a. Texts

FABIAN, Fr., ed. The Liturgy of the St. Thomas Christians of
Malabar; or, the Raza of the Syro-Malabar Rite. Mannanam:
St. Joseph's Press, 1954.

HOWARD, George Broadley. The Christians of St. Thomas and
their Liturgies: Comprising the Anaphorae of St. James, St.
Peter, the Twelve Apostles, Mar Dionysius, Mar Xystus, and
Mar Evannis, together with the Ordo Communis. Translated
from Syriac MSS. Oxford: J. & H. Parker, 1864.

Ordo celebrationis "Quddasa" iuxta usum ecclesiae Syro-Malabaren-
sis. Rome: Tipografia Pio X, 1959.

Syro-Malabar Missal. Ernakulam, 1963.

b. Studies

CONNOLLY, R. H. "The Work of Menezes on the Malabar Liturgy."
Journal of Theological Studies, 15 (1914):   396-425, 569-589;
"Addition" by Edmund Bishop. 15 (1914):   589-593.

MADEY, Johannes. "Die erneuerte syro-malabarische Liturgie der
Eucharistiefeier ('Qurbana')." Der christliche Osten, 26
(1971):   148-151.

MOOLAVEETIL, L. Yakobinre Annaphura: oru Pathanam. Kottayam: St. Thomas Apostolic Seminary, 1976.

PAKENHAM-WALSH, Herbert. A Devotional Study of the Holy Qurbana. 2d ed. Madras: Christian Literature Society, 1949.

PAYNGOT, Charles. "Liturgical Developments in Kerala." Diakonia, 8 (1973):   358-377.

PLACIDUS OF ST. JOSEPH. "The Present Syro-Malabar Liturgy:
Menezian or Rozian?" Orientalia Christiana Periodica, 23
(1957):   313-331.

PODIPARA, P. J. "Thomas-Christians and Adaptation." Eastern
Churches Review, 3 (1970):   171-177.

_____. "The Thomas Christians of Malabar and the Chaldean
Liturgy." In Die Einheit der Kirche, pp. 339-341. Herausgegeben von L. Hein. Wiesbaden: Steiner, 1977.

VAVANIKUNNEL, Georg. Die eucharistische Katechese der Anaphora der Apostel Mar Addai und Mar Mari in der syro-

malabarischen Kirche gestern und heute. OstC, n.F. 26.
Würzburg: Augustinus-Verlag, 1976.

_____, and MADEY, Johannes. "A 'Reform' of the Restored
Syro-Malabar Quarbana." Ostkirchliche Studien, 18 (1969):
172-181.

VERGHESE, Pathikulangara. "Communion of Churches according
to the Syro-Malabar Liturgical Traditions." Ostkirchliche
Studien, 27 (1978): 169-173.

3. The Malankara Church (Antiochene Rite)

a. Texts

The Order of the Holy Qurbana of the Orthodox Syrian Church of
Malabar: The Liturgy of St. James. Translated by Mar Ivanios. London: SPCK, 1934.

The Order of the Holy Qurbana of the Syro-Malankarese Rite.
Trivandrum, India: n.p., 1964.

b. Studies

MALANCHARUVIL, C. The Syro Malankara Church. Ernakulam,
1974.

MAR IVANIOS [PANIKERVIRTIS, Givergis Thomas]. A Handbook
of the Holy Mass according to the Malankara Rite. New York:
Catholic Near East Welfare Association, 1947.

4. The Orthodox Syrian Church of the East

Orthodox Syrian Church of the East. The Service Book of the
Holy Qurbana (Qurbanakramam). 2d ed. Translated and published by Mathews Athanasios. Kottayam: C. M. S. Press,
1970, c1966.

5. The Mar Thoma Church

a. Texts

The Mar Thoma Syrian Liturgy. Translated by George Kuttickal
Chacko. New York: Morehouse-Gorham, 1956.

b. Studies

KURUVILLA, K. K. A History of the Mar Thoma Church and Its

Doctrines.   Madras: Christian Literature Society for India,
1951.

VERGHESE, Paul. "Mar Thoma Church Worship." Dictionary of
Liturgy and Worship, pp. 251-253.

J. THE SLAVONIC (GLAGOLITIC) LITURGY

1. Texts

MOHLBERG, Cunibert. "Il Messale glagolitico di Kiew (sec. IX)
ed il suo prototypo Romano del sec. VI-VII." Memorie, 2
(1928):   207-320.

2. Studies

DOSTAL, Antonin. "The Origins of the Slavonic Liturgy." In
Dumbarton Oaks Papers, number 19, pp. 67-87. Washington,
DC: Trustees for Harvard University, The Dumbarton Oaks
Center for Byzantine Studies, 1965.

ERICSSON, K. "The Pope and the Controversy over the Slavonic
Books and Liturgy in the IXth Century." In La Chiesa greca
in Italia dall' VIII al XVI secolo, vol. 3, pp. 1223-1236.
Padoue: Antenore, 1972-1973.

GAMBER, Klaus. "Das glagolitische Sakramentar der Slavenapostel
Cyrill und Method und seine lateinische Vorlage." Ostkirchliche Studien, 6 (1957):   165-173.

GINZEL, Joseph A. Geschichte der Slawenapostel Cyril und Method
und der slawischen Liturgie. Vienna, 1861; reprint ed., Amsterdam: Rodopi, 1969.

LANCKORONSKA, Karolina. Studies on the Roman-Slavonic Rite in
Poland. OCA, 161. Rome: Pontificium Institutum Orientalium
Studiorum, 1961.

SMRZIK, Stephan. The Glagolitic or Roman-Slavonic Liturgy.
Cleveland, OH: Slovak Institute, 1959.

K. SPECIAL STUDIES

ARRANZ, M. "Le Sancta sanctis dans la tradition liturgique des
églises." Archiv für Liturgiewissenschaft, 15 (1973):   31-67.

BERTONIERE, Gabriel. The Historical Development of the Easter
     Vigil and Related Services in the Greek Church. OCA, 193.
     Rome: Pontificium Institutum Orientalium Studiorum, 1972.

BOTTE, Bernard. "Fragments d'une anaphora inconnue attribuée
     à S. Epiphane." Le Muséon, 73 (1960): 311-315.

BUCKEL, Albanus. Die Gottesbezeichnungen in den Liturgien der
     Ostkirchen. Würzburg: Triltsch, 1938.

GRAFFIN, F. "Recherches sur le thème de l'église-épouse dans
     les liturgies et la littérature de la langue syriaque." L'Orient
     syrien, 3 (1968): 317-334.

HOLLER, Joseph. Die Epiklese der griechisch-orientalischen Litur-
     gien: ein Beitrag zur Lösung der Epiklesisfrage. SMKS, 9.
     Wien: Mayer, 1912.

JOHN, Marquess of Bute, and BUDGE, E. A. Wallis, eds. The
     Blessing of the Waters on the Eve of Epiphany: The Greek,
     Latin, Syriac, Coptic, and Russian Versions edited or trans-
     lated from the Original Texts. London: Oxford University
     Press, 1901.

KERN, Cyprien. "En marge de l'épiclèse." Irénikon, 24 (1951):
     166-194.

_____, and CODRINGTON, H. W. "The Epiklesis." Eastern
     Churches Quarterly, 9 (1951-1952): 198-205.

Kirchlichen Aussenamt der Evangelischen Kirche in Deutschland.
     Die Anrufung des Heiligen Geistes im Abendmahl. Viertes the-
     ologisches Gespräch zwischen dem Okumenischen Patriarchat
     und der Evangelischen Kirche in Deutschland vom 6. bis 9.
     Oktober 1975 in der Evangelischen Sozialakademie Friedewald.
     BOR, 31. Frankfurt: Lembeck, 1977.

RIOS, Romanus. "The Liturgy and Reunion, III: The Words of
     Consecration in the Tradition of the Eastern Churches."
     Eastern Churches Quarterly, 4 (1940-1941): 97-104.

SCHWEIGL, J. "De Concilio Vaticano et de quaestione Liturgia
     Orientalis." Gregorianum, 21 (1940): 3-16.

SHEPHERD, Massey H., Jr. "Liturgical Expressions of the Constantine
     Triumph." In Dumbarton Oaks Papers, number 21, pp. 57-78.
     Washington, DC: Trustees for Harvard University, The Dum-
     barton Oaks Center for Byzantine Studies, 1967.

WALLACE-HADRILL, D. S. "Eusebius and the Institution Narrative
     in the Eastern Liturgies." Journal of Theological Studies, 4
     (1953): 41-42.

IX. THE LATIN CHURCHES

A. TEXTS

1. Collected Texts

AERTNYS, Joseph. Compendium liturgiae sacrae iuxta ritum romanum. Ed. 11 accommodata cura Adr Dankelman. Turin:
Marietti, 1943.

ASSEMANI, G. L., ed. Codex liturgicus ecclesiae universae in quo
continentur libri rituales, missales, pontificales, officia, dyp-
ticha, etc. ecclesiarum Occidentis et Orientis. 13 vols. Rome:
Komarek, 1749–1766; reprint eds., Paris: Huberti Welter, 1902;
Farnborough, Eng.: Gregg, 1968.

BRIGHT, William, ed. Ancient Collects and Other Prayers selected
for Devotional Use from Various Rituals. 8th ed. Oxford:
Parker, 1908.

BUGNINI, Annibale, ed. Documenta pontificia ad instaurationem
liturgicam spectantia. 2 vols. BEL, 6 & 9. Rome: Edizioni
Liturgiche, 1953, 1959.

Codices liturgici e Vaticanis praesertim delecti phototypice expressi.
Augsburg: Filser, 1929– .

DANIEL, Hermann Adalbert, ed. Codex liturgicus ecclesiae universae in epitomen redactus, vol. 1: Codex liturgicus ecclesiae
romano-catholicae. 4 vols. Lipsiae: Weigel, 1847; reprint
ed., Hildesheim: Olms, 1966.

Decreta authentica Congregationis Sacrorum Rituum ex actio eiusdam
collecta eiusque auctoritate promulgata sub auspiciis ss. domini
nostri Leonis Papae XIII. 7 vols. Rome: Typographia Polyglotta, 1898–1927.

GAVANTI, Bartolommeo, and MERATI, Cajetan Marcia. Thesaurus
sacrorum rituum, Editio novissima. 5 vols. in 2. Venice:
Typographia Balleoniana, 1823.

HAMMAN, Adalbert, ed. La Messe: liturgies anciennes et textes
patristiques. LC, 9. Paris: Grasset, 1964; The Mass: Ancient Liturgies and Patristic Texts. APL, 1. Staten Island,
NY: Alba House, 1967.

HATCHETT, Marion J. "Seven Pre-Reformation Eucharistic Liturgies: Historic Rites arranged for Contemporary Celebration."
St. Luke's Journal of Theology, 16 (1973): 43–115.

LIETZMANN, Hans, ed. Ordo Missae, secundum Missale Romanum.
Liturgische Texte, II. KT, 19. Bonn: Marcus & Weber, 1906.

_____. Ordo Missae Romanus et Gallicanus. 4. Aufl. Litur-
gische Texte, II. KT, 19. Bonn: Marcus & Weber, 1935.

MABILLON, Jean. Museum Italicum, vol. 2: Complectens antiquos
libros rituales sanctae Romanae Ecclesiae. Paris: Apud viduam
E. Martin, 1687-1689; reprint ed., Rome: Ristampe Offsett a
curia di Bibliopola, 1971?

MONE, Franz Joseph, ed. Lateinische und griechische Messen aus
dem zweiten bis sechsten Jahrhundert. Frankfurt am Main:
C. B. Lizius, 1850.

MURATORI, Ludovico Antonio, ed. Liturgia romana vetus. 2 vols.
Venice: Typis Jo. Baptistae Pasquali, 1748.

SALMON, Pierre, ed. Analecta liturgica: extraits des manuscrits
liturgiques de la Bibliothèque vaticane: contribution à l'histoire de la prière chrétienne. ST, 273. Città del Vaticano:
Biblioteca apostolica vaticana, 1974.

WEST, Ronald Cameron. Western Liturgies. London: SPCK, 1938.

2. Texts of the Roman Liturgy

a. Medieval Texts

ANDRIEU, Michel, ed. Les Ordines romani du haut moyen-âge.
5 vols. SSL, 11, 23, 24, 28, 29. Louvain: Spicilegium Sacrum Lovaniense, 1956-1961.

_____, ed. Le Pontifical romain au moyen-âge. 4 vols. ST,
86-88, 99. Città del Vaticano: Biblioteca Apostolica Vaticana,
1938-1941.
1. Le Pontifical romain du XIIe siècle. 1938.
2. Le Pontifical de la Curie romaine au XIIIe siècle. 1940.
3. Le Pontifical de Guillaume Durand. 1940.
4. Tables alphabétiques. 1941.

ATCHLEY, E. G., ed. Ordo Romanus Primus. LLE, 6. London:
Moring, 1905.

LIPPE, Robert, ed. Missale romanum Mediolani, 1474. 2 vols.
HBS, 17, 33. London: Harrison, 1899-1907.
1. Text. Introductory note by J. Wickham Legg. HBS, 17.
1899.
2. A Collation with Other Editions printed before 1570. Preface
by J. Wickham Legg. Indices by H. A. Wilson. HBS, 33.
1907.

Ordines of Haymo of Faversham. HBS, 85. London: Henry Brad-
    shaw Society, 1953.

STAPPER, Richard, ed. Ordo romanus primus de missa papali
    quem e cod. Wolfenbüttel. 4175. OTHE, 1. Münster:
    Aschendorff, 1933.

VAN DIJK, S. J. P., ed. Sources of the Modern Roman Liturgy:
    The Ordinals by Haymo of Faversham and Related Documents
    (1243-1307). 2 vols. SDF, 1-2. Leiden: E. J. Brill, 1963.
    1. Introduction; Description of Manuscripts. 1963.
    2. Texts. 1963.

VAN DIJK, S. J. P., and WALKER, Joan Hazelden, eds. The
    Ordinal of the Papal Court from Innocent II to Boniface VIII
    and Related Documents. Latin text. SF, 22. Fribourg:
    University Press, 1975.

VOGEL, Cyrille, and ELZE, Reinhard, eds. Le Pontifical romano-
    germanique du dixième siècle. 2 vols. ST, 226-227. Città
    del Vaticano: Biblioteca Apostolica Vaticana, 1963.

       b. Tridentine Texts

       (1). The Missal

Missale Romanum ex decreto sacrosancti Concilii Tridentini restitu-
    tum [1570]. Venetiis: Apud Ioannem Variscum, 1571.

_____. Editio typica. Rome: Typis polyglottis Vaticanis, 1920.

Ordo hebdomadae sanctae instauratus. Rome: Typis polyglottis
    Vaticanis, 1956; The Sacred Ceremonies of Holy Week. Edited
    by F. P. Prucha and Gerald Ellard. Washington, DC: Na-
    tional Catholic Welfare Conference, 1956.

BOTTE, Bernard, ed. Le Canon de la messe romaine: édition
    critique. TEL, 2. Louvain: Abbaye du Mont César, 1935.

BOTTE, Bernard, and MOHRMANN, Christine, eds. L'Ordinaire
    de la messe: texte critique, traduction et études. EL, 2.
    Paris: Cerf, 1953.

EISENHOFER, Leo, ed. Canon missae romanae. 2 vols. RED,
    subsidia studiorum, 1. Rome: Orbis Catholicus, 1954-1966.

O'CONNELL, J., and FINBERG, H. P. R., eds. The Missal in
    Latin and English. Translated by Ronald A. Knox. Westmin-
    ster, MD: Newman Press, 1960.

THOMPSON, Bard. "The Mass in Latin and English." In his

Liturgies of the Western Church, pp. 25-91. Cleveland, OH:
World, 1961; reprint ed., Philadelphia, PA: Fortress Press,
1981.

BOMM, Urbanus, ed. Lateinisch-deutsches Volksmessbuch. Einsiedeln: Benziger, 1944.

   (2). Pontifical Books

Pontificale Romanum. Rome: Apud Iacobum Lunam, Impensis
Leonardi Parasoli, 1595.

_____. Editio typica. Regensburg, New York: Pustet, 1888.

_____. Editio typica emendata. Città del Vaticano: Typis
polyglottis Vaticanis, 1962- .

Caeremoniale Episcoporum. Rome: Ex typographia linguarum ex-
ternarum, 1600.

_____. Editio typica. Ratisbonae: Pustet, 1886.

   (3). The Ritual

Rituale Romanum. Venetiis: Apud Juntas, 1614.

_____. Editio typica. Città del Vaticano: Typis polyglottis
Vaticanis, 1952.

WELLER, Philip T., ed. The Roman Ritual. 3 vols. Milwaukee:
Bruce, 1946-1952.
1. The Sacraments and Processions. 1950.
2. Christian Burial, Exorcism, Reserved Blessings, etc. 1946.
3. The Blessings. 2d ed. 1952.

Collectio Rituun, pro Diocesibus Civitatum Foederatarum Americae
septentrionalis. Ritual approved by the National Conference of
Catholic Bishops of the United States of America. Collegeville:
Liturgical Press; Milwaukee: Bruce; New York: Benziger,
1964.

Memoriale rituum pro aliquibus praestantioribus sacris functionibus
persolvendis in minoribus ecclesiis. Ed. 3. Taurini: Marietti,
1958.

   c. Post-Vatican II Texts

   (1). The Missal

Missale Romanum. Editio typica. Rome: Typis polyglottis
Vaticanis, 1969.

Missale Romanum cum Lectionibus. Editio iuxta typicam alteram.
4 vols. Rome: Typis polyglottis Vaticanis, 1977.

The Roman Missal. Revised by decree of the Second Vatican Ecu-
menical Council and published by authority of Pope Paul VI.
Washington, DC: International Committee on English in the
Liturgy, 1973.

Sacramentary. New York: Catholic Book Publishing Co., 1974.

The Book of Catholic Worship. Washington, DC: Liturgical Conference, 1966.

McNIERNEY, Stephen W., ed. The Underground Mass Book.
Baltimore, MD: Helicon, 1968.

PATINO, J. The New Order of Mass. Collegeville, MN: Liturgical Press, 1970.

        (2). The Pontifical and Ritual

Pontificale Romanum: De Ordinatione Diaconi, Presbyteri, et Episcopi. Rome: Typis polyglottis Vaticanis, 1968.

The Roman Pontifical. Revised by decree of the Second Vatican
Council and published by authority of Pope Paul VI. Washington, DC: National Conference of Catholic Bishops, 1973.

The Rites of the Catholic Church. Revised by decree of the Second Vatican Ecumenical Council and published by authority of
Pope Paul VI. 2 vols. Translated by the International Commission on English in the Liturgy. New York: Pueblo, 1976–
1980.

B. INTRODUCTIONS

BAUDOT, Jules. Notions générales de liturgie. 2. éd. Liturgie.
Paris: Bloud & Cie, 1908.

BOUYER, Louis. Eucharistie: théologie et spiritualité de la prière
eucharistique. Paris: Desclée, 1966; Eucharist: Theology and
Spirituality of the Eucharistic Prayer. Translated by Charles
Underhill Quinn. Notre Dame, IN: University of Notre Dame
Press, 1968.

CRICHTON, J. D. Christian Celebration: The Mass. London:
Chapman, 1971.

_____. Christian Celebration: The Prayer of the Church. Lon-
don: Chapman, 1976.

DALMAIS, Irénée H. Initiation à la liturgie. Paris: Desclée de
    Brouwer, 1958; Introduction to the Liturgy. Translated by
    Roger Capel. Baltimore, MD: Helicon, 1961.

DEISS, Lucien. Le Cène du Seigneur: eucharistie des chrétiens.
    Croire et comprendre. Paris: Centurion, 1975; It's the Lord's
    Supper: The Eucharist of the Christians. Translated by E.
    Bonin. New York: Paulist Press, 1976.

DIEKMANN, Godfrey. Come Let Us Worship. BS, 2. Baltimore:
    Helicon, 1961; paper ed., Garden City, NY: Image Books,
    1966.

EISENHOFER, L. "Liturgie" and "Liturgik." Lexikon für Theologie
    und Kirche (1st ed.): 6:605-615.

EMMINGHAUS, Johannes H. Die Messe: Wesen, Gestalt, Vollzug.
    Klosterneuburg: Osterreich katholisches Bibelwerke, 1976;
    The Eucharist: Essence, Form, Celebration. Collegeville,
    MN: Liturgical Press, 1978.

GALLEN, John, ed. Christians at Prayer. LS. Notre Dame, IN:
    University of Notre Dame Press, 1977.

GUARDINI, Romano. Besinnung vor der Feier der heiligen Messe.
    5. Aufl. Mainz: Matthias-Grünewald, 1954; Before Mass.
    Translated by Elinor Castendyk Briefs. London: Longmans,
    Green, 1957.

_____. Vom Geist der Liturgie. Freiburg: Herder, 1918; The
    Spirit of the Liturgy. London: Sheed & Ward, 1930.

JUGLAR, Jean. Le Sacrifice de louange. LO, 15. Paris: Cerf,
    1953.

LECLERCQ, Jean. La Liturgie et les paradoxes chrétiens. LO, 36.
    Paris: Cerf, 1963.

MARTIMORT, A. G., ed. L'Eglise en prière. 3. éd. Paris:
    Desclée, 1965; partial adaptations in two volumes: The Church
    at Prayer: Introduction to the Liturgy. Translated by Robert
    Fisher et al. English ed. edited by Austin Flannery and Vin-
    cent Ryan. New York: Desclée, 1968; and The Eucharist
    [The Church at Prayer, vol. 2]. Edited by Austin Flannery
    and Vincent Ryan. New York: Herder & Herder, 1973.

MARTIMORT, A. G. En mèmoire de moi; la prière de l'église et
    ses sacrements. Paris: Editions de l'Ecole, 1954; In Remem-
    brance of Me: The Prayer of the Church and the Sacraments.
    Translated by Aldhelm Dean. Collegeville, MN: Liturgical
    Press, 1958.

MILLER, John H. Fundamentals of the Liturgy. Notre Dame, IN:
Fides, 1960, c 1959.

MILNER, Paulinus. The Worship of the Church. NLCK, 9. London: Burns & Oates; New York: Hawthorn Books, 1964.

O'SHEA, William. The Worship of the Church: A Companion to
Liturgical Studies. Westminster, MD: Newman Press, 1957.

PEIL, Rudolf. Handbuch der Liturgik für Katecheten und Lehrer.
Freiburg: Herder, 1955; A Handbook of the Liturgy. Trans-
lated by H. E. Winstone. Freiburg: Herder; New York:
Herder & Herder, 1960.

ROGUET, A. M. La Messe, approaches du mystère. Nouvelle éd.
Paris: Editions du Seuill, 1971.

SCHUERMANS, Marie Philippe. Parole de Dieu et rite sacramentel.
Bruxelles: Lumen Vitae, 1963.

C. GENERAL HISTORIES AND
    CRITICAL STUDIES

AMIOT, François. Histoire de la messe. JSJC, 109. Paris: Fayard, 1956; History of the Mass. 2d ed. Translated by Lancelot Sheppard. TCEC, 110. London: Burns & Oates; New
York: Hawthorn Books, 1966.

BATIFFOL, Pierre. Leçons sur la messe. Paris: Gabalda, 1919.

BERNARD, Théophile. Cours de liturgie romaine, ou explication
historique, littérale et mystique des cérémonies de l'église.
5 vols. in 11. Paris: Berche & Tralin, 1887-1908.
1. Prolégomènes. La Messe. Nouv. éd. 1898.
2. La bréviaire. 1887.
3. Le rituel. 1893.
4. Le pontifical. 1902.
5. Cérémonial. 1908.

BISHOP, Edmund. Liturgica Historica: Papers on the Liturgy and
Religious Life of the Western Church. Oxford: Clarendon
Press, 1918; reprinted 1962.

BOGLER, Theodor. Eucharistiefeiern in der Christenheit: Gesammelte Aufsätze. LM, 26. Maria Laach: Ars Liturgica, 1960.

BOROVNITSKY, Ivan. The Origin and Composition of the Roman
Catholic Liturgy, and its Difference from that of the Orthodox
Church. 3d ed. Translated from the edition of Kiev:

University Press, 1857 by Basil Popoff. London: J. Masters, 1863.

BRINKTRINE, Johannes. Die heilige Messe in ihrem Werden und Wesen. 3. Aufl. Paderborn: Schöningh, 1950.

CABROL, Fernand. "Messe VIII: La Messe dans la liturgie." Dictionnaire de théologie catholique, 10:1346-1403.

_____. La Messe en Occident. BCSR. Paris: Bloud & Gay, 1932; The Mass of the Western Rites. Translated by Catherine M. Antony. London: Sands, 1934.

CALLEWAERT, Camillus Aloysius. Liturgicae institutiones. Ed. 3. Brugis: Beyaert, 1933- .

_____. Sacris erudiri: fragmenta liturgica collecta a monachis Sancti Petri de Aldenburgo in Steenbrugge ne pereant. Steenbrugge: Abbatia S. Petri de Aldenburgo, 1940; reprinted 1962.

CAPELLE, Bernard. Pour une meilleure intelligence de la messe. 2. éd. Louvain: Abbaye du Mont César, 1955; A New Light on the Mass. 2d ed. Translated by a monk of Glenstal. Dublin: Clonmore & Reynolds, 1961.

CASEL, Odo. Das christliche Kultmysterium. 4. Aufl. hrsg. von Burkhard Neunheuser. Regensburg: Pustet, 1960; The Mystery of Christian Worship and Other Writings. Edited by Burkhard Neunheuser. Preface by Charles Dairs. Westminster, MD: Newman Press, 1962.

_____. Die Liturgie als Mysterienfeier. EO, 9. Freiburg: Herder, 1918.

_____. "Das Mysteriengedächtnis der Messliturgie im Lichte der Tradition." Jahrbuch für Liturgiewissenschaft, 6 (1926): 113-204.

_____. "Neue Zeugnisse für das Kultmysterium." Jahrbuch für Liturgiewissenschaft, 13 (1933): 99-171.

_____. Vom christlichen Mysterium: Gesammelte Arbeiten zum Gedächtnis. Herausgegeben von Anton Mayer, Johannes Quasten und Burkhard Neunheuser. Düsseldorf: Patmos-Verlag, 1951.

Centre de pastorale liturgique. La messe et sa catéchèse: Vanves, 30 avril-4 mai 1946. LO, 7. Paris: Cerf, 1947.

CHAVASSE, Antoine. "Liturgie papale et liturgies presbytérales:

leurs zones d'influence." In Mélanges en l'honneur de Mgr
Michel Andrieu, pp. 103-112. Strasbourg: Palais Universitaire, 1956.

CRICHTON, James D. "An Historical Sketch of the Roman Liturgy."
In True Worship, pp. 45-82. Edited by L. Sheppard. Baltimore, MD: Helicon Press, 1963.

CROEGAERT, Augus Jan Marie Josef. Les rites et les prières du
saint sacrifice de la messe. 2. ed. 3 vols. in 2. Malines:
H. Dessain, 1948-1949; The Mass: A Liturgical Commentary.
2 vols. Translated by J. Holland Smith. London: Burns &
Oates, 1958-1959.

DENIS-BOULET, Noele Maurice, and BOULET, Robert. Eucharistie
ou la messe dans ses variétés: son histoire et ses origines.
Paris: Letouzey & Ané, 1953.

DE STEFANI, Gaspare. La sancta messa nella liturgia romana.
Turin: Berruti, 1935.

DUCHESNE, Louis M. O. Origines du culte chrétien. 5. éd.
Paris: Boccard, 1920; Christian Worship: Its Origin and
Evolution. 5th ed. Translated by M. L. McClure. London:
SPCK, 1956.

DURIG, Walter, ed. Liturgie: Gestalt und Vollzug. Munich:
Hueber, 1963.

EISENHOFER, Ludwig. Handbuch der katholischen Liturgik. 2.
Aufl. 2 vols. Freiburg: Herder, 1941.
--re-issue of Eisenhöfer's 1912 revision of Valentin Thalhofer's
Handbuch der katholischen Liturgik.

_____, and LECHNER, Joseph. Liturgik des römischen Ritus.
6. Aufl. Freiburg: Herder, 1953; The Liturgy of the Roman
Rite. Translated by A. J. and E. F. Peeler. Edited by
H. E. Winstone. New York: Herder & Herder, 1961.

FILTHAUT, Theodore. Die Kontroverse über die Mysterienlehre.
Warendorf: J. Schnell, 1947; La théologie des mystères: exposé de la controverse. Traduit par J.-C. Didier et A. Liefoognie. Paris: Desclée, 1954.

FISCHER, Balthasar. Signs, Words & Gestures: Short Homilies on
the Liturgy. Translated by Matthew J. O'Connell. New York:
Pueblo, 1981.

FORTESCUE, Adrian. The Mass: A Study in the Roman Liturgy.
2d ed. London: Longmans, Green, 1955.

GAMBER, Klaus. Liturgie Ubermorgen: Gedanken über die Geschichte und Zukunft des Gottesdienstes. Freiburg: Herder,
1966.

GIHR, Nikolaus. Das heilige Messopfer dogmatisch, liturgisch und
ascetisch erklärt. 6. Aufl. Freiburg: Herder, 1897; The
Holy Sacrifice of the Mass: Dogmatically, Liturgically and
Ascetically Explained. 8th ed. Translated from the 6th German edition. St. Louis, MO: B. Herder, 1929.

GUARDINI, Romano. Besinnung vor der Feier der heiligen Messe.
5. Aufl. Mainz: Matthias-Grünewald, 1954; Before Mass.
Translated by Elinor Castendyk Briefs. London, New York:
Longmans, Green, 1957.

GUERANGER, Prosper. Institutions liturgiques. 2. éd. 4 vols.
Paris: Société générale de Librairie catholique, 1878-1885.

HERWEGEN, Ildefons. Das Kunstprinzip der Liturgie. 4. und 5.
Aufl. Paderborn: Jungfermannschen Buchhandlung, 1929;
The Art-Principle of Liturgy. Translated by William Busch.
Collegeville, MN: Liturgical Press, 1931; reprinted as Litur-
gy's Inner Beauty. Collegeville, MN: Liturgical Press, 1955.

HILDEBRANDT, Franz. I Offered Christ: A Protestant Study of
the Mass. Philadelphia, PA: Fortress Press, 1967.

HUBERT, Martin Ph. La messe: histoire du culte eucharistique
en Occident. Paris: Publications filmées d'art et d'histoire,
1965?

ISERLOH, Erwin. "'Das Herrenmahl' im römischen und evangelisch-
lutherischen Gespräch." Theologische Revue, 3 (1979): 178-
182.

JOUBIER, Antoine. La notion canonique de rite: essai historico-
canonique. 2. ed. Rome: PP. Basiliani, 1961.

JUNGMANN, Josef Andreas. "Abendmahl als Name der Eucharistie."
Zeitschrift für katholische Theologie, 93 (1971): 91-94.

_____. "Das Gedächtnis des Herrn in der Eucharistie." Theo-
logische Quartalschrift, 133 (1953): 389-399.

_____. Gewordene Liturgie: Studien und Durchblicke. Inns-
bruck: F. Rauch, 1941.

_____. Glaubensverkündigung im Lichte der Frohbotschaft.
Innsbruck: Tyrolia Verlag, 1963; Announcing the Word of God.
Translated by Ronald Walls. New York: Herder & Herder,
1967.

_____ . Der Gottesdienst der Kirche: auf dem Hintergrund
seiner Geschichte kurz erläutert. Innsbruck: Tyrolia Verlag,
1955; Public Worship: A Survey. Translated by Clifford
Howell. London: Challoner, 1957; Collegeville, MN: Liturgical Press, 1958.

_____ . Der Gottesdienst der Kirche. 3. Aufl. Innsbruck:
Tyrolia-Verlag, 1962.

_____ . Die liturgische Feier: Grundsätzliches und Geschicht-
liches über Formgesetze der Liturgie. 2. Aufl. Regensburg:
Pustet, 1939; Liturgical Worship. Translated by a Monk of
St. John's Abbey, Collegeville, MN. New York: Pustet, 1941.

_____ . Die liturgische Feier. 3. Aufl. Regensburg: Pustet,
1961.

_____ . Liturgisches Erbe und pastorale Gegenwart. Innsbruck:
Tyrolia, 1960; Pastoral Liturgy. Translated by Ronald Walls.
London: Challoner; New York: Herder & Herder, 1962.

_____ . The Mass: An Historical, Theological, and Pastoral
Survey. Edited by Mary Ellen Evans. Translated by Julian
Fernandes. Collegeville, MN: Liturgical Press, 1976.

_____ . Missarum sollemnia: eine genetische Erklärung der
römischen Messe. 2 Bde. Wien: Herder, 1948; The Mass of
the Roman Rite: Its Origins and Development. 2 vols.
Translated by Francis A. Brunner. New York: Benziger,
1951-1955.

_____ . Missarum sollemnia. 2 Bde. 4. Aufl.. Freiburg: Herder, 1958; The Mass of the Roman Rite. New rev. and abridged
ed. Translated by Francis A. Brunner. Revised by K.
Riepe. New York: Benziger, 1959, 1961.

_____ . Missarum sollemnia. 2 Bde. 5. Aufl. Wien: Herder,
1962.

_____ . Die Stellung Christi im liturgischen Gebet. 2. Aufl.
LQF, 19-20. Münster: Aschendorff, 1962; The Place of Christ
in Liturgical Prayer. 2d ed. Translated by A. Peeler. Staten
Island, NY: Alba House, 1965.

KASPER, Walter. "Wort und Sakrament." In Martyria, Leiturgia,
Diakonia, pp. 260-285. Herausgegeben von Otto Semmelroth.
Mainz: Matthias-Grünewald, 1968.

KING, Archdale Arthur. Notes on the Catholic Liturgies. London:
Longmans, Green, 1930.

_____. Rites of Western Christendom. 4 vols. London: Long-
mans, Green; Milwaukee, WI: Bruce, 1955-1959.
1. Liturgies of the Religious Orders. 1955.
2. Liturgy of the Roman Church. 1957.
3. Liturgies of the Primatial Sees. 1957.
4. Liturgies of the Past. 1959.

KLAUSER, Theodor. Abendländische Liturgiegeschichte: For-
schungsbericht und Besinnung. Bonn: Hanstein, 1949; The
Western Liturgy and Its History: Some Reflections on Recent
Studies. Translated by F. L. Cross. London: Mowbray;
New York: Morehouse-Gorham, 1952.

_____. Kleine abendländische Liturgiegeschichte. Bonn: Han-
stein, 1965; A Short History of the Western Liturgy. 2d ed.
Translated by John Halliburton. New York: Oxford University Press, 1979.

MEGIVERN, James J. Concomitance and Communion: A Study in
Eucharistic Doctrine and Practice. New York: Herder, 1963.

MICHELL, G. A. Landmarks in Liturgy. London: Darton, Longman & Todd, 1961.

MICHELS, Thomas Aquinas. Sarmenta: Gesammelte Studien.
Herausgegeben von Norbert Brox und Ansgar Paus. Münster:
Aschendorff, 1972.

MILLER, John H. "Mass, Roman." New Catholic Encyclopedia,
9:414-426.

MOHRMANN, Christine. "Missa." Vigiliae Christianae, 12 (1958):
67-92, reprinted in her Etudes sur le latin des chrétiens, vol.
3, pp. 307-330. Roma: Edizioni di storia e letteratura, 1965.

NEUNHEUSER, Burkhard. Storia della liturgia attraverso le epoche
culturali. BEL, 11. Rome: Edizioni Liturgiche, 1977.

NOCILLI, Giuseppe. La messa romana, suo sviluppo nella liturgia
e nel canto. Venezia: Istituto per la Collaborazione Culturale,
1961.

OPPENHEIM, Philippus. Institutiones systematico-historicae in sacram liturgiam. 9 vols. Turin: Marietti, 1939-1947. Pars I.
Liturgia generalis.
1. Introductio historica in litteras liturgicas. 2. ed. 1945.
2-4. Tractatus de jure liturgico. 1939-1940.
5. Introductio in scientiam liturgicam. 1940.
6. Notions liturgiae fundamentales. 1941.
7. Principia theologiae liturgicae. 1947.
Pars II. Liturgia specialis.

Series 2:   Liturgia sacramentorum.
1. De fontibus et historia ritus baptismalis.   1943.
2. Jus liturgiae baptismalis.   1943.
3, part 1. Commentationes ad ritum baptismale, pars I: Ritus
    antebaptismales.   1943.
9. Sacramentum ordinis secundun Pontificale Romanum ... pars
    I: Notiones de ordine generatim inspecto.   1946.

OURY, Guy-Marie. La Messe romaine et les peuple de Dieu dans
    l'histoire. Sable-sur-Sarthe: Solesmes, 1981.

PASCHER, Joseph. Eucharistia: Gestalt und Vollzug. 2. Aufl.
    Freiburg: Wewel Verlag, 1953.

_____. Form und Formenwandel Sakramentaler Feier: ein Beit-
    rag zur Gestaltenlehre der heiligen Zeichen. Münster: As-
    chendorff, 1949.

_____. Die Liturgie der Sakramente. 3. Aufl. Münster: As-
    chendorff, 1961.

PIOLANTI, Antonio. Eucaristia: Il mistero dell' altare nel pensiero
    e nella vita della Chiesa. Rome: Desclée, 1957.

PUNIET, Jean de. La liturgie de la messe: ses origines et son
    histoire. 2. éd. Avignon: Aubanel Fils Aine, 1930; The Mass:
    Its Origin and History. Translated by the Benedictines of
    Stanbrook. New York: Longmans, Green, 1930.

RADO, P. Enchiridion Liturgicum. 2 vols. 2. ed. Rome:
    Herder, 1966.

REINHOLD, Hans Ansgar. The American Parish and the Roman
    Liturgy. New York: Macmillan, 1958.

_____. Bringing the Mass to the People. Introductin by F. R.
    McManus. Baltimore, MD: Helicon Press, 1960.

RIGHETTI, Mario. Manuale di storia liturgica. 4 vols. 3. ed.
    Milan: Editrice Ancora, 1959-1969.
    1. Introduzione generale. 1964.
    2. L'anno liturgico. Il Breviario.
    3. L'eucaristia.
    4. I sacramenti. I sacramentali.

ROGUET, A. M. Invitatoires, pour commenter la messe. 2. éd.
    Neuilly-sur-Seine: Centre de Pastorale liturgique, 1958.

SCHAEFFLER, Richard, and HUNERMANN, Peter. Ankunft Gottes
    und Handeln des Menschen: Thesen über Kult und Sakrament.
    QD, 77. Freiburg: Herder, 1977.

SCHMIDT, Herman A. P. Introductio in liturgiam occidentalem.
    Rome: Herder, 1960.

SHEPPARD, Lancelot. The Mass in the West. TCEC, 111. New
    York: Hawthorn Books, 1962.

STAPPER, Richard. Katholische Liturgik: zum Gebrauch bei
    Akademischen Vorlesungen sowie zum Selbstunterricht. 6.
    Aufl. Münster: Aschendorff, 1931.

THALHOFER, Valentin.
    --See IX. EISENHOFER above.

WAGNER, Johannes, and ZAHRINGER, D., eds. Eucharistiefeier
    am Sonntag: Reden und Verhandlungen des 1. deutschen
    liturgischen Kongresses. Trier: Paulinus Verlag, 1953.

D. STUDIES IN LITURGICAL THEOLOGY

ADAM, Karl. "Les bases dogmatiques de la liturgie." Questions
    liturgiques et paroissiales, 22 (1937): 3-18, 75-92, 147-158.

ARNOLD, Franz Xaver, and FISCHER, Balthasar, eds. Die Messe
    in der Glaubensverkündigung: kerygmatische Fragen. [Fest-
    schrift für P. Josef Andreas Jungmann, S.J., zu seinem 60.
    Geburtstag.] 2. Aufl. Freiburg: Herder, 1953.

BERGER, Rupert. "Die Terminologie der Nachfolge Christi in der
    römischen Liturgie." In Liturgie: Gestalt und Vollzug, pp.
    1-24. Herausgegeben von Walter Dürig. Münster: Hueber,
    1963.

BRINKTRINE, Johannes. "Der dogmatische Beweis aus der Litur-
    gie." In Scientia sacra: theologische Festgabe zugeeignet
    Seiner Eminenz dem hochwürdigsten Herrn Karl Joseph Kardinal
    Schulte, Erzbischof von Köln, zum fünfundzwanzigsten Jahre-
    stage der Bischofsweihe 19. März 1935, pp. 231-251. Köln:
    J. P. Bachem; Düsseldorf: L. Schwann, 1935.

_____. "Die Liturgie als dogmatische Erkenntnisquelle."
    Ephemerides liturgicae, 43 (1929): 44-51.

BROWE, Peter. "Die Entstehung der Sakramentsandachten." Jahr-
    buch für Liturgiewissenschaft, 7 (1927): 83-103.

BRUNNER, Peter. "Zur katholischen Sakramenten- und Eucharistie-
    lehre." Theologische Literaturzeitung, 88 (1963): 169-186.

CUVA, A. La presenza di Cristo nella liturgia. Rome: Edizioni
    Liturgiche, 1973.

DALMAIS, J. M. "Le mystère: Introduction à la théologie de la
    liturgie." La Maison-Dieu, 14 (1948): 67-98.

DEKKERS, Eligius. "La liturgie, mystère chrétien." La Maison-
    Dieu, 14 (1948): 30-64.

DE VRIES, W. "Lex supplicandi--lex credendi." Ephemerides
    liturgicae, 47 (1933): 48-58.

DURIG, Walter. Imago: Ein Beitrag zur Terminologie und Theo-
    logie der römischen Liturgie. MTS, 5. Münster: Zink, 1952.

FORTE, Bruno. La chiesa nell'eucharistia: per un' ecclesiologia
    eucaristica alla luce del Vaticano II. BTN, 6. Napoli: D'Auria,
    1975.

HERZ, Martin. Sacrum commercium: eine begriffsgeschichtliche
    Studie zur Theologie der römischen Liturgiesprache. MTS,
    15. Münster: Zink, 1958.

JUNGMANN, Josef Andreas. Die Stellung Christi im liturgischen
    Gebet. 2. Aufl. LQF, 19-20. Münster: Aschendorff, 1962;
    The Place of Christ in Liturgical Prayer. 2d ed. Translated
    by A. Peeler. Staten Island, NY: Alba House, 1965.

KASPER, Walter. "Wort und Sakrament." In Martyria, Leiturgia,
    Diakonia, pp. 260-285. Herausgegeben von Otto Semmelroth.
    Mainz: Matthias-Grünewald, 1968.

LUKKEN, G. M. Original Sin in the Roman Liturgy: Research into
    the Theology of Original Sin in the Roman Sacramentaria and
    the Early Baptismal Liturgy. Leiden: E. J. Brill, 1973.

McGRORY, W. Barry. The Mass and the Resurrection. Rome:
    Catholic Book Agency, 1964.

MOORE, Sebastian. "The Theology of the Mass and the Liturgical
    Datum." Downside Review, 61 (1951): 31-44.

NEUNHEUSER, Burkhard, ed. Opfer Christi und Opfer der Kirche:
    die Lehre vom Messopfer als Mysteriengedächtnis in der Theo-
    logie der Gegenwart. Düsseldorf: Patmos-Verlag, 1960.

SCHAEFFLER, Richard, and HUNERMANN, Peter. Ankunft Gottes
    und Handeln des Menschen: Thesen über Kult und Sakrament.
    QD, 77. Freiburg: Herder, 1977.

TIHON, P. "Theology of the Eucharistic Prayer." In The New
    Liturgy, pp. 174-193. Edited by Lancelot Sheppard. London:
    Darton, Longman & Todd, 1970.

VAGAGGINI, Cipriano. Il senso teologico della liturgia. 4. ed.
Rome: Edizioni Paoline, 1965; Theological Dimensions of the
Liturgy. Translated by L. J. Doyle and W. A. Jurgens.
Collegeville, MN: Liturgical Press, 1976.

VONIER, Anscar. "The Doctrinal Power of the Liturgy in the
Catholic Church." Clergy Review, 9 (1935): 1-8.

E. EARLY AND MEDIEVAL STUDIES

1. General Studies

BATIFFOL, Pierre. Etudes de liturgie et d'archéologie chrétienne.
Paris: Gabalda, 1919.

BROWE, Peter. Die eucharistische Wunder des Mittelalters. BSHT,
n.F. 4. Breslau: Müller & Seiffert, 1938.

_____. Die häufige Kommunion im Mittelalter. Münster: Regens-
burgsche Verlagsbuchhandlung, 1938.

_____. Die Pflichtkommunion im Mittelalter. Münster: Regens-
burgsche Verlagsbuchhandlung, 1940.

CABROL, Fernand. Le livre de la prière antique. 5. éd. Tours:
Mame, 1921; Liturgical Prayer: Its History and Spirit. Trans-
lated by a Benedictine of Stanbrook. London: Burns, Oates
& Washbourne, 1922; reprint ed., Westminster, MD: Newman
Press, 1950.

_____. La prière des premiers chrétiens. [6th ed. of Le livre
de la prière antique.] Paris: Grasset: 1929; The Prayer of
the Early Christians. Translated by Ernest Graf. London:
Burns, Oates & Washbourne, 1930.

_____. Les origines liturgiques. Paris: Letouzey & Ané, 1906.

ISERLOH, Erwin. "Der Wert der Messe in der Diskussion der
Theologen vom Mittelalter bis zum 16. Jahrhundert." Zeitschrift
für katholische Theologie, 83 (1961): 44-79.

LUBAC, Henri de. Corpus Mysticum: l'eucharistie et l'église au
moyen âge. 2. éd. Théologie, 3. Paris: Aubier, 1949.

PFAFF, Richard William. Medieval Latin Liturgy: A Select Bibliography. Toronto Medieval Bibliographies, 9. Toronto:
University of Toronto Press, 1982.

STEPHENSON, A. A. "Two Views of the Mass: Medieval Linguistic Ambiguities." Theological Studies, 22 (1961): 588-609.

VOGEL, Cyrille. Introduction aux sources de l'histoire du culte chrétien au moyen âge. 2. ed. BSM, 1. Spoleto: Centro italiano di studi sull'alto medioevo, 1975.

2. Studies of Early Latin Liturgies

a. Liturgical Books and Manuscripts

(See also sections IX. I, J, K, L, M, N, O, P, and Q.)

BENZ, Suitbert. Der Rotulus von Ravenna, nac seiner Herkunft und seiner Bedeutung für die Liturgiegeschichte kritisch untersucht. LQF, 45. Münster: Aschendorff, 1967.

BOURQUE, Emmanuel. Etude sur les sacramentaires romains. 3 vols. SAC, 20 & 25. Citta del Vaticano: Pontificio Instituto di Archeologia Cristiana, 1948-1958.
1. Pt. 1: Les Textes primitifs. 1948.
2. Pt. 2, t. 1: Les textes remaniés. Le Gélasien du VIIIe siècle. 1952.
3. Pt. 2, t. 2: Le sacramentaire d'Hadrien. Le supplement d'Alcuin et les Gregoriens mixtes. 1958.

CABROL, Fernand. "Autour de la liturgie de Ravenne: Saint Pierre Chrysologue et le Rotulus." Revue bénédictine, 23 (1906): 489-500.

CROSS, F. L. "Early Western Liturgical Manuscripts." Journal of Theological Studies, n.s. 16 (1965): 61-67.

DELISLE, Léopold. Mémoire sur d'anciens sacramentaires. Paris: Imprimerie nationale, 1886.

DOLD, Alban. Vom Sakramentar, Comes und Capitulare zum Missale: eine Studie über die Entstehungszeit der erstmals vollständig erschlossenen liturgischen Palimpsesttexte im Unziale aus Codex 271 von Monte Cassino. Mit Beiträgen von Anton Baumstark. TuA, 34. Beuron: Beuroner Kunstverlag, 1943.

EBNER, Adalbert. Quellen und Forschungen zur Geschichte und Kunstgeschichte des Missale Romanum im Mittelalter: Iter Italicum. Freiburg: Herder, 1896; reprint ed., Graz: Akademische Druch- und Verlagsanstalt, 1957.

EHRENSBERGER, Hugo. Bibliotheca liturgica manuscripta: nach Handschriften der Grossherzoglich Badischen Hof- und Landesbibliothek. Karlsruhe: C. T. Groos, 1889.

_____. Libri liturgici Bibliothecae Vaticanae manuscripti.
Freiburg: Herder, 1897.

FRERE, Walter Howard, ed. Bibliotheca musico-liturgica: A Descriptive Handlist of the Musical & Latin-liturgical mss. of the
Middle Ages preserved in the Libraries of Great Britain and
Ireland. 2 vols. London: B. Quaritch (for the Plainsong
and Medieval Music Society), 1901-1932.

GAMBER, Klaus. Codices liturgici latini antiquiores. 2. ed. SF
subsidia, 1. Freiburg (Schweiz): Universitätsverlag, 1968.

_____. Sakramentarstudien und andere Arbeiten zur frühen
Liturgiegeschichte. SPL, 7. Regensburg: Pustet, 1978.

_____. Sakramentartypen: Versuch einer Gruppierung der
Handschriften und Fragmente bis zur Jahrtausendwende.
TuA, 49-50. Beuron: Beuroner Kunstverlag, 1958.

GY, Pierre-Marie. "Typologie et ecclésiologie des livres liturgiques
médiévaux." La Maison-Dieu, 120 (1974): 7-21.

HUGHES, Andrew. Medieval Manuscripts for Mass and Office: A
Guide to their Organization and Terminology. Toronto: University of Toronto Press, 1982.

LADNER, Pascal, ed. Iter Helveticum. SF, 15. Freiburg
(Schweiz): Universitätsverlag, 1976- .

LAMPEN, Willibrord. Florilegium liturgicum medii aevi. Fulda:
In Monte Mariano, 1923.

MARTENE, Edmond. De antiquis ecclesiae ritibus libri. Ed. 2.
4 vols. Antverpiae: Joannis Baptistae de la Bry, 1736-1738.

MERCATI, Giovanni. Antiche reliquie liturgiche ambrosiane e
romane; con un excursus sui frammenti dogmatici ariani del
Mai. ST, 7. Rome: Tipografia vaticana, 1902; reprint ed.,
Brussels: Gregg, 1962.

SALMON, Pierre. Les manuscrits liturgiques latins de la Bibliothèque Vaticane. 2 vols. ST, 251. Città del Vaticano: Biblioteca Apostolica Vaticana, 1968-1969.

SIFFRIN, Petrus. Konkordanztabellen zu den lateinischen Sakramentarien. Rome: Herder, 1961.

_____. Konkordanztabellen zu den römischen Sakramentarien.
2 vols. Rome: Herder, 1958-1959.

VOS, Margriet. "A la recherche de normes pour les textes

liturgiques de la messe (Ve-VIIe siècles)." Revue d'histoire
ecclésiastique, 69 (1974): 5-37.

WEALE, William Henry James. Bibliographia Liturgica: catalogus
missalium ritus latini ab anno M.CCCC.LXXV impressorum.
London: B. Quaritch, 1886; new ed., edited by H. Bohatta.
London: B. Quaritch, 1928.

WILSON, H. A. A Classified Index to the Leonine, Gelasian and
Gregorian Sacramentaries according to the Text of Muratori's
Liturgia Roman Vetus. Cambridge: Cambridge University
Press, 1892.

        b. The Early Roman Mass

BAUMSTARK, Anton. Liturgia romana e liturgia dell'esarcato: Il
rito detto in seguito Patriarchino e le origini del canon missae
romano. Rome, 1904.

BISHOP, Edmund. "On the Early Texts of the Roman Canon."
Journal of Theological Studies, 4 (1903): 555-577; reprinted
in his Liturgica Historica, pp. 77-115. Oxford: Clarendon
Press, 1918.

CAGIN, P. L'euchologie latine étudiée dans la tradition de ses
formules et de ses formulaires, vol. 2: L'eucharistia: canon
primitif de la messe ou formulaire essentiel et premiere de
toutes les liturgies. Scriptorium Solesmense, 2. Rome, Paris,
Tournai: Desclée, 1912.

CASEL, Odo. Das Gedächtnis des Herrn in der altchristlichen
Liturgie: Die Grundgedanken des Messkanons. EO, 2.
Freiburg: Herder, 1918.

CLERCK, Paul de. La "Prière universelle" dans les liturgie latines
anciennes: tèmoignages patristiques et textes liturgiques.
LQF, 62. Münster: Aschendorff, 1977.

CROSS, F. L. "Pre-Leonine Elements in the Proper of the Roman
Mass." Journal of Theological Studies, 50 (1949): 191-197.

FRERE, Walter Howard. Studies in the Early Roman Liturgy. 3
vols. ACC, 28, 30, 32. London: Oxford University Press,
1930-1935.
   1. The Kalendar. ACC, 28. 1930.
   2. The Roman Gospel Lectionary. ACC, 30. 1934.
   3. The Roman Epistle Lectionary. ACC, 32. 1935.

GAMBER, Klaus. Liturgie und Kirchenbau: Studien zur Geschichte
der Messfeier und des Gotteshauses in der Frühzeit. SPOL, 6.
Regensburg: Pustet, 1976.

_____. Missa Romensis: Beiträge zur frühen römischen Liturgie und zu den Anfängen des Missale Romanum. SPL, 3. Regensburg: Pustet, 1970.

KEIFER, Ralph. "Oblation in the First Part of the Roman Canon: An Examination of a Primitive Eucharistic Structure and Theology in Early Italian and Egyptian Sources." Ph.D. dissertation, University of Notre Dame, 1972.

MAGANI, Francesco. L'antica liturgia romana. 3 vols. in 1. Milano: Tip. Pontificia S. Giuseppe, 1897-1899.

MORIN, G. "Le Te Deum, type anonyme d'anaphore latine préhistorique?" Revue bénédictine, 24 (1907): 180-223.

OPPENHEIM, Philipp. Canon Missae primitivus. Rome, 1948.

_____. De Canone Missae primitivo. [Torino]: Marietti, 1947.

RATCLIFF, E. C. "The Early Roman Canon Missae." Journal of Ecclesiastical History, 20 (1969): 211-224; reprinted in his Liturgical Studies, pp. 91-107. Edited by A. H. Couratin and D. H. Tripp. London: SPCK, 1976.

WILLIS, Geoffrey G. Essays in Early Roman Liturgy. ACC, 46. London: SPCK, 1964.

_____. Further Essays in Early Roman Liturgy. ACC, 50. London: SPCK, 1968.

_____. "The Roman Canon of the Mass at the End of the Sixth Century." Downside Review, 98 (1980): 124-137.

c. The African Liturgy

BISHOP, W. C. "The African Rite." Journal of Theological Studies, 13 (1911-1912): 250-277.

CASATI, G. "La liturgia della messa al tempo di S. Agostino." Augustinianum, 9 (1969): 484-514.

GAMBER, Klaus. "Ordo Missae Africanae. Der nordafrikanische Messritus zur Zeit des hl. Augustinus." Römische Quartalschrift, 64 (1969): 139-153.

d. Early Eucharistic Theology

GEISELMANN, Josef Rupert. Die Abendmahlslehre an der Wende der christlichen Spätantike zum Frühmittelalter: Isidor von Sevilla und das Sakrament der Eucharistie. Munich: Max Hueber Verlag, 1933.

_____. Die Eucharistielehre der Vorscholastik. FCLDG, 15/1-
3. Paderborn: Schöningh, 1926.

_____. "Zur Eucharistielehre der Frühscholastik." Theologische
Review, 29 (1930): 1-12.

MACY, Gary. The Theologies of the Eucharist in the Early Scholastic Period. A Study of the Salvific Function of the Sacrament According to the Theologians, c. 1080-c. 1220. Oxford:
Clarendon Press; New York: Oxford University Press, 1984.

SCHULTE, Raphael. Die Messe als Opfer der Kirche: Die Lehre
frühmittelalterischen Autoren über das eucharistische Opfer.
LQF, 47. Münster: Aschendorff, 1968.

e. Other Topics

ANDRIEU, Michel. Immixtio et consecratio: la consécration par
contact dans les documents liturgiques du moyen âge. Paris:
Picard, 1924.

ARBUSOW, L. Liturgie und Geschichtsschreibung im Mittelalter.
Bonn: Rohrscheid, 1951.

CHUPUNGCO, Anscar J. "Greco-Roman Culture and Liturgical
Adaptation." Notitiae, 15 (1979): 202-218.

DUMOUTET, Edouard. Le Crist selon la chair et la vie liturgique
au moyen-âge. Paris: Beauchesne, 1932.

_____. Le désir de voir l'hostie et les origines de la dévotion
au saint-sacrament. Paris: Beauchesne, 1926.

FRANZ, Adolf. Die kirchliche Benediktionen im Mittelalter. 2 vols.
Freiburg: Herder, 1909.

GAMBER, Klaus. "Conversi ad Dominum: Die Hinwendung von
Priester und Volk nach Osten bei der Messfeier im 4. und 5.
Jahrhundert." Römische Quartalschrift, 67 (1972): 49-64.

HARDERLIN, Alf. Aquae et Vini mysterium: Geheimnis der Erlö-
sung und Geheimnis der Kirche im Spiegel der mittelalterlichen
Auslegung des gemischten Kelches. LQF, 57. Münster:
Aschendorff, 1973.

HAFFNER, F. "Die Zeit der Messfeier bis zum 12. Jahrhundert."
In Miscellanea liturgica in onore di Sua Eminenza Cardinale
Giacomo Lercaro, vol. 1, pp. 133-142. Rome: Desclée, 1966.

KANTOROWICZ, Ernst H., and BUKOFZER, Manfred F. Laudes
regiae: A Study in Liturgical Acclamations and Medieval Ruler
Worship. Berkeley: University of California Press, 1946.

KLAUSER, Theodor. "Der Ubergang der römischen Kirche von der griechischen zur lateinischen Liturgiesprache." In Miscellanea Giovanni Mercati, vol. 1, pp. 467-482. Vatican City: Biblioteca Apostolica Vaticana, 1946.

KOTTJE, Raymund. Studien zum Einfluss des Alten Testamentes auf Recht und Liturgie des frühen Mittelalters (6.-8. Jahrhundert). 2. Aufl. BHF, 23. Bonn: Röhrscheid, 1970.

MICHELS, Thomas Aquinas. "Dedicatio und Consecratio in früher römischer Liturgie." In Enkainia: Gesammelte Arbeiten zum 800 jährigen Weihegedächtnis der Abteikirche Maria Laach am 24. August 1956, pp. 58-61. Herausgegeben von H. Emonds. Düsseldorf: Patmos-Verlag, 1956.

OPFERMANN, B. Die liturgischen Herrscherakklamationen im Sacrum Imperium des Mittelalters. Weimar: Böhlau, 1953.

SCHNITZLER, Theodor. "Das Konzil von Chalkedon und die westliche (römische) Liturgie." In Das Konzil von Chalkedon: Geschichte und Gegenwart, Bd. 2, pp. 735-755. Herausgegeben von Alois Grillmeier und Heinrich Bacht. Würzburg: Echter-Verlag, 1953.

3. The Carolingian Reforms and Alcuin

(See also IX. E. 7. a. Amalarius of Metz and Florus of Lyons, and IX.K. Gregorian Sacramentary, below.)

BARRE, Henri, and DESHUSSES, Jean. "A la recherche du missel d'Alcuin." Ephemerides liturgicae, 82 (1968): 3-44.

CAPELLE, Bernard. "Alcuin et l'histoire du symbole de la messe." Recherches de théologie ancienne et médiévale, 6 (1934): 249-260; reprinted in his Travaux liturgiques, vol. 2, pp. 211-221. Louvain: Centre liturgique, Abbaye du Mont César, 1962.

DESHUSSES, Jean. "Les messes d'Alcuin." Archiv für Liturgiewissenschaft, 14 (1972): 7-41.

ELLARD, Gerald. Master Alcuin, Liturgist: A Partner of Our Piety. Chicago: Loyola University Press, 1956.

NETZER, H. L'introduction de la messe romaine en France sous les carolingiens, Préface par A. Clerval. Paris: Picard, 1910.

NICKL, Georg. Der Anteil des Volkes und der Messliturgie im Frankenreiche von Chlodwig b is Karl der Grossen. Innsbruck: Rauch, 1930.

PORTER, Harry Boone, Jr. "The Liturgical Reforms of Charlemagne." D. Phil. dissertation, Oxford University, 1954.

VOGEL, Cyrille. "La réforme liturgique sous Charlemagne." In
Karl der Grosse: Lebenswerk und Nachleben, Bd. 2, pp. 217-
232. Unter Mitwirkung von Helmut Beumann et al. 2. Aufl.
Düsseldorf: L. Schwann, 1966-1967.

4. The Middle Centuries

DURIG, Walter. "Die Scholastiker und die communio sub una
specie." In Kyriakon: Festschrift Johannes Quasten, pp.
864-875. Münster: Aschendorff, 1970.

GHELLINCK, Joseph de. "Eucharistie au XIIe siècle en Occident."
Dcitionnaire de théologie catholique, 5:1233-1302.

MANGENOT, E. "Eucharistie du XIIIe au XVe siécle." Dictionnaire
de théologie catholique, 5:1302-1326.

REYNOLDS, Roger E. "Liturgical Scholarship at the Time of the
Investiture Controversy: Past Research and Future Opportunities." Harvard Theological Review, 71 (1978): 109-124.

SALMON, Pierre. "Les prières et les rites de l'offertoire de la
messe dans la liturgie romaine au XIIIe et XIVe siècle."
Ephemerides liturgicae, 43 (1929): 508-519.

VAN DIJK, S. J. P., and WALKER, J. Hazelden. The Origins of
the Modern Roman Liturgy: The Liturgy of the Papal Court
and the Franciscan Order in the Thirteenth Century. Westminster, MD: Newman Press, 1960.

5. The Late Middle Ages

KOTTER, Franz Joseph. Die Eucharistielehre in den katholischen
Katechismen des 16. Jh. bis zum Erscheinen des Catechismus
Romanus (1566). RST, 98. Münster: Aschendorff, 1969.

VARCA, V. "Le signe de la Messe d'après le 'De captivitate babylonica Ecclesiae praeludium' de Martin Luther." Ephemerides
liturgicae, 93 (1979): 81-122.

6. Papal Contributions (arranged chronologically)

a. General Studies

ANDRIEU, Michel. "La carrière ecclésiastique des papes et les

documents liturgiques du moyen âge." Revue des sciences religieuses, 21 (1947): 89-120.

b. Innocent I

CABIE, Robert, ed. La lettre du pape Innocent I à Décentius de
Gubbio, 19 mars 416. Texte critique, traduction et commentaire par Robert Cabié. BRHE, 58. Louvain: Publications
universitaires de Louvain, Bureau de la R. H. E., 1973.

CAPELLE, Bernard. "Innocent I et le canon de la messe." Recherches de théologie ancienne et médiévale, 19 (1952): 5-16;
reprinted in his Travaux liturgiques, vol. 2, pp. 236-247.
Louvain: Centre liturgique, Abbaye du Mont César, 1962.

c. Leo the Great

DEKKERS, Eligius. "Autour de l'oeuvre liturgique de S. Léon le
Grand." Sacris Erudiri, 10 (1958): 363-398.

HOLETON, D. R. "The Sacramental Language of S. Leo the Great:
A Study of the Words munus and oblata." Ephemerides liturgicae, 92 (1978): 115-165.

LANG, Arthur Paul. "Anklänge an liturgische Texte in Epiphanie-
sermonen Leos des Grossen." Sacris Erudiri, 10 (1958): 43-
126.

_____. "Anklänge an Orationen der Ostervigil in Sermonen Leos
des Grossen." Sacris Erudiri, 13 (1962): 281-325.

_____. "Leo der Grosse und die liturgischen Texte des Oktav-
tages von Epiphanie." Sacris Erudiri, 11 (1960): 12-135.

SOOS, Maris Bernard de. Le mystère liturgique d'après Saint
Léon le Grand. LQF, 34. Münster: Aschendorff, 1958.

d. Gelasius

CAPELLE, Bernard. "Le Kyrie de la messe et le pape Gélase."
Revue bénédictine, 46 (1934): 126-144; reprinted in his
Travaux liturgiques, vol. 2, pp. 116-135. Louvain: Centre
liturgique, Abbaye du Mont César, 1962.

_____. "L'oeuvre liturgique de S. Gélase." Journal of Theo-
logical Studies, 2 (1951): 129-144; reprinted in his Travaux
liturgiques, vol. 2, pp. 146-160. Louvain: Centre liturgique,
Abbaye du Mont César, 1962.

_____. "Le Pape Gélase et la messe romaine." Revue d'histoire

ecclésiastique, 35 (1939): 22-34; reprinted in his Travaux
liturgiques, vol. 2, pp. 135-145. Louvain: Centre liturgique,
Abbaye du Mont César, 1962.

e. Gregory the Great

CALLEWAERT, Camille. "L'ouevre liturgique de S. Grégoire: la
septuagésime et l'alleluia." In his Sacris Erudiri: fragmenta
liturgica collecta, pp. 635-653. Steenbrugge: Abbatia S. Petri
de Aldenburgo, 1940.

FROGER, J. "L'Alleluja dans l'usage romain et la réforme de saint
Grégoire." Ephemerides liturgicae, 62 (1948): 6-48.

GRIFFE, E. "Saint Grégoire le Grand et Mgr. Duchesne, à propos
de la récitation du Pater à la messe." Bulletin de littérature
ecclésiastique, 55 (1954): 164-166.

LAMBOT, C. "Le Pater dans la liturgie apostolique d'après Saint
Grégoire." Revue bénédictine, 42 (1930): 265-269.

MICHELS, T. "Woher nahm Gregor der Grosse die Kanonbitte
'diesque nostros in tua pace disponas'?" Jahrbuch für Liturgiewissenschaft, 13 (1935): 188-190.

WELLESZ, Egon. "Gregory the Great's Letter on the Alleluia."
Annales musicologiques, 2 (1954): 1-26.

WILLIS, G. G. "St. Gregory the Great and the Lord's Prayer in
the Roman Mass." In his Further Essays in Early Roman Liturgy, pp. 175-188. ACC, 50. London: SPCK, 1968.

f. Alexander III

ALEXANDER III. Die Sentenzen Rolands, nachmals Papstes Alexander III, pp. 214-237. Herausgegeben von A. M. Gietl.
Freiburg: Herder, 1891.

g. Innocent III

BARBERO, Giuseppe. La dottrina eucaristica negli scritti di papa
Innocenzo III. Roma: Edizione Paoline, 1953.

h. Clement V

DYKMANS, Marc. "Le missel de Clément V." Ephemerides liturgicae, 86 (1972): 449-473.

7. Medieval Writers (arranged chronologically)

a. Amalarius of Metz and Florus of Lyons

AMALARIUS OF METZ. Amalarii episcopi opera liturgica omnia. 3 vols. Edited by J. M. Hanssens. ST, 138-140. Città del Vaticano: Biblioteca apostolica vaticana, 1948-1950.

DUC, Paul. Etude sur l'Expositio missae de Florus de Lyon. Belley: Chaduc, 1937.

KOLPING, Adolf. "Amalar von Metz und Florus von Lyon: Zeugen eines Wandels im liturgischen Mysterienverständnis in der Karolingerzeit." Zeitschrift für katholische Theologie, 73 (1951): 424-464.

b. The Controversy at Corbie: Radbertus and Ratramnus

PASCHASIUS RADBERTUS. "The Lord's Body and Blood (Selections)." In Early Medieval Theology, pp. 94-108. Edited by George E. McCracken and Allen Cabaniss. LCC, 9. Philadelphia, PA: Westminster Press, 1957.

RATRAMNUS OF CORBIE. Ratramnus: De corpore et sanguine Domini--texte établi d'après les manuscrits et notice bibliographique. Edited by J. N. Bakhuizen van den Brink. Verhandlingen der koninklijke Nederlandse Akademie van Wetenschappen, Afd. Letterkunde, Nieuwe Reeks, Deel 71/1. Amsterdam: North-Holland Publishing Co., 1954.

_____. "Christ's Body and Blood." In Early Medieval Theology, pp. 118-147. Edited by George E. McCracken and Allen Cabaniss. LCC, 9. Philadelphia, PA: Westminster Press, 1957.

CHOISY, Eugène. Paschase Radbert: étude historique sur le IXe siècle et sur le dogme de la cène. Genève: Richter, 1888.

FAHEY, John F. The Eucharistic Teaching of Ratramn of Corbie. Pontificia Facultas Theologica Seminarii Sanctae Mariae ad Lacum, Dissertationes ad lauream, 72. Mundelein, IL: St. Mary of the Lake Seminary, 1951.

GLIOZZO, Calogero. La dottrina della conversione eucaristica in Pascasio Radberto e Ratramno, monaci di Corbia. Publicazioni dell' Ignatianum, Messina, serie teologica, 1. Palermo: Industrie riunite editoriale Siciliane, 1945.

c. Berengar of Tours and Lanfranc of Bec

BERENGAR OF TOURS. De sacra coena adversus Lanfrancum. Edited by W. H. Beekenkamp. KSNAK, 2. s'Gravenhage: Nijhoff, 1941.

GEISELMANN, Josef Rupert. "Abendmahlsstreit." Lexikon für
    Theologie und Kirche (2. Aufl.), 1:33-35.

_____. "Berengar von Tours." Lexikon für Theologie und
    Kirche (2. Aufl.), 2:213-214.

HODL, Ludwig. "Die confessio Berengarii von 1059: eine Arbeit
    zum frühscholastischen Eucharistietraktat." Scholastik, 37
    (1962): 370-394.

MacDONALD, A. J. Berengar and the Reform of Sacramental Doc-
    trine. London: Longmans, Green, 1930.

SHEEDY, Charles Edmund. The Eucharistic Controversy of the
    Eleventh Century against the Background of Pre-Scholastic
    Theology. SST, 2d ser., 4. Washington, DC: Catholic Uni-
    versity of America Press, 1947; reprint ed., New York: AMS
    Press, 1980.

SOUTHERN, R. W. "Lanfranc of Bec and Berengar of Tours." In
    Studies in Medieval History: Festschrift for F. M. Powicke,
    pp. 27-48. Edited by R. W. Hunt, W. A. Pantin, and R. W.
    Southern. Oxford: Clarendon Press, 1948.

        d. Hugh of St. Victor

HUGO OF ST. VICTOR. On the Sacraments of the Christian Faith
    (De Sacramentis). Translated by R. J. Deferrari. MAAP, 58.
    Cambridge, MA: Medieval Academy of America, 1951.

SCHLETTE, H. R. "Die eucharistielehre Hugos von St. Viktor."
    Zeitschrift für katholische Theologie, 81 (1959): 67-100, 163-
    210.

        e. Bernard of Clairvaux

BERTETTE, D. "La dottrina eucaristica di San Bernardo." Salesi-
    anum, 16 (1954): 258-292.

        f. Peter Lombard

PETRUS LOMBARDUS. Libri quatour sententiarum, lib. 4, d. 8-13.
    2. ed. Ed. Collegii S. Bonaventurae. Quaracchi: Coll. S.
    Bonaventurae, 1916.

ROGERS, Elizabeth Frances. Peter Lombard and the Sacramental
    System. Diss. Columbia U, 1917.

STEGMULLER, Friedrich, ed. Repertorium Commentariorum in Sen-
    tentias Petri Lombardi. 2 Bde. Würzburg: Schöningh, 1947.

g. Peter the Chanter and Stephen Langton

DUMOUTET, Edouard. "La théologie de l'Eucharistie à la fin du
XIIe siècle: le témoignage de Pierre le Chantre d'après la
Summa de Sacramentis." Archives d'histoire doctrinale et lit-
téraire du moyen-âge, 14 (1943-1945): 181-262.

MASI, Roberto. "La teologia della transustanziazione in Pietro
Cantore." Divinitas, 3 (1959): 451-475.

VEAL, J. F. The Sacramental Theology of Stephen Langton and
the Influence upon him of Peter the Chanter. Roma: Officium
Libri Catholici, 1955.

h. Albertus Magnus

ALBERTUS MAGNUS. B. Alberti Magni ... Opera Omnia. 38 vols.
Edited by Augusti Borgnet. Paris: Ludovicum Vivès, 1890-
1899.
--vol. 13. Sermones.
--vol. 38. Distinctiones in sacramentum eucharistiae.

JORISSEN, Hans. "Materie und Form der Sakramente im Verständnis Alberts der Grosse." Zeitschrift für Kirche und Theologie,
80 (1958): 267-315.

_____. "Messerklärung und Kommuniontraktat: Werke Alberts
der Grosse." Zeitschrift für Kirche und Theologie, 78 (1956):
41-97.

KOLPING, Adolf. "Eucharistia als Bona Gratia: Die Messauffasung
Alberts der Grosse an Hand seiner Messerklärung." In Studia
Albertina: Festschrift für Bernhard Geyer, pp. 249-278.
Herausgegeben von Heinrich Ostlender. BGPMA, Supplement-
band 4. Münster: Aschendorff, 1952.

SCHLETTE, H. R. Die Lehre von der geistlichen Kommunion bei
Bonaventura, Albert dem Grossen, und Thomas von Aquin.
MTS, 17. München: Hueber, 1959.

i. Thomas Aquinas

THOMAS AQUINAS. Opera omnia, vol. 10: In IV Sententiarum.
Edited by S. E. Fretté and P. Maré. Paris: Vives, 1873.

_____. Rites et prières de la messe [from Summa Theologica,
3, q. 83). Introduction by Joseph-Marie Parent. Montreal:
Editions de l'Arbre, 1944.

_____. Somme théologique. Paris: Société saint Jean l'evange-
liste, Desclée, 1945.

--Les Sacraments, 3a, q. 60-65. Traduction par A.-M. Roguet.
--Le baptême, la confirmation, 3a, q. 66-72. Traduction par
    A. B. Boulanger.
--L'eucharistie, 3a, q. 73-83. Traduction par A.-M. Roguet.
--La pénitence, 3a, q. 84-90; Supp., q. 1-20. Traduction par
    E. Hugueny. 1931, 1954.
--L'ordre, Suppl. q. 34-49. Traduction par M. J. Gerland.
--Le mariage, Suppl. q. 41-68. 3 vols. Traduction par L.
    Missery.

_____. Summa theologica, 3, q. 60-65, 66-72, 73-83. In his
Opera omnia iussu impensaque Leonis XIII edita, Bd. 12. Roma:
Typographia Polyglotta S. C. de Propaganda Fide, 1906.

_____. Summa Theologica, vol. 3 (III, q. 60-65, 73-83). Trans-
lated by Fathers of the English Dominican Province. London:
Burns & Oates; New York: Benziger, 1947-1948.

_____. Summa Theologiae. Cambridge: Blackfriars; New York:
McGraw-Hill; London: Eyre & Spottiswoode, 1975.
--Vol. 56: The Sacraments (3a. 60-65). Edited and translated
    by David Bourke, 1975.
--Vol. 57: Baptism & Confirmation (3a. 66-72). Edited and
    translated by James J. Cunningham. 1975.
--Vol. 58: The Eucharistic Presence (3a. 73-78). Edited and
    translated by W. Barden. 1975.
--Vol. 59: Holy Communion (3a. 79-83). Edited and translated
    by Thomas Gilby. 1975.

_____. The Three Greatest Prayers: Commentaries on the Our
Father, the Hail Mary, and the Apostles' Creed. Translated by
Lawrence Shapcote. Introduction by Thomas Gilby. London:
Burns, Oates & Washbourne, 1937.

_____. The Venerable Sacrament of the Altar. Translated by
J. M. Neale. London: J. T. Hayes, 1871.

BAUER, Georg Lorenz. "Das heiligen Messopfer im Licht der
    Grundsätze des hl. Thomas über das Opfer." Divus Thomas,
    28 (1950): 5-31.

NAU, Paul. Le mystére du corps et du sang du seigneur: la
    messe d'aprés Saint Thomas d'Aquin, son rite d'après l'histoire.
    Solesmes: Abbaye Saint-Pierre de Solesmes, 1976.

WINZEN, Damasus. "Kommentar." In Die deutsche Thomas-
    Ausgabe, Bd. 30: Das Geheimnis der Eucharistie, pp. 473-580.
    Salzburg: A. Pustet, 1938.

    j. Bonaventure

BONAVENTURA. "In IV Sententia." In Opera Omnia, vol. 4:

Sententiarum Petri Lombardi. Ed. PP. Collegii a S. Bonaventura. Quaracchi: Typ. Coll. S. Bonaventurae, 1889.

KATTUM, Franz Xaver. Die Eucharistielehre des heiligen Bonaventura. München: Datterer, 1920.

k. William Durandus

DURANTIS, Gulielmus. Rationale divinorum officiorum. Moguntini: J. Fust & P. Gernzeim, 1459.

_____. Rational; ou, Manuel des divins offices; ou, Raisons mystiques et historiques de la liturgie catholique, traduit pour la première fois du latine en français par Ch. Barthélemy; précédé d'une notice historique sur la vie et sur les écrits de Durand de Mende; suivi d'une bibliographie chronologique ... avec un grand nombre de notes à la suite de chaque volume. 5 vols. Paris: Vives, 1845.

_____. The Symbolism of Churches and Church Ornaments: A Translation of the First Book of the Rationale Divinorum Officiorum. With an introductory essay, notes, and illustrations, by John Mason Neale and Benjamin Webb. 3d ed. London: Gibbings & Co., 1906.

_____. The Sacred Vestments: An English Rendering of the Third Book of the Rationale divinorum officiorum of Durandus, Bishop of Mende. Translated, with notes, by T. H. Passmore. London: Sampson, Low, Marston, 1899.

l. Duns Scotus

DUNS SCOTUS, Joannes. "Quaestiones in IV Sententia (Lectura Oxoniensis)." In his Opera Omnia, Bd. 17. Edited by L. Wadding. Paris: Vivès, 1894.

m. William of Ockham

WILLIAM OF OCKHAM. The De sacramento altaris of William of Ockham. Edited by T. Bruce Birch. Latin text and English translation. Burlington, IA: Lutheran Literary Board, 1930.

BUESCHER, Gabriel Norbert. The Eucharistic Teaching of William Ockham. SST, 2d ser., 44. Washington, DC: Catholic University of America Press, 1950.

ISERLOH, Erwin. Gnade und Eucharistie in der philosophischen Theologie des Wilhelm von Ockham: ihre Bedeutung für das Ursachen der Reformation. VIEG, 8. Wiesbaden: Steiner, 1956.

LAMPEN, Willibrordus. "Doctrina Guillelmi Ockham de reali prae-
sentia et transsubstantiation." Antonianum, 3 (1928): 21-32.

        n. Gabriel Biel

BIEL, Gabriel. Canonis missae expositio. 4 vols. Edited by Heiko
A. Oberman and William J. Courtenay. Wiesbaden: Steiner,
1963-1967.
    --Supplementary volume: Dispositio et conspectus materiae cum
    indices. Edited by Wilfrid Werbeck. Wiesbaden: Steiner,
    1976.

_____. Epitome et collectorium ex Occamo circa quatour senten-
tiarum libros, 1486ff. Tübingen, 1501; reprint ed., Frankfurt:
Minerva, 1965.

ANATRIELLO, Pasquale. La dottrina di Gabriele Biel sull'Eucaristia. Milano: Tipografia delle Missioni, 1937.

CREHAN, J. H. "Biel and the Mass." Clergy Review, 43 (1958):
606-617.

DAMERAU, Rudolf. Die Abendmahlslehre des Nominalismus, insbesondere die des Gabriel Biel. SGR, 1. Giessen: Schmitz,
1964.

OBERMAN, Heiko Augustinus. The Harvest of Medieval Theology:
Gabriel Biel and Late Medieval Nominalism. Cambridge, MA:
Harvard University Press, 1963; reprint ed., Grand Rapids,
MI: Eerdmans, 1967.
    --see esp. Ch. 8, "Christ and the Eucharist." Revised ed.,
        pp. 249-280.

        o. Cajetan de Vio, Thomas

CAJETAN DE VIO, Thomas. De missae sacrificio et ritus adversus
Lutheranos. Rome, Paris, 1531.

_____. "The Celebration of the Mass." In Forerunners of the
Reformation, pp. 256-264. Edited by Heiko A. Oberman. New
York: Holt, Rinehart & Winston, 1966.

HALMER, Notker M. "Die Messopferspekulation von Kardinal Cajetan
und Ruard Tapper." Divus Thomas, 21 (1943): 187-212.

        p. Reformation Controversies: Hieronymus Emser,
        Johannes Cochlaeus, Johann Eck

COCHLAEUS, Johannes. Ernstliche Disputation vom heyligen Sakrament des Altars, von der Mess.... Dresden: Wolfgang Stöckel,
1530.

ECK, Johann. Enchiridion locorum communium adversus Lutteranos.
Landshut, 1525; Ingolstadt: Weisshorm, 1541.

EMSER, Hieronymus. Schriften zur Verteidigung der Messe. Herausgegeben von Theobald Freundenberger. CCath, 28. Münster: Aschendorff, 1959.

HEYNCK, Valens. "Die Verteidigung der Sakramentslehre des Duns
Scotus durch den hl. Johann Fischer gegen die Anschuldigun-
gen Luthers." Franziskanische Studien, 24 (1937): 165-175.

ISERLOH, Erwin. Die Eucharistie in der Darstellung des Johannes
Eck: ein Beitrag zur vortridentinischen Kontroverstheologie
über das Messopfer. RST, 73-74. Münster: Aschendorff,
1950.

    q. Other Tracts and Expositions

    (1). Texts

BECHOFFEN, Johann. Quadruplex Missalis expositio. Basilee
[Basel]: Michael Furter, 1505.

GHERIT VAN DER GOUDE. Dat boexken vander Missen: "The
Booklet of the Mass," 1507. Edited by Percy Dearmer. ACC,
5. London: Longmans, Green, 1903.

HITTORP, Melchior. De divinis catholicae ecclesiae officiis et mys-
steriis, varii vetustorum aliquot ecclesiae patrum ac scriptorum
ecclesiasticorum libri. Paris, 1624.

HOEN, Cornelisz. "A Most Christian Letter." In Forerunners of
the Reformation, pp. 268-278. Edited by Heiko A. Oberman.
New York: Holt, Rinehart & Winston, 1966. [on the Eucharist]

JEAN DE VIGNAY. Exposition de la messe from La Legende dorée
of Jean de Vignay. Edited by Walter Howard Frere. ACC, 2.
London: Longmans, Green, 1899.

LEGG, John Wickham, ed. Tracts on the Mass. HBS, 27. London:
Harrison, 1904.

PRIERIAS, Sylvester. "Word and Sacrament." In Forerunners of
the Reformation, pp. 265-267. Edited by Heiko A. Oberman.
New York: Holt, Rinehart & Winston, 1966.

    (2). Studies

BOUHOT, Jean-Paul. "Les sources de l'Expositio missae de Remi
d'Auxerre." Revue des études augustiniennes, 26 (1980):
118-169.

EYNDE, Damien van den. "On the Attribution of the Tractatus de
sacramento alteris to Stephen of Baugé." Franciscan Studies,
10 (1950): 33-45.

LECHNER, Josef. Die Sakramentenlehre des Richard von Mediavilla.
MSHT, 5. München: J. Kösel & F. Pustet, 1925.

MANN, Wolfgang. "Eine humanistische Schrift über die Messe
[Ambrosius Perlargus]." Archiv für mittelrheinische Kirchengeschichte, 13 (1961): 197-233.

F. TRENT TO THE EVE OF VATICAN II

1. Studies of the Roman Missal and
Other Liturgical Books

ALAMO, Mateo de. "La liturgia en el Concilio tridentino y el misal
restitudio por decreto del mismo." Apostolado Sacerdotal, 2
(1945): 365-371.

BAUDOT, Jules. Le missel romain: ses origines, son histoire.
2 vols. Liturgie. Paris: Bloud & Cie, 1912.

BAUMSTARK, Anton. Missale Romanum: seine Entwicklung, ihre
wichtigsten Urkunden und Probleme. Eindhoven-Nijmegen:
W. van Eupen, 1929.

CABROL, Fernand. Les livres de la liturgie latine. BCSR. Paris:
Bloud & Gay, 1930; The Books of the Latin Liturgy. CLRK,
22. St. Louis, MO: B. Herder, 1932.

FERRERES, Juan Bautista. Historia del misal romano. Barcelona:
Subirana, 1929.

GONI-GAZTAMBIDE, José. "El Concilio de Trento y la reforma del
Misal Romano." Liturgia, 2 (1945): 219-224.

GRISAR, Hartmann. Das Missale im Lichte römischer Stadtgeschichte:
Stationen, Perikopen, Gebräuche. Freiburg: Herder, 1925.

JEDIN, Hubert. "Das Konzil von Trient und die Reform der liturgischen Bücher." In Kirche des Glaubens, Kirche der Geschichte,
Bd. 2, pp. 499-525. Freiburg: Herder, 1966.

_____. "Das Konzil von Trient und die Reform des römischen
Messbuches." Liturgisches Leben, 6 (1939): 30-66.

SCHUSTER, Ildefonso. Liber Sacramentorum: note storiche e liturgiche sul Messale Romano. 5 vols. Rome: Marietti, 1919-1929;

The Sacramentary (Liber Sacramentorum): Historical and Liturgical Notes on the Roman Missal. 5 vols. Translated by Arthur Levelis-Marke and Mrs. W. Fairfax-Cholmeley. London: Burns, Oates & Washbourne; New York: Benziger, 1924-1930.

SHEPPARD, Lancelot. The Liturgical Books. TCEC, 109. New York: Hawthorn Books, 1962.

2. Studies of the Roman Canon
(Eucharistic Prayer)

BAUMSTARK, Anton. "Antik-römischer Gebetsstil im Messkanon." In Miscellanea in honorem L. Cuniberti Mohlberg, vol. 1, pp. 301-331. BEL, 22. Rome: Edizioni Liturgiche, 1948.

_____. "Das 'Problem' des römischen Messkanons: Eine Retractatio auf geistesgeschichtlichem Hintergrund." Ephemerides liturgicae, 53 (1939): 204-243.

BERTI, Corrado M., and CALABUIG, Ignacio M. Saggi de canone eucaristico per le messe delle ordinazioni, nozze, esequie e degli infermi. SFTM, 21. Rome: Edizioni Marianum, Desclée, 1968.

BORELLA, P. "Il canone della Messa Romana nella sua evoluzione storica." Ambrosius, 35 (1959): Suppl. (26)-(50).

BOTTE, Bernard. "Canon Missae." Reallexikon für Antike und Christentum, 2:842-845.

_____. "Excursus sur deux points obscurs du canon de la messe." La Maison-Dieu, 23 (1950): 49-53.

_____. "La prière du célébrant." La Maison-Dieu, 20 (1950): 133-152.

BOUMAN, C. A. "Variants in the Introduction of the Eucharistic Prayer." Verbum Caro, 4 (1950): 94-115.

BOURQUE, E. Pour l'histoire de la messe: Ordinaire de la messe et le canon des apôtres à nos jours. Bibliothèque Théologique de Laval. Quebec: Ed. de la Faculté de Théologie Université de Laval, 1946.

BOUYER, Louis. "The Different Forms of Eucharistic Prayer and Their Geneology." In Studia Patristica, vol. 8, pp. 156-170. Edited by F. L. Cross. TUGAL, 93. Berlin: Akademie-Verlag, 1966.

CABROL, Fernand. "Canon romain." Dictionnaire d'archéologie chrétienne et de liturgie, 3:1847-1905.

CASEL, Odo. Das christliche Opfermysterium: zur Morphologie
   und Theologie des eucharistischen Hochgebetes. Herausgegeben von Viktor Warnach. Graz: Styria, 1968.

CROSS, F. L. "Canon of the Mass." Oxford Dictionary of the
   Christian Church, pp. 228-229.

DREWS, Paul Gottfried. Zur Entstehungsgeschichte des Kanons in
   der römischen Messe. His Studien zur Geschichte des Gottesdienstes und des gottesdienstliche Lebens, 1. Tubingen:
   Mohr, 1902.

FRANK, H. "Beobachtungen zur Geschichte des Messkanons."
   Archiv für Liturgiewissenschaft, 1 (1950): 107-119.

GASSNER, Jerome. The Canon of the Mass: Its History, Theology
   and Art. St. Louis, MO: B. Herder, 1949.

JUNGMANN, Josef Andreas. Das eucharistische Hochgebet: Grundgedanken des Canon Missae. Würzburg: Werkbund-Verlag,
   1954; The Eucharistic Prayer: A Study of the Canon of the
   Mass. London: Burns & Oates; Chicago: Fides, 1956.

_____. The Eucharistic Prayer. Revised ed. Revised by George
   C. Davey. Wheathampstead, Eng.: A. Clarke, 1978.

_____. "Le canon romain, et les autres formes de la grande
   prière eucharistique." La Maison-Dieu, 87 (1966): 62-77.

_____. "Thèmes fondamentaux du canon de la messe." Questions
   liturgiques et paroissiales, 35 (1954): 123-132, 155-166, 207-
   217, 272-281.

KAVANAGH, Aidan. "Thoughts on the Roman Anaphora." Worship,
   39 (1965): 515-529; 40 (1966): 2-16.

LUYKX, B. De oorsprong van het gewone der Mis. Utrecht:
   Spectrum, 1955.

MAERTENS, Thierry. Pour une meilleure intelligence du canon de
   la messe. PL, 42. Bruges: Apostolat liturgique, 1959.

_____. Pour une meilleure intelligence de la prière eucharistique.
   2. éd. PL, 42. Bruges: Saint-André, 1963.

MOHRMANN, Christine. "Quelques observations sur l'évolution
   stylistique du canon de la messe romain." Vigiliae Christianae,
   4 (1950): 1-19/ reprinted in her Etudes sur le latin des
   chrétiens, vol. 3, pp. 227-244. Rome: Edizioni di storia e
   letteratura, 1965.

MURRAY, Placid. "The Canon of the Mass: The History and
Meaning of the Canon: A Translation of the Canon." In
Studies in Pastoral Liturgy, vol. 1, pp. 101-116. Edited by
Placid Murray. Maynooth, Ireland: The Furrow Trust, 1961.

SERAPHIM, Hans-Christian. "Von der Darbringung des Leibes
Christi in der Messe: Studien zur Auslegungsgeschichte des
römischen Messkanons." Dissertation, München, 1970.

3. Miscellaneous Studies

ALAMO, Mateo de. "Trento y la liturgia." In El Concilio de
Trento, pp. 293-318. Madrid: Razon y Fe, 1945.

ARNOLD, Franz Xaver. "Vorgeschichte und Einfluss des Trienter
Messopferdekrets auf die Behandlung des eucharistischen
Geheimnisses in der Glaubensverkündigung der Neuzit." In
Die Messe in der Glaubensverkündigung: Kerygmatische Fragen,
pp. 114-161. Herausgegeben von Franz Xaver Arnold und
Balthasar Fischer. 2. Aufl. Freiburg: Herder, 1953.

ASMUSSEN, Hans. Abendmahl und Messe: Was Papst Pius XII in
der Encyclica Mediator Dei von Abendmahl lehrt. ES, 5.
Stuttgart: Evangelisches Verlagswerk, 1949.

BEINERT, Wolfgang. "Neue Deutungsversuche der Eucharistielehre
und das Konzil von Trient." Theologie und Philosophie, 46
(1971): 342-364.

BUGNINI, Annibale. "Pius XII et Liturgia." Ephemerides liturgicae,
72 (1958): 375-383.

_____, ed. Documenta pontificia ad instaurationem liturgicam
spectantia. 2 vols. BEL, 6 & 9. Rome: Edizioni Liturgiche,
1953, 1959.

CUERVO, M. "Los theologos de la Escuela salmantina en las dis-
cusiones del Concilio de Trento sobre el sacrificio de la misa."
Cincia tomista, 74 (1948): 172-216.

DUVAL, A. "Le Concile de Trente et le culte eucharistique." In
Studia Eucharistica: DCC anni a condito festo sanctissimi Cor-
poris Christi (1246-1946), pp. 379-414. Antwerpen: De Nederlandsche Boekhandel, 1946.

GODEFROY, L. "Eucharistie d'après le Concile de Trente." Dictionnaire de théologie catholique, 5:1426-1356.

GY, Pierre-Marie. "La réforme liturgique de Trente et celle de
Vatican II." La Maison-Dieu, 128 (1976): 61-75.

————————. "L'unification liturgique de l'occident et la liturgie de la curie romaine." Revue des sciences philosophiques et théologiques, 59 (1975):   601-612.

ISERLOH, Erwin. Der Kampf um die Messe in den ersten Jahren der Auseinandersetzung mit Luther. Katholisches Leben und Kämpfen im Zeitalter der Glaubenspaltung, 10. Münster: Aschendorff, 1952.

————————. "Das tridentinische Messopferdekret in seinem Beziehungen zu der Kontroverstheologie der Zeit." In Il Concilio di Trento e la Riforma Tridentina, vol. 2, pp. 401-439. Edited by I. Rogger. Rome: Herder, 1965.

————————. "Der Wert der Messe in der Diskussion der Theologen vom Mittelalter bis zum Ausgang des 16. Jahrhunderts." Zeitschrift für katholische Theologie, 83 (1961):   44-79.

JUNGMANN, Josef Andreas. "Das Konzil von Trient und die Erneuerung der Liturgie." In Das Weltkonzil von Trient, Bd. 1, pp. 325-336. Herausgegeben von Georg Schreiber. Freiburg: Herder, 1951.

KLAUSER, Theodor. Die abendländische Liturgie von Aeneus Silvius Piccolomini bis heute: Erbe und Auftrage. Vorträge der Aeneus Silvius Stiftung an der Universität Basel, 1. Basel: Helbing & Lichtenhahn, 1962; The Western Liturgy Today. Translated by F. L. Cross. CST, 8. London: Mowbray, 1963.

LANDOTTI, Giuseppe. Le traduzioni del messale in lingua italiana anteriori al movimento liturgico moderno. BEL, 6. Rome: Edizione Liturgiche, 1976.

LE BRUN, Pierre. Explication littérale, historique et dogmatique des prières et des cérémonies de la messe suivant les anciens auteurs et les monuments de toutes les églises du monde chrétien. 4 vols. Paris: F. Delaulne, 1726; reprint ed., Farnborough, Eng.: Gregg, 1970.

————————. Explication de la messe. LO, 9. Paris: Cerf, 1949.

MICHEL, A. "Messe, V: La messe chez les théologiens postérieurs au Concile de Trente: essence et efficacité." Dictionnaire de théologie catholique, 10:1143-1316.

NOCENT, Adrien. La célébration eucharistique avant et après Saint Pie V. PT, 23. Paris: Beauchesne, 1977.

OURY, G. M. La Messe de Saint Pie V à Paul VI. Solesmes: Abbaye, Saint-Pierre, 1975.

REIFENBERG, H.   "Liturgie vom Trienter Konzil bis zum 2. Vatikan-
um."   Archiv für Liturgiewissenschaft, 16 (1974):   439-475.

RIVIERE, J.   "Messe, IV: La messe durant la période de la Réforme et du concile de Trente."   Dictionnaire de théologie
catholique, 10:1085-1142.

THEISEN, Reinhold.   Mass Liturgy and the Council of Trent.   Collegeville, MN: St. John's University Press, 1965.

VISMANS, T.   "Het concilie van Trente en de liturgie."   Tijdschrift
voor liturgie, 46 (1962):   109-122.

G.   VATICAN II TO PRESENT

1.   Documents

ABBOTT, Walter M., ed.   Documents of Vatican II.   Translated by
Joseph Gallager.   New York: Herder & Herder, 1966.

Apostolic Constitution (Missale Romanum) of Pope Paul VI; and General Instruction on the Roman Missal.   Translated by Clifford
Howell.   London: Catholic Truth Society, 1973.

BUGNINI, Annibale, ed.   Verso la riforma liturgica: documenti e
sussidi.   Città del Vaticano: Libreria Editrice Vaticana, 1965.

FLANNERY, Austin, ed.   Vatican Council II: The Conciliar and
Post Conciliar Documents.   Collegeville, MN: Liturgical Press,
1975.

HUCK, Gabe, ed.   The Liturgy Documents: A Parish Resource.
Chicago: Liturgy Training Program, 1980.

KACZYNSKI, Reiner, ed.   Enchiridion Documentorum Instaurationis
Liturgicae, I (1963-1973).   Torino: Marietti, 1976.

LENGELING, Emil Joseph, ed.   Die Konstitution des zweiten Vati-
kanischen Konzils über die heilige Liturgie.   Lateinisch-
Deutscher Text mit einem Kommentar.   2. Aufl.   LG, 5-6.
Münster: Regensburg, 1965.

MEGIVERN, James J., ed.   Worship and Liturgy.   Official Catholic
Teachings.   Wilmington, DE: Consortium Books, 1978.

O'BRIEN, Thomas C., ed.   Documents on the Liturgy 1963-1979:
Conciliar, Papal and Curial Texts.   Collegeville, MN: Liturgical
Press, 1983.

Selected Documentation from the New Sacramentary. Washington,
    DC: United States Catholic Conference Publications Office,
    1974.

SLOYAN, Gerard S.   The Constitution on the Sacred Liturgy of the
    Second Vatican Council. With a commentary by Gerard S.
    Sloyan.   Glen Rock, NJ: Paulist Press, 1964.

                        2.   General Studies

ADAM, Adolf.   Erneuerte Liturgie: Eine Sachbuch zum katholischer
    Gottesdienst.   Freiburg: Herder, 1972; 2d ed. as Erneuerte
    Liturgie: eine Orientierung über der Gottesdienst heute.
    Freiburg: Herder, 1975.

_____.   Die Messe in neuer Gestalt: ein Buch für Predigt,
    Katechese und Besinnung. PH, 10. Würzburg: Echter Ver-
    lag, 1974.

BARAUNA, G., ed.   The Liturgy of Vatican II: A Symposium.
    English ed. edited by Jovian Lang. 2 vols. Chicago: Fran-
    ciscan Herald Press, 1966.

Bishops' Committee on the Liturgy.   Study Texts. 10 vols. Wash-
    ington, DC: United States Catholic Conference Publications,
    1973-1985.
    1.   Holy Communion. 1973.
    2.   Anointing and the Pastoral Care of the Sick. 1973.
    3.   Ministries in the Church. 1974.
    4.   Rite of Penance. 1975.
    5.   Eucharistic Concelebration. 1978.
    6.   The Deacon, Minister of Word and Sacrament. 1979.
    7.   The Liturgy of the Hours. 1981.
    8.   Proclaim the Word: The Lectionary for Mass. 1982.
    9.   The Liturgical Year. 1985.
    10. Christian Initiation of Adults. 1985.

BOUYER, Louis.   The Liturgy Revived: A Doctrinal Commentary
    of the Conciliar Constitution on the Liturgy. Notre Dame, IN:
    University of Notre Dame Press, 1964.

BROCK, D.   "Die Einzelschritte der Liturgiereform seit Erscheinen
    der Konstitution über die heilige Liturgie." In Zum Gottesdienst
    morgen, pp. 259-269. Herausgegeben von Heinz G. Schmidt.
    Wuppertal: Jugenddeinst Verlag, 1969.

BUGNINI, Annibale, and BRAGA, Carlo, eds.   The Commentary on
    the Constitution and on the Instruction on the Sacred Liturgy,
    by a Committee of Experts. Translated by Vincent P. Mallon.
    New York: Benziger, 1965.

Congrés Liturgic de Montserrat. II. Congrés Liturgic de Montserrat. Montserrat: Monestir de Montserrat, 1966.

CRICHTON, J. D. Changes in the Liturgy. Staten Island, NY: Alba House, 1965.

_____. The Church's Worship: Considerations on the Liturgical Constitution of the Second Vatican Council. New York: Sheed & Ward, 1964.

_____, ed. The Liturgy and the Future. Techny, IL: Divine Word Publications, 1966.

DAVIES, Michael. Liturgical Revolution, vol. 2: Pope John's Council. New Rochelle, NY: Arlington House, 1977.

_____. Liturgical Revolution, vol. 3: Pope Paul's New Mass. New Rochelle, NY: Arlington House, 1979.

DIEKMANN, Godfrey L. "The Reform of Catholic Worship: Are We Too Late?" Worship, 41 (1967): 142-151.

EISENBACH, Franziskus. Die Gegenwart Jesu CHristi im Gottesdienst: systematische Studien zur Liturgiekonstitution des II. Vatikanischen Konzils. Mainz: Matthias-Grünewald Verlag, 1982.

ELLARD, Gerald. The Mass in Transition. Milwaukee, WI: Bruce, 1956.

FALSINI, Rinaldo, MORGENTI, Martimo, and PLACENTINI, Alberto. Perchè la riforma liturgica? Ragioni, difficoltà, prospective. Milan: Massimo, 1967.

FISCHER, Balthasar. "Catholic Liturgy in the Light of the Vatican Council and the Post-Conciliar Reform of the Liturgy." One in Christ, 13 (1977): 23-32.

GAMBER, Klaus. Ritus modernus: gesammelte Aufsätze zur Liturgiereform. SPL, 4. Regensburg: Pustet, 1972.

GELINEAU, Joseph. Demain la liturgie: essai sur l'evolution des assemblées chrétiennes. RS. Paris: Cerf, 1976; The Liturgy Today and Tomorrow. Translated by Dinah Livingstone. London: Darton, Longman & Todd, 1978.

HAUSSLING, Angelus. "Die Liturgie in der Theologie und im kirchlichen Leben nach dem 2. Vatikanischen Konzil." Archiv für Liturgiewissenschaft, 16 (1974): 324-357.

HENNIG, J. "Katholische Liturgiereform und Alter Bund." Una Sancta, 31 (1976): 236-244.

JOSSUA, Jean Pierre. La liturgie d'après Vatican II: bilans, études, prospectives, Par Y. Congar et al. US, 66. Paris: Cerf, 1967.

JOUNEL, Pierre. Les premières étapes de la réforme liturgiques. 3 vols. Paris: Desclée, 1965-1967.
1. L'Instruction du 26 septembre 1964. 1965.
2. Les rites de la Messe en 1965. 1965.
3. La concélébration. 1966; The Rite of Concelebration of Mass and of Communion under Both Species. New York: Desclée, 1967.

KEIFER, Ralph A. The Mass in Time of Doubt: The Meaning of the Mass for Catholics Today. Washington, DC: National Association of Pastoral Musicians, 1983.

_____. To Give Thanks and Praise: General Instruction of the Roman Missal, with Commentary. Washington, DC: National Association of Pastoral Musicians, 1980.

KLEINHEYER, Bruno. Liturgie nach dem Konzil. Kevelaer: Butzon & Bercker, 1967.

KRAUSE, Fred. Liturgy in Parish Life: A Study of Worship and the Celebrating Community. New York: Alba House, 1979.

KUNG, Hans. "The Mass of the Future." The Sign, 42 (1963): 18-21.

LODI, Enzo. E' cambiata la Messa in 2000 anni? Le lezioni della storia. Chiesa sotto inchiesta, 5. Torino: Marietta, 1975.

McMANUS, Frederick R. The Council and the Liturgy: A Commentary on the Constitution on the Sacred Liturgy. Washington, DC: National Catholic Welfare Conference, 1965.

_____, ed. The Revival of the Liturgy. New York: Herder & Herder, 1963.

_____. Sacramental Liturgy. New York: Herder & Herder, 1967.

McNASPY, Clement J. Our Changing Liturgy. Foreword by Godfrey Diekmann. New York: Hawthorn Books, 1966.

MAERTENS, Thierry. La Constitution de Vatican II sur la liturgie. Bruges: Biblica, 1964.

MITCHELL, Nathan, ed. Background and Directions. Washington, DC: Liturgical Conference, 1978.

SCHMIDT, Herman. Constitutie over de H. Liturgie. Bilthoven: Nelissen, 1964.

SCHNEIDER, Theodor. Gewandeltes Eucharistie-Verständnis? Einsiedeln: Benziger, 1969.

SHEPPARD, Lancelot. Blueprint for Worship. London: Darton, Longman & Todd, 1964.

_____, ed. The New Liturgy: A Comprehensive Introduction. London: Darton, Longman & Todd, 1970.

_____, ed. True Worship. Baltimore: Helicon Press, 1963.

SLOYAN, Gerard S. Worship in a New Key: What the Council Teaches on the Liturgy. Washington, DC: Liturgical Conference, 1965.

WAGNER, J., ed. Erneuerung der Liturgie. Trier: Paulinus Verlag, 1957.

3. Studies of the Order of Mass

ABEYASINGHA, N. "The New Rite of the Mass." Priest, 25 (1969): 617-621.

CABIE, Robert. "Le nouvel 'Ordo Missae.'" La Maison-Dieu, 100 (1969): 21-35.

COPPENS, J. "Le nouvel Ordo Missae." Ephemerides theologicae lovanienses, 46 (1970): 392-400.

COUGHLAN, Peter. "The New Order of Mass." The Furrow, 20 (June 1969): 294-301.

CRICHTON, J. D. Christian Celebration: The Mass, pp. 45-106. London: Geoffrey Chapman, 1971.

DALLEN, James. Worship in a New World. Cincinnati, OH: North American Liturgy Resources, 1972.

DEISS, Lucien. Christian Celebration. Chicago: World Library Publications, 1977.

HERTZSCH, Erich. "Die neue Ordnung der Eucharistiefeier." Theologische Lituraturzeitung, 98 (1973): 242-252.

JOHNSON, Lawrence. The Celebrating Community: Word and Eucharist. Wilmington, DE: Berakah Publications, 1977.

KEIFER, Ralph. To Give Thanks and Praise: General Instruction
    of the Roman Missal with Commentary for Musicians and Priests.
    Washington, DC: National Association of Pastoral Musicians,
    1980.

LENGELING, Emil J. Die neue Ordnung der Eucharistiefeier: All-
    gemeine Einführung in das römische Messbuch. 4. Aufl. LG,
    17-18. Münster: Regensburg, 1972.

McGOLDRICK, Patrick. "Aspects of the Order of Mass." The Fur-
    row, 20 (December 1969): 657-664.

McMANUS, Frederick R. "The Genius of the Roman Rite Revisited."
    Worship, 54 (1980): 360-378.

_____. "The New Order of the Mass." American Ecclesiastical
    Review, 161 (1969): 192-203, 396-409; 162 (1970): 47-56,
    186-197.

NEWNS, Brian. "The Institutio Generalis Missalis Romani." The
    Clergy Review, 54 (1969): 554-558.

O'CONNELL, J. B. "The General Instruction of the Roman Missal."
    The Clergy Review, 54 (1969): 817-821.

_____. "The Normative Mass." The Clergy Review, 54 (1969):
    884-894.

PATINO, J. Martin and others. The New Order of Mass: An Intro-
    duction and Commentary. Translated by Bruno Hecker and the
    Monks of Mt. Angel Abbey. Collegeville, MN: Liturgical Press,
    1970.

ROGUET, A.-M. "L'arriére-plan doctrinal de la nouvelle liturgie
    de la messe." La Maison-Dieu, 100 (1969): 72-88.

_____. Table ouverte, la messe d'aujourd'hui. Paris: Desclée,
    1969; The New Mass: A Clear and Simple Explanation of the
    Mass as Restored and Renewed in Accord with the Decrees of
    Vatican Council II. Translated by Walter van de Putts. New
    York: Catholic Book Publishing Co., 1970.

RYAN, Vincent. "The New Mass Rite." Doctrine and Life, 20
    (February 1970): 91-101.

RYDER, Andrew. "The Theology of the New Order of the Mass."
    The Clergy Review, 55 (1970): 101-111.

SHEPPARD, Lancelot. "The New Ordo Missae." In his The New
    Liturgy, pp. 19-40. London: Darton, Longman & Todd, 1970.

SIGLER, Gerald J., ed. Pastoral Commentary on the New Order of
Mass. New York: Benziger Brothers, 1970.

SMITS, Kenneth. "A Congregational Order of Worship." Worship,
54 (1980): 55-75; reprinted in The Assembly: A People Gathered in Your Name, pp. 33-39. Milwaukee, WI: Office of Worship, 1981.

"Sunday Eucharist." National Bulletin on Liturgy, 12 (71)
(November- December 1979): 206-231; 14 (77) (January-
February 1981): 4-36.

SWAYNE, Sean. Communion: The New Rite of Mass. Dublin:
Veritas Pubications, 1974.

TUCK, André. "Reflexions pastorales en marge du nouvel 'Ordo
Missae.'" Paroisse et liturgie, 51 (1969): 447-452.

4. Studies of the Missal

ASHWORTH, Henry. "Les sources patristiques du nouveau missel
romain." Questions liturgiques et paroissiales, 52 (1971):
295-304.

CRICHTON, J. D. Christian Celebration: The Mass, pp. 115-134.
London: Geoffrey Chapman, 1971.

DUMAS, Antoine. "Le missel romain, 1970." Paroisse et liturgie,
52 (1970): 291-296.

_____. "Les sources du nouveau missel romain." Notitiae, 60
(1971): 37-42; 61 (1971): 74-77; 62 (1971): 94-95; 63 (1971):
134-136; 65 (1971): 276-280.

GANTOY, Robert. "La présentation générale du missel de Paul VI."
Paroisse et liturgie, 51 (1969): 387-427.

JOUNEL, Pierre. "Le missel de Paul VI." La Maison-Dieu, 103
(1970): 16-45.

_____. "Les sources françaises du missel de Paul VI." Ques-
tions liturgiques et paroissiales, 52 (1971): 305-315.

McMANUS, Frederick. "Variety is the Chief Characteristic of the
New Missal." In Apostolic Constitution on the New Roman
Missal, pp. 6-11. Washington, DC: United States Catholic
Conference, 1969.

McNASPY, Clement J. "After 400 Years an Improved Missal."
America, 120 (May 17, 1969): 592-593.

"La mise en application du nouveau missel romain: état de la question." Notitiae, 77 (1972): 337-342.

NEWNS, Brian. "The New Missale Romanum." The Clergy Review, 55 (1970): 872-877.

RENIE, Jules. Missale romanum et missel romain: étude critique des traductions françaises du missel et des lectionnaires. Paris: Cèdre, 1975.

5. Studies of the Eucharistic Prayers

BIERITZ, Karl-Heinrich. "Oblatio Ecclesiae: Bemerkungen zu den neuen eucharistischen Hochgebeten der römischen Liturgie." Theologische Literaturzeitung, 94 (1969): 241-252.

BOTTE, Bernard. "The Short Anaphora." In The New Liturgy, pp. 194-199. Edited by Lancelot Sheppard. London: Darton, Longman & Todd, 1970.

BOUYER, Louis. Eucharist: Theology and Spirituality of the Eucharistic Prayer, pp. 446-461. Notre Dame, IN: University of Notre Dame Press, 1968.

_____. "The New Eucharistic Prayers of the Roman Rite." In Understanding the Eucharist, pp. 161-178. Edited by Patrick McGoldrick. Dublin: Gill and Macmillan, 1969.

_____. "The Third Eucharistic Prayer." In The New Liturgy, pp. 203-212. Edited by Lancelot Sheppard. London: Darton, Longman & Todd, 1970.

"Commentarium: De precibus eucharisticis." Notitiae, 84 (June 1973): 202-208.

Concilium for the Implementation of the Liturgy Constitution. "Guidelines on the Anaphoras of the Mass." American Ecclesiastical Review, 159 (1968): 358-367.

COSTELLOE, M. Joseph. "The New Eucharistic Prayers." Homiletic and Pastoral Review, 70 (1969): 171-179.

COUGHLAN, P. "The New Eucharistic Prayers." The Furrow, 19 (1968): 381-389.

CRICHTON, J. D. "The Eucharistic Prayers: Some Comments on the English Translation." Liturgy (England), 38, 1 (1969): 15-16.

_____. "The New Eucharistic Prayers." Liturgy (England), 37, 4 (1968): 89-101.

DALLEN, James. "The Congregation's Share in the Eucharistic Prayer." Worship, 52 (1978): 329-341.

DANNEELS, Godfried, and MAERTENS, Thierry. La prière euchar- istique: forms anciennes et conception nouvelle du canon de la messe. Paris: Centurion, 1967.

DELECLOS, Fabien. "Les nouvelles anaphores: réflexions pastor- ales." Paroisse et liturgie, 50 (1968): 454-461.

DENIS-BOULET, Noele Maurice. "Analysis of the Rites and Prayers of the Mass." In The Church at Prayer, vol. 2: The Euchar- ist, pp. 131-170. Edited by A.-G. Martimort. New York: Herder & Herder, 1973.

DUFRASNE, Dieudonne. "Les nouvelles prières eucharistiques: réflexions critiques et catéchèse." Paroisse et liturgie, 50 (1968): 433-453.

"Eucharistic Prayers and Prefaces: Texts, Melodies, and Transla- tor's Notes." National Bulletin on Liturgy, 3, 25 (November 1968).

FALSINI, Rinaldo. Le nuove preghiere eucaristiche. Introduzione e commento. 4. ed. Milan: O. R., 1969.

FINK, Peter. "Music and the Eucharistic Prayer." Pastoral Music, 6, 3 (February-March 1982): 47-49.

FREBURGER, William J. "Eucharistic Prayers for Children." Living Light, 12, 3 (1975): 450-456.

GANTOY, Robert. "Pour l'utilisation concrète des anaphores." Paroisse et liturgie, 50 (1968): 462-467.

GELINEAU, Joseph. "The Eucharistic Prayer." Music and Liturgy, 6, 1 (Winter 1980): 6-10.

_____. "The Fourth Eucharistic Prayer." In The New Liturgy, pp. 213-227. Edited by Lancelot Sheppard. London: Darton, Longman & Todd, 1970.

_____. "Les interventions de l'assemblée dans le canon de la messe." La Maison-Dieu, 87 (1966): 141-158.

_____. "Le mouvement interne de la prière eucharistique." La Maison-Dieu, 94 (1968): 114-124.

GRISBROOKE, W. Jardine. "The New Eucharistic Prayers: An Orthodox Comment." Liturgy (England), 38, 1 (1969): 6-12.

HENDERSON, Frank. "Participation in the Eucharistic Prayer."
National Bulletin on Liturgy, 11,65 (September-October 1978):
207-215.

HOWELL, Clifford. "The Canon of the Mass." The Clergy Review,
52 (1967): 786-791.

JOUNEL, Pierre. "La composition des nouvelles prières eucharistiques." La Maison-Dieu, 94 (1968): 38-76.

KAVANAGH, Aidan. "Thoughts on the New Eucharistic Prayers."
Worship, 43 (1969): 2-12.

KEIFER, Ralph A. "Eucharistic Prayers." New Catholic Encyclopedia, 17:213-214.

_____. "Eucharistic Prayers for Special Occasions." New
Catholic Encyclopedia, 17:214-215.

_____. "The Unity of the Roman Canon: An Examination of Its
Unique Structure." Studia Liturgica, 11 (1976): 39-58.

KLEINHEYER, Bruno. Erneuerung des Hochgebetes. Regensburg:
Pustet, 1969.

KUNG, Hans. "Das Eucharistiegebet: Konzil und Erneuerung der
römischen Messliturgie." Wort und Wahrheit, 18 (1963): 102-
107.

LENGELING, Emil. "De precibus eucharisticis." Notitiae, 8 (1972):
132-134.

_____. "Le problème des nouvelles prières eucharistiques dans
la liturgie romaine." Questions liturgiques et paroissiales, 53
(1972): 251.

LLEWELLYN, Robert. "The Congregation's Share in the Prayer of
the President." In The New Liturgy, pp. 103-112. Edited by
Lancelot Sheppard. London: Darton, Longman & Todd, 1970.

MAERTENS, Thierry. "Les nouvelles prières eucharistiques au service de l'assemblée." Liturgie et vie chrétienne, 65 (1968): 198-
202.

MALDONADO ARENAS, Luis. La plegeria eucaristica: estudios de
teologia biblica y liturgica sobre la misa. Madrid: Editorial
Católica, 1967.

MANDERS, H. "Tradition and Renewal: The New Roman Anaphoras." Worship, 42 (1968): 578-586.

McMANUS, Frederick R. "An Old-New Eucharistic Prayer--
Eucharistic Prayer II." American Ecclesiastical Review, 160
(1969): 116-124.

MENARD, Jacques. "La restauration de la bénédiction eucharistique." Liturgie et vie chrétienne, 65 (1968): 180-193.

MILNER, Paulinus. "Three New Eucharistic Prayers." New Blackfriars, 50 (1968): 38-40.

MOELLER, Eugène. "Pour une catéchèse des nouvelles prières
eucharistiques." Questions liturgiques et paroissiales, 49
(1968): 193-200.

MOSSI, John P. "The New Eucharistic Prayers of Reconciliation."
Folk Mass and Modern Liturgy, 3, 1 (January 1976): 28-29.

NEWNS, Brian. "The New Preces Eucharisticae." The Clergy Review, 52 (1968): 714-721.

_____. "The Roman Anaphora of St. Hippolytus." Liturgy
(England), 37 (1968): 13-14.

"Les Nouvelles prières eucharistiques." La Maison-Dieu, 94
(1968). [Special issue]

ORCHAMPT, Jean. "Valeur pastorale des nouvelles prières eucharistiques." La Maison-Dieu, 94 (1968): 103-113.

RAUCH, Laszio. "Eucharistic Prayers for Children." American
Ecclesiastical Review, 168 (1976): 185-195.

ROGUET, A.-M. "Les prières eucharistiques." Vie spirituelle,
118, 545 (January 1968): 70-87.

RYAN, John Barry. The Eucharistic Prayer: A Study in Contemporary Liturgy. New York: Paulist Press, 1974.

_____. "The Eucharistic Prayer Requires More than a Musical
Flourish." Pastoral Music, 1,4 (April-May 1977): 31-33; reprinted in Music in Catholic Worship: The NPM Commentary,
pp. 119-123. Edited by Virgil C. Funk. Washington, DC:
National Association of Pastoral Musicians, 1982.

Sacred Congregation for Divine Worship. "Indoles, structura et
elementa precis eucharisticae." Notitiae, 84 (1973): 209-213.

_____. "Litterae circulares ad conferentiarum episcopalium prae-
sides de precibus eucharisticis." Notitiae, 84 (1973): 193-201.

SCHMIDT-LAUBER, Hans-Christoph. "The Eucharistic Prayers in

the Roman Catholic Church Today." Studia Liturgica, 11
(1976): 159-176.

SCHMITZ, Walter. "Pastoral Insights: The New Eucharistic
Prayers." Priest, 25 (1969): 223-226.

SCHNITZLER, Theodore. "Die drei neuen eucharistischen Hochgebete und die neuen Präfationen." In Verkündigung und Betrachtung. Freiburg: Herder, 1968.

SHAUGHNESSY, James D. "The New Canons: Toward Greater
Flexibility." Homiletic and Pastoral Review, 68 (1968): 58-61.

SOUBIGOU, Louis. A Commentary on the Prefaces and the Eucharistic Prayers of the Roman Missal, pp. 247-261. Collegeville,
MN: Liturgical Press, 1969.

THURIAN, Max. "De novis precibus eucharisticis." Notitiae, 8
(1972): 132-134.

_____. "La théologie des nouvelles prières eucharistiques."
La Maison-Dieu, 94 (1968): 77-102.

VAGAGGINI, Cipriano. Il canone della messa e la riforma liturgica.
QRL, 4. Turin: Elle di Ci, 1966; The Canon of the Mass and
Liturgical Reform. Translation editor: Peter Coughlan. Staten
Island, NY: Alba House, 1967.

WILLIS, G. G. "The New Eucharistic Prayers: Some Comments."
The Heythrop Journal, 12 (1971): 5-28.

6. Miscellaneous Studies

BURROWS, Aelred. "The Ecumenical Significance of the New Canons."
Ampleforth Journal, 74 (1969): 217-228.

JORDAHN, Ottfried. "Die ökumenische Bedeutung der Hochgebete
in der erneuerten römischen Liturgie." Una Sancta, 31 (1976):
245-256; "The Ecumenical Significance of the New Eucharistic
Prayers of the Roman Liturgy." Studia Liturgica, 11 (1976):
101-117.

JUNGMANN, Josef Andreas. Messe im Gottesvolk: eine nachkonzili-
arer Durchblick durch Missarum Sollemnia. Freiburg: Herder,
1970.

KUNG, Hans. "Die Liturgiereform des Konzils und die Wiederver-
einigung." In Das Konzil im Spiegel der Presse, pp. 280-287.
Herausgegeben von Walther Kampe. Würzburg: Echter-Verlag,
1963; "Ecumenical Orientations." Worship, 37 (1962): 83-94.

McMANUS, Frederick R. "Ecumenical Import of the Constitution on
the Liturgy." Studia Liturgica, 4 (1965): 1-8.

MUHLEN, Heribert. "Gottesdienst-Ausdruck der Konziliarität unter
den Kirchen." Okumenische Rundschau, 22 (1973): 335-355.

ROGUET, A. M. Pourquoi le canon de la messe en français. Paris:
Cerf, 1967.

VAJTA, Vilmos. "The New Mass in Protestant Perspective." In
Vita laudanda: Essays in Memory of Ulrich S. Leupold, pp.
85-99. Edited by Erich R. W. Schultz. Waterloo, Ont.: Wilfrid Laurier University Press, 1976.

_____. "Renewal of Worship: De Sacra Liturgia." In Dialogue
on the Way, pp. 101-128. Edited by George A. Lindbeck.
Minneapolis, MN: Augsburg, 1965.

H. STUDIES OF THE PONTIFICAL

BATIFFOL, Pierre. Le pontifical romain: II. Le pontifical de
Guillaume Dirand, évêque de Mende. Paris: Firmin-Didot,
1900?

BAUDOT, Jules. Le pontifical. Liturgie. Paris: Bloud & Cie,
1910.

PUNIET, Pierre de. Le pontifical romain: histoire et commentaire.
2 vols. Paris: Desclée de Brouwer, 1929-1930; The Roman
Pontifical: A History and Commentary. Translated for the
Benedictines of Stanbrook by Mildred Vernon Harcourt. New
York: Longmans, Green, 1930.

VOGEL, Cyrille. "Le pontifical romano-germanique du Xe siècle:
éléments constitutifs avec indication des sections imprimées."
Revue des sciences religieuses, 32 (1958): 113-167.

I. LEONINE SACRAMENTARY

1. Texts

FELTOE, C. L., ed. Sacramentarium leonianum. Cambridge:
Cambridge University Press, 1896.

MOHLBERG, Cunibert, ed. Sacramentarium Veronense. RED, 1.
Rome: Herder, 1956.

_____, ed. Sacramentarium Veronense.   3. Aufl. von Leo Eizen-
höfer. Rome: Herder, 1978.

2. Studies

BRUYLANTS, Placide. Concordance verbale du sacramentaire léonien
(ms. Vérone, Bibliothèque capitulaire, LXXXV [80]). Louvain:
Abbaye du Mont César, 1950?

CALLEWAERT, Camillus A. "Saint Léon le Grand et les textes du
Léonien." Sacris Erudiri, 1 (1948): 35-122.

CAPELLE, Bernard. "Messes du Pape S. Gélase dans le sacramentaire léonien." Revue bénédictine, 56 (1945-1946): 12-41; reprinted in his Travaux liturgiques, vol. 2, pp. 79-105. Louvain: Centre liturgique, Abbaye du Mont César, 1962.

_____. "Retouches gélasiennes dans le sacramentaire léonien."
Revue bénédictine, 61 (1951): 3-14; reprinted in his Travaux
liturgiques, vol. 2, pp. 106-115. Louvain: Centre liturgique,
Abbaye du Mont César, 1962.

CHAVASSE, Antoine. "Messes du pape Vigile dans le sacramentaire
léonien." Ephemerides Liturgicae, 64 (1950): 161-213; 66
(1952): 145-219.

COEBERGH, C. "S. Gélase Ier auteur principal du soi-disant sacramentaire léonien." Ephemerides Liturgicae, 64 (1950): 214-
237.

_____. "S. Gélase auteur de plusieurs messes et prières du sac-
ramentaire léonien." Ephemerides Liturgicae, 65 (1951): 171-
181.

COLESS, Gabriel. "Theological Levels of the Sacramentarium Ver-
onese." In Studia Patristica, vol. 13, pp. 356-359. Edited by
Elizabeth A. Livingstone. TUGAL, 116. Berlin: Akademie-
Verlag, 1975.

HOPE, David M. The Leonine Sacramentary: A Reassessment of its
Nature and Purpose. London: Oxford University Press, 1971.

LUCCHESI, Giovanni. Nuove note agiografiche Ravennati: Santi e
riti del Sacramentario Leoniano a Ravenna. Faenza: Lega,
1943.

STUIBER, Alfred. Libelli sacramentorum romani: Untersuchungen
zur Entstehung des sogenannten Sacramentarium Leonianum.
Bonn: Hanstien, 1950.

J. GELASIAN SACRAMENTARY

1. Texts

DUMAS, A., and DESHUSSES, Jean, eds. Liber Sacramentorum
Gellonensis. 2 vols. CC, Ser. Catina, 159-159a. Turnhout:
Brepols, 1981.

MANZ, Georg, ed. Ein St. Galler Sakramentar-fragment (Cod.
Sangall. 348): als Nachtrag zum fränkischen Sacramentarium
Gelasianum. 2. Aufl. LQF, 31. Münster: Aschendorff,
1979.

MOHLBERG, Cunibert, ed. Das fränkische Sacramentarium Gelasianum in allemannischer Überlieferung. LQF, 1-2. 3. Aufl.
Münster: Aschendorff, 1971.

_____, ed. Liber sacramentorum romanae ecclesiae ordinis anni
circuli. 2. Aufl. RED, 4. Rome: Herder, 1968.

REHLE, Sieghild, ed. Sacramentarium Gelasianum mixtum von Saint-
Armand. Mit ein sakramentargeschichtliche Einführung von
Klaus Gamber. TPL, 10. Regensburg: Pustet, 1973.

WILSON, Henry A., ed. The Gelasian Sacramentary. Oxford:
Clarendon Press, 1894.

2. Studies

BISHOP, Edmund. "The Earliest Roman Mass Book (The Gelasianum)." In his Liturgica Historica, pp. 39-61. Oxford:
Clarendon Press, 1918, reprinted 1962.

BOURQUE, Emmanuel. Etude sur les sacramentaires romains. Pt.
2, t. 1: Les Textes remaniés. Le Gélasien du VIIIe siècle.
SAC, 25. Città del Vaticano: Pontificio Instituto di Archeologia
Cristiana, 1952.

CAGIN, P. "Note sur le sacramentaire de Gellone." In Mélanges
de littérature et d'histoire religieuses. Publiés à l'occasion du
jubilé épiscopal de Mgr de Cabrières, vol. 1, pp. 231-291.
Paris: Picard, 1899.

CHAVASSE, Antoine. Le Sacramentaire gélasien. BT, ser. 4, 1.
Tournai: Desclée, 1958.

DESHUSSES, J. "Le Sacramentaire de Gellone dans son contexte
historique." Ephemerides Liturgicae, 75 (1961): 193-210.

LANG, Arthur Paul. Leo der Grosse und die Texte des Altgelasi-
anums. Steyl: Steyler Verlag, 1957.

MORETON, Bernard. The Eighth-Century Gelasian Sacramentary:
A Study in Tradition. London: Oxford University Press, 1976.

PUNIET, Pierre de. Le Sacramentaire romain de Gellone. Rome:
Ephemerides Liturgicae, 1938.

K. THE GREGORIAN SACRAMENTARY

1. Texts

DESHUSSES, Jean, ed. Le Sacramentaire Grégorien: ses principales formes d'après les plus anciens manuscrits. 2 vols. 2.
éd. SF, 16 & 24. Fribourg (Suisse): Editions universitaires,
1971-1979.

GAMBER, Klaus, ed. Sacramentarium Gregorianum. 2 vols. TPL,
4 & 6. Regensburg: Pustet, 1966-1967.
1. Das Stationsmessbuch des Papstes Gregor: Versuch einer
Rekonstruktion nach hauptsächlich bayerischen Handschrift-
en. TPL, 4. 1966.
2. Appendix: Sonntags und Votivmessen. TPL, 6. 1967.

LIETZMANN, Hans, ed. Das Sacramentarium Gregorianum nach dem
Aachener Urexemplar. LQF, 3. Münster: Aschendorff, 1921.

_____. Mit Registern von Heinrich Bornkamm. 4. Aufl. LQF,
3. Münster: Aschendorff, 1968, c1967.

MOHLBERG, Cunibert, and BAUMSTARK, Anton, eds. Die älteste
erreichbare Gestalt des Liber sacramentorum anni circuli der
römischen Kirche. LQF, 11 & 12. Münster: Aschendorff,
1927; reprinted 1967.

WILSON, Henry A., ed. The Gregorian Sacramentary under Charles
the Great. HBS, 49. London: Harrison, 1915.

2. Studies

AMIET, Robert. "Le plus ancien temoin du supplément d'Alcuin:
le missel 'Excarpus' composé à Gellone vers 810." Ephemerides
Liturgicae, 72 (1958): 97-110.

_____. "Le prologue Hucusque et la table des Capitula du supplé-
ment d'Alcuin au sacramentaire grégorien." Scriptorum, 7 (1953):
177-209.

ASHWORTH, Henry. "Did St. Augustine bring the Gregorianum to England?" Ephemerides Liturgicae, 72 (1958): 39-43.

———. "The Influence of the Lombard Invasions on the Gregorian Sacramentary." Bulletin of the John Rylands Library, 36 (1954): 305-327.

———. "The Liturgical Prayers of St. Gregory the Great." Traditio, 15 (1959): 107-161.

BISHOP, Edmund. "On Some Early Manuscripts of the Gregorianum." In his Liturgica Historica, pp. 62-75. Oxford: Clarendon Press, 1918; reprinted 1962.

———. "On the Early Texts of the Roman Canon." In his Liturgica Historica, pp. 77-115. Oxford: Clarendon Press, 1918; reprinted 1962.

BOURQUE, Emmanuel. Etude sur les sacramentaires romains. Pt. 2, t. 2: Le Sacramentaire d'Hadrien. Le Supplement d'Alcuin et les Gregoriens mixtes. SAC, 25. Città del Vaticano: Pontificio Instituto di Archeologia Cristiana, 1958.

CABROL, F. "Grégorien (Le Sacramentaire)." Dictionnaire d'archéologie chrétien et de liturgie, 6:1766-1796.

CALLEWAERT, Camillus A. "S. Grégoire, les Scrutins et quelques messes quadragésimales." Ephemerides Liturgicae, 53 (1939): 191-203.

CAPELLE, Bernard. "La main de S. Grégoire dans le sacramentaire Grégorien." Revue bénédictine, 49 (1937): 13-28; reprinted in his Travaux liturgiques, vol. 2, pp. 161-175. Louvain: Centre liturgique, Abbaye du Mont César, 1962.

DESHUSSES, Jean. "Le 'Supplement' au sacramentaire grégorien: Alcuin ou saint Benoît d'Aniane?" Archiv für Liturgiewissenschaft, 9 (1965): 48-71.

GAMBER, Klaus. Wege zum Urgregorianum: Erörtung der Grundfragen und Rekonstruktionsversuch des Sakramentars Gregors des Grossen vom Jahre 592. TuA, 46. Beuron: Beuroner Kunstverlag, 1956.

L. THE AMBROSIAN (MILANESE) LITURGY

1. Texts

ATCHLEY, E. G., ed. The Ambrosian Liturgy. London: Cope & Fenwick, 1909.

FREI, Judith, ed.   Das ambrosianische Sakramentar D 3-3 aus dem
mailändischen Metropolitankapitel.   LQF, 56.   Münster: Aschendorff, 1974.

HEIMING, Odilo, ed.   Corpus Ambrosiano Liturgicum.   LQF, 49.
Münster: Aschendorff, 1968.

MAGISTRETTI, Marcus, ed.   Beroldus: sive, ecclesiae ambrosianae
Mediolanensis kalendarium et ordines saec. XII.   Mediolani: J.
Giovanola, 1894.

_____, ed.   Monumenta veteris liturgiae ambrosianae.   3 vols.
Mediolani: Apud Ulricum Hoepli, 1897-1905; reprint ed., 3
vols. in 2.   Nendeln, Liechtenstein: Kraus Reprint, 1971.
1.   Pontificale in usum Ecclesiae Mediolanensis necnon Ordines
    Ambrosiani ex codicibus saec. IX.-XV.   1897.
2-3.   Manuale Ambrosianum ex codice saec. XI olim in usum
    canonicae Vallis Travaliae.   1905.

Missale Ambrosianum.   5th ed.   Mediolani: Typis Ioannis Daverio,
1946.

PAREDI, Angelo, ed.   Sacramentarium Bergomense: maoscritto del
secolo IX della Biblioteca di S. Alessandro in Colonna in Bergamo.   MB, 6.   Bergamo: Edizioni "Monumenta Bergomensia,"
1962.

2.   Studies

BISHOP, William C.   The Mozarabic and Ambrosian Rites: Four Essays in Comparative Liturgiology.   Edited by Charles L. Feltoe.
ACT, 15.   London: Mowbray, 1924.

BORELLA, Pietro.   "Frazione, confractorium e commistione nell'-
antica messa Ambrosiana."   Ambrosius, 38 (1962):   303-311.

CERIANI, Antonio, ed.   Notitia liturgiae ambrosianae ante saeculum
XI medium et ejus concordia cum doctrina et canonibus Oecumen-
ici Concilii Tridentini de SS. Eucharistiae Sacramento et de
sacrificio missae.   Milan: Chirlanda, 1912.

Congresso Liturgico Diocesamo, 2d, MIlan, 1948.   Problemi di liturgica ambrosiana.   Milan: L Rivista Ambrosius, 1949.

KING, Archdale Andrew.   "Rite of Milan: Ambrosian Rite."   In his
Liturgies of the Primatial Sees, pp. 286-456.   London: Longmans, Green, 1957.

LEJAY, P.   "Ambrosienne (Liturgie)."   Dictionnaire d'archéologie
chrétienne et de liturgie, 1:1373-1442.

MERCATI, Giovanni. Antiche reliquie liturgiche ambrosiane e
    romane: con un excursus sui frammenti dogmatici ariani del
    Mai. ST, 7. Rome: Tipografia vaticana, 1902.

PAREDI, Angelo. "Messale antichi ambrosiani." Ambrosius, 35
    (1959): 1-25.

SAINT-LAURENT, George E. "St. Ambrose as Channel of Eastern
    Liturgical Customs to the West." Diakonia, 13 (1978):   101-110.

SCHMITZ, Josef. Gottesdienst in altchristlichen Mailand: eine lit-
    urgiewissenschaftliche Untersuchung über Initiation und Mess-
    feier während des Jahres zur Zeit des Bischofs Ambrosius.
    Köln: Hanstein, 1975.

TRIACCA, A. M. "Mater omnium viventium. Contributo metodologi-
    co ad una ecclesiologia liturgica dal nuovo Messale Ambrosiano."
    In In Ecclesia, pp. 353-384. Rome: Libreria Ateneo Salesiano,
    1977.

M. GALLICAN LITURGIES

1. Texts

BANNISTER, Henry Marriott, ed. Missale Gothicum: A Gallican
    Sacramentary. HBS, 52 & 54. London: Harrison, 1917-1919.

GAMBER, Klaus, ed. Ordo antiquus Gallicanus: der gallikanische
    Messritus des 6. Jahrhunderts. TPL, 3. Regensburg: Pustet,
    1965.

GERBERT, Martin, Freiherr von Hornau, ed. Monvmenta veteris
    litvrgiae alemannicae. 2 vols. St. Blasii in Hyrcinia Monast.:
    Typis San-Blasianis, 1777-1779; reprint ed., Hildesheim: Olms,
    1967.

LOWE, Elias A., ed. The Bobbio Missal: A Gallican Mass-Book.
    3 vols. HBS, 53, 58, 61. London: Harrison, 1917-1924.
    1. Facsimile. HBS, 53. 1917.
    2. Texts. HBS, 58. 1920.
    3. Notes. By A. Wilmart, E. A. Lowe, and H. A. Wilson.
    HBS, 61. 1924.

MOHLBERG, Cunibert, ed. Missale Francorum. RED, 2. Rome:
    Herder, 1957.

_____, ed. Missale Gallicanum vetus. RED, 3. Rome: Herder,
    1958.

_____, ed. Missale Gothicum. 2 vols. Augsburg: Filser Verlag,
    1929.

_____, ed. Missale Gothicum. RED, 5. Rome: Herder, 1961.

NEALE, John Mason, and FORBES, George Hay, eds. The Ancient
    Liturgies of the Gallican Church, now first collected, with an
    introductory Dissertation, Notes, and various Readings, together
    with parallel Passages from the Roman, Ambrosian, and Mozar-
    abic Rites. Burntisland, Scot.: Pitsligo Press, 1855-1857;
    reprint ed., New York: AMS Press, 1970.

                            2. Studies

ASHWORTH, Henry. "Gregorian Elements in Some Early Gallican
    Service Books." Traditio, 13 (1957): 431-443.

BECK, Henry G. J. The Pastoral Care of Souls in South-East
    France during the Sixth Century. AG, 51. Rome: Apud
    Aedes Universitais Gregorianae, 1950.

CABROL, Fernand. "Les origines de la liturgie gallicane." Revue
    d'histoire ecclésiastique, 30 (1930): 951-962.

DELAISSE, L. M. J. "A Liturgical Problem at the End of the Middle
    Ages: The 'Missale Gallicum.'" In Essays Presented to G. I.
    Lieftinck, vol. 4, pp. 16-27. Edited by J. P. Gumbert and
    M. J. M. de Haan. Amsterdam: Van Gendt, 1972-1976.

FRENDO, John A. The "Post Secreta" of the "Missale Gothicum"
    and Eucharistic Theology of the Gallican Anaphora. Malta, 1977.

GRIFFE, E. "Aux origines de la liturgie gallicane." Bulletin de
    littérature ecclésiastique, 52 (1951): 17-43.

LECLERCQ, H. "Gallicane (Liturgie)." Dictionnaire d'archéologie
    chrétienne et de liturgie, 6:473-493.

MARTIMORT, Aimée-Georges. "La liturgie de la messe en Gaule."
    Bulletin du Comité des études, Compagnie de Saint-Sulpice, 22
    (1958): 204-222.

MENSBRUGGHE, Alexis van der. "Pseudo-Germanus Reconsidered."
    In Studia Patristica, vol. 5, pp. 172-184. Edited by F. L.
    Cross. TUGAL, 80. Berlin: Akademie Verlag, 1962.

PINELL, J. "Legitima eucharistica: Cuestiones sobre la anamnesis
    y la epiclesis en el antiguo rito galicano." In Mélanges litur-
    giques offerts au R. P. Dom Bernard Botte, pp. 445-460.
    Louvain: Abbaye du Mont César, 1962.

PORTER, William Stevens. The Gallican Rite. London: Mowbray,
    1958.

RATCLIFF, E. C., ed. Expositio Antiquae liturgiae gallicanae.
    [Attr. to Germanus of Paris.] HBS, 98. London: Henry
    Bradshaw Society, 1971.

THIBAUT, Jean Baptiste. L'ancienne liturgie gallicane, son origine
    et sa formation en Provence aux Ve et VIe siècles sous l'influ-
    ence de Cassien et de Saint Césaire d'Arles. Paris: Maison
    de la Bonne Presse, 1929.

WILMART, A. "L'âge et l'ordre des messes de Mone." Revue
    bénédictine, 28 (1911): 377-390.

N. THE MOZARABIC LITURGY

1. Texts

EELES, F. C., ed. The Mozarabic Liturgy. London: Cope &
    Fenwick, 1909.

FEROTIN, Marius. Le Liber mozarabicus sacramentorum et les manu-
    scrits mozarabes. MEL, 6. Paris: Firmin-Didot, 1912; reprint
    ed., Farnborough, Eng.: Gregg, 1969.

_____. Le Liber ordinum en usage dans l'église wisigothique et
    mozarabe d'Espagne du cinquieme au onzieme siècle. MEL, 5.
    Paris: Firmin-Didot, 1904.

Missa gothica seu mozarabica, et officium itedem gothicum....
    Angelopoli: Typis Seminarii Palafoxiani, 1770.

Missae gothicae et officii muzarabici. Edited by Francisco Antonio
    Lorenzana and Francisco Fabian et Fuero. Editio novissima by
    Santos ab Arciniega. Toleti: S. Lopez Fando, 1875.

PEREZ DE URBEL, Justo, and GONZALEZ RUIZ-ZORILLA, Atilano,
    eds. Liber Commicus. 2 vols. MHS, 2-3. Madrid: Consejo
    Superior de Investigaciones Cientificas Escuela de Estudios
    Medievales, 1950-1955.

PRADO, German, ed. Textos inéditos de la liturgia mozarabe: rito
    solemne de la iniciacion cristiana, consagracion de las iglesias,
    uncion de los enfermos. Madrid: J. Gongora, 1926.

VIVES, José, and CLAVERAS, Jeronimo, eds. Oracional visigotico.
    MHS, 1. Barcelona: Biblioteca Balmes, 1946.

2. Studies

BAUMSTARK, Anton. "Orientalisches in altspanischer Liturgie."
Oriens Christianus, 7 (1935): 1-37.

BROU, Louis. "L'alleluia dans la liturgie mozarabe." Annuario musical, 6 (1951): 3-90.

CABROL, F. "Mozarabe (La Liturgie)." Dictionnaire d'archéologie
chrétienne et de liturgie, 12:390-491.

DIETZ, Matthias. Gebetsklänge aus Altspanien: Illationen (Präfationen) des altspanisch-westgotisch-mozarabischen Ritus mit
geschichtlicher und liturgischer Einführung. Bonn: Verlag
der Buchgemeinde, 1947.

JENNER, H. "Mozarabic Rite." Catholic Encyclopedia, 10:611-623.

KING, Archdale Andrew. "Rite of Toledo: Mozarabic Rite." In
his Liturgies of the Primatial Sees, pp. 457-631. London:
Longmans, Green, 1957.

MARTINEZ SAIZ, Pablo. El tiempo pascual en la liturgia hispanica.
Madrid: Instituto Superior de Pastoral, 1969.

PINELL, J. "La liturgia hispanica." [Instituto Historia de la teologia Española] Repertario de historica de la ciencias ecclesias-
ticas en España, 2 (1971): 29-68.

PORTER, A. W. S. "Studies in the Mozarabic Office." Journal of
Theological Studies, 35 (1934): 266-286.

PRADO, German. Historia del rito mozarabe y toledano. Burgos:
Abadia de Santo Domingo de Silos, 1928.

RAMOS, Manuel. Oratio admonitionis: contribucion al estudio de
la antigua misa española. BTG, 8. Granada: Facultad de
teologia, 1964.

RIVERA RECIO, Juan Francisco, ed. Estudios sobre la liturgia
mozarabe. Toledo: Diputacion Provincial, 1965.

THALER, Anton. Das Selbstverständnis der Kirche in den Gebets-
texten der altspanischen Liturgie. Bern: Lang, 1975.

O. CELTIC LITURGIES

1. Texts

DOLD, Alban, and EIZENHOFER, Leo, eds. Das Irische Palimp-

sestsakramentar in CLM 14429 der Staatsbibliothek München.
Mit einem Beitrag von David H. Wright. TuA, 53–54. Beuron:
Beuroner Kunstverlag, 1964.

FORBES, A. P., ed. Liber ecclesiae beati Terrenani de Arbuth-
nott; missale secundum usum ecclesiae sancti Andreae in Scotia.
Burntisland, Scot.: Pitsligo Press, 1864.

FORBES, G. H., ed. Missale drummondiense: The Ancient Irish
Missal, in the possession of the Baroness Willoughby de Eresby,
Drummond Castle, Perthshire. Burntisland, Scot.: Pitsligo
Press, 1882.

KUYPERS, Arthur Benedict, ed. The Prayer Book of Aedeluald
the Bishop, commonly called the Book of Cerne. Cambridge:
Cambridge University Press, 1902.

LAWLOR, Hugh Jackson, ed. The Rosslyn Missal: An Irish Manuscript in the Advocates' Library, Edinburgh. HBS, 15. London: Harrison, 1899.

PLUMMER, Charles, ed. Irish Litanies. HBS, 62. London: Harrison, 1925.

WARNER, George Frederic, ed. The Stowe Missal. 2 vols. HBS,
31–32. London: Harrison, 1906–1915.

WARREN, F. E., ed. The Manuscript Irish Missal belonging to the
President and Fellows of Corpus Christi College, Oxford. London: Pickering, 1879.

WORDSWORTH, Christopher, ed. Pontificale ecclesiae S. Andreae:
The Pontifical Offices used by David de Bernham, Bishop of S.
Andrews. Edinburgh: Pitsligo Press, 1885.

2. Studies

BAUMER, Suitbert. "Das Stowe-Missale aufs neue untersucht."
Zeitschrift für katholische Theologie, 16 (1892): 446–490.

BISHOP, Edmund. "The Litany of the Saints in the Stowe Missal."
Journal of Theological Studies, 7 (1906): 122–136; reprinted in
his Liturgica Historica, pp. 137–164. Oxford: Clarendon Press,
1918; reprinted 1962.

CREHAN, Joseph H. "The Theology of Eucharistic Consecration:
Role of the Priest in the Celtic Liturgy." Theological Studies,
40 (1979): 334–343.

GOUGAUD, L. "Celtique (Liturgie)." Dictionnaire d'archéologie
chrétien et de liturgie, 2:2969–3032.

HENNIG, John. "Sacramentaries of the Old Irish Church." Irish
    Ecclesiastical Record, 96 (1961): 23-28.

MacCARTHY, B. "On the Stowe Missal." Transactions of the Royal
    Irish Academy, 27 (1886): 135-268.

McROBERTS, David. Catalogue of Scottish Medieval Liturgical Books
    and Fragments. Glasgow: John S. Burns, 1953.

WARREN, Frederick E. The Liturgy and Ritual of the Celtic
    Church. Oxford: Clarendon Press, 1881.

P. LITURGIES USED IN ENGLAND
    (CHIEFLY MEDIEVAL)

1. General

a. Texts

MASKELL, William ed. The Ancient Liturgy of the Church of Eng-
    land according to the Uses of Sarum, York, Hereford and
    Bangor, and the Roman Liturgy, arranged in Parallel Columns.
    3d ed. Oxford: Clarendon Press, 1882; reprint ed., New
    York: AMS Press, 1973.

b. Studies

BRIDGETT, Thomas Edward. A History of the Holy Eucharist in
    Great Britain. 2 vols. London: C. K. Paul, 1881.

CRICHTON, James D., WINSTONE, H. E., and AINSLIE, J. R.,
    eds. English Catholic Worship: Liturgical Renewal in England
    Since 1900. London: Cassell, 1979.

CUTTS, Edward L. Parish Priests and Their People in the Middle
    Ages in England. London: SPCK, 1898; reprint ed., New
    York: AMS Press, 1970.

FRERE, W. H. "The Connexion between English and Norman Rites."
    Journal of Theological Studies, 4 (1903): 206-214.

GASQUET, Francis A. Parish Life in Medieval England. 3d ed.
    London: Methuen; New York: Benziger, 1906; reprint ed.,
    Freeport, NY: Books for Libraries Press, 1973.

MOORMAN, John R. H. Church Life in England in the Thirteenth
    Century. Cambridge: Cambridge University Press, 1945;
    reprint ed., New York: AMS Press, 1980.

SWETE, Henry Barclay. Church Services and Service-Books before
the Reformation. London: SPCK; New York: Young, 1896.

_____. _____. New ed., rev. by Arthur John Maclean. Lon-
don: SPCK; New York: Macmillan, 1930.

WORDSWORTH, Christopher. Notes on Medieval Services in England. London: T. Baker, 1898.

_____, and LITTLEHALES, Henry. The Old Service Books of the
English Church. London: Methuen, 1904.

2. Exeter

BARNES, Ralph, ed. Liber pontificalis of Edmund Lacy, Bishop of
Exeter. Exeter, Eng.: W. Roberts, 1847.

DALTON, John N., and DOBLE, G. H., eds. Ordinale Exon. 4
vols. HBS, 37, 38, 63, 79. London: Henry Bradshaw Society, 1909-1940.

TATLOCK, Richard. An English Benedictional. Translated and
adapted from the Leofric Missal. SCW, 2. Westminster: Faith
Press, 1964.

WARREN, F. E., ed. The Leofric Missal as used in the Cathedral
of Exeter during the Episcopate of its First Bishop, A.D. 1050-
1072. Together with some account of the Red Book of Derby,
the Missal of Robert of Jumièges, and a few other Early Manuscript Service Books of the English Church. Oxford: Clarendon
Press, 1883; reprint ed., Farnborough, Eng.: Gregg, 1968.

3. Hereford

HENDERSON, W. G., ed. Missale ad usum percelebris ecclesiae
herfordensis. Leeds, Eng.: McCorquodale, 1874; reprint ed.,
Farnborough, Eng.: Gregg, 1969.

4. Sarum (Salisbury)

a. Texts

COLLINS, A. Jeffries, ed. Manuale ad usum percelebris ecclesiae
Sarisburiensis. From the ed. printed at Rouen in 1543, compared
with those of 1506 (London), 1516 (Rouen), 1523 (Antwerp),
1526 (Paris). Chichester, Eng.: n.p., 1960.

COOKE, William, and WORDSWORTH, Christopher, eds. Ordinale

Sarum sive Directorium Sacerdotum: (Liber, quem Pica Sarum vulgo vocitat clerus) auctore Clemente Maydeston. 2 vols. HBS, 20, 22. London: Harrison, 1901-1902.

DICKINSON, Francis Henry, ed. Missale ad usum Insignis et Prae- clarae Ecclesiae Sarum. Burntisland, Scot.: Parker Society, 1861-1883; reprint ed.,, Farnborough, Eng.: Gregg, 1969.

FRERE, Walter H., ed. The Use of Sarum. 2 vols. Cambridge: Cambridge University Press, 1898-1901; reprint ed., Farn- borough, Eng.: Gregg, 1969.

LEGG, J. Wickham, ed. The Sarum Missal. Oxford: Clarendon Press, 1916.

MASKELL, William, ed. Monumenta ritualia Ecclesiae anglicanae: The Occasional Offices of the Church of England according to the Old Use of Salisbury. 3 vols. 2d ed. Oxford: Clarendon Press, 1882; reprint ed., Westmead, Eng.: Gregg, 1970.

PEARSON, A. Harford. The Sarum Missal Done into English. 2d ed. rev. and enl. London: The Church Printing Co., 1884.

WARREN, Frederick E., ed. The Sarum Missal in English. 2 vols. ACC, 11. London: Mowbray, 1913.

    b. Studies

BAILEY, Terence. The Processions of Sarum and the Western Church. STex, 21. Toronto, Ont.: Pontifical Institute of Mediaeval Studies, 1971.

WORDSWORTH, Christopher. Ceremonies and Processions of the Cathedral Church of Salisbury. Cambridge: Cambridge Univer- sity Press, 1901.

                              5. York

GREENWELL, William, ed. The Pontifical of Egbert, Archbishop of York, A.D. 732-766. SSP, 27. Durham, Eng.: Andrews, 1853.

HENDERSON, W. G., ed. Liber pontificalis Chr. Bainbridge, archi- episcopi eboracensis. SSP, 61. Durham, Eng.: Andrews, 1875.

_____, ed. Manuale et processionale ad usum insignis ecclesiae eboracensis. SSP, 63. Durham, Eng.: Andrews, 1875.

Missale ad usum insignis ecclesiae eboracensis. 2 vols. SSP, 59-60. Durham, Eng.: Andrews, 1874.

SIMMONS, Thomas Frederick, ed. The Lay Folks Mass Book, or
The Manner of Hearing Mass, with Rubrics and Devotions for
the People, in Four Texts, and Offices in English according to
the Use of York, from Manuscripts of the Xth to the XVth Century. With Appendix, Notes, and Glossary. EETS, Orig. Ser.,
71. London: Trubner, 1879.

6. Primers

a. Texts

BURTON, Edward, ed. Three Primers Put Forth in the Reign of
Henry VIII, viz., I. A goodly primer, 1535. II. The Manual
of Prayers or the Primer in English, 1539. III. King Henry's
Primer, 1545. 2d ed. Oxford: Oxford University Press, 1848.

DEWICK, E. S., ed. Facsimiles of Horae de Beata Maria Virgine
from English MSS. of the Eleventh Century. HBS, 21. London: Henry Bradshaw Society, 1902.

HOSKINS, Edgar P., ed. Horae Beatae Mariae Virginis, or Sarum
and York Primers, with Kindred Books and Primers of the Reformed Roman Use. London: Longmans, Green, 1901.

LITTLEHALES, Henry, ed. The Prymer or Lay-folks' Prayer Book.
2 vols. EETS, Original Ser., 105 & 109. London: Kegan Paul,
Trench, Trübner, 1895-1897; reprint ed., one vol. New York:
Kraus Reprint, 1973.

_____, ed. The Prymer or Prayer-Book of the Lay People in the
Middle Ages in English dating about 1400 A.D. 2 vols. London: Longmans, Green, 1891-1892.

The Primer, or Office of the Blessed Virgin Marie, in English (1615).
English Recusant Literature, 1558-1640, vol. 390. Ilkley, Eng.:
Scolar Press, 1978.

WORDSWORTH, Christopher, ed. Horae Eboracenses, the Prymer or
Hours of the Blessed Virgin Mary, according to the Illustrious
Church of York. SSP, 132. Durham, Eng.: Andrews; London:
Quaritch, 1920.

b. Studies

BISHOP, Edmund. "The Origin of the Prymer." In his Liturgica
Historica, pp. 211-227. Oxford: Clarendon Press, 1918; reprinted 1962.

BUTTERWORTH, Charles C. The English Primers (1529-1549):
Their Publication and Connection with the English Bible and

the Reformation in England. Philadelphia, PA: University of
    Pennsylvania Press, 1953; reprint ed., New York: Octagon
    Books, 1971.

WHITE, Helen C. The Tudor Books of Private Devotion. Madison,
    WI: University of Wisconsin Press, 1951; reprint ed., West-
    port, CT: Greenwood Press, 1979.

                    7. Other Texts and Studies

The Chichester Customary. The Rites of the Church as Observed
    throughout the Year in Chichester Cathedral. With an intro-
    ductory essay by A. S. Duncan-Jones. ACC, 36. London:
    SPCK, 1948.

DOBLE, G. H., ed. Pontificale Lanaletense (Bibliothèque de la
    Ville de Rouen A 27. Cat. 368): A Pontifical formerly in use
    at St. Germans, Cornwall. HBS, 74. London: Harrison,
    1937.

HUDSON, Anne. "A Lollard Mass." Journal of Theological Studies,
    n.s. 23 (1972): 407-419.

HUGHES, Anselm, ed. The Bec Missal. HBS, 94. London: Henry
    Bradshaw Society, 1963.

LEGG, J. Wickham, ed. Missale ad usum ecclesiae westmonasterien-
    sis. 3 vols. HBS, 1, 5, 12. London: Harrison, 1891-1897.

LITTLEHALES, Henry, ed. English Fragments from Latin Medieval
    Service-Books. EETS, Extra Ser., 90. London: Kegan Paul,
    Trench, Trübner, 1903; reprint ed., New York: Kraus Re-
    prints, 1973.

STEVENSON, Joseph, ed. Rituale ecclesiae Dunelmensis. SSP, 10.
    London: Nichols, 1840.

WARNER, G. F., and WILSON, H. A., eds. The Benedictional of
    Aethelwold. Oxford: Privately printed for the Roxburghe
    Club, 1910.

WILSON, H. A., ed. The Missal of Robert of Jumièges. HBS, 11.
    London: Harrison, 1896.

_____, ed. The Pontifical of Magdalen College. HBS, 39. Lon-
    don: Henry Bradshaw Society, 1910.

WOOLEY, Reginald Maxwell, ed. The Canterbury Benedictional.
    HBS, 51. London: Henry Bradshaw Society, 1917.

WORDSWORTH, Christopher, ed. The Tracts of Clement Maydeston, with the Remains of Caxton's Ordinale. HBS, 7. London:
Harrison, 1894.

Q. OTHER NATIONAL OR LOCAL LITURGIES

1. German and Central Europe

a. Texts

AMIET, Robert, ed. The Benedictionals of Freising (Munich, Bay-
erische Staatsbibliothek, Cod. Lat. 6430). With additional
material by C. Hohler and B. J. Wigan. HBS, 88. London:
Henry Bradshaw Society, 1974.

BRINKTRINE, Johannes, ed. Sacramentarium Rossianum. RQS,
25. Freiburg: Herder, 1930.

DOLD, Alban, ed. Die Konstanzer Ritualientexte in ihrer Entwicklung von 1482 bis 1721. LQ, 5-6. Münster: Aschendorff,
1923.

DOLD, Alban, and EIZENHOFER, Leo, eds. Das Prager Sakramentar (Cod. O.83 (fol. 1-120) der Bibliothek des Metropolitankapitel). TuA. Beuron: Beuroner Kunstverlag, n.d.

DOLD, Alban, FIALA, Virgil, and GAMBER, Klaus, eds. Das Sakramentar von Jena (Bud. M.f. 366 der Universitäts-Bibliothek).
TuA, 52. Beuron: Beuroner Kunstverlag, 1962.

DOLD, Alban, and GAMBER, Klaus, eds. Das Sakramentar von
Salzburg, seinem Typus nach auf Grund der erhaltenen Frag-
menten rekonstruiert, in seinem Verhältnis zum Paduanum untersucht. TuA, 4. Beuron: Beuroner Kunstverlag, 1960.

FRANZ, Adolf, ed. Das Rituale Bischof Heinrichs I. von Breslau.
Freiburg: Herder, 1912.

FRANZ, Adolf, ed. Das Rituale von St. Florian aus dem zwölften
Jahrhundert. Freiburg: Herder, 1904.

FREISEN, Joseph, ed. Liber agendarum ecclesiae et diocesis Slesz-
wicensis: katholisches Ritualbuch der Diözese Schleswig im
Mittelalter. Paderborn: Junfermannsche Buchhandlung, 1898.

REICHERT, Franz Rudolf, ed. Die älteste deutsche Gesamtauslegung
der Messe (erstausgabe ca. 1480). CCath, 29. Münster:
Aschendorff, 1967.

SCHONFELDER, Albert, ed. Liturgische Bibliothek: Sammlung
gottesdienstlicher Bücher aus dem deutschen Mittelalter. Paderborn: Schöningh, 1904- .

b. Studies

BISSIG, Hans. Das Churer Rituale, 1503-1927: Geschichte der
Agende, Feier der Sakramente. StF, n.F. 56. Freiburg:
Universitätsverlag, 1979.

FRANZ, Adolf. Die Messe im deutschen Mittelalter: Beiträge zur
Geschichte der Liturgie und des religiösen Volkslebens. Frei-
burg: Herder, 1902; reprint ed., Darmstadt: Wissenschaftliche
Buchgesellschaft, 1963.

GAMBER, Klaus. Ecclesia Reginensis: Studien zur Geschichte und
Liturgie der Regensburger Kirche im Mittelalter. SPL, 8.
Regensburg: Pustet, 1979.

GRUBER, Eugen. "Vergessene Konstanzer Liturgie." Ephemerides
liturgicae, 70 (1956): 229-237.

HUOT, François. L'Ordinaire de Sion: étude sur sa transmission
manuscrite, son cadre historique et sa liturgie. SF, 18.
Fribourg: Editions Universitaires, 1973.

HUPP, Otto. Ein Missale Speciale, Vorläufer des Psalteriums von
1457. München, Regensburg: Nationale Verlagsanstalt, Buch-
und Kunstdrukerei, 1898.

_____. Zum Streit um das Missale Speciale Constantiense.
Strassburg: J. H. E. Heitz, Heitz & Mündel, 1917.

KURZEJA, Adalbert. Der älteste Liber Ordinarius der Trierer Dom-
kirche: London, Brit. Mus., Harley 2958, Anfang 14. Jh.:
Ein Beitrag zur Liturgiegeschichte der deutschen Ortskirchen.
LQF, 52. Münster: Aschendorff, 1970.

PETERS, Franz Joseph. Beiträge zur Geschichte der kölnischen
Messliturgie: Untersuchungen über die gedruckten Messalien
des Erzbistums Köln. Colonia sacra, 2. Köln: Pick, 1951.

REIFENBERG, Hermann. Sakramente, Sakramentalien und Ritualien
im Bistum Mainz seit dem Spätmittelalter: unter besonderer
Berücksichtigung der Diözesen Würzburg und Bamberg. 2 vols.
LQF, 53-54. Münster: Aschendorff, 1971-1972.

SCHMIDT-KUNSEMULLER, F. A. "Der Streit um das Missale Speciale: ein Forschungsbericht." In Aus der Welt des Biblio-
thekars: Festschrift für Rudolf Juchhoff, pp. 51-89. Herausgegeben von Kurt Ohly und Werner Krieg. Köln: Greven
Verlag, 1961.

STEVENSON, Allan H. The Problem of the Missale Speciale. London: Bibliographical Society, 1967.

VIET, Ludwig Andreas. Volksfrommes Brauchtum und Kirche im deutschen Mittelalter. Freiburg: Herder, 1936.

2. Scandinavia

a. Texts

FRIESEN, Joseph, ed. Manuale curatorum secundum usum ecclesiae Roschildensis: katholisches Ritualbuch der dänischen Diözese Roskilde im Mittelalter. Paderborn: Junfermannsche Buchhandlung, 1898.

_____, ed. Manual Lincopense, Breviarium Scarense, Manuale Aboense: Katholische Ritualbücher Schwedens und Finnlands im Mittelalter. Paderborn: Junfermannsche Buchhandlung, 1904.

STROMBERG, Bengt, ed. Missale Lundense år 1514. LPSU, 4. Malmö: Kroon, 1946.

b. Studies

FAEHN, Helge. Fire Norske Messeordninger fra Middelalderen. Oslo: Jacob Dybwad, 1953.

JOHANSSON, Hilding. Bibel och liturgi: Med särskild hänsyn till svensk tradition under medeltiden och reformationstiden. STL, 4. Lund: Gleerup, 1953.

_____. Bidrag till den svenska manualetraditionen. Lund: Gleerup, 1951.

_____. Hemsjömanualet: en liturgi-historisk studie. SSSKH, 24. Stockholm: Svenska Kyrkans Diakonistyrelse, 1950.

LINDBERG, Gustaf. Die Schwedischen Missalien des Mittelalters: ein Beitrag zur Vergleichenden Liturgik. Uppsala: Almqvist & Wiksell, 1923- ; Berlin: Speyer & Peters, 1924- .

3. Italy

AMIET, Robert. Repertorium liturgicum Augustanum: les témoins de la liturgie d'Aoste. 2 vols. MLEA, 1-2. Aosta: Musumeci, 1974.

DOLD, Alban, and GAMBER, Klaus, ed. Das Sakramentar von Monza (im Cod. F1/101 der dortigen Kapitelsbibliothek): ein aus Einzel-Libelli redigiertes Jahresmessbuch. TuA, 3. Beuron:

Beuroner Kunstverlag, 1957.

GAMBER, Klaus. "Fragmente eines mittelitalienischen Plenarmissale aus dem 8. Jahrhundert." Ephemerides liturgicae, 76 (1962): 335-341.

LAMBOT, C., ed. North Italian Services of the Eleventh Century. HBS, 67. London: Harrison, 1931.

PAREDI, Angelo, and FASSI, Giuseppe, eds. Sacramentarium Bergomense, manuscritto del secolo IX della Biblioteca di S. Alessandro in Colonna in Bergamo. Bergamo: Edizioni "Monumenta Bergomensia," 1962.

TERRIZZI, Francesco, ed. Missale antiquum S. Panormitanae ecclesiae (Pa ASD 2). RED, 13. Roma: Herder, 1970.

4. Iberian Peninsula

a. Texts

Missale Bracarense. Rome: Typis Polyglottis Vaticanis, 1924.

OLIVAR, Alexandro, ed. Sacramentarium rivipullense, MHS, 7. Madrid: Consejo Superior de Investigaciones Cientificas, Instituto Enrique Flórez, 1964.

b. Studies

BRAGANCA, J. O. "A Liturgia de Braga." Hispania Sacra, 17 (1964): 259-281.

HUGHES, Andrew. "Medieval Liturgical Books at Arouca, Braga, Evora, Lisbon and Porto: Some Provisional Inventories." Traditio, 31 (1975): 369-384.

KING, Archdale Arthur. "Rite of Braga." In his Liturgies of the Primatial Sees, pp. 155-285. London: Longmans, Green, 1957.

VAZ, Antonio Luiz. O rito bracarense. Braga: J. de Portugal Fernandes Dias, 1970.

5. Lyons/France

BUENNER, D. L'ancienne liturgie romaine: le rite lyonnais. Lyon: Vitte, 1935; reprint ed., Farnborough: Gregg, 1969.

KING, Archdale A. "Rite of Lyons." In his Liturgies of the Primatial Sees, pp. 1-154. London: Longmans, Green, 1957.

6. Holland

SCHILLING, Alfred. Fürbitten und Kanongebete der höllandischen
Kirche: Materialen zur Diskussion um zeitgemässe liturgische
Texte. 2. Aufl. Essen: Driewer, 1968.

WEGMAN, H. A. J., ed. Goed or niet Goed? Het eucharistisch
gebed in Nederland. Hilversum: Gooi & Sticht, 1976.

7. Poland

(See also VIII. J. Slavonic (Glagolitic) Liturgy.)

ISNER, Jan. Joannis Isneri Expositio Missae. Primum Edidit Romanus Maria Zawadzki. Msza Swieta w Polsce przed Soborem
Trydenckhim w swietle rodzimych komentarzy: expositiones
missae. Warsaw: Akademia Teologii Katolickiej, 1971, 1972.

KOPEC, Jerzy Josef. Meka Panska w religijnej kulture polskiego
sredniowiecza: studium nad pasyjnymi motywami i tekstami lit-
urgicznymi. Warsaw: Akademia teologii Katholickiej, 1975.

RECHOWICZ, Marian, and SCHENK, Waclaw, eds. Studia z dziejów
liturgii w Polsche: Praca zbiorowa. Lublin: KUL, 1973.

8. Africa and the Far East

AMALORPAVADASS, D. S. "Indigenization and the Liturgy of the
Church." International Review of Mission, 65 (1976): 164-181.

_____. Post Vatican Liturgical Renewal in India. 3 vols. Banga-
lore: National Catechetical and Liturgical Centre, 1968-1972.

_____. Towards Indigenisation in the Liturgy: Theological Re-
flection, Policy, Programme, and Text. Mission Theology for
Our Times, 6. Bangalore: National Biblical, Catechetical and
Liturgical Centre, 1972.

_____, ed. Report of the Fourth All-India Liturgical Meeting,
2nd to 8th December 1973. Bangalore: National Biblical,
Catechetical and Liturgical Centre, 1976.

BONTINCK, F. La Lutte autour de la liturgie chinoise au XVIIe et
XVIIIe siècles. Louvain: Nauwelaerts, 1962.

CHUPUNGCO, Anscar J. Towards a Filipino Liturgy. Manila:
Benedictine Abbey, 1976.

LUYKX, Boniface. Culte chrétien en Afrique après Vatican II.

SNRSM, 22. Immensee: Nouvelle revue de science missionnaire,
1974.

_____. "Die Seele des Afrikaners und den christlicher Gottes-
dienst." Theologie und Kirche in Africa, pp. 265-276. Herausgegeben von Horst Bürkle. Stuttgart: Evangelisches
Verlagswerk, 1968.

PUTHANANGADY, Paul. "Inculturation of the Liturgy in India
since Vatican II." In Liturgy: A Creative Tradition, pp. 71-
77. Edited by Mary Collins and David Power. Concilium, 162.
New York: Seabury Press, 1983.

SANON, Titianma Anselme. "Cultural Rooting of the Liturgy in
Africa since Vatican II." In Liturgy: A Creative Tradition,
pp. 61-70. Edited by Mary Collins and David Power. Concilium, 162. New York: Seabury Press, 1983.

THURIAN, Max, and WAINWRIGHT, Geoffrey, eds. "New Orders
of the Mass for India." In Baptism and Eucharist: Ecumenical
Convergence in Celebration, pp. 186-198. Geneva: World
Council of Churches; Grand Rapids, MI: Eerdmans, 1983.

R. LITURGIES OF THE MONASTIC ORDERS

1. General Studies

DEKKERS, Eligius. "Les Anciens moines cultivaient-ils la liturgie?"
In Vom christlichen Mysterium, pp. 97-114. Herausgegeben
von Anton Mayer, Johannes Quasten und Burkhard Neunheuser.
Düsseldorf: Patmos, 1951.

HAUSSLING, Angelus. Mönchskonvent und Eucharistiefeier: einer
Studie über die Messe in der abendländischen Klosterliturgie
des frühen Mittelalters und zur Geschichte der Messhäufigkeit.
LQF, 58. Münster: Aschendorff, 1973.

KING, Archdale Arthur. Liturgies of the Religious Orders. London: Longmans, Green; Milwaukee: Bruce, 1955.

MARX, Michael. Incessant Prayer in Ancient Monastic Literature.
Rome: Facultas Theologica S. Anselmi de Urbe, 1946.

NUSSBAUM, Otto. Kloster, Priestermönch und Privatmesse: ihr
Verhältnis im Westen von Anfängen bis zum hohen Mittelalter.
Theophaneia, 14. Bonn: Hanstein, 1961.

SHEPHERD, Massey H., Jr. "The Development of Monastic Worship."
Ph.D. dissertation, University of Chicago, 1937.

2. Augustinian Canons

EELES, F. C., ed. The Holyrood Ordinale, a Scottish Version of
a Directory of English Augustinian Canons, with Manual and
Other Liturgical Forms. The Book of the Old Edinburgh Club,
7. Edinburgh: Constable, 1915.

JEBB, Philip, ed. Missale de Lesnes: MS L404 in the Library of
the Victoria and Albert Museum. HBS, 95. Worcester, Eng.:
Stanbrook Abbey Press, 1964.

3. Benedictines

ABBESS OF STANBROOK and TOLHURST, J. B. L., eds. The
Ordinal and Customary of the Abbey of Saint Mary, York (St.
John's College, Cambridge, MS. D. 27.). HBS, 73. London:
Harrison: 1936.

BROU, Louis, ed. The Monastic Ordinale of St. Vedast's Abbey,
Arras. 2 vols. HBS, 86-87. London: Henry Bradshaw Society, 1955.

RULE, Martin, ed. The Missal of St. Augustine's, Canterbury,
with excerpts from the Antiphonary and Lectionary of the same
Monastery. Cambridge: Cambridge University Press, 1896.

TOLHURST, J. B. L., ed. The Customary of the Cathedral Priory
Church of Norwich, ms. 465 in the Library of Corpus Christi
College, Cambridge. HBS, 82. London: Henry Bradshaw
Society, 1948.

_____, ed. The Ordinale and Customary of the Benedictine Nuns
of Barking Abbey (University College, Oxford, ms. 169). 2
vols. HBS, 65-66. London: Harrison, 1927-1928.

TURNER, D. H., ed. The Missal of the New Minster, Winchester:
Le Havre Bibliothèque Municipale, MS 330. HBS, 93. Leighton
Buzzard, Eng.: Faith Press, 1962.

4. Carmelites

FORCADELL, A. "Ritus Carmelitarum antiquae observantiae."
Ephemerides Liturgicae, 64 (1950): 5-52.

RICKERT, Margaret. The Reconstructed Carmelite Missal: An
English Manuscript of the Late XIV Century in the British Mu-
seum. London: Faber & Faber; Chicago: University of
Chicago Press, 1952.

WALL, Michael, ed. The Carmelite Rite for Altar Servers and Congregations. Faversham, Eng.: Carmelite Press, 1958.

ZIMMERMAN, Benedict, ed. Ordinaire de l'Ordre de Notre Dame du Mont Carmel par Sibert de Beka (vers 1312). BL, 13. Paris: Picard, 1910.

5. Carthusians

HOGG, James, ed. Mittelalterliche Caerimonialia der Kartäuser. Analecta Cartusiana, 2. Berlin: J. Hogg, 1971- .

SHEPPARD, L. C. "How the Carthusians Pray." Thought, 4 (1929): 294-311.

6. Cistercians

a. Texts

Missale Cisterciense, reformatum juxta decretum Sacrorum Rituum Congregationis diei 3 Julii 1869. Auctoritate Dominici Rogues editum. Westmalle: Ex typographia Ord. Cist. Strict. Obs., 1951.

b. Studies

CANIVEZ, Joseph-Marie. "Le Rite cistercien." Ephemerides Liturgicae, 63 (1949): 276-311.

MALET, André. La Liturgie cistercienne: ses origines, sa constitution, sa transformation, sa restauration. Westmalle: Typ. de l'Ordre des Cisterciens de l'étroite observance, 1921.

SCHNEIDER, Fulgence. L'Ancienne messe cistercienne. Tilbourg: Abbaye de N. D. de Koningshoeven, 1929.

WADDELL, Chrysogonus. "The Early Cistercian Experience of Liturgy." In Rule and Life: An Interdisciplinary Symposium, pp. 77-115. Edited by M. Basil Pennington. CS, 12. Spencer, MA: Cistercian Publications, 1971.

7. Dominicans

a. Texts

BONNIWELL, William R., ed. The Dominican Ceremonial for Mass and Benediction. New York: Comet Press, 1946.

Dominican Mass Book: The Ordinary of the Mass according to the
    Dominican Rite. By a Dominican of the Second Order, Caris-
    brooke. London: R. & T. Washbourne, 1914.

The Dominican Missal in Latin and English. Translated by Bruno
    Walkley. Rev. ed., revised by Hilary J. Carpenter. Oxford:
    Blackfriars, 1948.

    b. Studies

BONNIWELL, William R. A History of the Dominican Liturgy, 1215-
    1945. Introduction by Bartholomew J. Eustace. 2d ed. New
    York: Joseph F. Wagner, 1945.

SOLCH, G. "Die Liturgie des Dominikanerordens." Liturgische
    Zeitschrift, 3 (1930-1931): 306-314.

8. Franciscans

LEFEVRE, Placide. "La signification de la liturgie franciscaine."
    Revue d'histoire ecclesiastique, 58 (1963): 857-862.

9. Gilbertines

WOOLLEY, Reginald Maxwell, ed. The Gilbertine Rite. 2 vols.
    HBS, 59-60. London: Harrison, 1921-1922.

10. Premonstratensians

    a. Texts

LEFEVRE, Placide F., ed. Coutumiers liturgiques de Prémontré
    du XIIIe et du XIVe siècle. BRHE, 27. Louvain: Bureau de
    la Revue, 1953.

_____. L'Ordinaire de Prémontré d'après des manuscrits du XII.
    et du XIII. siècle. BRHE, 22. Louvain: Bureau de la Revue,
    1941.

Processionale ad usum sacri et canonici Ordinis Praemonstratensis.
    Paris, Tournai: Desclée, 1932.

Sacramentarium Praemonstratense. Edidit N. I. Weyns. BAP, 8.
    Averbode: Praemonstratensia, 1968.

    b. Studies

LEFEVRE, Placide F. La Liturgie et Prémontré: histoire, formulaire,
    chant et cérémonial. BAP, 1. Louvain: E. Warny, 1957.

LU YKX, Boniface. Essai sur les sources de l' 'Ordo Missae' prémontré. Tongerloo (Anvers):   Sint Norbertus-drukkerij, 1947.

————. Note sur l'étude de manuscrits liturgiques prémontrés.
n.p.:   Abbaye de Postel, 1952.

WAEFELGHEM, Raphaël van. Répertoire des sources imprimées et
manuscrits relatives à l'histoire et à la liturgie des monastères
de l'Ordre de Prémontré. Brussels: A. Dewit, 1930.

S. LITANIES

COENS, M. "Anciennes litanies des saints." Analecta Bollandiana,
54 (1936):   5-37; 55 (1937):   49-69; 59 (1941):   272-298; 62
(1944):   126-168.

MOELLER, D. E. "Litanies majeures et rogations." Questions liturgiques et paroissiales, 23 (1938):   75-91.

SAMSON, Heinrich. Die Allerheiligen-Litanei, geschichtlich, liturgisch und ascetisch erklärt. Paderborn: Bonifacius, 1894.

VAN DIJK, Stephen A. "The Litany of the Saints on Holy Satur-
day." Journal of Ecclesiastical History, 1 (1950):   51-62.

VANN, Gerald. "Notes on Our Lady's Litany." Worship, 30 (1955-
1956):   437-441.

T. PRONE

1. Latin Church Use

ALFONZO, Pio. Oration Fidelium. Finalpia, 1928.

ASHWORTH, Henry. "The Prayer of the Faithful." Liturgy (England), 37, 3 (1968):   67-72.

BORELLA, P. "L'oratio fidelium." Ambrosius, 40 (1964):   435-460;
41 (1965):   9-23.

————. "Oratio fidelium e dittici nelle segrete dell'offertorio."
Ambrosius, 36, 3, supplement (1960):   1-21.

CARMODY, J. "An American Use of the Prone." Theological
Studies, 19 (1958):   228-236.

————. "Prône." New Catholic Encyclopedia, 11:838-839.

Consilium. De oratione communi seu fidelium: natura, momentum
ac structura. Criteria atque speciminia coetibus territorialibus
episcoporum proposita. Vatican City, 1966.

GASTOUE, A. "Les prières du Prône à Paris au 14e siècle."
Questions liturgiques et paroissiales, 12 (1927): 240-249.

GATCH, Milton McC. "Basic Christian Education from the Decline
of Catechesis to the Rise of Catechisms." In A Faithful
Church. Edited by John H. Westerhoff III and O. C. Edwards, Jr. Wilton, CT: Morehouse-Barlow, 1981.

_____. Preaching and Theology in Anglo-Saxon England. Toron-
to, Ont.: University of Toronto Press, 1977.

GAUGHAN, Norbert F. "Prone and the Prayers of the Faithful."
Homiletic and Pastoral Review, 67 (1967): 385-390.

GRANCOLAS, Jean. Les anciennes liturgies, ou, la manière dont
on a dit la sainte messe dans chaque siècle, dans les églises
d'orient, & dans celles d'occident, vol. 1, pp. 525-526. Paris:
Jean de Nully, 1697.

JUNGMANN, Joseph Andreas. The Mass of the Roman Rite, vol. 1,
pp. 487-494. Translated by Francis A. Brunner. New York:
Benziger, 1951.

KUPPERS, Kurt. "Liturgie und Volksfrommigkeit." Archiv für
Liturgiewissenschaft, 25 (1983): 101-113.

LECLERCQ, H. "Prone." Dictionnaire d'archéologie chrétienne et
de liturgie, 14:1898-1907.

McMANUS, Frederick R. "Prayers of the Faithful." Worship, 35
(1961): 674-677.

MAERTENS, T. "Pour un renouveau des prières du prône."
Paroisse et Liturgie, 43 (1960-1961): 245-252.

MILLER, C. F. "Intercessory Prayer: History, Method, Subjects
and Theology." Studia Liturgica, 3 (1964): 20-29.

MOLIN, Jean-Baptiste. "L'Oratio fidelium et ses survivances."
Ephemerides liturgicae, 73 (1959): 130-137.

_____. "Les prières du Prône à Provins en XIVe siècle." Bulletin
de la Société d'histoire et d'archéologie de l'Arrondissement du
Provins, 114 (1960): 57-59; 116 (1962): 45-54.

MOLIN, Jean-Baptiste. "Les prières du Prône en Italie." Ephemerides liturgicae, 76 (1962):39-42.

NOCENT, Adrien. "La prière commune des fidèles." Nouvelle revue théologique, 86 (1964):   948-964.

OURY, G. "Les survivances de l'oratio fidelium au XIIe siècle."
Revue grégorienne, 40 (1962):   142-148.

SINCLAIR, K. V. "Anglo-Norman Bidding Prayers from Ramsey
Abbey." Medieval Studies, 42 (1980):   454-462.

2. Influence on Protestant Liturgies

BRIGHTMAN, F. E. "Appendix I: The Bidding of the Bedes."
In his The English Rite, vol. 2, pp. 1020-1045. 2d ed. Lon-
don: Rivington, 1921; reprint ed., Farnborough, Eng.:
Gregg, 1970.

COXE, H. Forms of Bidding Prayer with Introduction and Notes.
Oxford: J. H. Parker; London: J. G. F. and J. Rivington,
1840.

MAXWELL, William D. The Liturgical Portions of the Genevan Service Book. Westminster: Faith Press, 1931.

OLD, Hughes Oliphant. The Patristic Roots of Reformed Worship.
Zurich: Theologischer Verlag, 1970.

REED, Luther D. The Lutheran Liturgy, pp. 316-320 and passim.
Philadelphia, PA: Muhlenberg Press, 1947.

SCHMIDT-CLAUSING, Fritz. Zwingli als Liturgiker, pp. 54-66.
Berlin: Evangelische Verlagsanstalt, 1952.

THOMPSON, Bard. Liturgies of the Western Church, p. 143.
Cleveland, OH: World, 1961; reprint ed., Philadelphia, PA:
Fortress Press, 1981.

U.   CEREMONIAL AND PRACTICAL STUDIES

AHEARNE, Pierce, and LANE, Michael. Pontifical Ceremonies: A
Study of the Episcopal Ceremonies. London: Burns, Oates &
Washbourne, 1942.

Assemblée des Cardinaux et Archévêques. Directoire pour la pastorale de la messe à l'usage des diocèses de France. 2. éd.
Coutances: Editions Notre Dame, 1960.

BALDESCHI, Giuseppe. Esposizione delle sacre cerimonie. Ed. 2.
Rome: Nell' Ospizio de S. Maria degli Angela, 1839.

_____. Ceremonial According to the Roman Rite. Translated and edited by T. D. Hilarius Dale. London: n.p., 1853; 10th ed., London: Burns & Oates, 1907.

_____. Cérémonial selon le rit romain. Traduit et completée par Pierre Favrel. Paris: Lecoffre, 1847.

_____. Cérémonial selon le rit romain. 5. éd., entiere-refondue par Léon Le Vavasseur. Paris: Lecoffre, 1857.

LE VAVASSEUR, Léon Michel. Cérémonial selon le rit romain. 2 vols. 8. éd., rev. et augm. par le r. p. Haegy. Paris: Lecoffre, 1898.

_____. Manuel de liturgie et cérémonial selon le rit romain. 2 vols. 10. éd., rev. et augm. par Joseph Haegy. Paris: Lecoffre, 1909-1910.

_____, and HAEGY, Joseph. Manuel de liturgie et cérémonial selon le rit romain. 2 vols. 16. éd., rev. et mise à jour par Louis Stercky. Paris: Gabalda, 1935.

BAUDOT, Jules. Le Cérémonial. Paris: Bloud & Cie, 1913.

BROWE, P. "Die Elevation in der Messe." Jahrbuch für Liturgiewissenschaft, 9 (1929): 20-66.

CALLEWAERT, Camillus Aloysius. Ceremoniale in missa privata et solemni allisque frequentioribus functionibus liturgicis servandum. Ed. 5. denuo recognita. Bruges: Beyaert, 1948.

CAPELLE, Bernard. "Fraction et commixtion." La Maison-Dieu, 35 (1953): 79-94; reprinted in his Travaux liturgiques, vol. 2, pp. 319-331. Louvain: Centre liturgique, Abbaye du Mont César, 1962.

_____. "Le Rite de la fraction dans la messe romaine." Revue bénédictine, 53 (1941): 5-40; reprinted in his Travaux liturgiques, vol. 2, pp. 287-318. Louvain: Centre liturgique, Abbaye du Mont César, 1962.

CHANSON, A. Pour mieux administrer Baptême, Confirmation, Eucharistie, Extrême-Onction. 4. éd. Arras: Brunet, 1961.

CONNOLLY, P. "The Use of Incense in the Roman Liturgy." Ephemerides Liturgicae, 43 (1929): 171-176.

DOLGER, Franz Joseph. "Zu den Zeremonien der Messliturgie." In his Antike und Christentum, Bd. 1, pp. 236-240; Bd. 2, pp. 190-221; Bd. 6, pp. 81-132. Münster: Aschendorff, 1929-1950.

DYKMANS, Marc. "Aux origines de l'élévation eucharistique." In
Zetesis: Album amicorum door vrienden en collegas aangeboden
aan Prof. Dr. E. de Strycker ter gelegenheid van zijn 65e verjaardag, pp. 679-694. Antwerpen: De Nederlandsche Boekhandel, 1973.

FAVREL, Pierre. Cérémonial selon le rit romain.
--See BALDESCHI, Giuseppe, pp. 230-1.

FORTESCUE, Adrian. The Ceremonies of the Roman Rite Described. 8th ed. Westminster, MD: Newman Press, 1953.

GATTERER, Michael, ed. Praxis celebrandi functiones ordinarias
sacerdotales: regulae et ritus. Ed. 3a. Innsbruck (Deni-
ponte): Rauch, 1940.

GROMIER, L. Commentaire du Caeremoniale Episcorporum. Paris:
Editions de la Colombe, 1959.

HAEGY, Joseph. Cérémonial selon le rit romain.
--See LE VAVASSEUR, Léon Michel, p. 231.

HOVDA, Robert W. Strong, Loving and Wise: Presiding in Liturgy.
Foreword by Godfrey Diekmann. Washington, DC: Liturgical
Conference, 1976.

IRWIN, Kevin W. A Celebrant's Guide to the New Sacramentary.
New York: Pueblo, 1977.

_____. Sunday Worship: A Planning Guide to Celebration. New
York: Pueblo, 1983.

KAVANAGH, Aidan. Elements of Rite: A Handbook of Liturgical
Style. New York: Pueblo, 1982.

KENNEDY, Vincent Lorne. "The Date of the Parisian Decree on
the Elevation of the Host." Medieval Studies, 8 (1946): 87-96.

_____. "The Moment of Consecration and the Elevation of the
Host." Medieval Studies, 6 (1949): 121-150.

KIRCHGASSNER, Alfons, ed. Unser Gottesdienst: Uberlegungen
und Anregungen: ein Werkbuch. Freiburg: Herder, 1960;
Unto the Altar: The Practice of Catholic Worship. Translated
by Rosaleen Brennan. Freiburg: Herder; Montreal: Palm
Publishers; New York: Herder & Herder, 1963.

LERCARO, Giacomo. A messa figlioli! Direttorio liturgico per la
partecipazione attiva dei fedeli alla santa messa letta. 3. ed.
Bologna: Uficio tecnico organizzativo arcivescovile, 1956.

LE VAVASSEUR, Léon Michel. Cérémonial selon le rit romain.
--See BALDESCHI and LE VAVASSEUR, pp. 230-1.

_____. Les Fonctions pontificales selon le rit romain. 2 vols.
Revue et augmentée par le r. p. Haegy. 3. éd. Paris:
Lecoffre, 1904.

_____. _____. 6. éd., revue et mise à jour par le p. L.
Stercky. Paris: Gabalda, 1932.

McMANUS, Frederick R. Handbook for the New Rubrics. Baltimore, MD: Helicon Press, 1961.

MAERTENS, Thierry. La Pastorale de la messe à la lumière de la
tradition. 2. éd. PL, 32. Bruges: Publications de Saint-
André, 1964.

MEYER, H. B. "Das Elevation im deutschen Mittelalter und bei
Luther: eine Untersuchung zur Liturgie- und Frommigskeits-
geschichte des späten Mittelalters." Zeitschrift für katholische
Theologie, 85 (1963): 162-217.

MOSSI, John P. Modern Liturgy Handbook: A Study and Planning
Guide for Worship. Ramsey, NJ: Paulist Press, 1976.

MULLER, Johann Baptist. Zeremonienbüchlein für Priester und
Candidaten des Priestertums. 2. Aufl. Freiburg: Herder,
1904; Handbook of Ceremonies for Priests and Seminarians.
Translated by Andrew P. Ganss. Edited by W. H. W. Fanning.
St. Louis, MO: B. Herder, 1907.

_____. Handbook of Ceremonies for Priests and Seminarians.
18th English ed. Revised and edited by Adam C. Ellis. St.
Louis, MO: B. Herder, 1954.

O'CONNELL, J. B. The Celebration of Mass: A Study of the
Rubrics of the Roman Missal. 3 vols. Milwaukee, WI: Bruce,
1940-41; new ed., 1956.

O'CONNELL, Laurence J., and SCHMITZ, Walter J. The Book of
Ceremonies. Revised ed. Milwaukee, WI: Bruce, 1956.

Participation in the Mass. 20th North American Liturgical Week.
Washington, DC: Liturgical Conference, 1960.

Priest's Guide to Parish Worship. Preface by Frederick R. McManus. Introduction by Gerard S. Sloyan. Washington, DC:
Liturgical Conference, 1964.

"Processions." La Maison-Dieu, 43 (1955). [Special issue]

SALMON, Pierre. Etude sur les insignes du pontife dans le rite
    romain: histoire et liturgie. Rome: Officium Libri Catholici,
    1955.

SCHMITZ, Walter J., and TIERNEY, Terence E. Liturgikon: Pas-
    toral Ministrations. Huntingdon, IN: Our Sunday Visitor,
    1977.

SLOYAN, Virginia, ed. Touchstones for Liturgical Ministers.
    Collegeville, MN: Liturgical Press, 1978.

STERCKY, Louis. Manuel de liturgie et cérémonial selon le rit
    romain.
    --See LE VAVASSEUR, León Michel, p. 231.

SUNTRUP, Rudolf. Die Bedeutung der liturgischen Gebärden und
    Bewegungen in lateinischen und deutschen Auslegungen des 9.
    bis 13. Jahrhunderts. MMS, 37. München: Fink, 1978.

WISE, Joe. The Body at Liturgy. Cincinnati, OH: North American
    Liturgical Resources, 1975.

V.   OLD CATHOLIC LITURGIES

1.   Texts

Altkatholische Kirche in Deutschland. Altarbuch für die Feier der
    heiligen Eucharistie im katholischen Bistum der Alt-katholiken
    in Deutschland. Bonn, 1959.

Christkatholische Kirche der Schweiz. Gebetbuch der Christkatho-
    lischen Kirche der Schweiz. Solothurn, 1917.

_____. _____. Allschwil, 1968.

_____. (Old Catholic Church in Switzerland). "Liturgy of the
    Mass." Studia Liturgica, 5/4 (1966): II-6-1-24.

_____. Messliturgie der Christkatholischen Kirche der Schweiz.
    2. Aufl. Bern, 1905.

_____. Rituale der Christkatholischen Kirche der Schweiz. Her-
    ausgegeben von Bischof Dr. Adolf Küry in Verbindung mit der
    Geistlichkeit. 2. Aufl. Bern, 1940.

DE VOIL, Walter Harry, and WYNNE-BENNETT, Henry Douglas.
    Old Catholic Eucharistic Worship. With notes and translations
    of the Dutch, German, and Swiss Rites. London: Faith Press;
    New York: Morehouse, 1936.

MATTHEW, Arnold H., ed. The Old Catholic Missal and Ritual.
Prepared for the Use of English-speaking congregations ... in
communion with the ancient Catholic archepiscopal See of Utrecht. London: Cope & Fenwick, 1909.

Old Catholic Worship in the Netherlands. Amersfoort: Society of
St. Willibrord, 1961.

Polish National Catholic Church. A Book of Devotions and Prayers
according to the Use of the Polish National Catholic Church in
Polish and English. Scranton, PA: n.p., 1951.

_____. "The Polish National Catholic Liturgy." In The Polish
National Catholic Church in America and Poland, pp. 95-108.
By Theodore Andrews. London: SPCK, 1953.

_____. Prayer-Book of the Polish National Catholic Church.
Scranton, PA: n.p., 1939.

WARREN, F. E., ed. The Offices of the Old Catholic Prayer-Book,
done into English, and compared with the Offices of the Roman
and Old German Rituals. Oxford: Parker, 1876.

2. Studies

ALDENHOVEN, H. "Darbringung und Epiklese im Eucharistiegebet:
eine Studie über die Struktur des Eucharistiegebetes in den altkatholischen Liturgien im Lichte der Liturgiegeschichte." Internationale kirchliche Zeitschrift, 61 (1971): 90-111.

AMON, Karl. "Das eucharistische Hochgebet in den altkatholischen
Kirchen des deutschen Sprachgebiets." Liturgisches Jahrbuch,
18 (1968): 1-18.

ANDREWS, Theodore. The Polish National Catholic Church in America and Poland. London: SPCK, 1953.

FOX, Paul. The Polish National Catholic Church. Scranton, PA:
School of Christian Living, 1961?

KURY, Urs. Die altkatholische Kirche: Ihre Geschichte, ihre
Lehre, ihr Anliegen. Die Kirche der Welt, Bd. 3. Stuttgart:
Evangelisches Verlagswerk, 1966.

MOSS, C. B. The Old Catholic Movement: Its Origins and History.
2d ed. London: SPCK; New York: Morehouse-Barlow, 1964.

PURSCH, Kurt. "Das Opfermahl und die Neuordnung seiner Gestalt." Internationale Kirchliche Zeitung, 46 (1956): 214-226.

_____. "Die Probleme des Offertoriums und Versuche zu ihre Lösung." Internationale kirchliche Zeitung, 46 (1956): 1-27, 105-130.

_____. "Zur Neuordnung des eucharistischen Hochgebetes." Internationale kirchliche Zeitung, 58 (1968): 251-269; 59 (1969): 1-33.

RUTHY, Albert Emil. "Bemerkungen und Erwägungen zu den alt-katholischen Liturgien." Internationale kirchliche Zeitung, 47 (1957): 106-120; 48 (1958): 84-95; 50 (1960): 93-106, 225-238; 53 (1963): 40-50; 54 (1964): 83-96, 215-224; 56 (1966): 150-165; 57 (1967): 120-131; 58 (1968): 109-121; 60 (1970): 19-34.

_____. "The Place of the Old Catholic Church in the Liturgical Scene." Studia Liturgica, 2 (1963): 66-72.

SCHMID, Franz Xaver. Liturgik der christkatholischen Religion. 3 vols. 2. Aufl. Passau: Ambrosi, 1935.

W. OTHER SPECIAL STUDIES

ANDRIEU, Michel. "Aux origines du culte du Saint-Sacrament. Reliquaires et monstrances eucharistiques." Analecta Bollandiana, 68 (1950): 397-418.

BOULARAND, E. "La Vierge et l'eucharistie." Revue d'ascétique et de mystique, 34 (1958): 361-392.

CASEL, Odo. "Actio in liturgischer Verwendung." Jahrbuch für Liturgiewissenschaft, 1 (1921): 34-39.

COLLINS, Mary, and POWER, David, eds. Can We Always Celebrate the Eucharist? Concilium, 152. New York: Seabury Press, 1982.

DANIELOU, Jean. "Sacrements et histoire du salut." In Parole de Dieu et liturgie, pp. 51-69. Paris: Cerf, 1958.

DIEZINGER, Walter. Effectus in der römischen Liturgie: eine kult-sprachliche Untersuchung. Theophaneia, 15. Bonn: Hanstein, 1961.

DROSTE, Benedicta. "Celebrave" in der römische Liturgiesprache. MTS, 26. Munich: Hueber, 1963.

GRAEF, Hermann J. Palmenweihe und Palmenprozession in der lateinischen Liturgie. Kaldenkirchen: Steyler Verlagsbuchhandlung, 1959.

HAPPEL, Stephen. "Classicist Culture and the Nature of Worship."
Heythrop Journal, 21 (1980): 288-302.

HENNIG, J. "Alttestamentliche Personen in den liturgischen Büchern nach dem Konzil von Trient." Archiv für Liturgiewissenschaft, 17 (1976): 59-79.

IBANEZ, Javier, and MENDOZA RUIZ, Fernando. Maria en la liturgia hispana. Pamplona: Ediciones Universidad de Navarra, 1975.

ISERLOH, Erwin. "'Das Herrenmahl' im römisch-katholischen und evangelisch-lutherischen Gespräch." Theologische Revue, 3 (1979): 178-182.

JERG, E. "Die 'sustentatio' in der römischen Liturgie vor dem Hintergrund des kaiserlichen Hofzeremoniells." Zeitschrift für katholische Theologie, 8 (1958): 316-324.

JUNGMANN, Josef Andreas. "Abendmahl als Name der Eucharistie." Zeitschrift für katholische Theologie, 93 (1971): 91-94.

_____. "Das Gedächtnis des Herrn in der Eucharistia." Theologische Quartalschrift, 133 (1953): 385-399.

KAHLER, Ernst. Studien zum Te Deum und zur Geschichte des 24. Psalms in der alten Kirche. Göttingen: Vandenhoeck & Ruprecht, 1958.

KING, Archdale Arthur. Concelebration in the Christian Church. London: Mowbray, 1966.

LARGO, Gerald A. Community and Liturgy: An Historical Overview. Washington, DC: University Press of America, 1980.

LEWIS, Charles A. The Silent Recitation of the Canon of the Mass. Excerpt from a dissertation in the Gregorian University Theology Faculty. Bay St. Louis, MI: Divine Word Missionaries, 1962.

MARTIMORT, Aimé-Georges. La Documentation liturgique de Dom Edmond Martène: étude codicologique. ST, 279. Città del Vaticano: Biblioteca Apostolica Vaticana, 1978.

MERK, Carl Joseph. Abriss einer liturgiegeschichtlichen Darstellung des Mess-Stipendiums. Stuttgart: O. Scholz, 1928.

SCHAFER, Thomas. Die Fusswaschung im monastischen Brauchtum und in der lateinischen Liturgie: liturgiegeschichtliche Untersuchungen. TuA, 47. Beuron: Beuroner Kunstverlag, 1956.

SEARLE, Mark, ed. Parish: A Place for Worship. Collegeville:
Liturgical Press, 1981.

URBAN, Han-Jörg. "Der ökumenische Gottesdienst in katholischer
Sicht." Okumenische Rundschau, 29 (1980): 30-42.

X. STRUCTURAL ELEMENTS OF THE MASS

Note: This section follows, for the most part, the revised Roman order. Many of the elements, of course,
are shared by other liturgies, both Eastern and Western, and may appear in a different order in them.
All material specially devoted to the element under
discussion has been collected here, regardless of its
source. Many of the major books on particular liturgies, both eastern and western, also contain discussions
of these elements. A short list of some of the most
notable of these is included here. For the rest, see
general entries under the particular liturgical traditions.

AMIOT, François. Histoire de la messe. JSJC, 109. Paris: Fayard, 1956; History of the Mass. 2d ed. Translated by Lancelot Sheppard. TCEC, 110. London: Burns & Oates; New
York: Hawthorn Books, 1966.

BATIFFOL, Pierre. Leçons sur la messe. Paris: Gabalda, 1919;
8th ed., 1941.

BISHOP, Edmund. Liturgica Historica: Papers on the Liturgy and
Religious Life of the Western Church. Oxford: Clarendon
Press, 1918; reprinted 1962.

BOTTE, Bernard, and MOHRMANN, Christine. L'Ordinaire de la
messe. TEL, 2. Paris: Cerf, 1953.

BRINKTRINE, Johannes. Die heilige Messe in ihrem Werden und
Wesen. 3. Aufl. Paderborn: Schöningh, 1950.

CALLEWAERT, Camillus Aloysius. Sacris erudiri: fragmenta liturgica collecta a monachis Sancti Petri de Aldenburgo in Steenbrugge ne pereant. Steenbrugge: Abbatia S. Petri de Aldenburgo, 1940; reprinted 1962.

CAPELLE, Bernard. Travaux Liturgiques, vol. 2: La Messe.
Louvain: Centre liturgique, Abbaye du Mont César, 1962.

CRICHTON, J. D. Christian Celebration: The Mass. London:
Geoffrey Chapman, 1971.

_____, ed. The Mass and the People of God. London: Burns & Oates, 1966.

DALMAIS, Irénée-Henri. Les liturgies d'Orient. RS, 10. Paris: Cerf, 1980.

DEISS, Lucien, ed. Aux sources de la liturgie: textes choisis et traduits. VT, 3. Paris: Fleurus, 1963; Early Sources of the Liturgy. Translated by Benet Weatherhead. London: Geoffrey Chapman; Staten Island, NY: Alba House, 1967.

_____, ed. Printemps de la liturgie: Textes liturgiques des 4 premiers siècles. Paris: Levain, 1979; Springtime of the Liturgy: Liturgical Texts of the First Four Centuries. Translated by Matthew J. O'Connell. Collegeville, MN: Liturgical Press, 1979.

_____. Spirit and Song of the New Liturgy. Translated by Lyla L. Haggard and Michael L. Mazzarese. Cincinnati, OH: World Library of Sacred Music, 1970.

DELORME, J., et al. The Eucharist in the New Testament. Baltimore, MD: Helicon, 1964.

DIX, Gregory. The Shape of the Liturgy. 2d ed. Westminster: Dacre Press, 1945; reprint ed., London: A. & C. Black, 1975; New York: Seabury Press, 1982.

EMMINGHAUS, Johannes H. The Eucharist: Essence, Form, Celebration. Translated by Matthew J. O'Connell. Collegeville, MN: Liturgical Press, 1978.

EVERY, George. The Mass: Meaning, Mystery and Ritual. Huntington, IN: Our Sunday Visitor, 1980.

GIHR, Nikolaus. Das heilige Messopfer dogmatisch, liturgisch und ascetisch erklärt. 6. Aufl. Freiburg: Herder, 1897; The Holy Sacrifice of the Mass: Dogmatically, Liturgically and Ascetically Explained. 8th ed. Translated from the 6th German edition. St. Louis, MO: B. Herder, 1929.

HAMMAN, Adalbert, ed. La messe: liturgies anciennes et textes patristiques. LC, 9. Paris: Grasset, 1964; The Mass: Ancient Liturgies and Patristic Texts. English editorial Supervisor: Thomas Holton. APL, 1. Staten Island, NY: Alba House, 1967.

HATCHETT, Marion J. Commentary on the American Prayer Book. New York: Seabury Press, 1980.

HERWEGEN, Ildefons. Das Kunstprinzip der Liturgie. 4. und 5.

Aufl. Paderborn: Jungfermannschen Buchhandlung, 1929; The Art-Principle of Liturgy. Translated by William Busch. Collegeville, MN: Liturgical Press, 1931; reprinted as Liturgy's Inner Beauty. Collegeville, MN: Liturgical Press, 1955.

HOWELL, Clifford. Mean What You Say: The Short Responses in the Mass. Collegeville, MN: Liturgical Press, 1965.

JUNGMANN, Josef Andreas. The Early Liturgy to the Time of Gregory the Great. Translated by Francis A. Brunner. LS,6. Notre Dame, IN: University of Notre Dame Press, 1959.

_____. The Mass of the Roman Rite. 2 vols. Translated by Francis A. Brunner. New York: Benziger, 1951-1955; revised and abridged one-vol. ed. New York: Benziger, 1959, 1961.

KING, Archdale A. The Liturgy of the Roman Church. [Rites of Western Christendom, vol. 4.] London: Longmans, Green; Milwaukee, WI: Bruce, 1957.

_____. The Rites of Eastern Christendom. 2 vols. Rome: Catholic Book Agency, 1947-1948; reprint ed., New York: AMS Press, 1972.

KLAUSER, Theodor. Kleine abendländische Liturgiegeschichte. Bonn: Hanstien, 1965; A Short History of the Western Liturgy. 2d ed. Translated by John Halliburton. New York: Oxford University Press, 1979.

LIETZMANN, Hans. Messe und Herrenmahl. 3. Aufl. AK, 8. Berlin: De Gruyter, 1955; Mass and Lord's Supper. Translated by Dorothea H. G. Reeve. Leiden: Brill, 1953; reprinted with introduction and further inquiry by Robert Douglas Richardson. Leiden: Brill, 1979.

MARTIMORT, A. M., ed. L'Eglise en prière. 3. ed. Paris: Desclee, 1965; partial adaptation in two volumes: The Church at Prayer: Introduction to the Liturgy. Translated by Robert Fisher et al. English ed. edited by Austin Flannery and Vincent Ryan. New York: Desclee, 1968; and The Eucharist [The Church at Prayer, vol. 2]. Edited by Austin Flannery and Vincent Ryan. New York: Herder & Herder, 1973.

NOCENT, Adrien. La célébration eucharistique avant et après saint Pie V. PT, 23. Paris: Beauchesne, 1977.

REED, Luther Dotterer. The Lutheran Liturgy: A Study of the Common Service of the Lutheran Church in America. Revised ed. Philadelphia, PA: Muhlenberg Press, 1959.

RORDORF, Willy, et al. The Eucharist of the Early Christians.
    Translated by Matthew J. O'Connell. New York: Pueblo, 1978.

SALAVILLE, Sévérien. Liturgies orientales: notions générales,
    éléments principaux. BCSR, 47. Paris: Bloud & Gay, 1932;
    An Introduction to the Study of Eastern Liturgies. Adapted
    from the French with a preface and some additional notes by
    John M. T. Barton. London: Sands, 1938.

SHEPHERD, Massey H., Jr. The Oxford American Prayer Book
    Commentary. New York: Oxford University Press, 1950.

SHEPPARD, Lancelot, ed. The New Liturgy: A Comprehensive
    Introduction to the New Liturgy as a Whole and to its New
    Calendar, Order of Mass, Eucharistic Prayers, the Roman
    Canon, Prefaces and the New Sunday Lectionary. London:
    Darton, Longman & Todd, 1970.

A. MISCELLANEOUS AND GENERAL

1. Acclamations

KANTOROWICZ, Ernst H., and BUKOFZER, Manfred F. Laudes
    Regiae: A Study in Liturgical Acclamations and Medieval Ruler
    Worship. Berkeley: University of California Press, 1946.

KLAUSER, Theodor. "Akklamation." Reallexikon für Antike und
    Christentum, 1:216-233.

OPFERMANN, B. Die liturgischen Herrscherakklamationen im sacrum
    Imperium des Mittelalters. Weimar: Böhlau, 1953.

RAUCH, C. "La prière du peuple." La Maison-Dieu, 20 (1949):
    127-129.

THIBAULT, Jeannette. "Make His Praise Resound." Liturgy, 21,3
    (March 1976): 83-84.

THOMAS, I. "Acclamations." New Catholic Encyclopedia, 1:79-80.

2. Silent Prayer

BUGNINI, A. "Tibi silentium laus." Notitiae, 110 (October 1975):
    279-282.

CECCHETTI, I. "Tibi silentium laus." In Miscellanea liturgica in
    honorem L. Cuniberti Mohlberg, vol. 2, pp. 521-570. Rome:
    Edizioni Liturgiche, 1949.

GRISBROOKE, W. Jardine. "Silent Prayer." A Dictionary of Liturgy and Worship, p. 349.

O'SULLIVAN, Eugene. "Liturgy and Stillness." Doctrine and Life, 30 (1980): 461-469.

QUELLEC, Jean-Yves. "Le silence dans la liturgie." Communautés et liturgies, (1981); English excerpt in Symbol: The Language of Liturgy, pp. 65-68. Prepared and edited by a joint committee of the Liturgical Commissions of Brooklyn, New York and Rockville Center, 1982.

RICHSTATTER, Thomas. "Silence in Worship." New Catholic Encyclopedia, 17:610.

SHAUGHNESSY, James D. "Silence during Mass: Why? When?" Homiletic and Pastoral Review, 71,1 (October 1970): 51-54.

SMITH, Gregory. "Liturgical Silence." Carmelus, 23 (1976): 1-20.

_____. "Values and Uses of Silence as Part of Liturgical Action." Living Worship, 13,5 (May 1977).

3. Sign of the Cross

BERESFORD-COOKE, Ernest. The Sign of the Cross in the Western Liturgies. ACT,7. London: Longmans, Green, 1907.

BOTTE, Bernard. "Un passage difficile de la 'Tradition apostolique' sur le signe de la croix." Recherches de théologie ancienne et médiévale, 27 (1960): 5-19.

CROSS, F. L. "Sign of the Cross." The Oxford Dictionary of the Christian Church, p. 1255.

LECLERCQ, Henri. "Croix (signe de la)." Dictionnaire d'archéologie chrétienne et de liturgie, 3:3139-3144.

MILLER, John. "Cross." New Catholic Encyclopedia, 4:473-479.

THURSTON, H. "The Sign of the Cross." The Month, 118 (1911): 586-602.

4. Incensation

(See XLV. H--Incense, p. 649.)

5. Miscellaneous Ceremonial

DOLGER, F. J. "Der Altarküss." Antike und Christentum, 2 (1930): 190-221.

DUNLOP, Colin. Processions: A Dissertation together with Practical Suggestions. ACT, 20. London: Mowbray; London: Oxford University Press, H. Milford, 1932.

GRAEF, Hermann J. Palmenweihe und Palmenprozession in der lateinischen Liturgie. Kaldenkirchen: Steyler Verlagsbuchhandlung, 1959.

"Processions." La Maison-Dieu, 43 (1955). [Special issue]

B. INTRODUCTORY RITES

1. General Studies

HUCK, Gabe. "Introductory Rites at the Lord's Supper: The First, Best Moments." Liturgy, 1,4 (1981): 22-27.

KEIFER, Ralph. "Making the Gathered Assembly a Worshipping Community." Pastoral Music, 1,4 (April-May 1977): 21-24; reprinted in Music in Catholic Worship: The NPM Commentary, pp. 105-109. Edited by Virgil C. Funk. Washington, DC: National Association of Pastoral Musicians, 1982.

_____. "Our Cluttered Vestibule: The Unreformed Entrance Rite." Worship, 48 (1974): 270-277.

ROZIER, Claude. "Les rites d'ouverture de la messe." La Maison-Dieu, 100 (1969): 36-43.

2. Entrance Procession and Song (Introit)

CALLEWAERT, Camillus Aloysius. "Introitus." Ephemerides liturgicae, 52 (1938): 484-489.

CROSS, F. L. "Introit." Oxford Dictionary of the Christian Church, p. 698.

FROGER, J. "Le chant de l'introit." Ephemerides liturgicae, 62 (1948): 248-255.

HOWELL, Clifford. "The Introit." The Clergy Review, 54 (1966): 796-802.

LECLERCQ, Henri. "Introit." Dictionnaire d'archéologie chrétienne et de liturgie, 7:1212-1220.

SHAUGHNESSY, James D. "The Entrance Procession and Chants." Homiletic and Pastoral Review, 66 (1966): 326-328.

SHEPHERD, Massey H. "Antiphonal Psalmody: The Introit, Offertory and Communion." In his The Psalms in Christian Worship: A Practical Guide, pp. 40-43. Minneapolis, MN: Augsburg, 1976.

3. Greeting and Response (Dominus vobiscum...)

ASHWORTH, Henry. "'Et cum Spiritu tuo': An Inquiry into its Origin and Meaning." The Clergy Review, 51 (February 1966): 122-130.

CROSS, F. L. "Dominus vobiscum." Oxford Dictionary of the Christian Church, p. 414.

GRATSCH, E. J. "Dominus vobiscum." New Catholic Encyclopedia, 4:993.

HOWELL, Clifford. "Dominus vobiscum." Worship, 36 (1962): 462-465; reprinted in his Mean What You Say, pp. 23-28.

LECLERCQ, Henri. "Dominus vobiscum." Dictionnaire d'archéologie chrétienne et de liturgie, 4:1387.

MILNER, Paulinus. "Et cum Spiritu tuo." In Studies in Pastoral Liturgy, vol. 3, pp. 202-210. Edited by P. Murray. Dublin: Gill, 1967.

O'CONNELL, J. B. "Et cum Spiritu tuo." Priest, 22 (1966): 914-918.

VAN UNNIK, W. C. "Dominus vobiscum: The Background of a Liturgical Formula." In Studies in Memory of Th. W. Manson, pp. 270-305. Manchester, Eng.: Manchester University Press, 1959.

4. Penitential Rite

BEGHEYN, Paul. "Confession." Modern Liturgy, 7,8 (December 1980): 42.

Bishops' Committee on the Liturgy. "Penitential Rite: Form Three." Newsletter, 10,6-7 (June-July 1974).

BOUMAN, Walter R. "Confession-Absolution and the Eucharistic Liturgy." Lutheran Quarterly, 26 (1974): 204-220.

CALLEWAERT, Camillus. "'Confiteor' in missa et officio." In his Sacris Erudiri: fragmenta liturgica collecta, pp. 191-194. Steenbrugge: Abbatia S. Petri de Aldenburgo, 1940 (1962).

CROSS, F. L. "Confiteor." Oxford Dictionary of the Christian Church, p. 328.

DAVIES, David R. Down, Peacock's Feathers: Studies in the Contemporary Significance of the General Confession. Rev. ed. London: G. Bles; New York: Macmillan, 1961.

DOWNING, J. D. H. "Penitence at the Eucharist." Church Quarterly Review, 165 (1964): 209-218.

DUFRASNE, Dieudonne. "La 'préparation penitentielle' dans le nouveau missel des dimanches." Communautés et liturgies, 4 (1980): 296-319.

NOCENT, Adrien. "L'Acte penitentiel du nouvel 'Ordo missae': sacrement ou sacrementel?" Nouvelle revue théologique, 101 (1969): 956-971.

O'CALLAGHAN, Denis F. "The Confiteor-Indulgentiam and the Forgiveness of Sin." Irish Ecclesiastical Review, 106 (1966): 322-326.

5. Sunday Renewal of Baptism (Asperges)

CRICHTON, J. D. "Asperges." Dictionary of Liturgy and Worship, p. 42.

CROSS, F. L. "Asperges." Oxford Dictionary of the Christian Church, p. 95.

_____. "Vidi Aquam." Oxford Dictionary of the Christian Church, p. 1419.

GOEB, C. "The Asperges." Orate Fratres, 2 (1927-1928): 338-342.

KELLEHER, Margaret Mary. "The Rite of Sprinkling as an Invitation to Worship: The Church is a Community." Liturgy, 4, 1 (1981): 28-33.

LEFEVRE, Placide. "La bénédiction dominicale de l'eau, l'aspersion des fidèles et des lieux." Questions liturgiques et paroissiales, 51 (1970): 29-36.

6. Lord Have Mercy (Kyrie)

BISHOP, Edmund. "Kyrie Eleison: A Liturgical Consultation." In
his Liturgica Historica, pp. 116-136. Oxford: Clarendon Press,
1918.

CALLEWAERT, Camillus A. "Les étapes de l'histoire du Kyrie."
Revue d'histoire ecclésiastique, 38 (1942): 20-45.

CAPELLE, Bernard. "Le Kyrie de la messe et le Pape Gélase."
Revue bénédictine, 46 (1934): 126-144; reprinted in his Travaux liturgiques, vol. 2, pp. 116-134. Louvain: Centre liturgique, Abbaye du Mont César, 1962.

_____. "L'oeuvre liturgique de saint Gélase." Journal of Theo-
logical Studies, 52 (n.s. 2) (1951): 129-144; reprinted in his
Travaux liturgiques, vol. 2, pp. 146-160. Louvain: Centre
liturgique, Abbaye du Mont César, 1962.

_____. "Le Pape Gélase et la messe romaine." Revue d'histoire
écclésiastique, 35 (1939): 22-34; reprinted in his Travaux
liturgiques, vol. 2, pp. 135-145. Louvain: Centre liturgique,
Abbaye du Mont César, 1962.

CROSS, F. L. "Kyrie Eleison." Oxford Dictionary of the Christian
Church, p. 775.

GRISBROOKE, W. Jardine. "Kyrie." Dictionary of Liturgy and Worship, p. 209.

HOWELL, Clifford. "Kyrie Eleison." Worship, 36 (1962): 392-396;
reprinted in his Mean What You Say, pp. 17-22.

KELLY, C. "Kyrie Eleison." New Catholic Encyclopedia, 8:273-274.

MELNICKI, Margareta. Das einstimmige Kyrie des lateinischen Mittelalters. Regensburg: G. Bosse, 1955.

7. Glory to God (Gloria)

BAUMSTARK, Anton. "Die Textüberlieferung des Hymnus angelicus." In Hundert Jahre Markus-und-Weber-Verlag, pp. 83-87.
Bonn: Markus und Weber Verlag, 1909.

BLUME, Clemens. "Der Engelhymnus Gloria in Excelsis Deo: sein
Ursprung und seine Entwicklung." Stimmen aus Maria Laach,
73 (1907): 43-62.

BRINKTRINE, Johannes. "Zur Entstehung und Erklärung des Gloria
in Excelsis Deo." Römische Quartelschrift, 35 (1927): 303-315.

CAPELLE, Bernard. "Le texte du 'Gloria in Excelsis.'" Revue
d'histoire écclésiastique, 44 (1949): 439-457; reprinted in his
Travaux liturgiques, vol. 2, pp. 176-191. Louvain: Centre
liturgique, Abbaye du Mont César, 1962.

CROSS, F. L. "Gloria in Excelsis." Oxford Dictionary of the
Christian Church, p. 563.

FLUSSER, D. "Sanktus und Gloria." In Abraham unser Vater:
Festschrift für O. Michel, pp. 129-152. Edited by O. Betz et
al. Leiden: Brill, 1963.

KELLY, C. "Gloria in Excelsis Deo." New Catholic Encyclopedia,
6: 510-511.

LEBRETON, J. "La forme primitive du Gloria in excelsis: prière
au Fils ou prière au Père?" Recherches de science religieuse,
13 (1923): 322-329.

MARANGET, L. "Le Gloria in Excelsis." Cours et conférences des
semaines liturgiques, 6 (1927): 44.

MATEOS, Juan. "Le 'Gloria in Excelsis' de début des offices maronites." L'Orient Syrien, 12 (1967): 117-121.

PRADO, German. "Una nueva recension del himno 'Gloria in Excelsis.'" Ephemerides liturgicae, 46 (1932): 481-486.

STAPELMANN, W. Der Hymnus angelicus: Geschichte und Erklärung des Gloria. Heidelberg, 1948.

STEINHEIMER, M. Die doxa tou Theou in der römischen Liturgie.
Munich: Zink, 1951.

VERMEULEN, A. The Semantic Development of "Gloria" in Early
Christian Literature. Nijmegen: Dekker & Van de Vegt, 1956.

8. Opening Prayer, Collects

ASHWORTH, Henry. "Practical Commentaries on Some Prayers of
the Missal." In Studies in Pastoral Liturgy, vol. 2, pp. 74-
115. Edited by Vincent Ryan. Dublin: Gill, 1963.

BRUYLANTS, Placide. Les Oraisons du missel romain, texte et
histoire. 2 vols. EtL, 1. Louvain: Centre de documentation
et d'information liturgiques, 1952.

CAPELLE, Bernard. "Collecta." Revue bénédictine, 42 (1930):
197-204; reprinted in his Travaux liturgiques, vol. 2, pp. 192-
199. Louvain: Centre liturgique, Abbaye du Mont César, 1962.

_____. "Pour mieux comprendre les oraisons de missel." Cours et conférences des semaines liturgiques, 5 (1926): 135-145.

CAPPUYNS, M. "La portée religieuse des collects." Cours et conférences des semaines liturgiques, 6 (1928): 92-103.

CASEL, Odo. "Beiträge zu römischen Orationen." Jahrbuch für Liturgiewissenschaft, 11 (1931): 35-45.

COCHEZ, J. "La structure rhythmique des oraisons." Cours et conférences des semaines liturgiques, 6 (1928): 138-150.

CROSS, F. L. "Collect." Oxford Dictionary of the Christian Church, pp. 310-311.

DEARMER, Percy. The Art of Public Worship. London: Mowbray; Milwaukee, WI: Morehouse, 1919.

DEVEREAUX, James A. "The Primers and the Prayer Book Collects." Huntington Library Quarterly, 32 (1968): 29-44.

_____. "Reformed Doctrine in the Collects of the First Book of Common Prayer." Harvard Theological Review, 58 (1965): 49-68.

_____. "Translating the Orations of the Mass: Problems and Suggestions." American Ecclesiastical Review, 153 (1965): 399-410.

DUMAS, Antoine. "Les oraisons du nouveau missel romain." Questions liturgiques et paroissiales, 52 (1971): 263-270.

ELLEBRACHT, M. P. Remarks on the Vocabulary of the Ancient Orations in the Missale Romanum. (Latinitas Christianorum primaeva, 18). Nijmegen: Dekker & Van de Vegt, 1963.

GOULBOURN, Edward Meyrick. The Collects of the Day: An Exposition Critical and Devotional of the Collects appointed at the Communion, etc. 2 vols. London: Longmans, Green, 1897-1901.

GRISBROOKE, W. Jardine. "Collect." Dictionary of Liturgy and Worship, p. 139.

HAESSLY, Mary Gonzaga. Rhetoric in the Sunday Collects of the Roman Missal. St. Louis, MO: The Manufacturers Printery, 1938.

KIESLING, Christopher. Before His Majesty: A Study of the Spiritual Doctrine of the Sunday Orations of the Roman Missal. River Forest, IL: The Aquinas Library, 1965.

McMANUS, Frederick. "The Problem of the Roman Collect." American Ecclesiastical Review, 159 (1968): 270-275.

MITCHELL, Leonel L. "The Collects of the Proposed Book of Common Prayer." Worship, 52 (1978): 138-145.

PFLIEGER, A. Liturgicae orationis concordantia verbalia. Rome: Herder, 1964.

ROSE, André. "Les oraisons du Rotulus de Ravenne dans le nouveau missel romain." Questions liturgiques et paroissiales, 52 (1971): 271-292.

SALMON, Pierre. "Les protocoles des oraisons du missel romain." Ephemerides liturgicae, 45 (1931): 140-147.

SCHORLEMMER, Paul. Die Kollektengebete mit Texte, Ubersetzung und einem Glossar. Gütersloh: Bertelsmann, 1928.

SMET, S. de. "Les oraisons présidentielles." Questions liturgiques et paroissiales, 50 (1969): 223-234, 289-309.

STEPHENS-HODGE, L. E. H. The Collects, with the Litany and the Occasional Prayers: An Introduction and Commentary. London: Hodder & Stoughton, 1961.

STRODACH, Paul Zeller. The Collect for the Day. Philadelphia, PA: United Lutheran Publishing House, 1939.

WILLIS, G. G. "The Variable Prayers of the Roman Mass." In his Further Essays in Early Roman Liturgy, pp. 89-132. ACC, 50. London: SPCK, 1968.

C. LITURGY OF THE WORD

(See also The Bible in the Liturgy, p. 27; Lectionaries, p. 605.)

1. General Studies

ANTONSEN, Conrad. "The Liturgy of the Word." Pastoral Life, 24, 11 (December 1975): 14-18.

ASTING, Ragnar Kristian. Der Verkündigung des Wortes im Urchristentum. Stuttgart: Kohlhammer, 1939.

BARROIS, Georges. Scripture Readings in Orthodox Worship. Crestwood, NY: St. Vladimir's Seminary Press, 1977.

BAUER, Walter. Der Wortgottesdienst der ältesten Christen. SGVS, 148. Tübingen: Mohr, 1930.

BOUYER, Louis. "The Pauline Myst ery and Its Proclamation: From the Synagogal Service to the Missa Catechumenorum." In his Liturgical Piety, pp. 99-114. Notre Dame, IN: University of Notre Dame Press, 1955.

BURCHFIELD, Brian and Susan. "The Sunday Assembly as Gospel Event." Liturgy, 2,3 (Summer 1982): 9-13.

COLLINS, Patrick. "Establishing the Importance of What is Important: The Word." Pastoral Music, 1,4 (April-May 1977): 25-30; reprinted in Music in Catholic Worship: The NPM Commentary, pp. 111-117. Edited by Virgil C. Funk. Washington, DC: National Association of Pastoral Musicians, 1982.

CONSTANTELOS, Demetrios J. "The Holy Scriptures in Greek Orthodox Worship." The Greek Orthodox Theological Review, 12 (1966): 7-83.

CUNNINGHAM, Joseph. "Celebrating the Liturgy of the Word." In Celebrating the Word, pp. 75-86. Edited by James Schmeiser. Toronto, Ont.: Anglican Book Centre, 1977.

DALMAIS, Irénée-Henri. "Rites et prières accompagnant les lectures dans la liturgie eucharistique." In La Parole dans la liturgie, pp. 107-121. Paris: Cerf, 1970.

DEISS, Lucien. God's Word and God's People. Translated by Matthew J. O'Connell. Collegeville, MN: Liturgical Press, 1976.

DePRIEST, Ellis. "Music and the Liturgy of the Word." Pastoral Music, 6,3 (February-March 1982): 20-22.

GIBBARD, S. M. "Liturgy as Proclamation of the Word." Studia Liturgica, 1 (1962): 6-20.

GLAUE, Paul. Die Vorlesung der hl. Schriften im Gottesdienst, I: Bis zur Entstehung der altkatholischen Kirche. Berlin: Duncker, 1907.

GRISBROOKE, W. Jardine. "Synaxis." Dictionary of Liturgy and Worship, pp. 353-354.

HUCK, Gabe. "What is the Liturgy of the Word Supposed to Be?" Liturgy, 23,2 (March 1978): 19-21.

JOHNSON, Earl. "The Liturgy: Where Man is Confronted by God's Word." Liturgical Week Proceedings, 26 (1965): 174-179.

JUNGMANN, Josef Andreas. Wortgottesdienst im Licht von Theologie und Geschichte. 4. Aufl. Regensburg: Pustet, 1965; The

Liturgy of the Word. Translated by H. E. Winstone. London:
Burns & Oates, 1966.

KODELL, Jerome. "The Word in Christian Celebration." Liturgy,
2,3 (Summer 1982): 15-19.

LABIGNE, Jean. "L'eucharistie renouvelée par la liturgie de la
parole." La Maison-Dieu, 85 (1966): 155-167.

LEE, Charlotte I. Oral Reading of the Scriptures. Boston, MA:
Houghton Mifflin, 1974.

MACOMBER, William F. "The Liturgy of the Word according to the
Commentators of the Chaldean Mass." In The Word in the
World: Essays in Honor of Frederick L. Moriarty, pp. 179-190.
Edited by R. J. Clifford and G. MacRae. Cambridge, MA:
Weston College Press, 1973.

MARTIMORT, A.-G. et al. Parole de Dieu et liturgie. LO, 25.
Paris: Cerf, 1958; The Liturgy and the Word of God. Collegeville, MN: Liturgical Press, 1959.

_____. "Praesens adest in verbo suo." Acta congressus inter-
nationalis de theologia concilii Vaticani II, pp. 300-315. Vatican
City, 1968.

McBRIDE, Alfred. "The Understanding of Biblical Proclamation."
Liturgical Week Proceedings, 27 (1966): 129-131.

McNALLY, Robert E. "The Word of God and the Mystery of Christ."
Worship, 38 (1964): 392-401.

MILNER, Paulinus. "The Purpose and Structure of the Liturgy of
the Word." In The Ministry of the Word, pp. 11-26. London:
Burns & Oates, 1967.

La Parole dans la liturgie. Semaine liturgique de l'Institut Saint-
Serge. LO, 48. Paris: Cerf, 1970.

ROGUET, A.-M. "La présence active du Christ dans la Parole de
Dieu." La Maison-Dieu, 82 (1965): 8-28.

_____. "Lectures bibliques et mystère du salut." La Maison-
Dieu, 99 (1969): 2-27.

SCHLIER, Heinrich. "Die Verkündigung im Gottesdienst der Kirche."
In his Die Zeit der Kirche: Exegetische Aufsätze und Vorträge, pp. 244-265. 5. Aufl. Freiburg: Herder, 1972.

URNER, Hans. Die ausserbiblische Lesung im christlichen Gottesdienst: ihre Vorgeschichte und Geschichte bis zur Zeit

Augustins. VEGL, 6. Göttingen: Vandenhoeck & Ruprecht, 1952.

WICKER, Brian. "The Ministry of the Word." In The Mass and the People of God, pp. 84-95. Edited by J. D. Crichton. London: Burns & Oates, 1966.

_____. "The Ministry of the Word." New Blackfriars, 47 (1965): 61-67.

2. Old Testament Lesson

GUILLAUME, Paul-Marie. "The Reason for an Old Testament Lesson." In The New Liturgy, pp. 59-72. Edited by Lancelot Sheppard. London: Darton, Longman & Todd, 1970.

LIGHTBOURN, F. "Getting the Old Testament into the Liturgy." Anglican Theological Review, 43 (1961): 370-374.

NEWNS, Brian. "Lesson." Dictionary of Liturgy and Worship, pp. 214-215.

RAHLFS, Alfred. Die alttestamentlichen Lektionen der griechischen Kirche. Berlin: Weidmannsche Buchhandlung, 1915.

3. Psalm (Gradual, Tract)

(See also XL. B. Psalter.)

BATTEAUX, Jean. "Le psaume graduel." La Maison-Dieu, 99 (1969): 62-76.

BUGNINI, A. "Salmo responsoriale: recita o canto?" Notitiae, 102 (February 1975): 59-60; English translation in Bishops' Committee on the Liturgy Newsletter, 12 (April 1976): 15.

CROSS, F. L. "Gradual." Oxford Dictionary of the Christian Church, pp. 577-578.

_____. "Tract (Liturgical)." Oxford Dictionary of the Christian Church, pp. 1368-1369.

DEISS, Lucien. "The Gradual Psalm." In The New Liturgy, pp. 73-91. Edited by Lancelot Sheppard. London: Darton, Longman & Todd, 1970.

HOWELL, Clifford. "The Chants between the Readings." The Clergy Review, 52,2 (February 1967): 124-127.

HUGLO, M. "Gradual." New Catholic Encyclopedia, 6:685-687.

_____. "Tract." New Catholic Encyclopedia, 14:221-222.

KENNY, Colum. "Singing the Responsory." Worship, 38 (1964):
    169-173.

NEWNS, Brian. "Problems of the Liturgical Renewal: The Respon-
    sorial Psalm." The Clergy Review, 62,6 (June 1977): 247-251.

PALACHKOVSKY, V. "Les 'pneumatica' des antiphones graduelles."
    Ephemerides liturgicae, 90 (1976): 417-424.

SHEPHERD, Massey H. "Responsorial Psalmody: The Gradual."
    In his The Psalms in Christian Worship: A Practical Guide,
    pp. 36-39. Minneapolis, MN: Augsburg, 1976.

THOMPSON, Mikkel. "The Presence of Christ in the Word." Litur-
    gy, 2,3 (Summer 1982): 57-61.

THOMPSON, Robert J. "A New Musical Form." Liturgy, 2,3
    (Summer 1982): 37-41.

4. Epistle Reading

CROSS, F. L. "Epistle." Oxford Dictionary of the Christian
    Church, pp. 458-459.

FRERE, Walter H. Studies in the Early Roman Liturgy, vol. 3:
    The Roman Epistle-Lectionary. ACC, 32. London: Oxford
    University Press, 1935.

GODU, G. "Epîtres." Dictionnaire d'archeologie chretienne et de
    liturgie, 5:245-344.

NEWNS, Brian. "Epistle." Dictionary of Liturgy and Worship, pp.
    171-172.

ROUSSEAU, Oliver. "Lecture et présence de l'Apôtre à la liturgie
    de la messe." La Maison-Dieu, 62 (1960): 69-78.

5. Gospel Acclamation (Alleluia), Sequence

BLANCHARD, P. "Le correspondance apocryphe du pape S. Dam-
    ase et de S. Jerome sur le psautier et le chant de l'alleluia."
    Ephemerides liturgicae, 63 (1949): 376-388.

BROU, L. "L'alleluia dans la liturgie mozarabe." Annuario musical,
    6 (1951): 3-90.

CABROL, Fernand. "Alleluia." Dictionnaire d'archéologie chrétienne et de liturgie, 1:1226-1246.

CALLEWAERT, Camillus. "L'oeuvre liturgique de S. Grégoire:
La Septuagésime et l'alleluia." In his Sacris Erudiri: frag-
menta liturgica collecta, pp. 635-653. Steenbrugge: Abbatia
S. Petri de Aldenburgo, 1940.

CROSS, F. L. "Alleluia." Oxford Dictionary of the Christian
Church, p. 37.

_____. "Alleluyatic Sequence." Oxford Dictionary of the Chris-
tian Church, pp. 37-38.

_____. "Sequence." Oxford Dictionary of the Christian Church,
p. 1241.

DEISS, Lucien. "The Alleluia or the Processional for the Gospel."
In The New Liturgy, pp. 91-102. Edited by Lancelot Sheppard.
London: Darton, Longman & Todd, 1970.

DURST, L. "Sequence." New Catholic Encyclopedia, 17:603.

EIZENHOFER, Alfons. "Der allelujagesang vor dem Evangelium."
Ephemerides liturgicae, 45 (1931): 374-382.

ENGBERDING, H. "Alleluia." Reallexikon für Antike und Christentum, 1:293-299.

FROGER, J. "L'alleluia dans l'usage romaine et la réforme de saint
Grégoire." Ephemerides liturgicae, 62 (1948): 6-48.

GLIBOTIC, Ioannes. "De cantu alleluia in partibus saeculo VII
antiquioribus." Ephemerides liturgicae, 50 (1936): 99-123.

HOWELL, Clifford. "Before the Gospel." Worship, 36 (1962):
574-578; reprinted in his Mean What You Say, pp. 35-40.
Collegeville, MN: Liturgical Press, 1965.

LEAHY, E. "Sequence." New Catholic Encyclopedia, 13:100-104.

MARTIMORT, Aimée-Georges. "Origine et signification de l'alleluia
de la messe romaine." In Kyriakon: Festschrift Johannes
Quasten, vol. 2, pp. 811-834. Edited by Patrick Granfield
and Josef A. Jungmann. Münster: Aschendorff, 1970.

RODIMER, Frank J. "... And Alleluia is Our Song." Pastoral
Music, 4,5 (June-July 1980): 63-64.

STABLEIN, B. "Alleluia." In Die Musik in Geschichte und Gegenwart, vol. 1, pp. 331-350. Kasel and Basel: Bärenreiter, 1951.

THOMPSON, Mikkel. "The Presence of Christ in the Word." Liturgy, 2,3 (Summer 1982): 57-61.

WAGNER, Peter. "Alleluia." Dictionnaire d'archéologie chrétienne et de liturgie, 1:1226-1229.

WEAKLAND, Rembert G. "Alleluia." New Catholic Encyclopedia, 1:321-323.

WELLESZ, Egon. "Gregory the Great's Letter on the Alleluia." Annales musicologiques, 2 (1954): 1-26.

6. Gospel Reading

CROSS, F. L. "Gospel (in the Liturgy)." Oxford Dictionary of the Christian Church, p. 574.

GODU, G. "Evangiles." Dictionnaire d'archéologie chrétienne et de liturgie, 5:852-923.

NEWNS, Brian. "Gospel." Dictionary of Liturgy and Worship, p. 190.

7. Sermon, Homily

(See XXXVII--Liturgical Preaching, p. 566.)

8. Profession of Faith (Creed)

CAPELLE, Bernard. "Alcuin et l'histoire du symbole de la messe." Recherches de théologie ancienne et médiévale, 6 (1934): 249-260; reprinted in his Travaux liturgiques, vol. 2, pp. 211-221. Louvain: Centre liturgique, Abbaye du Mont César, 1962.

_____. "Le Credo." Cours et conférences des semaines liturgiques, 6 (1928): 171-184.

_____. "Le symbole de la messe est-il celui de Constantinople?" Questions liturgiques et paroissiales, 13 (1928): 65-73; reprinted in his Travaux liturgiques, vol. 2, pp. 204-210. Louvain: Centre liturgique, Abbaye du Mont César, 1962.

_____. "L'introduction du symbole à la messe." In Mélanges Joseph de Ghellinck, vol. 2, pp. 1003-1027. Gembloux: Duculot, 1951; reprinted in his Travaux liturgiques, vol. 3, pp. 60-81. Louvain: Centre liturgique, Abbaye du Mont César, 1967.

_____. "L'origine antiadoptioniste de notre texte du symbole de
la messe." Recherches de théologie ancienne et médiévale, 1
(1929): 7-10; reprinted in his Travaux liturgiques, vol. 3,
pp. 47-59. Louvain: Centre liturgique, Abbaye du Mont
César, 1967.

CAPIEU, Henri. "La confession de foi dans le culte réformé." La
Maison-Dieu, 134 (1978): 37-42.

CORNET, Léon. "Confesser la foi durant la célébration liturgique?
Les avatars d'une credo." Communautés et liturgies, 2 (1980):
93-112.

CROSS, F. L. "Nicene Creed." Oxford Dictionary of the Christian
Church, p. 952.

CULLMANN, Oscar. Les premières confessions de foi chrétiennes.
2. éd. CRHPR, 30. Paris: Presses universitaires de France,
1948; The Earliest Christian Confessions. Translated by
J. K. S. Reid. London: Lutterworth Press, 1949.

DALMAIS, Irénée-Henri. "Symbole et confession de la foi dans les
églises orientales." La Maison-Dieu, 134 (1978): 31-36.

DURST, L. "Profession of Faith (The Creed)." New Catholic Encyclopedia, 17:542.

HAMMAN, André. "Du symbole de la foi à l'anaphore eucharistique." In Kyriakon: Festschrift Johannes Quasten, vol. 2,
pp. 835-843. Edited by Patrick Granfield and Joseph A. Jungmann. Münster: Aschendorff, 1970.

HUCKE, H. "Credo." New Catholic Encyclopedia, 4:431-432.

KELLY, J. N. D. Early Christian Creeds. 3d ed. London: Longmans; New York: McKay, 1972.

MURPHY, F. X. "Creed." New Catholic Encyclopedia, 4:432-438.

RICHARDSON, Alan. "Creed, Creeds." Dictionary of Liturgy and
Worship, p. 156.

RORDORF, Willy. "La confession de foi et son 'Sitz im Leben' dans
l'Eglise ancienne." Novum Testamentum, 9 (1967): 225-238.

RYAN, T. "Nicene Creed." New Catholic Encyclopedia, 10:437-438.

9. General Intercessions

(See also IX. T--Prône, pp. 228-230.)

Bishops' Committee on the Liturgy. General Intercessions. Wash-
    ington, DC: USCC Publications Office, 1979; reprinted in BCL
    Newsletter 1976-1980.

BORELLA, P. "L'oratio super sindonem." Ambrosius, 34 (1958):
    173-176.

CAPPUYNS, M. "Les 'orationes solemnes' du vendredi saint."
    Questions liturgiques et paroissiales, 23 (1938): 18-31.

CHAVASSE, Antoine. "L'oraison 'super sindonem' dans la liturgie
    romaine." Revue bénédictine, 70 (1960): 313-323.

CLERCK, Paul de. La "prière universelle" dans les liturgies latines
    anciennes: témoignages patristiques et testes liturgiques.
    LQF, 62. Münster: Aschendorff, 1977.

CONNOLLY, H. "Liturgical Prayers of Intercession." Journal of
    Theological Studies, 21 (1920): 219-232.

COXE, H. Forms of Bidding Prayer with Introduction and Notes.
    Oxford: J. H. Parker; London: J. G. F. and J. Rivington,
    1840.

DENIS, Henri. "La prière universelle." La Maison-Dieu, 84 (1965):
    140-165.

GRISBROOKE, W. Jardine. "Intercessions at the Eucharist, I:
    The Intercession at the Synaxis." Studia Liturgica, 4, 3 (Au-
    tumn 1965): 129-155.

GY, Pierre-Marie. "Fonctionnement et signification de la prière uni-
    verselle en occident." La Maison-Dieu, 129 (1977): 148-152.

HOVDA, Robert. "The Prayer of General Intercession." Worship,
    44 (1970): 497-502.

KLAUSER, Theodore. "The Decline of the Prayer of the Faithful."
    In his A Short History of the Western Liturgy, pp. 47-54.
    New York: Oxford University Press, 1969.

O'CONNELL, J. B. "The Bidding Prayer." The Clergy Review, 50
    (1965): 685-690.

_____. "The Bidding Prayer." Priest, 21 (1965): 861-864.

_____. "The Prayer of the Faithful." Priest, 22 (1966): 409-412.

RICHSTATTER, Thomas. "General Intercessions." New Catholic
    Encyclopedia, 17:241.

SHAUGHNESSY, James D. "The Common Prayer--Prayer of the
    Faithful." Homiletic and Pastoral Review, 66 (1965): 55-58.

VASEY, Michael. Intercession in Worship. GBMW, 77. Bramcote,
    Eng.: Grove Books, 1981.

VEYS, Michel. "Note sur la prière universelle." Paroisse et litur-
    gie, 52 (1970): 511-516.

WHITAKER, E. C. "Bidding Prayer." Dictionary of Liturgy and
    Worship, p. 76.

_____. The Intercessions of the Prayer Book. London: SPCK,
    1956.

D. THE EUCHARISTIC LITURGY: PREPARATORY RITES

1. Preparation of the Gifts and Altar (Offertory)

BEAUDUIN, L. "L'offertoire, jadis et aujourd'hui." Questions lit-
    urgiques et paroissiales, 6 (1921): 30-45.

BRYCE, Glendon E. "Gifts and the Rite of Counter-Gifts." Litur-
    gy, 21,10 (December 1976): 312-315.

BUCHANAN, Colin O. The End of the Offertory: An Anglican
    Study. GLS, 14. Bramcote, Eng.: Grove Books, 1979.

CABROL, Fernand. "Offertoire." Dictionnaire d'archéologie chréti-
    enne et de liturgie, 12:1946-1962.

CALLEWAERT, Camille. "De offerenda et oblatione in missa."
    Periodica de re morali, canonica, liturgica, 33 (1944): 61-91.

CAPELLE, Bernard. "L'offertoire." Questions liturgiques et
    paroissiales, 17 (1932): 57-67.

CLARK, A. C. "Offertory." New Catholic Encyclopedia, 10:649-
    651.

_____. "The Function of the Offertory Rite in the Mass."
    Ephemerides liturgicae, 64 (1950): 309-344.

_____. "The Offertory Rite: A Recent Study." Ephermides
    liturgicae, 67 (1953): 242-247.

CLIFFORD, Elizabeth Ann. "The Rite of Preparation." Today's
    Parish, 7,8 (November-December 1975): 22.

COBB, Gerald T. "Preparing." Modern Liturgy, 7,8 (December 1980): 43.

COPPENS, J. "Les prières de l'offertoire." Cours et conférences des semaines liturgiques, 6 (1927): 185-196.

CROSS, F. L. "Offertory." Oxford Dictionary of the Christian Church, p. 978.

DANZE, Willy. "Des mots à échelle du vent: prières d'offrande." Paroisse et liturgie, 55 (1973): 54-60.

DUBA, Arlo D. "Gift Giving as Human and Liturgical Symbols." Liturgy, 21,10 (December 1976): 293-296.

_____. "Gifts in Worship: God's and Ours." Liturgy, 21,10 (December 1976): 297-299.

HESS, Charles. "Offering of the Faithful at Mass." Homiletic and Pastoral Review, 67 (1967): 382-384.

HOWELL, Clifford. "The Offertory." The Clergy Review, 52 (1967): 467-471.

KEIFER, Ralph. "Preparation of the Altar and the Gifts or Offertory?" Worship, 48 (1974): 595-600.

KENNEDY, V. L. "The Offertory Rite." Orate Fratres, 12 (1937-1938): 193-198.

LEBLANC, Paul J. "Preparation of Altar and Gifts: A Review." Liturgy, 21,10 (Decemberd 1976): 308-311.

LEGG, J. Wickham. "A Comparative Study of the Time in the Christian Liturgy at which the Elements Are Prepared and Set on the Holy Table." In his Ecclesiological Essays. LLE, 7. London: Moring, 1905.

MILLER, Charles E. "Explaining the New Offertory Rite." Homiletic and Pastoral Review, 69 (1969): 924-927.

NEWNS, Brian. "The New Ordo Missae: The Offertory." The Clergy Review, 55 (1970): 213-219.

PHELAN, Thomas. "Offertory." Dictionary of Liturgy and Worship, pp. 282-284.

PURSCH, K. "Die Probleme des Offertoriums und Versuche ihrer Lösung." International Kirchliche Zeitschrift, 46 (1956): 1-27, 105-130.

RASMUSSEN, Niels K. "Les rites de présentation du pain et du
vin." La Maison-Dieu, 100 (1969): 44-58.

SALMON, Pierre. "Les prières et les rites de l'offertoire de la
messe dans la liturgie romaine au XIIIe au XIVe siècles."
Ephemerides liturgicae, 43 (1929): 508-519.

SHAUGHNESSY, James D. "The Key to the Offertory." Homiletic
and Pastoral Review, 66 (1966): 411-413, 428.

WILLIS, G. G. "The Offertory Prayers and the Canon of the
Mass." In his Essays in the Early Roman Liturgy, pp. 107-110.
ACC, 46. London: SPCK, 1964.

2. Presentation of the Gifts (Offertory)

BOOTH, G. J. The Offertory Procession in the Ordo Romanus
Primus: A Study of Its Bearing on the So-Called "Offertory
Procession". SST, 2d ser., 13. Washington, DC: Catholic
University of America Press, 1948.

BUCKLEY, J. C. "Money and the Offertory." In The Mass and
the People of God, pp. 96-107. Edited by J. D. Crichton.
London: Burns & Oates, 1966.

CAPELLE, Bernard. "Quête et offertoire." La Maison-Dieu, 24
(1950): 121-138; reprinted in his Travaux liturgiques, vol. 2,
pp. 221-235. Louvain: Centre liturgique, Abbaye du Mont
César, 1962.

CLOUD, Duncan. "The Theology of the Offertory Collection: An
Historical Analysis with Some Practical Conclusions." In The
Mass and the People of God, pp. 108-121. Edited by J. D.
Crichton. London: Burns & Oates, 1966.

CONNOLLY, James. "The Collection: From Principles to Practice."
Homiletic and Pastoral Review, 71 (1971): 51-59.

COPPENS, J. "L'offrande des fidèles dans la liturgie eucharistique
ancienne." Cours et conférences des semaines liturgiques, 6
(1927): 99-123.

TAFT, Robert F. The Great Entrance: A History of the Transfer
of Gifts and Other Preanaphoral Rites of the Liturgy of St.
John Chrysostom. OCA, 200. Rome: Pontificium Institutum
Studiorum Orientalium, 1975.

_____. "Towards the Origins of the Offertory Procession in the
Syro-Byzantine East." Orientalia Christiana Periodica, 36
(1970): 73-107.

3. Offertory Song

BRINKTRINE, Johannes. "De origine offertorii in missa romana."
Ephemerides liturgicae, 40 (1926): 15-20.

HUGLO, M. "Offertory Antiphon." New Catholic Encyclopedia,
10:651-652.

KEIFER, Ralph A. "When You're Choosing Offertory Songs, Don't
Choose Songs of Offering." Pastoral Music, 1,1 (October-
November 1977): 11-15.

SHEPHERD, Massey H. "Antiphonal Psalmody: The Introit, Offertory, and Communion." In his The Psalms in Christian Worship:
A Practical Guide, pp. 40-43. Minneapolis, MN: Augsburg,
1976.

4. Mixing of Water and Wine

CROSS, F. L. "Mixed Chalice." Oxford Dictionary of the Christian
Church, p. 909.

DAVIES, J. G. "Mixed Chalice." Dictionary of Liturgy and Worship,
pp. 274-275.

5. Washing of the Hands (Lavabo)

DAVIES, J. G. "Lavabo." Dictionary of Liturgy and Worship, p.
210.

ROGUET, A.-M. "Purifications à la messe et désacralisation." La
Maison-Dieu, 103 (1970): 61-72.

6. Prayer over the Gifts (Secret)
and Invitation

CROSS, F. L. "Orate, Fratres." Oxford Dictionary of the Christian Church, p. 985.

_____. "Secret." Oxford Dictionary of the Christian Church,
p. 1235.

GRISBROOKE, W. Jardine. "Super oblata." Dictionary of Liturgy
and Worship, pp. 352-353.

O'SHEA, William J. "Secret Prayer." New Catholic Encyclopedia,
13:27.

RAFFA, V.   Commento alle orazioni sulle offerte.   Milan: Opera
della Regalita, 1965.

WILMART, A.   "Une curieuse expression pour désigner l'oraison
sécrète."   Bulletin de litterature écclésiastique, 26 (1925):
94-103.

E.   EUCHARISTIC PRAYER

1.   General Studies

(See entries for eucharistic prayers in the historical traditions
sections.)

GRISBROOKE, W. Jardine.   "Anaphora."   Dictionary of Liturgy and
Worship, pp. 10-17.

MORETON, M.   "The Anaphoral Prayer."   Church Quarterly Review,
168 (1967):   45-52.

POCKNEE, Cyril E.   "The Eucharistic Prayer."   Church Quarterly
Review, 169 (1968):   33-43.

2.   Preface

ASHWORTH, Henry.   "The New Prefaces."   The Clergy Review, 53
(1968):   839-860.

AVERY, Raymond.   "A Preview of the New Prefaces."   Worship, 42
(1968):   514-531, 587-608.

BOUMAN, C. A.   "Variants in the Introduction to the Eucharistic
Prayer."   Vigiliae Christianae, 4 (1950):   94-115.

BOUYER, Louis.   Eucharist: Theology and Spirituality of the
Eucharistic Prayer, pp. 227-230.   Notre Dame, IN: University
of Notre Dame Press, 1968.

_____.   "Le préface et le sanctus."   La Maison-Dieu, 87 (1966):
97-110.

BRUYLANTS, Placide.   "Les préfaces du missel romain."   La
Maison-Dieu, 87 (1966):   111-133.

BUGNINI, Annibale.   "Praefari = Praefatio."   Ephemerides liturgicae,
67 (1953):   247-249.

CAGIN, P.   "Les noms latins de la préface eucharistique."   Rassegna
gregoriana, 5 (1906):   321-358.

CAPELLE, Bernard. "Problèmes textuels de la préface romaine." In Mélanges Jules Lebreton, vol. 2, pp. 139-150. RSR, 40. 1952.

CROSS, F. L. "Preface." Oxford Dictionary of the Christian Church, p. 1100.

DEKKERS, Antoine. "Propheteia--Praefatio." In Mélanges offerts à Chr. Mohrmann, pp. 190-195. Utrecht: Spectrum, 1963.

DUMAS, Antoine. "Les nouvelles préfaces du missel romain." La Maison-Dieu, 94 (1968): 159-164.

"Eucharistic Prayers and Prefaces: Texts, Melodies, and Translator's Notes." National Bulletin on Liturgy, 3,25 (November 1968).

GRABNER, D. "Preface." New Catholic Encyclopedia, 17:532-533.

JUNGMANN, Josef A. "Praefatio und stiller Kanon." Zeitschrift für katholische Theologie, 53 (1929): 66-94, 247-271.

LHOIR, José. "Rendons grâce au Seigneur notre Dieu: L'importance et les lois de la préface." Paroisse et liturgie, 50 (1968): 215-225.

MOHRMANN, Christine. "Sur l'histoire de praefari-praefatio." Vigiliae Christianae, 7 (1953): 1-15.

MUNOZ, H., and ISAGUIRRE, R. Le misal de Pablo VI: Commentario espiritual y pastoral a los prefacios. Buenos Aires: Claretiana, 1977.

O'CONNELL, J. B. "The Angels of the Preface." Priest, 16 (1960): 530-535.

ROSE, André. "The New Prefaces." In The New Liturgy, pp. 244-258. Edited by Lancelot Sheppard. London: Darton, Longman & Todd, 1970.

SCHNITZLER, Theodore. "Die drei neuen eucharistischen Hochgebete und die neuen Präfationem." In Verkündigung und Betrachtung. Freiburg: Herder, 1968.

SOUBIGOU, L. A Commentary on the Prefaces and the Eucharistic Prayers of the Roman Missal, pp. 3-243. Collegeville, MN: Liturgical Press, 1971.

3. Holy, Holy, Holy (Sanctus)

BAUMSTARK, Anton. "Trishagion und Qeduscha." Jahrbuch für
    Liturgiewissenschaft, 3 (1923): 18-32.

BOTTE, Bernard. "A propos de virgules." La Maison-Dieu, 30
    (1952): 156-161.

BOUYER, Louis. "Le préface et le sanctus." La Maison-Dieu, 87
    (1966): 97-110.

CROSS, F. L. "Benedictus qui venit." Oxford Dictionary of the
    Christian Church, p. 156.

_____. "Sanctus." Oxford Dictionary of the Christian Church,
    p. 1213.

FLUSSER, D. "Sanktus und Gloria." In Abraham unser Vater:
    Festschrift O. Michel, pp. 129-152. Edited by O. Betz et al.
    Leiden: Brill, 1963.

GRISBROOKE, W. Jardine. "Trisagion." Dictionary of Liturgy and
    Worship, p. 358.

GY, Pierre-Marie. "Le sanctus romain et les anaphores orientales."
    In Mélanges liturgiques offerts au R. P. Dom Bernard Botte,
    O.S.B., pp. 167-174. Louvain: Abbaye du Mont César, 1972.

JOHN OF DAMASCUS. "Epistola de hymno Trisagio." In Die Schrif-
    ten de Johannes von Damaskos, Bd. 4, pp. 289-332. Edited by
    Bonifatius Kotter. PTS, 22. Berlin: De Gruyter, 1981.

LEVY, K. "The Byzantine Sanctus and Its Modal Tradition in East
    and West." Annales musicologiques, 6 (1963): 7-67.

MASTERMAN, M. R. E. "Hosanna." New Catholic Encyclopedia,
    7:153.

McILHAGGA, Donald. "Hosanna: Supplication and Acclamation."
    Studia Liturgica, 5,3 (Autumn 1966): 129-150.

RATCLIFF, E. C. "The Sanctus and the Pattern of the Early
    Anaphora." Journal of Ecclesiastical History, 1 (1950): 29-36,
    125-134; reprinted in his Liturgical Studies, pp. 18-40. Edited
    by A. H. Couratin and D. H. Tripp. London: SPCK, 1976.

SPINKS, Bryan D. "The Jewish Sources for the Sanctus." Hey-
    throp Journal, 21 (1980): 168-179.

VAN UNNIK, W. C. "I Clem. 34 and the 'Sanctus.'" Virgiliae
    Christianae, 5 (1951): 204-248.

WERNER, Eric. "The Genesis of the Liturgical Sanctus." In Essays Presented to Egon Wellesz, pp. 19-32. Edited by J. Westrup. Oxford: Clarendon Press, 1966.

4. Eucharistic Consecration and Manual Acts--General Studies

BOWMER, John C. "The Manual Acts in the Communion Office." London Quarterly and Holborn Review, 170, 4 (October 1945): 392-398; American revision, Religion in Life, 28 (1958-1959): 119-126.

CALCOTE, A. D. Word and Spirit: The Prayer of Consecration in Anglican Thought and Practice 1604-1740. S.T.M. thesis, General Theological Seminary, New York, 1963.

KAWERAU, Gustav. "Uber die liturgische Gestaltung der 'Konsekration' in der lutherischen Abendmahlsfeier." Theologische Studien und Kritiken, 69 (1896): 356-369.

MICHELL, Gilbert Arthur. Eucharistic Consecration in the Primitive Church. London: SPCK, 1948.

_____. "Firmilian and Eucharistic Consecration." Journal of Theological Studies, N.S. 5 (1954): 215-220.

RATCLIFF, E. C. "The English Usage of Eucharistic Consecration, 1548-1662." Theology, 60 (1957): 229-236, 273-280; reprinted in his Liturgical Studies of E. C. Ratcliff, pp. 203-221. Edited by A. H. Couratin and D. J. Tripp. London: SPCK, 1976.

5. Epiclesis

ADAMS, Ramond A. "The Holy Spirit and the Real Presence." Theological Studies, 29 (1968): 37-51.

ALBERTINE, R. "Selected Moments in the History of the Epiclesis in Anglican Liturgy." Ephemerides liturgicae, 92 (1978): 420-439.

ATCHLEY, E. G. C. F. On the Epiclesis of the Eucharistic Liturgy and in the Consecration of the Font. ACC. London: Oxford University Press, 1935.

BOTTE, Bernard. "L'épiclèse dans les liturgies syriennes orientales." Sacris erudiri, 6 (1954): 48-72.

_____. "L'épiclèse de l'anaphore d'Hippolyte." Recherches de théologie ancienne et médiévale, 14 (1947): 241-251.

BRINKTRINE, Johannes. De epiclesis eucharisticae origine. Rome,
     1923.

_____. "Zur Entstehung der morgenländischen Epiklese." Zeit-
     schrift für katholische Theologie, 42 (1918):   301-326, 483-518.

BUCHWALD, R. Die Epiklese in der römischen Messe. Weidenauer
     Studien, 1 (special printing). Vienna, 1907.

BURMESTER, O. "A Comparative Study of the Form of the Words
     of Institution and the Epiclesis in the Anaphorae of the Ethiopic
     Church." The Eastern Churches Quarterly, 13 (1959):   13-42.

_____. "The Epiclesis in the Eastern Church and the 'Heavenly
     Altar' of the Roman Canon." In Tome commémoratif du millén-
     aire de la Bibliothèque Patriarcale d'Alexandrie, pp. 277-296.
     Alexandria, 1953.

CABROL, Fernand. "Epiclèse." Dictionnaire d'archéologie chréti-
     enne et de liturgie, 5:142-184.

CALLEWAERT, Camille. "Histoire positive du canon romain: une
     épiclèse à Rome." Sacris erudiri, 2 (1949):   95-110.

CASEL, Odo. "Neue Beiträge zur Epiklesenfrage." Jahrbuch für
     Liturgiewissenschaft, 4 (1924):   169-178.

_____. "Zur Epiklese." Jahrbuch für Liturgiewissenschaft, 3
     (1923):   100-102.

CHAVASSE, Antoine. "L'épiclèse eucharistique dans les anciennes
     liturgies orientales: une hypothèse d'interprétation." Mélanges
     de science religieuse, 2 (1946):   197-206.

CODRINGTON, H. W. "The Heavenly Altar and the Epiclesis in
     Egypt." Journal of Theological Studies, 39 (1938):   141-150.

CONNOLLY, R. H. "The Meaning of epiklesis: A Reply." Journal
     of Theological Studies, 25 (1923-1924):   337-364.
     --Reply to X. TYRER, below (page 269).

CREHAN, Joseph H. "Eucharistic Epiclesis: New Evidence and a
     New Theory." Theological Studies, 41 (1980):   698-712.

CROSS, F. L. "Epiclesis." Oxford Dictionary of the Christian
     Church, p. 456.

DALMAIS, Irénée-Henri. "L'Esprit-Saint et le mystère de salut
     dans les épiclèses eucharistiques syriennes." Ephemerides litur-
     gicae, 90 (1976):   262-271.

DANZE, Willy. "Vienne ton Saint Esprit sur ces dons ... L'épiclèse hier et aujourd'hui." Communautés et liturgies, 5 (1980): 364-390.

DINESSEN, P. "Die Epiklese im Rahmen altkirchlicher Liturgien." Studia theologica, 16 (1962): 42-107.

DIX, Gregory. "The Origins of the Epiclesis." Theology, 28 (1936): 125-137, 187-202.

FISCHER, Balthasar. "Eine ausdrückliche Geistepiklese im bisherigen Missale Romanum." In Mélanges liturgiques offerts au R. P. Dom Bernard Botte, O. S. B., pp. 139-149. Louvain: Abbaye du Mont César, 1962.

HEBERT, Arthur Gabriel. The Meaning of the Epiclesis. London: SPCK, 1933.

HOLLER, Joseph. Die epiklese der griechisch-orientalischen Liturgien: ein Beitrag zur Lösung der Epiklesisfrage. SMKS, 9. Wien: Mayer, 1912.

HOPPE, Ludwig A. Die Epiklesis der griechischen und orientalischen Liturgien und der römische Consekrationskanon. Schaffhausen: F. Hurtersche Buchhandlung, 1864.

JONG, J. P. de. "La connexion entre le rite de la consignation et l'épiclèse dans saint Ephrem." In Studia Patristica, vol. 2, pp. 29-37. Edited by Kurt Aland and F. L. Cross. TUGAL, 64. Berlin: Akademie-Verlag, 1957.

_____. "Epiklese." Lexikon für Theologie und Kirche, pp. 933-937.

_____. "Der ursprungliche Sinn von Epiklese und Mischungsritus nach der Eucharistielehre des heiligen Irenäus." Archiv für Liturgiewissenschaft, 9 (1965): 28-47.

JUGIE, Martin. De forma eucharisticae: de epiclesibus eucharisticis. Rome: Officium Libri Catholici, 1943.

KERN, Cyprien. "En marge de l'epiclèse." Irénikon, 24 (1951): 166-194.

KERN, Cyprien, and CODRINGTON, H. W. "The Epiclesis." Eastern Churches Quarterly, 9 (1951-1952): 198-205.

Kirchlichen Aussenamt der Evangelischen Kirche in Deutschland. Die Anrufung des Heiligen Geistes im Abendmahl. Viertes theologisches Gespräch zwischen dem Okumenischen Patriarchat und der Evangelischen Kirche in Deutschland von 6. bis 9. Oktober

1975 in der Evangelischen Sozialakademie Friedewald. BOR, 31.
Frankfurt: Lembeck, 1977.

LAAGER, J. "Epiklesis." Reallexikon für Antike und Christentum,
5:577-599.

L'HUILLIER, P. "Théologie de l'epiclèse." Verbum Caro, 14
(1960): 307-327.

MALONEY, G. A. "Epiclesis." New Catholic Encyclopedia, 5:464-
466.

McKENNA, John H. "Epiclesis." New Catholic Encyclopedia, 16:
154-156.

_____. Eucharist and Holy Spirit: The Eucharistic Epiclesis in
Twentieth Century Theology (1900-1966). ACC, 57. Great
Wakering, Eng.: Published for the Alcuin Club by Mayhew-
McCrimmon, 1975.

_____. "Eucharistic Epiclesis: Myopia or Microcosm?" Theologi-
cal Studies, 36 (1975): 265-284.

_____. "The Eucharistic Epiclesis in Twentieth Century Theology
(1900-1966)." Ephemerides liturgicae, 90 (1976): 289-328.

MERCER, S. A. B. "The Epiclesis in the Ethiopic Liturgy." In
Oriental Studies dedicated to Paul Haupt, pp. 446-453. Baltimore, MD: The Johns Hopkins Press, 1926.

MITCHELL, Joseph. "The Epiclesis." The Clergy Review, 52 (1967):
203-207.

PINELL, J. "Legitima eucharistica: Cuestiones sobre la anamnesis
y la epiclesis en el antiguo rito galicano." In Mélanges liturgiques offerts au R. P. Dom Bernard Botte, O. S. B., pp.
445-460. Louvain: Abbaye du Mont César, 1972.

POCKNEE, Cyril E. "The Invocation of the Holy Spirit in the Eucharistic Prayer." Church Quarterly Review, 169 (1968): 216-
219.

RAES, Alphonse. "Les paroles de la consécration dans les anaphores syriennes." Orientalia Christiana Periodica, 3 (1937):
486-504.

RICHARDSON, C. C. "A Note on the Epiclesis in Hippolytus and
the Testamentum Domini." Recherches de théologie ancienne et
médiévale, 15 (1948): 357-359.

_____. "The Origin of the Epiclesis." Anglican Theological Re-
view, (1948): 148-153.

_____. "The So-Called Epiclesis in Hippolytus." Harvard Theo-
logical Review, 40 (1947): 101-108.

RIOS, Romanus. "The Liturgy and Reunion, III: The Words of
Consecration in the Tradition of the Eastern Churches." Eastern Churches Quarterly, 4 (1940-1941): 97-104.

SALAVILLE, Séverien. "La consécration eucharistique d'après
quelques auteurs grecs et syriens." Echos d'Orient, 13
(1910): 321-324.

SMIT, G. S. "Epiclèse et théologie des sacrements." Mélanges de
science religieuse, 15 (1958): 95-136.

SPINKS, Bryan D. "The Consecratory Epiclesis in the Anaphora of
St. James." Studia Liturgica, 11,1 (1976): 19-38.

TILLARD, J. M. R. "The Eucharist and the Holy Spirit." Theology Digest, 17,2 (Summer 1969): 133-138.

TYRER, John Walton. The Eucharistic Epiclesis. London, New
York: Longmans, Green, 1917.

_____. "The Meaning of epiklesis." Journal of Theological
Studies, 25 (1923-1924): 139-150.

VISCHER, Lukas. "The Epiclesis: Sign of Unity and Renewal."
Studia Liturgica, 6,1 (1969): 30-39.

WATTERICH, Johannes. Der Konsekrationsmoment im heiligen
Abendmahl und sein Geschichte. Heidelberg: C. Winter, 1896.

WEBB, Douglas. "La doctrine du Saint-Esprit dans la liturgie eucharistique d'après les théologiens anglais des 17e et 18e
siècles." Ephemerides liturgicae, 90 (1976): 272-288.

6. Institution Narrative and Elevation

BOTTE, Bernard. "Problèmes de l'anaphore syrienne des apôtres
Addai et Mari." L'Orient Syrien, 10 (1965): 89-106.

BROWE, Peter. "Die Elevation in der Messe." Jahrbuch für Liturgiewissenschaft, 9 (1929): 20-66.

BUXTON, Richard F. Eucharist and Institution Narrative: A Study
in the Roman and Anglican Traditions of the Consecration of
the Eucharist from the Eighth to the Twentieth Centuries. ACC,
58. Great Wakering, Eng.: Mayhew-McCrimmon, 1976.

CAPELLE, Bernard. "L'evolution du Qui Pridie de la messe romain."

Recherches de théologie ancienne et médiévale, 22 (1955):   5-16;
reprinted in his Travaux liturgiques, vol. 2, pp. 276-286.
Louvain: Centre liturgique, Abbaye du Mont César, 1962.

CROSS, F. L.   "Institution, Words of."   Oxford Dictionary of the
Christian Church, p. 696.

DRURY, Thomas W.   Elevation in the Eucharist: Its History and
Rationale.   Cambridge: Cambridge University Press, 1907.

DUMOUTET, E.   Le désir de voir l'hostie.   Paris: Beauchesne,
1926.

DURIG, Walter.   "Centrality of the Consecration."   Theology Digest,
21,2 (Summer 1973):   122-125.

DYKMANS, Marc.   "Aux origines de l'élévation eucharistiques."   In
Zetesis: Album amicorum door vrienden en collegas aangeboden
aan Prof. Dr. E. de Strycker ter gelegenheid van zijn 65e
verjaardag, pp. 679-694.   Antwerp: De Nederlandsche Boekhandel, 1973.

HAMM, F.   Die liturgischen Einsetzungsberichte im Sinne vergleichender Liturgie Forschung untersucht.   LQF, 23.   Münster:
Aschendorff, 1928.

KENNEDY, Vincent Lorne.   "The Date of the Parisian Decree on the
Elevation of the Host."   Medieval Studies, 8 (1946):   87-96.

_____.   "The Moment of Consecration and the Elevation of the
Host."   Medieval Studies, 6 (1944):   121-150.

L. K. L.   "De 'verbis institutionis' in anaphora."   Notitiae, 84
(1973):   228-230.

MANDERS, H.   "Sens et fonction du récit de l'institution."   Questions liturgiques et paroissiales, 53 (1972):   203-217.

MERK, Karl Josef.   Der Konsekrationstext der römischen Messe.
Rottenburg: A. N. W. Badern, 1915.

MEYER, H. B.   "Das Elevation im deutschen Mittelalter und bei
Luther: eine Untersuchung zur Liturgie- und Frommigskeit-
geschichte des späten Mittelalters."   Zeitschrift für katholische
Theologie, 85 (1963):   162-217.

MORIN, G.   "Une particularité inaperçue du 'Qui pridie' de la messe
romaine."   Revue bénédictine, 27 (1910):   513-515.

PITT, W. E.   "The Anamnesis and Institution Narrative in the Liturgy
of the Apostolic Constitutions Book 8."   Journal of Ecclesiastical
History, 9 (1958):   1-7.

RAES, Alphonse. "Les paroles de la consécration dans les anaphores syriennes." Orientalia christiana periodica, 3 (1937):
486-504.

RATCLIFF, E. C. "The Eucharistic Institution Narrative of Justin
Martyr's First Apology." Journal of Ecclesiastical History, 22
(1971): 97-102; reprinted in his Liturgical Studies, pp. 41-48.
Edited by A. H. Couratin and D. H. Tripp. London: SPCK,
1976.

_____. "The Institution Narrative of the Roman Canon Missae:
Its Beginnings and Early Background." In Studia Patristica,
vol. 2, pp. 64-82. Edited by Kurt Aland and F. L. Cross.
TUGAL, 64. Berlin: Akademie-Verlag, 1957; reprinted in his
Liturgical Studies, pp. 49-65. Edited by A. H. Couratin and
D. H. Tripp. London: SPCK, 1976.

RIOS, R. "The Liturgy and Reunion: The Words of Consecration
in the Tradition of the Eastern Churches." Eastern Churches
Quarterly, 4 (1940-1941): 97-104.

SALAVILLE, Sévérien. "La consecration eucharistique d'après quelques auteurs grecs et syriens." Echos d'Orient, 13 (1910):
321-324.

VAGAGGINI, C. "L'extension de la main au moment de la consécration: geste indicatif ou épiclètique?" Paroisse et liturgie, 51
(1969): 46-53.

WALLACE-HADRILL, D. S. "Eusebius and the Institution Narrative
in the Eastern Liturgies." Journal of Theological Studies, 4
(1953): 41-42.

ZERWICK, Max. "Pro vobis et pro multis effundetur." Notitiae,
53 (1970): 138-140.

7. Memorial Acclamation

BOTTE, Bernard. "Mysterium fidei." Bible et vie chrétienne, 80
(1968): 29-34.

BRINKTRINE, Johannes. "Mysterium fidei." Ephemerides liturgicae,
44 (1930): 493-500.

FUNK, Virgil C. "Why the Memorial Acclamation Matters So Much."
Pastoral Music, 1,3 (February-March 1977): 10-11.

GELINEAU, Joseph. "The Commemorative Acclamation." In The New
Liturgy, pp. 200-202. Edited by Lancelot Sheppard. London:
Darton, Longman & Todd, 1970.

MICHELS, Th. "Mysterium Fidei in Einsetzungsbericht." Catholica,
    6, 81-88.

8. Anamnesis

BOTTE, Bernard. "Problèmes de l'anamnèse." Journal of Ecclesi-
    astical History, 5 (1954): 16-24.

CHILDS, Brevard S. Memory and Tradition in Israel. London:
    SCM Press, 1962.

CROSS, F. L. "Anamnesis." Oxford Dictionary of the Christian
    Church, p. 47.

DAHL, Nils A. "Anamnesis: mémoire et commémoration dans le
    christianisme primitif." Studia Theologica (Lund), 1 (1948):
    69-95.

FAIVRE, B. "Eucharistie et mémoire." Nouvelle revue théologique,
    90 (1968): 278-290.

FRAIGNEAU-JULIEN, B. "Eléments de la structure fondamentale de
    l'Eucharistie, I: Bénédiction, anamnèse et action de grâces."
    Revue des sciences religieuses, 34 (1960): 35-61.

FULCO, William. "Jewish Storytelling and Anamnesis." Modern
    Liturgy, 3,8 (November-December 1976): 8-9.

HENDERSON, J. Frank. "... In Memory of Me." Liturgy, 23,2
    (March 1978): 23-25.

HICKLING, Colin. "The Eucharist and Time." Theology, 80
    (1977): 197-204.

HOOK, Norman. "Note on Anamnesis." In The Eucharist in the
    New Testament, pp. 144-150. London: Epworth Press, 1964.

JUNGMANN, Joseph A. "Das Gedächtnis des Herrn in der Euchar-
    istie." Theologische Quartelschrift, 133 (1953): 385-399.

KILPATRICK, G. D. "Anamnesis." Liturgical Review, 5 (May
    1975): 35-40.

LIGIER, Louis. "Célébration divine et anamnèse dans la première
    partie de l'anaphore ou canon de la messe orientale." Gregori-
    anum, 48 (1967): 225-252.

MARSILI, S. "Memoriale-Anamnesi." Notitiae, 84 (1973): 225-227.

MONTMINY, J. P. "L'offrande sacrificielle dans l'anamnèses des liturgies anciennes." Recherches des sciences philosophiques et théologiques, 50 (1966): 385-407.

PINELL, J. "Legitima eucharistica: Cuestiones sobre la anamnesis y la épiclesis en el antiguo rito galicano." In Mélanges liturgiques offerts au R. P. Dom Bernard Botte, O. S. B.,pp. 445-460. Louvain: Abbaye du Mont César, 1972.

PITT, William E. "The Anamnesis and Institution Narrative in the Liturgy of Apostolic Constitutions Book VIII." Journal of Ecclesiastical History, 7 (1958): 1-7.

RAUCH, C. "L'anamnèse de la messe." In La messe et sa catéchèse, pp. 312-319. LO, 7. Paris: Cerf, 1947.

THURIAN, Max. The Eucharistic Memorial. 2 vols. ESW, 7-8. Richmond, VA: John Knox Press, 1960-1961.

TILLARD, J. M. R. "Le mémorial dans la vie de l'Eglise." La Maison-Dieu, 106 (1971): 24-45.

9. Offering

BAUMSTARK, Anton. "Ein Ubersetzungsfehler im Messkanon." Studia Catholica, 5 (1929): 378-382.

BOTTE, Bernard. "L'ange du sacrifice." Cours et conférences des semaines liturgiques, 7 (1929): 209-221.

_____. "L'ange du sacrifice et l'épiclèse de la messe romaine au moyen âge." Recherches de théologie ancienne et médiévale, 1 (1929): 285-308.

FIALA, Virgil. "Les prières d'acceptation de l'offrande et le genre littéraire du canon romain." In Eucharisties d'Orient et d'Occident, pp. 117-133. LO, 46. Paris: Cerf, 1970.

LE DEAUT, R. "Le titre de 'summus sacerdos' donné à Melchisédech est-il d'origine juive?" Recherches de science religieuse, 50 (1962): 222-229.

MARSILI, S. "Offerta-sacrificia nella preghiera eucaristica." Notitiae, 84 (June 1973): 231-237.

MORIARITY, Frederick. "Abel, Melchizedech, Abraham." The Way, 5 (1965): 94-104.

SAGE, A. "Saint Augustine et la prière du canon 'Supplices te rogamus.'" Revue des études byzantines, 11 (1953): 252-265.

10. Prayers of Intercession

a. General Studies

BERGER, Rupert. Die Wendung "offere pro" in der römischen Liturgie. LQF, 41. Münster: Aschendorff, 1965.

CAPELLE, Bernard. "Innocent Ie et le canon de la messe." Recherches de théologie ancienne et médiévale, 19 (1952): 5-16; reprinted in his Travaux liturgiques, vol. 2, pp. 236-247. Louvain: Centre liturgique, Abbaye du Mont César, 1962.

_____. "L'intercession dans la messe romaine." Revue bénédictine, 65 (1955): 181-191; reprinted in his Travaux liturgiques, vol. 2, pp. 248-257. Louvain: Centre liturgique, Abbaye du Mont César, 1962.

CONNOLLY, R. H. "Liturgical Prayers of Intercession." Journal of Theological Studies, 21 (1920): 319-332.

ENGBERDING, Hieronymus. "Das anaphorische Fürbittgebet der älteren armenischen Basiliusliturgie." Oriens Christianus, 51 (1967): 29-50.

_____. "Das anaphorische Fürbittgebet der Basiliusliturgie." Oriens Christianus, 47 (1963): 16-52; 49 (1965): 18-37.

_____. "Das anaphorische Fürbittgebet der byzantinischen Chrysostomusliturgie." Oriens Christianus, 45 (1961): 20-29; 46 (1962): 33-60.

_____. "Das anaphorische Fürbittgebet der griechischen Markusliturgie." Orientalia Christiana Periodica, 30 (1964): 398-446.

_____. "Zum anaphorischen Fürbittgebet des ostsyrischen Liturgie Addaj und Mar(j)." Oriens Christianus, 41 (1957): 102-124.

GRISBROOKE, W. Jardine. "Intercession." Dictionary of Liturgy and Worship, p. 204.

_____. "Intercession at the Eucharist, II: The Intercession at the Eucharist Proper." Studia Liturgica, 5,1 (Spring 1966): 20-44; 5,2 (Summer 1966): 87-103.

LEBLANC, P. J. "A Consideration of Intercessory Prayer within the Eucharist." The Dunwoodie Review, 8 (1968): 115-132.

PALMER, R. F. "The Place of Intercession and Confession in the Eucharist." Anglican Theological Review, 44 (1962): 238-241.

SOTTOCORNOLA, F. "L'elemento di petizione nella preghiera eucharistica." Notitiae, 84 (1973): 238-241.

WINKLER, Gabriele. "Die Interzessionen der Chrysostomusanaphora in ihrer geschichtlichen Entwicklung." Orientalia Christiana Periodica, 36 (1970): 301-336; 37 (1971): 333-383.

b. The "Te Igitur" in the Roman Canon

CAPELLE, Bernard. "Et omnibus orthodoxis atque apostolicis fidei cultoribus." In Miscellanea historica in honorem Alberti de Meyer, pp. 137-150; reprinted in his Travaux liturgiques, vol. 2, pp. 258-268. Louvain: Centre liturgique, Abbaye du Mont César, 1962.

CROSS, F. L. "Te Igitur." Oxford Dictionary of the Christian Church, p. 1326.

EIZENHOFER, Ludwig. "Te Igitur und Communicantes im römischen Messkanon." Sacris Erudiri, 8 (1956): 14-75.

PETERSON, Erik. "Dona, munera, sacrificia." Ephemerides liturgicae, 46 (1932): 75-77.

c. The Memorial of the Living in the Roman Canon

BISHOP, Edmund. "The Diptychs." Appendix to The Liturgical Homilies of Narsai, pp. 97-117. Edited by R. H. Connolly. TaS, 8/1. Cambridge: Cambridge University Press, 1909; reprint ed., Nendeln: Kraus, 1967.

CABROL, Fernand. "Diptyques (Liturgie)." Dictionnaire d'archéologie chrétienne et de liturgie, 4: 1045-1094.

CROSS, F. L. "Diptychs." Oxford Dictionary of the Christian Church, p. 404.

GIBSON, A. G. "Diptychs." New Catholic Encyclopedia, 3:885-887.

GRISBROOKE, W. Jardine. "Diptychs." Dictionary of Liturgy and Worship, pp. 162-163.

LECLERCQ, Henri. "Diptyques (Archéologie)." Dictionnaire d'archéologie chrétienne et de liturgie, 4:1094-1170.

STEGMULLER, O. "Diptychon." Reallexikon für Antike und Christentum, 3:1143-1148.

STUIBER, Alfred. "Die Diptychon-Formel für die Nomina Offerentium im römischen Messkanon." Ephemerides liturgicae, 68 (1954): 127-146.

d. The "Communicantes" and the "Nobis Quoque"
in the Roman Canon

ABERCROMBIE, N. J. "Nobis Quoque in the Roman Canon Missae."
Journal of Theological Studies, 4 (1933): 49-50.

BAUMSTARK, Anton. "Das Communicantes und seine Heiligenliste."
Jahrbuch für Liturgiewissenschaft, 1 (1921): 5-33.

BORELLA, Pietro. "Memoriis sanctorum communicantes." Ambrosius,
27 (1951): 75-76.

_____. "S. Leone e il Communicantes." Ephemerides liturgicae,
60 (1946): 93-101.

BOTTE, Bernard. "Communicantes." Questions liturgiques et
paroissiales, 38 (1957): 119-123.

CALLEWAERT, Camille. "S. Léon, le 'Communicantes' et le 'Nobis
quoque peccatoribus.'" Sacris erudiri, 1 (1948): 123-164.

CAPELLE, Bernard. "Problèmes du 'Communicantes' de la messe."
Rivista liturgica (Finalpia), (1953): 187-195; reprinted in his
Travaux liturgiques, vol. 2, pp. 269-275. Louvain: Centre
liturgique, Abbaye du Mont César, 1962.

CROSS, F. L. "Communicantes." Oxford Dictionary of the Christian Church, p. 319.

_____. "Nobis Quoque Peccatoribus." Oxford Dictionary of the
Christian Church, p. 962.

EIZENHOFER, Ludwig. "Te Igitur und Communicantes im römischen
Messkanon." Sacris erudiri, 8 (1956): 14-75.

FRANK, H. "Beobachtungen zur Geschichte des Messkanons."
Archiv für Liturgiewissenschaft, 1 (1950): 111-119.

HOSP, E. Die Heiligen im Canon Missae. Graz, 1926.

JOUNEL, Pierre. "Les saints du canon de la messe." La Maison-
Dieu, 92 (1967): 35-42.

KENNEDY, Vincent Lorne. The Saints of the Canon of the Mass.
2d ed. SAC, 14. Vatican City: Pontificio Instituto di Archeologia Cristiana, 1963.

MAURICE, D. V. "Les saints du canon de la messe au moyen
âge." Ephemerides liturgicae, 52 (1938): 353-384.

RUSSMANN, C. L. "Die Heiligen des Messopfer Kanons."

Theologisch-Praktische Quartelschrift, 101 (1953):   1-15, 101-
113.

e. The "Hanc Igitur' in the Roman Canon

KENNEDY, Vincent L. "The Pre-Gregorian 'Hanc Igitur.'" Ephemerides liturgicae, 50 (1936):   349-358.

MICHELS, T. "Woher nahm Gregor d. Gr. die Kanonbitte 'diese
nostros in tua pace disponas?'" Jahrbuch für Liturgiewissenschaft, 13 (1935):   188-190.

f. The Memento of the Dead in the Roman Canon

ANDRIEU, Michel. Les Ordines romani du haut moyen-âge, vol. 2,
pp. 274-281. SSL, 23. Louvain: Spicilegium Sacrum Lovaniense, 1960.

_____. "L'insertion du memento des morts au canon romain de la
messe." Recherches de sciences religieuses, 1 (1921):   151-154.

DOLD, Alban. "Eine unbekannte Diptychenformel für das Memento
Defunctorum." Archiv für Liturgiewissenschaft, 1 (1950):
120-123.

MOHRMANN, Christine. "Locus refrigerii et pacis." Questions liturgiques et paroissiales, 39 (1958):   196-214.

11. Doxology

ALAMO, M. de. "La conclusion actuel del canon de la missa." In
Miscellanea liturgica in honorem L. Cuniberti Mohlberg, vol. 2,
pp. 107-113. BEL, 23. Rome: Edizioni Liturgiche, 1948.

BORELLA, P. "La dossologia finale." Ambrosius, 41 (1965):   183-
201.

BOTTE, Bernard. "In unitate Spiritus Sancti." La Maison-Dieu,
23 (1950):   49-53; reprinted in his L'Ordinaire de la messe,
pp. 133-139. EL, 2. Paris: Cerf, 1953.

BRINKTRINE, Johannes. "Uber die Herkunft und die Bedeutung
des Kanongebetes der römischen Messe 'Per quem haec omnia.'"
Ephemerides liturgicae, 62 (1948):   365-369.

CALLEWAERT, Camille. "La finale du canon de la messe." Revue
d'histoire écclésiastique, 39 (1943):   5-21.

JUNGMANN, Joseph A. "In der Einheit des Heiligen Geistes." In
his Gewordene Liturgie, pp. 190-205. Innsbruck: Rauch, 1941.

KREPS, J. "La doxologie du canon." Cours et conférences des
    semaines liturgiques, 7 (1929): 223-230.

PINELL, Jordi. "La grande conclusion du canon romain." La
    Maison-Dieu, 88 (1966): 96-115.

12. Amen

BRYCE, Mary Charles. "All in Favor Say Amen." Liturgy, 22,4
    (May 1977): 32-34.

CABROL, Fernand. "Amen." Dictionnaire d'archéologie chrétienne
    et de liturgie, 1:1554-1573.

CECCHETTI, I. L'amen nella scrittura e nella liturgia. Città del
    Vaticano: Tipografia Vaticana, 1942.

CROSS, F. L. "Amen." Oxford Dictionary of the Christian
    Church, p. 43.

DAVIES, J. G. "Amen." Dictionary of Liturgy and Worship, p. 10.

HOGG, H. W. "Amen: Notes on its Significance and Use in Bibli-
    cal and Post-Biblical Times." Jewish Quarterly Review, 9
    (1896): 1-23.

HOWELL, Clifford. "Amen." Worship, 36 (1962): 514-518; re-
    printed in his Mean What You Say, pp. 64-68. Collegeville,
    MN: Liturgical Press, 1965.

KROUSE, Dennis W. "The Historical Experience: A Review of the
    Great Amen in Christian Tradition." Chicago Studies, 16,1
    (Spring 1977): 135-156.

MASTERMAN, M. R. E. "Amen." New Catholic Encyclopedia,
    1:378.

ROXBURGH, Gilbert. "The Great Amen." The Bible Today, 25
    (October 1966): 1783-1787.

STUIBER, A. "Amen." Jahrbuch für Antike und Christentum,
    1:153-159.

F. COMMUNION RITE

1. General Studies

BERAUDY, R. "Les rites de préparation à la communion." La
    Maison-Dieu, 100 (1969): 59-71.

BROWE, Peter. "Mittelalterliche Kommunionriten." Jahrbuch für Liturgiewissenschaft, 15 (1941): 23-66.

CLIFFORD, Elizabeth Ann. "The Communion Rite." Today's Parish, 8,4 (April 1976): 43.

COLLINS, Mary. "L'Zikkaron." Liturgy, 21,2 (February 1976): 61-62.

DAVIES, J. G. "Communion." Dictionary of Liturgy and Worship, pp. 143-144.

HARBERT, Bruce. "The Church, the Kingdom, and the English Mass." The Clergy Review, 63,1 (January 1978): 2-8.

HOWELL, Clifford. "The Communion." The Clergy Review, 53,2 (February 1968): 135-141; 53,6 (June 1968): 441-446; 53,8 (August 1968): 626-631.

KAY, Melissa. It Is Your Own Mystery: A Guide to the Communion Rite. Washington, DC: Liturgical Conference, 1977.

KEIFER, Ralph. "Learning Liturgy from the Communion Rite." Pastoral Music, 2,3 (February-March 1978): 15-17.

KRANTZ, Carol. "Our Com(mon)union." Modern Liturgy, 7,8 (December 1980): 46.

McMANUS, Frederick R. "Word, Song and Gesture Articulate the Communion Rite." Pastoral Music, 1,4 (April-May 1977): 34-38; reprinted in Music in Catholic Worship: The NPM Commentary, pp. 125-131. Edited by Virgil C. Funk. Washington, DC: National Association of Pastoral Musicians, 1982.

NOTEBAART, James. "Music and the Communion Rite/Dismissal." Pastoral Music, 6,3 (February-March 1982): 50-53.

WHITAKER, E. C. "Ante-Communion." Dictionary of Liturgy and Worship, pp. 19-20.

2. Lord's Prayer

ARON, Robert. "Les origines juives du Pater." La Maison-Dieu, 85 (1966): 36-40.

BENOIT, Jean-Daniel. "Le Notre Père dans le culte et la prière des églises protestantes." La Maison-Dieu, 85 (1966): 101-116.

BROWN, R. E. "The Pater Noster as an Eschatalogical Prayer." Theological Studies, 22 (1961): 175-208.

BRUNNER, Francis A. "Embolism." New Catholic Encyclopedia,
5:299.

CROSS, F. L. "Embolism." Oxford Dictionary of the Christian
Church, p. 449.

_____. "Lord's Prayer, The." Oxford Dictionary of the Christian
Church, p. 821.

DALMAIS, Irénée-Henri. "L'introduction et l'embolisme de l'oraison
dominicale dans la célébration eucharistique." La Maison-Dieu,
85 (1966): 92-100.

EIZENHOFER, Ludwig. "Zum Pater Noster Einleitung der römischen
Messe." Archiv für Liturgiewissenschaft, 4 (1956): 325-340.

FISCHER, Balthasar. "Praeceptus salutaribus moniti." Archiv für
Liturgiewissenschaft, 1 (1950): 124-127.

FURBERG, I. Das Pater Noster in der Messe. BTP, 21. Lund:
Gleerup, 1968.

GRASSI, A. "Our Father, The." New Catholic Encyclopedia, 10:
829-831.

GRIFFE, E. "Saint Grégoire le Grand et Mgr. Duchesne, à propos
de la récitation du Pater à la messe." Bulletin de littérature
ecclésiastique, 55 (1954): 164-166.

GRISBROOKE, W. Jardine. "Lord's Prayer." Dictionary of Liturgy
and Worship, p. 246.

JUNGMANN, Joseph A. "Das Pater Noster im Kommunionritus." In
his Gewordene Liturgie, pp. 137-164. Innsbruck: Rauch, 1941.

LAMBOT, C. "Le Pater dans la liturgie apostolique d'après S.
Grégoire." Revue bénédictine, 42 (1930): 265-269.

LIGIER, Louis. "Le sens du Notre Père dans la liturgie de la
messe." Parole et pain, 12 (January 1966): 34-59.

PETUCHOWSKI, Jakob J. and BROCKE, Michael, eds. The Lord's
Prayer and Jewish Liturgy. New York: Seabury Press, 1978.

RORDORFF, Willy. "The Lord's Prayer in the Light of its Liturgical
Use in the Early Church." Studia Liturgia, 14,1 (1980-1981):
1-19.

ROUSSEAU, Oliver. "Le 'Pater' dans la liturgie de la messe."
Cours et conférences des semaines liturgiques, 7 (1929): 231-
241.

SCHURMANN, Heinz. Das Gebet des Herrn: als Schlüssel zum
    verstehen Jesu. 4. Aufl. Freiburg: Herder, 1981.

SOUBIGOU, Louis. A Commentary on the Prefaces and the Euchar-
    istic Prayers of the Roman Missal, pp. 319-337. Collegeville,
    MN: Liturgical Press, 1971.

_____. "The 'Our Father' in the New Order of Mass." The
    Bible Today, 60 (April 1972): 791-807.

WILLIS, G. G. "St. Gregory the Great and the Lord's Prayer in
    the Roman Mass." In his Further Essays in the Early Roman
    Liturgy, pp. 175-188. ACC, 46. London: SPCK, 1964.

3. The Peace

BIANCHI, S. "Offerte vobis pacem." Notitiae, 65 (August-
    September 1971): 273-275.

BROU, Louis. "L'oraison ad pacem dans les anciennes liturgies
    latines." In XXXV Congresso eucaristico internacional, sesiones
    de estudios, I, pp. 699-704. Barcelona, 1952.

CABROL, Fernand. "Baiser." Dictionnaire d'archéologie chrétienne
    et de liturgie, 2:117-130.

CLIFFORD, Elizabeth Ann. "Sign of Peace." Today's Parish, 8,3
    (March 1976): 40.

COLLINS, Mary. "The Sign of Peace." Liturgy, 21,1 (January
    1976): 20-21.

CROSS, F. L. "Kiss of Peace." Oxford Dictionary of the Christian
    Church, p. 771.

McNASPY, Clement J. "The Peace." Modern Liturgy, 4,7 (Novem-
    ber 1977): 30.

MULLAHY, B. I. "Kiss, Liturgical." New Catholic Encyclopedia,
    8:207.

THRAEDE, Klaus. "Friedenkuss." Reallexikon für Antike und
    Christentum, 8:505-519.

_____. "Ursprunge und Formen des 'Hl. Küsses' im frühen
    Christentum." Jahrbuch für Antike und Christentum, 11-12
    (1968-1969): 124-180.

4. Breaking of Bread (Fraction)

BERNAS, C. "Breaking of Bread." New Catholic Encyclopedia,
    2:779-780.

BORELLA, Pietro. "Frazione, confractorium e commistione
    nell'anticamessa Ambrosiana." Ambrosius, 38 (1962):   303-311.

CABROL, Fernand. "Fractio panis." Dictionnaire d'archéologie
    chrétienne et de liturgie, 5:2103-2116.

CAPELLE, Bernard. "Fraction et commixtion." La Maison-Dieu,
    35 (1953):   79-94; reprinted in his Travaux liturgiques, vol.
    2, pp. 319-331. Louvain: Centre liturgique, Abbaye du Mont
    César, 1962.

_____. "Le rite de la fraction dans la messe romaine." Revue
    bénédictine, 53 (1941):   5-40; reprinted in his Travaux litur-
    giques, vol. 2, pp. 287-318. Louvain: Centre liturgique,
    Abbaye du Mont César, 1962.

CROSS, F. L. "Fraction." Oxford Dictionary of the Christian
    Church, p. 517.

DAVIES, J. G. "Fraction." Dictionary of Liturgy and Worship,
    p. 184.

HABERSTROH, L. "Der Ritus der Brechung und Mischung nach
    dem Missale Romanum." St. Gabrieler Studien, 5 (1937):   11-
    33.

JANERAS, V. "El rito de la fraccion en la liturgia hispanica."
    Liturgica, 2, pp. 217-247. Scripta et documenta 10. Monser-
    rat, 1958.

MOSSI, John. "Breaking Bread." Folk Mass and Modern Liturgy,
    2,2 (February 1975):   27-29.

SCHERMANN, Theodore. "Das 'Brotbrechen' im Urchristentum."
    Biblische Zeitschrift, 8 (1910):   33-52, 162-183.

VON SEVERUS, E. "Brotbrechen." Reallexikon für Antike und
    Christentum, 2:620-626.

5. Lamb of God (Agnus dei)

CABROL, Fernand. "Agnus Dei." Dictionnaire d'archéologie
    chrétienne et de liturgie, 1:965-969.

CROSS, F. L. "Agnus Dei." Oxford Dictionary of the Christian
    Church, p. 26.

GRISBROOKE, W. Jardine. "Agnus Dei." Dictionary of Liturgy and Worship, p. 2.

HUGLO, M. "Antifone antiche per la 'fractio panis.'" Ambrosius, 31 (1955): 85-95.

KELLY, Columba. "Agnus Dei." New Catholic Encyclopedia, 1:209-210.

6. Commingling

CABROL, Fernand. "Fermentum." Dictionnaire d'archéologie chrétienne et de liturgie, 5:1371-1374.

CAPELLE, Bernard. "Fraction et commixtion." La Maison-Dieu, 35 (1953): 79-94; reprinted in his Travaux liturgiques, vol. 2, pp. 319-331. Louvain: Centre liturgique, Abbaye du Mont César, 1962.

_____. "L'oraison 'Haec commixtio et consecratio' de la messe romaine." In Mélanges en l'honneur de Mgr. Michel Andrieu, pp. 65-78. Strasbourg: Palais universitaire, 1956; reprinted in his Travaux liturgiques, vol. 2, pp. 332-343. Louvain: Centre liturgique, Abbaye du Mont César, 1962.

_____. "Le rite de la fraction dans la messe romaine." Revue bénédictine, 53 (1941): 5-40; reprinted in his Travaux liturgiques, vol. 2, pp. 287-318. Louvain: Centre liturgique, Abbaye du Mont César, 1962.

CROSS, F. L. "Fermentum." Oxford Dictionary of the Christian Church, p. 500.

DAVIES, J. G. "Commixture." Dictionary of Liturgy and Worship, p. 143.

HABERSTROH, L. "Der Ritus der Brechung und Mischung nach dem Missale Romanum." St. Gabrieler Studien, 5 (1937): 11-30.

JONG, J. P. de. "Commingling." New Catholic Encyclopedia, 4:11.

_____. "Fermentum." New Catholic Encyclopedia, 5:889.

_____. "L'arrière-plan dogmatique du rite de la commixtion dans la messe romaine." Archiv für Liturgiewissenschaft, 3 (1953): 15-37.

_____. "Le rite de la commixtion dans la messe romaine." Revue bénédictine, 61 (1951): 15-37.

_____. "Le rite de la commixtion dans la messe romaine dans ses
rapports avec les liturgies syriennes." Archiv für Liturgiewissenschaft, 4 (1956): 245-278; 5 (1957): 33-79.

JUNGMANN, Joseph A. "Fermentum: Ein Symbol kirchlicher Einheit und sein Nachleben im Mittelalter." In Colligere Fragmenta
(Festschrift A. Dold), pp. 185-190. Beuron: Beuroner Kunstverlag, 1952; "Fermentum: A Symbol of Church Unity and its
Observance in the Middle Ages." In his Pastoral Liturgy, pp.
287-295. New York: Herder & Herder, 1962.

VOLKL, L. "Apophoretum, Eulogie und Fermentum als Ausdrucks-
former der frühchristlichen Communio." In Miscellanea G.
Belvediri, pp. 391-414. Vatican City: Pontificio istituto di
archeologia cristiana, 1954.

7. Private Preparation of Priest and
People, Invitation

ARRANZ, Miguel. "Le 'sancta sanctis' dans la tradition liturgique
des églises." Archiv für Liturgiewissenschaft, 15 (1973):
31-67.

BROU, Louis. "Le 'sancta sanctis' en occident." Journal of Theological Studies, 46 (1946): 11-29.

HOWELL, Clifford. "A Prayer of Humble Access." In his Mean
What You Say, pp. 82-91. Collegeville, MN: Liturgical Press,
1972.

8. The Eucharistic Elements and Their Distribution

a. Words of Administration

Bishops' Committee on the Liturgy. "The Body of Christ." Newsletter, 12 (September 1976): 33-34.

CALDOGNETTO, Dominik. "Corpus Christi." Priest, 22 (July
1966): 568-569.

CAMELOT, Th. "Un texte de Tertullien sur l'amen de la communion." La Maison-Dieu, 79 (1964): 108-113.

DAVIES, J. G. "Words of Administration." Dictionary of Liturgy
and Worship, p. 385.

FLANNERY, Austin. "The New Formula for Holy Communion." In
Vatican II: The Liturgy Constitution, pp. 75-78. Dublin:
Scepter Books, 1964.

KRUGER, Friedrich. "Geschichte der Spendeformel bei der Feier des heiligen Abendmahls in den deutschen evangelischen Kirche." Monatsschrift für Gottesdienst und kirchliche Kunst, 16 (1911): 84–92, 117–125, 157–164, 198–205.

b. Communion Under Both Kinds

Bishops' Committee on the Liturgy. "Communion Under Both Kinds." Newsletter, 15 (January 1979): 145–147.

BRINKTRINE, Johannes. "Uber die Beziehung des eucharistlichen Kelches zum Glauben und zum Heiligen Geist." Ephemerides liturgicae, 80 (1966): 21–23.

Commission Interdiocésaine de Pastorale Liturgique. "La portée liturgique et spirituelle de la communion au calice." Notitiae, 65 (August–September 1971): 281–283; English translation in Bishops' Committee on the Liturgy Newsletter, 14 (October 1978): 135–136.

CROSS, F. L. "Communion Under Both Kinds." Oxford Dictionary of the Christian Church, pp. 320–321.

DANNEELS, Godfried. "Communion Under Both Kinds." Concilium, 2 (1968): 153–160.

DUBLANCHY, E. "Communion eucharistique (sous les deux espèces)." Dictionnaire de théologie catholique, 3:552–572.

DURIG, Walter. "Die Scholastiker und die Communion sub una Specie." In Kyriakon: Festschrift Johannes Quasten, vol. 2, pp. 864–875. Edited by Patrick Granfield and Joseph A. Jungmann. Münster: Aschendorff, 1970.

ELBERN, Victor H. Der eucharistische Kelch im frühen Mittelalter. Berlin: Deutscher Verein für Kunstwissenschaft, 1964.

FLYNN, Eugene. "The Eucharist Under Both Kinds." Doctrine and Life, 19 (1969): 399–410.

KILMARTIN, Edward J. "The Eucharistic Cup in the Primitive Liturgy." Catholic Biblical Quarterly, 24 (1962): 32–43.

KING, Archdale A. Reception of the Chalice: Its Revival. Carlow, Ireland: Liturgy Center, 1972.

MEGIVERN, J. J. "Communion Under Both Species." New Catholic Encyclopedia, 4:44–46.

_____. "Communion Under Both Species." Worship, 37 (1962–1963): 50–58.

_____. Concomitance and Communion. New York: Herder &
    Herder, 1963.

MICHEL, Jean-Charles. "La communion au calice." La Maison-
    Dieu, 85 (1966): 168-178.

MOUGEOT, Louis. "Quelques remarques en marge de l'instruction
    sur la communion sous les deux espèces." La Maison-Dieu,
    103 (1970): 91-95.

NEWNS, Brian. "Communion Under Both Kinds." The Clergy Re-
    view, 56 (1971): 373-380.

PASCHER, J. "Der Kelch in den Texten der römischen Messlitur-
    gie." Liturgische Jahrbuch, 10 (1960): 217-226.

POSPISHILL, Victor J. "Latin Rite Communion Under Both Species."
    Worship, 38 (1964): 224-228.

QUASTEN, Johannes. "Sobria ebrietas in Ambrosius, De Sacra-
    mentis." In Miscellanea liturgica in honorem L. Cuniberti
    Mohlberg, vol. 1, pp. 117-125. BEL, 22. Rome: Edizioni
    Liturgiche, 1948.

SCHLITZER, A. T. "The Sacramental Sign of the Eucharist."
    Yearbook of Liturgical Studies, 2 (1961): 3-31.

SHAUGHNESSY, James D. "Communion Under Both Kinds." Homi-
    letic and Pastoral Review, 65 (1965): 1036-1038.

_____. "Communion Under Both Kinds." Homiletic and Pastoral
    Review, 71 (1965): 456-459.

SMEND, Julius. Kelchversagung und Kelchspendung in der abend-
    ländischen Kirche: ein Beitrag zur Kultusgeschichte. Göttin-
    gen: Vandenhoeck, 1898.

VAN BILSEN, B. "The Lay Chalice." In Liturgy in Development,
    pp. 123-134. Edited by A. von Geusau. London: Sheed &
    Ward, 1965.

WINSTONE, H. E. "The Significance of Communion Under Both
    Kinds." Liturgy (England), 36,1 (1967): 1-6.

c. Communion in the Hand

Bishops' Committee on the Liturgy. The Body of Christ. Washing-
    ton, DC: Bishops' Committee on the Liturgy, 1977.

Federation of Diocesan Liturgical Commissions. Take and Eat. Chi-
    cago: Federation of Diocesan Liturgical Commissions, 1977.

FREBURGER, William J. "Do's and Don'ts of Communion in the Hand." Today's Parish, 9,8 (November–December 1977): 15.

HOVDA, Robert. "Communion in the Hand—A Small Gesture with a Potentially Large Significance." Living Worship, 13,7 (August–September 1977).

KRAUSE, F. J. "Intercommunion and Communion in the Hand: A Reply." Homiletic and Pastoral Review, 73, 11-12 (August–September 1973): 32-33.
--Reply to SOUTHARD, below.

KROSNICKI, Thomas A. "The Early Practice of Communion in the Hand." Review for Religious, 29 (1970): 669-676.

McKENNA, John H. "Communion in the Hand." New Catholic Encyclopedia, 17:143.

MEGIVERN, J. J. Concomitance and Communion. New York: Herder & Herder, 1963.

SHAUGHNESSY, James D. "Communion in the Hand." Homiletic and Pastoral Review, 70 (1970): 866-869.

SOUTHARD, R. E. "Intercommunion and Communion in the Hand." Homiletic and Pastoral Review, 73 (1973): 28-32.

VERHEUL, Ambroise. "La communion dans la main." Questions liturgiques et paroissiales, 50 (1969): 115-122.

WINZEN, Damasus. "Communion in the Hand." Homiletic and Pastoral Review, 71 (1971): 298-304.

d. The Bread of the Eucharist

ERICKSON, John H. "Leavened and Unleavened: Some Theological Implications of the Schism of 1054." St. Vladimir's Theological Quarterly, 14 (1970): 155-176.

SMITH, Mahlon H. And Taking Bread...: Cerularius and the Azyme Controversy of 1054. TH, 47. Paris: Beauchesne, 1978.

WOOLEY, Reginald Maxwell. The Bread of the Eucharist. ACT, 11. London: Mowbray; Milwaukee, WI: Young Churchman, 1913.

9. Communion Song

BORELLA, Pietro. "Il transitorium della messa ambrosiana." Ambrosius, 38 (1962): 231-238.

CROSS, F. L. "Communion Anthem." Oxford Dictionary of the
Christian Church, p. 319.

HUGLO, M. "Communion Antiphon." New Catholic Encyclopedia,
4: 39-41.

HURT, Helen Marie. "Restoring the Communion Song." Modern
Liturgy, 5, 2 (March 1978): 23.

LECLERCQ, Henri. "Communion (Rite et Antienne)." Dictionnaire
d'archéologie chrétienne et de liturgie, 3: 2427-2465.

ROSE, André. "Les antiennes et les psaumes de communion."
Revue diocésaine de Namur, 11 (1957): 280-286, 289-305, 420-
432, 539-548, 698-708; 12 (1958): 52-58.

SCHUERMANS, Marie Philippe. Parole de Dieu et rite sacramentel:
étude critique des antiennes de communion néotestamentaires.
Brussels: Lumen Vitae, 1963.

SHAUGHNESSY, James D. "The Communion Procession." Homiletic
and Pastoral Review, 67 (1966): 593-596.

SHEPHERD, Massey H. "Antiphonal Psalmody: The Introit, Offertory, and Communion." In The Psalms in Christian Worship:
A Practical Guide, pp. 40-43. Minneapolis, MN: Augsburg,
1976.

10. Purification of the Vessels (Ablutions)

CROSS, F. L. "Ablutions." Oxford Dictionary of the Christian
Church, pp. 5-6.

DAVIES, J. G. "Ablutions." Dictionary of Liturgy and Worship,
p. 1.

_____. "Disposal of the Eucharistic Remains." Dictionary of Lit-
urgy and Worship, p. 164.

LOCKTON, William. The Treatment of the Remains at the Eucharist
after Holy Communion and the Time of the Ablutions. Cambridge: Cambridge University Press, 1920.

ROGUET, A.-M. "Purifications à la messe et désacralisation." La
Maison-Dieu, 103 (1970): 61-72.

11. Prayer After Communion (Postcommunion)

CROSS, F. L. "Postcommunion." Oxford Dictionary of the Christian
Church, p. 1094.

FALSINI, Rinaldo. Commento alle Orazioni dopo la communione delle
    domeniche e feste. Sussidi liturgico-pastorali, 17. Milan,
    1967.

HONDERS, A. C. "Remarks on the Postcommunio in Some Reformed
    Liturgies." In The Sacrifice of Praise, pp. 143-160. Edited
    by Bryan D. Spinks. BEL, 19. Rome: Edizioni Liturgiche,
    1981.

KROSNICKI, Thomas A. Ancient Patterns in Modern Prayer. SCA,
    19. Washington, DC: Catholic University of America Press,
    1973.

_____. "The Prayer after Communion." National Bulletin on Lit-
    urgy, 11,65 (September-October 1978): 222-225.

MURRAY, Placid. "The Graces of the Eucharist Studied in the
    Post Communion Prayers." In Studies in Pastoral Liturgy,
    vol. 1, pp. 117-131. Edited by Placid Murray. Maynooth,
    Ireland: The Furrow Trust, 1961.

12. Concluding Rite: General Studies

CLIFFORD, Elizabeth Ann. "The Dismissal Rite." Today's Parish,
    8,5 (May-June 1976): 26.

MAUCK, Marchita. "Rites at the Closing of a Liturgy: When the
    End is the Beginning." Liturgy, 1,4 (1981): 73-77.

NOTEBAART, James. "Music and the Communion Rite/Dismissal."
    Pastoral Music, 6,3 (February-March 1982): 50-53.

SHAUGHNESSY, James D. "The Dismissal Rites." Homiletic and
    Pastoral Review, 66 (1966): 682-684.

13. Greeting and Blessing

BRUNNER, Peter. "Der Segen als dogmatisches und liturgisches
    Problem." In his Pro Ecclesia: Gesammelte Aufsätze zur dog-
    matischen Theologie, Bd. 2, pp. 339-351. Berlin: Lutherisches
    Verlag, 1966.

CALLEWAERT, Camille. "Qu'est-ce que l' 'oratio super populum?'"
    Ephemerides liturgicae, 51 (1937):310-318; reprinted in his
    Sacris erudiri: fragmenta liturgica collecta, pp. 687-696.
    Steenbrugge: Abbatia S. Petri de Aldenburgo, 1940.

EIZENHOFER, Ludwig. "Untersuchungen zum Stil und Inhalt der
    römischen 'Oratio super Populum.'" Ephemerides liturgicae, 52
    (1938): 258-311.

_____. "Zum Stil der Oratio super Populum des Missale Romanum."
    Liturgisches Leben, 5 (1938): 160-168.

HOWELL, Clifford. "The Blessing." Worship, 38 (1964): 91-94;
    reprinted in his Mean What You Say, pp. 98-102. Collegeville,
    MN: Liturgical Press, 1965.

JUNGMANN, Joseph A. "Oratio super Populum und altchristliche
    Büssersegnung." Ephemerides liturgicae, 52 (1938): 77-96.

KROSNICKI, Thomas A. "New Blessings in the Missal of Paul VI."
    Worship, 45 (1971): 199-205.

LECHNER, J. "Der Schlussegen der Priesters in der hl. Messe."
    In Festschrift Eduard Eichmann, pp. 654ff. Herausgegeben
    von Martin Grabmann und Karl Hoffmann. Paderborn: Schön-
    ingh, 1940.

MOELLER, E. "Les bénédictions solennelles du nouveau missel
    romain." Questions liturgiques et paroissiales, 52 (1971):
    317-325.

O'SHEA, William J. "Oratio super Populum." New Catholic Ency-
    clopedia, 10:713.

RICHSTATTER, Thomas. "Solemn Blessing and Prayer over the
    People." New Catholic Encyclopedia, 17:620.

WILLIMON, William H. "The Peace of God Go with You: Blessing
    in Worship." Liturgy, 1,4 (1981): 66-71.

14. Dismissal

ADAMS, Doug. "Direction in Moving Dismissals." Modern Liturgy,
    7,8 (December 1980): 47.

CROSS, F. L. "Benedicamus Domino." Oxford Dictionary of the
    Christian Church, pp. 151-152.

_____. "Ite, Missa est." Oxford Dictionary of the Christian
    Church, p. 707.

DAVIES, J. G. "Dismissal." Dictionary of Liturgy and Worship,
    pp. 163-164.

DOLGER, Franz Joseph. "Zu den Zeremonien der Messliturgie, III:
    Ite Missa est in kultur- und sprachgeschichtlicher Beleuchtung."
    In his Antike und Christentum, Bd. 6, pp. 81-132. Münster:
    Aschendorff, 1940; revised 1950.

KELLY, Columba. "Benedicamus Domino." New Catholic Encyclopedia, 2:270.

_____. "Ite, Missa est." New Catholic Encyclopedia, 7:772.

MICHELS, Thomas. Ite Missa Est. Deo Gratias. Per Hanc Lucis
Viam, 8. Salzburg, 1929.

MOHRMANN, Christine. "Missa." Vigiliae Christianae, 12 (1958):
67-92; reprinted in her Etudes sur le latin des chrétiens, vol.
3, pp. 351-376. Roma: Edizioni di storia e letteratura, 1965.

XI. FORERUNNERS OF THE REFORMATION

A. WYCLIFFE AND THE LOLLARDS

1. Sources

HUDSON, Anne, ed. Selections from English Wycliffite Writings,
esp. pp. 17-18, 110-115. Cambridge: Cambridge University
Press, 1978.

WYCLIF, John. Ioannis Wyclif De eucharistia tractatus maior.
Edited by Johann Loserth. London: Published for the Wyclif
Society by Trübner & Co., 1892; "On the Eucharist." Edited
and translated by Ford Lewis Battles. In Advocates of Reform:
From Wyclif to Erasmus, pp. 61-88. Edited by Matthew Spinka.
LCC, 14. Philadelphia, PA: Westminster Press, 1953.

2. Studies

HUDSON, Anne. "A Lollard Mass." Journal of Theological Studies,
N.S. 23 (1972): 407-419.

KNOX, D. Broughton. The Lord's Supper from Wycliffe to Cranmer.
Exeter, Eng.: Paternoster Press, 1983.

LECHLER, Gotthard Victor. Johann von Wiclif und die Vorgeschichte
der Reformation. 2 vols. Leipzig: Friedrich Fleischer, 1873;
John Wiclif and His English Precursors. Translated by Peter
Lorimer. London: C, K. Paul, 1878; New ed., John Wycliffe
and His English Precursors. Translated by Peter Lorimer.
London: Religious Tract Society, 1884.

McFARLANE, Kenneth Bruce. John Wycliffe and the Beginnings of
English Nonconformity. London: English Universities Press,
1952.

STACEY, John. John Wyclif and Reform. Philadelphia, PA:
Westminster Press, 1964.

WORKMAN, H. B. John Wyclif: A Study of the English Medieval
Church. 2 vols. Oxford: Clarendon Press, 1926.

B. HUS AND THE HUSSITES

1. Sources

HUS, John. Magistri Joannis Hus Tractatus de Ecclesia. Edited by
S. Harrison Thomson. Boulder, CO: University of Colorado
Press, 1956.

_____. The Church. Translated by David S. Schaff. New York:
Scribner, 1915; reprint ed., Westport, CT: Greenwood Press,
1974.

2. Studies

LOSERTH, Johann. Hus und Wiclif: Zur Genesis der husitischen
Lehre. Prag: F. Tempsky, 1884; Wiclif and Hus. Translated
by M. J. Evans. London: Hodder & Stoughton, 1884.

_____. Hus und Wiclif. 2. Aufl. München & Berlin: R. Olden-
bourg, 1925.

SEIBT, Ferdinand. "Hus." Lexikon für Theologie und Kirche (2.
Aufl.), 5:543-546.

_____. "Hussiten." Lexikon für Theologie und Kirche (2. Aufl.),
5:546-549.

SPINKA, Matthew. John Hus: A Biography. Princeton, NJ: Princeton University Press, 1968.

_____. John Hus' Concept of the Church. Princeton, NJ: Prince-
ton University Press, 1966.

VOOGHT, Paul de. L'hérésie de Jean Huss. Louvain: Publications
universitaires de Louvain, 1960.

_____. Hussiana. Louvain: Publications universitaires de Lou-
vain, 1960.

C. THE WALDENSES

Note: The modern Waldensian church is sometimes re-
ferred to as a "reformed" church in the narrower
sense. The prereformation roots of the Waldenses,
however, suggest a separate classification. The liturgical entries below represent the modern form of
Waldensian worship.

1. Texts

Eglise évangélique vaudoise. La liturgie vaudoise, ou la manière
de célébrer le service divin comme elle est établie dans l'église
évangélique des vallées de Piémont. Lausanne: Blanchard,
1842.

[Chiesa evangelica valdese] Eglise évangélique vaudoise. Liturgia.
2 vols. in 1. Torre Pelice: Claudiana, 1927-1934.

2. Studies

BOHMER, H., and CLOT, Alberto. "Waldenses." The New Schaff-
Herzog Encyclopedia of Religious Knowledge, 12:241-255.

MAITLAND, S. R. Facts and Documents Illustrative of the History,
Doctrine, and Rites of the Ancient Albigenses and Waldenses.
London: Rivington, 1832.

MONASTIER, Antoine. Histoire de l'église vaudois depuis son ori-
gine, et des Vaudois du Piémont jusqu'à nos jours. 2 vols.
Paris: Delay; Toulouse: Tartanac, 1847; A History of the
Vaudois Church from its Origin and of the Vaudois of Piedmont
to the Present Day. London: [Religious Tract Society], 1848;
Revised ed., New York: Lane & Scott, 1849.

XII. THE REFORMATION: GENERAL
AND COMPARATIVE WORKS

DANIEL, Hermann Adalbert, ed. Codex liturgicus ecclesiae universae in epitomen redactus, vol. 2: Codex liturgicus ecclesiae
lutheranae; and vol. 3: Codex liturgicus ecclesiae reformatae
atque anglicanae. Lipsiae: Weigel, 1848-1851; reprint ed.,
Hildesheim: Olms, 1966.

HERBST, Wolfgang, ed. Quellen zur Geschichte des evangelischen
Gottesdienstes von der Reformation bis zur Gegenwart. Göttingen: Vandenhoeck & Ruprecht, 1968.

HERMINJARD, Aime L., ed. Correspondance des Reformateurs
    dans les pays de la langue française. 9 vols. Geneva: H.
    Georg, 1866-1897; reprint ed., Nieuwkoop: De Graaf, 1965-
    1966.

NIESEL, Wilhelm. Die Bekenntnisschriften und Kirchenordnungen
    der nach Gottes Wort reformierten Kirche. 3. Aufl. Zurich:
    Evangelischer Verlag, 1938.

RICHTER, Aemilius L., ed. Die evangelischen Kirchenordnungen
    des 16. Jahrhunderts. 2 vols. Weimar: Land-Industriecomp-
    toir, 1846; reprint ed., Nieuwkoop: De Graaf, 1967.

SEHLING, Emil, ed. Die evangelischen Kirchenordnungen des 16.
    Jahrhunderts. 15 vols. Leipzig: Reisland, 1902-1913; reprint
    eds., Tübingen: Mohr, 1955; Aalen: Scientia Verlag, 1970.

SMEND, Julius, ed. Die evangelischen deutschen Messen bis zu
    Luthers deutscher Messe. Göttingen: Vandenhoeck & Rup-
    recht, 1896; reprint ed., Nieuwkoop: De Graaf, 1967.

XIII. THE LUTHERAN CHURCHES

A. GENERAL STUDIES

ALBRECHT, Christoph. Einführung in die Liturgik. Berlin:
    Evangelische Verlagsanstalt, 1964.

ALT, Heinrich. Der christliche Cultus. 2 vols. 2. Aufl. Berlin:
    Müller, 1851-1860.

BRUNNER, Peter. "Vom heiligen Abendmahl. Zum Verständnis des
    10. Artikels der Augsburgischen Konfession." In his Pro
    Ecclesia: Gesammelte Aufsätze zur dogmatischen Theologie,
    Bd. 1, pp. 183-202. Berlin: Lutherisches Verlag, 1962-1966.

BUSZIN, Walter. "The Genius of Lutheran Corporate Worship."
    Concordia Theological Monthly, (April 1950): 1-16.

EBELING, Gerhard. "Die Notwendigkeit des christlichen Gottes-
    dienstes." Zeitschrift für Theologie und Kirche, 67 (1970):
    232-249.

Essays Presented at the First Liturgical Institute, held under the
    auspices of Valparaiso University at Valparaiso, Indiana, June
    7th, 8th, and 9th, 1949. Valparaiso, IN: Valparaiso University
    Press, 1950.

FENDT, Leonhard. Einführung in die Liturgiewissenschaft. Berlin:
Töpelmann, 1958.

HERRLIN, Olle. Liturgiska perspektiv: några kapitel om kyrkans
gudstjänst. Stockholm: Svenska Kyrkans Diakonistyrelses
Bokförlag, 1960; Divine Service: Liturgy in Perspective.
Translated by Gene J. Lund. Philadelphia, PA: Fortress
Press, 1966.

JOHNSTAD, Johan. Kirkens gudstjenesteliv fra oldtiden til idag;
et liturgisk grunnriss. Oslo: Land og Kirke, 1953.

KALB, Friedrich. Grundriss der Liturgik: eine Einführung in die
Geschichte, Grundsätze und Ordnungen des lutherischen Gottesdienstes. Münich: Claudius Verlag, 1965.

KLIEFOTH, Theodor F. D. Liturgische Abhandlungen,   8 vols.
Schwerin: Stiller, 1854-1861.

_____. Theorie des Kultus der evangelischen Kirche. Parchim:
Hinstorff, 1844.

KOENKER, Ernest B. Worship in Word and Sacrament. St. Louis,
MO: Concordia, 1959.

KRESSEL, Hans. Von der rechten Liturgie: Prolegomena zu einer
Morphologie der Liturgie, zu ihrer Gestalt und Gestaltung.
Neuendettelsau: Freimund-Verlag, 1971.

KRUGER, Friedrich. "Geschichte der Spendeformel bei der Feier
des heiligen Abendmahls in den deutschen evangelischen Kirche."
Monatsschrift für Gottesdienst und kirchliche Kunst, 16 (1911):
84-92, 117-125, 157-164, 198-205.

LOCHNER, Friedrich. Der Hauptgottesdienst der evangelisch-
lutherischen Kirche. St. Louis, MO: Concordia, 1895.

MULLER, Karl Ferdinand, and BLANKENBURG, Walter, eds. Leiturgia: Handbuch des evangelischen Gottesdienstes. 5 vols.
Kassel: Stauda, 1954-1970.
    1. Geschichte und Lehre des evangelischen Gottesdienstes.
        1954.
    2. Gestalt und Formen des evangelischen Gottesdienstes, I:
        Der Hauptgottesdienst. 1955.
    3. Gestalt und Formen des evangelischen Gottesdienstes, II:
        Der Predigtgottesdienst und der tägliche Gottesdienst.
        1956.
    4. Die Musik des evangelischen Gottesdienstes. 1961.
    5. Der Taufgottesdienst. 1970.

NIEBERGALL, Alfred. "Agende." Theologische Realenzyklopädie,
1:755-784.

PIEPKORN, Arthur Carl. "The Lutheran Doctrine of the Sacrament
    of the Altar, Ecumenically Considered." National Liturgical
    Week, 25 (1964): 135-154.

_____. What the Symbolical Books of the Lutheran Church have
    to Say about Worship and the Sacraments. St. Louis, MO:
    Concordia, 1952.

PRENTER, Regin. "Die Realpräsenz als die Mitte des christlichen
    Gottesdienstes." In Gedankschrift für D. Werner Elert:
    Beiträge zur historischen und systematischen Theologie, pp.
    307-319. Herausgegeben von Friedrich Hübner. Berlin:
    Lutherisches Verlagshaus, 1955.

_____. Theologie und Gottesdienst: Gesammelte Aufsätze. Göttin-
    gen: Vandenhoeck & Ruprecht, 1977.

REED, Luther Dotterer. Worship: A Study of Corporate Devotion.
    Philadelphia, PA: Muhlenberg Press, 1959.

RENDTORFF, Franz M. Die Geschichte des christlichen Gottes-
    dienstes unter dem Gesichtspunkt der liturgischen Erbfolge.
    SPT, 7/1. Giessen: Töpelmann, 1914.

RIETSCHEL, Georg. Lehrbuch der Liturgik. 2 Bde. 2. Aufl.
    von Paul Graff. SLPT, 2-3. Göttingen: Vandenhoeck & Rup-
    recht, 1951-1952.

SCHLINK, Edmund. "Der Kult in der Sicht evangelischer Theol-
    ogie." In his Der kommende Christus und die kirchlichen
    Traditionen, pp. 116-125. Göttingen: Vandenhoeck & Rup-
    recht, 1961; "Worship from the Viewpoint of Evangelical Theol-
    ogy." In his The Coming Christ and the Coming Church, pp.
    132-143. Edinburgh: Oliver & Boyd; Philadelphia, PA:
    Fortress Press, 1967.

SMEND, Julius. Der evangelische Gottesdienst. Göttingen: Van-
    denhoeck & Ruprecht, 1904.

VAJTA, Vilmos. "Der Gottesdienst und das sakramentale Leben."
    In Die evangelisch-lutherische Kirche, pp. 135-160. Heraus-
    gegeben von Vilmos Vajta. Stuttgart: Evangelisches Verlags-
    werk, 1977; "Worship and the Sacramental Life." In The
    Lutheran Church: Past and Present, pp. 121-145. Edited by
    Vilmos Vajta. Minneapolis, MN: Augsburg, 1977.

_____, ed. Kirche und Abendmahl, Bd. 1: Studien und Docu-
    mente zur Frage der Abendmahlsgemeinschaft im Luthertum.
    Berlin: Lutherisches Verlagshaus, 1963.

WEBER, Edith. "La Liturgie luthérienne." Positions Luthériennes,
    21 (1973): 43-48.

B. LUTHER

1. Texts

Note: Abbreviated entries have been adopted from the
following sources:

LW -- Luther's Works. American Edition. 55 vols.
Edited by Jaroslav Pelikan and Helmut T. Lehmann.
St. Louis, MO: Concordia; Philadelphia, PA: Muhlenberg Press (later Fortress Press), 1955-1976.
PE -- Works of Martin Luther. The Philadelphia Edition. 6 vols. Philadelphia, PA: A. J. Holman, 1915-
1932; reprint eds., Philadelphia, PA: Muhlenberg
Press, 1943; Grand Rapids, MI: Baker, 1982.
WA -- D. Martin Luthers Werke. Kritische Gesamtausgabe. 57 vols. Weimar: Herman Böhlaus Nachfolger,
1883- .

LUTHER, Martin. "Allerliebsten freunde in Christo, 1525." WA,
Briefwechsel, vol. 3, pp. 462-463; "An Exhortation to the Communicants, 1525." LW, vol. 53, pp. 104-105; "A Preface Suggested for Use at the Holy Communion." PE, vol. 6, pp. 137-
138.

_____. "Ein Bericht an einen guten Freund von beider Gestalt
des Sakraments, 1528." WA, vol. 26, pp. 560-618.

_____. "Betbüchlein, 1522." WA, vol. 10/2, pp. 375-501; "Per-
sonal Prayer Book, 1522." LW, vol. 43, pp. 11-45.

_____. "Eine christliche Vermahnung von eusserlichem Gottesdienst
und eintracht, an die in Lieffland." WA, vol. 18, pp. 417-421;
"A Christian Exhortation to the Livonians Concerning Public
Worship and Concord, 1525." LW, vol. 53, pp. 45-50; "Exhortation to the Christians in Livonia Concerning Public Worship
and Unity." PE, vol. 6, pp. 144-150.

_____. "Dass diese Wort Christi 'Das is mein Leib' noch fest ste-
hen, wider die Schwarmgeister, 1527." WA, vol. 23, pp. 64-
230; "That These Words of Christ, 'This Is My Body,' etc.,
Still Stand Firm Against the Fanatics, 1527." LW, vol. 37, pp.
13-150.

_____. "De abroganda missa privata, 1521." WA, vol. 8, pp.
411-476.

_____. "De captivitate Babylonica ecclesiae praeludium, 1520."
WA, vol. 6, pp. 497-573; "The Babylonian Captivity of the
Church, 1520." LW, vol. 36, pp. 11-126; PE, vol. 2, pp. 170-
293.

_____. "The Collects." LW, vol. 53, pp. 131-146; PE, vol. 6, pp. 319-361.

_____. "Deutsche Litanei und Latina litania correcta, 1529." WA, vol. 30/3, pp. 29-42; "The German Litany and the Latin Litany Corrected, 1529." LW, vol. 53, pp. 153-170; "The Latin Litany Corrected" and "The German Litany." PE, vol. 6, pp. 262-266, 269-273.

_____. "Deutsche Messe und Ordnung Gottesdiensts, 1526." WA, vol. 19, pp. 72-113; "The German Mass and Order of Service, 1526." LW, vol. 53, pp. 61-90; PE, vol. 6, pp. 170-186; "Martin Luther, Formula Missae and Deutsche Messe." In Liturgies of the Western Church, pp. 93-137. By Bard Thompson. Cleveland, OH: World, 1961; reprint ed., Philadelphia, PA: Fortress Press, 1981.

_____. Martin Luthers Deutsche Messe, 1526. Herausgegeben von Hans Lietzmann. KT, 37. Liturgische Texte, V. Bonn: Marcus & Weber, 1909.

_____. "Exempel, einen rechten christlichen Bischof zu weihen, 1542." WA, vol. 53, pp. 231-260.

_____. "Formula Missae et communionis pro Ecclesia Vuittembergensi, 1523." WA, vol. 12, pp. 205-220; "An Order of Mass and Communion for the Church at Wittenberg, 1523." LW, vol. 53, pp. 19-40; "Formula of Mass and Communion for the Church at Wittenberg." PE, vol. 6, pp. 83-101; "Martin Luther, Formula Missae and Deutsche Messe." In Liturgies of the Western Church, pp. 93-137. By Bard Thompson. Cleveland, OH: World, 1961; reprint ed., Philadelphia, PA: Fortress Press, 1981.

_____. "Eine kurze weise zu beichten für die enfeltigen, dem Priester, 1529." WA, vol. 30/1, pp. 343-345; "A Short Order of Confession Before the Priest for the Common Man, 1529." LW, vol. 53, pp. 117-118; "A Short Method of Confessing to the Priest, for the Use of Simple Folk." PE, vol. 6, pp. 215-216.

_____. "Kurzes Bekenntnis vom heiligen Sakrament, 1544." WA, vol. 54, pp. 141-167; "Brief Confession Concerning the Holy Sacrament, 1544." LW, vol. 38, pp. 287-319.

_____. "Die Lieder Luthers" and the "Vorrheden" to the Hymn Books. WA, vol. 35, pp. 410-547; "The Liturgical Chants," "The Hymns," "Prefaces to Hymnals" and "A Motet." LW, vol. 53, pp. 147-341; "Hymn Book Prefaces," and "Luther's Hymns Briefly Annotated." PE, vol. 6, pp. 283-308.

_____ . Luthers Lieder und Gedichte. Mit Einleitung und Er-
läuterung von Wilhelm Stapel. Stuttgart: Evangelisches Verlagswerk, 1950.

_____ . "Das Marburger Gespräch und die Marburger Artikel,
1529." WA, vol. 30/3, pp. 110-171; "The Marburg Colloquy
and the Marburg Articles, 1529." LW, vol. 38, pp. 15-89.

_____ . "Das Ordinationsformular, 1535." WA, vol. 38, pp. 423-
433; "The Ordination of Ministers of the Word, 1539." LW,
vol. 53, pp. 124-126; PE, vol. 6, pp. 237-239.

_____ . "Ein Ratschlag, wie in der christlichen Gemeine eine
beständige Ordnung solle vorgenommen werden, 1526." WA,
vol. 19, pp. 440-446.

_____ . "Ein Sermon von dem Gebet und Procession in der Kreuz-
woche, 1519." WA, vol. 2, pp. 175-179; "On Rogationtide
Prayer and Procession, 1519." LW, vol. 42, pp. 87-93.

_____ . "Ein Sermon von dem heiligen hochwürdigen Sakrament
der Taufe, 1519." WA, vol. 2, pp. 727-737; "The Holy and
Blessed Sacrament of Baptism, 1519." LW, vol. 35, pp. 29-43;
"Treatise on Baptism (1519)." PE, vol. 1, pp. 56-71.

_____ . "Ein Sermon von dem hochwürdigen Sakrament des heiligen
Leichnams Christi und von den Bruderschaft, 1519." WA, vol.
2, pp. 742-758; "The Blessed Sacrament of the Holy and True
Body of Christ, and the Brotherhoods, 1519." LW, vol. 35,
pp. 49-73; "A Treatise Concerning the Blessed Sacrament and
Concerning the Brotherhoods (1519)." PE, vol. 2, pp. 9-31.

_____ . "Ein Sermon von dem neuen Testament, das ist von der
heiligen Messe, 1520." WA, vol. 6, pp. 353-378; "A Treatise
on the New Testament, that is, the Holy Mass, 1520." LW,
vol. 35, pp. 79-111.

_____ . "Ein Sermon von dem Sakrament der Busse, 1519." WA,
vol. 2, pp. 713-723; "The Sacrament of Penance, 1519." LW,
vol. 35, pp. 9-22.

_____ . "Sermon von dem Sakrament des Leibes und Blutes
Christi, wider die Schwarmgeister, 1526." WA, vol. 19, pp.
482-523; "The Sacrament of the Body and Blood of Christ--
Against the Fanatics, 1526." LW, vol. 36, pp. 335-361.

_____ . "Sermon von der würdigen Empfahnung des heiligen
wahren Leichnams Christi, gethan am Gründonnerstag, 1521."
WA, vol. 7, pp. 692-697; "Sermon on the Worthy Reception of
the Sacrament, 1521." LW, vol. 42, pp. 171-177.

_____. "Das Taufbüchlein verdeutscht, 1523." WA, vol. 12, pp. 42-48; The Order of Baptism, 1523." LW, vol. 53, pp. 96-103; PE, vol. 6, pp. 197-201.

_____. "Das Taufbüchlein aufs neue zugerichtet, 1526." WA, vol. 19, pp. 537-541; "The Order of Baptism Newly Revised, 1526." LW, vol. 53, pp. 107-109; PE, vol. 6, pp. 207-211.

_____. "Ein Traubüchlein für die einfältigen Pfarrherr, 1529." WA, vol. 30/3, pp. 74-80; "The Order of Marriage for Common Pastors, 1529." LW, vol. 53, pp. 111-115; "A Marriage Booklet for Simple Pastors." PE, vol. 6, pp. 225-230.

_____. "Vermahnung zum Sakrament des Leibes und Blutes Christi, 1530." WA, vol. 30/2, pp. 595-626; "Admonition Concerning the Sacrament of the Body and Blood of Our Lord, 1530." LW, vol. 38, pp. 97-137.

_____. "Vom Abendmahl Christi, Bekenntnis, 1528." WA, vol. 26, pp. 261-509; "Confession Concerning Christ's Supper, 1528." LW, vol. 37, pp. 161-372.

_____. "Vom Greuel der Stillmesse, 1525." WA, vol. 18, pp. 22-36; "The Abomination of the Secret Mass, 1521." LW, vol. 36, pp. 311-328; (excerpt) "The Canon of the Mass from Concerning the Abomination of Low Mass." PE, vol. 6, pp. 124-132.

_____. "Vom Missbrauch der Messe, 1521." WA, vol. 8, pp. 482-563; "The Misuse of the Mass, 1521." LW, vol. 36, pp. 133-230.

_____. "Von Anbeten des Sakraments des heiligen Leichnams Christi, 1523." WA, vol. 11, pp. 431-456; "The Adoration of the Sacrament, 1523." LW, vol. 36, pp. 275-305.

_____. "Von beiden Gestalt des Sakraments zu nehmen, 1522." WA, vol. 10/2, pp. 11-41; "Receiving Both Kinds in the Sacrament, 1522." LW, vol. 36, pp. 237-267.

_____. "Von der Wiedertaufe an zwei Pfarrherrn, 1528?" WA, vol. 26, pp. 144-174; "Concerning Rebaptism, 1528." LW, vol. 40, pp. 229-262.

_____. "Von der Winkelmesse und Pfarrenweihe, 1533" and "Ein Brief D. M. Luthers von seinem Buch der Winkelmessen, 1534." WA, vol. 38, pp. 195-256, 262-272; "The Private Mass and the Consecration of Priests, 1533" and "A Letter of Dr. Martin Luther Concerning His Book on the Private Mass, 1534." LW, vol. 38, pp. 147-214, 221-233.

_____. "Von Ordnung Gottesdiensts in der Gemeine, 1523." WA, vol. 12, pp. 35-37; "Concerning the Order of Public Worship, 1523." LW, vol. 53, pp. 11-14; "Concerning the Ordering of Divine Worship in the Congregation." PE, vol. 6, pp. 60-64.

_____. Martin Luthers 'Von Ordnung Gottesdiensts,' Taufbüchlein, Formula Missae et communionis, 1523. Herausgegeben von Hans Lietzmann. KT, 36. Liturgische Texte, IV. Bonn: Marcus & Weber, 1909; new ed., Berlin: De Gruyter, 1936.

_____. "Wider die himmlischen Propheten von den Bildern und Sakrament, 1525." WA, vol. 18, pp. 62-214; "Against the Heavenly Prophets in the Matter of Images and Sacraments, 1525." LW, vol. 40, pp. 79-223.

_____. "Wie man die Einfeltigen sol leren Beichten, 1531." WA, vol. 30/1, pp. 383-387; "How One Should Teach Common Folk to Shrive Themselves, 1531." LW, vol. 53, pp. 119-121.

_____. "Wie man recht und verständlich einen Menschen zum Christenglauben taufen soll, 1523." WA, vol. 12, pp. 51-52; "How One Shall Properly and Intelligibly Baptize a Person into the Christian Faith." PE, vol. 6, pp. 210-211. [Authorship doubtful]

2. Studies

ALLWOHN, Adolf. Gottesdienst und Rechtfertigungsglaube Luthers Grundlegung evangelischer Liturgik bis zum Jahre 1523. HF, 2. Göttingen: Vandenhoeck & Ruprecht, 1926.

ARMENTROUT, Don S., and LENHARDT, John E., II. "Martin Luther's Theology of Worship and a Reconstruction of His 1523 'Order of Mass and Communion.'" St. Luke's Journal of Theology, 16 (March 1973): 65-85.

BEUMER, Johannes. "Die deutsche Messe Martin Luthers und ihre Weiterentwicklung im Verlauf des 16. Jahrhunderts." Theologie und Glaube, 62 (1972): 339-354.

_____. "Der Minorit Thomas Murner und seine Polemik gegen die deutsche Messe Luthers." Franziskanische Studien, 54 (1972): 192-196.

BRAND, Eugene L. "Luther's Liturgical Surgery." In Interpreting Luther's Legacy, pp. 108-119. Edited by F. W. Meuser and S. D. Schneider. Minneapolis, MN: Augsburg, 1969.

CLEMEN, Otto. Luther und die Volksfrömmigkeit seiner Zeit. SRV, 6. Dresden-Leipzig: C. L. Ungelenk, 1938.

CLEVE, Fredric. Luthers nattvardslära mot bakgrunden av Gabriel
    Biels uppfattning av nattvard och sakrament. Abö: Akademien,
    1968.

CROCEN, Robert C. "Luther and the Eucharist: The Mass as
    Sacrifice." Ph.D. dissertation, Fordham University, 1972.

DREWS, Paul Gottfried. Beiträge zu Luthers liturgischen Reformen.
    2 vols. His Studien zur Geschichte des Gottesdienstes und des
    gottesdienstliche Lebens, 4-5. Tübingen: Mohr, 1910.
    1. Luthers lateinische und deutsche Litanei von 1529.
    2. Luthers deutsche Versikel und Kollekten.

FLEMMING, Friedrich. Die treibenden Kräfte in der lutherischen
    Gottesdienstreform. Leipzig: Deichert, 1926.

GOTTSCHICK, Johannes. Luthers Anschauungen vom christlichen
    Gottesdienst und seine thatsächliche Reform desselben. Giessen:
    C. von Münchow, 1887.

GRAEBKE, Friedrich. Die Konstruktion der Abendmahlslehre Luthers
    in ihrer Entwicklung dargestellt. Leipzig: Deichert, 1908.

GRASS, Hans. "Luther et la liturgie eucharistique." In Eucharis-
    ties d'Orient et d'Occident, vol. 1, pp. 151-170. Edited by B.
    Botte. LO, 46. Paris: Cerf, 1970.

HORN, Edward T. "Luther on the Principles and Order of Christian
    Worship." Lutheran Church Review, 10 (1891): 217-256.

JACOBY, Hermann. Die Liturgik der Reformatoren. 2 vols. Gotha:
    Perthes, 1871-1876.
    1. Liturgik Luthers.
    2. Liturgik Melanchthons.

LEFEBVRE, Marcel. La Messe de Luther. Martigny: Editions
    Saint-Gabriel, 1976?

MEYER, H. B. Luther und die Messe: eine liturgiewissenschaft-
    liche Untersuchung über das Verhältnis Luthers zum Messwesen
    des späten Mittelalters. KKS, 11. Paderborn: Bonifacius
    Druckerei, 1965.

PELIKAN, Jaroslav. "Luther and the Liturgy." In More About
    Luther, pp. 3-62. Decorah, IA: Luther College Press, 1958.

SENN, Frank C. "Martin Luther's Revision of the Eucharistic Canon
    in the Formula Missae of 1523." Concordia Theological Monthly,
    44 (1973): 101-118.

SOMMERLATH, Ernst. Der Sinn des Abendmahls nach Luthers

Gedanken über das Abendmahl 1527-1529. Leipzig: Dörffling & Franke, 1930.

SPINKS, Bryan. Luther's Liturgical Criteria and His Reform of the Canon of the Mass. GLS, 30. Bramcote, Eng.: Grove Books, 1982.

SUSS, Théobald. "L'Histoire du salut dans la théologie et la liturgie de Luther." Positions Luthériennes, 21 (1973): 1-11.

VAJTA, Vilmos. "Luther et la liturgie eucharistique." In Eucharisties d'Orient et d'Occident, vol. 1, pp. 135-150. Edited by B. Botte. Paris: Cerf, 1970.

_____. Die Theologie des Gottesdienstes bei Luther. 2. Aufl. FKD. Göttingen: Vandenhoeck & Ruprecht, 1954; Luther on Worship. Translated by Ulrich S. Leupold. Philadelphia, PA: Muhlenberg Press, 1958.

C. EARLY LUTHERANISM

ALTHAUS, Paul. Zur Einführung in die Quellengeschichte der kirchlichen Kollekten in den lutherischen Agenden des 16. Jahrhunderts. Leipzig: Edelmann, 1919.

BANGERTER, D. "History of the Protestant Liturgy in the Danube Area." Studia Liturgica, 9 (1973): 186-204.

BERGSMA, Johannes H. Die Reform der Messliturgie durch Johannes Bugenhagen (1485-1558). Kevelaer: Butzon & Bercker, 1966.

BIZER, Ernst. Studien zur Geschichte des Abendmahlsstreits im 16. Jahrhundert. BFCT, 2. Reihe, 46. Gütersloh: Bertelsmann, 1940; reprint ed., Darmstadt: Wissenschaftliche Buchgesellschaft, 1962.

BOES, Adolf. "Die reformatorischen Gottesdienste in der Wittenberger Pfarrkirche von 1523 an und die Ordnung der gesenge der Wittenbergischen Kirchen von 1543/44." Jahrbuch für Liturgik und Hymnologie, 4 (1958-1959): 1-40; 6 (1961): 49-61.

BRANDENBURG, Albert. "Liturgie im Zeitalter der Reformation." Archiv für Liturgiewissenschaft, 16 (1974): 433-438.

BRUNNER, Peter. "Die Wormser deutsche Messe." In Kosmos und Ekklesia: Festschrift für Wilhelm Stählin zu seinem siebzigsten Geburtstag 24. September 1953, pp. 106-162. Herausgegeben von Heinz-Dietrich Wendland. Kassel: Stauda, 1953.

DIETRICH, Viet.   Die Evangelien-Kollekten des Viet Dietrich.
Herausgegeben von Otto Dietz.   Leipzig: Wallmann, 1930.

DOLAN, John P.   "Liturgical Reform among the Irenicists."   Sixteenth Century Journal, 2 (1971):   72-94.

FENDT, Leonhard.   Der lutherische Gottesdienst des 16. Jahrhunderts.   Munich: Reinhardt, 1923.

FRANZEN, August.   Die Kelchbewegung am Niederrhein im 16.
Jahrhundert: ein Beitrag zum Problem der Konfessionsbildung
im Reformationszeitalter.   KLKZG, 13.   Münster: Aschendorff,
1955.

GOERTZ, Hansjosef.   Deutsche Begriffe der Liturgie im Zeitalter
der Reformation.   PSQ, 88.   Berlin: Schmidt, 1977.

GOLLWITZER, Helmut.   Coena Domini: die altlutherische Abendmahlslehre in ihrer Auseinandersetzung mit dem Calvinism dargestellt
an der lutherischen Frühorthodoxie.   Munich: Kaiser, 1937.

GRAFF, Paul.   Geschichte der Auflösung der alten gottesdienstlichen
Formen in der evangelischen Kirche Deutschlands.   2 vols.
Göttingen: Vandenhoeck & Ruprecht, 1937-1939.

HARDT, Tom G. A.   Venerabilis et adorabilis eucharistia: en studie
i den lutherska nattvardslären under 1500-talet.   SDCU, 9.
Uppsala: Universitetet, 1971.

HERMANN VON WIED, ed.   Von Gottes genaden unser Hermans,
Ertzbischoffs zu Cöln, einfältigs bedencken warauff ein christliche in dem Wort Gottes gegrünte Reformation an lehr, brauch
der Heyligen Sakramenten und Ceremonien, Seelsorg und and-
erem Kirchendienst...   Bonn: Von der Mülen, 1544; A Simple
and Religious Consultation....   London: Daye, 1547.

HEROLD, Max.   Alt-Nürnberg in seinen Gottesdiensten: ein Beitrag
zur Geschichte der Sitte und des Kultus.   Gütersloh: Bertelsmann, 1890.

JACOBS, Henry E.   "Archbishop Hermann of Cologne and his Consultation."   Lutheran Church Review, 11 (1892):   301-344.

JENNY, Markus.   Die Einheit des Abendmahlsgottesdienstes bei den
elsäsischen und schweizerischen Reformation.   SDST, 23.   Zürich: Zwingli-Verlag, 1968.

JUNG, Wolfgang.   Zur Geschichte des evangelischen Gottesdienstes
in der Pfalz.   Grünstadt, 1959- .

KLAUS, Bernhard.   "Die Nürnberger Deutsche Messe 1524."   Jahrbuch für Liturgik und Hymnologie, 1 (1955):   1-46.

KLIEFOTH, Theodor F. D. Die ursprüngliche Gottesdienstordnung in den deutschen Kirchen lutherischen Bekenntnisses, ihre Destruction und Reformation. 5 vols. in 2. 2. Aufl. Schwerin: Stiller, 1858-1863.

KNOPFLER, A. Die Kelchbewegung in Bayern unter Herzog Albrecht V: ein Beitrag zur Reformationsgeschichte des 16. Jahrhunderts aus archivalischen Quellen. München: E. Stähl, 1891.

LEEUWEN, Gerrit van. "Liturgische ziekenzorg in de reformatie." Tijdschrift voor Liturgie, 60 (1976): 51-61.

NEUSER, Wilhelm H. Die Abendmahlslehre Melanchthons in ihrer geschichtlichen Entwicklung (1519-1530). BGLRK, 26. Neukirchen: Neukirchener Verlag des Erziehungsvereins, 1968.

OLSEN, Oliver K. "Flacius Illyricus als Liturgiker." Jahrbuch für Liturgik und Hymnologie, 12 (1967): 45-69.

PAHL, I. "Das eucharistische Hochgebet in den Abendmahlsordnungen der Reformationskirchen." Questions liturgiques et paroissiales, 53 (1972): 219-250.

ROTH, Erich. Die Geschichte des Gottesdienstes der Siebenbürger Sachsen. FKD, 3. Göttingen: Vandenhoeck & Ruprecht, 1954.

SANDER, Hans Adolf. Beiträge zur Geschichte des lutherischen Gottesdienstes und der Kirchenmusik in Breslau. Breslau: Priebatsch, 1937.

SCHMID, Heinrich. Der Kampf der lutherischen Kirche um Luthers vom Abendmahl in Reformationszeitalter. Leipzig: Hinrichs, 1868.

SCHMIEDER, Paul H. C. "The Church Orders of the Sixteenth Century." Lutheran Church Review, 32 (1913): 361-372; 37 (1918): 195-199, 450-456.

SCHONE, Jobst. Um Christi sakramentale Gegenwart: Der saligersche Abendmahlsstreit, 1568/69. Berlin: Evangelische Verlagsanstalt, 1966.

VARRENTRAPP, Conrad. Hermann von Wied und sein Reformationsversuch in Köln: ein Beitrag zur deutschen Reformationsgeschichte. Leipzig: Duncker & Humblot, 1878.

WALDENMAIER, Hermann. Die Entstehung der evangelischen Gottesdienstordnungen Süddeutschlands im Zeitalter der Reformation. Leipzig: Verein für Reformationsgeschichte, 1916.

ZIEGER, Andreas. Die religiöse und kirchliche Leben im Preussen und Kurland im Spiegel der evangelischen Kirchenordnungen des 16. Jahrhunderts. Köln: Böhlau, 1967.

D. CONTINENTAL LUTHERAN CHURCHES FROM THE PERIOD OF ORTHODOXY TO THE PRESENT

1. Texts

Eglise evangelique lutherienne de France. Liturgie. 2 vols. Paris: Secrétariats généraux de l'Eglise, 1965-1966.

Evangelische Kirche der altpreussischen Union. Kirchenagende. Herausgegeben im Auftrag der liturgischen Ausschüsse von Rheinland und Westfalen in Gemeinschaft mit anderen von Joachim Beckmann. 3 vols. Gütersloh: Bertelsmann, 1949-1957.

_____. Kirchenbuch für evangelische Christen. Berlin: Deckersche Hofbuchdruckerei, 1854.

Evangelische Kirche von Westfalen. Kirchenordnung. Herausgegeben von Werner Danielsmeyer und Oskar Kuhn. 2. Aufl. Bielefeld: Bechauf, 1973.

Evangelische Landeskirche in Baden. Agende für die Evangelisch-Protestantische Kirche im grossherzogthume Baden. Karlsruhe: Groos, 1836.

Evangelisch-Lutherische Landeskirche des Königsreichs Sachsen. Agende für die Evangelisch-Lutherische Kirche Deutschlands. 2 vols. 2. Aufl. Leipzig: Pöschel, 1906.

FRANK, Johan, and WILKENS, Erwin, eds. Ordnungen und Kundgebungen der Vereinigten Evangelisch-Lutherischen Kirche Deutschlands. 2. Aufl. Berlin: Lutherisches Verlagshaus, 1966.

GREIFENSTEIN, Hermann, HARTOG, Hans, and SCHULZ, Frieder, eds. Allgemeine evangelisches Gebetbuch: Anleitung und Ordnung für das Beten des Einzelnen, der Familie und der Gemeinde. Mit einer ökumenischen Gebetsammlung. 2. Aufl. Hamburg: Furche-Verlag, 1965.

HEILER, Friedrich, ed. Deutsche Messe: oder, Feier des Herrenmahls nach altkirchlicher Ordnung im Auftrag der Evangelisch-ökumenischen Vereinigung des Augsburgischen Bekenntnisses. 2. Aufl. Munich: Federmann, 1948.

LIETZMANN, Hans, ed. Die preussische Agende im Auszug. KT,
70. Liturgische Texte, VII. Bonn: Marcus & Weber, 1911.

_____, ed. Die sächsische Agende im Auszug. KT, 75. Litur-
gische Texte, VIII. Bonn: Marcus & Weber, 1911.

LOEHE, Wilhelm, ed. Agende für christliche Gemeinden des luth-
erischen Bekenntnisses. 2 vols. in 1. 3. Aufl. Nördlingen:
Beck, 1884; Liturgy for Christian Congregations of the Luth-
eran Faith. 3d ed. Edited by J. Deinzer. Translated by
F. C. Longaker. With an introduction by Edward T. Horn.
Newport, KY: n.p., 1902.

MAHRENHOLZ, Christhard, and SCHADE, Herwarth von, eds.
Abendmahlsordinarien. Reihe Gottesdienst, 4. Hamburg:
Lutherisches Verlagshaus, 1972.

MAHRENHOLZ, Christhard. Kompendium der Liturgik des Haupt-
gottesdienstes: Agende I für evangelisch-lutherische Kirchen
und Agende I für die Evangelische Kirche der Union. Kassel:
Stauda, 1963.

MEYER, Johannes, ed. Die Hannoversche Agende im Auszug. KT,
125. Liturgische Texte, IX. Bonn: Marcus & Weber, 1913.

MULLER, Karl Ferdinand, and RITTER, Karl Bernhard, eds. Die
Ordnung der Messe: Ausgabe mit den musikalischen Formen
des Ordinariums für Pfarrer, Chor und Gemeinde. Kassel:
Stauda, 1950.

RITTER, Karl Bernhard, ed. Die eucharistische Feier: die Liturgie der evangelischen Messe und des Predigtgottesdienstes.
Herausgegeben in Verbindung mit der Evangelischen Michaelsbruderschaft. 3. Aufl. Kassel: Stauda, 1961.

Vereinigte Evangelisch-Lutherische Kirche Deutschlands. Agende
für evangelisch-lutherische Kirchen und Gemeinden. 2. Aufl.
4 vols. Berlin: Lutherisches Verlagshaus, 1963-1964.

2. Studies

ALBRECHT, Christoph. Schleiermachers Liturgik: Theorie und
Praxis des Gottesdienstes bei Schleiermacher und ihre geistes-
geschichtlichen Zusammenhänge. VEGL, 13. Göttingen: Vandenhoeck & Ruprecht, 1963.

ALTHAUS, Paul. Die lutherische Abendmahlslehre in der Gegenwart. SL, 6. München: Kaiser, 1931.

_____. Der Sinn der Liturgie: Leitsätze und Erlauterungen [and]

Ordnung einer Oster-Vesper von Georg Kempff. ELG, 2. Erlangen: Martin Luther-Verlag, 1937.

_____. Das Wesen des evangelischen Gottesdienstes. 2. Aufl.
Gütersloh: Bertelsmann, 1932.

ASMUSSEN, Hans. Gottesdienstlehre. 3 vols. München: Kaiser,
1936-1937.
1. Die Lehre vom Gottesdienst. 1937.
2. Das Kirchenjahr. 1937.
3. Ordnung des Gottesdienstes. 1936.

BECKMANN, Joachim, ed. Der Gottesdienst an Sonn- und Feier-
tagen: Untersuchungen zur Kirchenagende I, 1. Gütersloh:
Bertelsmann, 1949.

_____. Neuordnung der Evangelischen Kirche der altpreussischen
Union: Antwort an ihre Kritiker. Gütersloh: Bertelsmann,
1951.

BUCHRUCKER, Armin Ernst. "Das Abendmahlslied im Zeitalter des
Pietismus und der Aufklärung." Evangelisch-lutherische Kirch-
enzeitung, 5 (1951): 140-143, 156-157, 173-175, 187-188, 205-
208.

DIETZ, Otto. Die liturgischen Bewegung der Gegenwart im Licht
der Theologie Luthers. HF, 11. Göttingen: Vandenhoeck &
Ruprecht, 1932.

Die Eucharistie: Das Sagorsker Gespräch über das heilige Abendmahl zwischen Vertretern der Evangelischen Kirche in Deutschland und der russischen Orthodoxen Kirche. Herausgegeben
von Kirchlichen Aussenamt der Evangelische Kirche in Deutschland. Bielefeld: Luther-Verlag, 1974.

GOETZ, Karl Gerold. Die heutige Abendmahlsfrage in ihrer gescht-
liche Entwicklung. 2. Aufl. Leipzig: Hinrich, 1907.

HACKER, Josef. Die Messe in den deutschen Diözesan-Gesang- und
Gebetbüchern von der Aufklärungszeit bis zur Gegenwart.
MTS, 2/1. München: Zink, 1950.

HEILER, Friedrich. "The Catholic Movement in German Lutheranism." In Northern Catholicism: Centenary Studies in the Oxford and Parallel Movements, pp. 478-487. Edited by N. P.
Williams and Charles Harris. London: SPCK; New York:
Macmillan, 1933.

HERTZSCH, Erich. "Pläydoyer für die Messe." Theologische Literaturzeitung, 103 (1978): 402-410.

HOFLING, Johann W. F. Liturgisches Urkundenbuch enthaltend die Akte der Communion, der Ordination und Introduction und der Trauung. Herausgegeben von Gottfried Thomasius und Theodosius Harnack. Leipzig: Teubner, 1854.

HUPFELD, Renatus. Die Abendmahlsfeier: ihr ursprünglicher Sinn und ihre sinngemässe Gestaltung. Gütersloh: Bertelsmann, 1935.

JORDAHN, Ottfried. "Georg Friedrich Seiler, der Liturgiker der deutschen Aufklärung." Jahrbuch für Liturgik und Hymnologie, 14 (1969): 1-62.

KAHNIS, Karl Friedrich August. Die Lehre vom Abendmahle. Leipzig: Dörffling & Franke, 1851.

KALB, Friedrich. Die Lehre vom Kultus der lutherischen Kirche zur Zeit der Orthodoxie. AGTL, 3. Berlin: Lutherisches Verlagshaus, 1959; Theology of Worship in 17th Century Lutheranism. Translated by P. A. Hamann. St. Louis, MO: Concordia, 1965.

KAWERAU, Gustav. "Uber die liturgische Gestaltung der 'Konsekration' in der lutherischen Abendmahlsfeier." Theologische Studien und Kritiken, 69 (1896): 356-369.

KNOLLE, Theodor. Bindung und Freiheit in der Gestaltung: Vortrag auf der Vierten Haupttagung des Liturgisches Konferenz Niedersachsens zu Flensburg, 1931. HF, 12. Göttingen: Vandenhoeck & Ruprecht, 1932.

_____. Die Eucharistiefeier und der lutherische Gottesdienst. ELG, 4-5. Erlangen: Martin Luther-Verlag, 1939.

KRESSEL, Hans. Liturgie der evangelisch-lutherischen Kirche in Bayern. 2. Aufl. München: Evangelische Presseverband für Bayern, 1953.

_____. Die Liturgik der Erlanger Theologie, ihre Geschichte und ihre Grundsätze. 2. Aufl. Göttingen: Vandenhoeck & Ruprecht, 1948.

_____. Wilhelm Löhe als Liturg und Liturgiker. Neuendettelsau: Freimund-Verlag, 1952.

Lutherische Liturgische Konferenz Deutschlands. Versammelte Gemeinde: Struktur und Elemente des Gottesdienstes. Zur Reform des Gottesdienstes und die Agende. Hamburg: Lutherisches Verlagshaus, 1974.

MAYER, Anton L. "Liturgie, Aufklärung und Klassizismus." Liturgisches Jahrbuch, 9 (1929): 67-127.

MELAND, Bernard E. "The Modern Liturgical Movement in Germany." Journal of Religion, 11 (1931): 517-532.

MENSCHING, Gustav. Katholische Kultprobleme dargestellt in ihrem Verhältnis zur evangelischen Kultauffassung. Gotha: L. Klotz, 1927.

MUETHEL, Julius. Nochmals Sätze über unsere lutherische Consecrations-Liturgie im Abendmahls-Akte. Leipzig: Deichert, 1896.

_____. Ein Wunder Punkt in der lutherischen Liturgie: Beitrag zur Liturgie. Leipzig: Hartmann, 1895.

OTTO, Rudolf. Zur Erneuerung und Ausgestaltung des Gottesdienstes. Giessen: Töpelmann, 1925.

SASSE, Hermann, ed. Vom Sakrament des Altars: Lutherische Beiträge zur Frage des heiligen Abendmahls. Leipzig: Dörffling & Franke, 1941.

SCHMIDT, Martin. "Die spiritualistische Kritik Christian Hoburgs an der lutherischen Abendmahlslehre und ihre orthodoxen Abwehr." In Bekenntnis zur Kirche: Festgabe für Ernst Sommerlath, pp. 126-138. Berlin: Evangelische Verlagsanstalt, 1960.

SCHMIDT-LAUBER, Hans Christoph. Die Eucharistie als Entfaltung der Verba Testamenti: eine forgeschichtlich-systematische Einführung in die Probleme des lutherischen Gottesdienstes und seiner Liturgie. Kassel: Stauda, 1957.

SCHOBERLEIN, Ludwig. Uber den liturgische Ausbau des Gemeindegottesdienstes in der deutschen evangelischen Kirche. Gotha: Perthes, 1859.

SKIBBE, Eugene Moritz. "Das Proprium des Abendmahls." Kerygma und Dogma, 10 (1964): 78-112.

_____. "The Proprium of the Lord's Supper in the German Lutheran Theology of the 19th Century." Dissertation, Heidelberg, 1962.

VIERBACH, Albert. Die liturgischen Anschauungen des Vitus Anton Winter: ein Beitrag zur Geschichte der Aufklärung. MSHT, 9. München: J. Kösel & F. Pustet, 1929.

E. SCANDINAVIAN LUTHERAN CHURCHES

1. Texts

DANSKE FOLKEKIRKE. Den aeldste danske Alterbog 1556. Udgivet
efter originalen af Lis Jacobsen. Copenhagen: Gyldendalske
Boghandel, 1918.

_____. The Danish High Mass and a Selection of Hymns from the
Danish Hymn-Book. Copenhagen: Church of Denmark Council
on Inter-Church Relations, 1958.

_____. Danske messebøger fra Reformationstiden. Udgivet i fac-
simile af Universitets-Jubilaeets danske Samfund med en liturgi-
historisk redegørelse af S. H. Poulsen. Copenhagen: J. H.
Schultz, 1959.

_____. Forslag til ritualbog for den Danske evangelisklutherske
folkekirke: gudstjenester of kirkelige handlinger. Copenhagen:
Det Kgl. Vajsenhus'Forlag, 1965.

_____. Die lateinische Kirchenordnung König Christians III von
1537. Herausgegeben vom Verein für schleswigholsteinische
Kirchengeschichte. Kiel: In Kommission bei W. G. Mühlau,
1934.

HOLLOWAY, Henry, ed. The Norwegian Rite translated into English, with an Account of its History. With an appendix containing translations into English of Danish Services. London:
A. H. Stockwell, 1934.

NORSKE KIRKE. Alterbok for den Norske Kirke. Kristiania:
Kristeligi Andagtsbøkers Utgivelse, 1922.

_____. An English Translation of the Norwegian Høimesse, the
Regular Sunday Morning Worship Service of the Church of Norway. Translated by David Helgen. Oslo: Andaktsbokselskapet,
1952?

_____. Nynorsk Salmebok for kyrkja og heim og skule. Sjette
upplaget; kyrkjeutgaave. Oslo: Delt Norske Samlaget, 1961.

_____. Tekstbok for den Norske Kirke. Oslo: Andaktsboksel-
skapets Forlag, 1958.

_____. Liturgi-Kommisjonen av 1965. En prøveordning for Høy-
messen i den Norske Kirke. Oslo: Andaktsbokselskapet, 1969.

SUOMEN EVANKELISLUTERILAINEN KIRKKO. Kirkkok Asikirja. 4
vols. in 1. Helsinki: Suomen Kirkon Sisalahetysseura, 1969.

_____. Kyrkohandbok. Helsingsfors: Föbundet för svenskt
församlingsarbete i Finland, 1969.

SVENSKA KYRKAN. Handbok för Svenska Kyrkan, 1894. Lund:
Gleerup, 1900; The Swedish Rite, a translation of "Handbok
för Svenska Kyrkan". By Eric E. Yelverton. TCL, Ser. 3.
London: SPCK; New York: Macmillan, 1921.

_____. Kyrkoordning av är 1571: utgiven av samfundet pro fide
et christianismo. Med historisk inledning av Emil Färnström.
Stockholm: Svenska Kyrkans Diakonistyrelses Bokförlag, 1932.

_____. Missale för svenska kyrkan: innehållande ordningen vid
den allmänna gudstjänsten jämte kyrkoårets evangelier och
epistlar. Ny uppl. Lund: Gleerup, 1973.

_____. Reformationstidens svenska mässa. Kommentarhäfte till
en inspelning: St. Jakobs kyrkokör under ledning av Erick
Ericson, liturg Evert Palmer. Stockholm: Almqvist & Wiksell,
1966.

                        2. Studies

AGRICOLA, Michael Olavi. Mikael Agricolan Rukouskirja ja sen
l'ähteet. Essittänyt Jaakko Gummerus. Helsinki: Suomen
Kirkkohistoriallinen Seura, 1941-1955.

AHLBERG, Bo. Laurentius Petris nattvardsuppfattning: zusam-
menfassung Laurentius Petris Abendmahlsauffassung. STL, 26.
Lund: Gleerup, 1964.

ANDREN, Ake. Högmässa och nattvardsgäng i reformationstidens
svenska kyrkoliv. SSSKH, 32. Stockholm: Svenska Kyrkans
Diakonistyrelses Bokförlag, 1954.

_____. Nattvardsberedelsen i reformationstidens svenska kyrkoliv:
Skriftermål och fasta. SSSKH, 27. Stockholm: Svenska Kyrkans Diakonistyrelses Bokförlag, 1952.

ANDREN, Carl Gustaf. Renewal: A Central Concept in Gustaf
Aulén's Work with the Liturgy in Theory and Practice. Scripta
minora, 1978-1979, 4. Lund: Gleerup, 1979.

BARFOED, E. Christian N. Altar og praedikestol: Liturgiske skil-
dringer og betragtninger. Copenhagen: Lehmann & Stage,
1886.

BERGENDORFF, Conrad J. I. Olavus Petri and the Ecclesiastical
Transformation in Sweden, 1521-1552. New York: Macmillan,
1928; reprint ed., Philadelphia, PA: Fortress Press, 1965.

En bok om kyrkan, av svenska theologer. Stockholm: Svenska
Kyrkans Diakonistyrelses Bokförlag, 1943.

CLEVE, Fredric. Högmassan i församlingens liv. Avhandling
utarb. för synodalmötet i Borgå den 17-19 oktober 1967.
Helsingfors: Församlingsförbund, 1967.

ENGELSTOFT, Christian Thorning. Liturgiens eller alterbogens og
kirkeritualets historie i Danmark. Copenhagen: C. A. Reitzels
Forlag, 1840.

FAEHN, Helge. Høymessen igå og idag. Liturgiens struktur og
vekst. Vår høymesse fra reformasjonen til idag. 2. utg.
Oslo: Universitetsforlaget, 1968.

GUSTAFSSON, Berndt. "Kierkegaard und das Abendmahl."
Kerygma und Dogma, 3 (1957): 316-329.

KENT, Harald Knud Martin Jensen. Braendpunkter i reformationstiden gudstjeneste-ordning, med ny-udgivelse af 1539-
haandbogens gudstjenestedel og nodebilag samt ordinansens an-
visning og nodebilag. Copenhagen: Levin & Munksgaard, 1937.

KJOLLERSTROM, Sven, ed. Den Svenska Kyrkoordningen 1571
jämte studier kring till komst, innehall och anvandning. Lund:
H. Ohlsson, 1971.

LANDSTAD, Magnus Brostrup. Kirkesalmebog, efter offentlig foranstaltning. Kristiania: J. Dybwad, 1871.

LINDQUIST, David. Första-Mässan i Stockholm. En liturgihistorisk
studie. SSSKH, 12. Stockholm: Svenska Kyrkans Diakonistyrelses Bokförlag, 1945.

_____. Hovförsamlingens liturgiska tradition, 1614-1693. LUA,
n.f., 41/1. Lund: Gleerup, 1944.

_____. Nattvarden i svenskt kultliv: en liturgihistorisk studie.
LUA, n.f., 43/7. Lund: Gleerup, 1947.

_____. Stockholms liturgiska tradition: Högmässa och bigudst-
jänster. Stockholm: Svenska Kyrkans Diakonistyrelses Bokförlag, 1951.

NYMAN, Helge. Kyrkotjänarens nattrardsgang i lutherskt gudstjänstliv. AAAbo, 21/4. Abo: Abo akademi, 1955.

PRENTER, Regin. "Worship." In Scandinavian Churches: The
Development and Life of the Churches of Denmark, Finland,
Iceland, Norway and Sweden, pp. 85-103. Edited by Leslie
Stannard Hunter. Minneapolis, MN: Augsburg, 1965.

314   Two: Worship and the Liturgy

QUENSEL, Oscar. Bidrag till svenska liturgiens historia. 2 vols.
in 1. Uppsala: Berling, 1890-1893.

RODHE, Edvard Magnus. Svenskt gudstjänstliv. Historisk belys-
ning av den svenska kyrkohandboken. Stockholm: Svenska
Kyrkans Diakonistyrelses Bokförlag, 1923.

ROSENQUIST, Georg Olof. Det liturgiska arbetet i Finland efter
skilsmässan från Sverige. Abo: Abo Tidning och Tryyckeri,
1935- .

SCHNELL, Jenny. Die Danische Kirchenordnung von 1542 und der
Einfluss von Wittenberg. Breslau: Hirt, 1927.

SENN, Frank C. "Liturgia Svecanae Ecclesiae: An Attempt at
Eucharistic Restoration during the Swedish Reformation."
Studia Liturgica, 14 (1980): 20-36.

SERENIUS, Sigtrygg. Den heliga mässans liturgiska förnyelse
genom Johan III. Hangö: Föreningen Sanct Henriks-Kretsen,
1944.

_____. Liturgia Svecanae ecclesiae catholicae et orthodoxae con-
formis. Abo: Abo Akademi, 1966.

SILEN, Sven. Vi firar mässa: reflektioner och förslag. Stockholm: Verbum, 1975.

ULLMAN, Uddo Lechard. Evangelisk-luthersk liturgik med särskild
hänsyn till den Svenska kyrkans forhällanden framstäld. 2.
uppl. Lund: Gleerup, 1905.

YELVERTON, Eric Esskildsen. An Archbishop of the Reformation:
Laurentius Petri Nericius, Archbishop of Uppsala, 1531-1573:
A Study of his Liturgical Projects. Minneapolis, MN: Augs-
burg, 1959.

_____, ed. The Mass in Sweden: Its Development from the Latin
Rite from 1531 to 1917. HBS, 57. London: Harrison, 1920.

F. LUTHERAN CHURCHES IN THE UNITED STATES

1. Texts

American Lutheran Church. The Minister's Manual of the American
Lutheran Church. Columbus, OH: Lutheran Book Concern,
1940.

Augustana Evangelical Lutheran Church. The Hymnal and Order of
Service. Rock Island, IL: Augustana Book Concern, 1926.

DOBERSTEIN, John W., ed. A Lutheran Prayer Book. Philadel-
    phia, PA: Muhlenberg Press, 1960.

_____, ed. The Minister's Prayer Book: An Order of Prayers
    and Readings. Philadelphia, PA: Muhlenberg Press, 1959;
    London: Collins, 1964.

Evangelical Lutheran Church. The Lutheran Hymnary, including
    the Symbols of the Evangelical Lutheran Church. Revied ed.
    Minneapolis, MN: Augsburg, 1935.

General Council of the Evangelical Lutheran Church in North Amer-
    ica. Church Book for the Use of Evangelical Lutheran Con-
    gregations. Philadelphia, PA: Lutheran Book Store, 1868.

_____. Church Book for the Use of Evangelical Lutheran Con-
    gregations. With Music. Philadelphia, PA: J. K. Schryock,
    1893.

General Synod of the Evangelical Lutheran Church in the United
    States of America. Book of Worship with Hymns. Philadelphia,
    PA: Lutheran Publications Society, 1899.

Lutheran Book of Worship. Prepared by the churches participating
    in the Inter-Lutheran Commission on Worship. Minneapolis,
    MN: Augsburg, 1978.

Lutheran Church in America. Service Book and Hymnal of the
    Lutheran Church in America. Minneapolis, MN: Augsburg,
    1958.

Lutheran Church--Missouri Synod. Liturgy and Agenda. 2d ed.
    St. Louis, MO: Concordia, 1921.

_____. Lutheran Worship. St. Louis, MO: Concordia, 1982.

United Lutheran Church in America. Collects and Prayers for Use
    in Church. Philadelphia, PA: Board of Publication of the
    United Lutheran Church in America, 1935.

_____. The Common Service Book of the Lutheran Church. Au-
    thorized by the General Synod, the General Council, and the
    United Synod of the South. Philadelphia, PA: Lutheran Pub-
    lication Society, 1917.

_____. The Common Service Book of the Lutheran Church.
    Philadelphia, PA: Board of Publication of the United Lutheran
    Church in America, 1919.

_____. The Common Service Book of the Lutheran Church. Re-
    vised ed. Philadelphia, PA: Board of Publication of the United
    Lutheran Church in America, 1929.

_____. The Orisons: A Fellowship of Prayer. Philadelphia, PA:
United Lutheran Press, 1941.

United Synod of the Evangelical Lutheran Church in the South.
The Book of Worship. Columbia, SC: W. J. Duffie, 1888.

2. Studies

BROWN, Edgar S., ed。 Liturgical Reconnaissance: Papers. Inter-
Lutheran Consultaiton on Worship, Chicago, 1966. Philadelphia,
PA: Fortress Press, 1968.

COOPER, Frederick E. An Explanation of the Common Service.
Philadelphia, PA: United Lutheran Publication House, 1941.

EGGE, Mandus A., ed. Worship: Good News in Action. Minneapolis, MN: Augsburg, 1973.

General Council of the Evangelical Lutheran Church in North America. An Explanation of the Common Service, with appendices
on Christian Hymnody and Liturgical Colors. 2d ed. Philadelphia, PA: General Council Publication House, 1908.

HORN, Edward T. "The Lutheran Sources of the Common Service."
The Lutheran Quarterly, 21 (1891): 239-268.

_____, ed. Outlines of Liturgics, on the Basis of Harnack in
Zöckler's Handbuch der theologischen Wissenschaften. 2d ed.
Philadelphia, PA: Lutheran Publicaiton Society, 1912.

Inter-Lutheran Commission on Worship. The Great Thanksgiving.
CW, 1. New York: Inter-Lutheran Commission on Worship,
1975.

_____. Services: The Holy Communion. CW, 2. Minneapolis,
MN: Augsburg, 1970.

_____. Services of the Word. CW, 5. Minneapolis, MN: Augs-
burg, 1972.

JENSON, Robert W. "Concerning and Illustrating New Orders for
the Eucharist." Dialog, 10 (1971): 68-72.

JORDAHL, Leigh D. "A New Rite of Holy Communion for American
Lutherans." Worship, 44 (1970): 578-587.

_____. "New Winds of Liturgical Renewal in the USA." Lutheran
World, 21 (1974): 15-23.

_____, GREEN, Lowell C., and PFATTEICHER, Philip H. "The

New Holy Communion Rite." Lutheran Forum, 5, 4 (April 1971):
10-15.

LEHMANN, Helmut T., ed. Meaning and Practice of the Lord's
Supper. Philadelphia, PA: Muhlenberg Press, 1961.

LINDEMANN, Herbert F. The New Mood in Lutheran Worship.
Minneapolis, MN: Augsburg, 1971.

Lutheran Liturgical Association. Memoirs. ·7 vols. in 1. Edited
by Luther D. Reed. Pittsburgh, PA: Lutheran Liturgical Association, 1906-1907.

PFATTEICHER, Philip H., and MESSERLI, Carlos R. Manual on
the Liturgy: The Lutheran Book of Worship. Minneapolis, MN:
Augsburg, 1979.

REED, Luther Dotterer. "The Character and Claims of the Church
Book." Lutheran Church Review, 26 (1907): 689-700.

_____. "The Common Liturgy." Lutheran Quarterly, 1 (1949):
46-60.

_____. "The Common Service in the Life of the Church." Luth-
eran Church Quarterly, 12 (1939): 3-25.

_____. "Historical Sketch of the Common Service." Lutheran
Church Review, 36 (1917): 501-519.

_____. "Introduction to the New Common Liturgy." Lutheran
Quarterly, 2 (1950): 253-268.

_____. The Lutheran Liturgy: A Study of the Common Service
of the Lutheran Church in America. Revised ed. Philadelphia,
PA: Muhlenberg Press, 1959.

_____. "New Features of the Recent Lutheran Liturgy in Ameri-
ca." Studia Liturgica, 1 (1962): 21-30.

_____. "The Standard Manuscript of the Common Service and
Variata Editions." Lutheran Church Review, 20 (1901): 459-
473.

RICHARD, James William. "The Liturgical Question." Lutheran
Quarterly, 20 (1890): 103-185.

SCHMUCKER, Beale M. "The First Pennsylvania Liturgy Adopted
in 1748." Lutheran Church Review, 1 (1882): 16-27, 161-172.

SELTZER, George R. "The New Liturgy." Lutheran Quarterly,
5 (1953): 3-19.

SENN, Frank. The Pastor as Worship Leader. Minneapolis, MN:
Augsburg, 1977.

SMITH, Robert Morris, et al. "Liturgical Development within the
Evangelical Church in the United States." Lutheran Church
Review, 36 (1917): 469-500.

SPAETH, Adolph. "History of the Liturgical Development of the
Ministerium of Pennsylvania." Lutheran Church Review, 17
(1898): 93-119.

STRODACH, Paul Zeller. The Collect for the Day. Philadelphia,
PA: United Lutheran Publishing House, 1939.

_____. A Manual on Worship: Venite Adoremus! Revised ed.
Philadelphia, PA: Muhlenberg Press, 1946.

United Lutheran Church in America. An Explanation of the Common Service, with appendices on Christian Hymnody and Liturgical Colors and a Glossary of Liturgical Terms. Philadelphia,
PA: United Lutheran Publication House, 1941.

WENNER, George U. "An Answer to the Liturgical Question."
Lutheran Quarterly, 20 (1890): 299-342.

G. LUTHERAN CEREMONIAL

Basic Principles for the Ordering of the Main Worship Service in
the Evangelical Lutheran Church. Geneva: Lutheran World
Federation, 1958.

JORDAHL, Leigh D. "Liturgy and Ceremony: Catholic-Protestant
Cross Currents." Worship, 44 (1970): 578-587.

LANG, Paul H. D. Ceremony and Celebration: An Evangelical
Guide for Christian Practice in Corporate Worship. St. Louis,
MO: Concordia, 1965.

MEHL, Oskar Johannes. Das liturgische Verhalten: Beiträge zu
einem evangelischen Zeremoniale und Rituale. Göttingen:
Vandenhoeck & Ruprecht, 1927.

MEYER, H. B. "Das Elevation im deutschen Mittelalter und bei
Luther: Eine Untersuchung zur Liturgie- und Frömmigkeits-
geschichte des späten Mittelalters." Zeitschrift für katholische
Theologie, 85 (1963): 162-217.

H. SPECIAL STUDIES

BOSCH, Paul. The Sermon as Part of the Liturgy. St. Louis,
MO: Concordia, 1977.

BOUMAN, Walter R. "Confession-Absolution and the Eucharistic
Liturgy." Lutheran Quarterly, 26 (1974): 204-220.

BRUNNER, Peter. "Der Segen als dogmatisches und liturgisches
Problem." In his Pro Ecclesia: Gesammelte Aufsätze zur dogmatischen Theologie, Bd. 2, pp. 339-351. Berlin: Lutherisches Verlag, 1962-1966.

FURBERG, Ingemar. Das Pater Noster in der Messe. BTP, 21.
Lund: Gleerup, 1968.

KRESSEL, Hans. Wilhelm Löhe als Liturgik und Liturgiker. Neuendettelsau: Freimund Verlag, 1952.

KRETZMANN, Paul Edward. Christian Art in the Place and in the
Form of Lutheran Worship. St. Louis, MO: Concordia, 1921.

KUNNETH, F. W. "Roman Liturgical Reform and Lutheranism."
Lutheran World, 14 (1967): 204-209.

NAGEL, William. "Der Artikel von der Rechtfertigung in seiner
Bedeutung für die Entfaltung der Liturgik." Theologische
Literaturzeitung, 79 (1954): 526-531; Justification and the
Discipline of Liturgics." Lutheran Quarterly, 8 (February
1956): 43-50.

SEEMANN, Michael. Heilsgeschehen und Gottesdienst: Die Lehre
Peter Brunners in katholischer Sicht. Mit einem Geleitwort von
Peter Brunner. KKS, 16. Paderborn: Bonifacius Druckerei,
1965.

SENN, Frank C. "Lutheran and Anglican Liturgies: Reciprocal
Influences." Anglican Theological Review, 64 (1982): 47-60.

XIV. THE REFORMED CHURCHES

A. GENERAL STUDIES

ALLMEN, Jean-Jacques von. "Les liturgies Reformées et leur portée
pour l'oecumenisme." In Liturgie de l'église particulière et liturgie de l'église universelle, pp. 17-28. Rome: Edizioni Liturgiche, 1976.

ARNDT, Elmer J. F. The Font and the Table. ESW, 16. London:
    Lutterworth Press; Richmond, VA: John Knox Press, 1967.

BAIRD, Charles W. Eutaxia; or the Presbyterian Liturgies: His-
    torical Sketches. New York: M. W. Dodd, 1855.

_____. A Chapter on Liturgies: Historical Sketches. With an
    introductory preface, and an appendix touching the question
    "Are dissenters to have a liturgy?" by Thomas Binney. London:
    Knight & Son, 1856.

BARKLEY, John M. "'Pleading His Eternal Sacrifice' in the Re-
    formed Liturgy." In The Sacrifice of Praise, pp. 123-142.
    Edited by Bryan D. Spinks. BEL, 19. Rome: Edizioni Litur-
    giche, 1981.

BEARDSLEE, John W. "Some Implications for Worship in Traditional
    Reformed Doctrine." Reformed Review, 30, 3 (Spring 1977):
    210-215.

BENOIT, J. D. "Les Liturgies eucharistiques de l'Eglises de la
    Réforme." Etudes théologiques et religieuses, 37 (1962):   3-39.

BOSC, J. "L'Eucharistie dans les églises de la Réforme." Verbum
    Caro, 87 (1968):   36-47.

DAUERTY, J. S. "The Source of Reformed Worship." Journal of
    the Presbyterian Historical Society, 36 (1958):   217-253; 37
    (1959):   15-29; and "The Recovery of Worship." 37 (1959):
    91-103, 177-190.

DOUMERGUE, Emile. Essai sur l'histoire du culte réformé, princi-
    palement XVIe au XIXe siècle. Paris: Fischbacher, 1890.

ENGELBRECHT, Benjamin. Die vrye gebed en die formuliergebed in
    die Reformatoriese kerke. Free Prayer and Fixed Forms of
    Prayer in the Reformed Churches. With a Summary in English.
    Utrecht: Kemink, 1954.

GERRISH, Brian A. "The ord's Supper in the Reformed Confes-
    sions." Theology Today, 23 (1966-1967):   224-243.

HAGEMAN, Howard G. Pulpit and Table: Some Chapters in the
    History of Worship in the Reformed Churches. Richmond, VA:
    John Knox Press, 1962.

HARRIS, Thomas L. Christian Public Worship: Its History, De-
    velopment, and Ritual for To-day. Garden City, NY: Double-
    day, Doran, 1928.

HONDERS, A. C. "Remarks on the Postcommunio in Some Reformed

Liturgies." In The Sacrifice of Praise, pp. 143-160. Edited by
Bryan D. Spinks. BEL, 19. Rome: Edizioni Liturgiche, 1981.

JENNY, Markus. Die Einheit des Abendmahlsgottesdienstes bei den
elsässischen und schweizerischen Reformatoren. SDST, 23.
Zürich: Zwingli Verlag, 1968.

LAMB, J. A. "Liturgies: Reformed." A Dictionary of Liturgy and
Worship, pp. 242-244.

LEKKERKERKER, Arie Frederik Nelis. "Gereformeerde liturgiek in
de XVIe eeuw." Nederlands Theologisch Tijdschrift, 6 (1951-
1952): 72-89.

MACLEOD, Donald. Presbyterian Worship: Its Meaning and Method.
Revised ed. Richmond, VA: John Knox Press, 1980.

_____. Word and Sacrament: A Preface to Preaching and Worship.
Englewood Cliffs, NJ: Prentice-Hall, 1960.

MAXWELL, William D. "Reformed Worship." A Dictionary of Liturgy
and Worship, pp. 331-333.

NICHOLS, James H. Corporate Worship in the Reformed Tradition.
Philadelphia, PA: Westminster Press, 1968.

_____. "The Liturgical Tradition of the Reformed Churches."
Theology Today, 11 (1954): 210-224.

NIESEL, Wilhelm. "The Order of Public Worship in the Reformed
Churches." Scottish Journal of Theology, 2 (1949): 381-390.

OLD, Hughes O. The Patristic Roots of Reformed Worship. ZBR,
5. Zurich: Theologischer Verlag, 1975.

_____. Worship That is Reformed according to Scripture. Guides
to the Reformed Tradition. Atlanta, GA: John Knox Press,
1984.

SCHLEMMER, André, and CADIER, Jean. Le Culte réformé. Mont-
pelier: n.p., 1947.

STRACHAN, C. Gordon. "The Reformed Tradition and the Pentecostal Movement." Journal of the United Reformed Church Historical Society, 1, 4 (1974): 98-105.

B. THE REFORMERS

1. Zwingli

a. Texts

Note: Abbreviated entries have been adopted from the
following sources:

Bromiley--Zwingli and Bullinger. Edited by G. W.
Bromiley. LCC, 24. Philadelphia, PA: Westminster
Press, 1953.
Liturgies--Liturgies of the Western Church. By Bard
Thompson. Cleveland, OH: World, 1961; reprint ed.,
Philadelphia, PA: Fortress Press, 1981.
Werke--ZWINGLI, Ulrich. Sämtliche Werke. 14 vols.
Herausgegeben von Emil Egli, Georg Finsler, Walther
Köhler, Oskar Farner, Fritz Blanke, Leonhard von
Muralt, Edwin Künzli, Rudolf Pfister. CR, 88-101.
Berlin: C. A. Schwetschke; Leipzig: M. Heinsius;
Zurich: Verlag Berichthaus, 1905-1968.

ZWINGLI, Ulrich. "Ad Matthaeum Alberum de coena dominica epistola, 1524." Werke, vol. 3, pp. 322-354. CR, 90. 1914.

_____. "Aktion oder Brauch des Nachtmals, 1525." Werke, vol.
4, pp. 1-24. CR, 91. 1927; "Action or Use of the Lord's
Supper, 1525." Liturgies, pp. 149-156.

_____. "Amica Exegesis, id est: expositio eucharistiae negocii ad
Martinum Lutherum, 1527." Werke, vol. 5, pp. 548-758. CR,
92. 1934.

_____. "Antwort über Balthasar Hubmaiers Taufbüchlein, 1525."
Werke, vol. 4, pp. 577-647. CR, 91. 1927.

_____. "Antwort über Straussens Büchlein, das Nachtmahl Christi
betreffend, 1527." Werke, vol. 5, pp. 453-547. CR, 92. 1934.

_____. "Eine Aufzeichnung Zwinglis zum Marburger Religions-
gespräch, 1529." Werke, vol. 6, t. 2, pp. 524-531. CR, 93,
pars II. 1968.

_____. "Das diese Worte: Das ist mein Leib usw. ewiglich den
alten Sinn haven werden usw., 1527." Werke, vol. 5, pp. 795-
977. CR, 92. 1934.

_____. "De canone missae epichiresis, 1523." Werke, vol. 2, pp.
552-608. CR, 89. 1908.

_____. Kanonversuch. Eingeleitet übers. und kommentiert von
Fritz Schmidt-Clausing. Frankfurt: Lembeck, 1969.

_____. "De canone missae libelli apologia, 1523." Werke, vol. 2,
pp. 617-625. CR, 89. 1908.

_____. "Gutachten betreffend Taufe, 1526." Werke, vol. 5, pp.
448-452. CR, 92. 1934.

_____. "Eine klare Unterrichtung vom Nachtmahl Christi, 1526."
Werke, vol. 4, pp. 773-862. CR, 91. 1927; "On the Lord's
Supper." Bromiley, pp. 185-238.

_____. Liturgische Formulare. Eingeleitet übers. und kommentiert
von Fritz Schmidt-Clausing. Frankfurt: Lembeck, 1970.

_____. "Die Marburger Artikel, 1527." Werke, vol. 6, t. 2, pp.
510-523. CR, 93, pars II. 1968.

_____. "Notae Zuinglii. Randbemerkungen Zwinglis zu den Mar-
burger Artikeln von 1529, 1529." Werke, vol. 6, t. 2, pp.
532-551. CR, 93, pars II. 1968.

_____. "Ordnung der christlichen Kirche zu Zürich, 1525."
Werke, vol. 4, pp. 671-717. CR, 91. 1927; partial translation
(comprising "Ein Form dess Bittens nach der Leer Pauli 1. Thim.
2.", pp. 686-687) in "Liturgy of the Word, 1525." Liturgies,
pp. 147-148.

_____. "Ratschläge betreffend Messe und Bilder, 1523." Werke,
vol. 2, pp. 804-815. CR, 89. 1908.

_____. "Responsio ad epistolam Ioannis Bugenhagii, 1525." Werke,
vol. 4, pp. 546-576. CR, 91. 1927.

_____. "Subsidium sive coronis de eucharistia, 1525." Werke,
vol. 4, pp. 440-504. CR, 91. 1927.

_____. "Von dem Predigtamt, 1525." Werke, vol. 4, pp. 369-433.
CR, 91. 1927.

_____. "Von der Taufe, von der Wiedertaufe und von der Kinder-
taufe, 1525." Werke, vol. 4, pp. 188-337. CR, 91. 1927;
"Of Baptism." Bromiley, pp. 129-175.

_____. "Vorschlag wegen der Bilder und der Messe, 1524."
Werke, vol. 3, pp. 114-131. CR, 90. 1914.

b. Studies

BAUER, Johannes. "Einige Bemerkunger über die ältesten Züricher
Liturgien." Monatschrift für Gottesdienst und kirchliche Kunst,
17 (1912): 116-124, 152-161, 178-187.

CADOUX, Cecil J.   "Zwingli."   In Christian Worship, pp. 137-153.
   Edited by Nathaniel Micklem.   Oxford: Clarendon Press, 1936.

FARNER, Oskar.   Huldrych Zwingli der schweizerische Reformator.
   Emmishofen: J. Blanke, 1917; Zwingli the Reformer.   Translated by D. G. Sear.   New York: Philosophical Library, 1952.

GARSIDE, Charles.   Zwingli and the Arts.   YHP, 83.   New Haven,
   CT: Yale University Press, 1966; reprint ed., New York: Da
   Capo Press, 1981.

JENNY, Markus.   Zwinglis Stellung zur Musik im Gottesdienst.
   Zurich: Zwingli Verlag, 1966.

KREIENBUHLER, Johann.   Zwingli und das Messopfer.   Zurich:
   Müller, 1927.

LOCHER, G. W.   Im Geist und in der Wahrheit: Die reformatorische
   Wendung im Gottesdienst zu Zurich.   Neukirchen: Buchhand-
   lung des Erziehungsvereins, 1957; reprinted in his Huldrych
   Zwingli in neuer Sicht: Zehn Beiträge zur Theologie der
   Zürcher Reformation, pp. 21-54.   Zurich: Zwingli Verlag, 1969;
   "In Spirit and in Truth: How Worship in Zurich changed at the
   Reformation."   In his Zwingli's Thought: New Perspectives,
   pp. 1-30.   SHCT, 25.   Leiden: Brill, 1981.

PFISTER, Rudolf.   "Zwingli als Liturg."   Der Grundriss.   Schweizerische reformierte Monatsschrift, 5 (1943):   322-329.

POTTER, G. R.   Zwingli.   Cambridge: Cambridge University
   Press, 1976.

RICHARDSON, Cyril C.   Zwingli and Cranmer on the Eucharist.
   Evanston: Seabury-Western Theological Seminary, 1949.

SCHMIDT-CLAUSING, Fritz.   "Die liturgietheologische Arbeit
   Zwinglis am Sintflutgebet des Taufformulars."   Zwingliana, 13
   (1973):   591-615.

_____.   "Die Neudatierung der liturgischen Schriften Zwinglis."
   Theologische Zeitschrift, 25 (1969):   252-265.

_____.   Zwingli als Liturgiker.   Göttingen: Vandenhoeck & Rup-
   recht; Berlin: Evangelische Verlagsanstalt, 1952.

SCHWEIZER, Julius.   Reformierte Abendmahlsgestaltung in der Schau
   Zwinglis.   Basel: F. Reinhardt, 1952.

SOHNGEN, Oskar.   "Zwinglis Stellung zur Musik im Gottesdienst."
   In Theologie in Geschichte und Kunst, pp. 176-192.   Heraus-
   gegeben von Siegfried Herrmann und Oskar Söhngen.   Witten:
   Luther, 1968.

THOMPSON, Bard. "Reformed Liturgies in Translation, I. Ulrich Zwingli." Bulletin of the Theological Seminary of the Evangelical and Reformed Church, 27, 4 (October 1956): 1-13.

———. "Ulrich Zwingli." In Reformers in Profile, pp. 115-141. Edited by Brian A. Gerrish. Philadelphia, PA: Fortress Press, 1967.

———. "Zwingli's Eucharistic Doctrine." Theology and Life, 4, 2 (May 1961): 134-143.

2. Farel

a. Texts

FAREL, William. La Manière et fasson quon tient es lieux que Dieu de sa grâce a visités. Première liturgie des Eglises Réformées de France de l'an 1533. Publiée d'après l'original a l'occasion du troisième jubilé seculaire de la constitution de ces églises l'an 1599 par Jean-Guillaume Baum. Strassbourg: Treuttel & Wurtz, 1859; "The Manner Observed in Preaching When the People are Assembled to Hear the Word of God," and "Our Lord's Supper." In Liturgies of the Western Church, pp. 216-218, 219-224. By Bard Thompson. Cleveland, OH: World, 1961; reprint ed., Philadelphia, PA: Fortress Press, 1981.

b. Studies

BURGER, J. D. "La Conversion de Farel." Bulletin de la Société de l'histoire du protestantisme française, 111 (1965): 199-212.

———. "Le Pasteur Guillaume Farel." Theologische Zeitschrift, 21 (1965): 410-426.

Guillaume Farel: une biographie nouvelle. Neuchâtel: Delachaux & Niestlé, 1930.

"Guillaume Farel, 1489-1565." Kirchenblatt für die reformierte Schweiz, 121, 19 (1965): 292.

JACOBS, Elfriede. Die Sakramentslehre Wilhelm Farels. ZBR, 10. Zurich: Theologischer Verlag, 1978.

MacVICAR, Donald H. "William Farel, Reformer of the Swiss Romand." Ph.D. dissertation, Union Theological Seminary in the City of New York, 1954.

STAEDTKE, Joachim. "Wilhelm Farel: zum 400. Todestag (13. September 1565)." In Reformation und Zeugnis der Kirche, pp. 135-139. Herausgegeben von Dietrich Blaufuss. Zurich: Theologischer Verlag, 1978.

THOMPSON, Bard. "Reformed Liturgies in Translation, IV. William
Farel." Bulletin of the Theological Seminary of the Evangelical
and Reformed Church, 28, 4 (1957): 28-42.

VUILLEUMIER, Henri. Histoire de l'Eglise réformée du pays de
Vaud sous le regime bernois. Lausanne: Editions La Con-
corde, 1927.

3. Bucer

a. Texts

BUCER, Martin. Censura Martini Buceri super libro sacrorum.
Martin Bucer and the Book of Common Prayer. Edited by
E. C. Whitaker. ACC, 55. Great Wakering, Eng.: Mayhew-
McCrimmon, 1974.

_____. Common Places of Martin Bucer. Translated and edited
by D. F. Wright. CLRC, 4. Abingdon, Eng.: Sutton Courtenay Press, 1972.

_____. Martini Buceri Opera Omnia, Series I: Martin Bucers
Deutsche Schriften. Gütersloh: Mohn; Paris: Presses universitaires de France, 1960- . Partial contents relating to worship:
1. Frühschriften 1520-1524. Herausgegeben von Robert Stup-
    perich. 1960.
    Grund und Ursach auss gotlicher schrifft der neüwerungen
    an dem nachtmal des herren, so man die Mess nennet,
    Tauff, Feyrtagen, bildern und gesang in der gemein
    Christi, wann die zusammenkompt, durch und auff das wort
    gottes zů Strassburg fürgenommen, 1524. Pp. 185-278.
2. Schriften der Jahre 1524-1528. Herausgegeben von Robert
    Stupperich. 1962.
    Psalter wol verteutscht, 1526. Pp. 175-224. Gutachten und
    Eingaben um die Abschaffung der Messe und Neuordnung
    des kirchlichen Lebens, 1525-1529. Pp. 423-558.
5. Strassburg und Münster im Kampf um den rechten Glauben
    1532-1534. Herausgegeben von Robert Supperich. 1978.
    Kirchenordnung, 1534. Pp. 15-42.
7. Schriften der Jahre 1538-1539. Herausgegeben von Robert
    Stupperich. 1964.
    Ordenung der Kirchenůbunge. Für die Kirchen zu Cassel,
    1539. Pp. 279-318.
    Martin Bucers Vorrede zum Strassburger Gesangbuch. Pp.
    576-582.

_____. "Psalter mit aller Kirchenübung." In Die Strassburger
liturgischen Ordnungen im Zeitalter der Reformation, pp. 90-114.
Herausgegeben von Friedrich Hubert. Göttingen: Vandenhoeck

& Ruprecht, 1900; "Psalter with Complete Church Practice." In Liturgies of the Western Church, pp. 167-181. By Bard Thompson. Cleveland, OH: World, 1961; reprint ed., Philadelphia, PA: Fortress Press, 1981.

b. Studies

BORNERT, Rene. "Martin Bucer et la liturgie strassbourgeoise de 1537-1539." Archives de l'Eglise d'Alsace, 35 (1971): 105-125.

BUCHSENSCHUTZ, Louis. Histoire des liturgies en langue allemande dans l'Eglise de Strasbourg au XVIe siècle. Cahors: A. Coueslant, 1900.

CYPRIS, Ottomar F. "Basic Principles: Translation and Commentary of Martin Bucer's Grund und Ursach, 1524." Th.D. dissertation, Union Theological Seminary in the City of New York, 1971.

EELLS, Hastings. Martin Bucer. New Haven, CT: Yale University Press, 1931; reprint ed., New York: Russell & Russell, 1971.

ERICHSON, Alfred. Die Calvinische und die altstrassburgische Gottesdienstordnung. Strasbourg: J. H. E. Haitz, 1894.

FICKER, Johannes. "Das grösste Prachtwerk des Strassburger Buchdrucks." Archiv für Reformationsgeschichte, 38 (1941): 198-230.

GRESCHAT, Martin. "Die Anfange der reformatorischen Theologie Martin Bucers." In Reformation und Humanismus. Robert Stupperich zum 65. Geburtstag, pp. 124-140. Herausgegeben von Martin Greschat und J. F. G. Goeters. Witten: Luther Verlag, 1969.

HAZLETT, Ian. "The Development of Martin Bucer's Thinking on the Sacrament of the Lord's Supper in its Historical and Theological Context 1523-1534." Diss. Münster, 1975.

_____. "Zur Auslegung von Johannes 6 bei Bucer während der Abendmahlskontroverse." In Bucer und seine Zeit: Forschungsbeiträge und Bibliographie, pp. 74-87. Herausgegeben von Marijn de Kroon und Friedhelm Krüger. Wiesbaden: Steiner, 1976.

HOPF, Constantin. Martin Bucer and the English Reformation. Oxford: Basil Blackwell, 1946.

HUBERT, Friedrich H., ed. Die Strassburger liturgischen Ordnungen im Zeitalter der Reformation. Göttingen: Vandenhoeck & Ruprecht, 1900.

KITTELSON, James M. "Martin Bucer and the Sacramentarian Controversy: The Origins of his Policy of Concord." Archiv für Reformationsgeschichte, 64 (1973): 166-183.

KOHLS, Ernst-Wilhelm. "Die hessischen Kirchenordnungen des 16. Jahrhunderts." Jahrbuch für Liturgik und Hymnologie, 14 (1969): 120-122.

KROON, Marijn de. "Bemerkungen Martin Bucers über das Abendmahl in seinem Psalmenkommentar von 1529." In Bucer und seine Zeit: Forschungsbeiträge und Bibliographie, pp. 88-100. Herausgegeben von Marijn de Kroon und Friedhelm Krüger. Wiesbaden: Steiner, 1976.

KRUGER, Friedhelm. Bucer und Erasmus: eine Untersuchung zum Einfluss des Erasmus auf die Theologie Martin Bucers, esp. pp. 183-224. Wiesbaden: Steiner, 1970.

OLD, Hughes O. "Daily Prayer in the Reformed Church of Strasbourg, 1525-1530." Worship, 52 (1978): 121-138.

POLL, Gerrit Jan van de. Martin Bucer's Liturgical Ideas. Assen: Van Gorcum, 1954.

ROTT, Jean. "Bucer et des débuts de la querelle sacramentaire." Revue d'histoire et de philosophie religieuses, 34 (1954): 224-254.

SMEND, Julius. Der erste evangelische Gottesdienst in Strassburg. Strasbourg: Heitz & Muendel, 1897.

STEPHENS, W. P. The Holy Spirit in the Theology of Martin Bucer. Cambridge: Cambridge University Press, 1970.

THOMPSON, Bard. "Reformed Liturgies in Translation, II. Martin Bucer." Bulletin of the Theological Seminary of the Evangelical and Reformed Church, 28, 1 (January 1957): 1-18.

ZIPPERT, Christian. "Der Gottesdienst in der Theologie des jungen Bucer." Diss., Marburg, 1969.

4. Calvin

a. Texts

Note: Abbreviated entries have been adopted from the following sources:

Opera omnia--Ioannis Calvini Opera quae supersunt omnia. 34 vols. Ediderunt Gulielmus Baum, Eduardus

Cunitz, Eduardus Reuss. CR, 29-62. Brunswick:
C. A. Schwetschke, 1863-1900.
Opera selecta--Joannis Calvini Opera selecta. 5 vols.
Ediderunt Petrus Barth. Munich: Kaiser, 1926-1936.
Theological Treatises--Calvin: Theological Treatises.
Translated with introductions and notes by J, K. S.
Reid. LCC, 22. Philadelphia, PA: Westminster
Press, 1954.
Tracts--CALVIN, John. Tracts and Treatises in De-
fense of the Reformed Faith. 3 vols. Translated by
Henry Beveridge. Historical notes added to the pre-
sent edition by Thomas F. Torrance. Grand Rapids,
MI: Eerdmans, 1958.

CALVIN, John. "Articles concernant l'organisation de l'église et
du culte a Genève, proposés au Conseil par les ministres
(1537)." Opera omnia, vol. 10, 1, cols. 5-14. CR, 38. 1871;
Opera selecta, vol. 1, pp. 369-377; "Articles concerning the
Organization of the Church and of Worship at Geneva, 1537."
Theological Treatises, pp. 48-55.

_____. "Breve et clarum doctrinae de coena Domini compendium."
Opera omnia, vol. 9, cols. 677-688. CR, 37. 1870.

_____. "Confessio fidei de Eucharistia (1537)." Opera omnia,
vol. 9, cols. 711-712. CR, 37. 1870; Opera selecta, vol. 1,
pp. 433-436; "Confession of Faith concerning the Eucharist
(1537)." Theological Treatises, pp. 167-169.

_____. "Consensio mutua in re sacramentaria (1549)." Opera
omnia, vol. 7, cols. 693-748. CR, 35. 1868; Opera selecta,
vol. 2, pp. 241-253; "Mutual Consent in regard to the Sacraments." Tracts, vol. 2, pp. 199-244.

_____. "De fugiendis impiorum illicitis sacris et puritate christi-
anae religionis observanda (1537)." Opera omnia, vol. 5, cols.
239-278. CR, 33. 1866; Opera selecta, vol. 1, pp. 289-328;
"On Shunning the Unlawful Rites of the Ungodly, and Preserv-
ing the Purity of the Christian Religion." Tracts, vol. 3, pp.
360-411.

_____. "Defensio sanae et orthodoxae doctrinae de sacramentis
(1555)." Opera omnia, vol. 9, cols. 1-40. CR, 37. 1870;
Opera selecta, vol. 2, pp. 259-287.

_____. "Dilucida explicatio sanae doctrinae de vera participatione
carnis et sanguinis Christi in sacra coena (1561)." Opera omnia,
vol. 9, cols. 457-524. CR, 37. 1870; "The Clear Explanation
of Sound Doctrine Concerning the True Partaking of the Flesh
and Blood of Christ in the Holy Supper." Tracts, vol. 2, pp.
495-572; Theological Treatises, pp. 257-324.

_____. "La Forme des prières et chantz ecclésiastiques ... (1542)."
Opera omnia, vol. 6, cols. 161-210. CR, 34. 1867; Opera
selecta, vol. 2, pp. 1-58; "Forms of Prayer for the Church"
and "Forms of Administering the Sacraments." Tracts, vol. 2,
pp. 102-126; "The Form of Church Prayers and Hymns." In
Liturgies of the Western Church, pp. 197-210. By Bard
Thompson. Cleveland, OH: World, 1961; reprint ed., Philadelphia, PA: Fortress Press, 1981.

_____. La Forme des prières et chants ecclésiastiques Genève
1542. Edited by Pierre Pidoux. Kassel: Bärenreiter, 1959.

_____. La Forme des prières Ecclésiastiques et Catéchisme par
Jean Calvin. Genève: Crespin, 1552; facsimile ed., New
Brunswick, NJ: Friends of the Rutgers University Libraries,
1973.

_____. Institutio Religionis Christianae (Editio princeps, 1536),
cap. 4 & 5. In Opera omnia, vol. 1, cols. 102-195. CR, 29.
1863; Opera selecta, vol. 1, pp. 118-223.

_____. Institutio Christianae Religionis (1559), lib. 4, cap. 14-
19. In Opera omnia, vol. 2, cols. 941-1092. CR, 30. 1864;
Opera selecta, vol. 5, pp. 258-471; Institutes of the Christian
Religion, vol. 2, pp. 1276-1484. Edited by John T. McNeill.
Translated by Ford Lewis Battles. LCC, 21. Philadelphia, PA:
Westminster Press, 1960.

_____. "(Petit) Traicté de la Saincte Cene de Nostre Seigneur
Iesus Christ (1541)." Opera omnia, vol. 5, cols. 429-460.
CR, 33. 1866; Opera selecta, vol. 1, pp. 499-530; "Short
Treatise on the Holy Supper of Our Lord Jesus Christ."
Tracts, vol. 2, pp. 163-198; "Short Treatise on the Lord's
Supper (1541)." Theological Treatises, pp. 140-166.

_____. "Projet d'ordonnances ecclésiastiques (1541)." Opera
omnia, vol. 10/1, cols. 15-30. CR, 38. 1871; Opera selecta,
vol. 2, pp. 328-345; "Draft Ecclesiastical Ordinances (1541)."
Theological Treatises, pp. 58-72.

_____. "Secunda defensis piae et orthodoxae de sacramentis fidei
contra Ioachimi Westphali calumnias (1556)." Opera omnia, vol.
9, cols. 41-120. CR, 37. 1870; "Second Defense of the Pious
and Orthodox Faith Concerning the Sacraments." Tracts, vol.
2, pp. 245-345.

_____. "Summa doctrinae de ministerio verbi et sacramentorum."
Opera omnia, vol. 9, cols. 773-778. CR, 37. 1870; "Summary
of Doctrine Concerning the Ministry of the Word and the Sacraments." Theological Treatises, pp. 170-177.

_____. "Supplex exhortatio ad Caesarem Carolum Quintum et
Principes aliosque ordines Spirae nunc imperii conventum
agentes, ut restituendae ecclesiae curam serio velint suscipere
(1543)." Opera omnia, vol. 6, cols. 453-534. CR, 34. 1867;
"The Necessity of Reforming the Church." Tracts, vol. 1,
pp. 121-234; Theological Treatises, pp. 184-216.

_____. "Ultima admonitio ad Ioachimum Westphalum (1557)."
Opera omnia, vol. 9, cols. 137-252. CR, 37. 1870; "Last Admonition of John Calvin to Joachim Westphal." Tracts, vol. 2,
pp. 346-494.

b. Studies

BERGIER, Jean Francois, and KINGDON, Robert McCune, eds.
Registres de la compagnie des pasteurs de Genève au temps de
Calvin. Tome I: 1546-1553, par Jean François Bergier; and
Tome II: 1553-1564, par Robert M. Kingdon avec Jean Fran-
çois Bergier et Alain Dufour. Geneva: Droz, 1962- ; The
Register of the Company of Pastors of Geneva in the Time of
Calvin. Edited and translated by Philip Edgcumbe Hughes.
Grand Rapids, MI: Eerdmans, 1966.

CADIER, Jean. "La Doctrine calviniste de la saint cène." Etudes
théologiques et religieuses, 26, 1 & 2 (1951).

DOUMERGUE, Emile. Essai sur l'histoire du culte réformé. Paris:
Fischbacher, 1890.

_____. Jean Calvin. 7 vols. Lausanne: Bridel, 1899-1927.

FITZER, Joseph. "The Augustinian Roots of Calvin's Eucharistic
Thought." Augustinian Studies, 7 (1976): 69-98.

HARTVELT, Gerrit Pieter. Verum Corpus: een studie over een
centraal hoofdstuk uit de avondmaalsleer van Calvijn. Delft:
Meinema, 1960.

HOFFMANN, Gottfried. "Eine biblisch-theologische Begründung der
Liturgie im französischen Calvinismus." Liturgisches Jahrbuch,
68 (1956): 68-75.

McDONNELL, Kilian. "Calvin's Conception of the Liturgy and the
Future of the Roman Catholic Liturgy." In The Crisis of Litur-
gical Reform, pp. 87-97. Concilium, 42. New York: Paulist
Press, 1969.

_____. John Calvin, the Church, and the Eucharist. Princeton,
NJ: Princeton University Press, 1967.

MILNER, Benjamin Charles. Calvin's Doctrine of the Church. SHCT,
5. Leiden: Brill, 1970.

NIESEL, Wilhelm. Calvins Lehre vom Abendmahl im Lichte seiner
   letzten Antwort an Westphal. 2. Aufl. FGLP, 3. Reihe, 3.
   Munich: Kaiser, 1935.

PACHE, Edouard. "La Sainte Cène selon Calvin." Revue de théologie et de philosophie, 24 (1936): 308-327.

PARKER, Thomas H. L. The Oracles of God: An Introduction to
   the Preaching of John Calvin. London: Lutterworth Press,
   1947.

ROGGE, Joachim. Virtus und res: um die Abendmahlswirklichkeit
   bei Calvin. AZT, 1. Reihe, 18. Stuttgart: Calwer Verlag,
   1965.

SCHADE, Herwarth von. "Das fünfte Verbrechen: Joachim Westphal, Johannes Calvin und die Perikopenfrage im 16. Jahrhundert." Jahrbuch für Liturgik und Hymnologie, 22 (1978):
   124-129.

SCHEUNER, Dora. "Calvins Genfer Liturgie und seine Strassburger
   Liturgie textgeschichtlich dargestellt." In Festschrift für D.
   Albert Schädelin, pp. 79-85. Bern: Lang, 1950.

SCHOLL, Hans. Der Dienst des Gebetes nach Johannes Calvin.
   SDST, 22. Zurich: Awingli Verlag, 1968.

THOMPSON, Bard. "Reformed Liturgies in Translation, III. John
   Calvin." Bulletin of the Theological Seminary of the Evangelical
   and Reformed Church, 28, 3 (1957): 42-62.

TYLENDA, Joseph N. "Calvin and Christ's Presence in the Supper
   --True or Real." Scottish Journal of Theology, 27 (1974):
   65-75.

_____. "A Eucharistic Sacrifice in Calvin's Theology?" Theologi-
   cal Studies, 37 (1976): 456-466.

_____. "A Study in the Eucharistic Theologies of John Calvin,
   Reformer of Geneva and of Max Thurian, Monk of Taizé."
   Diss., Pontificia Universitas Gregoriana, 1964.

WALKER, G. M. "The Lord's Supper in the Theology and Practice
   of Calvin." In John Calvin, pp. 131-148. Edited by G. E.
   Duffield. CSRT, 1. Abingdon, Eng.: Sutton Courtenay
   Press; Grand Rapids, MI: Eerdmans, 1966.

WALLACE, R. S. Calvin's Doctrine of the Word and Sacrament.
   Grand Rapids, MI: Eerdmans, 1957.

WEBER, A. S. "Doctrine of the Lord's Supper in Calvin's System

of Thought." Reformed Church Review, Fourth Series, 13
(1909): 209-228.

WHALE, J. S. "Calvin." In Christian Worship: Studies in Its
History and Meaning, pp. 152-171. Edited by Nathaniel Micklem. Oxford: Clarendon Press, 1936.

WILL, Robert. "Les Origines de la liturgie protestante de Strasbourg." Revue d'histoire et de philosophie religieuses, 9 (1929):
479-486; 11 (1931): 521-537.

_____. "La Première liturgie de Calvin." Revue d'histoire et de
philosophie religieuses, 18 (1938): 523-529.

ZEEDEN, Ernest Walter. "Calvinistische Elemente in de kurpfal-
zischen Kirchenordnung von 1563." In Existenz und Ordnung,
pp. 183-214. Frankfurt: Klostermann, 1962.

5. Other Continental Reformers

a. Texts

LASKI, Jan. [John a Lasco]. "Forma ac Ratio tota ecclesiastici
ministerii." In Joannis a Lasco Opera tam edita quam inedita,
recensuit, vitam auctoris enarravit A. Kuyper, vol. 2, pp. 1-
277. Amsterdam: F. Muller, 1866.

MICRONIUS, Martin. Die christliche ordinancien der nederlantschen
ghemeinten te Londen. Opniew uitgegeven en van een inleiding
voorzien door W. F. Dankbaar. KSNAK, 7. The Hague: Nijhoff, 1956.

OECOLAMPADIUS, John. Form und gstalt Wie des Herren Nachtmal/
Der kinder Tauff/ Der Krancken haymsüchung/ zu Basel ge-
braucht vnd gehalten werden. 1525?; "Form and Manner of the
Lord's Supper, Infant Baptism, and the Visitation of the Sick
as They are Used and Observed in Basel." In Liturgies of the
Western Church, pp. 211-215. By Bard Thompson. Cleveland,
OH: World, 1961; reprint ed., Philadelphia, PA: Fortress
Press, 1981.

POLLANUS, Valerandus. Liturgia Sacra (1551-1555). Opniew uitgegeven A. C. Honders. Kerkhistorische Bijdragen, 1. Leiden:
Brill, 1970.

b. Studies

KOCH, Ernst. "Die Grundzüge der Liturgik Heinrich Bullingers."
Jahrbuch für Liturgik und Hymnologie, 10 (1965): 22-34.

KRUSKE, Karl A. R. Johannes à Lasco und der Sakramentsstreit.
SGTK, 7/1. Leipzig: Deiterich'sche Verlags-buchhandlung,
T. Weicher, 1901.

McLELLAND, Joseph C. The Visible Words of God: An Exposition
of the Sacramental Theology of Peter Martyr Vermigli, 1500–
1562. Edinburgh: Oliver & Boyd; Grand Rapids, MI: Eerdmans, 1957.

SPRENGLER-RUPPENTHAL, Anneliese. Mysterium und Riten nach
der Londoner Kirchenordnung der Niederländer (ca. 1550 bis
1566). FKRK, 7. Köln: Böhlau, 1967.

STAEHELIN, Ernst. Das theologische Lebenswerk Johannes Oekolampads. QFR, 21. Leipzig: M. Heinsius, 1939.

6. Knox

a. Texts

KNOX, John. The Forme of Prayers and Ministration of the Sacraments, &c. Vsed in the Englishe Congregation at Geneua: and
approued by the Famous and Godly Learned Man, Iohn Caluyn.
Geneva: John Crespin, 1556; "The Forms of Prayers and Ministration of the Sacraments." In Liturgies of the Western Church,
pp. 295-307. By Bard Thompson. Cleveland, OH: World,
1961; reprint ed., Philadelphia, PA: Fortress Press, 1981.

_____. John Knox's History of the Reformation in Scotland. 2
vols. Edited by William Croft Dickinson. London: Thomas
Nelson; New York: Philosophical Library, 1950.

_____. The Works of John Knox. 6 vols. Edited by David Laing.
Edinburgh: Printed for the Woodrow Society, 1846-1864; Edin-
burgh: J. Thin, 1854-1895; reprint ed., New York: AMS
Press, 1966.

MAXWELL, William D., ed. John Knox's Genevan Service Book,
1556: The Liturgical Portions of the Genevan Service Book
used by John Knox while a Minister of the English Congregation of Marian Exiles at Geneva, 1556-1559. Edinburgh: Oliver
& Boyd, 1931; reprint ed., London: Faith Press, 1965.

b. Studies

(See also XIV. E.1., Scotland, p. 338.)

DONALDSON, Gordon. The Scottish Reformation. Cambridge: Cambridge University Press, 1960.

GREAVES, Richard L. "John Knox, the Reformed Tradition, and
    the Sacrament of the Lord's Supper." Archiv für Reformations-
    geschichte, 66 (1975): 238-255.

LANG, August. "Genfer Liturgie des J. Knox." Reformierte
    Kirchenzeitung, 81 (1931): 315.

REID, W. Stanford. Trumpeter of God: A Biography of John
    Knox. New York: Scribner, 1974.

C. THE PALATINATE

1. Texts

THOMPSON, Bard, ed. "Palatinate Liturgy, Heidelberg, 1563."
    Theology and Life, 6 (1963): 49-67.
    --Translated from Bekenntnisschriften und Kirchenordnungen,
        pp. 187-205. Edited by Wilhelm Niesel. Zürich: Evan-
        gelischer Verlag, 1938.
    Note: J. H. A. Bomberger translated the Palatinate Liturgy
    (1563) into English in The Mercersburg Review, II (1860), 81-
    96, 265-286; III (1851), 97-128.

2. Studies

THOMPSON, Bard. "Heidelberg Catechism and the Mercersburg
    Theology." Theology and Life, 6 (1963): 225-238.

_____. "The Palatinate Church Order of 1563." Church History,
    23 (1954): 339-354. (See also XIV. B. 4. ZEEDEN above.)

D. POST-REFORMATION CONTINENTAL
    REFORMED CHURCHES

1. Texts

BERSIER, Eugène Arthur Francois. Liturgie à l'usage des églises
    réformées. Nouvelle ed. Paris: Fischbacher, 1876.

_____. Project de revision de la liturgie. Paris: n.p., 1888.

EBRARD, Johannes H. A., ed. Reformirtes Kirchenbuch. Zurich,
    1847.

Eglise nationale évangélique réformée du canton de Vaud. Liturgie.
    Vevey: Klausfelder, 1964.

Eglise nationale protestante de Genève.   Liturgie de l'Eglise de
Genève.   Geneva: n.p., 1945.

Eglise réformée Neuchâteloise.   La Liturgie; ou la manière de célébrer le service divin dans l'Eglise réformée Neuchâteloise.
6. éd.   Neuchâtel: James Attiner, 1873.

Eglises réformées de France.   La manier et fasson quon tient es
lieux que Dieu de sa grace a visites.   Première liturgie des
églises réformées de France de l'an 1533, publiée d'après l'original à l'occasion du troisième jubilé séculaire de la constitution
de ces églises l'an 1559.   Par Jean-Guillaume Baum.   Strasbourg: n.p., 1859.

Eglises réformées évangéliques de France.   Liturgie des églises réformées de France, revisée par le Synod Général officieux.
Nouvelle ed.   Paris: Editions Berger Levrault, 1931.

Evangelisch-reformierte Kirche des Kantons Bern.   Liturgie pour
les paroisses de langue française.   Moutier: M. Robert, 1955.

Evangelisch-reformierte Kirche in Nordwestdeutschland.   Kirchenbuch: Gebete und Ordnungen für die unter dem Wort versammelte Gemeinde.   Herausgegeben vom Moderamen des Reformierten Bundes.   2. Aufl.   Neukirchen: Moers, 1956.

Evangelische-reformierte Landeskirche des Kantons Aargau.   Liturgie.   2 vols.   2. Au fl.   Zofingen: Kuhn, 1959.

Evangelisch-reformierte Landeskirche des Kantons Zürich.   Züricher
Gottesdienstordnung: Entwurf zu einer Ordnung für den
Gottesdienst mit Predigt, Abendmahl, Taufe und Konfirmation.
Herausgegeben von Kirchenrat des Kantons Zürich.   Zurich:
Zwingli Verlag, 1965.

_____.   Liturgiekomission.   Kirchenbuch: Ordnungen und Texte
für den Gottesdienst der Gemeinde.   2 vols.   Zurich: Kirchenrat des Kantons, 1969.

Evangelisch-reformierten Kirchen in der deutschsprachigen Schweiz.
Liturgie.   2 vols.   Bern: Stämpfli, 1964.

Gereformeerde Kerken in Nederland.   Kerkorde van de Gereformeerde Kerken in Nederland.   Kampen: Kok, 1971 [1972].

_____.   Orden voor de eredienst van de Gereformeerde Kerken
in Nederland.   2. druk.   Kampen: Kok, 1967.

Liturgie des temps de fête à l'usage des Eglises réformées de la
Suisse Romande.   Lausanne: Communauté de travail des Commissions romandes de liturgie, 1979.

Nederlandse Hervormde Kerk. Dienstboek voor de Nederlandse
Hervormde Kerk in Ontwerp. The Hague: Boekcentrum, 1955.

OSTERWALD, Jean Frédéric, ed. La Liturgie, ou la manière de
célébrer le service divin. Basel: Jean Pistorius, 1713.

_____. _____. 2. éd. Neufchâtel: Jonas Galandre, 1737.

_____. _____. 4. éd. Neufchâtel: George Sinnet, 1751.

2. Studies

DANKBAAR, W. F. "Middeleeuwse oorsprongen van Gereformeerde
Liturgie." Nederlands Theologisch Tijdschrift, 30 (1976):
1-16.

FARNER, Oskar. Wegmarken zur Besinnung über den Dienst der
Kirche im Auftrag des Zürcherischen Kirchenrates. 3. Aufl.
Zürich: Zwingli Verlag, 1962.

Handboek voor den eeredienst in de Nederlandse Hervormde Kerk.
Samengesteld door den Liturgischen Kring. Baarn: Voor
Adoremus door Bosch & Keuning, 1934.

KRUIJF, Ernst Frederik. Liturgiek: ten dienste van dienaren der
Nederlandsche Hervormde Kerk. Groningen: J. B. Wolters,
1901.

KUYPER, Abraham. Onze Eeredienst. Kampen: Kok, 1911.

LACHERET, E. La Liturgie Wallonne: étude historique et pratique
suivie des textes anciens et d'un projet de revision. Paris:
La Haye, 1890.

LEEUW, Gerhardus van der. Liturgiek. Nijkerk: Callenbach,
1946.

LEKKERKERKER, Arie Frederik Nelis. Kanttekeningen bij het
Hervormde Dienstboek. 4 vols. in 1. The Hague: Boekencentrum, 1952-1956.

_____. De liturgische situatie in de Nederlandse Hervormde
Kerk. Wageningen: H. Veenman, 1952?

LESCRAUWAET, Josephus Franciscus. De liturgische beweging onder de Nederlandse Hervormden in oecumenisch perspectief:
een fenomenologische en kritische studie. Bussum: Paul
Brand, 1957.

LUTHI, Walter, and THURNEYSEN, Edward. Predigt; Beichte;

Abendmahl: ein Wort an unsere Gemeinden. Zollikon: Evan-
gelischer Verlag, 1957; Preaching, Confession, the Lord's
Supper. Translated by Francis J. Brooke III. Richmond, VA:
John Knox Press, 1960.

MENSINGA, Johannes Aleta Marinus. Verhandeling over de liturgische schriften der Nederlandsche Hervormde. The Hague:
Erven Thierry en Mensing, 1851.

MEULENBELT, H. H. Onze onderlinge bijeenkomst. Utrecht:
G. J. A. Ruys, 1918.

MOREL, Bernard. "Les Origines liturgiques du culte réformé de
langue française." Foi et Vie, 52 (1954): 1-17.

OBERMAN, G. W. "The High Church Movement in the Dutch Re-
formed Church." In Northern Catholicism, pp. 488-500.
Edited by N. P. Williams and Charles Harris. London: SPCK;
New York: Macmillan, 1933.

SCHOOT, Ebel van der. Hervormde eredienst. The Hague: Boekcentrum, 1950.

SCHOTEL, Gilles Dionsius Jacobus. De openbare eeredienst der
Nederlandse Hervormde Kerk in de zestiende, zeventiende en
achttiende eeuw. 2. uitg. door H. C. Rogge. Leiden: A. W.
Sijthoff, 1906.

SNOEKS, Remi. L'argument de tradition dans la controverse eucharistique entre catholiques et réformés français au XVII siècle.
Louvain: Presses universitaires de Louvain, 1951.

E. REFORMED CHURCHES OF THE UNITED KINGDOM,
   AUSTRALIA, AND SOUTH AFRICA

1. Scotland

(See also XIV. B. 6. Knox, p. 334.)

a. Texts

CAIRNS, David, ed. Worship Now: A Collection of Services and
Prayers for Public Worship. Edinburgh: St. Andrews Press,
1972.

Church of Scotland. The Book of Common Order (1979). Edinburgh: Saint Andrew Press, 1979.

_____. Book of Common Order of the Church of Scotland. Edin-
burgh: Oxford University Press, 1940.

_____. The Book of Common Order of the Church of Scotland commonly known as John Knox's Liturgy. With Historical Introduction and Illustrative Notes by G. W. Sprott. Edinburgh: W. Blackwood, 1901.

_____. Euchologion. A Book of Common Order: Being Forms of Prayer, and Administration of the Sacraments, and Other Ordinances of the Church. 7th ed. rev. Edinburgh: W. Blackwood, 1896.

_____. Euchologion. A Book of Common Order, etc. Edited by George W. Sprott. Edinburgh: W. Blackwood, 1905.

_____. Manual of Church Praise, according to the Use of the Church of Scotland. Edinburgh: Church of Scotland Committee on Publications, 1932.

_____. Ordinal and Service Book for Use in Courts of the Church. 2d ed. London: Oxford University Press, 1954; 3d ed., 1962.

_____. Prayers for the Christian Year. London: Oxford University Press, 1935.

_____. Prayers for the Christian Year. 2d ed. London: Oxford University Press, 1952.

_____. Prayers for Divine Service in Church and Home. Edinburgh: Blackwood, 1923.

_____. Prayers for Divine Service. 2d ed. Edinburgh: Blackwood, 1929.

_____. The Scotch Minister's Assistant; or, a Collection of Forms, for Celebrating the Ordinances of Marriage, Baptism, and the Lord's Supper, according to the Usage of the Church of Scotland, with Suitable Devotions for Church and Family Worship. Inverness, Scot.: Young & Imray, 1802.

_____. The Scottish Collects of 1595. Edinburgh: Church of Scotland, Committee on Publications, 1933.

_____. Committee on Public Worship and Aids to Devotion. The Divine Service: Three Orders for the Celebration of the Lord's Supper. London: Oxford University Press, 1973.

_____. _____. New Ways to Worship. Edinburgh: St. Andrew Press, 1980.

_____. _____. Prayers for Contemporary Worship. Edinburgh: St. Andrew Press, 1977.

_____. _____. Prayers for Sunday Services. Edinburgh:
    St. Andrew Press, 1980.

HURLBUT, Stephen A., ed. The Liturgy of the Church of Scot-
    land since the Reformation. 4 vols. Washington, DC: St.
    Albans, 1944-1952.

SPROTT, George W., ed. The Book of Common Prayer and Ad-
    ministration of the Sacraments of the Church of Scotland as it
    was sett downe at first etc. Edinburgh: Edmonston & Doug-
    las, 1871.

_____, ed. Scottish Liturgies of the Reign of James VI. Lon-
    don: Blackwood, 1901.

United Free Church of Scotland. Book of Common Order, 1928,
    for Use in Services and Offices of the Church. London: Ox-
    ford University Press, 1928.

_____. Church Worship Association. Anthology of Prayers for
    Public Worship. Edinburgh: Macniven & Wallace, 1907.

_____. _____. Directory and Forms for Public Worship.
    Edinburgh: Macniven & Wallace, 1909; New ed., 1920.

United Presbyterian Church (Scotland). Presbyterian Forms of
    Service. 3d ed. Edinburgh: Macniven, 1899.

WOTHERSPOON, H. J. The Divine Service ('H θεια λειτουργία):
    A Eucharistic Office according to the Forms of the Primitive
    Church. 2d ed. London: Hodder & Stoughton, 1929.

b. Studies

AVERY, W. L. "Biblical Warrants: An Examination of the Scrip-
    tural and Early Patristic Basis for the Major Liturgical Practices
    of the Church of Scotland." Ph.D. dissertation, University of
    Glasgow, 1969.

BARKLEY, John M. "The Renaissance of Public Worship in the
    Church of Scotland, 1865-1905." In Studies in Church History,
    vol. 14: Renaissance and Renewal in Christian History, pp.
    339-350. Edited by Derek Baker. Oxford: Blackwell, 1977.

_____. The Worship of the Reformed Church: An Ex-
    position and Critical Analysis of the Eucharistic, Baptismal, and
    Confirmation Rites in the Scottish, English-Welsh, and Irish
    Liturgies. ESW, 15. London: Lutterworth, 1966; Richmond,
    VA: John Knox Press, 1967.

BRUCE, Robert. Sermons. Reprinted from the original edition of

M.D.XC. and M.D.XCI by Robert Wodrow. Edited by William Cunningham. Wodrow Society Publications. Edinburgh: Wodrow Society, 1843. [In Scots dialect]

_____. The Mysterie of the Lord's Supper. Translated by M. S. Mitchell. London: Thomas Man, 1614. [English]

_____. Sermons on the Sacrament. Translated by John Laidlau. Edinburgh: Oliphant, Anderson & Ferrier, 1901.

_____. The Mystery of the Lord's Supper: Sermons on the Sacrament preached in the Kirk of Edinburgh by Robert Bruce in A.D. 1589. Translated and edited by Thomas F. Torrance. London: James Clarke; Richmond, VA: John Knox Press, 1958.

BURNET, George B. The Holy Communion in the Reformed Church of Scotland. Edinburgh: Oliver & Boyd, 1960.

CAIRNS, David. "The Holy Communion in the Presbyterian Churches." In The Holy Communion: A Symposium, pp. 67-84. Edited by Hugh Martin. London: SCM Press, 1947.

CHEYNE, A. C. "Worship in the Kirk: Knox, Westminster and the 1940 Book." In Reformation and Revolution, pp. 70-81. Edited by Duncan Shaw. Edinburgh: St. Andrew Press, 1967.

COWAN, William. A Bibliography of the Book of Common Order and Psalm Book of the Church of Scotland, 1556-1644. Edinburgh: [Edinburgh Bibliographic Society], 1913.

FORRESTER, Duncan, and MURRAY, Douglas, eds. Studies in the History of Worship in Scotland. Edinburgh: T. & T. Clark, 1984.

LEISHMAN, Thomas. "The Ritual of the Church of Scotland." In The Church of Scotland, Past and Present: Its History, Its Relation to the Law and the State, Its Doctrine, Ritual, Discipline and Patrimony, vol. 5, pp. 307-426. Edited by Robert Herbert Story. London: W. Mackenzie, 1890-1891.

McMILLAN, William. The Worship of the Scottish Reformed Church, 1550-1638. London: J. Clarke, 1931.

MAXWELL, William D. A History of Worship in the Church of Scotland. London: Oxford University Press, 1955.

ROSS, J. M. Four Centuries of Scottish Worship. New ed. Edinburgh: St. Andrew Press, 1972.

SPROTT, George W. The Worship and Offices of the Church of Scotland. Edinburgh: Blackwood, 1882.

_____. The Worship of the Church of Scotland during the Cov-
enanting Period, 1638-61. Edinburgh: n.p., 1893.

_____. The Worship, Rites and Ceremonies of the Church of
Scotland Compared with those of the other Reformed Churches
and of the Primitive Church. Edinburgh: Blackwood, 1863.

2. England, Ireland, and Wales

OWEN, David M., ed. Praise and Prayer: For Use in Worship by
Minister and Congregation. Reigate, Eng.: Reigate Park
Church, 1979. [United Reformed Church]

Presbyterian Church in Ireland. Book of Public Worship of the
Presbyterian Church in Ireland. Belfast: B. N. L. Printing
Co., 1965.

Presbyterian Church of England. The Presbyterian Service Book.
London: Publications Committee of the Presbyterian Church of
England, 1968.

United Reformed Church in England and Wales. Book of Order for
Worship. London: United Reformed Church, 1974.

_____. Doctrine and Worship Committee. A Book of Services.
Edinburgh: St. Andrew Press, 1980.

3. Australia

Presbyterian Church of Australia. Book of Common Order of the
Presbyterian Church of Australia. 2d ed. London: Oxford
University Press, 1965.

4. South Africa

Presbyterian Church of Southern Africa. Service Book and Ordinal
of the Presbyterian Church of Southern Africa. London: Oxford University Press, 1969.

F. REFORMED CHURCHES OF THE UNITED STATES
AND CANADA

1. General Studies

COFFIN, Henry Sloane. The Public Worship of God: A Source
Book. Philadelphia, PA: Westminster Press, 1946.

DANIELS, Harold M., ed. Worship in the Community of Faith:
Liturgical Studies from the Perspective of the Contemporary
Reformed Tradition. Louisville, KY: The Joint Office of Wor-
ship, 1982.

HAGEMAN, Howard G. "The Need and Promise of Reformed Preaching." Reformed Review, 28 (1974-1975): 75-84.

_____. Pulpit and Table: Some Chapters in the History of Wor-
ship in the Reformed Churches. Richmond, VA: John Knox
Press, 1962.

_____. "Three Reformed Liturgies." Theology Today, 15 (1959):
507-520.

MELTON, Julius. Presbyterian Worship in America: Changing Patterns Since 1787. Richmond, VA: John Knox Press, 1967.

_____. "Presbyterian Worship in Twentieth Century America."
In The Divine Drama in History and Liturgy, pp. 179-199.
Edited by John E. Booty. Allison Park, PA: Pickwick Pub-
lications, 1984.

2. Christian Reformed Church

CHRISTIAN REFORMED CHURCH. The Psalter, with the Doctrinal
Standards and Liturgy of the Christian Reformed Church.
Grand Rapids, MI: Eerdmans-Sevensma, 1916?

_____. The Psalter, Doctrinal Standards, Liturgy and Church
Order of the Christian Reformed Church in America. Grand
Rapids, MI: Eerdmans, 1927.

_____. Psalter Hymnal, Doctrinal Standards and Liturgy of the
Christian Reformed Church. 3d ed. Grand Rapids, MI: Publication Committee of the Christian Reformed Church, 1934.

_____. Service of Word and Sacrament. Grand Rapids, MI:
Board of Publications of the Christian Reformed Church, [1978].
[Trial liturgy]

_____. Liturgical Committee. Service Book. Grand Rapids, MI:
Board of Publications of the Christian Reformed Church, 1981-
1984.
Part 1: Liturgical Forms for Baptism and the Lord's Supper.
    1981.
Part 2: Liturgical Forms (Non-Sacramental). 1981.
Part 3: Service of Word and Sacrament. 1981.
Part 4: Prayers and Responsive Readings of the Law. 1981.
Part 5: Heidelberg Catechism. 1981.
Part 6: Belgic Confession. 1984.

3. Orthodox Presbyterian Church

ORTHODOX PRESBYTERIAN CHURCH. The Standards of Govern-
ment, Discipline, and Worship of the Orthodox Presbyterian
Church: Including also Suggested Forms for Use in Connection
with the Book of Discipline, and Suggested Forms for Particular
Services. 3d ed. Philadelphia, PA: Committee on Christian
Education, Orthodox Presbyterian Church, 1980.

4. Presbyterian Church in Canada

PRESBYTERIAN CHURCH IN CANADA. Aids for Social Worship:
Being Short Services of Prayer and Praise. Toronto, Ont.,
1900.

_____. Book of Common Order. Rev. ed. Toronto, Ont.:
Presbyterian Publications, 1964.

5. Presbyterian Church in the U.S.

PRESBYTERIAN CHURCH IN THE U.S. The Directory for the Worship of God in the Presbyterian Church in the United States.
Richmond, VA: Presbyterian Committee of Publication, 1889.

6. Presbyterian Church in the U.S.A.

PRESBYTERIAN CHURCH IN THE U.S.A. The Book of Common
Prayer as Amended by the Westminster Divines, A.D. 1661.
Edited by Charles W. Shields, with a historical and liturgical
treatise. Philadelphia, PA: J. S. Claxton, 1867.

_____. The Directory for the Worship of God in the Presbyterian
Church in the United States of America. Philadelphia, PA:
Presbyterian Board of Publication and Sabbath-School Work,
1893.

_____. The Book of Common Worship. Philadelphia, PA:
Presbyterian Board of Publication and Sabbath-School Work,
1906.

_____. The Book of Common Worship. Revised ed. Philadel-
phia, PA: Presbyterian Board of Christian Education, 1932.

_____. The Book of Common Worship. Philadelphia, PA:
Published for the Office of the General Assembly by the Publication Division of the Board of Christian Education, 1946.

7. Reformed Church in America

a. Texts

REFORMED CHURCH IN AMERICA. *The Psalms of David with Hymns and Spiritual Songs; Also the Catechism, Confession of Faith and Liturgy of the Reformed Church in the Netherlands.* For the Use of the Reformed Dutch Church in North America. New York: Printed by Hodge & Campbell, 1792.

_____. *The Liturgy of the Reformed Protestant Dutch Church in North America.* New York: Board of Publication of the Reformed Protestant Dutch Church, 1857.

_____. *The Liturgy of the Reformed Church in America.* New York: Board of Publications, 1873.

_____. *The Liturgy of the Reformed Church in America together with the Book of Psalms.* New York: n.p., 1882.

_____. *The Liturgy of the Reformed Church in America together with the Psalter.* New York: Board of Education, 1968.

_____. *Our Song of Hope: A Provisional Confession of Faith of the Reformed Church in America.* With Commentary and Appendixes by Eugene P. Heideman. Grand Rapids, MI: Eerdmans, 1975, c1974.

_____. *Proposed Alternate Orders of Worship 1981.* n.p.: Reformed Church in America, 1981.

b. Studies

HAGEMAN, Howard G. "The Eucharistic Prayer in the Reformed Church in America." *Reformed Review*, 30, 3 (Spring 1977): 166-179.

_____. "Liturgical Development in the Reformed Church of America: 1868-1947." *Journal of Presbyterian History*, 47 (1969): 262-289.

ROORDA, Garrett C., ed. *A Companion to the Liturgy: A Guide to Worship in the Reformed Church in America.* New York: Half Moon Press, 1971.

8. Reformed Church in the United States
(German Reformed Church)

(See also XXIII. The Mercersburg Tradition, p. 427, and XXV. E. United Church of Christ, p. 451.)

a. Texts

REFORMED CHURCH IN THE UNITED STATES. Liturgy for the
Use of Congregations of the German Reformed Church in the
United States of North America. Chambersburg, PA: Publi-
cation Office of the German Reformed Church, 1841.

_____ . A Liturgy: or, Order of Christian Worship. Philadelphia, PA: Lindsay & Blakiston, 1857.

_____ . Order of Worship for the Reformed Church in the United
States. Philadelphia, PA: Publication and Sunday School
Board of the Reformed Church in the United States, 1866;
Philadelphia, PA: S. R. Fisher, 1867.

_____ . A Liturgy: or, Order of Worship for the Reformed
Church. Cincinnati, OH: T. P. Bucher, 1869.

_____ . The Directory of Worship for the Reformed Church in
the United States. Reading, PA: Daniel Miller, 1884.

_____ . The Book of Worship for the Reformed Church in the
United States. Philadelphia, PA: Publication and Sunday
School Board of the Reformed Church in the United States,
1923.

b. Studies

GOOD, James Isaac. History of the Reformed Church in the U.S.,
in the Nineteenth Century. New York: Board of Publication
of the Reformed Church in America, 1911.

SLIFER, M. D. "The Liturgical Tradition of the Reformed Church
in the U.S.A." Studia Liturgica 1 (1962): 228–240.

9. United Presbyterian Church in the U.S.A.

(For texts and studies of the Worshipbook, see 10. Joint Commission on Worship, below.)

UNITED PRESBYTERIAN CHURCH IN THE U.S.A. The Directory
for Worship. Philadelphia, PA: United Presbyterian Church
in the U.S.A., 1961.

10. Joint Commissions on Worship [Presbyterian]

a. Texts

The Worshipbook. Prepared by the Joint Commission on Worship for

the Cumberland Presbyterian Church, Presbyterian Church in
the United States, and United Presbyterian Church in the
U.S.A. Philadelphia, PA: Westminster Press, 1970.

The Worshipbook: Services and Hymns. Philadelphia, PA: Westminster Press, 1972.

JOINT OFFICE OF WORSHIP FOR THE PRESBYTERIAN CHURCH
(U.S.A.) AND THE CUMBERLAND PRESBYTERIAN CHURCH.
The Service for the Lord's Day: The Worship of God. SLR,
1. Philadelphia, PA: Westminster Press, 1984.

   b. Studies

HAGEMAN, Howard G. "Old and New in the Worshipbook." Theology Today, 31 (1974): 207-213.

ROUTLEY, Erik. "A British Look at the Worshipbook." Theology
Today, 31 (1974): 214-219.

_____. "A New Book of Worship for a New Church." Worship,
48 (1974): 413-420.

11. Other Texts

French Protestant Church, Charleston, S.C. The Liturgy of the
French Protestant Church. Translated from the editions of
1737 and 1772, published at Neuchatel, with additional prayers,
carefully selected, and some alterations. Arranged for the
Use of the Congregation in the City of Charleston, S.C.
Charleston, SC: James S. Burges, 1836.

HODGE, Archibald Alexander. Manual of Forms for Baptism, Admission to Communion, Administration of the Lord's Supper,
Marriage, and Funerals. New ed. Philadelphia, PA: Presbyterian Board of Publication, 1883.

KIRK, James G. When We Gather: A Book of Prayers for Worship.
2 vols. Philadelphia, PA: Geneva Press, 1983-1984.
1. Year A. 1983.
2. Year B. 1984.

McCABE, Joseph. Service Book for Ministers. Philadelphia, PA:
Westminster Press, 1961.

XV. THE RADICAL REFORMATION AND ITS OFFSPRING

A. GENERAL STUDIES

WILLIAMS, George Huntston. The Radical Reformation. Philadelphia, PA: Westminster Press, 1962.

B. HUBMAIER

HUBMAIER, Balthasar. Schriften. Herausgegeben von Gunnar
Westin und Torsten Bergsten. QGT, 9 (QFR, 29). Gütersloh:
Mohn, 1962.
--"Etliche Schlussreden vom Unterricht der Messe, 1525."
Pp. 101-104.
--"Von der christlichen Taufe der Gläubigen, 1525." Pp. 116-
163.
--"Ein Gespräch auf Zwinglis Taufbüchlein, 1525-1526." Pp.
164-214.
--"Von der Kindertaufe, 1525-1526." Pp. 256-269.
--"Grund und Ursach, 1526." Pp. 327-336.
--"Eine Form zu taufen, 1526." Pp. 347-352.
--"Eine Form des Nachtmahls Christi, 1526." Pp. 353-365.

HUBMAIER, Balthasar. "Form for the Celebration of the Lord's
Supper." Translated by W. J. McGlothlin. Review and Ex-
positor, 3 (1906): 82-97; reprinted as "An Anabaptist Liturgy
of the Lord's Supper." In Great Voices of the Reformation:
An Anthology, pp. 311-315. Edited by H. E. Fosdick. New
York: Random House, 1952.

SACHSSE, Carl. D. Balthasar Hubmaier als Theologe. NSGTK,
20. Berlin: Trowitzsch, 1914.

C. MUNTZER

MEHL, Oscar Johannes, ed. Thomas Müntzers deutsche Messen und
Kirchenämter, mit Singnoten und liturgischen Abhandlungen.
Grimmen: Waberg, 1937.

MUNTZER, Thomas. "Deutsch-evangelische Messe." In his Schriften und Briefe: Kritische Gesamtausgabe, pp. 157-206. Unter
mitarbeit von Paul Kirn, herausgegeben von Günther Franz.
QFR, 33. Gütersloh: Mohn, 1968.

_____. "Deutsches Kirchenamt." In his Schriften und Briefe:

Kritische Gesamtausgabe, pp. 25-156. Unter mitarbeit von Paul Kirn, herausgegeben von Günther Franz. QFR, 33. Gütersloh: Mohn, 1968.

SCHULZ, Karl. "Thomas Müntzerts liturgische Bestrebungen." Zeitschrift für Kirchengeschichte, 47 (n.F. 10) (1928): 369-401.

D. SCHWENCKFELD

LOETSCHER, Frederick William. Schwenckfeld's Participation in the Eucharistic Controversy of the Sixteenth Century. Philadelphia, PA: MacCalla, 1906.

SCHULTZ, Selina Gerhard. Caspar Schwenckfeld von Ossig (1489-1561). 4th ed. Pennsburg, PA: Board of Publication of the Schwenckfelder Church, 1977.

SCHWENCKFELD, Caspar. Corpus Schwenckfeldianorum. 19 vols. Leipzig: Breitkopf & Härtel, 1907-1961.

E. THE MENNONITES

1. Texts

ALGEMEENE DOOPSGEZINDE SOCIETEIT. Commissie tot de Liturgie. Kanselboek: ten dienste van de Doopsgezinde Gemeenten in Nederland. Amsterdam: Algemeene Doopsgezinde Sociëteit, 1948.

CHURCH OF GOD IN CHRIST, MENNONITE. The Confession of Faith and Minister's Manual of the Church of God in Christ, Mennonite. 3d ed. Lahoma, OK: Publication Board of the Church of God in Christ, Mennonite, 1962.

COFFMAN, John S., and FUNK, John F., eds. Confession of Faith and Minister's Manual. Elkhart, IN: Mennonite Publishing Co., 1890; 8th ed., Scottdale, PA: Mennonite Publishing House, 1925.

NAFFZIGER, Johannes. Ein Alter Brief. Elkhart, IN: Mennonite Publishing Co., 1916; reprinted Kutztown, PA, 1926. [Amish]

UMBLE, John. "An Amish Minister's Manual." Mennonite Quarterly Review, 15 (1941): 95-117. [Text of a manual by Joseph Unzicker]

2. Historical Sources and Studies

BEACHY, Alvin J. Worship as Celebration of Covenant and Incarnation. Newton, KS: Faith & Life Press, 1968.

BENDER, Harold S. Conrad Grebel, c. 1498-1526: The Founder of the Swiss Brethren sometimes called Anabaptists. SAMH, 6/1. Goshen, IN: Mennonite Historical Society, Goshen College, 1950.

_____. "Minister's Manuals." Mennonite Encyclopedia, 3:696-697.

_____, ZIJPP, N. van der, and KRAHN, Cornelius. "Worship, Public." Mennonite Encyclopedia, 4:984-988.

FRIEDMANN, Robert. "Hutterite Worship and Preaching." Mennonite Quarterly Review, 40 (1966): 5-26.

HOFER, Peter. The Hutterian Brethren and Their Beliefs. Starbuck, Man. Hutterian Brethren of Manitoba, 1955.

KRAHN, Cornelius. "Communion." Mennonite Encyclopedia, 1:651-655.

_____. "Communion Call." Mennonite Encyclopedia, 1:655.

LEHMAN, Jacob S., and LEHMANN, Abraham, eds. Christianity Defined: A Manual of New Testament Teaching on the Unity of the Church, Nonresistance of Evil, Nonconformity to the World in Deportment and Dress, the Proper Observance of the Ordinances, Separation from All Unfaithful Worship; Dissertation on Marriage, the Millenium, and Beneficiary Organizations. Lancaster, PA: Reformed Mennonite Church, 1958.

MILLER, Paul M. "An Investigation of the Relationship between Mennonite Theology and Mennonite Worship." Th.D. dissertation, Southern Theological SEminary, 1961.

_____. "Worship Among the Early Anabaptists." Mennonite Quarterly Review, 30 (1956): 235-246.

NEFF, Christian. "Abendmahl." Mennonitisches Lexikon, 1:6-9.

_____. "Abendmahlsfeier." Mennonitisches Lexikon, 1:9-10.

RIEDEMANN, Peter. Rechenschaft unserer Religion, Lehre und Glaubens. 1565; An Account of Our Religion, Doctrine and Faith. London: Hodder & Stoughton in conjunction with Plough Publishing House, 1950; 2d ed., Rifton, NY: Plough Publishing House, 1970.

SCHOWALTER, Otto. "Gottesdienst." Mennonitisches Lexikon,
    2:148-150.

SIMONS, Menno. The Complete Works of Menno Simons. Elkhart,
    IN: John F. Funk, 1871.
    --"Concerning Baptism." First Part, pp. 24-40.
    --"The Lord's Holy Supper." First Part, pp. 40-52.
    --"An Explanation of Christian Baptism in the Water, from the
        Word of God." Second Part, pp. 189-231.
    --"A Fundamental and Clear Confession of the Poor and Dis-
        tressed Christians concerning Justification, the Preachers,
        Baptism, the Lord's Supper, and the Swearing of Oaths."
        Second Part, pp. 257-276.

TOEWS, Abraham P. American Mennonite Worship: Its Roots, De-
    velopment and Application. New York: Exposition Press,
    1960.

UMBLE, John. "Manuscript Amish Minister's Manuals in the Goshen
    College Library." Mennonite Quarterly Review, 15 (1941):
    243-253.

WENGER, J. C. The Mennonite Church in America, Sometimes
    Called Old Mennonites. Scottdale, PA: Herald Press, 1966.

WEST, W. M. S. "The Anabaptists and the Rise of the Baptist
    Movement." In Christian Baptism, pp. 223-272. Edited by
    A. Gilmore. London: Lutterworth Press, 1959.

XVI. THE MORAVIANS

A. TEXTS

MORAVIAN CHURCH. Acta Fratrum Unitatis in Anglia. London,
    1749.

MORAVIAN CHURCH (GREAT BRITAIN). A Collection of Hymns,
    for the Use of the Protestant Church of the United Brethren.
    London, 1789; Bath, Eng. 1801; Manchester, Eng.: Dean,
    1809; Ashton-under-Lyne, Eng.: Cunningham, 1826.

_____. Hymns for the Use of the Protestant Church of the
    United Brethren. London, 1836.

_____. Liturgy and Hymns for the Use of the Protestant Church
    of the United Brethren. London: Mallalieu, 1838; 1844; 1849;
    1854; 1869; 1886.

_____. The Liturgy and Hymns authorised for Use in the Mora-
vian Church (Unitas Fratrum) in Great Britain and Ireland.
London: Moravian Publication Office, 1911.

MORAVIAN CHURCH (U.S.). A Collection of Hymns for the Use
of the Protestant Church of the United Brethren. Philadelphia,
PA: Zentler, 1813; Philadelphia, PA: Ashmead, 1832.

_____. Liturgy and Hymns for the Use of the Protestant Church
of the United Brethren. Philadelphia, PA: Crissy, 1842;
Bethlehem, PA: Held, 1851.

_____. Liturgy and Hymns of the American Province of the
Unitas Fratrum, or the Moravian Church. Bethlehem, PA:
Moravian Publication Office, 1876.

_____. Offices of Worship and Hymns (with Tunes) published
by authority of the American Province of the Unitas Fratrum,
or the Moravian Church. 3d ed. Bethlehem, PA: Moravian
Publication Office, 1891.

_____. Liturgy and the Offices and Hymns of the American
Province of the Unitas Fratrum, or Moravian Church. Bethlehem, PA: Moravian Publication Office, 1908.

_____. Hymnal and Liturgies of the Moravian Church (Unitas
Fratrum). Bethlehem, PA: Provincial Synod, 1920; 1969.

B. STUDIES

DE SCHWEINITZ, Edmund Alexander. History of the Church
known as the Unitas Fratrum. Bethlehem, PA: Moravian
Publishing Office, 1885.

_____. The Moravian Manual; containing an Account of the
Moravian Church or Unitas Fratrum. 3d ed. Bethlehem, PA:
Times Publishing Co., 1901.

FOY, J. H. "Moravian Worship." Dictionary of Liturgy and Worship, pp. 276-277.

HAMILTON, J. Taylor, and Kenneth G. History of the Moravian
Church: The Renewed Unitas Fratrum, 1722-1957. New York:
Interprovincial Board of Christian Education, Moravian Church
in America, 1967.

HICKEL, Helmut. Das Abendmahl zu Zinzendorfs Zeiten. Herrn-
huter Hefte, 9. Hamburg: L. Appel, 1956.

HUTTON, Joseph Edmund. A History of the Moravian Church.
2d ed. London: Moravian Publication Office, 1909.

KORTZ, Edwin. "The Liturgical Development of the American
Moravian Church." Transactions of the Moravian Historical
Society, 17, part 2 (1962): 267-302.

LANGTON, Edward. History of the Moravian Church: The Story
of the First International Protestant Church. London: Allen
& Unwin, 1956.

LEWIS, Arthur James. Zinzendorf, the Ecumenical Pioneer: A
Study in the Moravian Contribution to Christian Mission and
Unity. London: SCM Press; Philadelphia, PA: Westminster
Press, 1962.

PEASTON, A. Elliott. "The Moravians." In his The Prayer Book
Tradition in the Free Churches, pp. 91-106. London: James
Clarke, 1964.

WETTACH, Theodor. Kirche bei Zinzendorf. Wuppertal: Brockhaus, 1971.

ZEMAN, Jarold Knox. The Anabaptists and the Czech Brethren in
Moravia 1526-1628: A Study of Origins and Contacts. SEH,
20. The Hague: Mouton, 1969.

XVII. THE ANGLICAN CHURCHES

A. WORSHIP IN THE ANGLICAN COMMUNION

1. Collections of Texts

ARNOLD, John H., ed. Anglican Liturgies. ACT, 22. London:
Oxford University Press, 1939.
--replaced by WIGAN, below.

BUCHANAN, Colin O., ed. Modern Anglican Liturgies, 1958-1968.
New York: Oxford University Press, 1968.

_____, ed. Further Anglican Liturgies, 1968-1975. Bramcote,
Eng.: Grove Books, 1975.

GRISBROOKE, W. Jardine. Anglican Liturgies of the Seventeenth
and Eighteenth Centuries. ACC, 40. London: SPCK, 1958.

HATCHETT, Marion J. The Eucharistic Liturgies of Historic
    Prayer Books: Historic Rites arranged for Contemporary Cele-
    bration. Sewanee, TN: St. Luke's Journal of Theology Occa-
    sional Publications, 1980.

SUTER, John Wallace, ed. The Book of English Collects, from the
    Prayer Books of the Anglican Communion: England, Scotland,
    Ireland, Canada, South Africa and the United States of America.
    New York: Harper, 1940.

WIGAN, Bernard, ed. The Liturgy in English. 2d ed. London:
    Oxford University Press, 1964.
    --replaces ARNOLD, above; supplemented by BUCHANAN,
        above.

                          2. General Studies

CLARKE, William K. L., and HARRIS, Charles, eds. Liturgy and
    Worship: A Companion to the Prayer Book of the Anglican
    Communion. London: SPCK, 1932.

ECHLIN, Edward P. The Anglican Eucharist in Ecumenical Per-
    spective. New York: Seabury Press, 1968.

GWYNN, Walker. Primitive Worship and the Prayer Book: Ration-
    ale, History and Doctrine of the English, Irish, Scottish and
    American Books. New York: Longmans, Green, 1917.

HETTLINGER, R. F. "Worship in the Anglican Communion."
    Anglican Theological Review, 40 (1958): 169-181.

MAXWELL, William D. The Book of Common Prayer and the Worship
    of the Non-Anglican Churches. London: Oxford University
    Press, 1950.

MUSS-ARNOLT, William. The Book of Common Prayer among the
    Nations of the World: A History of Translations of the Prayer
    Book of the Church of England and of the Protestant Episcopal
    Church of America. London: SPCK; New York: Gorham,
    1914.

PEASTON, A. Elliott. The Prayer Book Tradition in the Free
    Churches. London: James Clarke, 1964.

B. THE CHURCH OF ENGLAND

1. Texts

a. Collections

BRIGHTMAN, Francis E., ed. The English Rite: Being a Synopsis of the Sources and Revisions of the Book of Common Prayer
with an Introduction and an Appendix. 2 vols. 2d ed. London: Rivingtons, 1921; reprint ed., Farnborough, Eng.:
Gregg, 1970.

HALL, Peter, ed. Fragmenta Liturgica: Documents Illustrative of
the Liturgy of the Church of England. 7 vols. Bath, Eng.:
Binns & Goodwin, 1848.
1. The Puritan Prayer Book; The New Book of Scotland; Communion Office of King Edward VI; Bishop Rattray's Liturgy
   of Jerusalem.
2. Stephens' Liturgy of the Ancients and Liturgy of Ancient
   Christians; Scougal's Aberdeen Service; Deacon's Litany
   and Prayers.
3. Whiston's Primitive Liturgy.
4. Henley's Liturgy of the Oratory.
5. The Nonjuror's Offices; The Scottish Communion Office;
   Bishop Skinner's Aberdeen Prayers and Forms of Prayer
   and Thanksgiving.
6. Deacon's Devotions.
7. The Dunkirk Prayer-Book.

_____, ed. Reliquae Liturgicae: Documents Connected with the
Liturgy of the Church of England. 5 vols. Bath, Eng.:
Binns & Goodwin, 1847.
1. A Booke of the forme of common prayer, 4th ed. Middel-
   burgh, 1602.
2. The Booke of common prayer for the use of the Church of
   Scotland, 1637.
3. Directory for Public Worship, 1644.
4. The Savoy Liturgy, 1661.
5. Book of Common Prayer for the Episcopal Church of New
   York, 1786.

HURLBUT, Stephen A., ed. The Liturgy of the Church of England before and after the Reformation; together with the Service of the Holy Communion of the Episcopal Church in the
United States. Washington, DC: St. Albans Press, 1941;
reprint eds., Grand Rapids, MI: Eerdmans, [1941]; Charleston, SC: St. Albans Press, 1950.

KEELING, William, ed. Liturgiae Britannicae, or, the Several Editions of the Book of Common Prayer of the Church of England,

from its Compilation to the Last Revision, together with the
Liturgy set forth for the Use of the Church of Scotland, arranged to show their Respective Variations. 2d ed. London:
Pickering, 1851; reprint ed., Farnsborough, Eng.: Gregg,
1969.

SANDERSON, Robert, and WREN, Matthew. Fragmentary Illustrations of the History of the Book of Common Prayer, from
Manuscript Sources. Edited by William Jacobson. London:
John Murray, 1874; reprint ed., Farnborough, Eng.: Gregg,
1969.

  b. Texts, chiefly of the Book of Common Prayer
      (arranged chronologically)

HUNT, John Eric, ed. Cranmer's First Litany, 1544, and Merbecke's Book of Common Prayer Noted, 1550. London: SPCK;
New York: Macmillan, 1939.

LEGG, J. Wickham, ed. Cranmer's Liturgical Projects. HBS, 50.
London: Harrison, 1915.

WILSON, H. A., ed. The Order of the Communion, 1548: A Facsimile of the British Museum Copy C. 25, f. 15. HBS, 34.
London: Harrison, 1908.

LEGG, J. Wickham, ed. The Clerk's Book of 1549. HBS, 25.
London: Henry Bradshaw Society, 1903.

The Two Liturgies, A.D. 1549, and 1552, with Other Documents set
forth by authority in the Reign of King Edward VI, viz., The
Order of Communion, 1548; The Primer, 1553; The Catechism
and Articles, 1553; Catechismus Brevis, 1553. Edited by
Joseph Ketley. PS, 29. Cambridge: Cambridge University
Press, 1844.

CARDWELL, Edward, ed. The Two Books of Common Prayer set
forth in the Reign of Edward VI, compared with each other.
3d ed. Oxford: Oxford University Press, 1852.

The First and Second Prayer Books of Edward VI. EL. London:
Dent; New York: Dutton, 1910; many reprints to 1952.

The Book of Common Prayer, printed by Whitchurch March 1549.
Commonly called the First Book of Edward VI. [Facsimile.]
London: W. Pickering, 1844.

PARKER, James, ed. The First Prayer Book of Edward VI compared with the Successive Revisions of the Book of Common
Prayer. 2d ed. Oxford: J. Parker, 1883.

"The Booke of the Common Prayer," 1549. In Liturgies of the
    Western Church, pp. 245-268. By Bard Thompson. Cleve-
    land, OH: ·World, 1961; reprint ed., Philadelphia, PA:
    Fortress Press, 1981.

The Book of Common Prayer Noted by John Merbecke, 1550. [Fac-
    simile.] London: W. Pickering, 1844.

FELLOWES, E. H., ed. The Office of the Holy Communion as set
    by John Merbecke. New York: Oxford University Press,
    1949.

The Book of Common Prayer, printed by Whitchurch 1552. Com-
    monly called the Second Book of Edward VI. [Facsimile.]
    London: W. Pickering, 1844.

The Second Prayer Book of King Edward the Sixth (1552) with
    Historical Introduction and Notes by H. J. Wotherspoon, and
    The Liturgy of Compromise used in the English Congregation
    at Frankfort, from an unpublished ms. edited by George W.
    Sprott. Edinburgh: Blackwood, 1905.

"The Book of Common Prayer," 1552. In Liturgies of the Western
    Church, pp. 245-268. By Bard Thompson. Cleveland, OH:
    World, 1961; reprint ed., Philadelphia, PA: Fortress Press,
    1981.

Liturgical Services: Liturgies and Occasional Forms of Prayer set
    forth in the Reign of Queen Elizabeth. Edited by William
    Keatinge Clay. PS, 30. Cambridge: Cambridge University
    Press, 1847.
    --includes Book of Common Prayer, 1559; Godley Prayers; The
    Ordinal, 1559; New Calendar, etc.

The Boke of Common Praier and administration of the Sacramentes.
    London: R. Grafton, 1559; facsimile ed., London: W. Picker-
    ing, 1844.

BOOTY, John E., ed. The Book of Common Prayer, 1559: The
    Elizabethan Prayer Book. FDTSC, 22. Charlottesville, VA:
    Published for the Folger Shakespeare Library by the University
    Press of Virginia, 1976.

Private Prayers, put forth by Authority during the Reign of Queen
    Elizabeth: The Primer of 1559; The Orarium of 1560; The
    Preces Privatae of 1564; The Book of Christian Prayers of 1578;
    with an appendix containing the Litany of 1544. Edited by
    William Keatinge Clay. PS, 37. Cambridge: Cambridge Univer-
    sity Press, 1851.

The Booke of Common Prayer and Administration of the Sacraments

and Other Rites and Ceremonies of the Church of England.
London: R. Barker, 1604; facsimile ed., London: W. Pickering, 1844.

Facsimile of the Black Letter Prayer-Book [i.e. that of 1636] containing Manuscript alterations and Additions made in 1661, "out
of which was fairly written" the Book of Common Prayer sub-
scribed, December 20, A.D. 1661, etc. London: Longmans
and Pickering; Oxford: Parker; Cambridge: Macmillan, 1871.

The Book of Common Prayer ... for the Church of Scotland [Laud's
Liturgy], 1637.
--See both COOPER and SPROTT under Scotland, Texts, page
384.

CUMING, G. J., ed. The Durham Book, Being the First Draft of
the Book of Common Prayer in 1661. London: Oxford University Press, 1961; reprint ed., Westport, CT: Greenwood
Press, 1979.

Facsimile of the Original Manuscript of the Book of Common Prayer;
signed by Convocation December 20th, 1661, and Attached to
the Act of Uniformity, 1662 (13 & 14 Charles II. Cap. 4).
["The Annexed Book."] London: Eyre & Spottiswoode, 1891.

CLAY, W. K., ed. The Book of Common Prayer [1662]. Illustrated; so as to show its various Modifications, Date of its
several Parts, and Authority on which they Rest. London,
1841.

The Book of Common Prayer as Revised and Settled at the Savoy
Conference, anno 1662, 14 Charles II. Reprinted from the
Sealed Book in the Tower of London. London: W. Pickering,
1844.

BLACK, Henry, ed. The Alterations in the Book of Common
Prayer ... for the Revision of the Liturgy in 1689. By order
of the House of Commons, 1854.

TAYLOR, John, ed. The Revised Liturgy of 1689, being the Book
of Common Prayer, interleaved with the Alterations prepared
for Convocation by the Royal Commissioners, in the first year
of the Reign of William and Mary. London: Bagster, 1855.

The Book of Common Prayer and Administration of the Sacraments
and Other Rites and Ceremonies, etc. [1844.] London: William Pickering, 1844.

The Convocation Prayer Book, being The Book of Common Prayer
and Administration of the Sacraments, and Other Rites and
Ceremonies of the Church, according to the Use of the Church

of England: With altered Rubrics, showing what would be the
condition of the Book if amended in conformity with the recommendations of the Convocations of Canterbury and York, contained in Reports presented to Her Majesty, the Queen, in the
Year 1879. London: Murray, 1907.

The Book of Common Prayer and Administration of the Sacraments,
etc. ["Prayer Book of King Edward VII."] London: Eyre &
Spottiswoode, 1901-1903; New York: M. W. Dunne, 1904.

ENGLISH CHURCH UNION. A Suggested Prayer Book: Being the
Text of the English Rite, altered and enlarged in accordance
with the Prayer Book Revision Proposals made by the English
Church Union. ["The Green Book."] London: Oxford University Press, 1923.

A New Prayer Book: Proposals for the Revision of the Book of
Common Prayer and for additional Services and Prayers, drawn
up by a Group of Clergy. ["The Grey Book."] London:
Oxford University Press, 1923.

A Survey of the Proposals for the Alternative Prayer Book. ["The
Orange Book."] 3 vols. ACP, 12-14. London: Mowbray;
Milwaukee, WI: Morehouse, 1923-1924.
1. The Order of Holy Communion. ACP, 12. 1923.
2. Occasional Offices. ACP, 13. 1924.
3. The Calendar--The Collects, Epistles and Gospels--The
   Ordination Services. ACP, 14. 1924.

STONE, Darwell, ed. The Deposited Prayer Book. By a group of
Priests, with an introduction. London: Allan, 1927.

The Book of Common Prayer, [etc.]: The Book of 1662 with Permissive Additions and Deviations Approved in 1927. Oxford:
Oxford University Press, 1927.

The Book of Common Prayer with the Additions and Deviations Proposed in 1928. Oxford: Oxford University Press, 1928.

COPE, Gilbert F., DAVIES, John G., and TYTLER, D. A. An Ex-
perimental Liturgy. ESW, 3. London: Lutterworth Press;
Richmond, VA: John Knox Press, 1958.

CHURCH OF ENGLAND. Liturgical Commission. Alternative Services: First Series. London: SPCK, 1965.

_____. Alternative Services: Second Series. London: SPCK,
1965.

_____. Modern Liturgical Texts. London: SPCK, 1968.

_____. Alternative Services: Series 3. London: SPCK, 1971.

_____. The Alternative Service Book, 1980. Cambridge: Cambridge University Press; Oxford: Mowbray; London: SPCK, 1980.

AKEHURST, Peter R., and BISHOP, Anthony J. Collects with the New Lectionary: A Compilation for the Christian Year. 4th ed. Bramcote, Eng.: Grove Books, 1974.

2. General Histories and Introductions

ALBERTINE, R. "Selected Moments in the History of the Epiclesis in Anglican Liturgy." Ephemerides liturgicae, 92 (1978): 420-439.

BURGESS, Francis G. The Romance of the Book of Common Prayer. 5th ed. New York: Morehouse-Gorham, 1947.

CUMING, Geoffrey. The Godly Order: Texts and Studies Relating to the Book of Common Prayer. ACC, 65. London: SPCK, 1983.

CUMING, G. J. A History of Anglican Liturgy. London: Macmillan; New York: St. Martin's, 1969.

_____. _____. 2d ed. London: Macmillan, 1982.

_____. "Eastern Liturgies and Anglican Divines, 1510-1662." In The Orthodox Church and the West, pp. 231-238. Edited by Derek Baker. Oxford: Basil Blackwell, 1976.

DANIEL, Evan. The Prayer Book: Its History, Language and Contents. London: Gardner, 1877; 26th ed., Redhill, Eng.: Gardner, Darton, 1948.

DAVIES, Horton. Worship and Theology in England. 5 vols. Princeton, NJ: Princeton University Press, 1961-1975.
1. From Cranmer to Hooker, 1534-1603. 1970.
2. From Andrewes to Baxter and Fox, 1603-1690. 1975.
3. From Watts and Wesley to Maurice, 1690-1850. 1961.
4. From Newman to Martineau, 1850-1900. 1962.
5. The Ecumenical Century, 1900-1965. 1965.

DEARMER, Percy. Everyman's History of the Prayer Book. London: Mowbray; Milwaukee, WI: Young Churchman, 1912.

_____. _____. New American ed., revised and edited for American use by Frederic Cook Morehouse. Milwaukee, WI: Morehouse, 1931.

_____. The Story of the Prayer Book in the Old and New World and throughout the Anglican Church. Based upon the author's Everyman's History of the Prayer Book. London: Oxford University Press, 1933.

DIX, Gregory. The Shape of the Liturgy. 2d ed. Westminster: Dacre Press, 1945; reprint ed., London: A. & C. Black, 1975; New York: Seabury Press, 1982.

DUFFIELD, G. E. Admission to Holy Communion: Two Essays in the Historical Tradition of the Church of England and Its Underlying Theology. Abingdon, Eng.: Marcham Manor Press, 1964.

DUGMORE, Clifford W. "The Development of Anglican Worship." In Aspects de l'Anglicanisme, pp. 123-143. Paris: Presses Universitaires de France, 1974.

DUNLOP, Colin. Anglican Public Worship. Rev. ed. London: SCM Press, 1961.

FABRICUS, Cajus. Die Kirche von England, ihr Gebetbuch, Bekenntnis und kanonisches Recht. Corpus Confessionum, 17/1. Berlin: De Gruyter, 1937.

HARRISON, D. E. W. Common Prayer in the Church of England. Rev. ed., with new title. London: SPCK, 1969.

_____, and SANSOM, Michael C. Worship in the Church of England. London: SPCK, 1982.

LAMBURN, Edward Cyril Russell. The Liturgy Develops. London: W. Knott, 1960.

LATHBURY, Thomas. A History of the Book of Common Prayer. 3d ed. Oxford: Parker, 1875.

LEGG, J. Wickham. English Church Life from the Restoration to the Tractarian Movement, considered in some of its Neglected or Forgotten Features. London: Longmans, Green, 1914.

MORISON, Stanley. English Prayer Books: An Introduction to the Literature of Christian Public Worship. ACT, 23. Cambridge: Cambridge University Press, 1943.

NEILL, Stephen. "The Holy Communion in the Anglican Church." In The Holy Communion: A Symposium, pp. 49-66. Edited by Hugh Martin. London: SCM Press, 1947.

PROCTOR, Francis, and FRERE, William H. A New History of the Book of Common Prayer. Rev. ed. London: Macmillan, 1905.

PULLAN, Leighton.   The History of the Book of Common Prayer.
3d ed.   OLPT.   New York: Longmans, Green, 1914.

VROOM, Fenwick Williams.   An Introduction to the Prayer-Book.
London: SPCK; New York: Macmillan, 1930.

3.   Documents

BAYNE, Peter, and GOULD, Geo., eds.   Documents Relating to the
Settlement of the Church of England by the Act of Uniformity
of 1662.   London: W. Kent, 1862.

GEE, Henry, and HARDY, William John, eds.   Documents Illustrative of English Church History.   London: Macmillan, 1910;
reprint ed., New York: Kraus Reprint, 1966.

POCOCK, Nicholas, ed.   Troubles Connected with the Prayer Book
1549:   Documents.   Camden Society, n.s. 37.   Westminster,
Eng.:   Printed for the Camden Society, 1884.

4.   Prayer Book History (chiefly to 1662)

BALL, Frank E.   "A Liturgical Colloquy: An Examination of the
Savoy Conference, 1661."   B. Litt., Oxford University, 1958.

BEESLEY, Alan.   "An Unpublished Source of the Book of Common
Prayer: Peter Martyr Vermigli's Adhortatio ad Coenam Domini
mysticam."   Journal of Ecclesiastical History, 19 (1968):   83-88.

BOSHER, R. S.   The Making of the Restoration Settlement: The
Influence of the Laudians 1649-1662.   New York: Oxford University Press; Westminster, Eng.:   Dacre Press, 1951; reprint
ed., Westminster, Eng.:   Dacre Press; New York: Barnes &
Noble, 1957.

CALCOTE, A. D.   Word and Spirit: The Prayer of Consecration
in Anglican Thought and Practice 1604-1740.   S.T.M. thesis,
General Theological Seminary, New York, 1963.

CARDWELL, Edward.   A History of Conferences and Other Pro-
ceedings connected with the Revision of the Book of Common
Prayer, from the Year 1558 to the Year 1690.   3d ed.   Oxford:
Oxford University Press, 1849; reprint ed., Ridgewood, NJ:
Gregg Press, 1966.

COURATIN, A. H.   "The Holy Communion 1549."   Church Quarterly
Review, 164 (1963):   148-159; and "The Service of Holy Communion, 1552-1662."   Church Quarterly Review, 163 (1962):
431-442.

_____. The Service of Holy Communion, 1549-1662. London:
SPCK, 1963.

CUMING, G. J. "The Making of the Durham Book." Journal of
Ecclesiastical History, 6 (1955): 60-72.

_____. "The Prayer Book in Convocation, November 1661."
Journal of Ecclesiastical History, 8 (1957): 182-192.

DAVIES, John G. "The 1662 Book of Common Prayer: Its Virtues
and Vices." Studia Liturgica, 1 (1962): 167-174.

DEVEREAUX, James A. "The Primers and the Prayer Book Collects." Huntington Library Quarterly, 32 (1968): 29-44.

The English Prayer Book, 1549-1662. By the Archbishop of Canterbury and Others. London: SPCK, 1963.

GEE, Henry. The Elizabethan Prayer Book and Ornaments. London: Macmillan, 1902.

GRISBROOKE, W. Jardine. "The 1662 Book of Common Prayer:
Its History and Character." Studia Liturgica, 1 (1962): 146-
166.

KING, Peter. "The Reasons for the Abolition of the Book of Common Prayer in 1645." Journal of Ecclesiastical History, 21
(1970): 327-339.

LUCKOCK, Herbert Mortimer. Studies in the History of the Book
of Common Prayer: The Anglican Reform, the Puritan Innova-
tions, the Elizabethan Reaction, the Caroline Settlement. 4th
ed. London: Longmans, Green, 1894.

MacCOLL, Malcolm. The Royal Commission and the Ornaments
Rubric. London: Longmans, Green, 1906.

MEYER, Carl S. Elizabeth I and the Religious Settlement of 1559.
St. Louis, MO: Concordia, 1960.

RATCLIFF, Edward Cradock. The Booke of Common Prayer of the
Churche of England: Its Making and Revisions M.D.XLIX-
M.D.CLXI. Set Forth in Eighty Illustrations with Introduction
and Notes. ACC, 37. London: SPCK, 1949.

_____. "The English Usage of Eucharistic Consecration, 1548-
1662." Theology, 60 (1957): 229-236, 273-280; reprinted in
his Liturgical Studies of E. C. Ratcliff, pp. 203-221. Edited by
A. H. Couratin and D. J. Tripp. London: SPCK, 1976.

_____. "The Savoy Conference and the Revision of the Book of

Common Prayer." In From Uniformity to Unity 1662-1962, pp.
89-148. Edited by G. F. Nuttall and Owen Chadwick. London:
SPCK, 1962.

TOMLINSON, John Tomlinson. The Prayer Book Articles and Homilies: Some Forgotten Facts in their History which may decide
their Interpretation. London: E. Stock, 1897.

5. Reformers

a. General Studies

BRIGHTMAN, F. E. "The Litany Under Henry VIII." English Historical Review, 29 (1909): 101-104.

BUTTERWORTH, Charles C. The English Primers, 1529-1545: Their
Publication and Connection with the English Bible and the Reformation in England. Philadelphia, PA: University of Pennsylvania Press, 1953; reprint ed., New York: Octagon Books,
1971.

DUGMORE, Clifford W. The Mass and the English Reformers. London: Macmillan; New York: St. Martin's Press, 1958.

HOPF, Constantin. Martin Bucer and the English Reformation.
Oxford: Basil Blackwell, 1946.

HUGHES, Philip E. Theology of the English Reformers, pp. 119-
222. Grand Rapids, MI: Eerdmans, 1965; new ed., Grand
Rapids, MI: Baker, 1980.

KNOX, D. Broughton. The Lord's Supper from Wycliffe to Cranmer. Exeter, Eng.: Paternoster Press, 1983.

b. Collected Letters

ROBINSON, Hastings, ed. Original Letters Relative to the English
Reformation written during the Reigns of King Henry VIII.,
King Edward VI., and Queen Mary. 2 vols. PS, 53-54.
Cambridge: Cambridge University Press, 1846-1847.

_____, ed. The Zurich Letters, comprising the Correspondence
of Several English Bishops and Others, with some of the Hel-
vetian Reformers, during the Early Part of the Reign of Queen
Elizabeth. 2 vols. PS, 50-51. Cambridge: Cambridge University Press, 1842-1845.

c. Cranmer and the First Two Prayer Books

(1). Sources

CRANMER, Thomas. Miscellaneous Writings and Letters of Thomas
Cranmer. Edited by John Edmund Cox. PS, 16. Cambridge:
Cambridge University Press, 1846.
--"Some Queries concerning Confirmation, with Cranmer's An-
swers." P. 80.
--"Questions and Answers concerning the Sacraments &c.,
1540." Pp. 115-117.
--"Questions concerning some Abuses of the Mass." Pp. 150-
151.
--[Appendix contains numerous documents pertaining to worship
and sacraments]

_____. The Works of Thomas Cranmer. Edited by G. E. Duf-
field. CLRC, 2. Appleford, Eng.: Sutton Courtenay Press,
1964.

_____. Writings and Disputations of Thomas Cranmer ... Rela-
tive to the Sacrament of the Lord's Supper. Edited by James
Edmund Cox. PS, 15. Cambridge: Cambridge University
Press, 1844.
--"An Answer to a Crafty and Sophistical Cavillation devised
by Stephen Gardiner." Pp. 1-367.
[Contains text of Gardiner's "An Explication and Assertion
of the True Catholic Faith, touching the Most Blessed
Sacrament of the Altar."]
--"Answer to Smith's Preface." Pp. 368-379.
--"Matters wherein the Bishop of Winchester varied from other
Papists, &c." Pp. 380-388.
--"Disputations at Oxford." Pp. 389-430.
--"Defensio Verae et Catholicae Doctrinae de Sacramento."
[Latin version of "Answer to Gardiner."] Appendix, pp.
1-98.

(2). Studies

BROOKES, T. H. "The First Prayer-book of Edward VI." Contemporary Review, 175 (1949): 348-351.

DAVIES, Michael. Liturgical Revolution, vol. 1: Cranmer's Godly
Order: The Destruction of Catholicism through Liturgical
Change. New Rochelle, NY: Arlington House, 1977.

DEVEREAUX, James A. "Reformed Doctrine in the Collects of the
First Book of Common Prayer." Harvard Theological Review,
58 (1965): 49-68.

DIX, Morgan. Lectures on the First Prayer Book of King Edward
VI. 4th ed. New York: E. & J. B. Young, 1883.

GASQUET, Francis Aidan, and BISHOP, Edmund. Edward VI and
the Book of Common Prayer. London: J. Hodges, 1890.

KAVANAGH, Aidan. The Concept of Eucharistic Memorial in the
    Canon Revisions of Thomas Cranmer, Archbishop of Canterbury
    1533-1556. Bonn: Roesberg, 1982.

LEWIS, C. S. English Literature in the Sixteenth Century, Ex-
    cluding Drama, pp. 215-221. OHEL. Oxford: Clarendon
    Press, 1954.

NIJENHUIS, Willem. "Sporen van een Lutherse avondmaalsleer bij
    Thomas Cranmer." Nederlands Archief voor Kerkgeschiedenis,
    45 (1963): 129-151; "Traces of a Lutheran Eucharistic Doctrine
    in Thomas Cranmer." In his Ecclesia Reformata: Studies on
    the Reformation, pp. 1-22. Leiden: Brill, 1972.

"Preparations for the First Prayer Book of Edward VI." Church
    Quarterly Review, 35 (1892): 33-68.

"Preparations for the Second Prayer Book of Edward VI." Church
    Quarterly Review, 37 (1893): 137-166.

PRUETT, Gordon E. "Thomas Cranmer and the Eucharistic Con-
    troversy in the Reformation." Ph.D. dissertation, Princeton
    University, 1968.

RATCLIFF, Edward Cradock. "The Liturgical Work of Archbishop
    Cranmer." Journal of Ecclesiastical History, 7 (1956): 189-
    203; reprinted in his Liturgical Studies of E. C. Ratcliff, pp.
    184-202. Edited by A. H. Couratin and D. J. Tripp. London:
    SPCK, 1962.

SMYTH, C. H. Cranmer and the Reformation under Edward VI.
    Cambridge: Cambridge University Press, 1926; reprint ed.,
    London: SPCK, 1973.

SYMONDS, H. Edward. "Cranmer and the Edwardine Prayer
    Books." Theology, 49 (June–July 1946): 171-176, 200-204.

        (3). The Dix Controversy (Cranmer's Doctrine
              of the Eucharist)

DIX, Gregory. The Shape of the Liturgy, esp. pp. 640-674. 2d
    ed. Westminster: Dacre Press, 1945; reprint ed., London:
    A. & C. Black, 1975; New York: Seabury Press, 1982.

RATCLIFF, E. C. "The Shape of the Liturgy." Theology, 48
    (1945): 127-131 (esp. p. 130).

DUGMORE, Clifford W. [Review of The Shape of the Liturgy.]
    Journal of Theological Studies, 47 (1946): 107-113 (esp. p.
    111).

TIMMS, G. B. Dixit Cranmer: A Reply to Dom Gregory. Alcuin
    Club Papers. London: Mowbray, 1946; reprinted in Church
    Quarterly Review, 143 (1947): 217-234; 144 (1947): 33-51.

DIX, Gregory. "Dixit Cranmer et Non Timuit." Church Quarterly
    Review, 145 (1948): 145-176; 146 (1948): 44-60; reprint ed.,
    London: Dacre Press, 1948.

RICHARDSON, Cyril C. Zwingli and Cranmer on the Eucharist
    [Cranmer Dixit et Contradixit]. Evanston, IL: Seabury-
    Western Theological Seminary, 1949.

COURATIN, A. H. The Service of Holy Communion, 1549-1662,
    pp. 3-5, 8-12. London: SPCK, 1963.

BROOKS, Peter. Thomas Cranmer's Doctrine of the Eucharist: An
    Essay in Historical Development. New York: Seabury Press,
    1965.

CUMING, G. J. A History of Anglican Liturgy, pp. 109-110. Lon-
    don: Macmillan; New York: St. Martin's, 1969.

DAVIES, Horton. Worship and Theology in England, vol. 1: From
    Cranmer to Hooker, 1534-1603, pp. 178-194. Princeton, NJ:
    Princeton University Press, 1970.

BUCHANAN, Colin. What Did Cranmer Think He Was Doing? GLS,
    7. Bramcote, Eng.: Grove Books, 1976.

STEVENSON, Kenneth W. Gregory Dix--Twenty-Five Years On.
    GLS, 10. Bramcote, Eng.: Grove Books, 1977.

     d. Other Reformers

BECON, Thomas. The Catechism of Thomas Becon, etc., pp. 199-
    301. Edited by John Ayre. PS, 3. Cambridge: Cambridge
    University Press, 1844.

_____. Prayers and Other Pieces of Thomas Becon. Edited by
    John Ayre. PS, 4. Cambridge: Cambridge University Press,
    1844.
    --"The Displaying of the Popish Mass." Pp. 251-286.
    --"A Comparison between the Lord's Supper and the Pope's
        Mass." Pp. 351-395.
    --"Certain Articles of Religion Proved and Confirmed." Pp.
        396-483.

BRADFORD, John. The Writings of John Bradford, containing Ser-
    mons, Meditations, Examinations, etc. Edited by Aubrey Town-
    send. PS, 5. Cambridge: Cambridge University Press, 1848.
    --"Sermon on the Lord's Supper." Pp. 82-110.

_____ . The Writings of John Bradford, ... containing Letters,
Treatises, Remains. Edited by Aubrey Townsend. PS, 6.
Cambridge: Cambridge University Press, 1953.
--"Confutation of Four Romish Doctrines." Pp. 267-296.
--"Hurt of Hearing Mass." Pp. 297-351.

BULL, Henry. Christian Prayers and Holy Meditations, as well for
Private as Public Exercise. PS, 38. Cambridge: Cambridge
University Press, 1842.

_____ . "Bishop Bull on the Ancient Liturgies (from his XIIIth
Sermon)." In Tracts for the Times, vol. 2, Tract 64. London:
Rivington, 1834-1841.

COVERDALE, Miles. "Ghostly Psalms and Spiritual Songs." In
Remains of Myles Coverdale, pp. 536-590. Edited by George
Pearson, PS, 14. Cambridge: Cambridge University Press,
1846.

_____ . Writings and Translations of Myles Coverdale. Edited
by George Pearson. PS, 13. Cambridge: Cambridge Univer-
sity Press, 1844.
--"A Treatise on the Sacrament of the Body and Blood of
Christ, translated from Calvin" and "Additions to the
Translator's Preface, from the Second Edition." Pp. 425-
466, 530-535.
--"The Order of the Church in Denmark, and in Many Places
of Germany, for the Lord's Supper, Baptism, and Holy
Wedlock." Pp. 469-483.

GRINDAL, Edmund. The Remains of Edmund Grindal. Edited by
William Nicholson. PS, 19. Cambridge: Cambridge University
Press, 1843.
--"Occasional Services for the Plague." Pp. 75-120.
--"Disputation at Cambridge, A.D. 1549, about the Sacrament
of the Lord's Supper." Pp. 193-198.

HOOPER, John. Early Writings of John Hooper. Edited by Samuel
Carr. PS, 20. Cambridge: Cambridge University Press, 1943.
--"A Declaration of Christ and His Office," chs. 8 & 10. Pp.
60-71, 73-78.
--"Answer to the Bishop of Winchester's Book." Pp. 97-247.

_____ . Later Writings of Bishop Hooper. Edited by Charles
Nevinson. PS, 21. Cambridge: Cambridge University Press,
1852.
--"Copy of Bishop Hooper's Visitation Book." Pp. 117-156.
--"Hyperaspismus de vera doctrina et usu coenae Domini."
Pp. 399-541.

JEWEL, John. The Works of John Jewel, vol. 2. Edited by John

Ayre. PS, 24. Cambridge: Cambridge University Press, 1847.
--"The Reply to Harding's Answer." Vol. 2, pp. 553-800.
--"A Treatise of the Sacraments." Vol. 2, pp. 1099-1139.

_____. The Works of John Jewel. Edited by R. W. Jelf. Oxford: Oxford University Press, 1848.
--"The Reply to Harding's Answer." Vol. 1, pp. 157-440; vol. 2, pp. 1-443; vol. 3, pp. 1-500.
--"A Treatise of the Sacraments." Vol. 8, pp. 1-72.

RIDLEY, Nicholas. A Brief Declaration of the Lord's Supper. Edited by H. C. G. Moule. London: Seeley; New York: Whittaker, 1895.

_____. "Reply of Bishop Ridly to Bishop Hooper on the Vestment Controversy, 1550." In The Writings of John Bradford ... containing Letters, Treatises, Remains, pp. 375-395. Edited by Aubrey Townsend. PS, 6. Cambridge: Cambridge University Press, 1853.

_____. The Works of Nicholas Ridley. Edited by Henry Christmas. PS, 39. Cambridge: Cambridge University Press, 1841.
--"Brief Declaration or Treatise against Transubstantiation." Pp. 1-45.
--"Treatise against Image Worship." Pp. 81-96.
--"A Determination concerning the Sacrament." Pp. 167-179.
--"Disputation at Oxford." Pp. 187-252.
--"Ridley's Account of his Disputation at Oxford." Pp. 303-306.
--"The Theological Variations of Stephen Gardiner." Pp. 307-315.
--"Answers to Certain Queries touching the Abuses of the Mass." Pp. 316-318.
--"Injunctions to the Diocese of London." Pp. 319-321.
--"Reasons Why the Lord's Board Should Be in the Form of a Table." Pp. 321-324.

SANDYS, Edwin. The Sermons of Edwin Sandys. Edited by John Ayre. PS, 41. Cambridge: Cambridge University Press, 1841.
--"The Fourth Sermon," par. 19-24. Pp. 81-91.
--"Advice concerning Rites and Ceremonies in the Synod 1562." P. 433.

TYNDALE, William. "A Brief Declaration of the Sacraments." In Doctrinal Treatises and Introductions to Different Portions of the Holy Scriptures, pp. 345-388. Edited by Henry Walter. PS, 42. Cambridge: Cambridge University Press, 1848.

_____. "The Supper of the Lord." In An Answer to Sir Thomas More's Dialogue, The Supper of the Lord, etc., pp. 222-268.

Edited by Henry Walter.   PS, 44.   Cambridge: Cambridge
University Press, 1850.

WHITGIFT, John.   "The Defence of the Answer to the Admonition,
against the Reply of Thomas Cartwright."   In The Works of
John Whitgift, vols. 1-3.   Edited by John Ayre.   PS, 46-48.
Cambridge: Cambridge University Press, 1851-1853.   See
especially:
--"Tract. 7: Of the Apparel of Ministers." Vol. 2, pp. 1-76.
--"Tract. 9: Of the Communion-Book." Vol. 2, pp. 438-564.
--"Tract. 10: Of Holy-days." Vol. 2, pp. 565-595.
--"Tract. 12: Of Preaching before the Administration of the
    Sacrament." Vol. 3, pp. 14-27.
--"Tract. 15: Of Matters touching Communion." Vol. 3, pp.
    73-108.
--"Tract. 16: Of Matters touching Baptism." Pp. 109-149.

WHITTINGHAM, William [supposed author].   A Brief Discourse of
the Troubles begun at Frankfort in the Year 1554, about the
Book of Common Prayer and Ceremonies.   Reprinted from the
Black-Letter edition of 1575, with an introduction.   London:
J. Petheram, 1846.

_____. _____. New ed., edited by Edward Arber.   London:
Stock, 1908.

WYCLIF, John.   "On the Eucharist."   Edited and translated by
Ford Lewis Battles.   In Advocates of Reform: From Wyclif to
Erasmus, pp. 61-88.   Edited by Matthew Spinks.   LCC, 14.
Philadelphia, PA: Westminster Press, 1953.

        6. Seventeenth and Eighteenth Centuries

    a. Collections

BROGDEN, James, ed.   Illustrations of the Liturgy and Ritual of
the United Church of England and Ireland, being Sermons and
Discourses selected from the Works of Eminent Divines who
lived in the Seventeenth Century.   London: J. Murray, 1842.

MORE, Paul Elmer, and CROSS, Frank Leslie, eds.   Anglicanism:
The Thought and Practice of the Church of England, Illustrated
from the Religious Literature of the Seventeenth Century.
London: SPCK, 1935.
--especially pp. 345-638.

    b. General and Miscellaneous Studies

ADDLESHAW, George W. O.   The High Church Tradition: A Study
in the Liturgical Thought of the Seventeenth Century.   London:
Faber & Faber, 1944.

BROXAP, Henry. The Later Non-Jurors. Cambridge: Cambridge University Press, 1924.

DAVIES, Horton. "Prière liturgique et prière spontanée dans le débat entre anglicans et puritans." La Maison-Dieu, 111 (1972): 31-42.

DUGMORE, Clifford W. Eucharistic Doctrine in England from Hooker to Waterland. London: SPCK; New York: Macmillan, 1942.

EVERY, George. The High Church Party, 1688-1718. London: Published for the Church Historical Society by SPCK, 1956.

FAWCETT, T. J. The Liturgy of Comprehension 1689: An Abortive Attempt to revise the Book of Common Prayer. ACC, 54. Great Wakering, Eng.: Mayhew-McCrimmon, 1973.

GRISBROOKE, W. Jardine. Anglican Liturgies of the Seventeenth and Eighteenth Centuries. ACC, 40. London: SPCK, 1958.

LATHBURY, Thomas. A History of the Nonjurors: Their Controversies and Writings, with Remarks on some of the Rubrics in the Book of Common Prayer. London: Pickering, 1845.

OVERTON, J. H. The Nonjurors: Their Lives, Principles, and Writings. New York: Whittaker, 1903.

PEASTON, A. Elliott. The Prayer Book Reform Movement in the XVIIIth Century. Oxford: Basil Blackwell, 1940.

WEBB, Douglas. "La doctrine du Saint-Esprit dans la liturgie eucharistique d'après les théologiens anglais des 17e et 18e siècles." Ephemerides liturgicae, 90 (1976): 272-288.

c. Andrewes

ANDREWES, Lancelot. The Works of Lancelot Andrewes. 11 vols. Edited by J. P. Wilson and J. Bliss. LACT. Oxford: J. H. Parker, 1841-1854.
--"Discourse of Ceremonies Retained and Used in Christian Churches." Vol. 6, pp. 363-392.
--"Form of Consecration of a Church and Churchyard." Vol. 6, pp. 309-333.
--"Notes on the Book of Common Prayer" and "Form of Consecration of Church Plate." Vol. 11, pp. 141-163.

_____. Preces privatae quotidianae, Graece et latine. Editio altera. London: Pickering, 1828.

_____. "The Greek Devotions of Bishop Andrews, Translated and Arranged." [By J. H. Newman.] In Tracts for the Times,

vol. 5, tract 88. London: Rivington, 1834-1841; new edition
published as Private Prayers. Edited by Hugh Martin. London: SCM Press, 1957.

_____. The Preces Privatae of Lancelot Andrewes, Bishop of
Winchester. Translated with introduction and notes by F. E.
Brightman. London: Methuen, 1903.

d. Durel

DUREL, John. The Liturgy of the Church of England Asserted in
a Sermon. London: Printed for R. Royston, 1662.

MARSHALL, Charles and William W. The Latin Prayer Book of
Charles II; or, An Account of the Liturgia of Dean Durel
(1670). Oxford: Thornton, 1882.

e. Hooker

HOOKER, Richard. Of the Laws of Ecclesiastical Polity, Book V.
In The Works of that Learned and Judicious Divine, Mr. Richard
Hooker, vol. 2. New ed. Edited by John Keble. Oxford:
Oxford University Press, 1836.

_____. Of the Laws of Ecclesiastical Polity, vol. 2, Book 5.
EL. London: Dent; New York: Dutton, 1907; many reprints.

_____. Of the Laws of Ecclesiastical Polity, Book 5. In The
Folger Library Edition of the Works of Richard Hooker, vol. 2.
Edited by W. Speed Hill. Cambridge: Belknap Press of Har-
vard University Press, 1977.

BOOTY, John E. "Hooker's Understanding of the Presence of Christ
in the Eucharist." In The Divine Drama in History and Liturgy,
pp. 131-148. Edited by John E. Booty. Allison Park, PA:
Pickwick Publications, 1984.

LOYER, Olivier. L'Anglicanisme de Richard Hooker. 2 vols.
Lille: Université de Lille; Paris: Champion, 1979.

MARSHALL, John S. Hooker's Theology of Common Prayer: The
Fifth Book of the Polity Paraphrased and Expanded into a Commentary on the Prayer Book. Sewanee, TN: University Press
of the University of the South, 1956.

PAGET, Francis. An Introduction to the Fifth Book of Hooker's
Treatise Of the Laws of Ecclesiastical Polity. 2d ed. Oxford:
Clarendon Press, 1907.

PARRIS, J. R. "Hooker's Doctrine of the Eucharist." Scottish
Journal of Theology, 16 (1963): 151-165.

f. Laud

LAUD, William. The Works of ... William Laud. 7 vols. in 9.
    LACT. Oxford: J. H. Parker, 1847-1860.
    --"Answer to Lord Say's Speech touching the Liturgy." Vol.
      6, part 1, pp. 83-146.
    --"A Form of Penance and Reconciliation." Vol. 5, part 2,
      pp. 372-376.
    --"The History of the Troubles and Trial of William Laud."
      Vol. 3, pp. 273-463; vol. 4, pp. 1-461.
    --"A Speech at the Censure of Bastwick, Burton and Prynne."
      Vol. 6, part 1, pp. 35-70.

BOURNE, E. C. E. The Anglicanism of William Laud. London:
    SPCK, 1947.

g. Taylor

(See also BOLTON under Ireland, Studies, page 386.)

TAYLOR, Jeremy. The Whole Works of the Right Rev. Jeremy
    Taylor. 15 vols. London: Rivington, etc., 1828.
    --"An Apology for Authorized and Set Forms of Liturgy." Vol.
      7, pp. 277-390.
    --"A Collection of Offices, or Forms of Prayer in Cases Ordi-
      nary and Extraordinary...." Vol. 15, pp. 237-389.
    --"The Real Presence and Spiritual of Christ in the Blessed
      Sacrament." Vol. 9, pp. 403-512; vol. 10, pp. 1-108.

_____. The Whole Works of the Right Rev. Jeremy Taylor. 10
    vols. Edited by Reginald Heber; revised by Charles Eden
    Page. London: Longmans, etc., 1849.
    --"Apology for Authorized and Set Forms of Liturgy." Vol. 5,
      pp. 229-314.
    --"Collection of Offices, or Forms of Prayer." Vol. 8, pp.
      573-701.
    --"A Discourse of Confirmation." Vol. 5, pp. 609-669.
    --"Festival Hymns." Vol. 7, pp. 649-662.
    --"On the Reverence Due to the Altar." Vol. 5, pp. 317-338.
    --"The Real Presence and Spiritual of Christ in the Blessed
      Sacrament." Vol. 6, pp. 3-168.
    --"The Worthy Communicant." Vol. 8, pp. 3-239.

PORTER, Harry Boone. Jeremy Taylor, Liturgist (1613-1667).
    ACC, 61. London: SPCK, 1979.

h. Other Writers

BEVERIDGE, William. The Theological Works of William Beveridge.
    12 vols. LACT. Oxford: J. H. Parker, 1842-1848.
    --"The Great Necessity and Advantage of Public Prayer." Vol.
      8, pp. 477-531.

--"The Great Necessity and Advantage of Frequent Communion."
   Vol. 8, pp. 532-611.
--"Sermon 1 [from Five Sermons, etc.]:   The Excellency and
   Usefulness of the Common Prayer."   Vol. 6, pp. 367-398.
--"Sermon 2:   The Institution of Ministers."   Vol. 1, pp. 26-43.
--"Sermon 3:   Manner of their Institution with us."   Vol. 1,
   pp. 44-58.
--"Sermon 5:   The True Notion of Religious Worship to be Paid
   by Ministers."   Vol. 1, pp. 88-107.
--"Sermon 12:   The Sacerdotal Benediction in the Name of the
   Trinity."   Vol. 1, pp. 210-231.
--"Sermon 58:   The Advantage of Public Worship."   Vol. 3,
   pp. 109-125.
--"Sermon 59:   The Duty of Public Thanksgiving."   Vol. 3,
   pp. 126-143.
--"Sermon 121:   The Presence of Christ in Religious Assemblies
   of Christians."   Vol. 5, pp. 313-329.
--"Sermon 130:   The Worthy Communicant."   Vol. 6, pp. 20-41.

_____.   "Bishop Beveridge: The Great Necessity and Advantage
of Public Prayer."   In Tracts for the Times, vol. 1, tract 25.
London: Rivington, 1834.

_____.   "Bishop Beveridge on the Necessity and Advantage of
Frequent Communion."   In Tracts for the Times, vol. 1, tract
26.   London: Rivington, 1834.

COMBER, Thomas.   A Companion to the Temple; or a Help to Devotion in the Use of the Common Prayer.   7 vols.   Oxford: Oxford University Press, 1841.

COSIN, John.   A Collection of Private Devotions.   Edited by P. G.
Stanwood.   Oxford: Clarendon Press, 1967.

_____.   "Bishop Cosin: The History of Popish Transubstantia-
tion."   In Tracts for the Times, vol. 1, tracts 27-28.   London:
Rivington, 1834.

_____.   Notes and Collections on the Book of Common Prayer.
In The Works of ... John Cosin, vol. 5 [entire volume].
LACT.   Oxford: J. H. & J. Parker, 1855.

HAMMOND, Henry.   A View of the New Directory, and a Vindication of the Ancient Liturgy of the Church of England.   2d ed.
Oxford: H. Hall, printer to the University, 1646.

JOHNSON, John.   The Unbloody Sacrifice, and Altar, Unveiled and
Supported, etc.   In The Theological Works of the Rev. John
Johnson, vols. 1 & 2.   LACT.   Oxford: J. H. Parker, 1847.

L'ESTRANGE, Hamon.   The Alliance of the Divine Offices.   4th ed.
LACT.   Oxford: J. H. Parker, 1846.

NICHOLLS, William. A Comment on the Book of Common Prayer, and Administration of the Sacraments, &c. 2d ed. London: Printed for R. Bonwicke, 1712.

SECKER, Thomas. The Works of Thomas Secker, vol. 3. London: Rivington, etc., 1811.
--"On the Lawfulness and Expediency of Forms of Prayer" (Sermon 24). Vol. 3, pp. 380-394.
--"An Explanation and Defense of the Liturgy of the Church of England" (Sermons 25-29). Vol. 3, pp. 395-481.

SHARP, Thomas. The Rubric in the Book of Common Prayer and the Canons of the Church of England, so far as they Relate to the Parochial Clergy. London: J. & P. Knapton, 1753; reprint ed., Oxford: Oxford University Press, 1834.

SHEPHERD, John. A Critical and Practical Elucidation of the Book of Common Prayer ... according to the Use of the United Church of England and Ireland. 2 vols. London: Rivington, 1797.

_____. _____. 2 vols. 5th ed. of vol. 1, 4th ed. of vol. 2. London: Rivington: 1828.

SPARROW, Anthony. A Rationale upon the Book of Common Prayer of the Church of England. New ed. Oxford: J. H. Parker, 1839.
--First published in 1655

THORNDIKE, Herbert. Of Religious Assemblies and the Publick Service of God. Cambridge: R. Daniel, 1642.

_____. _____. In The Theological Works of Herbert Thorndike, vol. 1, pp. 99-394. LACT. Oxford: J. H. Parker, 1844.

WATERLAND, Daniel. The Works of the Rev. Daniel Waterland. 6 vols. 2d ed. Oxford: Oxford University Press, 1843.
--"An Inquiry Concerning the Antiquity of the Practice of Infant-Communion." Vol. 6, pp. 39-72.
--"Letters on Lay-Baptism." Vol. 6, pp. 73-233.
--"The Nature, Obligation, and Efficacy of the Christian Sacraments considered" and "Supplement." Vol. 4.
--"A Review of the Doctrine of the Eucharist" and "Charges [to the Clergy of Middlesex]." Vol. 4, pp. 459-802; vol. 5, pp. 105-296.

_____. A Review of the Doctrine of the Eucharist: With Four Charges to the Clergy of Middlesex connected with the Same Subject. Oxford: Clarendon Press, 1868.

WHEATLY, Charles. The Church of England Man's Companion; or,
A Rational Illustration of the Harmony, Excellency, and Usefulness of the Book of Common Prayer. [1st ed.] Oxford, 1710.

_____. A Rational Illustration of the Book of Common Prayer.
[Of the long history of editions and reprints, the following are
representative:]
--Oxford: Clarendon Press, 1794.
--Oxford: Oxford University Press, 1846.
--Bohn's Standard Library. London: Bohn, 1850.
--Cambridge: Cambridge University Press, 1858.
--London: Bell, 1890.

_____. A Rational Illustration of the Book of Common Prayer
... adapting this Edition to the Present State of the Protestant
Episcopal Church in America.... [1st American ed.] Boston,
MA: R. P. & C. Williams, 1825.

WILSON, Thomas. The Works of ... Thomas Wilson. 7 vols.
LACT. Oxford: J. H. Parker, 1847-1863.
--[Liturgical Offices:] "Excommunication," "A Form of Receiv-
ing Penitents," "A Form of Prayer," "A Form of Consecrat-
ing Churches, etc." and "Consecration of a Churchyard."
Vol. 7, pp. 8-27.
--"Sermon 58: On the Due Observance of the Sabbath." Vol.
3, pp. 77-86.
--"Sermon 76: The Lord's Supper Practically Explained." Vol.
3, pp. 273-287.
--"Sermon 77: A Frequent Receiving of the Lord's Supper
Recommended and Enforced." Vol. 3, pp. 288-302.
--"A Short and Plain Instruction for the Better Understanding
of the Lord's Supper." Vol. 4, pp. 331-423.

_____. "Bishop Wilson's Form of Excommunication." In Tracts
for the Times, vol. 1, tract 37. London: Rivington, 1834.

_____. "Bishop Wilson's Form of Receiving Penitents." In
Tracts for the Times, vol. 1, tract 39. London: Rivington,
1834.

7. Nineteenth Century, Including the
Oxford Movement

a. Sources

BRICKNELL, W. S., ed. The Judgment of the Bishops upon
Tractarian Theology. Oxford: J. Vincent, 1845.

BURBIDGE, Edward. Liturgies and Offices of the Church for the
Use of English Readers, in Illustration of the Book of Common
Prayer. London: Bell, 1885; New York: Whittaker, 1886.

FORBES, A. P. A Primary Charge Delivered to the Clergy of His Diocese at the Annual Synod. 2d ed. London: Joseph Masters, 1858. [On the Eucharist]

FREEMAN, Philip. The Principles of Divine Service: An Enquiry Concerning the True Manner of Understanding the Order for Morning and Evening Prayer and for the Administration of the Holy Communion in the English Church. 2 vols. 2d ed. Oxford: J. H. & J. Parker, 1863-1866; reprint ed., London: J. Parker, 1893.

JEBB, John. Choral Service of the United Church of England and Ireland: Being an Inquiry into the Liturgical System of the Cathedral and Collegiate Foundations of the Anglican Communion. London: Parker, 1843.

_____. The Ritual Law and Custom of the Church Universal. A sermon preached in Aug. 29, 1865 [on I Cor. XI.16] ... 2d ed. London: n.p., 1866.

KEBLE, John. On Eucharistic Adoration. 2d ed. Oxford: J. H. & J. Parker, 1859.

MAURICE, Frederick Denison. The Prayer-Book Considered especially in reference to the Romish System. 3d ed. London: John W. Parker, 1852; reprint ed. published as The Prayer Book. Foreword by the Archbishop of Canterbury. London: James Clarke, 1966.

PALMER, William. Origines liturgicae; or, Antiquities of the English Ritual; and a Dissertation on Primitive Liturgies. 2 vols. 2d ed. Oxford: Oxford University Press, 1836.

PARKER, James. An Introduction to the History of the Successive Revisions of the Book of Common Prayer. Oxford: J. H. Parker, 1877.

PUSEY, E. B. The Doctrine of the Real Presence as Contained in the Fathers. Oxford: J. H. Parker, 1855.

QUARITCH, Bernard. A Short Sketch of Liturgical History and Literature, Illustrated by Examples Manuscript and Printed. London: C. W. H. Wyman, 1887.

SCUDAMORE, W. E. Notitia Eucharistica: A Commentary, Explanatory, Doctrinal, and Historical, on the Order for the Administration of the Lord's Supper or Holy Communion according to the Use of the Church of England. 2d ed. London: Rivingtons, 1876.

SELBORNE, Roundell Palmer [Lord]. Notes on Some Passages in

the Liturgical History of the Reformed English Church. London: J. Murray, 1878.

Tracts for the Times. By members of the University of Oxford
[J. H. Newman, J. Keble, W. Palmer, R. H. Froude, E. B.
Pusey, I. Williams, and others]. 6 vols. London: Rivington,
1834-1841.
--Tract 3.   "Thoughts Respectfully Addressed to the Clergy
on Alterations in the Liturgy." [By J. H. Newman.]
Vol. 1.
--Tract 9.   "On Shortening the Church Services." [By R. H.
Froude.] Vol. 1.
--Tract 13. "Sunday Lessons." [By John Keble.] Vol. 1.
--Tract 14. "The Ember Days." [By A. Menzies.] Vol. 1.
--Tract 16. "Advent." [By Benjamin Harrison.] Vol. 1.
--Tract 25. "Bishop Beveridge: The Great Necessity and
Advantage of Public Prayer." Vol. 1.
--Tract 26. "Bishop Beveridge on the Necessity and Advantage
of Frequent Communion." Vol. 1.
--Tracts 27-28. "Bishop Cosin: The History of Popish Tran-
substantiation." Vol. 1.
--Tract 32. "The Standing Ordinances of Religion." Vol. 1.
--Tract 34. "Rites and Customs of the Church." [By J. H.
Newman.] Vol. 1.
--Tract 37. "Bishop Wilson's Form of Excommunication." Vol.
1.
--Tract 39. "Bishop Wilson's Form of Receiving Penitents."
Vol. 1.
--Tract 52. "Sermons for Saints' Days." [By John Keble.]
Vol. 2.
--Tract 56. "Holy Days Observed in the English Church."
Vol. 2.
--Tract 63. "The Antiquity of the Existing Liturgies." [By
R. H. Froude.] Vol. 2.
--Tract 64. "Bishop Bull on the Ancient Liturgies (from his
XIIIth Sermon)." Vol. 2.
--Tracts 67-69. "Scriptural Views of Holy Baptism." [By
E. B. Pusey.] Vol. 2.
--"Note to the Advertisement." By E. B. Pusey. Vol. 3.
--Tract 75. "On the Roman Breviary as Embodying the Sub-
stance of the Devotional Services of the Church Catholic."
[By J. H. Newman.] Vol. 3.
--Tract 76. "Catena Patrum, No. II: Testimony of Writers in
the Later English Church, to the Doctrine of Baptismal Re-
generation." Vol. 3.
--Tract 81. "Catena Patrum, No. IV. Testimony of Writers of
the Latern English Church to the Doctrine of the Eucharis-
tic Sacrifice, with an account of the Changes made in the
Liturgy as to the Expression of that Doctrine." Vol. 4.
--[Tract 82.] "Letter to a Magazine on the Subject of Dr.
Pusey's Tract on Baptism." [By J. H. Newman.] Vol. 4.

--Tract 84. "Whether a Clergyman of the Church of England Be Now Bound to have Morning and Evening Prayers Daily in his Parish Church?" Vol. 5.

--Tract 86. "Indications of a Superintending Providence in the Preservation of the Prayer Book and in the Changes which it has Undergone." [By Isaac Williams.] Vol. 5.

--Tract 88. "The Greek Devotions of Bishop Andrews, Translated and Arranged." [By J. H. Newman.] Vol. 5.

--Tract 90. "Remarks on Certain Passages in the Thirty-Nine Articles." [By J. H. Newman.] Vol. 6.

--"A Letter Addressed to the Rev. R. W. Jelf ... in Explanation of No. 90 in the Series called The Tracts for the Times." [By J. H. Newman.] Vol. 6.

--"The Articles Treated on in Tract 90 Reconsidered and their Interpretation vindicated in a Letter to the Rev. R. W. Jelf." [By E. B. Pusey.] Vol. 6.

The Tractarian Doctrine of the Mass. From the Tracts for the Times, nos. 26, 27, 52, 81, 90. Anglican's Library, 1. London: Faith Press, 1928.

WILBERFORCE, Robert Isaac. The Doctrine of Holy Baptism. 3d ed. London: John Murray, 1850.

_____. The Doctrine of the Holy Eucharist. 3d ed. London: Mozley, 1854.

WOODD, Basil. The Excellence of the Liturgy; sermon in the parish church of St. Mary, Pylesbury, June 27, 1810. London: n.p., [1810].

b. Studies

BENTLEY, James. Ritualism and Politics in Victorian Britain. New York: Oxford University Press, 1978.

BERESFORD-HOPE, A. J. B. Worship and Order. London: Murray, 1883.

BRILIOTH, Yngve. The Anglican Revival: Studies in the Oxford Movement. London: Longmans, Green, 1925.

CHURCH, Richard William. The Oxford Movement: Twelve Years, 1833-1845. London: Macmillan, 1891; reprint ed., edited by Geoffrey Best. Chicago: University of Chicago Press, 1970.

GASELEE, S. "The Aesthetic Side of the Oxford Movement." In Northern Catholicism, pp. 423-445. Edited by N. P. Williams and C. Harris. London: SPCK; New York: Macmillan, 1933.

JASPER, R. C. D. Prayer Book Revision in England, 1800-1900. London: SPCK, 1954.

PEASTON, A. Elliott. The Prayer Book Revisions of the Victorian
    Evangelicals. Dublin: APCK, 1963.

WHITE, James F. The Cambridge Movement: The Ecclesiologists
    and the Gothic Revival. New York: Cambridge University
    Press, 1979.

WILLIAMS, N. P., and HARRIS, C., eds. Northern Catholicism:
    Centenary Studies in the Oxford and Parallel Movements. Lon-
    don: SPCK; New York: Macmillan, 1933.

8. Twentieth Century

CLARKE, William K. Lowther. The New Prayer Book Explained.
    London: SPCK, 1927.

_____. The Prayer Book of 1928 Reconsidered. London:
    SPCK, 1943.

COIT, Stanton. National Idealism and the Book of Common Prayer:
    An Essay in Re-interpretation and Revision. London: Williams
    & Norgate, 1908.

FRERE, Walter Howard. Some Principles of Liturgical Reform. 2d
    ed. London: John Murray, 1914.

_____. Walter Howard Frere: A Collection of his Papers on
    Liturgical and Historical Subjects. Edited by J. H. Arnold
    and E. G. P. Wyatt. ACC, 35. London: Oxford University
    Press, 1940.

_____. Walter Howard Frere: His Correspondence on Liturgical
    Revision and Construction. Edited by R. C. D. Jasper. ACC,
    39. London: SPCK, 1954.

HEBERT, Arthur Gabriel, ed. The Parish Communion: A Book of
    Essays. London: SPCK; New York: Macmillan, 1937.

JOYNSON-HICKS, William. The Prayer Book Crisis. London:
    Putnam, 1928.

THE LAMBETH CONFERENCE, 1958. The Encyclical Letter from
    the Bishops, together with the Resolutions and Reports. Lon-
    don: SPCK; Greenwich, CT: Seabury Press, 1958.

MACKENZIE, Kenneth, ed. The Liturgy: Papers Read at the
    Priest's Convention, Tewkesbury, May, 1938. London: SPCK,
    1962.

PATON, David M., ed. The Parish Communion Today: The Report

of the 1962 Conference of Parish and People. London: SPCK,
1962.

RELTON, H. Maurice, ed. The New Prayer Book. London: Allen
& Unwin, 1927.

STEWART, M. E. "Anglican Eucharistic Theology in the Twentieth
Century." Ph.D. dissertation, Queen's University, Belfast,
1975.

TEMPLE, William. The Prayer Book Crisis: A Reply to the Rt.
Hon. Sir William Joynson-Hicks. London: SPCK, 1928.

9. Recent Liturgical Revision

BAKER, Tom. "New Testament Scholarship and Liturgical Revision."
In What about the New Testament: Essays in Honour of Chris-
topher Evans, pp. 187-197. Edited by Morna Hooker and Colin
Hichling. London: SCM Press, 1975.

BECKWITH, Roger T. The Service of Holy Communion and Its Revision. LatM, 3. Abingdon, Eng.: Marcham Manor Press,
1972.

_____, ed. Towards a Modern Prayer Book: The New Services
Examined. Abingdon, Eng.: Marcham Manor Press, 1966.

_____. "A Turning Point in Prayer Book Revision." The
Churchman, 89 (1975): 120-129.

BROOKS, Cleanth. "Prayer Book Revision: Literary Style."
Anglican Theological Review, 44 (1962): 18-33.

BUCHANAN, Colin O. , ed. The Development of the New Eucharistic
Prayers of the Church of England. GLS, 20. Bramcote, Eng.:
Grove Books, 1979.

_____. The End of the Offertory: An Anglican Study. GLS,
14. Bramcote, Eng.: Grove Books, 1978.

_____. Recent Liturgical Revision in the Church of England.
4 vols. GBMW, 14. Bramcote, Eng.: Grove Books, 1973-1978.

Church of England. Liturgical Commission. Prayer Book Revision
in the Church of England. London: SPCK, 1957.

FROST, David L. The Language of Series 3: An Essay on Modern
Liturgical Language, with an Account of the Debate on Series 3
Communion Service, and an Analysis of the Language of the
Congregational Text. GBMW, 12. Bramcote, Eng.: Grove
Books, 1973.

_____. "Liturgical Language from Canmer to Series 3." In
The Eucharist Today: Studies on Series 3, pp. 142-167.
Edited by R. C. D. Jasper. London: SPCK, 1974.

JASPER, R. C. D., ed. The Eucharist Today: Studies on Series
3. London: SPCK, 1974.

MARSHALL, Michael. Renewal in Worship. London: Marshall,
Morgan & Scott, 1982; revised American ed., Wilton, CT:
Morehouse-Barlow, 1985.

MARTIN, David, and MULLEN, Peter, eds. No Alternative: The
Prayer Book Controversy. Oxford: Basil Blackwell, 1981.

MORETON, Michael. Consecrating, Remembering, Offering: Catholics and Series 3, 2, and 1, and 1662. London: Church Literature Association, 1976.

SPENCER, Bonnell. "A Functional Liturgy." Anglican Theological
Review, 43 (1961): 333-369.

SPINKS, Bryan D. "Christian Worship or Cultural Incantations?"
Studia Liturgica, 12 (1977): 1-19.

10. Commentaries

ATCHLEY, Edward G. C. F. The People's Prayers: Being Some
Considerations on the Use of the Litany in Public Worship.
ACT, 6. London: Longmans, Green, 1906.

BATE, Herbert Newell, and EELES, Francis C. Thoughts on the
Shape of the Liturgy. ACT, 24. London: Mowbray, 1946.

BLOMFIELD, John. The Eucharistic Canon, with Suggestions for
a Possible Revision. London: SPCK, 1930.

BLUNT, John Henry, ed. The Annotated Book of Common Prayer:
Being an Historical, Ritual, and Theological Commentary on the
Devotional System of the Church of England. London: Riving-
ton, 1866; many editions up to 1907.

BROOK, Stella. The Language of the Book of Common Prayer.
New York: Oxford University Press, 1965.

BUXTON, Richard F. Eucharist and Institution Narrative: A
Study in the Roman and Anglican Traditions of the Consecration of the Eucharist from the Eighth to the Twentieth Centuries. ACC, 58. Great Wakering, Eng.: Mayhew-McCrimmon,
1976.

CLARKE, William K. L. The English Liturgy in the Light of the
   Bible. New York: Macmillan, 1940.

DAVIES, David R. Down, Peacock's Feathers: Studies in the
   Contemporary Significance of the General Confession. Rev. ed.
   London: G. Bles; New York: Macmillan, 1961.

DEARMER, Percy. The Art of Public Worship. London: Mowbray;
   Milwaukee, WI: Morehouse, 1919.

Deviations of Modern Editions of the Prayer Book from the Text of
   the Sealed Book: Report of the Committee of the Lower House
   of Convocation of the Province of York. London: Christian
   Knowledge Society, 1892.

DOWDEN, John. Further Studies in the Prayer Book. London:
   Methuen, 1908.

_____. The Workmanship of the Prayer Book. 3d ed. London:
   Methuen, 1904.

EVERY, George. Basic Liturgy: A Study in the Structure of the
   Eucharistic Prayer. London: Faith Press, 1961.

GORE, Charles. Reflections on the Litany. London: Mowbray;
   Milwaukee, WI: Morehouse, 1932.

GOULBOURN, Edward Meyrick. The Collects of the Day: An Exposition Critical and Devotional of the Collects Appointed at the
   Communion, with Preliminary Essays on their Structure, Sources,
   and General Character, and Appendices containing Expositions
   of the Discarded Collects of the First Prayer Book of 1549, and
   of the Collects of Morning and Evening Prayer. 2 vols. [Last
   ed.] London: Longmans, Green, 1897-1901.

HALL, A. C. A. An Exposition of the Litany. Milwaukee, WI:
   Young Churchman, 1914.

HARFORD, George, STEVENSON, Morley, and TYRER, J. W. The
   Prayer Book Dictionary. London: I. Pitman; New York:
   Longmans, Green, 1912.

KARSLAKE, W. H. The Litany of the English Church Considered
   in its History, its Plan, and the Manner in which it is Intended
   to be Used. London: Pickering, 1876.

KONSTANT, David. The Bidding Prayer for the Church's Year.
   Rev. ed. Great Wakering, Eng.: Mayhew-McCrimmon, 1982.

LEGG, J. Wickham. Some Principles and Services of the Prayer-
   Book Historically Considered. London: Rivington, 1899.

LUCKOCK, Herbert Mortimer. The Divine Liturgy: Being the Order of the Administration of Holy Communion Historically, Doc-
trinally and Devotionally Set Forth. New ed. London: Longmans, Green, 1902.

MINCHIN, Basil. Covenant and Sacrifice. His Worship in the
Body of Christ. London: Longmans, Green, 1958.

PEPPER, George Wharton. An Analytical Index to the Book of
Common Prayer and a Brief Account of its Evolution; Together
with a Revision of Gladstone's Concordance to the Psalter.
Philadelphia, PA: J. C. Winston, 1948.

SIMPSON, W. J. Sparrow. The Prayer of Consecration. Introduction by Charles Gore. London: Scott, 1916.

STALEY, Vernon. The Holy Communion: Addresses and Instructions, Doctrinal, Practical, and Ceremonial concerning the
Sacrament of the Body and Blood of Christ. Oxford: Mowbray,
1905.

STEPHENS-HODGE, L. E. H. The Collects, with the Litany and
the Occasional Prayers: An Introduction and Commentary.
London: Hodder & Stoughton, 1961.

VASEY, Michael. Intercessions in Worship. GBMW, 77. Bramcote, Eng.: Grove Books, 1981.

WARREN, F. E., ed. The Book of Comm on Prayer, with Commentary for Teachers and Students. 2d ed. London: SPCK,
1922.

WHITAKER, E. C. The Intercessions of the Prayer Book. London:
SPCK, 1956.

C. SCOTLAND

1. Texts (arranged chronologically)

(See also HALL [1,2, & 5] and HALL [2] on page 355.)

LEMPRIERE, Philip A. Scottish Communion Offices of 1637, 1735,
1755, 1764 and 1889, together with the English Liturgy of 1549,
arranged to show their Variations. Edinburgh: R. Grant,
1909.

SPROTT, George W., ed. The Booke of Common Prayer and Administration of the Sacraments, with Other Rites and Ceremonies of the Church of Scotland as it was Sett Downe at First,

before the change thereof made by ye Archbishop of Canter-
burie, and sent back to Scotland.... Edinburgh: Edmonston
& Douglas, 1871.

The Book of Common Prayer as printed at Edinburgh, 1637. Commonly called Archbishop Laud's. [Facsimile ed.] London:
W. Pickering, 1844.

COOPER, James, ed. The Book of Common Prayer and Administration of the Sacraments, with Other Parts of Divine Service for
the Use of the Church of Scotland, commonly known as Laud's
Liturgy (1637). With historical introduction and illustrative
notes. Edinburgh: Blackwood, 1904.

EPISCOPAL CHURCH IN SCOTLAND. The Book of Common Prayer,
and Administration of the Sacraments and Other Rites and
Ceremonies of the Church according to the Use of the Church
of England. Together with the Psalter ... and the Scottish
Liturgy, and the Permissible Additions to and Deviations from
the Service Books of the Scottish Church as Canonically Sanc-
tioned. Edinburgh: Cambridge University Press, 1912.

_____. The Scottish Book of Common Prayer, and Administra-
tion of the Sacraments and Other Rites and Ceremonies of the
Church, etc. Edinburgh: Cambridge University Press, 1929.

_____. The Liturgy. Auchterarder, Scot.: Representative
Church Council of Scottish Episcopal Church, 1970.

2. Studies

DON, Alan Campbell. The Scottish Book of Common Prayer, 1929:
Notes on Its Origin and Growth with Illustrations from Original
Documents. London: SPCK, 1949.

DONALDSON, Gordon. The Making of the Scottish Prayer Book of
1637. Edinburgh: Edinburgh University Press, 1954.

DOWDEN, John. The Scottish Communion Office 1764. New ed.
seen through the press by H. A. Wilson. Oxford: Clarendon
Press, 1922.

PERRY, William. The Scottish Liturgy: Its Value and History.
2d ed. London: Mowbray, 1922.

_____. The Scottish Prayer Book. Cambridge: Cambridge
University Press, 1929.

D. IRELAND

1. Texts

CHURCH OF IRELAND. The Book of Common Prayer, and Administration of the Sacraments and Other Rites and Ceremonies of
the Church, according to the Use of the Church of Ireland,
etc. Dublin: APCK, 1878.

_____. The Book of Common Prayer, etc. Dublin: APCK, 1927.

_____. The Book of Common Prayer, etc. Dublin: APCK, 1953.

2. Studies

BOLTON, Frederick R. The Caroline Tradition of the Church of
Ireland, with Particular Reference to Bishop Jeremy Taylor.
London: Published for the Church Historical Society by SPCK,
1958.

E. WALES

1. Texts

CHURCH IN WALES. Additional Collects, Epistles and Gospels for
Use with the Revised Calendar. Penarth, Wales: Church in
Wales Publications, 1965.

_____. An Order for the Celebration of the Holy Eucharist and
the Administration of the Holy Communion with additional Propers. Penarth, Wales: Church in Wales Publications, 1966?

_____. Trefn Gwasanaeth, yr Offeren, a Gweinyddu'r, Cymun
Bendigaid, Gyda'r, Colectau, Llithiau o'r hen Destament, Epis-
tolau, Salmau, ac Efengylau. Awdurdodwyd gan Gorff Llywo-
draethol yr Eglwys yng Nghymru i'w harfer ar brawf, Medi
1966. Penarth, Wales: Gwasg yr Eglwys yng Nghymru, 1971?

2. Studies

CHURCH IN WALES. The Constitution of the Church in Wales.
Revised 1956. Cardiff, Wales: Western Mail & Echo, 1956.

_____. A Guide to the Parish Eucharist. By W. U. Jacob and
others. Penarth, Wales: Church in Wales Publications for the
Standing Liturgical Commission, 1969.

_____. Report of the Liturgical Congress, Carmarthen, 1965.
Cardiff, Wales, 1965.

_____. Worship and Life: A Manual for Communicants of the
Church in Wales. By T. J. Morris. Penarth, Wales: Church
in Wales Publications, 1970?

LEWIS, Ewart. Prayer Book Revision in the Church of Wales.
Penarth, Wales: Church of Wales Provincial Council for Education, 1958.

THOMAS, David Richard. The Life and Work of Bishop Davies and
Williams Salesbury, with an Account of Some Early Translations
into Welsh of the Holy Scriptures and the Prayer Book. Os-
westry, Eng.: Caxton Press, 1902.

F. THE PROTESTANT EPISCOPAL CHURCH IN THE
    UNITED STATES OF AMERICA

1. Texts

a. Book of Common Prayer (arranged chronologically)

McGARVEY, William. Liturgicae Americanae; or the Book of Common
Prayer as Used in the United States of America as Compared
with the Proposed Book of 1786 and with the Prayer Book of
the Church of England, and an Historical Account and Documents. Philadelphia, PA: Church Publishing Co., 1907.

Bishop Seabury's Communion Office, reprinted in Facsimile. With
an historical sketch and notes by Samuel Hart. 2d ed. New
York: Whittaker, 1883.

The Book of Common Prayer ... as Revised and Proposed to the
Use of the Protestant Episcopal Church ... in ... 1785.
Philadelphia, PA: Hall & Sellers, 1786.

PROTESTANT EPISCOPAL CHURCH IN THE U.S.A. The Book of
Common Prayer, and Administration of the Sacraments and
Other Rites and Ceremonies of the Church, according to the
Use of the Protestant Episcopal Church in the United States
of America. Philadelphia, PA: Hall & Sellers, 1790.

_____. The Book of Common Prayer, etc. New York: Eyre &
Spottiswoode; New York: Stanford & Swords; Philadelphia,
PA: Lippincott, 1850.

_____. The Book of Common Prayer ...: The Book Annexed to
the Report of the Joint Committee on the Book of Common Prayer

as modified by the Action of the General Convention of 1883.
New York: E. & J. B. Young, 1884.

_____. The Book of Common Prayer, etc. New ed. Oxford:
Oxford University Press; New York: Thomas Nelson, 1892.

PERRY, William Stevens, ed. The Changes, Additions, and Omis-
sions of the Standard Book of Common Prayer of 1892, as
Compared with the Standard of 1871. Davenport, IA: n.p.,
1893.

PROTESTANT EPISCOPAL CHURCH IN THE U.S.A. Prayer Book
Alterations, finally adopted or ratified by the General Conven-
tion of 1925. Edited by Charles L. Pardee and Carroll M.
Davis. Milwaukee, WI: Morehouse, 1925.

_____. The Book of Common Prayer, etc. [1928 revision.]
New York: Oxford University Press; New York: Thomas
Nelson, 1929.

_____. A Short Book of Common Prayer of the Episcopal Church
in the Common Speech of Today. Provisional ed. New York:
Church Hymnal Corp., 1970.

_____. Services for Trial Use. New York: Church Hymnal
Corp., 1971. [The Greek Book]

_____. Authorized Services--1973. New York: Church Hymnal
Corp., 1973.

_____. The Draft Proposed Book of Common Prayer, etc. New
York: Church Hymnal Corp., 1976.

_____. (Proposed) The Book of Common Prayer, etc. New York:
Church Hymnal Corp., 1977.

_____. The Book of Common Prayer, etc. New York: Church
Hymnal Corp., 1979.

b. Other Liturgical Texts

HOBART, John Henry, ed. The Clergyman's Companion, containing
the Occasional Offices of the Protestant Episcopal Church, with
Prayers Suitable to be Used by the Clergy. New York: P. A.
Mesier, 1806; Revised (4th) ed., New York: Whittaker, 1893.

PROTESTANT EPISCOPAL CHURCH IN THE U.S.A. A Book of Offices: Services for Occasions not provided for in the Book of
Common Prayer. Milwaukee, WI: Young Churchman, 1914.

_____. The Book of Offices: Services for Certain Occasions

not provided for in the Book of Common Prayer. New York:
Church Pension Fund, 1940.

_____. _____. 2d ed. New York: Church Pension Fund,
1949.

_____. The Book of Occasional Services. New York: Church
Hymnal Corp., 1979.

_____. Lesser Feasts and Fasts. Rev. ed. New York: Church
Hymnal Corp., 1973.

CARLOZZI, Carl G., ed. Prayers for Pastor and People. New York:
Church Hymnal Corp., 1984.

Word and Action: New Forms of the Liturgy. With an introduction
by John C. Kirby. New York: Seabury Press, 1969.

2. Historical Studies

ADDISON, Charles Morris, and SUTER, John Wallace. The People's
Book of Worship: A Study of the Book of Common Prayer.
New York: Macmillan, 1919.

CALCOTE, A. Dean. "The Proposed Prayer Book of 1785." Historical Magazine of the Protestant Episcopal Church, 46 (1977):
275-295.

CHORLEY, E. C. Men and Movements in the American Episcopal
Church. New York: Scribner, 1946; reprint ed., Hamden,
CT: Archon Books, 1961.

_____. The New American Prayer Book: Its History and Con-
tents. New York: Macmillan, 1929.

CLARK, Thomas M. Reminiscences. New York: Whittaker, 1895.

DEMILLE, George E. The Catholic Movement in the American Episcopal Church. 2d ed. CHSP, 12. Philadelphia, PA: Church
Historical Society, 1950.

DIX, Morgan. "Revision of the Common Prayer." American Church
Review, No. 136 (January 1882): 41-71.

FRERE, Walter Howard, ed. Russian Observations upon the American Prayer Book. Translated by Wilfrid J. Barnes. ACT, 12.
London: Mowbray; Milwaukee, WI: Young Churchman, 1917.

HATCHETT, Marion J. The Making of the First American Book of
Common Prayer, 1776-1789. New York: Seabury Press, 1982.

_____. "A Sunday Service in 1776 or Thereabouts." Historical
    Magazine of the Protestant Episcopal Church, 45 (1976): 369-
    385.

HUNTINGTON, William R. The Book Annexed: Its Critics and
    Its Prospects. Three Papers reprinted from the Church Re-
    view. New York, 1886.

_____. "The Revision of the American Common Prayer." Ameri-
    can Church Review, 34, 2 (April 1881): 11-58.

_____. A Short History of the Book of Common Prayer together
    with Certain Papers Illustrative of Liturgical Revision 1878-
    1892. New York: Thomas Whittaker, 1893.

LANGSTAFF, John Brett. The American Communion Service: Its
    Order and History. 2d ed. Milwaukee, WI: Morehouse, 1931.

LOVELAND, Clare O. The Critical Years: The Reconstitution of
    Anglican Church in the United States of America, 1780-1789.
    Greenwich, CT: Seabury Press, 1956.

MANROSS, William Wilson. The Episcopal Church in the United
    States 1800-1840: A Study in Church Life. SHEPL, 441.
    New York: Columbia University Press, 1938; reprint ed.,
    New York: AMS Press, 1967.

PARSONS, Edward Lambe, and JONES, Bayard H. The American
    Prayer Book: Its Origins and Principles. New York: Scrib-
    ner, 1937.

STEVENS, C. Ellis, ed. The Genesis of the American Prayer Book:
    A Survey of the Origin and Development of the Liturgy of the
    Church in the United States. New York: Potts, 1893.

SUTER, John Wallace, and CLEAVELAND, George Julius. The
    American Book of Common Prayer: Its Origins and Develop-
    ment. New York: Oxford University Press, 1949.

SYDNOR, William. The Real Prayer Book: 1549 to the Present.
    Wilton, CT: Morehouse-Barlow, 1978.

WHITE, William. Memoirs of the Protestant Episcopal Church. 3d
    ed. Edited by B. F. DeCosta. New York: E. P. Dutton,
    1880.

WOOLVERTON, John. "W. R. Huntington: Liturgical Renewal and
    Church Unity in the 1880's." Anglican Theological Review, 48
    (1966): 175-199.

WRIGHT, John. Early Prayer Books of America: Being a Descriptive

Account of Prayer Books Published in the United States, Mexico and Canada. St. Paul, MN: privately printed, 1896.

3. Recent Liturgical Revision

BABIN, David E. The Celebration of Life: Our Changing Liturgy. New York: Morehouse-Barlow, 1969.

CRAIGHILL, Peyton Gardner. "Liturgy and Piety: A Study of Three Trial Eucharistic Rites in the Episcopal Church." Ph.D. dissertation, Princeton Theological Seminary, 1973.

EVANS, H. Barry, ed. Prayer Book Renewal: Worship and the New Book of Common Prayer. Foreword by Charles M. Guilbert, introduction by William S. Pregnall. New York: Seabury Press, 1978.

HATCHETT, Marion J. "The First American Trial Liturgy." St. Luke's Journal of Theology, 14 (September 1971): 20-29.

MARSHALL, Michael. Renewal in Worship. Revised American ed., Wilton, CT: Morehouse-Barlow, 1985.

PARSONS, Donald J. The Holy Eucharist, Rite Two: A Devotional Commentary. New York: Seabury Press, 1976.

PROTESTANT EPISCOPAL CHURCH IN THE U.S.A. Liturgical Commission. Prayer Book Studies. 29 vols. New York: Church Pension Fund, 1950-1970; New York: Church Hymnal Corp., 1970-1976.
1.   Baptism and Confirmation. 1950.
2.   The Liturgical Lectionary. 1950.
3.   The Order for the Ministration to the Sick. 1951.
4.   The Eucharistic Liturgy. 1953.
5.   The Litany. 1953.
6.   Morning and Evening Prayer. 1957.
7.   The Penitential Office. 1957.
8.   The Ordinal. 1957.
9.   The Calendar. 1957.
10-11. The Solemnization of Matrimony and A Thanksgiving for the Birth of a Child. 1958.
12.   The Propers for the Minor Holy Days. 1958.
13-14. The Order for the Burial of the Dead and An Office of Institution of Rectors into Parishes. 1959.
15.   The Problem and Method of Prayer Book Revision. 1961.
16.   The Calendar and the Collects, Epistles, and Gospels for the Lesser Feasts and Fasts. 1963.
17.   The Liturgy of the Lord's Supper; A Revision of Prayer Book Studies 4. 1966.
18.   On Baptism and Confirmation. 1970.

19. The Church Year. 1970.
20. The Ordination of Bishops, Priests, and Deacons. 1970.
21. The Holy Eucharist. 1970.
22. The Daily Office. 1970.
23. The Psalter, Part I. 1970.
24. Pastoral Offices. 1970.
25. Prayers, Thanksgivings, and Litanies. 1973.
26. Holy Baptism, together with a Form for Confirmation....
     1973.
26, Supplement. Holy Baptism, together with a Form for the
     Affirmation of Baptismal Vows. By Daniel B. Stevick.
     1973.
27. The Daily Office Revised. 1973.
28. Dedication and Consecration of a Church. Celebration of
     a New Ministry. 1973.
29. Introducing the Draft Proposed Book: A Study of the
     Significance of the Draft Proposed Book of Common Prayer
     for the Doctrine, Discipline, and Worship of the Episcopal
     Church. By Charles P. Price. 1976.

SENN, Frank C. "Lutheran and Anglican Liturgies: Reciprocal
     Influences." Anglican Theological Review, 64 (1982): 47-60.

SHANDS, Alfred R., and EVANS, H. Barry. How & Why: An
     Introduction to the Three New Trial Eucharists and the Daily
     Office of the Episcopal Church. New York: Seabury Press,
     1971.

4. Commentaries

BURNETT, Charles P. A. A Ritual and Ceremonial Commentary
     on the Occasional Offices of Holy Baptism, Matrimony, Penance,
     Communion of the Sick, and Extreme Unction. New York:
     Longmans, 1907.

COXE, A. Cleveland. Thoughts on the Services: Designed as an
     Introduction to the Liturgy, and an Aid to its Devout Use.
     Philadelphia, PA: Lippincott, 1860.

_____. _____. Revised and enlarged by Cortlandt Whitehead.
     Philadelphia, PA: Lippincott, 1900.

GUMMEY, Henry Riley, Jr. The Consecration of the Eucharist: A
     Study of the Prayer of Consecration in the Communion Office
     from the Point of View of the Alterations and Amendments
     established therein by the Revisers of 1789. Philadelphia, PA:
     H. F. Anners Press, 1908.

HART, Samuel. The Book of Common Prayer. 2d ed. Sewanee,
     TN: The University Press at the University of the South, 1913.

HATCHETT, Marion J. Commentary on the American Prayer Book. New York: Seabury Press, 1980.

HOBART, John Henry. A Companion for the Altar. New York: P. A. Mesier, 1804.

_____. _____. 24th ed. New York: Swords, 1857.

_____. A Companion for the Book of Common Prayer, containing an Explanation of the Service. 2d ed. New York: n.p., 1805.

_____. _____. 4th ed. New York: Protestant Episcopal Tract Society, printed by T. & J. Swords, 1827.

HUGGETT, Milton, ed. A Concordance to the American Book of Common Prayer. New York: Church Hymnal Corp., 1970.

HUNTER, George W. On the Divine Liturgy in the Book of Common Prayer. Philadelphia, PA: J. McCauley, 1881.

HUNTINGTON, William R. "The Book of Common Prayer." In Christian Worship: Ten Lectures delivered in the Union Theological Seminary, New York, in the Autumn of 1896, pp. 211-245. New York: Scribner, 1897.

JONES, Bayard Hale. Dynamic Redemption: Reflections on the Book of Common Prayer. Greenwich, CT: Seabury Press, 1961.

LADD, W. P. Prayer Book Interleaves: Some Reflections on How the Book of Common Prayer might be made more Influential in our English-speaking World. New York: Oxford University Press, 1942; reprint ed., Greenwich, CT: Seabury Press, 1957.

LOWRIE, Walter. The Lord's Supper and the Liturgy. New York: Longmans, Green, 1943.

MITCHELL, Leonel L. "The Collects of the Proposed Book of Common Prayer." Worship, 52 (1978): 138-145.

_____. Praying Shapes Believing: A Theological Commentary on the Book of Common Prayer. Minneapolis, MN: Winston Press, 1985.

MULLER, James Arthur. Who Wrote the New Prayers in the Prayer Book? Philadelphia, PA: Church Historical Society, 1946.

PRICE, Charles P., and WEIL, Louis. Liturgy for Living. New York: Seabury Press, 1979.

SHEPHERD, Massey H., Jr. The Liturgy and the Christian Faith.
Greenwich, CT: Seabury Press, 1957.

_____. The Living Liturgy. New York: Oxford University
Press, 1946.

_____. The Oxford American Prayer Book Commentary. New
York: Oxford University Press, 1950.

_____. The Worship of the Church. Greenwich, CT: Seabury
Press, 1952.

G. CANADA

1. Texts

CHURCH OF ENGLAND IN CANADA. Book of Common Prayer, etc.
Toronto, Ont.: General Board of Religious Education of the
Church of England in Canada, 1918.

ANGLICAN CHURCH OF CANADA. The Book of Common Prayer,
etc. Toronto, Ont.: Anglican Book Centre, 1959.

_____. The Book of Common Prayer. [1962.] Toronto, Ont.:
Anglican Book Centre, 1962.

2. Studies

ANGLICAN CHURCH OF CANADA. Committee on Public Worship.
Experiment and Liturgy. Toronto: Anglican Church of Canada,
1969.

_____. Doctrine and Worship Committee. The Holy Eucharist.
CALS, 4. Toronto, Ont.: Anglican Book Centre, 1974.

_____. General Synod. Committee on Prayer Book Revision.
A Statement on Prayer Book Revision in Canada. Toronto,
Ont.: n.p., 1957?

ARMITAGE, W. J. The Story of the Canadian Revision of the
Prayer Book. Cambridge: Cambridge University Press; Toronto, Ont.: McClelland & Stewart, 1922.

PALMER, Roland F. His Worthy Praise: On Worship According to
the Book of Common Prayer (Canada, 1959). Toronto, Ont.:
Anglican Church of Canada, 1959.

H. OTHER ANGLICAN CHURCHES

1. Africa

BROWN, L. W. "A Liturgy for Africa." In his Relevant Liturgy, pp. 67-87. New York: Oxford University Press, 1965.

CHURCH OF ENGLAND. A Liturgy for Africa. London: SPCK, 1965, c1964.

2. Australia

CHURCH OF ENGLAND IN AUSTRALIA. A Service of Holy Communion for Australia, 1969. East Malvern, Vic., Aust.: G.B.R.E., 1969.

_____. An Australian Prayer Book 1978: for use together with the Book of Common Prayer, 1662. Sydney, Aust.: Anglican Information Office, 1978.

CHURCH OF ENGLAND IN AUSTRALIA AND TASMANIA. Prayer Book Revision in Australia: Report of a Commission of the General Synod appointed to explore the possibilities of revision of, and addition to, the Book of Common Prayer for the Church of England in Australia, 1966. 2d ed. Sydney, Aust.: Standing Committee of the General Synod, 1966.

3. Ghana

ANGLICAN CHURCH OF GHANA. Book of Common Prayer. Cambridge: Cambridge University Press, 1964?

4. India, Pakistan, Burma and Ceylon

The Eucharist in India: A Plea for a Distinctive Liturgy for the Indian Church. With a suggestion form by J. C. Winslow, J. E. G. Festing, D. R. Athavale, and E. C. Ratcliff. Foreword by the Bishop of Bombay. London: Longmans, Green, 1920.
--commonly called "The Bombay Liturgy"

CHURCH OF INDIA, BURMA AND CEYLON. An Order for the Administration of the Holy Communion, commonly known as the Indian Liturgy. Revised ed. Bombay: Oxford University Press, 1948.

CHURCH OF INDIA, PAKISTAN, BURMA AND CEYLON. A

Proposed Prayer Book containing Forms of Worship, supplementary and alternative to the Book of Common Prayer, authorized by the Episcopal Synod of the Church of India, Pakistan, Burma and Ceylon in 1951. Madras: SPCK, 1952.

_____. Principles of Prayer Book Revision. The Report of a Select Committee of the Church of India, Pakistan, Burma, and Ceylon appointed by the Metropolitan to review the principles of Prayer Book revision in the Anglican Communion. London: SPCK, 1957.

5. Japan

NIHON SEIKOKAI. The Holy Communion as Revised and Authorized for Permissive Use by the General Synod Nippon Sei Ko Kai 1953. Tokyo: Kasai Pub. & Printing Co., 1953.

6. Korea

ANGLICAN CHURCH IN KOREA. The Order for the Celebration of the Holy Eucharist, according to the Use of the Anglican Church in Korea. Original Korean text and authorized English version. Seoul, 1962.

_____. The Korean Liturgy; being an Order for the Celebration of Mass and the Holy Eucharist. Authorized English version. Seoul: Anglican Church in Korea Publication Board, 1966.

7. Melanesia

MELANESIAN BROTHERHOOD [Church of the Province of Melanesia]. Offices and Other Services of the Melanesian Brotherhood. Honiara, Solomon Islands: Church of Melanesia, 1975.

8. South Africa

a. Texts

CHURCH OF THE PROVINCE OF SOUTH AFRICA. An Alternative Form of the Order for the Administration of the Holy Communion. London: SPCK, 1927.

_____. An Alternative Form of the Calendar and Occasional Offices of the Church. London: SPCK, 1930.

_____. A Book of Common Prayer. Set forth by authority for use in the Church of the Province of South Africa. London: Oxford University Press; London, SPCK, 1954.

_____. Worship: A Book of Devotion for the Church in South Africa. London: SPCK, 1959.

b. Studies

HINCHLIFF, Peter. The South African Liturgy: The Story of the Revision of the Rite and its Consecration Prayer. Cape Town: Oxford University Press, 1959.

_____. The South African Rite and the 1928 Prayer Book. ACP, 17. London: Mowbray, 1960.

_____. "The Theory and Practice of Prayer Book Revision in South Africa." Journal of Ecclesiastical History, 11 (1960): 87-97.

9. West Indies

CHURCH IN THE PROVINCE OF THE WEST INDIES. An Order for the Celebration of the Holy Eucharist and the Administration of the Holy Communion. For use in the Diocese of Jamaica. London: SPCK, 1959.

CHURCH OF ENGLAND. Diocese of Nassau and the Bahamas. The People's Order of the Mass and Other Prayers. London: SPCK, 1965.

I. ANGLICAN CEREMONIAL

1. General and English

ATCHLEY, E. G. C. F., BISHOP, E., DEARMER, Percy, and LEGG, J. W. Essays on Ceremonial. LLE, 4. London: De La More Press, 1904.

AUSTERBERRY, David. Celebrating the Liturgy: A Guide for Priest and People. London, Oxford: Mowbray, 1980.

BRADSHAW, Paul F., and JENNINGS, Robert, eds. Episcopal Services. ACM, 2. London: Church Literature Association, Alcuin Club/SPCK, 1980.

[BULSTRODE, Edward Gordon, ed.] Sunday Morning, the New Way: Papers on the Parish Communion. London: SPCK; New York: Macmillan, 1938.

CHURCH OF ENGLAND. Liturgical Commission. The Presentation of the Eucharist. London: SPCK, 1971.

COBB, Cyril S., ed. The Rationale of Ceremonial, 1540-1543.
ACC, 18. London: Longmans, Green, 1910.

DEARMER, Percy. The Parson's Handbook containing Practical Directions both for Parsons and Others as to the Management of
the Parish Church and its Services according to the English
Use, as set forth in the Book of Common Prayer. 1st ed.
London: Grant Richards, 1899.

_____. _____. 4th ed. London: Grant Richards; Milwaukee,
WI: Young Churchman, 1902.

_____. _____. 6th ed. London: Oxford University Press,
1907.

_____. The Parson's Handbook. 8th ed. London: Oxford
University Press, 1913.

_____. _____. 11th ed. London: Oxford University Press,
1928.

_____. _____. 12th ed. London: Oxford University Press,
1931.

_____. The Parson's Handbook: Practical Directions for Parsons
and Others according to the Anglican Use, as set forth in the
Book of Common Prayer on the Basis of the Twelfth Edition by
Percy Dearmer. 13th ed. Revised and Rewritten by Cyril E.
Pocknee. London: Oxford University Press, 1965.

_____. The Server's Handbook: Being a Guide to the Duties of
the Clerk at a Plain Celebration of Holy Communion, at the Administration of Holy Baptism, the Solemnisation of Matrimony,
the Visitation of the Sick, the Churching of Women, and the
Burial of the Dead, with the Text of the Liturgy and Private
Prayers arranged for Use throughout the Anglican Church.
3d ed. London: Oxford University Press, 1950.

_____. A Short Handbook of Public Worship in the Churches of
the Anglican Communion. London: Oxford University Press,
1931.

A Directory of Ceremonial. 2 vols. ACT, 13 & 19. London: Mowbray, 1921-1930.

_____. 2 vols. ACT, 13 & 19. Part 1, 4th ed. London: Mow-
bray, 1947; Part 2, 2d ed. London: Mowbray, 1950.

EELES, F. C. Notes on Episcopal Ornament and Ceremonial. ACT,
25. London: Mowbray, 1948.

_____. Traditional Ceremonial and Customs connected with the Scottish Liturgy. ACC, 17. London: Longmans, Green, 1910.

FEASEY, Henry John. Ancient English Holy Week Ceremonial. London: T. Baker, 1897.

FERGUSON-DAVIE, Patrick. The Bishop in the Church. Published in conjunction with the Church Union. London: SPCK, 1961.

FRERE, Walter Howard. The Principles of Religious Ceremonial. 2d ed. OLPT. London: Mowbray, 1928.

JASPER, R. C. D., ed. Getting the Liturgy Right; Essays by the Joint Liturgical Group on Practical Liturgical Principles for Today. London: SPCK, 1982.

LAMBURN, Edward Cyril Russell. Anglican Services: A Book Concerning Ritual and Ceremony in the Anglican Communion. 2d ed. London: W. Knott, 1963.

_____. Behind Rite and Ceremony: An Historical Survey of their Development in the English Church. London: W. Knott, 1961.

LOWRIE, Walter. Action in the Liturgy: Essential and Unessential. New York: Philosophical Library, 1953.

MICKLETHWAITE, J. T. The Ornaments of the Rubric. ACT, 1. London: Longmans, Green, 1897.

_____. _____. 3d ed., with supplement. London: Longmans, Green, 1901.

MINCHIN, Basil. Outward and Visible. From his Worship in the Body of Christ. London: Darton, Longman & Todd, 1961.

PERHAM, Michael. The Eucharist. ACM, 1. London: SPCK, 1978.

_____. Liturgy Pastoral and Parochial. London: SPCK, 1984.

PURCHAS, John, and LEE, Frederick George, eds. The Directorium Anglicanum: Being a Manual of Directions for the Right Celebration of Holy Communion, for the Saying of Matins and Evensong, and for the Performance of Other Rites and Ceremonies of the Church. 4th ed. London: Hogg, 1879.

Ritual Notes on the Order of Divine Service. By the editors of 'The Order of Divine Service.' Revised and complete ed. Oxford: Mowbray, 1894.

Ritual Notes: A Comprehensive Guide to the Rites and Ceremonies
of the Book of Common Prayer of the English Church interpreted in accordance with the latest revisions of the Western
Use. Compiled by the present editor of 'The Order of Divine
Service' and 'Anglican Services.' 10th ed. London: W. Knott,
1956.

_____. 11th ed. Edited and largely rewritten by E. C. R.
Lamburn. London: W. Knott, 1964.

SPENCE, Horace. The Anglican Use: Five Outlines of Ceremonial,
Alike in Purpose, Different in Treatment for the Service of
Holy Communion as set forth in the Book of Common Prayer.
London: SPCK, 1930.

STALEY, Vernon. The Ceremonial of the English Church. 4th ed.
Oxford: Mowbray, 1927.

_____. The Manual Acts: Prescribed in the Rubrics of the
Prayer of Consecration of the Eucharist, according to the Ang-
lican Rite. ACP, 4. London: Mowbray; Milwaukee, WI:
Young Churchman, 1913.

_____, ed. Hierurgia Anglicana: Documents and Extracts Illus-
trative of the Ceremonial of the Anglican Church after the
Reformation. 3 vols. New ed. LLE, 1, 3 & 5. London:
De La More Press, 1902-1904.

TOMLINSON, J. T. Collected Tracts on Ritual. 2 vols. London:
Church Association, 1877-1907.

WILLIAMS, William Samuel. The Lay Ministry of the Church: The
History of Acolytes and Servers, and of What They have done
for the Church Down the Centuries. Chatham, Eng.: Parrett
& Neves, 1938.

2. American

BURNETT, Charles P. A. "The Ceremonies of High Mass." In
The Ceremonies of the Mass, Pt. 2. By the Clerical Union for
the Maintenance and Defense of Catholic Principles. New York,
1905.

_____. Low Mass Ceremonial: In Accordance with the English
Rite as Set Forth in the Book of Common Prayer. New York:
Green, 1921.

GENT, Barbara, and STURGES, Betty. The Altar Guild Book.
Wilton, CT: Morehouse-Barlow, 1982.

HATCHETT, Marion J. A Manual for Clergy and Church Musicians.
Prepared for the Standing Commission on Church Music. New
York: Church Hymnal Corp., 1980.

_____. "A Manual of Ceremonial." St. Luke's Journal of The-
ology, 17 (March 1974): 19-84; offprint ed., A Manual of
Ceremonial for the New Prayer Book. Sewanee, TN: St.
Luke's Journal of Theology, 1977.

A Manual for Priests of the American Church, Complementary to the
Occasional Offices of the Book of Common Prayer. Edited by
E. H. Maddux. Cambridge, MA: Society of St. John the
Evangelist, 1944.

_____. 5th ed. Cambridge, MA: Society of St. John the
Evangelist, 1970.

MICHNO, Dennis G. A Priest's Handbook: The Ceremonies of the
Church. Wilton, CT: Morehouse-Barlow, 1983.

A Prayer Book Manual. Prepared by the Boston Clergy Group of
the Episcopal Evangelical Fellowship. Louisville, KY: Cloister
Press, 1943.

SHEPHERD, Massey H., Jr., KEENE, John H., PATTERSON, John
O., and BILL, John R., eds. Before the Holy Table: A Guide
to the Celebration of the Holy Eucharist, Facing the People,
according to the Book of Common Prayer. Greenwich, CT:
Seabury Press, 1956.

J. INDEPENDENT CHURCHES RELATED TO OR
    DERIVED FROM THE ANGLICAN CHURCHES

1. African Orthodox Church

AFRICAN ORTHODOX CHURCH. The Divine Liturgy and Other
Rites and Ceremonies of the Church, according to the Use of
the African Orthodox Church, together with Selections from the
Psalter. New York: n.p., 1947.

2. The Countess of Huntingdon's Connexion

The Free Church Prayer Book, being the Public Services of the
Book of Common Prayer of the Established Church of England,
revised and enlarged by James Mountain. London, 1897.

HARDING, Alan. "The Anglican Prayer Book and the Countess of
Huntingdon's Connexion." Transactions of the Congregational
Historical Society, 20 (1970): 364-367.

PEASTON, A. Elliott. "The Countess of Huntingdon's Connexion."
In his The Prayer Book Tradition in the Free Churches, pp.
66-69. London: James Clarke, 1964.

3. Reformed Episcopal Churches

a. The Free Church of England (Reformed Episcopal Church in the United Kingdom of Great Britain and Ireland)

FREE CHURCH OF ENGLAND. The Book of Common Prayer, and
Administration of the Sacraments and Other Rites and Cere-
monies of the Church, according to the Use of the Reformed
Episcopal Church in the United Kingdom of Great Britain and
Ireland. London: J. F. Shaw, 1878.

ELDRIDGE, Philip. The Origin, Orders, Organisation, and Worship
of the Reformed Episcopal Church in the United Kingdom. London: Marlborough, 1899.

PEASTON, A. Elliott. "The Free Church of England." In his
The Prayer Book Tradition in the Free Churches, pp. 70-88.
London: James Clarke, 1964.

b. The Reformed Episcopal Church in the United States of America

REFORMED EPISCOPAL CHURCH IN THE UNITED STATES OF
AMERICA. The Book of Common Prayer according to the use
of the Reformed Episcopal Church in the United States of America. Philadelphia, PA: Reformed Episcopal Publication Society,
1930.

_____. _____. 6th ed. Philadelphia, PA: Reformed Epis-
copal Publication Society, 1963.

4. Philippine Independent Church

IGLESIA FILIPINA INDEPENDIENTE. The Filipino Missal (Book of
Divine Office): The Liturgy for the Holy Mass according to
the Use of the Iglesia Filipina Independiente, including the
Pontifical, Ordinal and Articles of Religion. Manila: Supreme
Council of Bishops, 1961.

_____. The Filipino Ritual: The Administration of the Sacra-
ments and Other Rites and Ceremonies of the Church, according to the Use of the Iglesia Filipina Independiente, together
with the Morning and Evening Prayer and the Psalter. Manila:
Supreme Council of Bishops, 1961.

_____. "The Ordinary of the Mass." Studia Liturgica, 5, 4 (1966): II-b-1-20.

CHANDLEE, H. Ellsworth. "The Liturgy of the Philippine Independent Church." Studia Liturgica, 3 (1964): 88-106.

XVIII. PURITANISM

A. LITURGICAL TEXTS AND DOCUMENTS

(See also HALL [1] and HALL [1 & 3] on page 355.)

BAXTER, Richard. "The Reformation of the Liturgy." In Reliquae Liturgicae: Documents Connected with the Liturgy of the Church of England, vol. 4, pp. 9-33, 55-79. Edited by Peter Hall. Bath: Binns & Goodwin, 1847; "The Reformation of the Liturgy." In Liturgies of the Western Church, pp. 385-405. By Bard Thompson. Cleveland, OH: World, 1961; reprint ed., Philadelphia, PA: Fortress Press, 1981.

A Booke of the Forme of Common Prayers, Administration of the Sacraments, &c. agreable to Gods Worde, and the vse of the Reformed Churches. Middleburg: Richard Schilders, 1586; " A Booke of the Forme of Common Prayers." In Liturgies of the Western Church, pp. 322-341. By Bard Thompson. Cleveland, OH: World, 1961; reprint ed., Philadelphia, PA: Fortress Press, 1981.

"A Directory for the Publique Vvorship of God throughout the Three Kingdoms of England, Scotland, and Ireland." In Liturgies of the Western Church, pp. 354-371. By Bard Thompson. Cleveland, OH: World, 1961; reprint ed., Philadelphia, PA: Fortress Press, 1981.

LEISHMAN, Thomas, ed. The Westminster Directory. London: Blackwood, 1901.

MITCHELL, Alexander F., and STRUTHERS, John, eds. Minutes of the Sessions of the Westminster Assembly of Divines. Edinburgh: W. Blackwood, 1874.

SHIELDS, Charles Woodruff, ed. The Book of Common Prayer and Administration of the Sacraments and Other Rites and Ceremonies of the Church as Amended by the Presbyterian Divines in the Royal Commission of 1661. New York: Scribner, 1897.

B. ENGLAND

1. Historical Sources

BARROW, Henry. Writings, 1587-1590. Edited by Leland H. Carl-
    son. ENT, 3. London: Published for the Sir Halley Stewart
    Trust by Allen & Unwin, 1962.

CARTWRIGHT, Thomas. Cartwrightiana. Edited by Albert Peel
    and Leland H. Carlson. ENT, 1. London: Published for the
    Sir Halley Stewart Trust by Allen & Unwin, 1951.

FRERE, Walter H., and DOUGLAS, Charles E., eds. Puritan Mani-
    festoes. London: SPCK, 1907; reprinted 1954.

GREENWOOD, John. The Writings of John Greenwood, 1587-1590.
    Together with the Joint Writings of Henry Barrow and John
    Greenwood, 1587-1590. Edited by Leland H. Carlson. ENT, 4.
    London: Published for the Sir Halley Stewart Trust by Allen
    & Unwin, 1962.

HARRISON, Robert, and BROWNE, Robert. The Writings of Robert
    Harrison and Robert Browne. Edited by Albert Peel and Leland
    H. Carlson. ENT, 2. London: Published for the Sir Halley
    Stewart Trust by Allen & Unwin, 1953.

OWEN, John. "A Discourse concerning Liturgies, and their Im-
    position." In The Works of John Owen, vol. 15, pp. 3-55.
    Edited by W. H. Goold. London: Johnstone & Hunter, 1851.

PERKINS, William. The Work of William Perkins. CLRC, 3. Apple-
    ford, Eng.: Sutton Courtenay Press, 1970.

TRINTERUD, Leonard J., ed. Elizabethan Puritanism. LPT.
    New York: Oxford University Press, 1971.

2. Studies

BURRAGE, Champlin. The Early English Dissenters in the Light
    of Recent Research (1550-1641). 2 vols. Cambridge: Cam-
    bridge University Press, 1912; reprint ed., New York: Rus-
    sell & Russell, 1967.

CARRUTHERS, Samuel W. The Everyday Work of the Westminster
    Assembly. Philadelphia, PA: Presbyterian Historical Society
    of America and the Presbyterian Historical Society of England,
    1943.

COLLINSON, Patrick. The Elizabethan Puritan Movement. London:

J. Cape; Berkeley, CA: University of California Press, 1967; reprint ed., London: Methuen, 1982.

DAVIES, Horton. The Worship of the English Puritans. Westminster, Eng.: Dacre Press, 1948.

HILL, Christopher, and DELL, Edmund, eds. The Good Old Cause: The English Revolution of 1640-1660, Its Causes, Course, and Consequences: Extracts from Contemporary Sources. 2d ed. London: Cass; New York: Kelley, 1969.

HINSON, E. Glenn. "Reassessing the Puritan Heritage in Worship and Spirituality: A Search for a Method." Worship, 53 (1979): 318-326.

HOLIFIELD, E. Brooks. The Covenant Sealed: The Development of Puritan Sacramental Theology in Old and New England, 1570-1720. New Haven, CT: Yale University Press, 1974.

KNAPPER, Marshall M. Tudor Puritanism. Chicago: University of Chicago Press, 1939.

McGEE, James Sears. The Godly Man in Stuart England: Anglicans, Puritans, and the Two Tables, 1620-1670. YHP, 110. New Haven, CT: Yale University Press, 1976.

McGRATH, Patrick. Papists and Puritans under Elizabeth I. New York: Walker, 1967.

MAYOR, Stephen. The Lord's Supper in Early English Dissent. London: Epworth Press, 1972.

MORGAN, Irvonwy. The Nonconformity of Richard Baxter. London: Epworth Press, 1946.

NEW, John F. H. Anglican and Puritan: The Basis of the Opposition, 1558-1640. Stanford: Stanford University Press, 1964.

NUTTALL, Geoffrey F. Richard Baxter. London: Nelson, 1965.

PAUL, Robert S. The Lord's Assembly. Edinburgh: T. & T. Clark, 1985. [Westminster Assembly]

PEASTON, A. Elliott. "The Puritans." In his The Prayer Book Tradition in the Free Churches, pp. 16-34. London: James Clarke, 1964.

PEEL, Albert, ed. Essays Congregational and Catholic. London: Congregational Union of England and Wales, 1931.

PORTER, Harry C. Reformation and Reaction in Tudor Cambridge. Cambridge: Cambridge University Press, 1958.

POWICKE, Frederick J. A Life of the Reverend Richard Baxter.
London: J. Cape, 1924.

RATCLIFF, E. C. "Puritan Alternatives to the Prayer Book. The
'Directory' and Richard Baxter's 'Reformed Liturgy.' In The
English Prayer Book, 1549-1662. By the Archbishop of Canter-
bury and others. London: SPCK, 1963; reprinted in his Lit-
urgical Studies of E. C. Ratcliff, pp. 222-243. Edited by
A. H. Couratin and D. J. Tripp. London: SPCK, 1976.

SPINKS, Bryan D. From the Lord and "The Best Reformed
Churches": A Study of the Eucharistic Liturgy in the English
Puritan and Separatist Traditions. Vol. 1. BEL, 33. Rome:
Edizione Liturgiche, 1984.

_____. "The Supply of Prayer for Ships: A Forgotten Puritan
Liturgy." Journal of the United Reformed Church Historical
Society, 1, 5 (1975): 139-148.

WHITE, B. R. The English Separatist Tradition: From the Marian
Martyrs to the Pilgrim Fathers. London: Oxford University
Press, 1971.

C. NEW ENGLAND

1. Historical Sources

CHAUNCY, Charles. Breaking of Bread in Remembrance of the
Dying Love of Christ, a Gospel Institution: Five Sermons on
the Lord's Supper. Boston, MA: Printed by D. Kneeland for
T. Leverett, 1772.

COTTON, John. A Modest and Cleare Answer to Mr. Ball's Discourse of Set Formes of Prayer. London: Printed for H.
Overton, 1642.

_____. The True Constitution of a Particular Visible Church,
Proved by Scripture. London: Printed for S. Satterthwaite,
1642.

_____. The Way of the Churches of Christ in New England.
London: Printed by M. Simmons, 1645.

MATHER, Increase. The Order of the Gospel, Professed and
Practiced by the Churches of Christ in New England, Justified.
Boston, MA: B. Green & J. Allen for Benjamin Eliot, 1700.

STODDARD, Solomon. The Inexcusableness of Neglecting the Worship of God. Boston, MA: B. Glen, 1708.

TAYLOR, Edward. Edward Taylor vs. Solomon Stoddard: The
    Nature of the Lord's Supper. Unpublished Writings of Edward
    Taylor, vol. 2. Edited by Thomas M. and Virginia L. Davis.
    Boston, MA: Twayne, 1981.

_____. Treatise Concerning the Lord's Supper. Edited by Nor-
    man S. Grabo. East Lansing, MI: Michigan State University
    Press, 1966.

2. Studies

BEEBE, David Lewis. "The Seals of the Covenant: The Doctrine
    and Place of the Sacraments and Censures in the New England
    Puritan Theology Underlying the Cambridge Platform of 1648."
    Th.D. dissertation, Pacific School of Religion, 1966.

SOLBERG, Winton U. Redeem the Time: The Puritan Sabbath in
    Early America. Cambridge, MA: Harvard University Press,
    1977.

XIX. THE CONGREGATIONAL CHURCHES

(See also XVIII. Puritanism, p. 403; XXV. E. United Church of
Christ, p. 451.)

A. TEXTS

1. United Kingdom

CONGREGATIONAL CHURCH IN ENGLAND AND WALES. An Order
    of Public Worship. London: Oxford University Press, 1970.

CONGREGATIONAL UNION OF ENGLAND AND WALES. Book of
    Congregational Worship. London: Congregational Union of
    England and Wales, 1920.

_____. A Book of Services and Prayers. London: Independent
    Press, 1959.

The Congregational Service Book: A Form of Public Worship de-
    signed for the Use of Independent and Other Nonconformist
    Bodies in Great Britain. London: Ward, 1847.

A Free Church Book of Common Prayer, and of the Administration
    of the Sacraments and Other Rites, Ceremonies and Services of
    the Christian Church. London: Dent; New York: Dutton,
    1929.

HORNE, C. S., and DARLOW, T. H. Let Us Pray. 2d ed. London: J. Clarke, 1897.

HUNTER, John. Devotional Services for Public Worship. 8th rev. ed. London: Dent, 1901; many reprints to 1943.

HUXTABLE, William John, MARSH, John, MICKLEM, Romilly, and TODD, James, eds. A Book of Public Worship Compiled for the Use of Congregationalists. London: Oxford University Press, 1948; 2d ed., 1949.

A Manual for Ministers. London: Independent Press, 1936.

MICKLEM, Caryl, et al. Contemporary Prayers for Public Worship. London: SCM Press, 1967.

MICKLEM, E. R., and COOPER, I. M. S., eds. Responsals: Acts of Prayer and Worship for Congregational Use. London: J. Clarke, 1947.

MICKLEM, Nathaniel, ed. Prayers and Praises. 2d rev. ed. London: Independent Press, 1954; reprint ed., Edinburgh: St. Andrews Press, 1977.

ORCHARD, William Edwin, ed. The Order of Divine Service for Public Worship, the Administration of the Sacraments and Other Rites and Ceremonies and a Selection from the Daily Offices compiled from Ancient and Modern Devotions together with an abridged and revised Psalter and Canticles pointed for Chanting. 2d ed. London: Oxford University Press, 1926.

THOMAS, David, ed. Biblical Liturgy for the Use of Evangelical Churches and Homes. 5th ed. London: Ward, 1855.

TODD, James Moody. Prayers and Services for Christian Festivals. London: Oxford University Press, 1951.

WATSON, C. E., ed. The Rodborough Bede Book: Offices for Free Churches. London: Independent Press, 1943.

2. United States

GENERAL COUNCIL OF THE CONGREGATIONAL AND CHRISTIAN CHURCHES OF THE UNITED STATES. A Book of Worship for Free Churches. New York: Oxford University Press, 1948.

_____. Manual of the Congregational Christian Churches: A Compendium of Information, Forms and Services. Edited by Oscar E. Maurer. Boston, MA: Pilgrim Press, 1947.

NATIONAL COUNCIL OF THE CONGREGATIONAL CHURCHES OF
THE UNITED STATES. Book of Church Services with Orders
of Worship, Prayers and Other Aids of Devotion. Boston, MA:
Pilgrim Press, 1922.

RICHARDS, Charles Herbert, ed. Christian Praise: A Manual of
Worship for Public, Social and Private Devotion. New York:
Taintor Bros., Merrill & Co., 1880.

B. STUDIES

CONGREGATIONAL UNION OF ENGLAND AND WALES. The Meaning of the Communion Service. A Church and Kingdom Pamphlet. London: Independent Press, 1952.

_____. Our Heritage of Free Prayer. A Church and Kingdom
Pamphlet. London: Independent Press, 1952?

_____. Worship. A Church and Kingdom Pamphlet. London:
Independent Press, 1952.

DAVIES, Horton M. "Books, Liturgical, Congregational." Dictionary of Liturgy and Worship, pp. 85-86.

_____. "Congregational Worship." Dictionary of Liturgy and
Worship, pp. 149-150.

_____. "Liturgical Reform in Nineteenth Century Congregational-
ism." Transactions of the Congregational Historical Society, 17,
3 (1954): 73-82.

_____. "Liturgies. Congregational." Dictionary of Liturgy and
Worship, pp. 234-235.

FORSYTH, P. T. The Church and the Sacraments. London:
Longmans, 1917.

GREGORY, J. K. "The Understanding of the Lord's Supper among
English Congregationalists, 1850-1950." D.Phil. thesis, University of Oxford, 1956.

HAMILTON, Herbert Alfred. The Family Church, in Principle and
Practice. 3d ed. Wallington, Eng.: Religious Education Press,
1960.

HANBURY, Benjamin. Historical Memorials Relating to the Indepen-
dents, or Congregationalists. 3 vols. London: Congregational
Union of England and Wales, 1839-1844.

HUNTER, Leslie S. John Hunter, D.D.: A Life. London: Hodder & Stoughton, 1921.

LORD, F. Townley. "The Holy Communion in Congregational and Baptist Churches." In The Holy Communion: A Symposium, pp. 85-98. Edited by Hugh Martin. London: SCM Press, 1947.

MANNING, B. L. Essays in Orthodox Dissent. London: Independent Press, 1939.

MAYOR, Stephen. The Lord's Supper in Early English Dissent. London: Epworth Press, 1972.

MICKLEM, Edward Romilly. Our Approach to God: A Study in Public Worship. London: Hodder & Stoughton, 1934.

PEASTON, A. Elliott. "The Congregationalists." In his The Prayer Book Tradition in the Free Churches, pp. 107-121. London: James Clarke, 1964.

SPINKS, Bryan D. Freedom or Order?: The Eucharistic Liturgy in English Congregationalism, 1645-1980. Allison Park, PA: Pickwick Publications, 1984.

_____. From the Lord and "The Best Reformed Churches": A Study of the Eucharistic Liturgy in the English Puritan and Separatist Traditions 1550-1633. Vol. 1. BEL, 33. Rome: Edizioni Liturgiche, 1984.

WALKER, Williston. The Creeds and Platforms of Congregationalism. New York: Scribner, 1893; reprint ed., Philadelphia, PA: Pilgrim Press, 1969.

XX. THE SOCIETY OF FRIENDS (QUAKERS)

A. EARLY WRITERS

BARCLAY, Robert. Theologiae Verè Christianae apologia. London, 1676; An Apology for the True Christian Divinity, as the Same is Held Forth, and Preached, by the People, called in scorn, Quakers. London, 1678; dozens of reprints up to 1908.

_____. Barclay in Brief: A Condensation of Robert Barclay's Apology for the True Christian Divinity, being an Explanation of the Principles and Doctrines of the People called Quakers, first published in 1676. By Eleanore Price Mather. With a

Preface by Howard H. Brinton. Pendle Hill Historical Studies,
3. Wallingford, PA: Pendle Hill Press, 1942.

FOX, George. Gospel Truth Demonstrated, in a Collection of Doc-
trinal Books. London: T. Sowle, 1706; republished as The
Works of George Fox, vols. 4-6. Philadelphia, PA: Marcus
T. C. Gould, 1831.

GURNEY, Joseph John. Brief Remarks on the History, Authority,
and Use, of the Sabbath. 3d ed. London: J. & A. Arch,
1832.

_____. Observations on the Religious Peculiarities of the Society
of Friends. 4th ed. London: Arch, 1824; 1st American from
the 4th London ed., Philadelphia, PA: Potter, 1825.

_____. Observations on the Distinguishing Views and Practices
of the Society of Friends. 7th ed. London: Arch, 1834; 2d
American from the 7th London ed., New York: Wood, 1854.

_____. On Silent Worship. Ipswich Series of Friends' Tracts,
4. Ipswich, Eng.: Burton, n.d.

KEITH, George. The Benefit, Advantage, and Glory of Silent Meetings. London, 1670.

PENINGTON, Isaac. The Works of the Long-Mournful and Sorely-
Distressed Isaac Penington. 2 vols. London: Clark, 1681.

PENN, William. A Collection of the Works of William Penn. 2 vols.
London: J. Sowle, 1726.

WOOLMAN, John. "On Silent Worship." In The Journal and Essays
of John Woolman, pp. 508-510. Edited by Amelia Mott Gunmere.
New York: Macmillan, 1922.

B. OFFICIAL DOCUMENTS

SOCIETY OF FRIENDS. Faith and Practice: Unofficial Statement
and Official Provisions for Organization and Procedures of the
Friends United Meeting. Richmond, IN: Friend Book & Supply
House, 1966.

_____. London Yearly Meeting. Christian Practice: Being the
Second Part of Christian Discipline of the Religious Society of
Friends in Great Britain. London: Friends Book Centre,
1925.

_____. Christian Faith and Practice in the Experience of the

Society of Friends. [Part of the Book of Christian Discipline
of the London Yearly Meeting of the Society of Friends.]
London: Headley Bros., 1960.

_____. Worship and Ministry: A Letter from London Yearly
Meeting on Ministry and Oversight, 1899. London: Newman,
1899?

_____. Committee on Ministry. Ministry and Our Meetings for
Worship. London: Headley Bros., 1911.

_____. Philadelphia Yearly Meeting. Faith and Practice of the
Philadelphia Yearly Meeting of the Religious Society of Friends:
A Book of Christian Discipline. Revised ed. Philadelphia, PA:
Philadelphia Yearly Meeting of the Religious Society of Friends,
1965.

C. STUDIES

BRAITHWAITE, William C. The Beginnings of Quakerism. Introduction by Rufus M. Jones. London: Macmillan, 1912.

_____. _____. 2d ed., revised by Henry J. Cadbury. Cam-
bridge: Cambridge University Press, 1961.

_____. The Second Period of Quakerism. 2d ed. prepared by
Henry J. Cadbury. Cambridge: Cambridge University Press,
1961.

BRINTON, Howard H. Creative Worship and Other Essays. London: Allen & Unwin, 1931; reprint ed., Wallingford, PA:
Pendle Hill, 1957.

COLLIER, Howard. The Quaker Meeting. London: Friends Home
Service Committee, 1949.

CREASEY, M. A. "Quaker Worship." A Dictionary of Liturgy and
Worship, pp. 328-330.

GORMAN, George H. The Amazing Fact of Quaker Worship. London: Friends' Home Service Committee, 1973.

GRAHAM, William John. The Lord's Supper: A Historical Study
from the Standpoint of the Society of Friends. London: Clarke,
1900.

GREEN, Thomas F. Preparation for Worship. London: Allen &
Unwin, 1952.

HARVEY, T. Edmund. Silence and Worship: A Study in Quaker Experience. New York: Doran, 1924.

HAYMAN, Eric. Worship and the Common Life. Cambridge: Cambridge University Press, 1944.

HEPHER, Cyril, ed. The Fellowship of Silence: Being Experiences in the Common Use of Prayer without Words. Narrated and interpreted by Thomas Hodgkin, Percy Dearmer, L. V. Hodgkin, J. C. Fitzgerald. London: Macmillan, 1915.

HIBBERT, Gerald K. Friends and the Sacraments. London: Friends Home Service Committee, 1944.

HODGKIN, L. Violet. Silent Worship: The Way of Wonder. 2d ed. London: Swarthmore Press, 1919.

HOWE, Ronald. "The Holy Communion and the Society of Friends." In The Holy Communion: A Symposium, pp. 99-112. Edited by Hugh Martin. London: SCM Press, 1947.

JANNEY, Samuel M. Extracts from a Dissertation on the Views of George Fox Concerning Christian Ministry and Divine Worship. Philadelphia, PA: Friends' Book Assoc., 1884.

JONES, Rufus M. The Faith and Practice of the Quakers. 2d ed. London: Methuen, 1927; reprint ed., Richmond, IN: Friends United Press, 1980.

_____. The Later Periods of Quakerism. 2 vols. London: Macmillan, 1921; reprint ed., Westport, CT: Greenwood Press, 1970.

[KIMBER, Thomas]. The Baptism and the Supper of Our Lord. New York: Friend's Book and Tract Committee, 1885.

RHOADS, James E. "Christian Worship and Ministry." In Four Lectures on Some of the Distinguishing Views of Friends, pp. 75-100. Philadelphia, PA: [Friends' Institute], 1890.

ROWNTREE, John Stephenson. The Society of Friends: Its Faith and Practice. 6th ed. London: Friends' Book Centre, 1935.

ROWNTREE, John Wilhelm. Essays and Addresses. 2d ed. Edited by Joshua Rowntree. London: Headley Bros., 1906.

SCULL, David. "The Ordinances." In Four Lectures on Some of the Distinguishing Views of Friends, pp. 33-74. Philadelphia, PA: [Friends' Institute], 1890.

STEERE, Douglas V. Where Words Come From: An Interpretation

of the Ground and Practice of Quaker Worship and Ministry.
London: Allen & Unwin, 1955.

WILSON, Gladys. Quaker Worship: An Introductory Historical
Study of the English Friends' Meeting. London: Bannisdale
Press, 1952.

"Worship and Ministry." In Principles of Quakerism: A Collection
of Essays, pp. 103-124. By representatives of the Religious
Society of Friends for Pennsylvania, New Jersey and Delaware.
Philadelphia, PA: Friends' Book Store, 1908.

"Your Local Meeting." Friends' Quarterly, 22 (July 1980).

XXI. THE METHODIST CHURCHES

A. GENERAL STUDIES

BISHOP, John. Methodist Worship in Relation to Free Church Worship. London: Epworth Press, 1950.

_____. _____. Revised ed. New York: Scholars Studies
Press, 1975.

BOWMER, John C. "Communion Tokens." Encyclopedia of World
Methodism, 1:557.

_____. "The History of Holy Communion in Methodism." London
Quarterly and Holborn Review, 184 (1959): 97-102.

_____. The Lord's Supper in Methodism, 1791-1960. London:
Epworth Press, 1961.

_____. "Methodist Liturgies." Methodist Magazine, (December
1964): 457-463.

CUSHMAN, Robert E. "Worship as Acknowledgment." In Worship
in Scripture and Tradition, pp. 9-43. Edited by Massey H.
Shepherd. New York: Oxford University Press, 1963.

FLEW, R. N. "The View of the Methodists." In The Ministry and
the Sacraments, pp. 230-243. Edited by Roderic Dunkerley.
London: SCM Press, 1937.

GEORGE, A. Raymond. "The Eucharist in Relation to the Total
Worship of the Church." London Quarterly and Holborn Review,
189 (1964): 217-223.

_____. "The Lord's Supper." In The Doctrine of the Church, pp. 150-160. Edited by Dow Kirkpatrick. New York: Abingdon Press, 1964.

_____. "Private Devotion in the Methodist Tradition." Studia Liturgica, 2 (1963): 223-236.

_____. "The Real Presence and the Lord's Supper." Proceedings of the Wesley Historical Society, 34, 8 (December 1964): 181-187.

GOODLOE, Robert W. The Sacraments in Methodism. Nashville, TN: Methodist Publishing House, 1953.

HARMON, Nolan B. "Methodist Worship: Practice and Ideals." In Methodism, pp. 229-239. Edited by William K. Anderson. Nashville, TN: Methodist Publishing House, 1947.

LAWSON, John. "Eucharistic Doctrine and Devotion." Encyclopedia of World Methodism, 1:797-801.

"Lord's Supper." McClintock and Strong, Cyclopedia, 5:509-515.

MASER, Frederick E. "Communion Tickets." Encyclopedia of World Methodism, 1:557.

NELSON, Robert. "Pulpit and Table in Methodism." In Church and Eucharist, pp. 98-114. Edited by Michael Hurley. Dublin: Gill, 1966.

PEASTON, A. Elliott. "The Methodists." In his The Prayer Book Tradition in the Free Churches, pp. 35-65. London: James Clarke, 1964.

PLUNKETT, Hedley W. "Doctrine and Practice of the Lord's Supper in Methodism." In Church and Eucharist, pp. 115-147. Edited by Michael Hurley. Dublin: Gill, 1966.

QUILLIAN, Joseph D. "Methodist Worship in the Light of Article XIII." Perkins School of Theology Journal, 13, 2 (Winter 1960): 15-20.

_____, and HARMON, Nolan B. "Communion, The Holy." Encyclopedia of World Methodism, 1:555-557.

QUEEN, Vergil E. "Methodism and the Holy Communion." Versicle, 13, 3 (July-September 1963): 5-12.

"Report and Recommendations of the First World Methodist Consultation on Worship, Denver, Colorado, USA, August 26-29, 1971." Studia Liturgica, 8 (1971-1972): 119-123.

RUPP, E. Gordon. "The Finished Work of Christ in Word and
    Sacrament." In The Finality of Christ, pp. 175-192. Edited
    by Dow Kirkpatrick. Nashville, TN: Abingdon Press, 1966.

_____. "Holy Communion in the Methodist Church." In The
    Holy Communion: A Symposium, pp. 113-126. Edited by Hugh
    Martin. London: SCM Press, 1947.

SHIPLEY, David C. "The Holy Communion and the Wesleyan Heri-
    tage." Perkins School of Theology Journal, 11, 1 (Fall 1957):
    4-7.

VOIGHT, Edwin. Methodist Worship in the Church Universal.
    Nashville, TN: Graded Press, 1965.

WAINWRIGHT, Geoffrey. "In Praise of God." Worship, 53 (1979):
    496-511.

WHITE, James F. "Traditions of Protestant Worship." Worship, 49
    (1975): 272-282.

B. THE WESLEYS AND EARLY METHODISM

1. Texts

    Note: Abbreviated entries have been adopted from the
    following source:

    Works--The Works of the Rev. John Wesley. 14 vols.
    London: Wesleyan-Methodist Book Room, 1872; reprint
    ed., Grand Rapids, MI: Zondervan, 1958; reprinted
    as Wesley's Works. Grand Rapids, MI: Baker, 1979.

HOBBS, Edward C., ed. The Wesley Orders of Common Prayer.
    Nashville, TN: National Methodist Student Movement, 1957.

HODGES, H. A., and ALCHIN, A. M., eds. A Rapture of Praise:
    Hymns of John and Charles Wesley. London: Hodder &
    Stoughton, 1966.

KAY, J. Alan, ed. Wesley's Prayers and Praises. London: Ep-
    worth Press, 1958.

WESLEY, Charles. Representative Verse. Edited by Frank Baker.
    London: Epworth Press, 1962.

WESLEY, John. "A Collection of Forms of Prayer, for Every Day
    in the Week." In his Works, vol. 11, pp. 203-237.

_____. "A Collection of Prayers for Families." In his Works,
vol. 11, pp. 237-259.

_____. "The Duty of Constant Communion" [Sermons, Second
Series, 101]. In his Works, vol. 7, pp. 147-157.

_____. [Journal, Nov. 1, 1739-Sept. 31, 1741.] In The Journal
of the Rev. John Wesley, vol. 2, pp. 309-500. Edited by
Nehemiah Curnock. London: Epworth Press, 1911; also in
his Works, vol. 1, pp. 241-335.

_____. "On Attending the Church Service" [Sermons, Second
Series, 104]. In his Works, vol. 7, pp. 174-185.

_____. "A Roman Catechism, faithfully drawn out of the allowed
writings of the Church of Rome: with a Reply thereto." In
his Works, vol. 10, pp. 86-128.

_____. The Sunday Service of the Methodists in North America.
London: Strahan, 1784.

_____. "The Sunday Service of the Methodists in North Amer-
ica." In Liturgies of the Western Church, pp. 415-433. By
Bard Thompson. Cleveland, OH: World, 1961; reprint ed.,
Philadelphia, PA: Fortress Press, 1981.

_____. The Sunday Service of the Methodists in North America.
Introduction by James F. White. Nashville, TN: United
Methodist Publishing House, 1984.

_____. "To Thomas Church." In his The Letters of the Rev.
John Wesley, vol. 2, pp. 175-211. Edited by John Telford.
London: Epworth Press, 1931.

_____. "Upon Our Lord's Sermon on the Mount. Discourse VI."
In his Works, vol. 5, pp. 327-342.

2. Studies

BAKER, Frank. "The Beginnings of the Methodist Covenant Service." London Quarterly and Holborn Review, 180, 3 (July
1955): 215-220.

_____. Charles Wesley's Verse. London: Epworth Press, 1964.

_____. Methodism and the Love Feast. London: Epworth Press;
New York: Macmillan, 1957.

_____. "The Prayer Book Revised." In John Wesley and the
Church of England, pp. 234-255. Nashville, TN: Abingdon
Press, 1970.

BARRATT, Thomas H. "The Place of the Lord's Supper in Early
Methodism." The London Quarterly Review, 139 (July 1923):
56-73.

BARTON, J. Hamby. "The Sunday Service of the Methodists."
Proceedings of the Wesley Historical Society, 32, 1 (March
1960): 97-101.

BORGEN, Ole E. John Wesley on the Sacraments. Nashville, TN:
Abingdon Press, 1973.

BOWMER, John C. "A Converting Ordinance and the Open Table."
Proceedings of the Wesley Historical Society, 34, 5 (March
1964): 109-113.

_____. The Sacrament of the Lord's Supper in Early Methodism.
Westminster, Eng.: Dacre Press, 1951.

_____. "Some Non-Wesleyan Service Books." Proceedings of the
Wesley Historical Society, 32, 5 (September 1960): 145-152.

_____. "Wesley's Revision of the Communion Service." London
Quarterly and Holborn Review, 176, 3 (July 1951): 230-237.

CHURCH, Leslie F. "Worship--Public and Private." In More About
the Early Methodist People, pp. 210-288. London: Epworth
Press, 1949.

COLE, Richard L. Love-Feasts: A History of the Christian Agape.
London: C. H. Kelly, 1916.

GEORGE, A. Raymond. "The Sunday Service." Proceedings of the
Wesley Historical Society, 40, 4 (February 1976): 102-105.

GRISLIS, Egil. "The Wesleyan Doctrine of the Lord's Supper."
Duke Divinity School Review, 28, 2 (May 1963): 99-110.

HARMON, Nolan B. "John Wesley's Sunday Service and Its American Revision." Proceedings of the Wesley Historical Society,
39, 5 (June 1974): 137-144.

HUNTER, Frederick. "Sources of Wesley's Revision of the Prayer
Book in 1784-8." Proceedings of the Wesley Historical Society,
23, 6 (June 1942): 123-133; and "Note on Article on 'Sources
of Wesley's Revision of the Prayer Book in 1784-8.'", 23, 8
(December 1942): 173-175.

MAYOR, Stephen. The Lord's Supper in Early English Dissent.
London: Epworth Press, 1972.

MUMFORD, Norman W. "The Administration of the Sacrament of the

Lord's Supper in the Methodist Church after the Death of John
Wesley." London Quarterly and Holborn Review, 176, 1
(January 1951): 61-70.

PARRIS, John R. John Wesley's Doctrine of the Sacraments. London: Epworth Press, 1963.

RATTENBURY, John E. The Eucharistic Hymns of John and
Charles Wesley. London: Epworth Press, 1948.

ROTH, Herbert John. "A Literary Study of the Calvinistic and
Deistic Implications in the Hymns of Isaac Watts, Charles Wes-
ley, and William Cowper." Ph.D. dissertation, Texas Christian
University, 1978.

ROUTLEY, Erik. The Musical Wesleys. New York: Oxford University Press, 1968; reprint ed., Westport, CT: Greenwood
Press, 1976.

SANDERS, Paul S. "An Appraisal of John Wesley's Sacramentalism
in the Evolution of American Methodism." Th.D. dissertation,
Union Theological Seminary in the City of New York, 1954.

_____. "Wesley's Eucharistic Faith and Practice." Anglican
Theological Review, 48 (1966): 157-174.

SELLECK, Jerald Brian. "The Book of Common Prayer in the Theology of John Wesley." Ph.D. dissertation, Drew University,
1983.

STOCKTON, C. R. "The Origin and Development of Extra-
Liturgical Worship in 18th Century Methodism." D. Phil. dissertation, Oxford University, 1970.

SWIFT, Wesley F. "Methodism and the Book of Common Prayer."
Proceedings of the Wesley Historical Society, 27, 2 (June 1949):
33-41.

_____. "The Sunday Service of the Methodists." Proceedings of
the Wesley Historical Society, 29, 1 (March 1953): 12-20.

TRIPP, David. The Renewal of the Covenant in the Methodist
Tradition. London: Epworth Press, 1969.

C. LATER ENGLISH METHODISM

1. Texts (arranged chronologically)

WESLEYAN METHODIST CHURCH (ENGLAND). The Book of Public
Prayer and Services for the Use of the People called Methodists.

London: Methodist Publishing House, 1846; new eds., 1864, 1882.

METHODIST CHURCH (ENGLAND). Divine Worship, Approved by the Conference for Optional Use in Methodist Churches. London: Methodist Publishing House, 1935.

_____. The Book of Offices; being the Orders of Service Authorized for Use in the Methodist Church, together with the Order of Morning Prayer. London: Methodist Publishing House, 1936.

_____. The Sunday Service. London: Methodist Publishing House, 1968.

_____. The Covenant Service. London: Methodist Publishing House, 1969.

_____. The Methodist Service Book. London: Methodist Publishing House, 1975.

2. Studies

BILLINGTON, Raymond J. The Liturgical Movement and Methodism. London: Epworth Press, 1969.

BISHOP, John. Methodist Worship in Relation to free Church Worship. London: Epworth Press, 1950.

_____. _____. Rev. ed. New York: Scholar's Studies Press, 1975.

BOWMER, John C. "The Manual Acts in the Communion Office." London Quarterly and Holborn Review, 170, 4 (October 1945): 392-398.

CLARKE, Adam. A Discourse on the Nature, Design, and Institution of the Holy Eucharist, commonly called the Sacrament of the Lord's Supper. London: J. Butterworth, 1808; reprint ed., New York: Published by G. Lane and P. P. Sandford for the Methodist Episcopal Church, 1842.

CLAY, Arnold. What is the Lord's Supper? London: Epworth Press, 1979.

COURATIN, Arthur H. "The Methodist Sunday Service" [1968]. Church Quarterly, 2, 1 (July 1969): 31-38.

DAVIES, Rupert E. "The History and Theology of the Methodist Covenant Service." Theology, 64 (February 1961): 62-68.

_____. "The History of Holy Communion." London Quarterly and Holborn Review, 184 (1959): 91-96.

DEARING, Trevor. Wesleyan and Tractarian Worship. London: Epworth Press, 1966.

DIXON, Neil. At Your Service: A Commentary on the Methodist Service Book (1975). London: Epworth Press, 1976.

GEORGE, A. Raymond. "The Changing Face of Methodism: I. The Methodist Service Book." Proceedings of the Wesley Historical Society, 41 (1977-1978): 65-72.

_____. "The Means of Grace." In A History of the Methodist Church in Great Britain, vol. 1, pp. 257-273. Edited by Rupert Davies and E. Gordon Rupp. London: Epworth Press, 1965.

GRAYSTON, Kenneth. "The Function of the Book of Offices." London Quarterly and Holborn Review, 189, 3 (July 1964): 212-216.

JONES, Clifford. A Companion to the Sunday service (1975). London: Methodist Publishing House, 1976.

RATTENBURY, John E. Thoughts on Holy Communion. London: Epworth Press, 1958.

_____. Vital Elements of Public Worship. 3d ed. London: Epworth Press, 1954.

STACEY, John. In Church: An Introduction to Worship and Preaching. London: Local Preachers' Department of the Methodist Church, 1971.

SWIFT, Wesley F. "The Sunday Service of the Methodists: A Study of 19th Century Liturgy." Proceedings of the Wesley Historical Society, 31, 1 (March 1958): 112-118; 31, 2 (June 1958): 133-143.

TIBBETTS, Kenneth. "The Revision of the Methodist Book of Offices." London Quarterly and Holborn Review, 187 (October 1962): 270-276.

WAINWRIGHT, Geoffrey. "The Methodist Service Book, 1975." Epworth Review, 3, 1 (January 1976): 110-118.

WAKEFIELD, Gordon S. "The Methodist Service Book, 1975." Epworth Review, 2, 3 (September 1975): 19-28.

_____. On the Edge of Mystery. London: Epworth Press, 1971.

_____. Our Different Ways of Worship. London: Epworth
Press, 1968.

_____. "Worship, British Methodist." Encyclopedia of World
Methodism.

WESTBROOK, Francis B. The Holy Communion Service: Explanatory Notes. London: Epworth Press, 1959.

D. LATER AMERICAN METHODISM

1. Texts (arranged chronologically
within each subgroup)

a. Methodist Churches

METHODIST EPISCOPAL CHURCH. The Ritual of the Methodist
Episcopal Church. New York: Carlton & Porter, 1864, 1865.

_____. _____. New York: Nelson & Phillips, 1872.

_____. _____. New York: Eaton & Mains; Cincinnati, OH:
Jennings & Graham, 1908.

_____. _____. New York: Methodist Book Concern, 1916,
1924, 1928, 1932.

_____. Book of Service: Orders of Worship, the Ritual and
Responsive Readings. New York: Methodist Book Concern,
1932.

_____. Commission on Worship and Music. Choral Responses,
including Opening Sentences, Prayer Responses, Offertory and
Closing Sentences. New York: J. Fischer, 1932.

METHODIST EPISCOPAL CHURCH, SOUTH. Ritual of the Methodist
Episcopal Church, South. Published by J. Early for the
Methodist Episcopal Church South, 1851.

_____. _____. Rev. ed. Nashville, TN: Publishing House
of the Methodist Episcopal Church, South, 1910.

METHODIST CHURCH (U.S.). General Conference. Commission on
Worship. The Book of Worship for Church and Home. Nashville, TN: Methodist Publishing House, 1945.

_____. Proposed Revisions for the Book of Worship for Church
and Home. Nashville, TN: Methodist Publishing House, 1960.

_____. The Book of Worship for Church and Home. Nashville,
TN: Methodist Publishing House, 1965.

UNITED METHODIST CHURCH (U.S.). Commission on Worship.
The Sacrament of the Lord's Supper: An Alternate Text.
SWR, 1. Nashville, TN: United Methodist Publishing House,
1972.

_____. Ritual in a New Day: An Invitation. Nashville, TN:
Abingdon Press, 1976.

_____. Word and Table: A Basic Pattern of Sunday Worship
for United Methodists. SWR, 3. Nashville, TN: Abingdon
Press, 1976.

_____. _____. Rev. ed. Nashville: Abingdon Press, 1980.

_____. A Service of Baptism, Confirmation, and Renewal: An
Alternate Text, 1976. Nashville, TN: United Methodist Publishing House, 1976.

_____. A Service of Christian Marriage. SWR, 5. Nashville,
TN: Abingdon Press, 1979.

_____. Seasons of the Gospel: Resources for the Christian
Year for the Use of United Methodists. SWR, 6. Nashville,
TN: Abingdon Press, 1979.

_____. Commission on Worship. A Service of Death and Resur-
rection: The Ministry of the Church at Death. SWR, 7.
Nashville, TN: Abingdon Press, 1979.

_____. From Ashes to Fire: Services of Worship for the Seasons
of Lent and Easter. SWR, 8. Nashville, TN: Abingdon Press,
1981.

_____. At the Lord's Table: A Communion Service Book for
Use by the Minister. SWR, 9. Nashville, TN: Abingdon
Press, 1981.

_____. We Gather Together: Services for Public Worship.
SWR, 10. Nashville, TN: United Methodist Publishing House,
1980.

b. Evangelical United Brethren Church

KOONTZ, Paul Rodes, ed. The Minister's Companion: A Compendium of Rituals of the Evangelical United Brethren Church.
Dayton, OH: Otterbein Press, 1947.

c. Other Texts

THIRKIELD, Wilbur Patterson, ed. Services and Prayers for
Church and Home. New York: Methodist Book Concern, 1928.

WILLMAN, Leon Kurtz. The Pastor's Vade Mecum: Containing the
Ritual for the Sacrament of the Lord's Supper, the Sacrament
of Baptism, Reception of Members, Matrimony, and Burial of
the Dead. Rev. ed. New York: Methodist Book Concern,
1933.

BURGESS, Stephen W., and RIGHTER, James D. Celebrations for
Today: Acts of Worship in Modern English Language. Nashville, TN: Abingdon Press, 1977.

2. Studies

BEDELL, Kenneth B. Worship in the Methodist Tradition. Nashville, TN: Tidings, 1976.

BOWMER, John C. "The Manual Acts in the Communion Office."
Religion in Life, 28 (1958-1959): 119-126.

BUCKS, Fladger Levon. Increasing the Understanding and Appreciation of the Celebration of the Lord's Supper in Bailey Memorial, a Small United Methodist Church located in a Small Southern Textile Mill Town. Ann Arbor, MI: University Microfilms,
1982.

COOKE, Richard J. History of the Ritual of the Methodist Episcopal Church. New York: Eaton & Mains, 1900.

DUNKLE, W. F., and QUILLIAN, J. D., eds. Companion to the
Book of Worship. Nashville, TN: Abingdon Press, 1970.

GIBSON, Samuel N. The Sacrament of the Lord's Supper: A
Commentary. State College, PA: n.p., 1965.

HARDIN, H. Grady. The Leadership of Worship. Nashville, TN:
Abingdon Press, 1980.

_____, QUILLIAN, Joseph D., and WHITE, James F. The Cele-
bration of the Gospel: A Study in Christian Worship. Nashville, TN: Abingdon Press, 1964.

HARMON, Nolan B. The Rites and Ritual of Episcopal Methodism.
Nashville, TN: Publishing House of the Methodist Episcopal
Church, South, 1926.

HICKMAN, Hoyt L. The Holy Meal. Nashville, TN: Tidings, 1974?

_____. A Primer for Church Worship. Nashville, TN: Abingdon Press, 1984.

NATIONAL METHODIST CONVOCATION ON WORSHIP. Addresses delivered at the First National Methodist Convocation on Worship, Baltimore, Maryland, April 19-21, 1966. Dallas, TX: Perkins School of Theology, 1966.

NELSON, J. Robert. "Methodist Eucharistic Usage: From Constant Communion to Benign Neglect to Sacramental Recovery." Journal of Ecumenical Studies, 13 (1976): 88-93.

_____. "Notes Toward a United Methodist Liturgical Theology." Nexus 57, 22, 2 (Spring 1979): 35-44.

_____. "What Methodists Think of Eucharistic Theology." Worship, 52 (1978): 409-424.

PEMBROKE, Maceo D. "Black Worship Experience in the United Methodist Church." Religion in Life, 44 (1975): 309-317.

SANDERS, Paul S. "The Methodist Communion Order [1784-1939]." The Pastor, 11, 10 (May 1948): 25-27.

_____. "Toward an Orderly Sunday service [1939-1948]." The Pastor, 11, 11 (June 1948): 26-28.

SUMMERS, Thomas G. Commentary on the Ritual of the Methodist Episcopal Church, South. Nashville, TN: A. H. Redford for the Methodist Episcopal Church, South, 1873.

TREADWAY, John Thomas. "The Lord's Supper in American Methodism." In his "Eucharistic Theology in American Protestantism 1820-1860," pp. 228-253. Ph.D. dissertation, Northwestern University, 1964.

VOIGHT, Edwin E. "Worship in American Methodism." Encyclopedia of World Methodism.

WADE, William Nash. "A History of Public Worship in the Methodist Episcopal Church and Methodist Episcopal Church, South, from 1784 to 1905." Ph.D. dissertation, University of Notre Dame, 1981.

WATSON, Richard. The Sacraments: Baptism and the Lord's Supper from "Theological Institutes." New York: Hunt, 1893.

WHITE, James F. "Liturgy, Theology of the Laity: The Case of the 1972 Methodist Communion Service." Duke Divinity School Review, 43 (1978): 33-43.

_____. "The New American Methodist Communion Order." Wor-
ship, 41 (1967): 552-560.

_____. "The Sacrament of the Lord's Supper: The New Alter-
nate Rite." Christian Advocate, 16, 21 (September 14, 1972):
13-14.

WILLIMON, William H. Sunday Dinner: The Lord's Supper and
the Christian Life. Nashville: Upper Room, 1981.

_____. Worship as Pastoral Care. Nashville, TN: Abingdon
Press, 1979.

XXII. THE CATHOLIC APOSTOLIC CHURCH

A. TEXTS

CATHOLIC APOSTOLIC CHURCH. The Liturgy and Other Divine
Offices of the Church. London, 1843.
--New editions in 1847, 1851, 1853, 1856, 1863, 1869 and 1880.

_____. _____. [Last reprint ed.] London: H. J. Glaisher,
1927.

_____. The Christian Liturgy, and Book of Common Prayer
... for Use of the Church in America. Boston, MA: Ticknor,
1846, 1861.

B. STUDIES

BUTLER, Pierce. "Irvingism as an Analogue of the Oxford Movement." Church History, 6 (1937): 101-113.

CARDALE, John Bate [supposed author]. Readings Upon the Liturgy and Other Divine Offices of the Church. 2 vols. London: G. J. W. Pitman, 1893-1899.

DAVIES, Horton. Worship and Theology in England, vol. 4: From
Newman to Martineau, 1850-1900, pp. 153-164. Princeton:
Princeton University Press, 1962.

DRUMMOND, Henry. The Rationale of Liturgies and of Public Worship. London, 1857.

LANCASTER, John. "John Bate Cardale, Pillar of Apostles: A

Quest for Catholicity." Ph.D. dissertation, St. Andrews University, Scotland, 1978.

NEWMAN-NORTON, Seraphim. The Time of Silence: A History of the Catholic Apostolic Church, 1901-1971. 3d ed. ASP, 2. Stoneygate, Eng.: Albury Society, 1975, c1974.

MAST, Gregg Alan. "The Eucharistic Service of the Catholic Apostolic Church and Its Influence on Reformed Liturgical Renewals of the Nineteenth Century." Ph.D. dissertation. Drew University, 1985.

PEASTON, A. Elliott. "The Catholic Apostolic Church." In his The Prayer Book Tradition in the Free Churches, pp. 161-170. London: James Clarke, 1964.

SHAW, P. E. The Catholic Apostolic Church, sometimes called Irvingite: A Historical Study. New York: King's Crown Press, 1946; reprint ed., Freeport, NY: Books for Libraries Press, 1972.

STEVENSON, Kenneth W. "The Catholic Apostolic Church--Its History and Its Eucharist." Studia Liturgica, 13 (1979): 21-45.

_____. "The Catholic Apostolic Eucharist." Ph.D. dissertation, Southhampton University, 1975.

TRIPP, David. "The Liturgy of the Catholic Apostolic Church." Scottish Journal of Theology, 22 (1969): 437-454.

WHITLEY, H. C. Blinded Eagle: An Introduction to the Life and Teaching of Edward Irving. London: SCM Press; Chicago: Allenson, 1955.

WORSFOLD, J. E. A History of the Charismatic Movements in New Zealand; including a Pentecostal Perspective and a Breviate of the Catholic Apostolic Church in Great Britain. Bradford, Eng.: Julian Literature Trust, 1974.

XXIII. THE MERCERSBURG TRADITION

A. LITURGICAL TEXTS

GERMAN REFORMED CHURCH IN THE U.S. Liturgy for the Use of the Congregations of the German Reformed Church in the United States. Chambersburg: Publications Office of the German Reformed Church, 1841.

_____. A Liturgy; or, Order of Christian Worship. Philadel-
phia, PA: Lindsay & Blakiston, 1857. [The Provisional Lit-
urgy]

"Kirchenordnung: Wie es mit der Christlichem Lehre/ heiligen
Sacramenten/ vnnd Ceremonien/ inn des Durchleuchtigsten
Hochgebornen Fürsten/ vnnd Herren/ Herrn Friderichs
Pfaltzgrauen bey Rhein/ des heiligen Römischen Reichs
Ertzdruchsessen vnnd Churfürsten/ Hertzogen inn Bayern
und Churfürstenthumb bey Rhein/ gehalten wirdt." In
Bekenntnisschriften und Kirchenordnungen der nach Gottes
Wort reformierten Kirche, pp. 136-218. Herausgegeben von
Wilhelm Niesel. 3. Aufl. Zollikon-Zürich: Evangelischer
Verlag, 1938; "The Old Palatinate Liturgy of 1563." Trans-
lated by J. H. A. Bomberger. Mercersburg Review, 2, 1
(January 1850): 81-96; 2, 3 (May 1850): 265-286; 3, 2
(March 1851): 97-128.

B. HISTORICAL SOURCES

BOMBERGER, John H. A. Reformed Not Ritualistic; Apostolic Not
Patristic: A Reply to Dr. Nevin's "Vindication." Philadelphia,
PA: J. B. Rodgers, 1867.

_____. The Revised Liturgy: A History and Criticism of the
Ritualistic Movement of the German Reformed Church. Philadelphia, PA: J. B. Rodgers, 1867.

DORNER, Isaak August. The Liturgical Conflict in the Reformed
Church. Philadelphia, PA: Loag, 1868.

GERHART, E. V. "The Sacramental Theory of the Heidelberg
Catechism." Mercersburg Review, 19 (October 1872): 534-563.

HARBAUGH, Henry. "Christian Cultus: Its Nature, History and
Relations." Mercersburg Quarterly Review, 6 (October 1854):
573-600; 7 (January 1855): 116-135.

_____. "Creed and Cultus: With Special Reference to the Re-
lation of the Heidelberg Catechism to the Palatinate Liturgy."
In Tercentenary Monument in Commemoration of the Three
Hundredth Anniversary of the Heidelberg Catechism, pp. 231-
295. Chambersburg, PA: M. Kieffer, 1863.

_____. "Reverence in Worship." Mercersburg Review, 1 (1849):
424-443.

KRAUTH, Charles Porterfield. "The Liturgical Movement in the
Presbyterian and Reformed Churches." Mercersburg Review,
16 (October 1869): 599-647.

_____. "The Western Liturgy." Mercersburg Review, 18 (January 1871): 92-114.

"Liturgical Contributions." Mercersburgh Quarterly Review, 6 (April 1854): 187-205; 6 (July 1854): 355-398; 6 (October 1854): 554-572; 8 (January 1856): 152-158; 8 (July 1856): 415-536.

NEVIN, John Williamson. Address on Sacred Music. Princeton, NJ: D. A. Borrenstein, 1827.

_____. The Anxious Bench. 2d rev. ed. Chambersburg, PA: Publication Office of the German Reformed Church, 1844.

_____. Catholic and Reformed: Selected Theological Writings of John Williamson Nevin. Edited by Charles Yrigoyen, Jr. and George H. Bricker. POTTS, 3. Pittsburgh, PA: Pickwick Press, 1978.

_____. "The Church Year." Mercersburg Review, 8 (January 1856): 456-478.

_____. "Doctrine of the Reformed Church on the Lord's Supper." Mercersburg Review, 2 (September 1850): 421-548.

_____. Liturgical Discussion. Philadelphia, PA: Fisher, 1868.

_____. "The Liturgical Movement." Mercersburg Review, 1 (November 1849): 608-612.

_____. The Liturgical Question, with Reference to the Provisional Liturgy of the German Reformed Church. Philadelphia, PA: Lindsay, 1862.

_____. The Mystical Presence: A Vindication of the Reformed or Calvinistic Doctrine of the Holy Eucharist. Philadelphia, PA: Lippincott, 1846; reprint ed., Hamden, CT: Archon Books, 1963.

_____. The Mystical Presence and Other Writings on the Eucharist. Edited by Bard Thompson and George H. Bricker. LSMT, 4. Philadelphia, PA: United Church Press, 1966.

_____. "Theology of the New Liturgy." Mercersburg Review, 14 (January 1867): 23-66.

_____. Vindication of the Revised Liturgy. Philadelphia, PA: J. B. Rodgers, 1867.

NICHOLS, James H., ed. The Mercersburg Theology. LPT. New York: Oxford University Press, 1966.

SCHAFF, David S. The Life of Philip Schaff, in Part Autobio-
graphical. New York: Scribner, 1897.

SCHAFF, Philip. "The New Liturgy." Mercersburg Review, 10
(April 1858): 199-227.

C. STUDIES

APPEL, Theodore. The Life and Work of John Williamson Nevin.
Philadelphia, PA: Reformed Church Publication House, 1889.

BARKER, V. L. "John W. Nevin: His Place in American Intellectual Thought." Ph.D. dissertation, St. Louis University,
1970.

BINKLEY, Luther. The Mercersburg Theology. Manheim, PA:
Sentinel Printing House, 1953.

BRENNER, Scott F. "Nevin and the Mercersburg Theology."
Theology Today, 12 (1955): 43-56.

_____. "Philip Schaff the Liturgist." Christendom, 11, 4
(Autumn 1946): 443-456.

CORDOUE, John T. "The Ecclesiology of John Williamson Nevin:
A Catholic Appraisal." Ph.D. dissertation, Catholic University
of America, 1968.

GERRISH, Brian A. "The Flesh of the Son of Man: John Williamson Nevin on the Church and the Eucharist." In his Tradition
and the Modern World, pp. 49-70. Chicago: University of
Chicago Press, 1978.

MAXWELL, Jack Martin. Worship and Reformed Theology: The
Liturgical Lessons of Mercersburg. Pittsburgh, PA: Pickwick
Press, 1976.

MITCHELL, Nathan D. "Church, Eucharist and Liturgical Reform
at Mercersburg, 1843-1857." Ph.D. dissertation, University of
Notre Dame, 1978.

NICHOLS, James H. Romanticism in American Theology: Nevin and
Schaff at Mercersburg. Chicago: University of Chicago Press,
1961.

SCHNEIDER, Carl E. The German Church on the American Frontier.
St. Louis, MO: Eden Publishing House, 1939.

THOMPSON, Bard. "The Catechism and the Mercersburg Theology."

In Essays on the Heidelberg Catechism, pp. 53-74. Philadelphia, PA: United Church Press, 1963.

_____. "Reformed Liturgies: An Historical and Doctrinal Inter-
pretation of the Palatinate Liturgy of 1563, Mercersburg Provisional Liturgy of 1858, Evangelical and Reformed Order of
1944, and their Sources." B.D. thesis, Union Theological
Seminary in the City of New York, 1949.

XXIV. FREE CHURCHES *

A. GENERAL TEXTS

CHRISTENSEN, James L. The Minister's Church, Home, and Community Services Book. Old Tappan, NJ: Revell, 1980.

_____. The Minister's Service Handbook. Westwood, NJ:
Revell, 1960.

HUTTON, Samuel Ward. Minister's Service Manual. Grand Rapids,
MI: Baker, 1958.

MOUNTAIN, J. The Free Church Prayer Book. London: n.p.,
1897.

WALLIS, Charles L., ed. The Table of the Lord: A Communion
Encyclopedia. New York: Harper, 1958; reprinted as A Com-
plete Source Book for the Lord's Supper. Grand Rapids, MI:
Baker, 1978.

_____. Worship Resources for the Christian Year. New York:
Harper, 1954.

B. GENERAL STUDIES

ABBA, Raymond. Principles of Christian Worship: With Special
Reference to the Free Churches. London: Oxford University
Press, 1957.

---

*Some of the churches already covered in this bibliography, e.g.
some Puritans, Congregationalists or Methodists, may be considered "free churches" in addition to those covered in this section.

ADAMS, Doug. "Free Church Worship in America from 1620 to 1835." Worship, 55 (1981): 436-440.

_____. Meeting House to Camp Meeting: Toward a History of American Free Church Worship from 1620 to 1835. Saratoga: Modern Liturgy resource Publications; Austin, TX: The Sharing Company, 1981.

BLAKEMORE, W. B. "Unity in Our Diversity of Worship." In The Challenge of Christian Unity, pp. 76-96. Edited by W. B. Blakemore. St. Louis, MO: Bethany Press, 1963.

JONES, Ilion T. A Historical Approach to Evangelical Worship. Nashville, TN: Abingdon Press, 1954.

PAYNE, Ernest A. "The Free Church Tradition and Worship." Baptist Quarterly, 21 (April 1965): 51-63.

PEASTON, A. Elliott. The Prayer Book Tradition in the Free Churches. London: James Clarke, 1964.

RAYBURN, Robert G. O Come, Let Us Worship: Corporate Worship in the Evangelical Church. Grand Rapids, MI: Baker, 1980.

SKOGLUND, John. "Free Churches (Worship in a Free Assembly)." In Liturgy: Self-Expression of the Church, pp. 107-111. Edited by Herman Schmidt. Concilium, 72. New York: Herder & Herder, 1972.

_____. Worship in the Free Churches. Valley Forge, PA: Judson Press, 1965.

WATKINS, Keith. "Liturgy and the Free Church." Encounter, 23 (1962): 196-203.

WHITE, James. "Creativity: The Free Church Tradition." In Liturgy: A Creative Tradition, pp. 47-52. Edited by Mary Collins and David Power. Concilium, 162. New York: Seabury Press, 1983.

C. THE BAPTIST CHURCHES

1. United Kingdom

a. Texts

AUBREY, M. E., ed. A Minister's Manual: Containing Orders of Service for Marriage, Dedication of Infants, Baptism, Communion, and Burial. London: Kingsgate Press, 1927; reprints, 1946, 1952.

BONNER, Henry. Services for Public Worship. Rev. ed. Birmingham, Eng.: Hall & English, 1900.

GILMORE, A., SMALLEY, E., and WALKER, M., eds. Praise God: A Collection of Resource Material for Christian Worship. London: Baptist Union, 1980.

JONES, John Isaiah. Readings for Worship. London: National Sunday School Union, 1937.

PATTERSON, David Tait, ed. The Call to Worship: A Book of Services for Ministers and Congregations, brought together from Various Sources. The music selected and arranged by George Dyson. London: Carey Press, 1930.

_____. _____. Rev. ed. London: Carey Press, 1947.

PAYNE, Ernest A., and WINWARD, Stephen F., eds. Orders and Prayers for Church Worship: A Manual for Ministers. London: Carey Kingsgate Press, 1960; 2d ed., 1962.

_____, _____, and COX, James W., eds. Minister's Worship Manual. New York: World, 1969.

SPURR, Frederick C., ed. Come, Let Us Worship: A Book of Common Worship for Use in Free Churches. London: Kingsgate Press, 1930.
--a revision of BONNER, above

WINWARD, Stephen F. Responsive Praises and Prayers for Minister and Congregation. London: Hodder & Stoughton, 1958.

_____. Responsive Service Book. London: Hodder & Stoughton, 1965.

b. Studies

CLARK, Neville. An Approach to the Theology of the Sacraments. SBT, 17. London: SCM Press, 1956.

_____. Call to Worship. SMW, 15. London: SCM Press, 1960.

CLIFFORD, Paul Rowntree. "Baptist Forms of Worship." Foundations, 3 (1960): 221-233.

_____. "The Structure and Ordering of Baptist Worship." Foundations, 3 (1960): 348-361.

GRANT, John Webster. Free Churchmanship in England (1870–
1940). London: Independent Press, 1955.

PAYNE, Ernest A. The Fellowship of Believers: Baptist Thought
and Practice Yesterday and Today. Enlarged ed. London:
Carey Kingsgate Press, 1952.

_____. Free Churchmen, Unrepentant and Repentant. London:
Carey Kingsgate Press, 1965.

PEASTON, A. Elliott. "The Baptists." In his The Prayer Book
Tradition in the Free Churches, pp. 122–130. London: James
Clarke, 1964.

ROBINSON, H. Wheeler. The Life and Faith of the Baptists.
London: Methuen, 1927.

_____. _____. 2d ed. London: Carey Kingsgate Press,
1946.

SKOGLUND, John E. "Baptist Worship." A Dictionary of Liturgy
and Worship, pp. 64–68.

SMYTH, John. The Works of John Smyth, vol. 1. Edited by
W. T. Whitley. Cambridge: Cambridge University Press,
1915.

WINWARD, Stephen. "Books, Liturgical. Baptist." A Dictionary
of Liturgy and Worship, pp. 84–85.

_____. The Reformation of Our Worship. London: Carey
Kingsgate Press, 1964; Richmond, VA: John Knox Press,
1965.

2. United States

a. Texts

COOK, Paul E. Communion Handbook. Valley Forge, PA: Judson
Press, 1980.

FOSHEE, Howard B. Broadman Church Manual. Nashville, TN:
Broadman Press, 1973.

HOBBS, James Randolph. The Pastor's Manual. Nashville, TN:
Broadman Press, 1934.

HUDSON, Winthrop S., and MARING, Norman H. A Baptist Manual
of Polity and Practice. Valley Forge, PA: Judson Press, 1963.

KEIGHTON, Robert E. The Minister's Communion Service Book.
Philadelphia, PA: Judson Press, 1940.

McNEIL, Jesse J. Minister's Service Book for Pulpit and Parish.
Grand Rapids, MI: Eerdmans, 1961.

PAYNE, Ernest A., WINWARD, Stephen F., and COX, James W.,
eds. Minister's Worship Manual. New York: World, 1969.

SEGLER, Franklin M. The Broadman Minister's Manual. Nashville,
TN: Broadman Press, 1968.

SKOGLUND, John E. A Manual of Worship. Valley Forge, PA:
Judson Press, 1968.

  b. Studies

ANDREWS, Charles R. "Public Worship in a Secular Age."
Foundations, 10 (1967): 123-136.

BRISTOL, Lyle O. "The Lord's Supper in the New Testament."
Foundations, 1, 4 (October 1958): 16-23.

BRUSH, John W. "Baptists and the Lord's Supper." Foundations,
1, 4 (October 1958): 7-15.

CARLTON, John. "The Lord's Supper in Worship." Review and
Expositor, 66 (Winter 1969): 67-74.

DALTON, Wayne A. "Worship and Baptist Ecclesiology." Foundations, 12 (1969): 7-18.

DAY, Judson LeRoy, II. "Spiritual Worship in Baptist Churches."
Foundations, 14 (1971): 271-283.

DEWEESE, Charles W. A Community of Believers. Valley Forge,
PA: Judson Press, 1978.

DOBBINS, Gaines Stanley. The Church at Worship. Nashville,
TN: Broadman Press, 1962.

EDWARDS, Morgan. The Customs of Primitive Churches; or, A
Set of Propositions Relative to the Name, Materials, Constitu-
tion, Power, Officers, Ordinances, Rites, Business, Worship,
Discipline, Government, etc., of a Church. Philadelphia, 1774;
microfilm copy, by the Historical Commission, Southern Baptist
Convention, 1958.

HINSON, E. Glenn. The Reaffirmation of Prayer. Nashville, TN:
Broadman Press, 1979.

_____. "Traditional Prayer Forms and the Recycling of Our
    Understanding." Spiritual Life, 27 (Spring 1981): 35-41.

HUDSON, Fred M. "Worship in a Secular Age." Foundations, 7
    (1964): 316-334.

LAHRSON, Gordon R. "Preaching and the Lord's Supper."
    Foundations, 12 (1969): 19-33.

McGLOTHLEN, Gaye L. "Worship Services, Baptist." Encyclopedia
    of Southern Baptists, 2: 1548-1550.

McGLOTHLIN, W. J. Baptist Confessions of Faith. Philadelphia,
    PA: American Baptist Publication Society, 1911.

MILLER, Samuel H. "Reducing the Reality of the Lord's Supper."
    Foundations, 1, 4 (October 1958): 24-29.

_____. "Worship and the Arts." Foundations, 3 (1960): 198-
    204.

MITCHELL, Carlton Turner. "Baptist Worship in Relation to Bap-
    tist Concepts of the Church." Thesis, New York University,
    1962.

MORTON, Hugh Q. "Worship in a Contemporary Church." Founda-
    tions, 12 (1969): 34-46.

PATTISON, T. Harwood. Public Worship. Philadelphia, PA:
    American Baptist Publication Society, 1900.

POLLEY, George W., Jr. "Toward a More Biblical View of the
    Lord's Supper." Foundations, 7 (1964): 335-340.

"Public Worship." Review and Expositor, 62, 3 (Summer 1965).

SEGLER, Franklin M. Christian Worship: Its Theology and Prac-
    tice. Nashville, TN: Broadman Press, 1967.

_____. "Worship, Christian." Encyclopedia of Southern Bap-
    tists, 2:1547-1548.

SKOGLUND, John E., ed. Worship and Renewal. Rochester, NY:
    Colgate-Rochester Divinity School, 1965.

SPIKE, Robert W. "The Growing Unity of Christian Worship."
    Foundations, 3 (1960): 205-213.

"Worship." Review and Expositor, 80, 2 (Winter 1983).

D. CHURCH OF THE BRETHREN

1. Texts (arranged chronologically)

CHURCH OF THE BRETHREN. Minister's Manual, Church of the
   Brethren. By H. L. Hartsough, Raymond R. Peters, M. R.
   Zigler, Foster B. Statler. Authorized by General Ministerial
   Board, Church of the Brethren. Elgin, IL: Brethren Pub-
   lishing House, 1946.

_____. Manual of Worship and Polity. Elgin, IL: Brethren
   Publishing House, 1953.

_____. Book of Worship. Elgin, IL: Brethren Press, 1964.

_____. Pastor's Manual. Elgin, IL: Brethren Press, 1978.

_____. We Gather Together: Worship Resources for the Church
   of the Brethren. Elgin, IL: Brethren Press, 1979.

ZEIGLER, Edward K. A Book of Worship for Village Churches.
   New York: Agricultural Missions Foundation, 1939.

2. Studies

ADAMS, C. D. Brethren Worship in the Spirit of '76. n.p., 1976.

ALLISON, Richard E. "Feetwashing." The Brethren Encyclopedia,
   1:481-482.

BENEDICT, F. W. A Brief Account of the Origins and a Description of the Brethren Love Feast. Pendleton, IN: Old Brotherhood Publishers, 1967.

BROWN, Dale W. "Liturgy." In The Church of the Brethren:
   Past and Present, pp. 53-65. Edited by Donald F. Durn-
   baugh. Elgin, IL: Brethren Press, 1971.

DENLINGER, Carolyn T. "Lord's Supper, Foot at." The Brethren
   Encyclopedia, 2:757-758.

ELLER, Vernard M. In Place of Sacraments. Grand Rapids, MI:
   Eerdmans, 1972.

FISHER, Nevin W. The History of Brethren Hymnbooks. Bridge-
   water, VA: Beacon Publishers, 1980.

FLORA, Delbert B. "Ordinances." The Brethren Encyclopedia,
   2:976-980.

GRAFF, Warren F. "Ordination." The Brethren Encyclopedia, 2:
    980.

KREIDER, D. "Leitourgia--A Forgotten Facet." Brethren Life and
    Thought, 10 (Spring 1965): 27-32.

MORSE, Kenneth I. "Worship, Public." The Brethren Encyclo-
    pedia, 2:1373-1379.

SCHULTZ, Joseph R. "Lord's Supper." The Brethren Encyclo-
    pedia, 2:757.

_____. The Soul of the Symbols: A Theological Study of Holy
    Communion. Grand Rapids, MI: Eerdmans, 1966.

SNYDER, Graydon F. "Love Feast." The Brethren Encyclopedia,
    2:762-765.

WEIMER, Glen E. "Christian Worship." Brethren Life and Thought,
    1 (Autumn 1955): 32-44.

_____. "The Nurture of the Church through Worship." Breth-
    ren Life and Thought, 6 (Summer 1961): 22-36.

_____. "Symbols in Religious Practice." Brethren Life and
    Thought, 4 (Autumn 1959): 23-28.

YODER, Charles F. God's Means of Grace: A Discussion of the
    Various Helps Divinely Given as Aids to Christian Character
    and a Plea for Fidelity to their Scriptural Form and Use.
    Elgin, IL: Brethren Publishing House, 1908; reprint ed.,
    Winona Lake, IN: BMH Books, 1979.

ZEIGLER, Edward K. Country Altars: Worship in the Country
    Church. New York: Commission on Worship, Federal Council
    of Churches of Christ in America, 1942.

_____. Rural People at Worship. New York: Agricultural Mis-
    sions Foundation, 1943.

E. CHURCH OF THE NAZARENE

CHURCH OF THE NAZARENE. Manual of the History, Doctrine,
    Government and Ritual of the Church of the Nazarene. 3d ed.
    Kansas City, MO: Nazarene Publishing House, 1924.

_____. Manual of the Church of the Nazarene: History, Con-
    stitution, Government, Ritual. 3d ed. Kansas City, MO:
    Nazarene Publishing House, 1964.

_____ . Manual, 1976, Church of the Nazarene: History, Constitution, Government, Ritual. Kansas City, MO: Nazarene
Publishing House, 1976.

F. CHURCHES OF CHRIST (DISCIPLES)

1. Texts

AINSLIE, Peter, and ARMSTRONG, H. C. A Book of Christian
Worship for Voluntary Use among Disciples of Christ and other
Christians. Baltimore, MD: Seminary House Press, 1923.

CAMPBELL, A. Order of Worship. Compiled by C. M. Stubble-
field. Cincinnati, OH: F. L. Rowe, 1915.

CAVE, R. C. A Manual for Ministers. Cincinnati, OH: Standard,
1918.

GREEN, Francis M. The Christian Minister's Manual: for the Use
of Church Officers in the Various Relations of Evangelists,
Pastors, Bishops, and Deacons. St. Louis, MO: John Burns,
1883.

HARRISON, Russell F. Brief Prayers for Bread and Cup: For
Elders at the Communion Table. St. Louis, MO: Bethany
Press, 1976.

HOPPER, Myron T. The Candle of the Lord. Rev. ed. St. Louis,
MO: Bethany Press, 1957.

HUTTON, Samuel W. Service Manual for Ministers of Non-Liturgical
Churches. Fort Worth, TX: Texas Convention of Christian
Churches, 1932, 1958.

_____ . Worship and Hymns for Church and Church School.
St. Louis, MO: Bethany Press, 1930.

HUTTON, Samuel W., and KEITH, Noel L. Worship Highways:
Guideposts for Spiritual Engineers. St. Louis, MO: Bethany
Press, 1943.

MURCH, James DeForest. Christian Minister's Manual. Cincinnati,
OH: Standard, 1937.

OSBORN, George Edwin. Christian Worship: A Service Book.
St. Louis, MO: Christian Board of Publication, 1953.

_____ . _____ . 2d ed. St. Louis, MO: Christian Board of
Publication, 1958.

SMITH, Benjamin L. A Manual of Forms for Ministers. St. Louis,
MO: Bethany Press, 1919.

THORNTON, E. W., ed. Lord's Day Worship Services. Cincinnati,
OH: Standard, 1930.

WATKINS, Keith. "An Order of Celebration of the Great Thanksgiving." Encounter, 24, 3 (1963): 310-313.

_____. "An Order of Holy Communion for Use Every Sunday."
Encounter, 24, 3 (1963): 303-309.

2. Studies

ABBOTT, B. A. "The Lord's Supper, the Love Ordinance." In
his The Disciples, an Interpretation, pp. 131-145. St. Louis,
MO: Bethany Press, 1924; reprinted 1964.

BAIRD, William. "The Problem of Worship." In his The Corinthian
Church: A Biblical Approach to Urban Culture, pp. 119-158.
New York: Abingdon Press, 1964.

BLAKEMORE, W. B. "Disciples of Christ Worship from 1925 to the
Present." The Scroll, 58 (Autumn 1966): 29-42.

_____. "Worship and the Lord's Supper." In The Renewal of
the Church: The Panel Reports, vol. 3: The Revival of the
Churches, pp. 227-250. St. Louis, MO: Bethany Press, 1963.

CAMPBELL, Alexander. The Christian System in Reference to the
Union of Christians and Restoration of Primitive Christianity
as Plead in the Current Reformation. Cincinnati, OH: Standard, 1835.

_____. _____. 5th ed. Cincinnati, OH: Standard, 1901.

COWDEN, John B. Christian Worship. Cincinnati, OH: Standard,
1920.

_____. Worshipping Toward Christian Unity. West Nashville,
TN: Christian Unity Evangelism, 1930.

CROW, P. A., Jr. "The Disciples, Reunion, and the Worship of
the Church." The Scroll, 59 (1967): 50-61.

FORTUNE, A. W. "The Disciples and the Communion Service."
Shane Quarterly, 2, 2-3 (1941): 280-288.

GARRIOTT, Christopher Troy. "The Role of Public Worship in a
Disciples Church." Ph.D. dissertation, University of Chicago,
1944.

HOGUE, Harland E. "Worship and the Non-Theological Factor."
Encounter, 24, 3 (1963): 379-385.

HOON, Paul Waitman, MacGREGOR, Geddes, PAUL, Robert S.,
SHEPHERD, Massey H., Jr., STECKEL, Clyde J., OSBORN,
G. Edwin, and JARMAN, William Jackson. "A Symposium on
[Keith Watkins'] 'An Order of Holy Communion for Use Every
Sunday.'" Encounter, 24 (1963): 314-329.

HUMBERT, Royal. A Compend of Alexander Campbell's Theology.
St. Louis, MO: Bethany Press, 1961.

JARMAN, William Jackson. "The Context of Preaching. Part 2:
The Worship Service." Encounter, 24, 2 (1963): 144-152.

KOENKER, Ernest B. "The Word and Liturgy." Encounter, 20
(1959): 252-256.

LESSLEY, George D. "The Development of Formal Worship Among
the Disciples of Christ." M.A. thesis, Yale University, 1933.

LOCKHART, W. S. The Ministry of Worship: A Study of the
Need, Psychology and Technique of Worship. St. Louis, MO:
Christian Board of Publication, 1927.

LUNGER, I. E. "O Come Let Us Worship." The Scroll, 45 (1953):
3-11.

MILLER, Samuel H. "The Nature of the Congregation in Worship."
Encounter, 20 (1959): 244-251.

MORRISON, Charles Clayton. The Social Gospel and the Christian
Cultus. New York: Harper, 1933.

OSBORN, G. Edwin. "The Glory of Christian Worship." Encounter, 20 (1959): 172-243.

_____. The Glory of Christian Worship. Indianapolis, IN:
Christian Theological Seminary Press, 1960.

_____. "Redeeming the Time." Encounter, 24 (1963): 330-347.

ROBINSON, William. The Administration of the Lord's Supper.
Birmingham, Eng.: Berean Press, 1947; reprinted 1959.

_____. A Companion to the Communion Service: A Devotional
Manual. London: Oxford University Press, 1942.

_____. Holy Baptism and Holy Communion. Birmingham, Eng.:
Berean Press, 1952.

_____. The Sacraments and Life. Birmingham, Eng.: Christian Action Fellowship, 1949.

ROTHERHAM, Joseph Bryant. Let Us Keep the Feast: Being Plain Chapters on the Lord's Supper. Cincinnati, OH: Standard, 1917.

SHORT, Howard E. "The Lord's Supper." In his The Doctrine and Thought of the Disciples of Christ, pp. 33-39. St. Louis, MO: Bethany Press, 1951.

TOLER, Thomas W. The Elder at the Lord's Table. St. Louis, MO: Bethany Press, 1954.

WATKINS, Keith. "Books, Liturgical. Christian Church." A Dictionary of Liturgy and Worship, p. 85.

_____. The Breaking of Bread: An Approach to Worship for the Christian Churches (Disciples of Christ). St. Louis, MO: Bethany Press, 1966.

_____. "Christian Church (Disciples of CHrist) Worship." A Dictionary of Liturgy and Worship, pp. 133-134.

_____. The Feast of Joy: The Lord's Supper in Free Churches. St. Louis, MO: Bethany Press, 1977.

_____. "Liturgies. Christian Church (Disciples of Christ)." A Dictionary of Liturgy and Worship, pp. 233-234.

_____. Liturgies in a Time When Cities Burn. Nashville, TN: Abingdon Press, 1969.

_____. "Ministers and Elders as Leaders of Worship in the Christian Church." Encounter, 39 (1978): 305-320.

_____. Worship and You. St. Louis, MO: Christian Board of Publication, 1971.

_____. "Worship in the Christian Church (Disciples of Christ)." Worship, 51 (1977): 486-496.

Worship in the Christian CHurch: The Common Worship of the Church. St. Louis, MO: Christian Board of Publication, 1969.

G. EVANGELICAL CATHOLIC CHURCH

Evangelical Catholic Church. The Order of the Ministration of the Lord's Supper or Mass, for the Use of Evangelical Catholics and Others. Oxford: Blackwell, 1920.

H. EVANGELICAL COVENANT CHURCH OF AMERICA

Evangelical Covenant Church of America. A Book of Worship for
Covenant Churches. Chicago: Covenant Press, 1964.

_____. The Covenant Book of Worship. 3 vols. Chicago:
Covenant Press, 1976-1978; one vol. ed., 1980.

I. EVANGELICAL FREE CHURCH OF AMERICA

Evangelical Free Church of America. Minister's Service Manual.
Minneapolis, MN: Free Church Publications, 1973.

J. THE LIBERAL CATHOLIC CHURCH

Liberal Catholic Church. The Liturgy according to the Use of the
Liberal Catholic Church. London: St. Alban Press, 1924.

_____. _____. 3d ed. London: St. Alban Press, 1942.

_____. _____. 4th ed., rev. & enlarged. London: St.
Alban Press, 1967.

_____. A Shorter Form for the Celebration of the Holy Euchar-
ist ... according to the Use of the Liberal Catholic Church.
London: St. Alban Press, 1966.

UDNY, E. Francis. A Help to Worship in the Liberal Catholic
Church: Being a Study of Her Eucharistic Service and of the
Nicene Creed. London: Theosophical Publishing House, 1927.

K. PENTECOSTAL AND HOLINESS CHURCHES

1. General Studies

BITTLINGER, Arnold. "The Charismatic Worship Service in the
New Testament and Today." Studia Liturgica, 9 (1973):
215-229.

BLOCH-HOELL, Nils. Pinsebevegelsen: en undersøkelse av pinse-
befegelsens tilblivelse, utvikling og saerpreg med saerlig hen-
blikk på bevegelsens utforming i Norge. Oslo: Universitetsforlaget, 1956; The Pentecostal Movement: Its Origin, Development, and Distinctive Character. Oslo: Universitetsforlaget;

London: Allen & Unwin; New York: Humanities Press,
1964.

EPINAY, Christian Lalive d'. Haven of the Masses: A Study of
the Pentecostal Movement in Chile. Translated from the
French ms. by Marjorie Sandle. London: Lutterworth Press,
1969.

GEE, Donald. "How to Lead a Meeting: The Breaking of Bread
Service." Study Hour, 5, 2 (February 15, 1946): 27-29.

HOLLENWEGER, Walter J. Enthusiastisches Christentum: Die
Pfingstbewegung in Geschichte und Gegenwart. Wuppertal:
Theologischer Verlag; Zurich: Zwingli Verlag, 1969; The
Pentecostals: The Charismatic Movement in the Churches.
Translated by R. A. Wilson. London: SCM Press; Minneap-
olis, MN: Augsburg, 1972.

_____. "Gottesdienst: Tote Tradition oder Ort des Lebens?"
In Notstand der Kirche: Gemeinde zwischen Tradition und
Auftrag, pp. 67-94. Herausgegeben von H. J. Girock.
Gütersloh: Gütersloher Verlagshaus, 1969.

_____. "Liturgies. Pentecostal." A Dictionary of Liturgy and
Worship, p. 241.

_____. "Pentecostal Worship." A Dictionary of Liturgy and
Worship, pp. 311-312.

_____. Die Pfingstkirchen: Selbstdarstellungen, Dokumente,
Kommentar. Die Kirchen der Welt, 7. Stuttgart: Evange-
lishes Verlagswerk, 1971.

_____. "The Social and Ecumenical Significance of Pentecostal
Liturgy." Studia Liturgica, 8 (1972): 207-215.

McCREADY, William. "The Pentecostals: A Social Analysis." In
Liturgy: Self-Expression of the Church, pp. 112-116. Edited
by Herman Schmidt. Concilium, 72. New York: Herder &
Herder, 1972.

McDONNELL, Kiliam. "Books, Liturgical. Pentecostal." A Dictionary of Liturgy and Worship, pp. 90-92.

NICHOL, John Thomas. Pentecostalism. New York: Harper &
Row, 1966.

2. Apostolic Church (Great Britain)

Apostolic Church (Great Britain). The Minister's Manual. Bradford, Eng.: Puritan Press, n.d.

3. Assemblies of God

a. Texts

PEARLMAN, Myer, ed. The Minister's Service Book. Springfield, MO: Gospel Publishing House, 1942?

PICKTHORN, W. E., ed. Minsiter's Manual. 3 vols. Springfield, MO: Gospel Publishing House, 1965.

b. Studies

MASSERANO, Frank C. "A Study of Worship Forms in the Assemblies of God Denomination." Th.M. thesis, Princeton Theological Seminary, 1966.

ZIMMERMAN, Thomas F. "Assemblies of God Churches' Worship." A Dictionary of Liturgy and Worship, pp. 42-43.

4. Assembly of the Associated Churches of Christ (Holiness)

ASSEMBLY OF THE ASSOCIATED CHURCHES OF CHRIST (HOLINESS). Manual of the History, Doctrine, Government and Ritual of the Associated Churches of Christ (Holiness). San Pedro, CA: Assembly of the Associated Churches of Christ (Holiness), 1953.

5. Church of Christ (Holiness)

CHURCH OF CHRIST (HOLINESS) U.S.A. Manual of the History, Doctrine, Government, and Ritual of the Church of Christ (Holiness) U.S.A., 1926. Norfolk: Guide Publishing Co., 1928.

6. Church of God in Christ

CHURCH OF GOD IN CHRIST. Manual of the Church of God in Christ. 4th ed. Memphis, TN: O. T. Jones, J. E. Bryant, 1947.

_____. _____. 7th ed. Memphis, TN: The Church of God in Christ, 1957.

7. Pentecostal Holiness Church

PENTECOSTAL HOLINESS CHURCH. Discipline of the Pentecostal Holiness Church. Franklin Springs, GA: Board of Publication, Pentecostal Holiness Church, 1902-1965.

_____. The Pentecostal Holiness Church Manual. Franklin
    Springs, GA: [Pentecostal Holiness Church], 1969- .

8. United Pentecostal Church

UNITED PENTECOSTAL CHURCH. Manual, United Pentecostal
    Church. St. Louis, MO: Pentecostal Publishing House, 1964.

L. THE PLYMOUTH BRETHREN

BRUCE, F. F. "Books, Liturgical. Plymouth Brethren." A Dic-
    tionary of Liturgy and Worship, p. 92.

    _____. "Liturgies. Plymouth Brethren." A Dictionary of Litur-
    gy and Worship, pp. 241-242.

    _____. "Plymouth Brethren Worship." A Dictionary of Liturgy
    and Worship, pp. 313-314.

COAD, F. Roy. A History of the Brethren Movement: Its Origins,
    Its Worldwide Development, and Its Significance for the Present
    Day. Exeter, Eng.: Paternoster Press; Grand Rapids, MI:
    Eerdmans, 1968.

DARBY, J. N. "On Worship." In his Collected Writings of J. N.
    Darby, vol. 7: Doctrinal No. 2, pp. 87-126. Edited by
    William Kelly. Oak Park, IL: Bible Truth Publishers, n.d.

NEATBY, William Blair. A History of the Plymouth Brethren. Lon-
    don: Hodder & Stoughton, 1901.

ROWDEN, Harold H. The Origins of the Brethren, 1825-1850.
    London: Pickering & Inglis, 1967.

WALLS, R. C. "A Visit to the Brethren: A Lesson in Liturgy."
    Theology, 60 (1957): 265-266.

WILSON, Bryan R., ed. Patterns of Sectarianism: Organisation
    and Ideology in Social and Religious Movements. London:
    Heinemann Educational Books, 1967.

M. THE SALVATION ARMY

Salvation Army. General Orders for Conducting Salvation Army
    Ceremonies. London: Salvationist Publishing and Supplies,
    1966.

_____. The Salvation Army Handbook of Doctrine. 4th ed.
London: International Headquarters of the Salvaiton Army,
1935; reprinted 1965.

N. THE SEVENTH DAY ADVENTIST CHURCH

BEACH, B. B. "Books, Liturgical. Seventh-day Adventist." A
Dictionary of Liturgy and Worship, pp. 94-95.

_____. "Liturgies. Seventh-day Adventist (Communion Serv-
ice)." A Dictionary of Liturgy and Worship, pp. 244-245.

_____. "Seventh-day Adventist Worship." A Dictionary of Lit-
urgy and Worship, pp. 345-346.

PEASE, Norval F. And Worship Him. Nashville, TN: Southern
Pub. Association, 1967.

XXV. UNITED CHURCHES AND THE
"YOUNG CHURCHES"

A. THE CHURCH OF SOUTH INDIA

1. Texts (arranged chronologically)

CHURCH OF SOUTH INDIA. The Service of the Lord's Supper or
the Holy Eucharist. Bombay: Oxford University Press, 1950.

_____. _____. 2d ed. Bombay: Indian Branch, Oxford
University Press, 1952.

_____. _____. Revised ed. Bombay: Indian Branch, Ox-
ford University Press, 1954.

_____. An Order for the Lord's Supper or the Holy Eucharist.
3d ed. London: Oxford University Press, 1962.

_____. The Liturgy of the Church of South India, with Notes.
Bangalore: Christian Literature Society Press, 1955; reprinted
1958.

_____. An Order for Holy Baptism [1954]. Madras: Published
for the Church of South India by the Oxford University Press,
1955.

_____. _____. Revised ed. Madras: Oxford University Press, 1960.

_____. Order of Service for Such as would Enter into or Renew their Covenant with God for Use on the First Sunday of the Year or Other Occasions. London: Oxford University Press, 1956.

_____. An Order for Morning and Evening Prayer and a Service of Worship with an Outline for Public Worship. London: Published for the Church of South India by the Oxford University Press, 1958.

_____. The Ordinal. Madras: Published for the Church of South India by the Oxford Unviersity Press, 1958.

_____. _____. 2d [1962] ed. London, New York: Published for the Church of South India by the Oxford University Press, 1964.

_____. Daily Bible Readings. Revised [1959] ed. Madras: Published for the Church of South India by the Oxford University Press, 1960.

_____. The Burial Service. Madras: Published for the Church of South India by the Oxford University Press, 1960.

_____. Commemorable Names: Notes for an Indian Christian Calendar. Madras: Christian Literature Society, 1960.

_____. The Marriage Service. Madras: Published for the Church of South India by the Oxford University Press, 1960.

_____. _____. 2d [1962] ed. Madras: Published for the Church of South India by the Oxford University Press, 1963.

_____. Order of Service for the Reception of Baptized Persons into the Full Fellowship of the Church, commonly called Confirmation. Revised ed. London: Published for the Church of South India by the Oxford University Press, 1960.

_____. The Propers: Bible Readings, Collects and Prefaces Proper for Sundays and Special Days, Seasons and Occasions. London: Published for the Church of South India by the Oxford University Press, 1962.

_____. The Book of Common Worship [1962]. London, New York: Oxford University Press, 1963 [1964].

_____. Book of Common Worship Supplement. London: Oxford University Press, 1967.

_____. The Lord's Supper, or the Holy Eucharist. Revised
version. Madras: Published for the Church of South India
by the Christian Literature Society, 1972.

2. Studies

BROWN, L. W. "The Making of a Liturgy." Scottish Journal of
Theology, 4 (1951): 55-63.

CHANDRAN, J. R., and LASH, William Q., eds. Worship in India.
Bangalore: Indian Continuation Committee on Worship, East
Asia Theological Commission, World Council of Churches, 1961.

Church of South India. Ways of Worship: How the Holy Communion
is Celebrated by Different Branches of the Church in South India. Madras: Christian Literature Society, 1950.

GARRETT, T. S. Christian Worship: An Introductory Outline.
2d ed. New York: Oxford University Press, 1963.

_____. The Liturgy of the Church of South India: An Intro-
duction to and Commentary on "The Service of the Lord's Supper." Madras: Oxford University Press, 1952.

_____. _____. 2d ed., commenting on the 1954 revision.
Madras: Oxford University Press, 1955.

_____. Worship in the Church of South India. New ed. ESW,
2. London: Lutterworth Press, 1965.

GIBBARD, S. Mark. "Liturgical Life in the Church of South India:
The Book of Common Worship in Practice." Studia Liturgica,
3 (1964): 193-209.

MacPHAIL, James Russell. Notes on the Daily Bible Readings of
the Church of South India. Madras: Indian Branch, Oxford
University Press, 1961.

_____. "The Order for the Lord's Supper of the Church of
South India." Expository Times, 69 (1958): 315-318.

RATCLIFF, E. C. "The Ordinal of the Church of South India."
Theology, 63 (1960): 7-15; reprinted in his Liturgical Studies
of E. C. Ratcliff, pp. 173-182. Edited by A. H. Couratin and
D. J. Tripp. London: SPCK, 1976.

B. UNION CHURCHES IN NORTH INDIA,
    PAKISTAN, AND CEYLON

NEGOTIATING COMMITTEE FOR CHURCH UNION IN CEYLON.
    Proposed Scheme of Church Union in Ceylon. 3d rev. ed.,
    amended. Madras: Published for the Negotiating Committee
    by the Christian Literature Society, 1964.

NEGOTIATING COMMITTEE FOR CHURCH UNION IN NORTH INDIA
    AND PAKISTAN. Plan of Church Union in North India and
    Pakistan. 3d rev. ed. Madras: Christian Literature Society,
    1957.

_____. Services Proposed for Use at the Inauguration of the
    Church of North India and the Church of Pakistan, and the
    Service for the Ordination of Presbyters in these United
    Churches. 2d rev. ed. Madras: Christian Literature Society,
    1960.

UNITED CHURCH OF NORTHERN INDIA. United Church Worship.
    Madras: Christian Literature Society, 1962.

BAYNE, Stephen F., Jr., ed. Ceylon, North India, Pakistan:
    A Study in Ecumenical Decision. London: SPCK, 1960.

C. L'EGLISE REFORMEE DE FRANCE

1. Texts

EGLISE REFORMEE DE FRANCE. Cinq projets de liturgies: mari-
    age, fête de la réformation, service d'offrande, culte commémor-
    atif, service liturgique de sainte cène. Paris: Editions Berger-
    Levrault, 1951.

_____. Liturgie du culte dominical. Paris: Editions Berger-
    Levrault, 1948.

_____. _____. Nouvelle éd., mise à jour. Paris: Editions
    Berger-Levrault, 1950.

_____. Liturgie. Paris: Editions Berger-Levrault, 1955.

_____. Liturgie de l'église réformée de France. Paris: Editions
    Berger-levrault, 1963.

_____. "Ordination of a Pastor" (Bi-lingual text). Studia Lit-
    urgica, 4, 4 (1965): II-b-1-21.

2. Studies

BENOIT, J. D. Initiation à la liturgie de l'église réformée de France. Paris: Editions Berger-Levrault, 1956.

BOURGUET, Pierre. Culte public: le culte, le baptême, la communion et le mariage dans l'Eglise réformée de France. Paris: S. C. E., 1965.

D. THE UNITED CHURCH OF CANADA

UNITED CHURCH OF CANADA. Book of Common Order. Toronto, Ont.: United Church Publishing House, 1932.

_____. _____. 2d rev. ed. Toronto, Ont.: United Church Publishing House, 1950.

_____. Service Book for the Use of Minsiters conducting Public Worship. Toronto, Ont.: Published for the United Church of Canada by the Ryerson Press, 1969.

_____. Service Book for the Use of the People. Toronto, Ont.: [United Church of Canada], 1969.

PLATO, William R. "The United Church of Canada and Eucharistic Worship." Bulletin of the Committee on Archives of the United Church of Canada, no. 22 (1973): 16-20.

E. THE UNITED CHURCH OF CHRIST
(Including the Evangelical and Reformed Church)

1. The Evangelical and Reformed Church

a. Texts

EVANGELICAL AND REFORMED CHURCH. General Synod. Book of Worship. Cleveland, OH: Central Publishing House, 1942.

_____. _____. St. Louis, MO: Eden Publishing House, 1947.

Evangelical Synod of North America. Evangelical Book of Worship. St. Louis, MO: Eden Publishing House, 1916.

b. Studies

BRENNER, Scott F. A Handbook on Worship: An Interpretation of the Book of Worship of the Evangelical and Reformed Church. Philadelphia, PA: Heidelberg Press, 1941.

_____. Ways of Worship. New York: Macmillan, 1944.

EVANGELICAL AND REFORMED CHURCH. "Report of the Committee on Liturgics." In Acts and Proceedings of the Eleventh Meeting of the General Synod of the Evangelical and Reformed Church held in Finney Chapel, Oberlin College, Oberlin, Ohio, July 1-5, 1959, pp. 383-426. n.p., 1959.

2. United Church of Christ

a. Texts

UNITED CHURCH OF CHRIST. The Lord's Day Service. Philadelphia, PA: United Church Press, 1965, 1964.

_____. Services of the Church. New York: United Church of Christ, 1969.

_____. Services of Word and Sacrament. Philadelphia, PA: United Church Press, 1966.

b. Studies

DAVIES, Horton. "Reshaping the Worship of the United Church of Christ." Worship, 41 (1967): 542-551.

GUNNEMANN, Louis H. "Liturgical Developments in the United Church of Christ." Worship, 50 (1976): 426-434.

O'DAY, Rey, and POWERS, Edward. Theatre of the Spirit: A Worship Handbook. New York: Pilgrim Press, 1980.

F. THE UNITED CHURCH OF CHRIST IN THE PHILIPPINES

UNITED CHURCH OF CHRIST IN THE PHILIPPINES. Book of Government and Book of Common Worship. Manila, n.d.

_____. The Book of Common Worship for Pulpit and Parish Use. Quezon City, 1962.

XXV. United Churches

453

G. THE YOUNG CHURCHES

(See also XXV. A. Church of South India, p. 447; B. Union
Churches in North India, etc., p. 450; IX.Q.8. Africa and the
Far East, p. 223; and XVII.J.4. Philippine Independent Church,
p. 402.)

1. General and Miscellaneous Studies

ABINENO, Johannes Ludwig Chrysostomus. Liturgische Vormen en
Patronen in de Evangelische Kerk op Timor: Liturgical Forms
and Patterns in the Evangelical Church in Timor. 's-Gravenhage, 1956.

AMALORPAVADASS, D. S. "Indigenization and the Liturgy of the
Church." International Review of Mission, 65 (1976): 164-181.

_____. Towards Indigenisation in the Liturgy: Theological Re-
flection, Policy, Programme, and Texts. Mission Theology for
Our Times, 6. Bangalore: National Biblical, Catechetical and
Liturgical Centre, 1972?

ENKLAAR, Ido Hendricus. De scheiding de sacramenten op het
zendingsveld. Amsterdam: Drukkerij Holland, 1947.

GABLER, Paul. "Die nichttheologischen Faktoren in ihrer Bedeutung für Wesen und Gestalt der Jungen Kirchen." Evangelische
Theologie, 16 (1956): 504-530.

HAAS, Harry. In Seinem Namen versammelt: Erlebnisberichte
lebendiger Liturgie. Graz: Styria; Göttingen: Vandenhoeck
& Ruprecht, 1972.

HOLSTEN, Walter. "Gottesdienst in den jungen Kirchen." Die
Religion in Geschichte und Gegenwart (3d ed.), 2:1783-1784.

IDOWU, E. Bolaji. "Indigenization." Dictionary of Liturgy and
Worship, pp. 198-203.

KRAEMER, Hendrik. From Missionfield to Independent Church:
Report on a Decisive Decade in the Growth of Indigenous
Churches in Indonesia. The Hague: Boekencentrum; London:
SCM Press, 1958.

VICEDOM, George. "Die Liturgie der jungen Kirchen." Evangelische Missionszeitung, n.s. 8 (1951): 129-141.

WALDENFELS, Hans, ed. Theologen der Dritten Welt: elf bio-
graphische Skizzen aus Afrika, Asien und Lateinamerika.
München: C. H. Beck, 1982.

ZIEGLER, Edward Krusen. A Book of Worship for Village Churches.
New York: Agricultural Missions Foundation, 1939.

_____. Country Altars: Worship in the Rural Church. New
York: Commission on Worship, Federal Council of the Churches
of Christ in America, 1942.

_____. Rural People at Worship. New York: Agricultural Mis-
sion Foundation, 1943.

2. African Churches

BURKI, Bruno. L'assemblée dominicale: Introduction à la liturgie
des églises protestantes d'Afrique. Immensee: Nouvelle revue
de science missionaire, 1976.

CHURCH OF NIGERIA. The Lord's Supper: With Two Additional
Orders of Morning Worship. Ibadan: Daystar Press, 1965.

EAST AFRICAN CHURCH UNION CONSULTATION. Liturgy and
Doctrine Committee. "A United Liturgy for East Africa."
Studia Liturgica, 6, 3 (1969): II-c-1-16.

_____. Dodoma Conference Report. (2d Church Union Confer-
ence, Dodoma, Tanzania, 1965.) English version. n.p., 1965.

GARRETT, T. S. "Products of Nigeria's Liturgy Committee."
Studia Liturgica, 5 (1966): 183-186.

POBEE, John S. "The Skenosis of Christian Worship in Africa."
Studia Liturgica, 14 (1980): 37-52.

SHORTER, Aylward. Prayer in the Religious Traditions of Africa.
Nairobi: Oxford University Press, 1975.

XXVI. INTER-CHURCH BODIES AND ECUMENICAL COMMUNITIES

A. THE CONSULTATION ON CHURCH UNION

CONSULTATION ON CHURCH UNION. An Order of Worship for the
Proclamation of the Word of God and the Celebration of the
Lord's Supper. Cincinnati, OH: Forward Movement Publica-
tions, 1968.

_____. Guidelines for Interim Eucharist Fellowship. Princeton,
NJ: Consultation on Church Union, 1973.

_____. An Order for the Celebration of Holy Baptism. Cincinnati, OH: Forward Movement Publications, 1973.

_____. Word, Bread, Cup. Cincinnati, OH: Forward Movement Publications, 1978.

_____. An Order for and Affirmation of the Baptismal Covenant (also called Confirmation). Princeton, NJ: Consultation on Church Union, 1980.

_____. An Order of Thanksgiving for the Birth or Adoption of a Child. [Princeton, NJ:] Consultation on Church Union, 1980.

BUCHANAN, Colin O. "An Order of Worship: The American C.O.C.U. Eucharistic Rite." Studia Liturgica, 8 (1971): 61-64.

B. THE WORLD COUNCIL OF CHURCHES

1. Liturgical Texts

WORLD'S STUDENT CHRISTIAN FEDERATION. Venite Adoremus I. 2d ed. Geneva: World's Student Christian Federation, 1951.

_____. Venite Adoremus II: Prayers and Services for Students. Geneva: World's Student Christian Federation, 1967?

WORLD COUNCIL OF CHURCHES. Let's Worship. Geneva: World Council of Churches, 1975; 2d ed., 1977. [Worship book for 5th Assembly, Nairobi, Kenya, 1975]

_____. Cantate Domino: An Ecumenical Hymnbook. Oxford: Oxford University Press, 1980.

2. Statements

WORLD COUNCIL OF CHURCHES. Commission on Faith and Order. One Lord, One Baptism. SMW, 17. London: SCM Press; Minneapolis: Augsburg, 1960.

WORLD CONFERENCE ON FAITH AND ORDER, 4th, Montreal, 1963. Report of the Theological Commission on Worship. Geneva: World Council of Churches, Commission on Faith and Order, 1963; also published in Faith and Order Findings: The Final Report of the Theological Commissions to the Fourth World Conference on Faith and Order, Montreal, 1963. London: SCM Press, 1963.

WORLD COUNCIL OF CHURCHES. Commission on Faith and Order.
One Baptism, One Eucharist, and a Mutually Recognized Ministry. Geneva: World Council of Churches, 1975.

"Louisville Consultation on Baptism." FOP, 97. Review and Expositor, 77, 1 (Winter 1980).

WORLD COUNCIL OF CHURCHES. Baptism, Eucharist and Ministry.
FOP, 111. Geneva: World Council of Churches, 1982. [The
Lima text]

3. Studies

KINNAMON, Michael. Why It Matters: A Popular Introduction to
the Baptism, Eucharist and Ministry Text. Risk Book, 25.
Geneva: World Council of Churches, 1985.

LAZARETH, William H. Growing Together in Baptism, Eucharist
and Ministry: A Study Guide. FOP, 114. Geneva: World
Council of Churches, 1982.

THURIAN, Max, ed. Ecumenical Perspectives on Baptism, Eucharist
and Ministry. FOP, 116. Geneva: World Council of Churches,
1983.

VISCHER, Lukas. Ye are Baptised: A Study of Baptism and Confirmation Liturgies as the Initiation to the Ministry of the Laity.
2d ed. Geneva: Department on the Laity, World Council of
Churches, 1964.

C. COMMUNAUTE DE TAIZE

1. Texts

Communauté de Taizé. Eucharistie à Taizé. Taizé: Presses de
Taizé, 1963; The Eucharistic Liturgy of Taizé. With an intro-
ductory essay by Max Thurian. Translated by John Arnold.
London: Faith Press, 1962.

_____. Eucharistie à Taizé. Nouvelle éd. Taizé: Presses de
Taizé, 1971.

_____. Liturgies pascales à Taizé. Taizé: Presses de Taizé,
1971.

_____. Office de Taizé. 2d éd. revue. Taizé: Presses de
Taizé, 1963; The Taizé Office. London: Faith Press, 1966.

_____. La Louange des jours. 6. éd. entièrement rev. Taizé: Presses de Taizé, 1977, c1971; Praise in All Our Days: Common Prayer at Taizé. Leighton Buzzard, Eng.: Faith Press, 1975; Praise God: Common Prayer at Taizé. New York: Oxford University Press, 1977.

_____. Respons de l'office de Taizé. Tournai: Desclée, 1968.

2. Studies

BRUNNER, Peter. "Aufbruch einer neuen Dimension in der evangelischen Abendmahlslehre? Geleitwort zu Max Thurians Buch Eucharistie." In his Pro Ecclesia: Gesammelte Aufsätze zur dogmatischen Theologie, Bd. 2, pp. 325-334. Berlin: Lutherisches Verlag, 1962-1966.

DAVIES, Horton. "Worship at Taizé: A Protestant Monastic Servant Community." Worship, 49 (1975): 23-34.

THURIAN, Max. "L'Anamnèse du Christ." In L'Evangile, hier et aujourd'hui: mélanges offerts au Franz J. Leenhardt, pp. 263-276. Geneva: Editions Labor et Fides, 1968.

_____. L'Eucharistie: mémorial du Seigneur. Neuchâtel: Delachaux & Niestlé, 1959; The Eucharistic Memorial. Translated by J. G. Davies. ESW, 7-8. Richmond, VA: John Knox Press, 1961.

_____. L'Eucharistie: mémorial du Seigneur, sacrifice d'action de grâce et d'intercession. 2. éd. Neuchâtel: Delachaux & Niestlé, 1963.

_____. The Mystery of the Eucharist. Grand Rapids, MI: Eerdmans, 1984.

_____. Le Pain unique: simple réflexion sur l'eucharistie et le ministère. Taizé: Presses de Taizé, 1967; The One Bread. Translated by Theodore DuBois. New York: Sheed & Ward, 1969.

PART THREE:

WORD AND SACRAMENTS--THEOLOGY, LITURGY,
AND SPIRITUALITY

XXVII. GENERAL SACRAMENTAL THEOLOGY

A. GENERAL STUDIES

BAIL, Paul. Die Haupttypen der neuen Sakramentslehre: die Sakramente als Sinnegung in der Kreaturlichen Welf. Leipzig: Klein, 1926.

BOUYER, Louis. Parole, église et sacrements dans le protestantisme et le catholicisme. Paris[?]: Desclée de Brouwer, 1960; The Word, Church and Sacraments in Protestantism and Catholicism. Translated by A. V. Littledale. New York: Desclée, 1961.

DAVIES, John G. The Spirit, the Church, and the Sacraments. London: Faith Press, 1954.

FINKENZELLER, Josef. Die Lehre von den Sakramenten in allgemeinen. 2 vols. HD, 4/1a & b. Freiburg: Herder, 1980-1981.
1. Von der Schrift bis zur Scholastik. HD, 4/1a. 1980.
2. Von der Reformation bis zu Gegenwart. HD, 4/1b. 1981.

GENNEP, Arnold van. Les Rites de passage: étude systematique des rites de la porte et du seuil, de l'hospitalité, de l'adoption, de la grossesse et de l'accouchement, de la naissance, de l'enfance, de la puberté, de l'initiation, de l'ordination, du couronnement des fiançailles et du mariage, des funerailles, des saisons, etc. Paris: Nourry, 1909; reprint eds., New York: Johnson Reprint, 1969; Paris: Picard, 1981; The Rites of Passage. Translated by Monika K. Vizedom and Gabrielle L. Caffe. Introduction by Solon T. Kimball. London: Routledge & Kegan Paul; Chicago: University of Chicago Press, 1960.

HODGSON, Leonard. Church and Sacraments in Divided Christendom. London: SPCK, 1959.

HOTZ, Robert. Sakramente, im Wechselspiel zwischen Ost und
West. OT, 2. Zurich: Benziger; Gütersloh: Mohn, 1979.

KIRCHGASSNER, Alfons. Heilige Zeichen der Kirche. Der Christ
in der Welt, eine Enzyklopaedie, 7. Reihe, 9. Bd. Aschaffenburg: Pattloch, 1961.

Oecumenica, 1970: Gospel and Sacrament. Edited in the Institute
for Ecumenical Research in Strasbourg by Günther Gassmann
and Vilmos Vajta. Minneapolis, MN: Augsburg, 1970.

PALMER, Paul F., ed. Sacraments and Worship: Liturgy and Doc-
trinal Development of Baptism, Confirmation, and the Eucharist.
SCT, 1. London: Longmans, Green, 1957; Westminster, MD:
Newman Press, 1963.

PAUL, Robert S. The Atonement and the Sacraments. London:
Hodder & Stoughton, 1961; New York: Abingdon Press, 1970.

RUNYON, Theodore. "The World as the Original Sacrament." Worship, 54 (1980): 495-511.

The Sacraments: An Ecumenical Dilemma. Concilium, 24. New
York: Paulist Press, 1967, c1966.

VILLETTE, Louis. Foi et sacrement. 2 vols. TICP, 5 & 6. Paris:
Bloud & Gay, 1959-1964.
1. Du Nouveau testament à saint Augustin. TICP, 5. 1959.
2. De saint Thomas à Karl Barth. TICP, 6. 1964.

WAND, J. W. C. The Development of Sacramentalism. London:
Methuen, 1928.

WEGENAER, Polykarpus. Heilsgegenwart: Das Heilswerk Christi
und die Virtus Divina in den Sakramenten unter besonderer
Berücksichtigung von Eucharistie und Taufe. LQF, 33. Münster: Aschendorff, 1958.

B. EARLY CHURCH

GHELLINCK, Joseph de. Pour l'histoire du mot Sacramentum. SSL,
3. Paris: E. Champion, 1924.

MOULE, C. F. D. "The Judgment Theme in the Sacraments." In
The Background of the New Testament and Its Eschatology, pp.
464-481. Edited by W. D. Davies and D. Daubé. Cambridge:
Cambridge University Press, 1956.

PROBST, Ferdinand. Sakramente und Sakramentalien in den drei
ersten christlichen Jahrhunderten. Tübingen: Laupp, 1872.

SMULDERS, P. "A Preliminary Remark on Patristic Sacramental
Doctrine: The Unity of the Sacramental Idea." Bijdragen, 15
(1954): 25-30.

STENDAHL, Krister. "The New Testament Background for the
Doctrine of the Sacraments." In Gospel and Sacrament, pp.
41-60. Edited by Günther Gassmann and Vilmos Vajta. Minneapolis, MN: Augsburg, 1970.

WORDEN, T., ed. Sacraments in Scripture: A Symposium. London: Chapman, 1966.

C. EASTERN CHURCHES

CABASILAS, Nicholas. The Life in Christ. Translated by Carmino
J. de Catanzaro. Introduction by Boris Bobrinskoy. Crestwood, NY: St. Vladimir's Seminary Press, 1974; reprinted
1982.

LAMPERT, Evgueny. The Divine Realm: Towards a Theology of
the Sacraments. London: Faber & Faber, 1944.

SCHMEMANN, Alexander. "Sacrament and Symbol." In his For
the Life of the World: Sacraments and Orthodoxy, pp. 135-151.
Crestwood, NY: St. Vladimir's Seminary Press, 1973.

SHERRARD, Philip. "The Sacrament." In The Orthodox Ethos:
Essays in honour of the Centenary of the Greek Orthodox
Archdiocese of North and South America, pp. 133-139. Edited
by A. J. Philippou. Oxford: Holywell Press, 1964.

SPACIL, Bohumil. Doctrina theologiae orientis separati de sacramentis in genere. OCA, 113. Rome: Pontificium Institutum
Orientalium Studiorum, 1937.

VRIES, Wilhelm de. Sakramententheologie bei den Nestorianern.
OCA, 133. Rome: Pontificium Institutum Orientalium Studiorum,
1947.

_____. "Théologie des sacraments chez les Syriens monophysites."
Orient Syrien, 8 (1963): 261-288.

_____. "La théologie sacramentaire chez les Syriens orientaux."
Orient Syrien, 4 (1959): 471-494.

D. LATIN CHURCHES

BACIOCCHI, Joseph de. La vie sacramentaire de l'église. FV. Paris: Cerf, 1958.

BAUSCH, William J. A New Look at the Sacraments. Notre Dame, IN: Fides/Claretian, 1977.

_____. _____. Rev. ed. Mystic, CT: Twenty-Third Publications, 1983.

BRETT, Lawrence F. X. Redeemed Creation: Sacramentals Today. MS, 8. Wilmington, DE: Michael Glazier, 1984.

CONGAR, Yves. "The Notion of 'Major' or 'Principal' Sacraments." In The Sacraments in General: A New Perspective, pp. 21-32. Edited by Edward Schillebeeckx and Boniface Willems. Concilium, 31. New York: Paulist Press, 1968.

COOKE, Bernard J. Christian Sacraments and Christian Personality. New York: Holt, Rinehart & Winston, 1965.

_____. Sacraments and Sacramentality. Mystic, CT: Twenty-Third Publications, 1983.

CRICHTON, J. D. Christian Celebration: The Sacraments. 2d ed. London: Chapman, 1980.

DANIELOU, Jean. "Sacrements et histoire du salut." In Parole de Dieu et liturgie, pp. 51-69. LO, 25. Paris: Cerf, 1958.

DUFFY, Regis A. Real Presence: Worship, Sacraments, & Commitment. San Francisco, CA: Harper & Row, 1982.

GALLAGHER, J. F. Significando Causant: A Study in Sacramental Efficiency. SF, 40. Fribourg: University Press, 1965.

GANOCZY, Alexandre. Einführung in die katholische Sakramentenlehre. Die Theologie: Einführungen in Gegenstand, Methoden und Ergebnisse ihrer Disziplinen und Nachbarwissenschaften. Darmstadt: Wissenschaftliche Buchgesellschaft, 1979; An Introduction to Catholic Sacramental Theology. Translated by William Thomas with the assistance of Anthony Sherman. New York: Paulist Press, 1984.

GIHR, Nikolaus. Die heiligen Sakramente der katholischen Kirche. 2 vols. TB, 2. Ser. Freiburg: Herder, 1897-1899.

GUARDINI, Romano. Von heiligen Zeichen. 2 vols. 2. Aufl.

Rothenfels: Deutsches Quickbornhaus, 1922-1923; Sacred Signs.
Translated by G. C. H. Pollen. London: Sheed & Ward, 1930.

_____. Von heiligen Zeichen. Basel: Hess, 1944.

GUZIE, Tad. The Book of Sacramental Basics. New York: Paulist
Press, 1981.

HARING, Bernard. Gabe und Auftrag der Sakramente. Salzburg:
Müller, 1962; The New Covenant. Translated by R. A. Wilson.
London: Burns & Oates, 1965.

_____. The Sacraments in a Secular Age. Slough, Eng.: St.
Paul Publications, 1976.

HELLWIG, Monika. The Meaning of the Sacraments. Foreword by
Robert W. Hovda. Dayton, OH: Pflaum/Standard, 1972.

HILL, Brennan. Rediscovering the Sacraments: Approaches to the
Sacred. New York: Sadlier, 1982.

LEEMING, Bernard. Principles of Sacramental Theology. New ed.
London: Longmans; Westminster, MD: Newman Press, 1960.

MARTIMORT, A. G. Les signes de la nouvelle alliance. Nouvelle
éd. Paris: Ligel, 1966; The Signs of the New Covenant.
Collegeville, MN: Liturgical Press, 1967.

MARTOS, Joseph. The Catholic Sacraments. MS, 1. Wilmington,
DE: Michael Glazier, 1983.

O'CONNELL, Matthew J. "New Perspectives in Sacramental Theology." Worship, 39 (1965): 195-206.

PIOLANTI, Antonio. De sacramentis. Ed. 3. CTR, 6. Torino:
Marietti, 1951.

POWER, David, and MALDONADO, Luis, eds. Liturgy and Human
Passage. Concilium, 112. New York: Seabury Press, 1979.

RAHNER, Karl. Kirche und Sakramente. QD, 10. Freiburg:
Herder, 1960; The Church and the Sacraments. Translated by
W. J. O'Hara. Freiburg: Herder; New York: Herder &
Herder, 1963; reprint ed., London: Burns & Oates; Westmin-
ster, MD: Christian Classics, 1974.

RATZINGER, Joseph. Die sakramentale Begründung christlicher
Existenz. Freising: Kyrios, 1966.

SASSE, Johann Baptist. Institutiones theologicae de sacramentis
ecclesiae. 2 vols. Freiburg: Herder, 1897-1898.

SCHANZ, John. Introduction to the Sacraments. New York:
    Pueblo, 1983.

_____. The Sacraments of Life and Worship. Milwaukee, WI:
    Bruce, 1966.

SCHILLEBEECKX, Edward. Christus, Sacrament van de Godsont-
    moeting. Bilthoven: Nelissen, 1960; Christ the Sacrament of
    the Encounter with God. New York: Sheed & Ward, 1963.

_____. De sacramentele Heilseconomie: theologische bezinning
    op S. Thomas' sacramentenleer in het licht van de traditie en
    van de hedendaagse sacramentsproblematiek. Antwerp: Nelis-
    sen, 1952.

_____, and WILLEMS, Boniface, eds. The Sacraments in General:
    A New Perspective. Concilium, 31. New York: Paulist Press,
    1968.

SEGUNDO, Juan Luis. Los sacramentos hoy. Teologia abierta
    para el laico adulto, vol. 4. Buenos Aires: Ediciones Carlos
    Lohle, 1971; The Sacraments Today. A Theology for Artisans
    of a New Humanity, vol. 4. Maryknoll, NY: Orbis Books,
    1974.

SULLIVAN, C. Stephen, ed. Readings in Sacramental Theology.
    Englewood Cliffs, NJ: Prentice-Hall, 1964.

TAYLOR, Michael J., ed. The Sacraments: Readings in Contempo-
    rary Sacramental Theology. Staten Island, NY: Alba House,
    1981.

TILLARD, J. M. R. "La triple dimension du signe sacramentel (a
    propos de Sum. Theol. III, 60, 3)." Nouvelle revue théologique,
    83 (1961): 225-254.

VAILLANCOURT, Raymond. Vers un renouveau de la théologie
    sacramentaire. Montreal, PQ: Fides, 1977; Toward a Renewal
    of Sacramental Theology. Translated by Matthew J. O'Connell.
    Collegeville, MN: Liturgical Press, 1979.

VILLIEN, Antoine. Les sacrements: histoire et liturgie. Paris:
    Gabalda, 1931; The History and Liturgy of the Sacraments.
    Translated by H. W. Edwards. London: Burns, Oates & Wash-
    bourne; New York: Benziger, 1932.

WINKLHOFER, Alois. Kirche in den Sakramenten. Frankfurt:
    Knecht, 1968.

WORGUL, George S. From Magic to Metaphor: A Validation of
    Christian Sacraments. New York: Paulist Press, 1980.

E. LUTHERAN AND REFORMED CHURCHES

BAILLIE, Donald M. The Theology of the Sacraments and Other
Papers. London: Faber & Faber; New York: Scribner, 1957.

BECKMANN, Joachim. Vom Sakrament bei Calvin: Die Sakramentslehre Calvins in ihren Beziehungen zu Augustin. Tübingen:
Mohr, 1926.

BERKOUWER, G. C. De sacramenten. His Dogmatische Studien.
Kampen: Kok, 1954; The Sacraments. His Studies in Dog-
matics. Translated by Hugo Bekker. Grand Rapids, MI:
Eerdmans, 1969.

BRING, Ragnar. "On the Lutheran Concept of the Sacrament."
in World Lutheranism of Today: A Tribute to Anders Nygren,
pp. 36-55. Stockholm: Svenska Kyrkans Diakonistyrelses
Bokförlag; Rock Island, IL: Augustana Book Concern, 1950.

BROMILEY, G. W. Sacramental Teaching and Practice in the Reformation Churches. Grand Rapids, MI: Eerdmans, 1957.

JENSON, Robert W. Visible Words: The Interpretation and Practice of Christian Sacraments. Philadelphia, PA: Fortress
Press, 1978.

KERR, Hugh T. The Christian Sacraments: A Source Book for
Ministers. Philadelphia, PA: Westminster Press, 1944.

LEENHARDT, Franz J. Parole visible: pour une évaluation nouvelle du sacrement. CTAP, 63. Neuchâtel: Delachaux &
Niestlé, 1971.

LEEUW, Gerardus van der. Sacramentstheologie. Nijkerk: G. F.
Callenbach, 1949.

METZKE, Erwin. Sakrament und Methaphysik: ein Lutherstudie
über das Verhältnis des christlichen Denkens zum Leiblich-
Materiellen. SLW, 9. Stuttgart: Kreuz-Verlag, 1948.

PELIKAN, Jaroslav. "The Theology of the Means of Grace." In
Accents in Luther's Theology, pp. 124-147. Edited by Heino
O. Kadai. St. Louis, MO: Concordia, 1967.

PRENTER, Regin. "Luther on Word and Sacrament." In More
About Luther, pp. 65-124. Decorah, IA: Luther College
Press, 1958.

ROTH, Erich. Sakrament nach Luther. TBT, 3. Berlin: Topel-
mann, 1952.

SCHWAB, Wolfgang. Entwicklung und Gestalt der Sakramententheologie bei Martin Luther. EHT, 79. Frankfurt am Main:
Lang, 1977.

STOCK, Ursula. Die Bedeutung der Sakramente in Luthers Sermonen von 1519. SHCT, 27. Leiden: Brill, 1982.

WOTHERSPOON, H. J. Religious Values in the Sacraments. Edinburgh: T. & T. Clark, 1928.

F. ANGLICAN AND METHODIST CHURCHES

BECKWITH, Roger T. Priesthood and Sacraments: A Study in the
Anglican-Methodist Report. LatM, 1. Appleford, Eng.:
Marcham Manor Press, 1964.

BUCHANAN, Colin, ed. Evangelical Essays on Church and Sacraments. London: SPCK, 1972.

COLET, John. A Treatise on the Sacraments of the Church.
Edited by J. H. Lupton. London: Bell & Daldy, 1867; reprint
ed., Ridgewood, NJ: Gregg Press, 1966.

GOODLOE, Robert W. The Sacraments in Methodism. Nashville,
TN: Methodist Publishing House, 1953.

MOZLEY, J. K. The Gospel Sacraments. London: Hodder &
Stoughton, 1933.

QUICK, Oliver Chase. The Christian Sacraments. New ed. London: Nisbet, 1932; reprinted 1955.

SMITH, C. Ryder. The Sacramental Society. London: Epworth
Press, 1927.

TAIT, Arthur J. The Nature and Functions of the Sacraments.
London, New York: Longmans, Green, 1917.

WEIL, Louis. Sacraments and Liturgy: The Outward Signs. Oxford: Basil Blackwell, 1983.

G. FREE CHURCHES

CLARK, Neville. An Approach to the Theology of the Sacraments.
SBT, 17. London: SCM Press, 1956. [Baptist]

FORSYTH, P. T. Lectures on the Church and the Sacraments.

London, New York: Longmans, Green, 1917; reprinted as <u>The</u>
<u>Church and the Sacraments</u>. London: Independent Press,
1953; reprinted 1964. [Congregational]

GRAUER, Gerhard, and JARMAN, W. J. "The Sacraments (including the Problem of Authority)." <u>Mid-Stream</u>, 3, 3 (1964):
32-52. [Disciples]

WILBURN, Ralph G. "A Theology of the Sacraments." <u>Encounter</u>,
24, 3 (1963): 280-302. [Disciples]

XXVIII. THE EUCHARIST

A. GENERAL STUDIES

BAMMEL, Fritz. <u>Das heilige Mahl im Glauben des Völker: eine</u>
<u>religionsphänomenologische Untersuchung</u>. Gütersloh: Bertels-
mann, 1950.

CLEMENTS, R. E., et al. <u>Eucharistic Theology Then and Now</u>.
Theological Collections, 9. London: SPCK, 1968.

CORBLET, Jules. <u>Histoire dogmatique, liturgique et archéologique</u>
<u>du sacrement de l'Eucharistie</u>. 2 vols. Paris: Société générale
de librairie catholique, 1885-1886.

DUSSAUT, Louis. <u>L'Eucharistie, pâques de toute la vie: diachronie</u>
<u>symbolique de l'Eucharistie</u>. LD, 74. Paris: Cerf, 1972.

HEDLEY, John Cuthbert. <u>The Holy Eucharist</u>. Westminster Library. London: Longmans, Green, 1907.

HURLEY, Michael, ed. <u>Church and Eucharist</u>. Dublin: Gill, 1966.

JONG, J. P. de. <u>De eucharistie, symbolische werkelijkheid</u>. Hilversum: Gooi & Sticht, 1966; enlarged French ed., <u>L'Eucharis-</u>
<u>tie: réalité symbolique, sacrement de l'unité</u>. Traduction du
néerlandais et de l'allemand par Antoine Freund. Cogitatio
fidei, 65. Paris: Cerf, 1972.

LASH, Nicholas. <u>His Presence in the World: A Study of Eucharistic</u>
<u>Worship and Theology</u>. London: Sheed & Ward; Dayton, OH:
Pflaum Press, 1968.

MARTIN, Hugh, ed. <u>The Holy Communion: A Symposium</u>. London:
SCM Press, 1947.

SARTORY, Thomas Aquinas, ed. Die Eucharistie im Verständnis der Konfessionen. Recklingshausen: Paulus, 1961.

STONE, Darwell. History of the Doctrine of the Holy Eucharist. 2 vols. New York: Longmans, 1909.

SUSS, Théobald. La communion au corps du Christ: études sur les problèmes de la sainte cène et les paroles d'institution. Bibliothèque théologique. Neuchâtel: Delachaux & Niestlé, 1968.

B. ECUMENICAL STUDIES

AFANASSIEV, Nikolai. "L'eucharistie, principal lien entre les catholiques et les orthodoxes." Irénikon, 38 (1965): 337-339.

BAILLIE, Donald, and MARSH, John, eds. Intercommunion: The Report of the Continuation Committee of the World Conference on Faith and Order, together with a Selection from the Material presented to the Commission. London: SCM Press; New York: Harper, 1952.

BENCKERT, Heinrich. Die Stofflichkeit der Abendmahlsgabe: zum Gespräch über die Arnoldshainer Abendmahlsthesen. UC, 2. Witten: Luther Verlag, 1961.

CHURCH OF ENGLAND. Archbishop's Commission on Intercommunion. Intercommunion Today. London: Church Information Office, 1968.

CLARK, Neville, and JASPER, R. C. D., eds. Initiation and Eucharist: Essays on their Structure by the Joint Liturgical Group. London: SPCK, 1972.

A Critique of Eucharistic Agreement. London: SPCK, 1975. [Critique of XXVIII, p. 468, Modern Eucharistic Agreement, below]

EMPIE, P. C., and MURPHY, T. A., eds. Eucharist and Ministry. Lutherans and Catholics in Dialogue, vol. 4. Washington, DC: United States Catholic Conference, 1970.

"The Eucharist in the Life of the Church, an Ecumenical Concensus, 1970." The Ecumenist, 8, 6 (September-October 1970): 9-93.

FELMY, Karl Christian. "Eucharistie, Gemeinde, Amt: Ein Neuansatz in russischen Orthodoxie und Luthertum." Kerygma und Dogma, 18 (1972): 139-160.

GRESHAM, Perry E. "Issues in Intercommunion." Ecumenical Review, 4 (1952): 252-258.

Groupe des Dombes. Vers une même foi eucharistique? Accord
entre catholiques et protestants. Taizé: Presses de Taizé,
1972.

HERON, Alasdair I. C. Table and Tradition: Toward an Ecumenical Understanding of the Eucharist. Edinburgh: Handsel
Press; Philadelphia, PA: Westminster Press, 1983.

ISERLOH, Erwin. "'Das Herrenmahl' im römisch-katholischen und
evangelisch-lutherischen Gespräch." Theologische Revue, 3
(1979): 178-182.

KOCH, Reinhold. Erbe und Auftrag: das Abendmahlsgespräch in
der Theologie des 20. Jahrhunderts. FGLP, 10/9. München:
Kaiser, 1957.

Modern Eucharistic Agreement. London: SPCK, 1973.

NELSON, J. Robert, and SLOYAN, Gerard S. "The Eucharist in
Ecumenical Dialogue: Methodist-Catholic." Journal of Ecumenical Studies, 13, 2 (Spring 1976): 88-103.

NISSIOTIS, Nikos A. "Worship, Eucharist and 'Intercommunion':
An Orthodox Reflection." Studia Liturgica, 2 (1963): 193-222.

REPORT OF THE JOINT COMMISSION BETWEEN THE ROMAN
CATHOLIC CHURCH AND THE WORLD METHODIST COUNCIL,
1967-1970. "Eucharist." In Proceedings of the Twelfth World
Methodist Conference, Denver, Colorado, August 18-26, 1971,
pp. 56-58. Edited by Lee F. Tuttle. Nashville, TN: Abingdon Press, 1972.

_____. "Roman Catholic-Methodist Statement on the Eucharist,
1971." In The Common Catechism: A Book of Christian Faith,
pp. 670-671. Edited by Johannes Feiner. New York: Seabury
Press, 1975. [Excerpt of above]

SASSE, Hermann. Corpus Christi: Ein Beitrag zum Problem der
Abendmahlskonkordie. Lutherische Blätter, 31. Herausgegeben
von Friedrich Wilhelm Hopf. Erlangen: Verlag der Evangelisch-
lutherische Mission, 1979.

SCHMAUS, Michael, ed. Aktuelle Fragen zur Eucharistie. München:
Hueber, 1960.

SCHULZ, Hans-Joachim. Ökumenische Glaubenseinheit aus euchar-
istischer Überlieferung. KKS, 39. Paderborn: Bonifacius-
Druckerei, 1976.

SWIDLER, Leonard, ed. "The Eucharist in Ecumenical Dialogue."
Journal of Ecumenical Studies, 13, 2 (Spring 1976). [Special
issue]

TORRANCE, Thomas F. "The Paschal Mystery of Christ and the Eucharist." In his Theology in Reconciliation, pp. 106-138. Grand Rapids, MI: Eerdmans, 1975.

WAINWRIGHT, Geoffrey. "Conciliarity and Eucharist." One in Christ, 14 (1978): 30-49.

_____. "Eucharist as an Ecumenical Sacrament of Reconciliation and Renewal." Studia Liturgica, 11 (1976): 1-18.

_____. "Recent Thinking on Christian Beliefs: Baptism and Eucharist." Expository Times, 88 (1976-1977): 132-137.

WHITLEY, Oliver Read. "The Lord's Supper: Challenge to Divided Christendom." Religion in Life, 18 (1949): 352-362.

WRIGHT, Nathan. One Bread, One Body. Greenwich, CT: Seabury Press, 1962.

ZIZIOULAS, Jean, TILLARD, J. M. R., and ALLMEN, J. J. von. L'eucharistie. Eglises en dialogue, 12. Paris: Mame, 1970.

C. EARLY CHURCH

(See Eucharist entries in Section VII.)

D. EASTERN CHURCHES

(See also Eucharist entries in Section VIII.)

AFANASSIEV, Nikolai. "Le sacrament de l'assemblée." International kirchliche Zeitung, 46 (1956): 200-214.

SPACIL, Bohumil. Doctrina theologiae orientis separati de ss. eucharistia. 2 vols. OC, 48 & 50. Rome: Pontificium Institutum Orientalium Studiorum, 1928-1929.

E. LATIN CHURCHES

(See also Eucharist entries in Section IX.)

BACIOCCHI, Joseph de. L'Eucharistie. MCTS, 3. Tournai: Desclée, 1964.

BRUNNER, Peter. "Zur katholischen Sakramenten- und Eucharistielehre." Theologische Literaturzeitung, 88 (1963): 169-186.

COLLINS, Mary. "Eucharistic Proclamation of God's Presence."
Worship, 41 (1967):   531–541.

F. L. K. "De communione cum Ecclesia in prece eucharistica."
Notitiae, 84 (1973):   242–246.

GERKEN, Alexander. "Dogmengeschichtliche Reflexion über heutige
Wende in der Eucharistielehre." Zeitschrift für katholische
Theologie, 94 (1972):   199–226.

_____. Theologie der Eucharistie. München: Kösel, 1973.

GLASSER, Alfred. "Eucharistieverständnis zwischen Ideologie und
Glaube." In Begegnung: Beiträge zu einer Hermeneutik des
theologischen Gesprächs, pp. 311–325. Herausgegeben von Max
Seckler, Otto H. Pesch, Johannes Brosseder, Wolfhart Pannenberg. Graz: Styria, 1972.

KEIFER, Ralph A. Blessed and Broken: An Exploration of the
Contemporary Experience of God in Eucharistic Celebration.
MS, 3. Wilmington, DE: Michael Glazier, 1982.

KELLY, George A., ed. The Sacrament of the Eucharist in Our
Time. Boston, MA: St. Paul Editions, 1978.

KILMARTIN, Edward J. Church, Eucharist, and Priesthood: A
Theological Commentary on "The Mystery and Worship of the
Most Holy Eucharist". New York: Paulist Press, 1981.

LANNE, E. "La relazione dell'anafora eucaristica alla confessione
di fede." Sacra doctrina, 12 (1967):   383–396.

LA TAILLE, Maurice de. Mysterium fidei: de augustissimo cor-
poris et sanguinis Christi sacrificio atque sacramento. 2. ed.
Paris: Beauchesne, 1924; The Mystery of Faith: Regarding
the Most August Sacrament and Sacrifice of the Body and
Blood of Christ. New York, London: Sheed & Ward, 1940.

LECUYER, Joseph. Le sacrifice de la nouvelle alliance. Le Puy:
Mappus, 1962.

MAERTENS, Thierry. C'est fête en l'honneur de Yahvé. Bruges:
Desclée de Brouwer, 1961; A Feast in Honor of Jahweh. Translated by Kathryn Sullivan. Notre Dame, IN: Fides, 1965.

MITCHELL, Nathan. Cult and Controversy: The Worship of the
Eucharist Outside Mass. SRR, 4. New York: Pueblo, 1982.

NEUNHEUSER, Burkhard. Eucharistie in Mittelalter und Neuzeit.
HD, 4/4b. Freiburg: Herder, 1963.

O'KEEFE, Bernard J. "Casel and Calvin on the Eucharist."
Canadian Journal of Theology, 11 (1965): 8-24.

Das Opfer der Kirche: Exegetische, dogmatische und pastoral-
theologische Studien zum Verständnis der Messe. Dargeboten
von R. Erni u. a. LTS, 1. Lucerne: Rex-Verlag, 1954.

PASCHER, Josef. Die christliche Eucharistiefeier als dramatische
Darstellung des geschichtlichen Abendmahles. MU, n.F., 24.
München: Hueber, 1958.

PIOLANTI, Antonio. Il mistero eucaristico. 2. ed. NCTC, 8.
Florence: Libreria Editrice Fiorentina, 1955.

POWERS, Joseph M. Eucharistic Theology. New York: Herder &
Herder, 1967.

_____. "Mysterium Fidei and the Theology of the Eucharist."
Worship, 40 (1966): 17-35.

RAHNER, Karl. Die vielen Messen und das eine Opfer. 2.
neubearb. und erw. Aufl. bearb. von Angelus Hässling. QD,
31. Freiburg: Herder, 1966; The Celebration of the Eucharist.
Translated by W. J. O'Hara. New York: Herder & Herder,
1968.

_____. "Wort und Eucharistie." In his Schriften zur Theologie,
Bd. 4, pp. 313-356. Einsiedeln: Benziger, 1960; "The Word
and the Eucharist." In his Theological Investigations, vol. 4,
pp. 253-286. Translated by Kevin Smyth. Baltimore, MD:
Helicon; London: Darton, Longman & Todd, 1966.

SAURAS, E. "La eucaristica y el misterio de la communidad liturgica." Teologia Espiritual, 2 (1958): 359-394.

SCHILLEBEECKX, Edward. Christus' tegenwoordigheid in de eucharistie. Bilthoven: Nelissen, 1967; The Eucharist. Translated by N. D. Smith. London, New York: Sheed & Ward,
1968.

SEASOLTZ, R. Kevin, ed. Living Bread, Saving Cup: Readings
on the Eucharist. Collegeville, MN: Liturgical Press, 1982.

SWAYNE, Sean, ed. Eucharist for a New World: A Selection of
Homilies, Addresses and Conferences from the 42nd Interna-
tional Eucharistic Congress, Lourdes, 1981. Carlow, Ireland:
Irish Institute of Pastoral Liturgy, 1981.

TILLARD, J. M. R. L'eucharistie, pâque de l'église. US, 44.
Paris: Cerf, 1964; The Eucharist: Pasch of God's People.
Translated by Dennis L. Wienk. Staten Island, NY: Alba
House, 1967.

VAJTA, Vilmos. "Eucharistic Faith and Practice in the Encyclical
Mysterium Fidei." In Oecumenica, 1966, pp. 179-226. Edited
by Friedrich Wilhelm Katzenbach and Vilmos Vajta. Minneapolis,
MN: Augsburg, 1966.

VONIER, Anscar. A Key to the Doctrine of the Eucharist. London:
Burns, Oates & Washbourne, 1925; reprint ed., Westminster,
MD: Newman Bookshop, 1946.

F.   GENERAL AND COMPARATIVE PROTESTANT STUDIES

BARCLAY, Alexander. The Protestant Doctrine of the Lord's Supper: A Study in the Eucharistic Teaching of Luther, Zwingli
and Calvin. Glasgow, Scot.: Jackson & Wylie, 1927.

BIZER, Ernst, and KRECK, Walter. Die Abendmahlslehre in den
reformatorischen Bekenntnisschriften. TEH, n.F., 47. Münch-
en: Kaiser, 1955.

DUGMORE, C. W. "The Eucharist in the Reformation Era." In
Eucharistic Theology Then and Now. London: SPCK, 1968.

EMPIE, Paul C., and McCORD, James I., eds. Marburg Revisited:
A Re-examination of Lutheran and Reformed Traditions. Minneapolis, MN: Augsburg, 1966.

GRASS, Hans. Die Abendmahlslehre bei Luther und Calvin: eine
kritische Untersuchung. 2. Aufl. BFCT, 2. Reihe, 47. Gütersloh: Bertelsmann, 1954.

KOCH, Reinhold. Erbe und Auftrag: Das Abendmahlsgespräch
in der Theologie des 20. Jahrhunderts. FGLP, 10/9. München:
Kaiser, 1957.

SKIBBE, Eugene M. Protestant Agreement on the Lord's Supper.
Minneapolis, MN: Augsburg, 1968.

G.   LUTHERAN CHURCHES

ASMUSSEN, Hans, et al. Abendmahlsgemeinschaft? 2. Aufl.
Evangelische Theologie, Beiheft, 3. München: Kaiser, 1938.

BARTH, Karl. "Anfass und Absicht in Luthers Abendmahlslehre."
In his Die Theologie und die Kirche, pp. 26-75. Gesammelte
Vorträge, Bd. 2. München: Kaiser, 1928; "Luther's Doctrine
of the Eucharist: Its Basis and Purpose (1923)." In his
Theology and Church: Shorter Writings, 1920-1928, pp. 74-111.

Translated by Louise Pettibone Smith. New York: Harper & Row, 1962.

BOELENS, Wim L. Die Arnoldshainer Abendmahlsthesen: die Suche nach einem Abendmahlskonsens in der Evangelischen Kirche in Deutschland 1947-1957 und eine Würdigung aus katholischer Sicht. Assen: Van Gorcum, 1964.

KANDLER, Karl-Hermann. Die Abendmahlslehre des Kardinals Humbert und ihre Bedeutung für das gegenwärtige Abendmahlsgespräch. AGTL, 24. Berlin: Lutherische Verlagshaus, 1971.

KRETSCHMAR, Georg. "Die Eucharistie in liturgischen Vollzug und in der kirchlichen Lehre." In Die Eucharistie, pp. 75-119. Herausgegeben vom Kirchlichen Aussenamt der Evangelischen Kirche in Deutschland. Bielefeld: Luther-Verlag, 1974.

LOEWENICH, Walther von. Vom Abendmahl Christi: eine historisch-systematische Untersuchung zum Abendmahlsproblem der Gegenwart. Furche-Studien, 18. Berlin: Furche-Verlag, 1938.

SASSE, Hermann. Kirche und Herrenmahl: Ein Beitrag zum Verständnis des Altarsakraments. Bekennende Kirche, 59-60. München: Kaiser, 1938.

H. REFORMED CHURCHES

(See also Eucharist entries in Section XIV.)

BARTH, Markus. Das Abendmahl: Passamahl, Bundesmahl und Messiasmahl. TS, 18. Zürich: Evangelischer Verlag, 1945.

BARTH, Peter. "Calvin zum Abendmahlsstreit." Christliche Welt, 43 (1929): 817-823, 922-929.

GERRISH, Brian A. "The Lord's Supper in the Reformed Confessions." Theology Today, 23 (1966-1967): 224-243.

I. ANGLICAN CHURCHES

(See also Eucharist entries in Section XVII.)

EVERY, George. The Mass. London: Gill & Macmillan, 1978; American ed., The Mass: Meaning, Mystery and Ritual. Huntington, IN: Our Sunday Visitor, 1978.

GORE, Charles. The Body of Christ: An Enquiry into the Insti-
     tution and Doctrine of Holy Communion. 4th ed. London:
     John Murray, 1907.

MASCALL, Eric Lionel. Corpus Christi: Essays on the Church and
     the Eucharist. London: Longmans, Green, 1953.

Thinking about the Eucharist: Essays by Members of the Arch-
     bishops' Commission on Christian Doctrine. Preface by Ian T.
     Ramsey. London: SCM Press, 1972.

WRIGHT, J. Robert, ed. A Communion of Communions: One Eu-
     charistic Fellowship. The Detroit Report and Papers of the
     Triennial Ecumenical Study of the Episcopal Church, 1976-1979.
     New York: Seabury Press, 1979.

J. METHODIST CHURCHES

(See Eucharist entries in Section XXI.)

K. FREE CHURCHES

(See also entries in Section XXIV.)

FEY, Harold. The Lord's Supper: Seven Meanings. New York:
     Harper, 1948; reprinted 1965.

L. SPECIAL TOPICS

1. Reservation

BUCHANAN, Colin O., ed. Reservation and Communion of the
     Sick. With R. T. Beckwith and J. I. Packer. GBMW, 4.
     Bramcote, Eng.: Grove Books, 1972.

DIX, Gregory. A Detection of Aumbries: With Other Notes on the
     History of Reservation. London: Dacre Press, 1942.

FREESTONE, W. H. The Sacrament Reserved: A Survey of the
     Practice of Reserving the Eucharist, with Special Reference to
     the Communion of the Sick, during the First Twelve Centuries.
     ACC, 21. London: Mowbray; Milwaukee, WI: Young Church-
     man, 1917.

KING, Archdale A. Eucharistic Reservation in the Western Church.
     New York: Sheed & Ward, 1965.

LOCKTON, William. The Treatment of the Remains at the Eucharist after Holy Communion and the Time of the Ablutions. Cambridge: Cambridge University Press, 1920.

MAFFEI, E. La Reservation eucharistique jusqu'à la renaissance. Bruxelles: Vromant, 1942.

STONE, Darwell. The Reserved Sacrament. 2d ed. London: Scott, 1918.

VAN DIJK, Stephen J. P., and WALKER, Joan Hazelden. The Myth of the Aumbry: Notes on Medieval Reservation Practice and Eucharistic Devotion. London: Burns & Oates, 1957.

2. The Presence of Christ in the Eucharist

BATIFFOL, Pierre. L'Eucharistie; la présence réelle et la transsubstantiation. His Etudes d'histoire de théologie positive, 2. Ser. 10. éd. Paris: Lecoffre, 1930.

BOBRINSKOY, Boris. "Présence réelte et communion eucharistique." Revue de science philosophique et théologique, 53 (1969): 402-420.

BRUNNER, Peter. "Realpräsenz und Transsubstantiation: Ist die Lehre von der eucharistischen Gegenwart Christi zwischen Katholiken und Lutheranern moch kirchentrennend?" In Begegnung: Beiträge zu einer Hermeneutik des theologischen Gesprächs, pp. 291-310. Herausgegeben von Max Seckler, Otto H. Pesch, Johannes Brosseder, Wolfhart Pannenberg. Graz: Styria, 1972.

COLOMBO, Carlo. "Teologia, filosofia e fisica nella dottrina della transustanziazione." Scuola cattolica, 83 (1955): 89-124.

DURRWELL, F. X. L'Eucharistie: présence du Christ. Paris: Editions ouvrières, 1971; The Eucharist: Presence of Christ. Denville, NJ: Dimension Books, 1974.

FORELL, George W. "Eucharistic Presence as the Key to Theological Understanding." In Vierhundertfunfzig Jahre lutherische Reformation: Festschrift für Franz Lau, pp. 90-98. Göttingen: Vandenhoeck & Ruprecht, 1967.

GHELLINCK, Joseph de. "A propos du premier emploie du mot 'transsubstantiatio.'" Revue des sciences religieuses, 1 (1911): 466-469, 570-572; 2 (1912): 255-259.

HITZ, Paul. "The Lord's Eucharistic Presence." Lumen Vitae, 22 (1967): 303-340.

JACOBS, Paul. "Pneumatische Realpräsenz bei Calvin." Revue
d'histoire et de philosophie religieuse, 44 (1964): 389-401.

JORISSEN, Hans. Die Entfaltung der Transsubstantiationslehre
bis zum Beginn der Hochscholastik. MBT, 28/1. Münster:
Aschendorff, 1965.

KATTENBUSCH, Ferdinand. "Luthers Idee der Konsubstantiation
im Abendmahl." In Forschungen zur Kirchengeschichte und
zur christlichen Kunst [Ficker Festschrift], pp. 62-86. Herausgegeben von Walter Elliger. Leipzig: Dieterich, 1931.

KLEMM, David E. "'This is my Body': Hermeneutics and Eucharistic Language." Anglican Theological Review, 64 (1982):
293-310.

LEENHARDT, Franz J. "La Présence eucharistique." Irénikon,
33 (1960): 146-172.

McCUE, James F. "The Doctrine of Transubstantiation from Berengar to Trent: The Point at Issue." Harvard Theological Review, 61 (1968): 385-430.

MICHEL, A. "Transsubstantiation." Dictionnaire de théologie
catholique, 15/1: 1396-1406.

PETERS, Albrecht. Realpräsenz: Luthers Zeugnis von Christi
Gengenwart im Abendmahl. 2. Aufl. AGTL, 5. Berlin:
Lutherisches Verlagshaus, 1966.

PUSEY, E. B. The Doctrine of the Real Presence as Contained in
the Fathers. London: J. H. Parker, 1855.

QUERE, Ralph W. Melanchthon's Christum Cognoscere: Christ's
Efficacious Presence in the Eucharist Theology of Melanchthon.
BHR, 22. Nieuwkoop: De Graaf, 1977.

RAHNER, Karl. "Die Gegenwart Christi im Sakrament des Herrenmahles." In his Schriften zur Theologie, Bd. 4, pp. 357-386.
Einsiedeln: Benziger, 1960; "The Presence of Christ in the
Sacrament of the Lord's Supper." In his Theological Investigations, vol. 4, pp. 287-311. Translated by Kevin Smyth.
Baltimore, MD: Helicon; London: Darton, Longman and Todd,
1966.

SALA, G. B. "Transubstantiation oder Transignifikation?" Zeitschrift für katholische Theologie, 92 (1970): 1-34.

SASSE, Hermann. This is My Body: Luther's Contention for the
Real Presence in the Sacrament of the Altar. Minneapolis, MN:
Augsburg, 1959; revised Australian ed., Adelaide: Lutheran
Publishing House, 1977.

SCHILLEBEECKX, Edward. "Transubstantiation, Transfinalization, Transignification." Worship, 40 (1966): 324-338.

SCHOONENBERG, P. "Presence and the Eucharistic Presence." Cross Currents, 17 (1967): 39-54.

SMITS, Luchesius. Actuele vragen rondom de transsubstantiatie en de tegenwoordigheid des Heren in de Eucharistie. Roermond: Romen, 1965.

SOHNGEN, Gottlieb. Christi Gegenwart in Glaube und Sakrament. München: Pustet, 1967.

STRONG, Thomas B. The Doctrine of the Real Presence. London: Longmans, Green, 1899.

STROTTMANN, T. "L'orthodoxie orientale dans le debat sur la transsubstantiation." Irénikon, 32 (1959): 295-308.

STRUCKMANN, Adolf. Die Gegenwart Christi in der heiligen Eucharistie nach den schriftlichen Quellen der vornizänischen Zeit. TSL, 12. Wien: Mayer, 1905.

SUSS, Théobald. "Dans quelle mesure la doctrine de la présence eucharistique sépare-t-elle encore les Eglises luthériennes et réformée?" Positions Luthériennes, 18 (1970): 91-107.

THOMAS AQUINAS. Summa Theologiae, Vol. 58: The Eucharistic Presence (3a. 73-78). Edited and translated by W. Barden. Cambridge, Eng.: Blackfriars; New York: McGraw-Hill; London: Eyre & Spottiswoode, 1975.

TYLENDA, Joseph N. "Calvin and Christ's Presence in the Supper --True or Real." Scottish Journal of Theology, 27 (1974): 65-75.

VOLLERT, Cyril. "The Eucharist: Controversy on Transsubstantiation." Theological Studies, 22 (1961): 391-425.

WETTER, Friedrich. "Die eucharistische Gegenwart des Herrn." In Geheimnis des Glaubens, pp. 9-35. By Hermann Volk and Friedrich Wetter. Mainz: Grünewald, 1968.

WOHLMUTH, Josef. Realpräsenz und Transsubstantiation im Konzil von Trient: eine historisch-kritische Analyse der Canones 1-4 der Sessio XIII. 2 vols. EH, 23/37. Bern: Lang, 1975.

3. The Eucharistic Offering or Sacrifice

ALLCHIN, A. M. "The Eucharistic Offering." Studia Liturgica, 1 (1962): 101-114.

AULEN, Gustaf. För eder utgiven. Stockholm: Diakonistyrelses
  Bokförlag, 1956; Eucharist and Sacrifice. Translated by Eric
  H. Wahlstrom. Philadelphia, PA: Muhlenberg Press, 1958.

AVERBECK, W. Der Opfercharakter des Abendmahles in der
  neueren evangelischen Theologie. KKS, 19. Paderborn:
  Bonifacius Druckerei, 1967.

BETZ, Johannes. "Messopfer." Lexikon für Theologie und Kirche
  (2. Aufl.), 7:343-350.

_____. "Der Opfercharakter des Abendmahls im interkonfes-
  sionellen Dialog." In Theologie im Wandel, pp. 469-491. Herausgegeben von der katholisch-theologischen Fakultät an der
  Universität Tübingen. München: Erich Wewel Verlag, 1967.

BRINKTRINE, Johannes. Der Messopferbegriff in den ersten zwei
  Jahrhunderten: eine biblisch-patristische Untersuchung. FTS,
  21. Freiburg: Herder, 1918.

BRINKTRINE, Johannes. Das Opfer der Eucharistie: dogmatische
  Untersuchungen über des Wesen des Messopfers. Paderborn:
  Schöningh, 1938.

CLARK, Francis. Eucharistic Sacrifice and the Reformation. 2d
  ed. with a Foreword by Cardinal John Heenan. Oxford: Blackwell, 1967.

DALY, Robert J. The Origins of the Christian Doctrine of Sacrifice. Philadelphia, PA: Fortress Press, 1978.

DANDEV, F. "Destruktionstheorien," and "Oblationstheorien."
  Lexikon für Theologie und Kirche (2. Aufl.), 3:253-254; 7:
  1088.

DOWD, Edward Francis. A Conspectus of Modern Catholic Thought
  on the Essence of the Eucharistic Sacrifice. SST, 1st Ser.,
  47. Washington, DC: Catholic University of America Press,
  1937.

EMERY, Pierre-Yves. "The Teaching of Calvin on the Sacrificial
  Element in the Eucharist." The Reformed and Presbyterian
  World, 26 (1960): 109-114.

The Eucharist as Sacrifice. Lutherans and Catholics in Dialogue,
  vol. 3. Edited by P. C. Empie and T. A. Murphy. Washington, DC: United States Catholic Conference, 1967.

FANDAL, Damian C. The Essence of the Eucharist Sacrifice. River
  Forest, IL: Aquinas Library, 1960.

GRISBROOKE, W. Jardine. "Oblation at the Eucharist, II: The Liturgical Issues." Studia Liturgica, 4 (1965): 37-55.

JOURNET, Charles. La Messe: présence du sacrifice de la Croix. 3. éd. TET. Bruges: Desclée de Brouwer, 1961.

JUNGMANN, Josef Andreas. "Oblatio und Sacrificium in der Geschichte des Eucharistieverständnisses." Zeitschrift für katholische Theologie, 92 (1970): 342-350.

_____. Vom Sinn der Messe als Opfer der Gemeinschaft. Einsiedeln: Johannes Verlag, 1954; The Sacrifice of the Church: The Meaning of the Mass. Translated by Clifford Howell. Collegeville, MN: Liturgical Press, 1956.

KIDD, B. J. Later Medieval Doctrine of the Eucharistic Sacrifice. London: SPCK, 1898; reprinted 1958.

LEPIN, Marius. L'Idée du sacrifice de la messe, d'après les théologiens, depuis l'origine jusqu'à nos jours. 2. éd. Paris: Beauchesne, 1926.

McCUE, James F. "Luther and Roman Catholicism on the Mass as Sacrifice." Journal of Ecumenical Studies, 2 (1965): 205-233.

MASURE, Eugène. Le Sacrifice du chef. 2. éd. Paris: Beauchesne, 1932; The Christian Sacrifice. Translated by Illtyd Trethowan. London: Burns, Oates & Washbourne, 1944.

_____. Le Sacrifice du chef. 9. éd. Paris: Beauchesne, 1944.

_____. Le Sacrifice du corps mystique. Paris: Desclée de Brouwer, 1950; The Sacrifice of the Mystical Body. Translated by Anthony Thorold. London: Burns & Oates, 1954.

MEINHOLD, Peter, and ISERLOH, Erwin. Abendmahl und Opfer. Stuttgart: Schwabenverlag, 1960.

MOLL, Helmut. Die Lehre von der Eucharistie als Opfer: eine dogmengeschichtliche Untersuchung vom Neuen Testament bis Irenäus von Lyon. Theophaneia, 26. Bonn: Hanstein, 1975.

MULLER, Otfried. "Die Eucharistie als Mahlopfer und Opfermahl." In Gott in Welt: Festgabe für Karl Rahner, Bd. 2, pp. 121-134. Herausgegeben von Johannes Baptist Metz, Walter Kern, Adolf Darlapp, Herbert Vorgrimler. Freiburg: Herder, 1964.

NEUNHEUSER, Burkhard. "Messopfertheorien." Lexikon für Theologie und Kirche (2. Aufl.), 7:350-352.

PACKER, J. I., ed. Eucharistic Sacrifice. London: Church Book Room Press, 1962.

PRATZNER, Ferdinand. Messe und Kreuzesopfer: Die Krise der
sakramentalen Idee bei Luther und in der mittelalterlichen
Scholastik. WBT, 29. Wien: Herder, 1970.

PRENTER, Regin. "Das Augsburger Bekenntnis und die römisch-
katholische Messopferlehre." Kerygma und Dogma, 1 (1955):
42-58.

RENZ, Franz Ser. Die Geschichte des Messopfer-begriffs, oder
der alte Glaube und die neuen Theorien das Wesen des unbluti-
gen Opfers. 2 vols. Freising: Datterer, 1901-1902.

RINGGREN, Helmer. Sacrifice in the Bible. New York: Association Press, 1962.

RUPPRECHT, Placidus. "Una eademque hostia--idem offerens: das
Verhältnis von Kreuz- und Messopfer nach dem Tridentinum."
Theologische Quartalschrift, 120 (1939): 1-36.

SCHULTE, Raphael. Die Messe als Opfer der Kirche: Die Lehre
frühmittelalterlicher Autoren über das eucharistische Opfer.
LQF, 35. Münster: Aschendorff, 1959.

SOHNGEN, Gottlieb. Das Sakramentale Wesen des Messopfers.
Essen: Wibbelt, 1946.

SPENCER, Bonnell. Sacrifice of Thanksgiving. West Park, NY:
Holy Cross Publications, 1965.

TYLENDA, Joseph N. "A Eucharistic Sacrifice in Calvin's Theology?" Theological Studies, 37 (1976): 456-466.

UNDERHILL, Evelyn. The Mystery of Sacrifice: A Meditation on
the Liturgy. London: Longmans, Green, 1938.

WISLOFF, Carl F. The Gift of Communion: Luther's Controversy
with Rome on the Eucharistic Sacrifice. Translated by Joseph
M. Shaw. Minneapolis, MN: Augsburg, 1964.

4. Other Special Studies

BACIOCCHI, J. de. "Eglise et Trinité dans le mystère eucharistique." In L'Evangile, hier et aujourd'hui: mélanges offerts
au Professeur Franz J. Leenhardt, pp. 241-249. Genève:
Editions Labor et Fides, 1968.

CANGH, Jean-Marie van. La Multiplication des pains et l'eucharistie. LD, 86. Paris: Cerf, 1975.

COLE, Richard L. Love-Feasts: A History of the Christian Agape.
London: C. H. Kelly, 1916.

GRISBROOKE, W. Jardine. "Intercession at the Eucharist."
Studia Liturgica, 4 (1965): 129-155; 5 (1966): 20-44.

HANSON, R. P. C. "The Liberty of the Bishop to Improvise
Prayer in the Eucharist." Vigiliae christianae, 15 (1961):
173-176.

KEATING, J. F. The Agapé and the Eucharist in the Early Church.
London: Methuen, 1901.

MARTELET, Gustave. Résurrection, eucharistie et genèse de
l'homme. Paris: Desclée, 1972; The Risen Christ and the
Eucharistic World. London: Collins; New York: Seabury
Press, 1976.

PITTENGER, Norman. Life as Eucharist. Grand Rapids, MI:
Eerdmans, 1973.

SCHWEIZER, Eduard. "Das Abendmahl eine Vergegenwärtigung des
Todes Jesu oder ein eschatologisches Freudenmahl?" Theologische Zeitschrift, 2 (1946): 81-101.

SLOYAN, Gerard S. "The Holy Eucharist as an Eschatalogical
Meal." Worship, 36 (1962): 444-451.

TILLARD, J. M. R. "L'Eucharistie et la fraternité." Nouvelle revue théologique, 91 (1969): 113-135.

_____. "L'Eucharistie et le Saint-Esprit." Nouvelle revue thé-
ologique, 90 (1968): 363-387.

TORRANCE, Thomas F. "Eschatology and the Eucharist." In Intercommunion, pp. 303-350. Edited by Donald Baillie and John
Marsh. London: SCM Press; New York: Harper, 1952.

WAINWRIGHT, Geoffrey. Eucharist and Eschatology. 2d ed.
London: Epworth Press, 1978; reprint ed., with new preface
and appendix. New York: Oxford University Press, 1981.

XXIX. CHRISTIAN INITIATION
(BAPTISM & CONFIRMATION)

A. COLLECTED TEXTS

FISCHER, J. D. C. Christian Initiation: Baptism in the Medieval
West. ACC, 47. London: SPCK, 1965.

_____. Christian Initiation: The Reformation Period.   ACC, 51.
London: SPCK, 1970.

JAGGER, Peter J.   Christian Initiation, 1552-1969:   Rites of Baptism and Confirmation since the Reformation Period.   ACC, 52.
London: SPCK, 1970.

PRICKETT, John, ed.   Initiation Rites.   Living Faiths.   London:
Lutterworth Press, 1978.

WHITAKER, E. C., ed.   Documents of the Baptismal Liturgy.   2d
ed.   ACC, 42.   London: SPCK, 1970.

B. GENERAL STUDIES

"Christian Initiation."   Studia Liturgica, 10, 1-2 (1974).

"Christian Initiation."   Studia Liturgica, 12, 2-3 (1977).

CORBLET, Jules.   Histoire dogmatique, liturgique et archéologique
du sacrement de baptême.   2 vols.   Paris: Victor Palmé, 1881-
1882.

CREHAN, Joseph.   "Ten Years' Work on Baptism and Confirmation,
1945-1955."   Theological Studies, 17 (1956):   494-515.

DANIELOU, Jean.   "Le Symbolisme des rites baptismaux."   Dieu
vivant, 1 (1945):   17-43.

ELIADE, Mircea.   Naissances mystiques: essai sur quelques types
d'initiation.   Paris: Gallimard, 1959; Birth and Rebirth: The
Religious Meanings of Initiation in Human Culture.   Translated
by Willard R. Trask.   New York: Harper, 1958; reprint ed.,
Rites and Symbols of Initiation: The Mysteries of Birth and
Rebirth.   New York: Harper Torchbooks, 1965.

KRETSCHMAR, Georg.   "Recent Research on Christian Initiation."
Studia Liturgica, 12 (1977):   87-106.

LEENHARDT, Franz J.   Le Baptême chrétien: son origine, sa
signification.   CTAP, 4.   Neuchâtel: Delachaux & Niestlé,
1944.

PORTER, H. B.   "Baptism: Its Paschal and Ecumenical Setting."
Worship, 42 (1968):   205-214.

SEARLE, Mark.   "The Journey of Conversion."   Worship, 54 (1980):
35-54.

SEGOND, Albert. Le Baptême chrétien: ses origines et sa pratique actuelle avec trois formulaires liturgiques. CFV, 28.
Genève: Cahiers de "Foi et Vérité," 1954.

STEVICK, Daniel. "Types of Baptismal Spirituality." Worship,
47 (1973): 11-26.

STONE, Darwell. Holy Baptism. 4th ed. London: Longmans,
Green, 1905.

WAINWRIGHT, Geoffrey. Christian Initiation. ESW, 10. London:
Lutterworth Press; Richmond, VA: John Knox Press, 1969.

WARNS, Johannes. Die Taufe. Bad Hamburg: W. Wiegand, 1913;
Baptism: Studies in the Original Christian Baptism, Its History
and Conflicts, Its Relation to a State or National Church, and
Its Significance for the Present Time. Translated by G. H.
Lang. London: Paternoster Press, 1957; Grand Rapids, MI:
Kregel, 1958.

WHITAKER, E. C. The Baptismal Liturgy: An Introduction to
Baptism in the Western Church. SCW, 5. London: Faith
Press, 1965.

_____. _____. 2d ed. London: SPCK, 1981.

_____. "The History of the Baptismal Formula." Journal of Ec-
clesiastical History, 16 (1965): 1-12.

WHITE, R. E. O. The Biblical Doctrine of Initiation. London:
Hodder & Stoughton; Grand Rapids, MI: Eerdmans, 1960.

WILLIMON, William H. Remember Who You Are: Baptism, a Model
for Christian Life. Nashville, TN: The Upper Room, 1980.

C. ECUMENICAL STUDIES

BENOIT, André, BOBRINSKOY, Boris, and COUDREAU, François.
Baptême, sacrement d'unité. Tours: Mame, 1971.

BRIDGE, Donald, and PHYPERS, David. The Water That Divides:
The Baptism Debate. Downers Grove, IL: InterVarsity Press,
1977.

CLARK, Neville, and JASPER, R. C. D., eds. Initiation and
Eucharist: Essays on their Structure by the Joint Liturgical
Group. London: SPCK, 1972.

EMPIE, Paul C., and BAUM, William W., eds. One Baptism for the

Remission of Sins. Lutherans and Catholics in Dialogue, vol. 2. New York: Lutheran World Federation, 1966.

HURLEY, Michael, ed. Ecumenical Studies: Baptism and Marriage. Dublin: Gill, 1968.

KINNAMON, Michael. Why It Matters: A Popular Introduction to the Baptism, Eucharist and Ministry Text. Risk Book, 25. Geneva: World Council of Churches, 1985.

LAZARETH, William H. Growing Together in Baptism, Eucharist and Ministry: A Study Guide. FOP, 114. Geneva: World Council of Churches, 1982.

"Louisville Consultation on Baptism." FOP, 97. Review and Expositor, 77, 1 (Winter 1980).

"A Lutheran-United Methodist Statement on Baptism." Quarterly Review, 1 (Fall 1980): 59-68; comments, pp. 69-79.

"Lutheran-United Methodist Papers on Baptism." Perkins Journal, 34 (Winter 1981): 1-56. [Special issue]

MOODY, Dale. Baptism: Foundation for Christian Unity. Philadelphia, PA: Westminster Press, 1967.

MOSS, Basil S., ed. Crisis for Baptism. The Report of the 1965 Ecumenical Conference sponsored by the Parish and People Movement. London: SCM Press, 1965.

RATSCHOW, Carl Heinz. Die eine christliche Taufe. Gütersloh: Mohn, 1972.

THURIAN, Max, ed. Ecumenical Perspectives on Baptism, Eucharist and Ministry. FOP, 116. Geneva: World Council of Churches, 1983.

TORRANCE, Thomas F. "The One Baptism Common to Christ and His Church." In his Theology in Reconciliation, pp. 82-105. Grand Rapids, MI: Eerdmans, 1975.

VISCHER, Lukas. Ye are Baptised: A Study of Baptism and Confirmation Liturgies as the Initiation to the Ministry of the Laity. 2d ed. Geneva: Department on the Laity, World Council of Churches, 1964.

WAINWRIGHT, Geoffrey. "Christian Initiation in the Ecumenical Movement." Studia Liturgica, 12 (1977): 67-86.

_____. "Développements baptismaux depuis 1967." Etudes théologiques et religieuses, 49 (1974): 67-93.

WORLD COUNCIL OF CHURCHES. Commission on Faith and Order.
One Lord, One Baptism. SMW, 17. London: SCM Press;
Minneapolis, MN: Augsburg, 1960.

WORLD COUNCIL OF CHURCHES. One Baptism, One Eucharist,
and a Mutually Recognized Ministry. Geneva: World Council
of Churches, 1975.

_____. Baptism, Eucharist and Ministry. FOP, 111. Geneva:
World Council of Churches, 1982.

D. EARLY CHURCH

1. Liturgical Texts

ADAM, Alfred, ed. Zur Geschichte der orientalischen Taufe und
Messe im II. und IV. Jahrhundert. Auf Grund der Auswahl
von Hans Lietzmann neubearbeitet und erweitert von Alfred
Adam. 3. Aufl. Liturgische Texte, 1. KT, 5. Berlin: De
Gruyter, 1960.

HAMMAN, Adalbert, ed. La Baptême d'après les pères de l'Eglise.
LC, 5. Paris: B. Grasset, 1962; Baptism: Ancient Liturgies
and Patristic Texts. APL, 2. English editorial supervisor:
Thomas Halton. Staten Island, NY: Alba House, 1967.

KRAFT, Heinrich, ed. Texte zur Geschichte der Taufe, besonders
der Kindertaufe in der alten Kirche. 2. Aufl. KT, 174. Berlin: De Gruyter, 1969.

SALLES, A., ed. Trois antiques rituels du baptême. SC, 59.
Paris: Cerf, 1958.

2. Studies

ALTHAUS, Paul. Die Heilsbedeutung der Taufe im Neuen Testament. Gütersloh: Bertelsmann, 1897.

BAMMEL, E. "Die Täufertradition bei Justin." In Studia Patristica,
vol. 8, pp. 287-290. Edited by F. L. Cross. TUGAL, 93.
Berlin: Akademie-Verlag, 1966.

BARTH, Gerhard. Die Taufe in frühchristlicher Zeit. BTS, 4.
Neukirchen: Neukirchen Verlag des Erziehungsvereins, 1981.

BEASLEY-MURRAY, G. R. Baptism in the New Testament. London:
Macmillan; New York: St. Martin's Press, 1962; reprint ed.,
Grand Rapids, MI: Eerdmans, 1973.

BENOIT, André. Le Baptême chrétien au 2e siècle: la théologie des pères. EHPRC, 43. Paris: Presses universitaires de France, 1953.

BEUS, Charles de. De oudchristelijke doop en zijn voorgeschiedenis. 2 vols. Haarlem: H. D. Tjeenk Willink, 1945-1948.

BIEDER, Werner. Die Verheissung der Taufe im Neuen Testament. Zürich: EVZ-Verlag, 1966.

BOISMARD, M.-E. "Une liturgie baptismale dans la Prima Petri." Revue biblique, 63 (1956): 182-208; 64 (1957): 161-183.

BORNEMANN, W. "Der erste Petrusbrief--eine Taufrede des Silvanus?" Zeitschrift für die neutestamentliche Wissenschaft, 19 (1919-1920): 143-165.

BOTTE, Bernard. "Note sur le symbole baptismal de saint Hippolyte." In Mélanges Joseph de Ghellinck, vol. 1, pp. 189-200. Gembloux: J. Duculot, 1951.

CREHAN, Joseph. Early Christian Baptism and the Creed: A Study in Ante-Nicene Theology. Bellarmine Series, 13. London: Burns, Oates & Washbourne, 1950.

CULLMANN, Oscar. Die Tauflehre des Neuen Testaments. ATANT, 12. Zürich: Zwingli-Verlag, 1948; Baptism in the New Testament. Translated by J. K. S. Reid. SBT, 1. London: SCM Press; Chicago: Henry Regnery, 1950.

DE JONG, J. P. "La connexion entre le rite de la consignation et l'Epiclèse dans Saint Ephrem." In Studia Patristica, vol. 2, pp. 29-34. Edited by Kurt Aland and F. L. Cross. TUGAL, 64. Berlin: Akademie-Verlag, 1957.

DELLING, Gerhard. Die Taufe im Neuen Testament. Berlin: Evangelische Verlagsanstalt, 1963.

_____. Die Zueignung des Heils in der Taufe: eine Untersuchung zum neutestamentlichen "taufen auf den Namen." Berlin: Evangelische Verlagsanstalt, 1961.

DIX, Gregory. "The Seal in the Second Century." Theology, 51 (1948): 7-12.

DOLGER, Franz. Die Sonne der Gerechtigkeit und der Schwarze: eine religionsgeschichtliche Studie zum Taufgelöbnis. LF, 2. Münster: Aschendorff, 1918.

DUNN, James D. G. Baptism in the Holy Spirit. SBT, 2d Ser., 15. London: SCM Press, 1970.

ELFERS, H. "Gehört die Salbung mit Chrisma im ältesten Initiations-
ritus zur Taufe oder zur Firmung?" Theologie und Glaube, 34
(1942): 334-341.

EYNDE, D. van den. "Baptême et confirmation d'après les Constitutiones Apostoliques VII, 44, 3." Recherches de science
religieuse, 27 (1937): 196-212.

FINN, Thomas M. "Baptismal Death and Resurrection: A Study
in Fourth Century Eastern Baptismal Theology." Worship, 43
(1969): 175-189.

_____. The Liturgy of Baptism in the Baptismal Instructions of
St. John Chrysostom. SCA, 15. Washington, DC: Catholic
University of America Press, 1967.

FLEMINGTON, W. F. The New Testament Doctrine of Baptism.
London: SPCK, 1957.

FORD, Steven R. "The Place of Catechesis in the Early Church:
Its Implications for Christian Initiation Today." St. Luke's
Journal of Theology, 24, 3 (June 1981): 175-199.

FRIEDRICH, Gerhard. "Ein Tauflied hellenisticher Judenchristen:
I Thess. 1:9f." Theologische Zeitschrift, 21 (1965): 502-16.

GEORGE, A., et al. Baptism in the New Testament: A Symposium.
Translated by David Askew. London: G. Chapman; Baltimore,
MD: Helicon, 1964.

GREEN, H. Benedict. "The Significance of the Pre-Baptismal Seal
in St. John Chrysostom." In Studia Patristica, vol. 6, pp.
84-90. Edited by F. L. Cross. TUGAL, 81. Berlin:
Akademie-Verlag, 1962.

HARKINS, P. W. "Pre-Baptismal Rites in Chrysostom's Baptismal
Catecheses." In Studia Patristica, vol. 8, pp. 219-238.
Edited by F. L. Cross. TUGAL, 93. Berlin: Akademie-
Verlag, 1966.

KASEMANN, Ernst. "Eine urchristliche Taufliturgie." In his
Exegetische Versuche und Besinnungen, Bd. 1, pp. 34-51.
2. Aufl. Göttingen: Vandenhoeck & Ruprecht, 1960; "A
Primitive Christian Baptismal Liturgy." In his Essays on New
Testament Themes, pp. 149-168. Translated by W. J. Monta-
gue. London: SCM Press; Naperville, IL: Allenson, 1964.

KIRBY, John C. Ephesians, Baptism and Pentecost: An Inquiry
into the Structure and Purpose of the Epistle to the Ephesians.
London: SPCK, 1968.

KIRSTEN, Hans. Die Taufabsage: eine Untersuchung zu Gestalt
und Geschichte der Taufe nach den altkirchlichen Tauflitur-
gien. Berlin: Evangelische Verlagsanstalt, 1959.

KLAUSER, Theodor. "Taufet in lebendigem Wasser! Zum religions-
und kulturgeschichtlichen Verständnis von Didache 7, 1-3."
In Pisciculi: Studien zur Religion und Kultur des Altertums,
Franz Joseph Dölger zum sechzigsten Geburtstage dargeboten
von Freunden, Verehren und Schülern, pp. 157-164. Herausgegeben von Theodor Klauser und Adolf Rücker. Münster:
Aschendorff, 1939.

KRETSCHMAR, G. "Die Geschichte des Taufgottesdienstes in der
alten Kirche." In Leiturgia: Handbuch des evangelischen
Gottesdienstes, Bd. 5: Der Taufgottesdienst, pp. 1-349.
Edited by K. F. Müller and Walter Blankenburg. Kassel:
Stauda, 1970.

LAMPE, G. W. H. The Seal of the Spirit: A Study in the Doctrine
of Baptism and Confirmation in the New Testament and the
Fathers. 2d ed. London: SPCK, 1967.

LUNDBERG, Per. La Typologie baptismale dans l'ancienne église.
Leipzig: A. Lorentz, 1942.

MANSON, T. W. "Entry into Membership of the Early Church."
Journal of Theological Studies, 48 (1947): 25-33.

MICHIELS, D. "L'Initiation chrétienne selon saint Ambroise." Les
Questions liturgiques et paroissiales, 34 (1953): 109-114, 164-
169.

MILLER, Ronald Homer. "Enlightenment through the Bath of Rebirth: The Experience of Christian Initiation in Late Fourth-
Century Jerusalem." Ph.D. dissertation, Fordham University,
1972.

MITCHELL, Leonel L. "The Baptismal Rite in Chrysostom." Anglican Theological Review, 43 (1961): 397-403.

MOZLEY, J. B. The Primitive Doctrine of Baptismal Regeneration.
London: J. Murray, 1856.

OULTON, J. E. L. "Second Century Teaching on Holy Baptism."
Theology, 50 (1947): 86-91.

QUASTEN, Johannes. "Baptismal Creed and Baptismal Act in St.
Ambrose's De mysteriis and De sacramentis." In Mélanges
Joseph de Ghellinck, vol. 1, pp. 223-234. Gembloux: J.
Duculot, 1951.

REITZENSTEIN, Richard. Die Vorgeschichte der christlichen Taufe.
Leipzig: Teubner, 1929; reprint ed., Stuttgart: Teubner,
1967.

RILEY, Hugh M. Christian Initiation: A Comparative Study of the
Baptismal Liturgy in the Mystagogical Writings of Cyril of
Jerusalem, John Chrysostom, Theodore of Mopsuestia, and Ambrose of Milan. SCA, 17. Washington, DC: Catholic University of America Press, 1974.

SCHLIER, Heinrich. "Die Taufe. Nach dem 6. Kapitel des Römer-
briefes." In his Die Zeit der Kirche: Exegetische Aufsätze
und Vorträge, pp. 47-56. 5. Aufl. Freiburg: Herder, 1972.

SCHNACKENBURG, Rudolf. Das Heilsgeschehen bei der Taufe nach
dem Apostel Paulus: eine Studie zur paulinischen Theologie.
MTS, 1. München: Zink, 1950; Baptism in the Thought of St.
Paul: A Study in Pauline Theology. Translated by G. A.
Beasley-Murray. Oxford: Blackwell; New York: Herder &
Herder, 1964.

SCHNEIDER, Johannes. Die Taufe im Neuen Testament. Stuttgart:
Kohlhammer, 1952.

_____. Baptism and Church in the New Testament. Translated
(from a lecture based on Die Taufe) by Ernest A. Payne.
London: Carey Kingsgate Press, 1957.

STANLEY, David. "The New Testament Doctrine of Baptism." In
The Apostolic Church in the New Testament, pp. 140-194.
Westminster, MD: Newman Press, 1963.

WAINWRIGHT, Geoffrey. "Baptismal Eucharist before Nicaea: An
Essay in Liturgical History." Studia Liturgica, 4 (1965): 9-36.

WINDISCH, Hans. Taufe und Sünde im ältesten Christentum bis
auf Origines. Tübingen: Mohr, 1908.

WINKLER, Gabriele. "The Original Meaning and Implications of the
Prebaptismal Anointing." Worship, 52 (1978): 24-25.

YARNOLD, Edward. The Awe-Inspiring Rites of Initiation: Baptismal Homilies of the Fourth Century. Slough, Eng.: St.
Paul Publications, 1972.

_____. "Baptism and the Pagan Mysteries in the Fourth Cen-
tury." Heythrop Journal, 13 (1972): 247-267.

_____. "The Ceremonies of Initiation in the De Sacramentis and
De Mysteriis of St. Ambrose." In Studia Patristica, vol. 10,
pp. 453-463. Edited by F. L. Cross. TUGAL, 107. Berlin:
Akademie-Verlag, 1970.

YSEBAERT, Joseph. Greek Baptismal Terminology: Its Origins
and Early Development. GCP, 1. Nijmegen: Dekker & Van
de Vegt, 1962.

E. EASTERN CHURCHES

1. Texts

COPTIC CHURCH. La Liturgie des sacrements du baptême et de
la confirmation. Traduit du copte en français par Cyrille Salib.
Le Caire: n.p., 1968.

_____. The Rites of the Coptic Church: The Order of Baptism
and the Order of Matrimony according to the Use of the Coptic
Church. Translated by B. J. A. Evetts. London: Nutt,
1888.

EASTERN ORTHODOX CHURCH. The Sacrament of Holy Baptism.
London: Williams & Norgate, 1928.

I'SO'YABH III. Nestorianische Taufliturgie. Ins Deutsch über-
setzt und unter Verwertung der neusten handschriftlichen
Funde historisch-kritisch erforscht von G. Diettrich. Giessen:
Ricker, 1903.

2. Studies

BOTTE, Bernard. "Le Baptême dans l'église syrienne." L'Orient
syrien, 1 (1956): 137-155.

BROCK, Sebastian. "Studies in the Early History of the Syrian
Orthodox Baptismal Liturgy." Journal of Theological Studies,
N.S., 23 (April 1972): 16-64.

_____. "The Syrian Baptismal Ordines." Studia Liturgica, 12
(1977): 177-183.

BURMESTER, O. H. E. "The Baptismal Rite of the Coptic Church
(A Critical Study)." Bulletin de la Société d'archéologie copte,
11 (1945): 27-86.

ELENJIKAL, Mathew. Baptism in the Malankara Church: A Study
on the Baptismal Ritual of the Malankara Church. Bangalore:
Dharmaram College, 1974.

FENOYL, M. de. "Les Sacrements de l'initiation chrétienne dans
l'église copte." Proche-Orient Chrétien, 7 (1957): 7-25.

GREBAUT, S. "Ordre du baptême et de la confirmation dans l'église éthiopienne." Revue de l'Orient chrétien, 26 (1927-1928): 105-189.

GRISBROOKE, W. Jardine. "Baptism. Orthodox." Dictionary of Liturgy and Worship, pp. 45-47.

MADEY, Johannes, and VAVANIKUNNEL, Georg. Taufe, Firmung und Busse in den Kirchen des ostsyrischen Ritenkreises. Einsiedeln: Benziger, 1971.

MOUHANNA, Augustin. Les Rites de l'initiation dans l'église maronite. Christianismos, 1. Rome: Pontificium Institutum Orientalium Studiorum, 1978.

QUASTEN, Johannes. "The Blessing of the Baptismal Font in the Syrian Rite of the Fourth Century." Theological Studies, 7 (1946): 309-313.

RAES, Alphonse. "Où se trouve la confirmation dans le rite syro-oriental?" L'Orient syrien, 1 (1956): 239-254.

RATCLIFF, E. C. "The Old Syrian Baptismal Tradition and Its Resettlement under the Influence of Jerusalem in the Fourth Century." In Studies in Church History, vol. 2, pp. 19-37. Edited by G. J. Cuming. London: Nelson, 1965; reprinted in his Liturgical Studies of E. C. Ratcliff, pp. 135-154. Edited by A. H. Couratin and D. J. Tripp. London: SPCK, 1976.

SAUGET, J. M. "Le Codex liturgicus de J. L. Assémani et ses sources manuscrites pour les Ordines de l'initiation chrétienne selon la tradition syro-occidentale." Gregorianum, 54 (1973): 339-352.

SCHMEMANN, Alexander. Of Water and the Spirit: A Liturgical Study of Baptism. Crestwood, NY: St. Vladimir's Seminary Press, 1974.

SPACIL, Bohumil. Doctrina theologiae orientis separati de sacramento baptismi. OC, 25. Rome: Pontificium Institutum Orientalium Studiorum, 1926.

VELLIAN, Jacob. Studies on Syrian Baptismal Rites. Kottayam: J. Vellian, 1973.

VERGHESE, Paul. "Relation between Baptism, 'Confirmation' and the Eucharist in the Syrian Orthodox Church." Studia Liturgica, 4 (1965): 81-93.

WHITAKER, E. C. "The Baptismal Formula in the Syrian Rite." Church Quarterly Review, 161 (1960): 346-352.

F. LATIN CHURCHES

1. Texts

a. Pre-Vatican II

Catholic Church, Milan. "The Order of Baptism." Studia Liturgica,
4, 4 (1965): I-a-(1-10).

HERWEGEN, Ildefons, ed. Taufe und Firmung, nach dem römischen
Missale, Rituale und Pontificale. Liturgische Texte, 11. KT,
144. Bonn: Marcus & Weber, 1920.

b. Post-Vatican II

Ordo Baptismi Parvulorum. Rome: Typis Polyglottis Vaticanis,
1969; The Rite of Baptism for Children. New York: Catholic
Book Publishing Co., 1969.

Ordo Initiationis Christianae Adultorum. Rome: Typis Polyglottis
Vaticanis, 1972; Rite of Christian Initiation of Adults. Washington, DC: United States Catholic Conference, 1974.

2. Studies

a. Pre-Vatican II

AKELEY, T. C. Christian Initiation in Spain, c. 300-1100. London: Darton, Longman & Todd, 1967.

ALES, Adhémar d'. Prima lineamenta tractatus dogmatici de bap-
tismo et confirmatione. Paris: Beauchesne, 1927; Baptême et
confirmation. Paris: Bloud & Gay, 1927; Baptism and Confirmation. Translated by Joseph H. Howard. London: Sands,
1929.

CAMELOT, Thomas. Spiritualité du baptême. LO, 30. Paris:
Cerf, 1960.

CAPELLE, Bernard. "L'introduction du catéchumenat à Rome."
Recherches de théologie ancienne et médiévale, 5 (1933): 129-
154; reprinted in his Travaux liturgiques, vol. 3, pp. 186-210.
Louvain: Centre liturgique, Abbaye du Mont César, 1967.

DELUZ, G. "Le baptême de l'eau et d'Esprit ou le problème de la
confirmation." Etudes théologiques et religieuses (Montpellier),
22 (1947): 201-235.

DUJARIER, Michel. A History of the Catechumenate: The First
Six Centuries. New York: Sadlier, 1979.

FISCHER, Balthasar. "Formes de la commémoration du baptême
    en Occident." La Maison-Dieu, 58 (1959): 111-134.

MAERTENS, Thierry. Histoire et pastorale du rituel du catéchu-
    menat et du baptême. PL, 56. Bruges: Biblica, Publications
    de Saint André, 1962.

MITCHELL, Leonel L. "Ambrosian Baptismal Rites." Studia Litur-
    gica, 1 (1962): 241-253.

_____. "Mozarabic Baptismal Rites." Studia Liturgica, 3 (1964):
    78-87.

MULLER, Alfons. Die Lehre von der Taufe bei Albert dem Grossen.
    VGI, n.F., 2. München: Schöningh, 1967.

NEUNHEUSER, Burkhard. "De benedictione aquae baptismalis."
    Ephemerides liturgicae, 44 (1930): 194-207, 258-281, 369-412,
    455-492.

_____. Taufe und Firmung. HD, 4/2. Freiburg: Herder,
    1956; Baptism and Confirmation. Herder History of Dogma.
    Translated by John Jay Hughes. Freiburg: Herder, 1964.

SPITAL, Hermann Josef. Der Taufritus in den deutschen Ritualien
    von den ersten Drucken bis zur Einführung des Rituale Roman-
    um. LQF, 47. Münster: Aschendorff, 1968.

STENZEL, Alois. Die Taufe: eine genetische Erklärung der Tau-
    fliturgie. FGTIL, 7-8. Innsbruck: Rauch, 1957.

STOMMEL, Eduard. Studien zur Epiklese der römischen Taufwasser-
    weihe. Theophaneia, 5. Bonn: Hanstien, 1950.

THOMAS AQUINAS. Summa Theologiae, vol. 57: Baptism and Con-
    firmation (3a. 66-72). Edited and translated by James J. Cun-
    ningham. Cambridge: Blackfriars; New York: McGraw-Hill;
    London: Eyre & Spottiswoode, 1975.

    b. Post-Vatican II (with special reference to
        the Rite of Christian Initiation of Adults)

Adult Baptism and the Catechumenate. Concilium, 22. New York:
    Paulist Press, 1967.

AUF DER MUR, H., and KLEINHEYER, B., eds. Zeichen des
    Glaubens: Studien zu Taufe und Firmung. Zürich: Benziger,
    1972.

Bishops' Committee on the Liturgy. Christian Initiation of Adults.
    Study Texts, 10. Washington, DC: United States Catholic
    Conference Publications, 1985.

BOYACK, Kenneth. A Parish Guide to Adult Initiation. Ramsey,
NJ: Paulist Press, 1979.

BROCKETT, Lorna. The Theology of Baptism. Notre Dame, IN:
Fides, 1971.

BROCKOPP, Daniel C., HELGE, Brian L., and TRUEMPER, David
G., eds. Christian Initiation: Reborn of Water and the Spirit.
ILSOP, 1. Valparaiso: Institute of Liturgical Studies, 1981.

"Christian Initiation: Into Full Communion." National Bulletin on
Liturgy (Canada), 64 (May-June 1978).

DANIELOU, Jean. L'entrée dans l'histoire du salut: baptême et
confirmation. FV, 36. Paris: Cerf, 1967.

DAVIS, Charles. The Making of a Christian. London: Sheed &
Ward, 1964; American ed., Sacraments of Initiation, Baptism
and Confirmation. New York: Sheed & Ward, 1964.

DUGGAN, Robert. "Implementing the Rite of Christian Initiation of
Adults: Pastoral-Theological Reflections." The Living Light,
17, 4 (Winter 1980): 327-333.

DUJARIER, Michel. The Rites of Christian Initiation: Historical
and Pastoral Reflections. New York: Sadlier, 1979.

DUNNING, James B. "The Rite of Christian Initiation of Adults:
Model of Adult Growth." Worship, 53 (1979): 142-156.

_____. New Wine, New Wineskins: Exploring the RCIA. New
York: Sadlier, 1981.

EASTMAN, A. Theodore. The Baptizing Community. New York:
Seabury Press, 1982.

GY, Pierre Marie. "La notion chrétienne d'initiation." La Maison-
Dieu, 132 (1977): 33-54.

HAMMAN, Adalbert. Le baptême et la confirmation. MCTS. Paris:
Desclée, 1969.

_____, ed. L'initiation chrétienne. Introduction de Jean Dan-
iélou. Nouvelle éd. Bruxelles: Desclée de Brouwer, 1980.

"L'initiation chrétienne." La Maison-Dieu, 132 (1977). [Special
issue]

KAVANAGH, Aidan. The Shape of Baptism: The Rite of Christian
Initiation. New York: Pueblo, 1978.

_____. "Unfinished and Unbegun Revisited: The Rite of Christian Initiation of Adults." Worship, 53 (1979): 327-340.

KEMP, Raymond B. A Journey in Faith: An Experience of the Catechumenate. New York: Sadlier, 1979.

LECUYER, Joseph. "Rapport entre foi et baptême dans la liturgie." Ephermides theologicae lovanienses, 49 (1973): 87-99.

McCORMACK, Arthur. Christian Initiation. TCEC, 50. New York: Hawthorn Books, 1969.

MALDONADO, Luis, and POWER, David, eds. Structures of Initiation in Crisis. Concilium, 122. New York: Seabury Press, 1979.

MARSH, Thomas. Gift of Community: Baptism and Confirmation. MS, 2. Wilmington, DE: Michael Glazier, 1984.

Modern Liturgy, 7, 7 (November 1980). [Special issue on RCIA]

Murphy Center for Liturgical Research. Made, Not Born: New Perspectives on Christian Initiation and the Catechumenate. LS. Notre Dame, IN: University of Notre Dame Press, 1976.

New Catholic World, 222, 1329 (July-August 1979). [Special issue on RCIA]

O'SHEA, William J. Sacraments of Initiation. Englewood Cliffs, NJ: Prentice-Hall, 1966.

REEDY, William, ed. Becoming a Catholic Christian: A Symposium on Christian Initiation. New York: Sadlier, 1978.

SAGOVSKY, Nicholas. Modern Roman Catholic Worship: Baptism and Penance. GBMW, 43. Bramcote, Eng.: Grove Books, 1976.

SCHLIER, Heinrich. "Zur kirchlichen Lehre von der Taufe." In his Die Zeit der Kirche: Exegetische Aufsätze und Vorträge, pp. 107-129. 5. Aufl. Freiburg: Herder, 1972.

SEARLE, Mark. Christening: The Making of Christians. Collegeville, MN: Liturgical Press, 1980.

STOOKEY, Laurence H. "Three New Initiation Rites." Worship, 51 (1977): 33-49.

_____. Baptism: Christ's Act in the Church. Nashville, TN: Abingdon Press, 1982.

3. Old Catholic Churches

PURSCH, Kurt, RUTHY, A. E., and TOL, C. "Baptism. Old
Catholic." Dictionary of Liturgy and Worship, pp. 56-58.

G. LUTHERAN CHURCHES

1. Texts

Inter-Lutheran Commission on Worship. Holy Baptism. CW, 7.
Minneapolis: Augsburg, 1974.

2. Studies

ALTHAUS, Paul. Die historische und dogmatische Grundlagen der
lutheranischen Taufliturgie. Hannover: Fische, 1893.

BECKMANN, Joachim. Die Heilsnotwendigkeit der Taufe. SBK, 8.
Stuttgart: Evangelisches Verlagswerk, 1951.

_____. Die kirchliche Ordnung der Taufe. SBK, 7. Stuttgart:
Evangelisches Verlagswerk, 1950.

BRAND, Eugene. Baptism: A Pastoral Perspective. Minneapolis,
MN: Augsburg, 1975.

BRUNNER, Peter. Die evangelisch-lutherische Lehre von der Taufe:
eine kontroverstheologische Anfrage an das Dogma und die Dogmatik der römisch-katholischen Kirche. Luthertum, 4. Berlin:
Lutherisches Verlagshaus, 1951.

GRUENAGEL, Friedrich, ed. Was ist Taufe? Ein Auseinandersetzung mit Karl Barth. Stuttgart: Evangelisches Verlagswerk,
1951.

JETTER, Werner. Die Taufe beim jungen Luther: eine Untersuchung über das Werden der reformatorischen Sakraments- und
Taufanschauung. BHT, 18. Tübingen: Mohr, 1954.

JOSEFSON, Ruben. Luthers lära om depet. Stockholm: Svenska
Kyrkans Diakonistyrelsis Bokförlag, 1944; Luther on Baptism.
Translated by Gustav Carlberg. Hong Kong: Lutheran Theo-
logical Seminary, 1952.

SCHLINK, Edmund. Die Lehre von der Taufe. Kassel: Stauda,
1967; The Doctrine of Baptism. Translated by Herbert J. A.
Bouman. St. Louis, MO: Concordia, 1972.

VICEDOM, Georg F. Die Taufe unter den Heiden. München: Kaiser, 1960.

H. REFORMED CHURCHES

1. Texts

Communauté de Taizé. Liturgie du baptême. Macon: Combier, 1957?

2. Studies

BAILLIE, John. Baptism and Conversion. New York: Scribner, 1963; London: Oxford University Press, 1964.

Le Baptême dans l'église réformée: textes commentés par un groupe de pasteurs. Neuchâtel: Imprimerie P. Attinger, 1954.

BARKLEY, John. "Baptism. Reformed." Dictionary of Liturgy and Worship, pp. 60-63.

BARTH, Karl. Die kirchliche Dogmatik, IV: Die Lehre von der Versöhnung, 4: Das christliche Leben (Fragment): Die Taufe als Begründung des christlichen Lebens. Zürich: Evangelischer Verlag, 1967; Church Dogmatics. Edited by G. W. Bromiley and T. F. Torrance. Vol. 4: The Doctrine of Reconciliation, Part 4: Baptism as the Foundation of the Christian Life. Translated by G. W. Bromiley. Edinburgh: T. & T. Clark, 1969.

_____. Die kirchliche Lehre von der Taufe. 2. Aufl. TS, 14. Zürich: Evangelischer Verlag, 1943; The Teaching of the Church Regarding Baptism. Translated by Ernest A. Payne. London: SCM Press, 1948.

_____. Die kirchliche Lehre von der Taufe. 4. Aufl. Zürich: Evangelischer Verlag, 1953.

BARTH, Markus. Die Taufe, ein Sakrament? Ein exegetischer Beitrag zum Gespräch über die kirchliche Taufe. Zürich: Evangelischer Verlag, 1951.

CHURCH OF SCOTLAND. The Biblical Doctrine of Baptism. Edinburgh: St. Andrew Press, 1958.

GRISLIS, Egil. "Calvin's Doctrine of Baptism." Church History, 31 (1962): 46-65.

JUNGEL, Eberhard. Karl Barths Lehre von der Taufe. TS, 98.
Zürich: EVZ-Verlag, 1968.

KRECK, Walter. "Die Lehre von der Taufe bei Calvin." Evangelische Theologie, 8 (1948-1949): 237-254.

MURRAY, John. Christian Baptism. Philadelphia, PA: Presbyterian and Reformed Publishing Co., 1962.

TORRANCE, T. F. "L'Enseignement baptismal de Calvin." Revue
de théologie et de philosophie, 9 (1959): 141-152.

USTERI, Joh. Martin. "Calvins Sakraments- und Tauflehre."
Theologische Studien und Kritiken, 57 (1884): 417-456.

_____. "Darstellung der Tauflehre Zwinglis." Theologische
Studien und Kritiken, 55 (1882): 205-284.

_____. "Oekolampads Stellung zur Kindertaufe." Theologische
Studien und Kritiken, 56 (1883): 155-174.

_____. "Die Stellung der Strassburger Reformatoren Bucer und
Capito zur Tauffrage." Theologische Studien und Kritiken, 57
(1884): 456-525.

_____. "Vertiefung der zwinglischen Sakraments- und Tauflehre
bei Bullinger." Theologische Studien und Kritiken, 56 (1883):
730-758.

_____. "Weitere Beiträge zur Geschichte der Tauflehre der re-
formierte Kirche." Theologische Studien und Kritiken, 56
(1883): 610-620.

VIERING, Fritz C., ed. Zu Karl Barths Lehre von der Taufe.
Gütersloh: Mohn, 1971.

I. ANGLICAN CHURCHES

1. Anglican Church of Canada

ANGLICAN CHURCH OF CANADA. Doctrine and Worship Committee.
Christian Initiation. CALS, 1. Toronto, Ont.: Anglican Book
Centre, 1974.

_____. Institution and Induction. CALS, 3. Toronto, Ont.:
Anglican Book Centre, 1974.

_____. Membership, Its Meaning and Expression. CALS, 2.
Toronto, Ont.: Anglican Book Centre, 1975.

SCHMEISER, James, ed. Initiation Theology. Toronto, Ont.:
Anglican Book Centre, 1978.

2. Church of England

BAILEY, Derrick Sherwin. Sponsors at Baptism and Confirmation:
An Historical Introduction to Anglican Practice. London:
SPCK, 1952; New York: Macmillan, 1953.

BROMILEY, Geoffrey W. Baptism and the Anglican Reformers.
London: Lutterworth Press, 1953.

CHILD, Robert Leonard. A Conversation about Baptism. London:
SCM Press, 1963.

CHURCH OF ENGLAND. The Theology of Christian Initiation. Being the Report of a Theological Commission appointed by the
Archbishops of Canterbury and York to advise on the relations
between Baptism, Confirmation and Holy Communion. London:
SPCK, 1948.

_____. Baptism Today. Being the scheduled attached to the
Second Interim Reports of the Joint Committees on Baptism,
Confirmation, and Holy Communion, as presented to the Convo-
cations of Canterbury and York in October, 1949. London:
Press and Publications Board, 1949.

_____. Convocations of Canterbury and York. Baptism and
Confirmation Today. London: SPCK, 1955.

_____. Liturgical Commission. Baptism and Confirmation. A
Report submitted by the Church of England Liturgical Commission to the Archbishops of Canterbury and York in November
1958. London: SPCK, 1959.

_____. Baptism and Confirmation. A Report submitted by the
Church of England Liturgical Commission to the Archbishops
of Canterbury and York December 1966. London: SPCK,
1967.

EVERY, George. The Baptismal Sacrifice. SMW, 14. London:
SCM Press, 1959.

HATCHETT, Marion J. "Thomas Cranmer and the Rites of Christian
Initiation." S.T.M. thesis, General Theological Seminary,
New York, 1967.

HEBERT, Arthur Gabriel. An Essay in Baptismal Revision. Westminster, Eng.: Dacre Press, 1947.

POCKNEE, Cyril E. The Rites of Christian Initiation: Their Revision and Reform. CST, 5. London: Mowbray, 1962.

RAWLINSON, A. E. J. Christian Initiation. London: SPCK, 1947.

SOUTHCOTT, E. W. Receive This Child: Constructive Thinking on Baptism. London: Mowbray, 1951.

THOMPSON, T. The Offices of Baptism and Confirmation. Cambridge: Cambridge University Press, 1914.

VIDLER, Alec R. "Baptismal Disgrace." Theology, 41 (1940): 1-9.

WHITAKER, E. C. The Proposed Services of Baptism and Confirmation Reconsidered. London: SPCK, 1960.

_____. Sacramental Initiation Complete in Baptism. GLS, 1. Bramcote, Eng.: Grove Books, 1975.

3. Protestant Episcopal Church in the United States of America

HINES, John M. By Water and the Holy Spirit: New Concepts of Baptism, Confirmation, and Communion. Foreword by Alfred R. Shands. New York: Seabury Press, 1973.

Ministry I: Holy Baptism. Alexandria, VA: Associated Parishes, 1978.

MITCHELL, Leonel L. "The Theology of Christian Initiation and the Proposed Book of Common Prayer." Anglican Theological Review, 60 (1978): 399-419.

[Prayer Book Studies.] Baptism and Confirmation. PBS, 1. New York: Church Pension Fund, 1950.

[_____.] On Baptism and Confirmation. PBS, 18. New York: Church Pension Fund, 1970.

[_____.] Holy Baptism, together with a Form for Confirmation. PBS, 26. New York: Church Hymnal Corp., 1973.

[_____.] Holy Baptism, together with a Form for the Affirmation of Baptismal Vows. PBS, 26, supplement. New York: Church Hymnal Corp., 1973.

WEIL, Louis. "Christian Initiation: A Theological and Pastoral Commentary on the Proposed Rites." St. Luke's Journal of

Theology, 18 (March 1975):   95-112; offprint ed., Alexandria, VA: Associated Parishes, 1977.

WOLF, Frederick B.   "Christian Initiation." In Prayer Book Renewal. Edited by H. Barry Evans. New York: Seabury Press, 1978.

J. METHODIST CHURCHES

1. Texts

UNITED METHODIST CHURCH. A Service of Baptism, Confirmation, and Renewal. Nashville, TN: United Methodist Publishing House, 1980.

2. Studies

CUSHMAN, Robert E.   "Baptism and the Family of God." In The Doctrine of the Church, pp. 79-102. Edited by Dow Kirkpatrick. Nashville, TN: Abingdon Press, 1964.

ENGLISH, John C.   The Heart Renewed: John Wesley's Doctrine of Christian Initiation. Macon, GA: Wesleyan College, 1967.

_____. "The Sacrament of Baptism according to the Sunday Service of 1784." Methodist History, 5 (1967):   10-16.

GUETTSCHE, Walter Louis.   "Background for United Methodist Baptismal Doctrine and Practice: The Wesleyan Tradition." D. Min. thesis, Perkins School of Theology, Southern Methodist University, 1974.

HOLLAND, Bernard G. Baptism in Early Methodism. London: Epworth Press, 1970.

"A Lutheran-United Methodist Statement on Baptism." Quarterly Review, 1 (Fall 1980):   59-68; comments pp. 69-79.

"Lutheran-United Methodist Papers on Baptism." Perkins Journal, 34 (Winter 1981):   1-56. [Special issue]

METHODIST CHURCH (ENGLAND). Entry into the Church: Baptism and Reception into Full Membership (or Confirmation). London: Methodist Publishing House, 1967.

_____. Ministry, Baptism and Membership in the Methodist Church. London: Methodist Publishing House, 1962.

NAGLEE, David Ingersoll. "The Significance of the Relationship
    of Infant Baptism and Christian Nurture in the Thought of
    John Wesley." Ph.D. dissertation, Temple University, 1966.

RANDOLPH, David J. "Baptism, Historical, Theological and Prac-
    tical Considerations." In Companion to the Book of Worship,
    pp. 44-50. Edited by William F. Dunkle, Jr., and Joseph D.
    Quillian, Jr. Nashville, TN: Abingdon Press, 1970.

ROSSER, Leonidas. Baptism: Its Nature, Obligation, Mode, Sub-
    jects, and Benefits. 4th ed. Richmond, VA: Published by
    the Author, 1854.

SUMMERS, Thomas O. Baptism: A Treatise on the Nature, Per-
    petuity, Subjects, Administrator, Mode, and Use of the Initiat-
    ing Ordinance of the Christian Church. Richmond, VA: J.
    Early, 1852; new ed., Nashville, TN: Publishing House of the
    Methodist Episcopal Church, South, 1906.

TRIPP, David. "Entry into the Church." Methodist Sacramental
    Fellowship Bulletin, no. 95 (Pentecost 1975): 6-9.

WAINWRIGHT, Geoffrey. "The Need for a Methodist Service for the
    Admission of Infants to the Catechumenate." London Quarterly
    and Holborn Review, 193 (1968): 51-60.

WARD, A. Marcus. "The Methodist Orders of Service for Baptism
    and the Public Reception of New Members." London Quarterly
    and Holborn Review, 187, 3 (July 1962): 207-212.

WATSON, Richard. The Nature, Subjects, and Mode of Christian
    Baptism. New York: Mason & Lane, 1837.

WESLEY, John. "A Treatise on Baptism." In The Works of the
    Rev. John Wesley, vol. 10, pp. 188-201. London: Wesleyan-
    Methodist Book Room, 1872; reprint ed., Grand Rapids, MI:
    Zondervan, 1958; reprinted as Wesley's Works, Grand Rapids,
    MI: Baker, 1979.

WILLIMON, William H. Remember Who You Are: Baptism, a Model
    for Christian Life. Nashville, TN: Upper Room, 1980.

WOLF, Milton. "History of the Baptismal Ritual in the Evangelical
    United Brethren Church." B.D. thesis, Evangelical Theological
    Seminary, 1964.

K. FREE CHURCHES

1. Anabaptists

ARMOUR, Rollin S. Anabaptist Baptism: A Representative Study. SAMH, 11. Scottdale, PA: Herald Press, 1966.

BENDER, H. S. "Baptism." Mennonite Encyclopedia, 1:224-228.

GEISER, Samuel, BENDER, H. S., and HEIN, Gerhard. "Taufe." Mennonitisches Lexikon, 4:283-288.

JESCHKE, Marlin. Believer's Baptism for Children of the Church. Scottdale, PA: Herald Press, 1983.

URNER, Hans. "Die Taufe bei Caspar Schwenckfeld." Theologische Literaturzeitung, 73 (1948): 329-342.

WINDHORST, Christof. Täuferisches Taufverständnis: Balthasar Hubmaiers Lehre zwischen traditioneller und reformatorischer Theologie. SMRT, 16. Leiden: Brill, 1976.

2. Puritan and Congregational Churches

Congregational Union of England and Wales. The Sacrament of Baptism. A Church and Kingdom Pamphlet. London: Independent Press, 1952?

DAVIES, Horton. "Baptism. Congregationalist." Dictionary of Liturgy and Worship, pp. 52-53.

ENGLISH, John C. "The Puritan Doctrine of Christian Initiation." Studia Liturgica, 6 (1969): 158-170.

3. Baptists

BEASLEY-MURRAY, G. R. "Baptism in the New Testament." Foundations, 3 (1960): 15-31.

_____. Baptism, Today and Tomorrow. London: Macmillan; New York: St. Martin's Press, 1966.

CARR, Warren. Baptism: Conscience and Clue for the Church. New York: Holt, Rinehart, & Winston, 1964.

CLARK, Neville. "Christian Initiation: A Baptist Point of View." Studia Liturgica, 4 (1965): 156-165.

GILL, Athol, ed. A Bibliography of Baptist Writings on Baptism,
    1900-1968. Rüschlikon-Zurich: Baptist Theological Seminary,
    1969.

GILMORE, Alec, ed. Christian Baptism: A Fresh Attempt to Un-
    derstand the Rite in Terms of Scripture, History, and Theology.
    Introduction by E. A. Payne. London: Lutterworth Press;
    Chicago: Judson Press, 1959.

HARDON, John A. "Believers' Baptism and the Sacrament of Con-
    firmation." Foundations, 11 (1968): 127-135.

HUGHEY, J. D., Jr. "Baptism in Baptist Theory and Practice."
    Foundations, 3 (1960): 7-14.

LUMPKIN, William L. A History of Immersion. Nashville, TN:
    Broadman Press, 1962.

MIDDLETON, Robert G. "Believers' Baptism and the Sacrament of
    Confirmation." Foundations, 11 (1968): 136-147.

PAYNE, Ernest A. "Baptists and Christian Initiation." Baptist
    Quarterly, 26 (1975): 147-157.

_____. "Believers' Baptism in Ecumenical Discussion." Founda-
    tions, 3 (1960): 32-39.

SAVORY, Jerold J. "Baptismal Hymns and Theological Restora-
    tion." Foundations, 3 (1960): 46-52.

WALKER, Michael. "Baptism: Doctrine and Practice among Bap-
    tists in the United Kingdom." Worship, 52 (1978): 46-57;
    reprinted in Foundations, 22 (1979): 72-80.

WINWARD, S. "Baptism. Baptist." Dictionary of Liturgy and
    Worship, pp. 50-51.

4. Christian Church (Disciples of Christ)

ABBOTT, B. A. "Baptism, the Faith Ordinance." In his The
    Disciples, an Interpretation, pp. 106-117. St. Louis, MO:
    Bethany Press, 1924; reprinted 1964.

BELCASTRO, Joseph. The Relationship of Baptism to Church Mem-
    bership. St. Louis, MO: Bethany Press, 1963.

CAMPBELL, Alexander. Christian Baptism: With Its Antecedents
    and Consequents. Bethany, VA: A. Campbell, 1851; rev.
    ed., Nashville, TN: Gospel Avocate, 1951.

_____. A Debate between Rev. A. Campbell and Rev. N. L.
Rice, on the Action, Subject, Design and Administration of
Christian Baptism. Reported by Marcus T. C. Gould. Lex-
ington, KY: Skillman, 1844.

CAMPBELL, Alexander. A Public Debate on Christian Baptism,
between Rev. W. L. MacCalla and Alexander Campbell. 2d ed.
Pittsburgh, PA: Eichbaum & Johnston, 1882; reprint ed.,
Kansas City, KS: Old Paths Book Club, 1948.

Encounter. 21, 3 (1960). [Special issue on baptism]

ENGLAND, Stephen Jackson. The One Baptism: Baptism and
Christian Unity, with Special Reference to the Disciples of
Christ. St. Louis, MO: Bethany Press, 1960.

SMITH, T. K. "Catholic and Apostolic Baptism." Shane Quarterly,
2, 2-3 (1941): 250-263.

WATKINS, Keith. "Baptism. Christian Church (Disciples of
Christ)." Dictionary of Liturgy and Worship, pp. 51-52.

5. Pentecostal Churches

McDONNELL, Kilian. "Baptism. Pentecostal." Dictionary of Liturgy and Worship, pp. 58-59.

RANAGHAN, Kevin M. "Conversion and Baptism: Personal Experience and Ritual Celebration in Pentecostal Churches." Studia
Liturgica, 10 (1974): 65-76.

SYNAN, Vinson. "Christian Initiation in the Pentecostal Holiness
Church." Studia Liturgica, 10 (1974): 56-64.

6. Other Free Churches

BEACH, B. B. "Baptism. Seventh-Day Adventist." Dictionary
of Liturgy and Worship, pp. 63-64.

BRUCE, F. F. "Baptism. Plymouth Brethren." Dictionary of
Liturgy and Worship, p. 59.

L. STUDIES OF INFANT BAPTISM

ALAND, Kurt. Die Säuglingstaufe im Neuen Testament und in der
alten Kirche. TEH, n.F., 86. München: Kaiser, 1961; Did
the Early Church Baptize Infants? Translated with an

introduction by G. R. Beasley-Murray. London: SCM Press;
Philadelphia, PA: Westminster Press, 1963.

_____. Die Stellung der Kinder in den frühen christlichen
Gemeinden--und ihre Taufe. TEH, n.F., 138. München:
Kaiser, 1967.

_____. Taufe und Kindertaufe: 40 Sätze zur Aussage des
Aussage des Neuen Testaments und dem historischen Befund,
zur modernen Debatte darüber und den Folgerungen daraus
für die kirchliche Praxis, zugleich eine Auseinandersetzung
mit Karl Barths Lehre von der Taufe. Gütersloh: Mohn, 1971.

ALTING VON GEUSAU, Leo George Marie. Die Lehre von der
Kindertaufe bei Calvin, gesehen im Rahmen seiner Sakraments-
und Tauftheologie. Bilthoven: Nelissen, 1963.

BENOIT, André. "Le problème du pédobaptisme." Revue d'histoire et de philosophie religieuse, 28 (1948-1949): 132-141.

BENOIT, Jean D. "Calvin et le baptême des enfants." Revue
d'histoire et de philosophie religieuse, 17 (1937): 457-473.

BERKOUWER, G. C. Karl Barth en de kinderdoop. Kampen:
Kok, 1947.

BRAND, E. L. "Baptism and Communion of Infants: A Lutheran
View." Worship, 50 (1976): 29-42.

BRINKEL, Karl. Die Lehre Luthers von der fides infantium bei der
Kindertaufe. ThA, 7. Berlin: Evangelische Verlagsanstalt,
1958.

BROMILEY, Geoffrey. Children of Promise: The Case for Baptizing Infants. Grand Rapids, MI: Eerdmans, 1979.

BUCHANAN, Colin O. A Case for Infant Baptism. 2d ed. GBMW,
20. Bramcote, Eng.: Grove Books, 1978.

COVINO, Paul F. X. "The Postconciliar Infant Baptism Debate in
the American Catholic Church." Worship, 56 (1982): 240-260.

CRYER, Neville. By What Rite? Infant Baptism in a Missionary
Situation. Oxford: Mowbray, 1969.

HOLLAND, Bernard G. The Doctrine of Infant Baptism in Non-
Wesleyan Methodism. London: Wesley Historical Society, 1970.

HUBERT, Hans. Der Streit um die Kindertaufe: eine Darstellung
der von Karl Barth 1943 ausgelösten Diskussion um die Kindertaufe und ihrer Bedeutung für die heutige Tauffrage. EH,
23/10. Bern: Herbert Lang; Frankfurt: Peter Lang, 1972.

HUCK, Gabe. Infant Baptism in the Parish. Chicago: Liturgy Training Program, 1979.

JEREMIAS, Joachim. Die Kindertaufe in den ersten vier Jahrhunderten. Göttingen: Vanderhoeck & Ruprecht, 1958; Infant Baptism in the First Four Centuries. Translated by David Cairns. London: SCM Press; Philadelphia, PA: Westminster Press, 1960.

_____. Nochmals: Die Anfänge der Kindertaufe. TEH, n.F., 101. München: Kaiser, 1962; The Origins of Infant Baptism: A Further Study in Reply to Kurt Aland. Translated by Dorothea M. Barton. London: SCM Press; Naperville, IL: Allenson, 1963.

JEWETT, Paul K. Infant Baptism and the Covenant of Grace. Grand Rapids, MI: Eerdmans, 1978.

KASPER, Walter, ed. Christsein ohne Entscheidung, oder soll die Kirche Kinder taufen? Mainz: Matthias-Grünewald, 1970.

KIESLING, C. "Infant Baptism." Worship, 42 (1968): 617-626.

LUSCHER, Albert. Grosstaufe oder Kindertaufe? Langenthal: Pflug, 1964.

MARCEL, Pierre Charles. "Le baptême, sacrement de l'alliance de grâce." La revue réformée, nos. 2-3 (October 1950); The Biblical Doctrine of Infant Baptism: Sacrament of the Covenant of Grace. Translated by Philip Edgcumbe Hughes. London: J. Clarke, 1953.

MARXSEN, Willi. Darf man kleine Kinder taufen? Eine Falsche Fragestellung. AMT, 12. Gütersloh: Mohn, 1969.

OEPKE, Albrecht. "Urchristentum und Kindertaufe." Zeitschrift für die neutestamentlichen Wissenschaft, 29 (1930): 81-111.

_____. "Zur Frage nach dem Ursprung der Kindertaufe." In Das Erbe Martin Luthers und die gegenwartige theologische Forschung: theologische Abhandlungen d. Ludwig Ihmels zum siebzigsten Geburtstage, pp. 84-100. Edited by R. Jelke. Leipzig: Dörffling & Franke, 1928.

POCKNEE, Cyril E. Infant Baptism, Yesterday and Today: The Case for Baptismal Reform in the Church of England. CST, 10. London: Mowbray, 1966.

PREISS, T. "Le baptême des enfants et le Nouveau Testament." Verbum Caro, 1 (1947): 113-122.

REDMOND, Richard X. "Infant Baptism: History and Pastoral
    Problems." Theological Studies, 30 (1969): 79-89.

SCHENCK, Lewis Bevens. The Presbyterian Doctrine of Children
    in the Covenant: An Historical Study of the Significance of
    Infant Baptism in the Presbyterian Church in America. New
    Haven, CT: Yale University Press; London: Oxford Univer-
    sity Press, 1940.

SMALL, Dwight Harvey. The Biblical Basis for Infant Baptism:
    Children in God's Covenant Promises. Westwood, NJ: Revell,
    1957.

UPTON, Julia Ann. "A Solution to the Infant Baptism Problem."
    Living Light, 16, 4 (Winter 1979): 484-496.

WALL, William. The History of Infant Baptism. 2 vols. London,
    1705.

_____. _____. New ed., by Henry Cotton. 4 vols. Oxford:
    Oxford University Press, 1835-1836.

WARNS, J., and BENDER, H. S. "Infant Baptism." Mennonite
    Encyclopedia, 3:34-38.

M. SPECIAL BAPTISMAL STUDIES

AUBRY, André. "Faut-il re-baptiser? Enquête historique et in-
    terrogations théologiques." Nouvelle revue théologique, 89
    (1967): 183-201.

BAILEY, Derrick Sherwin. Sponsors at Baptism and Confirmation.
    London: SPCK, 1952.

BURKI, Bruno. "Traditional Initiation in Africa." Studia Liturgica,
    12 (1977): 201-206.

DAVIES, John G. The Architectural Setting of Baptism. London:
    Barrie & Rockcliff, 1962.

DOLGER, Franz Josef. Der Exorcismus im altchristlichen Taufrituel.
    SGKA, 3/1-2. Paderborn: Schöningh, 1909.

GENSICHEN, Hans Werner. Das Taufproblem in der Mission.
    Gütersloh: Bertelsmann, 1951.

HATCHETT, Marion J. "Initiation: Baptism or Ordination?" St.
    Luke's Journal of Theology, 12 (September 1969): 17-22.

HUBER, Max. Taufe in der Eucharistiefeier: thematische Gottesdienst. Regensburg: Pustet, 1978.

LWAKALE, Celestin Mubengayi. Initiation africaine et initiation
chrétienne. Léopoldville (Kinshasa): Editions du C. E. P.,
1966.

MARSH, Thomas. "The History and Significance of the Post-
Baptismal Rites." Irish Theological Quarterly, 29 (1962):
175-206.

MAXWELL, William D. "Holy Baptism and Resurrection." Studia
Liturgica, 1 (1962): 175-181.

MITCHELL, Leonel L. Baptismal Anointing. ACC, 48. London:
SPCK, 1966; reprint ed., Notre Dame, IN: University of
Notre Dame Press, 1977.

MORIN, G. "La Sputation: rite baptismal de l'église de Milan au
IVe siècle, d'après un passage corrigé du De mysteriis de S.
Ambroise." Revue bénédictine, 16 (1899): 414-418.

RISSI, Mathis. Die Taufe für die Toten: ein Beitrag zur paulinischen Tauflehre. ATANT, 42. Stuttgart: Zwingli Verlag,
1962.

ROGERS, Clement F. Baptism and Christian Archaeology. Oxford:
Clarendon Press, 1903.

SCHEIDT, Hubert. Die Taufwasserweihegebete im Sinne vergleichender Liturgieforschung untersucht. LQF, 29. Münster:
Aschendorff, 1945.

TRIPP, David. "Initiation Rites of the Cathari." Studia Liturgica,
12 (1977): 184-194.

VAN UNNIK, W. C. "Les Cheveux défaits des femmes baptisées:
un rite de baptême dans l'ordre ecclésiastique d'Hippolyte."
Vigiliae Christianae, 1 (1947): 77-100.

WHITAKER, E. C. "The Baptismal Interrogations." Theology, 59
(1956): 103-112.

N. CONFIRMATION

1. General and Ecumenical Studies

[Confirmation--special issue]. Pastoral Music, 5, 2 (December 1980/
January 1981).

CULLY, Kendig Brubaker, ed. Confirmation: History, Doctrine
and Practice. Greenwich, CT: Seabury Press, 1962.

DOLGER, Franz Josef. Das Sakrament der Firmung historisch-
dogmatisch dargestellt. Wien: Mayer, 1906.

FISHER, J. D. C. Confirmation Then and Now. ACC, 60. London: SPCK, 1978.

FROR, Kurt, ed. Confirmatio; Forschungen zur Geschichte und
Praxis der Konfirmation. München: Evangelischer Presseverband für Bayern, 1959.

HALL, A. C. A. Confirmation. OLPT. London: Longmans,
Green, 1900.

HUGHES, Philip Edgcumbe. Confirmation in the Church Today.
Grand Rapids, MI: Eerdmans, 1973.

JACKSON, William. The History of Confirmation. Oxford: Parker,
1877.

KEIFER, R. "Confirmation and Christian Maturity: The Deeper
Issue." Worship, 46 (1972): 601-608.

LIGIER, Louis. La Confirmation: sens et conjoncture oecuménique
hier et aujourd'hui. TH, 23. Paris: Beauchesne, 1973.

THURIAN, Max. La Confirmation, consécration des laïcs. Neuchâtel: Delachaux & Niestlé, 1957; Consecration of the Layman:
New Approaches to the Sacrament of Confirmation. Translated
by W. J. Kerrigan. Baltimore, MD: Helicon, 1963.

VISCHER, Lukas. Die Geschichte der Konfirmation: ein Beitrag
zur Diskussion über das Konfirmationsproblem. Zürich:
Evangelischer Verlag, 1958.

2. Early Church

BOTTE, Bernard. "Le Vocabulaire ancien de la confirmation."
La Maison-Dieu, 54 (1958): 5-22.

CHASE, Frederic Henry. Confirmation in the Apostolic Age. London: Macmillan, 1909.

COURATIN, A. H. "Justin Martyr and Confirmation—a Note."
Theology, 55 (1950): 458-460.

LECUYER, J. "La Confirmation chez les pères." La Maison-Dieu,
54 (1958): 23-52.

MASON, Arthur James. The Relation of Confirmation to Baptism
as Taught in the Holy Scriptures and the Fathers. 2d ed.
London: Longmans, Green, 1893.

NEUMANN, Johannes. Der Spender der Firmung in der Kirche des
Abendlandes bis zum Ende des kirchlichen Altertums. Meitin-
gen: Kyrios, 1963.

RATCLIFF, E. C. "Justin Martyr and Confirmation." Theology,
51 (1948): 133-139; reprinted in his Liturgical Studies of
E. C. Ratcliff, pp. 110-117. Edited by A. H. Couratin and
D. J. Tripp. London: SPCK, 1976.

SHEPHERD, Massey H., Jr. "Confirmation: The Early Church."
Worship, 46 (1972): 15-21.

WELTE, Bernhard. Die postbaptismale Salbung: ihr symbolischer
Gehalt und ihre sakramentale Zugehörigkeit nach den Zeugnis-
sen der alten Kirche. FTS, 51. Freiburg: Herder, 1939.

3. Latin Churches

ADAM, Adolf. Das Sakrament der Firmung nach Thomas von Aquin.
FTS, 73. Freiburg: Herder, 1958.

AMOUGOU-ATANGANA, Jean. Ein Sakrament des Geistempfangs?
Zum Verhältnis von Taufe und Firmung. OF, 3/1. Freiburg:
Herder, 1974.

AUSTIN, Gerard. "What Has Happened to Confirmation?" Worship,
50 (1976): 420-426.

BOHEN, Marian. The Mystery of Confirmation: A Theology of the
Sacrament. New York: Herder & Herder, 1963.

BOTTE, Bernard. "A propos de la confirmation." Nouvelle revue
théologique, 88 (1966): 848-852.

BOUHOT, Jean Paul. La confirmation, sacrement de la communion
ecclésiale. CPT. Lyon: Chalet, 1968.

BOUYER, Louis. "Que signifie la confirmation?" Paroisse et liturgie, 34 (1952): 3-12.

BRINKTRINE, Johannes. "Zur Entstehung der lateinischen Firm-
formel." Theologie und Glaube, 44 (1954): 51-53.

CAPRIOLI, A. "Rassegna de Teologia sul sacramento della cresima."
Scuola Cattolica, Supp. Bib., 91 (1963): 131-146.

"La Confirmation." La Maison-Dieu, 54 (1958). [Special issue]

CREHAN, J. "The Sealing at Confirmation." Theological Studies,
    14 (1953):   273-279.

EYNDE, D. van den. "Les rites liturgiques latins de la confirma-
    tion." La Maison-Dieu, 54 (1958):   53-78.

FITZGERALD, Timothy. Confirmation, a Parish Celebration. Chi-
    cago: Liturgy Training Publications, 1983.

KIESLING, Christopher. Confirmation and Full Life in the Spirit.
    Cincinnati, OH: St. Anthony Messenger Press, 1973.

KUNG, Hans. "Confirmation as the Completion of Baptism." In
    Experience of the Spirit, pp. 79-99. Edited by Peter Huizing
    and William Bassett. Concilium, 99. New York: Seabury
    Press, 1974.

LAROS, Matthias. Pfingstgeist über uns: die heilige Firmung als
    Sakrament der Persönlichkeit, des allgemeinen Priestertums und
    des apostolischen Geistes hier und heute. Regensburg: Pus-
    tet, 1935; Confirmation in the Modern World. Translated by
    George Sayer. New York: Sheed & Ward, 1938.

LEVET, R. "L'âge de la confirmation." La Maison-Dieu, 54 (1958):
    118-142.

LUYKX, B. "Théologie et pastorale de la confirmation." Paroisse
    et liturgie, 39 (1957):   180-201, 263-278.

LYNCH, Kilian F. The Sacrament of Confirmation in the Early-
    Middle Scholastic Period, vol. 1: Texts. FIPT, 5. St. Bona-
    venture, NY: Franciscan Institute, 1957.

MARSH, Thomas. "Confirmation in its Relation to Baptism." Irish
    Theological Quarterly, 27 (1960):   259-293.

_____. "A Study of Confirmation, II." Irish Theological Quar-
    terly, 39 (1972):   319-336.

MARTIMORT, A. G. "La confirmation." In Communion solennelle
    et profession de foi, Vanves 4-7 avril 1951, pp. 159-201.
    Paris: Cerf, 1952.

MILNER, Austin P. The Theology of Confirmation. Notre Dame,
    IN: Fides, 1972, c1971.

O'DOHERTY, Michael Kevin. The Scholastic Teaching on the Sacra-
    ment of Confirmation. SST, 2d Ser., 23. Washington, DC:
    Catholic University of America Press, 1949.

RATCLIFF, E. C. "The Relation of Confirmation to Baptism in the Early Roman and Byzantine Liturgies." Theology, 49 (1946): 258-265, 290-295; reprinted in his Liturgical Studies of E. C. Ratcliff, pp. 118-134. Edited by A. H. Couratin and D. J. Tripp. London: SPCK, 1976.

TETTAMANZI, D. "L'età della cresima nel pensiero teologico contemporaneo." Scuola Cattolica, 95 (1967): 62-79.

_____. "L'età della cresima nella disciplina della chiesa latina." Scuola Cattolica, 95 (1967): 34-61.

"Um den rechten Zeitpunkt der Firmspendung." Diakonia, 1 (1966): 285-291.

4. Lutheran and Reformed Churches

ALLMEN, J.-J. von. "La confirmation." In his Prophétisme sacrementel, pp. 141-182. Neuchâtel: Delachaux & Niestlé, 1964.

FROR, Kurt, ed. Zur Geschichte und Ordnung der Konfirmation in den lutherischen Kirchen. München: Claudius Verlag, 1962.

HAREIDE, Bjarne. Konfirmasjonen i reformasjonstiden: en undersøkelse av den lutherske konfirmasjon i Tyskland 1520-1585. BTP, 20. Oslo: Universitets forlaget, 1966; Die Konfirmation in der Reformationszeit: eine Untersuchung der Lutherischen Konfirmation in Deutschland 1520-1585. Translated by Karin Krideland. AP, 8. Göttingen: Vandenhoeck & Ruprecht, 1971.

Inter-Lutheran Commission on Worship. Affirmation of the Baptismal Covenant. CW, 8. Minneapolis, MN: Augsburg, 1975.

REPP, Arthur C. Confirmation in the Lutheran Church. St. Louis, MO: Concordia, 1964.

SCHUTZEICHEL, Heribert. "Calvins Kritik an der Firmung." In Zeichen des Glaubens: Studien zu Taufe und Firmung, pp. 123-135. Herausgegeben von H. Auf der Mur und B. Kleinheyer. Zürich: Benziger, 1972.

5. Anglican Churches

CHURCH OF ENGLAND. Confirmation Today. Being the schedule attached to the Interim Reports of the Joint Committees on Baptism, Confirmation, and Holy Communion, as presented to the Convocations of Canterbury and York in October, 1944. London: Press and Publications Board, 1944.

Confirmation; or, the Laying on of Hands. 2 vols. London:
   SPCK, 1926-1933.

CULLY, Kendig Brubaker, ed. Confirmation Re-examined. Wilton,
   CT: Morehouse-Barlow, 1982.

DIX, Gregory. Confirmation, or the Laying on of Hands? London:
   SPCK, 1936.

_____. The Theology of Confirmation in Relation to Baptism.
   Westminster: Dacre Press, 1946.

"Documentation and Reflection: Confirmation Today." Anglican
   Theological Review, 54 (1972): 106-119.

HATCHETT, Marion J. "The Rite of 'Confirmation' in the Book of
   Common Prayer and in Authorized Services 1973." Anglican
   Theological Review, 56 (1974): 292-310.

HOLMES, Urban T. Confirmation: The Celebration of Maturity in
   Christ. New York: Seabury Press, 1975.

MITCHELL, Leonel L. "What is Confirmation?" Anglican Theological Review, 55 (1973): 201-212.

Protestant Episcopal Church in the U.S.A. Confirmation Crisis.
   New York: Seabury Press, 1968.

THORNTON, L. S. Confirmation: Its Place in the Baptismal Mystery. Westminster, Eng.: Dacre Press, 1954.

WEIL, Louis. "Confirmation: Some Notes on Its Meaning." Anglican Theological Review, 59 (1977): 220-224.

XXX.   ORDINATION

A. GENERAL STUDIES

FERGUSON, Everett. "Laying on of Hands: Its Significance in
   Ordination." Journal of Theological Studies, N.S. 26 (1975):
   1-12.

HANSON, Anthony Tyrell. The Pioneer Ministry. London: SCM
   Press; Philadelphia, PA: Westminster Press, 1961; reprint ed.,
   London: SPCK, 1975.

KIRK, Kenneth E., ed. The Apostolic Ministry: Essays on the

History and Doctrine of Episcopacy. London: Hodder &
Stouthton, 1946.

LEMAIRE, André. Les ministères dans l'Eglise. Paris: Centurion,
1974; Ministry in the Church. Translated by C. W. Danes.
London: SPCK, 1977.

LINE, John. The Doctrine of the Christian Ministry. London:
Lutterworth Press, 1959.

MANSON, Thomas Walter. The Church's Ministry. London: Hodder & Stoughton; Philadelphia, PA: Westminster Press, 1948.

_____. Ministry and Priesthood: Christ's and Ours. London:
Epworth Press; Richmond, VA: John Knox Press, 1958.

"Ordination Rites." Studia Liturgica, 13, 2-4 (1979). [Special
issue]

PALMER, Paul F. Sacraments of Healing and Vocation. FCT.
Englewood Cliffs, NJ: Prentice-Hall, 1963.

PAUL, Robert S. Ministry. Grand Rapids, MI: Eerdmans, 1965.

TELFER, William. The Office of a Bishop. London: Darton, Longman & Todd, 1962.

WARKENTIN, Marjorie. Ordination: A Biblical-Historical View.
Grand Rapids, MI: Eerdmans, 1982.

B. ECUMENICAL STUDIES

(See also XXVI. B. 2. & 3. [pages 455-456] for World Council documents on the mutual recognition of ministry.)

IERSEL, Bas van, and MURPHY, Roland, eds. Ministries in the
Church. Concilium, 80. New York: Herder & Herder, 1972.

KUNG, Hans, ed. Apostolic Succession: Rethinking a Barrier to
Unity. Concilium, 34. New York: Paulist Press, 1968.

KUNG, Hans, and KASPER, Walter, eds. Mutual Recognition of
Ecclesial Ministries? Concilium, 74. New York: Herder &
Herder, 1972.

McADOO, H. R., and CLARK, Alan C. Ministry and Ordination:
A Statement on the Ministry Agreed on by the Anglican-Roman
Catholic Internation Commission, Canterbury, 1973. London:
SPCK; New York: Morehouse-Barlow, 1973.

Modern Ecumenical Documents on the Ministry. London: SPCK,
     1975.

SCHMIDT, Herman, ed. Liturgy and the Ministry. Concilium, 72.
     New York: Herder & Herder, 1972.

SIMPSON, E. P. Y. Ordination and Christian Unity. Valley
     Forge, PA: Judson Press, 1966.

WRIGHT, J. Robert. "Ordination in the Ecumenical Movement."
     Review and Expositor, 78 (1981): 497-514.

C. THE REVIVAL OF THE DIACONATE

BARNETT, James M. The Diaconate: A Full and Equal Order.
     New York: Seabury Press, 1981.

BISHOPS' COMMITTEE ON THE LITURGY. The Deacon, Minister
     of Word and Sacrament. Study Texts, 6. Washington, DC:
     United States Catholic Conference Publications, 1979.

BISHOPS' COMMITTEE ON THE PERMANENT DIACONATE, NA-
     TIONAL CONFERENCE OF CATHOLIC BISHOPS. Permanent
     Deacons in the U.S.: Guidelines on their Formation and Min-
     istry. 1984 revision. Washington, DC: United States Catho-
     lic Conference, 1985.

Diaconal Reader: Selected Articles from the Diaconal Quarterly.
     Washington, DC: United States Catholic Conference, 1985.

ECHLIN, Edward P. The Deacon in the Church: Past and Future.
     Staten Island: Alba House, 1971.

McCASLIN, Patrick, and LAWLER, Michael G. Sacrament of Serv-
     ice: A Vision of the Permanent Diaconate Today. New York:
     Paulist Press, 1986.

WORLD COUNCIL OF CHURCHES. The Ministry of Deacons. WCC
     Studies, 2. Geneva: World Council of Churches, 1965.

D. ORDINATION OF WOMEN

ALLWORTHY, Thomas Bateson. Women in the Apostolic Church.
     Cambridge: Heffer, 1917.

BAM, Brigalia, ed. What is Ordination Coming To? Geneva: World
     Council of Churches, 1971.

BEDALE, Stephen. "The Meaning of Kephale in the Pauline Epistles." Journal of Theological Studies, 5 (1954): 211-215.

BILEZEKIAN, Gilbert G. Beyond Sex Roles: A Guide for the
Study of Female Roles in the Bible. Grand Rapids, MI:
Baker, 1985.

BLATTENBERGER, Ruth, ed. Women Ministers: A Quaker Contribution. Wallingford, PA: Pendle Hill Publications, 1979.

BLISS, Kathleen. The Service and Status of Women in the
Churches. London: SCM Press, 1952.

BLOESCH, Donald G. Is the Bible Sexist? Beyond Feminism and
Patriarchalism. Westchester, IL: Crossway Books, 1982.

BOLDREY, Richard & Joyce. Chauvinist or Feminist? Paul's View
of Women. Grand Rapids, MI: Baker, 1976.

BOOTH, Catherine. Female Ministry; or, Woman's Right to Preach
the Gospel. London: Morgan & Chase, 1859.

BOUYER, Louis. Women in the Church. Translated by Marilyn
Teichert. San Francisco, CA: Ignatius Press, 1979.

BOZARTH-CAMPBELL, Alla. Womanpriest: A Personal Odyssey.
New York: Paulist Press, 1978.

BROTHERS, Joan. "Women in Ecclesial Office." In Ministries in
the Church, pp. 109-122. Edited by Bas van Iersel and Roland
Murphy. Concilium, 80. New York: Herder & Herder, 1972.

BRUCE, Michael, and DUFFIELD, G. E., eds. Why Not? Priesthood and the Ministry of Women: A Theological Study. Rev.
& augm. ed., prepared by R. T. Beckwith. Abingdon, Eng.:
Marcham Manor Press, 1976.

BRUNNER, Peter. The Ministry and the Ministry of Women. Contemporary Theology Series. St. Louis, MO: Concordia, 1971.

BUSHNELL, Katherine C. God's Word to Women. Oakland, CA:
Katherine C. Bushnell, 1923; reprint ed., North Collins, NY:
Ray B. Munson, n.d.

CANHAM, Elizabeth. Pilgrimage to Priesthood. Minneapolis, MN:
Winston Press, 1985.

CARROLL, Jackson W., and HARGROVE, Barbara J. Women of the
Cloth: New Opportunities for the Churches. San Francisco,
CA: Harper & Row, 1983.

CHITTISTER, Joan. Women, Ministry and the Church. Ramsey,
    NJ: Paulist Press, 1983.

Concerning the Ordination of Women. Geneva: World Council of
    Churches, 1964.

CUNNINGHAM, Agnes, et al. Women in Ministry: A Sisters' View.
    Chicago: National Association of Women Religious, 1972.

DALY, Mary. Beyond God the Father: Toward a Philosophy of
    Women's Liberation. Boston, MA: Beacon Press, 1973.

_____. The Church and the Second Sex. New York: Harper
    & Row, 1968.

DANIELOU, Jean. The Ministry of Women in the Early Church.
    London: Faith Press, 1961.

DENIS, Henri, and DELORME, Jean. "La participation des femmes
    aux ministères." In Ministère et les ministères selon le Nou-
    veau Testament, pp. 505-515. Edited by Jean Delorme. Paris:
    Editions du Seuil, 1974.

ELDRED, O. John. Women Pastors: If God Calls, Why Not the
    Church? Valley Forge, PA: Judson Press, 1981.

ERMARTH, Margaret Sittler. Adam's Fractured Rib: Observations
    on Women in the Church. Philadelphia, PA: Fortress Press,
    1970.

EYDEN, René van. "The Place of Women in Liturgical Functions."
    In Liturgy and the Ministry, pp. 68-71. Edited by Herman
    Schmidt. Concilium, 72. Edinburgh: T. & T. Clark, 1972.

FORD, Josephine M. "Biblical Material Relevant to the Ordination
    of Women." Journal of Ecumenical Studies, 10 (1973): 669-694.

GOSSMAN, Elizabeth. "Women as Priests?" In Apostolic Succession:
    Rethinking a Barrier to Unity, pp. 115-125. Edited by Hans
    Küng. Concilium, 34. New York: Paulist Press, 1968.

GUTHRIE, Harvey H., Jr. "The Bible, the Nature of the Church
    and the Ordination of Women." In To Be a Priest: Perspectives
    on Vocation and Ordination, pp. 155-162. Edited by Robert E.
    Terwilliger and Urban T. Holmes, III. New York: Seabury
    Press, 1975.

HAMILTON, Michael P., and MONTGOMERY, Nancy S., eds. The
    Ordination of Women: Pro and Con. New York: Morehouse-
    Barlow, 1975.

HARKNESS, Georgia. Women in Church and Society: A Historical and Theological Inquiry. Nashville, TN: Abingdon Press, 1971, c1972.

HEWITT, Emily C., and HIATT, Suzanne R. Women Priests: Yes or No? New York: Seabury Press, 1973.

HEYER, Robert J., ed. Women and Orders. New York: Paulist Press, 1974.

HEYWARD, Carter. A Priest Forever. New York: Harper & Row, 1976.

HODGSON, Leonard. "Theological Objections to the Ordination of Women." Expository Times, 77 (1965-1966): 210-213.

HOPKO, Thomas, ed. Women and the Priesthood: Essays from the Orthodox Tradition. Crestwood, NY: St. Vladimir's Seminary Press, 1982.

HOWE, E. Margaret. Women and Church Leadership. Contemporary Evangelical Perspectives. Grand Rapids, MI: Zondervan, 1982.

ISAKSSON, Abel. Marriage and Ministry in the New Temple. ASNU, 24. Lund: Gleerup, 1965.

JEWETT, Paul K. Man as Male and Female. Grand Rapids, MI: Eerdmans, 1975.

_____. The Ordination of Women: An Essay on the Christian Ministry. Grand Rapids, MI: Eerdmans, 1980.

KNIGHT, George W., III. The New Testament Teaching on the Role Relationship of Men and Women. Grand Rapids, MI: Baker, 1977.

KUBO, Sakae. "The Bible and the Ordination of Women." Spectrum, 7, 2 (n.d.): 29-33. [Bibliographic essay]

KUHNS, Dennis R. Women in the Church. Scottdale, PA: Herald Press, 1978.

LEE, Luther. Woman's Right to Preach the Gospel. Syracuse, NY: Luther Lee, 1853.

LEWIS, C. S. "Notes on the Way." Time & Tide, 29 (14 August 1948): 830-831; reprinted as "Priestesses in the Church?" In his God in the Dock: Essays on Theology and Ethics, 234-239. Edited by Walter Hooper. Grand Rapids, MI: Eerdmans, 1970.

LUTGE, H. Karl, ed. Sexuality--Theology--Priesthood: Reflections on the Ordination of Women to the Priesthood. San
  Gabriel, CA: Concerned Fellow Episcopalians, 1973.

MAERTENS, Thierry. The Advancing Dignity of Woman in the
  Bible. Edited by Lisa McGaw. Translated by Sandra Dibbs.
  De Pere, WI: St. Norbert Abbey Press, 1969.

MAITLAND, Sara. A Map of the New Country: Women and Christianity. London: Routledge & Kegan Paul, 1983.

MALONE, David M. The Church Cannot Ordain Women to the
  Priesthood. Chicago: Franciscan Herald Press, 1978.

MARSHALL, Michael. "The Re-ordering of the Ministry." In To
  Be a Priest: Perspectives on Vocation and Ordination, pp.
  163-172. Edited by Robert E. Terwilliger and Urban T.
  Holmes, III. New York: Seabury Press, 1975.

MASCALL, E. L. Women and the Priesthood of the Church. London: Church Literature Assoc., n.d.

McCORMICK, Richard A., and DYER, George J., eds. Future
  Forms of Ministry. Chicago: National Federation of Priests'
  Councils, 1971.

MEER, Haye S. van der. Priestertum der Frau? QD, 42. Freiburg: Herder, 1969; Women in the Catholic Church? A
  Theological-Historical Investigation. Translated by Leonard
  Swidler and Arlene Swidler. Philadelphia, PA: Temple University Press, 1973.

MICKS, Marianne H., and PRICE, Charles P., eds. Toward a New
  Theology of Ordination: Essays on the Ordination of Women.
  Alexandria, VA: Virginia Theological Seminary; Somerville,
  MA: Greeno, Hadden, 1976.

MONTEFIORE, Hugh, ed. Yes to Women Priests. Great Watering,
  Essex, Eng.: Mayhew-McCrimmon, in association with Mowbray; Greenwood, SC: Attic Press, 1978.

MOORE, Peter, ed. Man, Woman, and Priesthood. London:
  SPCK, 1978.

MORRIS, Joan. The Lady was a Bishop: The Hidden History of
  Women with Clerical Ordination and the Jurisdiction of Bishops.
  New York: Macmillan, 1973.

PARVEY, Constance F., ed. The Community of Women and Men in
  the Church. Philadelphia, PA: Fortress Press, 1983.

_____, ed. Ordination of Women in Ecumenical Perspective:
Workbook for the Church's Future. FOP, 105. Geneva:
World Council of Churches, 1980.

PETERS, Jan. "Is There Room for Women in the Functions of the
Church?" In Apostolic Succession: Rethinking a Barrier to
Unity, pp. 126-138. Edited by Hans Küng. Concilium, 34.
New York: Paulist Press, 1968.

PINL, Claudia et al. Frauen auf neuen Wegen: Studien und Prob-
lemberichte zur Situation der Frauen in Gesellschaft und Kirche.
Kennzeichen, 3. Gelnhausen, Berlin: Burckhardthaus Verlag,
1978.

PROHL, Russell C. Woman in the Church: A Restudy of Woman's
Place in Building the Kingdom. Grand Rapids, MI: Eerdmans,
1957.

REUMANN, John. "What in Scripture Speaks to the Ordination of
Women?" Concordia Theological Monthly, 44 (January 1973):
1-30.

ROBERTS, Benjamin Titus. Ordaining Women. Rochester, NY:
Earnest Christian, 1891.

RUETHER, Rosemary Radford, and McLAUGHLIN, Eleanor, eds.
Women of Spirit: Female Leadership in the Jewish and Christian
Traditions. New York: Simon & Schuster, 1979.

RUTLER, George William. Priest and Priestess. Ambler, PA:
Trinity Press, 1973.

RYRIE, Charles C. The Place of Women in the Church. New
York: Macmillan, 1958.

SCHALLER, Lyle E., ed. Women as Pastors. Nashville, TN:
Abingdon Press, 1982.

SPENCER, Aida B. Beyond the Curse: Women Called to Ministry.
Nashville, TN: Thomas Nelson, 1985.

STENDAHL, Brita. The Force of Tradition: A Case Study of
Women Priests in Sweden. Philadelphia, PA: Fortress Press,
1985.

STENDAHL, Krister. "Bibelsynen och kvinnan." In Kvinnan,
Sambällat, Kyrkan, pp. 138-167. Stockholm: Svenska Kyrkans
Diakonistyrelses Bokförlag, 1958; The Bible and the Role of
Women: A Case Study in Hermeneutics. Translated by Emilie
T. Sander. Facet Book, Biblical Series, 15. Philadelphia, PA:
Fortress Press, 1966.

SWIDLER, Leonard, and SWIDLER, Arlene, eds. Women Priests:
A Catholic Commentary on the Vatican Declaration. New York:
Paulist Press, 1977.

TAVARD, George H. Woman in Christian Tradition. Notre Dame,
IN: University of Notre Dame Press, 1973.

TETLOW, Elisabeth M. Women and Ministry in the New Testament:
Called to Serve. Lanham, MD: University Press of America,
1985.

THOMAS, Hilah F., and KELLER, Rosemary Skinner, eds. Women
in New Worlds: Historical Perspectives on the Wesleyan Tradition. 2 vols. Nashville, TN: Abingdon Press, 1981-1982.

THRALL, Margaret E. The Ordination of Women to the Priesthood:
A Study of the Biblical Evidence. SMW, 7. London: SCM
Press, 1958.

TIEMEYER, Raymond. The Ordination of Women. Minneapolis, MN:
Augsburg, 1970.

VERDESI, Elizabeth H. In But Still Out: Women in the Church.
Philadelphia, PA: Westminster Press, 1976.

VOS, Clarence J. Woman in Old Testament Worship. Delft: Judels
& Brinkman, 1968.

WEIDMAN, Judith L., ed. Women Ministers: How Women are Re-
defining Traditional Roles. San Francisco, CA: Harper &
Row, 1981.

WILKINSON, Gregorius. Why Women Could Not and Should Not Be-
come Priests in the Catholic Church. Major Currents in the
Contemporary World Library. Albuquerque, NM: American
Classical College Press, 1981.

"Women's Place in the Ministry of Non-Catholic Christian Churches."
In Apostolic Succession: Rethinking a Barrier to Unity, pp.
163-177. Edited by Hans Küng. Concilium, 34. New York:
Paulist Press, 1968.

WORLD COUNCIL OF CHURCHES. Report on Women in the Ministry, and Summary of Facts about the Ordination of Women in
the Member Churches of the World Council of Churches.
Geneva: World Council of Churches, 1958.

ZERBST, Fritz. The Office of Woman in the Church. St. Louis,
MO: Concordia, 1955.

E. EARLY CHURCH

1. Texts

PORTER, Harry Boone, ed. The Ordination Prayers of the Ancient Western Churches. ACC, 49. London: SPCK, 1967.

2. Studies

BENEDEN, Pierre van. Aux origines d'une terminologie sacramentelle: "ordo," "ordinare," "ordinatio" dans la litterature chrétienne avant 313. SSL, 38. Louvain: Spicilegium Sacrum Lovaniense, 1974.

BOTTE, Bernard. "Le Rituel d'ordination des Statuta ecclesiae antiqua." Recherches de théologie ancienne et médiévale, 11 (1939): 223-241.

BRADSHAW, P. F. "Ordination." In Essays on Hippolytus, pp. 33-38. Edited by G. J. Cuming. GLS, 15. Bramcote, Eng.: Grove Books, 1978.

BROWN, Raymond E. Priest and Bishop: Biblical Reflections. Paramus, NJ: Paulist Press, 1970.

CAMPENHAUSEN, Hans von. Kirchliches Amt und geistliche Vollmacht in den ersten drei Jahrhunderten. BHT, 14. Tübingen: Mohr, 1953; Ecclesiastical Authority and Spiritual Power in the Church of the First Three Centuries. Translated by J. A. Baker. London: A. & C. Black; Stanford, CA: Stanford University Press, 1969.

COPPENS, Joseph. L'Imposition des mains et les rites connexes dans le Nouveau Testament et dans l'église ancienne: étude de théologie positive. UCLD, 2/15. Paris: Gabalda, 1925.

CULPEPPER, R. Alan. "The Biblical Basis of Ordination." Review and Expositor, 78 (1981): 471-484.

EHRHARDT, Arnold. "Jewish and Christian Ordination." Journal of Ecclesiastical History, 5 (1954): 125-138.

FERGUSON, Everett. "Eusebius and Ordination." Journal of Ecclesiastical History, 13 (1962): 139-144.

_____. "Jewish and Christian Ordination: Some Observations." Harvard Theological Review, 56 (1963): 13-19.

FRERE, Walter Howard.   Early Forms of Ordination.   London:
   Macmillan, 1921.

_____ .   "Early Ordination Services."   Journal of Theological
   Studies, 16 (1915):   323-372.

GY, Pierre-Marie.   "La Théologie des prières anciennes pour l'ordination des évêques et des prêtres."   Revue des sciences
   philosophiques et théologiques, 58 (1974):   599-617.

KASEMANN, Ernst.   "Das Formular einer neutestamentlichen Or-
   dinationsperänese."   In his Exegetische Versuche und Besinnungen, Bd. 1, pp. 101-109.   2. Aufl.   Göttingen: Vandenhoeck & Ruprecht, 1960.

LECUYER, J.   "Episcopat et presbytérat dans les écrits d'Hippolyte de Rome."   Recherches de science religieuse, 41 (1953):
   30-50.

LEMAIRE, André.   Les Ministères aux origines de l'Eglise, naissance de la triple hierarchie: évêques, presbytres, diacres.
   LD, 68.   Paris: Cerf, 1971.

LOHSE, Eduard.   Die Ordination im Spätjudentum und im Neuen
   Testament.   Berlin: Evangelische Verlagsanstalt, 1951.

MACLEAN, Arthur John.   The Ancient Church Orders.   CHLS.
   Cambridge: Cambridge University Press, 1910.

MAGNE, Jean.   "Tradition apostolique sur les charismes" et "Diataxeis des saints apôtres":   identification des documents et
   analyse du rituel des ordinations.   His Origines chrétiennes,
   1.   Paris: Magne, 1975.

REYNOLDS, Roger E.   The Ordinals of Christ from Their Origins
   to the Twelfth Century.   BGQM, 7.   Berlin, New York: De
   Gruyter, 1978.

SEGELBERG, E.   "The Ordination Prayers in Hippolytus."   In
   Studia Patristica, vol. 13, pp. 397-408.   Edited by Elizabeth
   A. Livingstone.   TUGAL, 116.   Berlin: Akademie-Verlag, 1975.

SWETE, Henry B., ed.   Essays on the Early History of the Church
   and the Ministry.   2d ed.   London: Macmillan, 1921.

F.   EASTERN CHURCHES

KNETES, C.   "Ordination and Matrimony in the Eastern Orthodox
   Church."   Journal of Theological Studies, 11 (1910):   348-400,
   481-513.

KOKKINAKIS, Athenagoras. Parents and Priests as Servants of
Redemption: An Interpretation of the Doctrines of the Eastern
Orthodox Church on the Sacraments of Marriage and Priesthood.
New York: Morehouse-Gorham, 1958.

LAZOR, Paul. "Ordination. Orthodox." A Dictionary of Liturgy
and Worship, pp. 287-288.

RAES, Alphonse. "Les Ordinations dans le pontifical chaldéen."
L'Orient Syrien, 5 (1960): 63-80.

G. LATIN CHURCHES

BLIGH, John. Ordinaiton to the Priesthood. London: Sheed &
Ward, 1956.

BOTTE, Bernard. "Le Sacre episcopal dans le rite romain."
Questions liturgiques et paroissiales, 25 (1940): 22-32.

BROWN, Raymond E. Priest and Bishop. New York: Paulist
Press, 1970.

Centre de pastorale liturgique, Strasbourg. Etudes sur le sacrement de l'ordre. Paris: Cerf, 1957; The Sacrament of Holy
Orders. Collegeville, MN: Liturgical Press, 1962.

CLANCY, Walter B. The Rites and Ceremonies of Sacred Ordination (canons 1002-1005): A Historical Conspectus and a Canonical Commentary. CLS, 394. Washington, DC: Catholic University of America Press, 1962.

COOKE, Bernard J. Ministry to Word and Sacraments. Philadelphia, PA: Fortress Press, 1976.

CREHAN, Joseph. "Ministerial Priesthood: A Survey of Work Since
the Council." Theological Studies, 32 (1971): 489-499.

_____. "The Seven Orders of Christ." Theological Studies, 19
(1958): 81-93.

CRUMB, Lawrence N. "Presbyteral Ordination and the See of
Rome." Church Quarterly Review, 164 (1963): 19-31.

FINK, Peter E. "The Sacrament of Orders: Some Liturgical Reflections." Worship, 56 (1982): 482-502.

GASPARRI, Pietro. Tractatus canonicus de sacra ordinatione. 2
vols. Paris: Delhomme & Briguet, 1893-1894.

GRELOT, Pierre. Le Ministère de la nouvelle alliance. FV, 37.
Paris: Cerf, 1967.

KLEINHEYER, Bruno. Die Priesterweihe im römischen Ritus: eine
liturgie-historische Studie. TTS, 12. Trier: Paulinus-
Verlag, 1962, c1961.

LECUYER, Joseph. Prêtres du Christ: le sacrement de l'ordre.
JSJC, 53. Paris: Fayard, 1957; What is a Priest? Translated
by Lancelot C. Sheppard. TCEC, 53. New York: Hawthorn
Books, 1959.

_____. Le Sacerdoce dans le mystère du Christ. LO, 24.
Paris: Cerf, 1957.

MITCHELL, Nathan. Mission and Ministry: History and Theology
in the Sacrament of Order. Message of the Sacraments, 6.
Wilmington: Michael Glazier, 1982.

MOHLER, James A. The Origin and Evolution of the Priesthood:
A Return to the Sources. Staten Island, NY: Alba House,
1969.

MOLITOR, Raphael. Vom Sakrament der Weihe: Erwägungen nach
dem Pontificale Romanum. 2. Bde. Regensburg: Pustet,
1938.

"Les Ordinations." La Maison-Dieu, 138-139 (1979).

OTT, Ludwig. Das Weihesakrament. HD, 4/5. Freiburg: Herder, 1969.

POWER, David N. Gifts that Differ: Lay Ministries Established
and Unestablished. New York: Pueblo, 1980.

_____. Ministers of Christ and His Church: The Theology of
Priesthood. London: Geoffrey Chapman, 1969.

PURSCH, Kurt, RUTHY, A. E., and TOL, C. "Ordination. Old
Catholic." A Dictionary of Liturgy and Worship, p. 295.

TIXERONT, Joseph. L'Ordre et les ordinations: étude de théologie historique. Paris: Lecoffre, 1925; Holy Orders and
Ordination: A Study in the History of Dogma. Authorized
translation by S. A. Raemers. St. Louis, MO: Herder, 1928.

H. LUTHERAN CHURCHES

1. Texts

Inter-Lutheran Commission on Worship. Commissioning Service for Lay Ministries. Minneapolis, MN: Augsburg, 1977.

_____. The Rite for Installation of a Pastor. Minneapolis, MN: Augsburg, 1977.

_____. The Rite for Ordination. Minneapolis, MN: Augsburg, 1977.

2. Studies

BRUNOTTE, Wilhelm. Das geistliche Amt bei Luther. Berlin: Lutherisches Verlagshaus, 1959.

HEUBACH, Joachim. Die Ordination zum Amt der Kirche. AGTL, 2. Berlin: Lutherisches Verlagshaus, 1956.

LIEBERG, Helmut. Amt und Ordination bei Luther und Melanchthon. FKD, 11. Göttingen: Vandenhoeck & Ruprecht, 1962.

LINDROTH, Hjalmar, ed. En bök om Kyrkans ämbete. Uppsala: Almqvist & Wiksell, 1951.

PIEPKORN, Arthur Carl. "The Sacred Ministry and Holy Ordination in the Symbolical Books of the Lutheran Church." Concordia Theological Monthly, 40 (1969): 553-573.

RIETSCHEL, Georg. Luther und die Ordination. 2. Aufl. Wittenberg: R. Herrosé, 1889.

SICARD, E. J. R. H. S. von. "Ordination. Lutheran." A Dictionary of Liturgy and Worship, pp. 293-294.

I. REFORMED CHURCHES

AINSLIE, James L. The Doctrines of Ministerial Order in the Reformed Churches of the 16th and 17th Centuries. Edinburgh: T. & T. Clark, 1940.

ALLMEN, J.-J. von. "Ministry and Ordination according to Reformed Theology." Scottish Journal of Theology, 25 (1972): 75-88.

_____ . Le Saint ministère selon la conviction et la volonté des
Réformés du XVIe siècle. Bibliothèque théologique. Neuchâtel:
Delachaux & Niestlé, 1968.

BARKLEY, John M. "Ordination. Reformed." A Dictionary of
Liturgy and Worship, pp. 296-300.

DONALDSON, Gordon. "Scottish Ordinations in the Restoration
Period." Scottish Historical Review, 33 (1954):   169-175.

FOSTER, Walter Roland. Bishop and Presbytery: The Church of
Scotland, 1661-1688. London: Published for the Church Historical Society by SPCK, 1958.

SHAW, Duncan. "The Inauguration of Ministers in Scotland:
1560-1620." Records of the Scottish Church History Society,
16 (1966):   35-62.

TORRANCE, Thomas F. "Consecration and Ordination." Scottish
Journal of Theology, 11 (1958):   225-253.

J. ANGLICAN CHURCHES

1. Studies

BRADSHAW, Paul F. The Anglican Ordinal: Its History and Development from the Reformation to the Present Day. ACC, 53.
London: SPCK, 1971.

CAREY, Kenneth Moir, ed. The Historic Episcopate in the Fullness
of the Church: Seven Essays by Priests of the Church of
England. London: Dacre Press, 1954.

ECHLIN, Edward P. The Story of Anglican Ministry. Slough,
Eng.: St. Paul Publications, 1974.

GORE, Charles. The Church and the Ministry. New ed. revised
by C. H. Turner. London: Longmans, Green, 1919; reprint
ed., London: SPCK; New York: Macmillan, 1936.

GREAVES, Richard L. "The Ordination Controversy and the Spirit
of Reform in Puritan England." Journal of Ecclesiastical History, 21 (1970):   225-241.

JASPER, R. C. D. "Ordination. Anglican." A Dictionary of Liturgy and Worship, pp. 289-290.

MINCHIN, Basil. Every Man in His Ministry. His Worship in the
Body of Christ. London: Darton, Longman & Todd, 1960.

MOBERLY, R. C. Ministerial Priesthood: Chapters (Preliminary to a Study of the Ordinal) on the Rationale of Ministry and the Meaning of Christian Priesthood. 2d ed. London: John Murray, 1899; reprint ed., London: SPCK, 1969.

TERWILLIGER, Robert E., and HOLMES, Urban T., III, eds. To Be a Priest: Perspectives on Vocation and Ordination. New York: Seabury Press, 1975.

2. The Anglican-Roman Controversy on Anglican Orders

BARNES, Arthur Stapylton, ed. The Popes and the Ordinal: A Collection of Documents Bearing on the Question of Anglican Orders. 2d ed. London: Robert Browning, 1898.

CLARK, Francis. Anglican Orders and Defect of Intention. London: Longmans, Green, 1956.

HUGHES, John Jay. Absolutely Null and Utterly Void: The Papal Condemnation of Anglican Orders, 1896. London: Sheed & Ward; Washington, DC: Corpus Books, 1968.

_____. Stewards of the Lord: A Reappraisal of Anglican Orders. London: Sheed & Ward, 1970.

MASCALL, E. L. "Intention and Form in Anglican Orders." The Church Quarterly Review, 158 (1957): 4-20.

PULLER, Frederick W. The Bull Apostolicae Curae and the Edwardine Ordinal. CHS, 16. London: SPCK, 1896.

K. METHODIST CHURCHES

BOWMER, John C. Pastor and People: A Study of Church and Ministry in Wesleyan Methodism from the Death of John Wesley (1791) to the Death of Jabez Bunting (1858). London: Epworth Press, 1975.

GEORGE, A. Raymond. "Ordination. Methodist." A Dictionary of Liturgy and Worship, pp. 294-295.

LAWSON, Albert Brown. John Wesley and the Christian Ministry. London: SPCK, 1963.

Methodist Church (England). Ministry, Baptism and Membership in the Methodist Church. London: Methodist Publishing House, 1962.

MOEDE, Gerald F. The Office of Bishop in Methodism: Its His-
    tory and Development. New York: Abingdon Press, 1964.

OUTLER, Albert C. "The Ordinal." In Companion to the Book of
    Worship, pp. 103-133. Edited by William F. Dunkle and Joseph
    D. Quillian. Nashville, TN: Abingdon Press, 1970.

WATSON, Philip S. "Ordination and the Ministry in the Church."
    In The Doctrine of the Church, pp. 121-139. Edited by Dow
    Kirkpatrick. Nashville, TN: Abingdon Press, 1964.

WESLEY, John. "The Ministerial Office" [Sermons, Third Series,
    115]. In his The Works of the Rev. John Wesley, vol. 7, pp.
    273-281. London: Wesleyan-Methodist Book Room, 1872; re-
    print ed., Grand Rapids, MI: Zondervan, 1958; reprinted as
    Wesley's Works. Grand Rapids, MI: Baker, 1979.

L. FREE CHURCHES

BEACH, B. B. "Ordination. Seventh-day Adventist." Dictionary
    of Liturgy and Worship, pp. 300-301.

DAVIES, Horton. "Ordination. Congregationalist." Dictionary of
    Liturgy and Worship, pp. 291-292.

Foundations, 12, 2 (April-June 1969). [Baptist--special issue on
    ordination]

HOLLENWEGER, W. J. "Ordination. Pentecostal." Dictionary of
    Liturgy and Worship, pp. 295-296.

LEONARD, Bill J. "The Ordination Service in Baptist Churches."
    Review and Expositor, 78 (1981): 549-562.

McEACHERN, Alton H. Set Apart for Service. Nashville, TN:
    Broadman, 1980. [Baptist]

"Ordination." Review and Expositor, 78, 4 (Fall 1981). [Baptist--
    Special issue]

PAYNE, Ernest A. The Meaning and Practice of Ordination among
    Baptists. London: Carey Kingsgate Press, 1957.

"A Service of Ordination." Foundations, 7 (1964): 311-312.
    [Baptist]

TAYLOR, John H. "Ordination among Us." Transactions of the
    Congregational Historical Society, 20 (1968): 210-222. [Con-
    gregational]

M. UNION CHURCHES

1. Church of South India

GARRETT, T. S. "The Ordinal of the Church of South India."
Scottish Journal of Theology, 12 (1959): 400-413.

RATCLIFF, E. C. "The Ordinal of the Church of South India."
Theology, 63 (1960): 7-15; reprinted in his Liturgical Studies
of E. C. Ratcliff, pp. 173-182. Edited by A. H. Couratin and
D. J. Tripp. London: SPCK, 1976.

2. L'Eglise réformée de France

"The Ordination of Ministers." Studia Liturgica, 5 (1966): 166-
175.

N. OTHER SPECIAL STUDIES

KLAUSER, Theodor. Der Ursprung der bischöflichen Insignien und
Ehrenrecht. 2. Aufl. BAR, 1. Krefeld: Scherpe-Verlag,
1953.

RATCLIFF, E. C. "On the Rite of the Inthronization of Bishops
and Archbishops." Theology, 45 (1942): 71-82.

XXXI. MATRIMONY

A. GENERAL STUDIES

ALLMEN, J.-J. von. Maris et femmes d'après saint Paul. CTAP,
29. Neuchâtel: Delachaux & Niestlé, 1951; Pauline Teaching
on Marriage. London: Faith Press; New York: Morehouse-
Barlow, 1963.

BAILEY, Derrick Sherwin. The Man-Woman Relation in Christian
Thought. London: Longmans, 1959; Sexual Relation in Christian Thought. New York: Harper, 1959.

BINDER, Basilius. Geschichte des feierlichen Ehesegens, von der
Entstehung der Ritualien bis zur Gegenwart, mit Berücksichtigung damit zusammenhängender Riten, Sitten und Bräuche:
eine liturgiegeschichtliche Untersuchung. Metten: Abtei, 1938.

HOWARD, George Elliott.   A History of Matrimonial Institutions
    Chiefly in England and the United States, with an Introductory
    Analysis of the Literature and the Theories of Primitive Mar-
    riage and the Family. 3 vols. Chicago: University of Chi-
    cago Press, Callaghan & Company, 1904; reprint ed., New
    York: Humanities Press, 1964.

JOYCE, George Hayward.   Christian Marriage: An Historical and
    Doctrinal Study. 2d ed. London: Sheed & Ward, 1948.

KASPER, Walter.   Zur Theologie der christlichen Ehe.   Mainz:
    Grünewald, 1977; Theology of Christian Marriage.   Translated
    by David Smith. London: Burns & Oates; New York: Sea-
    bury Press, 1980.

KERNS, Joseph E.   The Theology of Marriage: The Historical De-
    velopment of Christian Attitudes toward Sex and Sanctity in
    Marriage. New York: Sheed & Ward, 1964.

LACEY, T. A.   Marriage in Church and State.   London: R. Scott,
    1912.

_____.   _____. Fully revised and supplemented by R. C.
    Mortimer. London: SPCK, 1947.

PALMER, Paul F.   "Christian Marriage: Contract or Covenant?"
    Theological Studies, 33 (1972):   617-665.

RICHTER, Klemens.   "The Liturgical Celebration of Marriage: The
    Problems Raised by Changing Theological and Legal Views of
    Marriage." In The Future of Christian Marriage, pp. 72-87.
    Edited by William Bassett and Peter Huizing. Concilium, 87.
    New York: Herder & Herder, 1973.

RITZER, Korbinian.   Formen, Riten und religiöses Brauchtum der
    Eheschliessung in den christlichen Kirchen des ersten Jahr-
    tausends. LQF, 38. Münster: Aschendorff, 1962.

RONDET, Henri.   Introduction à l'étude de la théologie du mariage.
    TPS, 6. Paris: Lethielleux, 1960.

RORDORF, Willy.   "Marriage in the New Testament and in the Early
    Church." Journal of Ecclesiastical History, 20 (1969):   193-
    210.

SCHILLEBEECKX, Edward.   Het huwelijk: aardse werkelijkheid en
    heilsmysterie. Bilthoven: Nelissen, 1963; Marriage: Secular
    Reality and Saving Mystery. 2 vols. Translated by N. D.
    Smith. London: Sheed & Ward, 1965; Marriage: Human Real-
    ity and Saving Mystery. New York: Sheed & Ward, 1966,
    c1965.

STEVENSON, Kenneth J. Nuptial Blessing: A Study of Christian
Marriage Rites. ACC, 64. London: SPCK, 1982.

B. ECUMENICAL

1. Texts

Deutsche Bischofskonferenz und dem Rat der Evangelische Kirche
in Deutschland. Gemeinsame kirchliche Trauung: Ordnung
der kirchlichen Trauung für konfessionsverschiedene Paare
unter Beteiligung der Pfarrer beider Kirchen. 4. Aufl.
Regensburg: Pustet; Kassel: Stauda, 1977.

Evangelisch-katholischen Arbeitsgemeinschaft für Mischehen-
Seelsorge der Deutschen Schweiz. Okumenische Trauung.
Zürich: Benziger, 1973.

2. Studies

GREEVEN, Heinrich, et al. Theologie der Ehe. Veröffentlichung
des ökumenischen Arbeitskreises Evangelischer und Katholischer
Theologen. Regensburg: Pustet, 1969.

C. EASTERN CHURCHES

1. Texts

Coptic Church. The Rites of the Coptic Church: The Order of
Baptism and the Order of Matrimony according to the Use of
the Coptic Church. Translated by B. T. A. Evetts. London:
Nutt, 1888.

The Sacrament of Holy Matrimony. London: Williams & Norgate,
1929. [Eastern Orthodox]

2. Studies

EVDOKIMOV, Paul. Sacrement de l'amour: le mystère conjugal à
la lumière de la tradition orthodoxe. 2. éd. Paris: Epi, 1962.

LAZOR, Paul. "Matrimony. The Orthodox Church." A Dictionary
of Liturgy and Worship, pp. 257-258.

MEYENDORFF, John. Marriage: An Orthodox Perspective. 2d ed.
Crestwood, NY: St. Vladimir's Seminary Press, 1975.

_____ . The Sacraments of Holy Matrimony. OW, 4. Tuckahoe,
NY: St. Vladimir's Seminary Press, n.d.

RAES, Alphonse. Le Mariage: sa célébration et sa spiritualité
dans l'église d'orient. CI. Chevetogne: Editions de Chevetogne, 1959.

SMIRENSKY, Alvian N. "The Evolution of the Present Rite of
Matrimony and Parallel Canonical Developments." St. Vladimir's
Seminary Quarterly, 8 (1964): 38-47.

ZHISHMAN, Joseph. Das Eherecht der orientalischen Kirche. Wien:
Braumüller, 1864.

D. LATIN CHURCHES

ADNES, Pierre. Le Mariage. MCTS, 5. Tournai: Desclée, 1963.

BASSETT, William, and HUIZING, Peter, eds. The Future of
Christian Marriage. Concilium, 87. New York: Herder &
Herder, 1973.

BOCKLE, Franz, ed. The Future of Marriage as Institution. Concilium, 55. New York: Herder & Herder, 1970.

CLERCK, P. de. "Le Mariage, événement, célébration." Paroisse
et Liturgie, 52 (1970): 408-413.

COUNE, M. "Le Mariage dans le rayonnement de Vatican II."
Paroisse et Liturgie, 52 (1970): 397-407.

DOMINIAN, J. Christian Marriage: The Challenge of Change.
London: Darton, Longman & Todd, 1967.

GASPARRI, Pietro. Tractatus canonicus de matrimonio. 2 vols.
Ed. nova. Città del Vaticano: Typis Polyglottis Vaticanis,
1932.

HUARD, J. "La liturgie nuptiale dans l'église romaine: les grandes
étapes de sa formation." Questions liturgiques et paroissiales,
38 (1957): 197-205.

HUIZING, P. J. "Kirchliche und standesamtliche Trauung." Liturgisches Jahrbuch, 22 (1972): 137-147.

JONG, P. de. "Brautsegen und Jungfrauenweihe." Zeitschrift für
katholische Theologie, 84 (1962): 300-322; 86 (1964): 442-449.

KOTHEN, Robert. Vers une mystique familiale. Louvain: E.

Warny, 1944; Marriage, the Great Mystery. Translated and arranged by E. J. Ross. Westminster, MD: Newman Bookshop, 1947.

LECLERCQ, Jacques. Le Mariage chrétien. Tournai, Paris: Casterman, 1947; Marriage: A Great Sacrament. Translated by the Earl of Wicklow. New York: Macmillan, 1951.

"Liturgie et pastorale du mariage." La Maison-Dieu, 50 (1957).

Il matrimonio cristiano: studi biblici, teologici e pastorali, Il nuovo rituale. QRL, n.s., 4. Turin: Leumann, 1978.

MAZZARELLO, S. "De novo ordine celebrandi matrimonium." Ephemerides Liturgicae, 83 (1969): 251-277.

MOLIN, Jean Baptiste, and MUTEMBE, Protais. Le Rituel du mariage en France du XIIe au XVI e siècle. TH, 26. Paris: Beauchesne, 1974.

NIEBERGALL, A. "Die Bedeutung der neuen römisch-katholischen Trauordnung 1969." In Kerygma und Melos: Christhard Mahrenholz 70 Jahre, pp. 178-199. Herausgegeben von Walter Blankenburg. Kassel: Bärenreiter, 1970.

"Le Nouveau rituel du mariage." La Maison-Dieu, 99 (1969): 124-209.

RAHNER, Karl. "Die Ehe als Sakrament." In his Schriften zur Theologie, Bd. 8, pp. 519-540. Einsiedeln: Benziger, 1967.

RINKEL, A. "Ehe und Sakrament." Internationale kirchliche Zeitschrift, 31 (1941): 1-28.

SCHLECK, Charles A. The Sacrament of Matrimony: A Dogmatic Study. Milwaukee, WI: Bruce, 1964.

THOMAS, David M. Christian Marriage: A Journey Together. MS, 5. Wilmington, DE: Michael Glazier, 1983.

WAGNER, Johannes. "Zum neuen deutschen Trauungsritus." Liturgisches Jahrbuch, 11 (1961): 164-171.

E. PROTESTANT CHURCHES

1. Texts

BIDDLE, Perry H., Jr. Abingdon Marriage Manual. Nashville, TN: Abingdon Press, 1974.

CHRISTENSEN, James L. The Minister's Marriage Handbook.
    Westwood, NJ: Revell, 1974.

HUTTON, Samuel Ward. Minister's Marriage Manual. Grand
    Rapids, MI: Baker, 1968.

Inter-Lutheran Commission on Worship. The Marriage Service.
    CW, 3. Minneapolis, MN: Augsburg, 1972.

KIRSCHENBAUM, Howard, and STENSRUD, Rockwell. The Wed-
    ding Book: Alternative Ways to Celebrate Marriage. New
    York: Seabury Press, 1974.

LEACH, William H., ed. The Cokesbury Marriage Manual. 2d. ed.
    New York: Abingdon-Cokesbury Press, 1945; revised ed.,
    New York: Abingdon Press, 1973.

VINCENT, Arthur M. Join Your Right Hands: Addresses and
    Worship Aids for Weddings. St. Louis, MO: Concordia, 1965.

2. Studies

BEACH, B. B. "Matrimony. Seventh-day Adventist." Dictionary
    of Liturgy and Worship, pp. 268-269.

BRUCE, F. F. "Matrimony. Plymouth Brethren." Dictionary of
    Liturgy and Worship, pp. 266-267.

CUMING, G. J. "Matrimony. Anglican." Dictionary of Liturgy
    and Worship, p. 259.

DAVIES, Horton. "Matrimony. Congregationalist." Dictionary of
    Liturgy and Worship, pp. 260-261.

DOMBOIS, Hans Adolf, and SCHUMANN, Friedrich Karl, eds.
    Familierechts-Reform: Dokumente und Abhandlungen. GF, 8.
    Witten: Luther-Verlag, 1955.

_____, eds. Weltliche und kirchliche Eheschliessung: Beiträge
    zur Frage des Eheschliessungsrechtes. GF, 6. Gladbeck:
    Freizeiten-Verlag, 1953.

EASTON, Burton Scott, and ROBBINS, Howard Chandler. The
    Bond of Honour: A Marriage Handbook. New York: Macmil-
    lan, 1938.

HOON, Paul W. "The Order for the Service of Marriage." In
    Companion to the Book of Worship, pp. 72-89. Edited by Wil-
    liam F. Dunckle and Joseph D. Quillian. Nashville, TN:
    Abingdon Press, 1970.

LAMB, J. A. "Matrimony. Reformed." Dictionary of Liturgy and
    Worship, pp. 267-268.

NIEBERGALL, Alfred. "Matrimony. Lutheran." Dictionary of
    Liturgy and Worship, pp. 261-265.

PARKE, Hervey C. The Marriage Service and After. Milwaukee,
    WI: Morehouse, 1928.

[Prayer Book Studies.] The Solemnization of Matrimony and A
    Thanksgiving for the Birth of a Child. PBS, 10-11. New
    York: Church Pension Fund, 1958.

SCHUBERT, Hans von. Die evangelische Trauung: ihre geschicht-
    liche Entwicklung und gegenwärtige Bedeutung. Berlin:
    Reuther, 1890.

WATKINS, Oscar D. Holy Matrimony. London: Rivington, 1895.

WHITE, J. F. "Matrimony. Methodist." Dictionary of Liturgy and
    Worship, pp. 265-266.

WINWARD, S. "Matrimony. Baptist." Dictionary of Liturgy and
    Worship, pp. 259-260.

XXXII. PENANCE/RECONCILIATION

A. GENERAL STUDIES

GALTIER, Paul. De paenitentia tractatus dogmatico historicus.
    3. ed. Rome: Universitas Gregoriana, 1957.

GY, Pierre-Marie. "Histoire liturgique du sacrement de pénitence."
    La Maison-Dieu, 56 (1958): 5-21.

HARING, Bernard. Shalom: Peace; The Sacrament of Reconcilia-
    tion. New York: Farrar, Straus & Giroux; revised paper ed.,
    Garden City, NY: Image Books, 1969.

McNEILL, John Thomas. A History of the Cure of Souls. New
    York: Harper, 1951; reprinted 1965.

PALMER, Paul F., ed. Sacraments and Forgiveness: History and
    Doctrinal Development of Penance, Extreme Unction and Indul-
    gences. SCT, 2. Westminster, MD: Newman Press; London:
    Longmans, Green, 1959.

POSCHMANN, Bernhard. Die abendländische Kirchenbusse im Ausgang des christlichen Altertums. München: J. Kösel & F.
Pustet, 1928.

_____. Der Ablass im Licht der Bussgeschichte. Theophaneia,
4. Bonn: Hanstein, 1948.

TELFER, William. The Forgiveness of Sins: An Essay in the History of Christian Doctrine and Practice. London: SCM Press,
1959; Philadelphia, PA: Muhlenberg Press, 1960.

THURIAN, Max. La Confession. Neuchâtel: Delachaux & Niestlé,
1953; Confession. Translated by Edwin Hudson. London:
SCM Press, 1958.

_____. La Confession. 3. éd. Neuchâtel: Delachaux &
Niestlé, 1966; reprint ed., Taizé: Presses de Taizé, 1977.

TILMANN, K. Die Führung zu Busse, Beichte, und christlichen
Leben. Würzburg: Echter Verlag, 1961.

WATKINS, Oscar D. A History of Penance. 2 vols. London:
Longmans, Green, 1920; reprint ed., New York: Burt Franklin, 1961.

B. EARLY CHURCH

D'ALES, A. L'Edit de Calliste: étude sur les origines de la
pénitence chrétienne. BTH. Paris: Beauchesne, 1914.

BATIFFOL, Pierre. "Les Origines de la pénitence." In his Etudes
d'histoire et de théologie positive, vol. 1, pp. 43-222. Paris:
V. Lecoffre, 1902.

DALY, C. B. "The Sacrament of Penance in Tertullian." Irish
Ecclesiastical Record, 69 (1947):   693-707, 815-821; 70 (1948):
731-746, 832-848.

GALTIER, Paul. Aux origines du sacrement de pénitence. AG,
54. Rome: Apud Aetes Universitatis Gregorianae, 1951.

_____. L'Eglise et la rémission des péchés aux premiers siècles.
BETH. Paris: Beauchesne, 1932.

GIET, S. "L'Apocalypse d'Hermas et la pénitence." In Studia
Patristica, vol. 8, pp. 214-218. Edited by F. L. Cross.
TUGAL, 78. Berlin: Akademie-Verlag, 1961.

GROTZ, Joseph. Die Entwicklung des Bussstufenwesens in der
vornicänischen Kirche. Freiburg: Herder, 1955.

KARPP, Heinrich, ed. Die Busse: Quellen zur Entstehung des altkirchlichen Busswesens. TC, 1. Zürich: EVZ-Verlag, 1969.

KOCH, Hugo. "Die Bussfrage bei Cyprian." In his Cyprianische Untersuchungen, pp. 211-285. AK, 4. Bonn: Marcus & Weber, 1926.

LATKO, Ernest Francis. Origen's Concept of Penance. Quebec, PQ: Faculté de théologie, Univ. Laval, 1949.

LIPINSKI, E. La Liturgie pénitentielle dans la Bible. LD, 52. Paris: Cerf, 1969.

MARSHALL, Nathaniel. The Penitential Discipline of the Primitive Church. LACT. New ed. Oxford: J. H. Parker, 1844; reprint ed., New York: AMS Press, 1973.

POSCHMANN, Bernhard. Paenitentia secunda: die kirchliche Busse im ältesten Christentum bis Cyprian und Origenes. Theophaneia, 1. Bonn: Hanstein, 1940.

RAHNER, Karl. "Die Busslehre des hl. Cyprian von Karthago." Zeitschrift für katholischen Theologie, 74 (1952): 257-276, 381-438.

_____. "Die Busslehre im Hirten des Hermas." Zeitschrift für katholischen Theologie, 77 (1955): 385-431.

_____. "Busslehre und Busspraxis der Didascalia Apostolorum." Zeitschrift für katholische Theologie, 72 (1950): 257-281.

_____. "Zur Theologie der Busse bei Tertullian." In Abhandlungen über Theologie und Kirche: Festschrift für Karl Adam, pp. 139-167. Herausgegeben von Marcel Reding. Düsseldorf: Patmos, 1952.

VALGIGLIO, Ernesto. Confessio nella bibbia e nella letteratura cristiana antica. Torino: Giapichelli, n.d.

VOGEL, Cyrille. La Discipline pénitentielle en Gaule des origines à la fin du VIIe siècle. Paris: Letouzey & Ané, 1952.

_____. Le Pécheur et la pénitence dans l'église ancienne. Chrétiens de tous les temps, 15. Paris: Cerf, 1966.

C. EASTERN CHURCHES

ALMAZOV, A. Tainaia Ispovied' v pravoslavnoi vostochnoi tserkvi:

opyt vnieshnei istorii. 3 vols. Odessa: Tipo-litografiia
Shtaba Odesskago voennago akruga, 1894.

CARR, Ephrem. "Penance amon the Armenians: Notes on the
History of Its Practice and Theology." Studia Liturgica, 11
(1976): 65-100.

HOLL, Karl. Enthusiasmus und Bussgewalt beim griechischen
Mönchtum: eine Studie zu Symeon dem Neuen Theologen.
Leipzig: Hinrich, 1898; reprint ed., Hildesheim: Olms, 1969.

KIRK, David. "Penance in the Eastern Churches." Worship, 40
(1966): 148-155.

LIGIER, L. "Pénitence et Eucharistie en orient." Orientalia
Christiana Periodica, 29 (1963): 5-78.

_____. "Le Sacrement de pénitence selon la tradition orientale."
Nouvelle revue théologique, 89 (1967): 940-967.

VOSTE, J. M. "La Confession chez les Nestoriens." Angelicum,
7 (1930): 17-26.

D. LATIN CHURCHES

1. Historical Texts

ALAIN DE LILLE. Liber poenitentialis. 2 vols. Edited by J.
Longère. AMN, 17-18. Louvain: Nauwelaerts, 1965.

BIELER, Ludwig, ed. The Irish Penitentials. SLH, 5. Dublin:
Dublin Institute for Advanced Studies, 1963.

McNEILL, John T., and GAMER, Helena M., eds. Medieval Handbooks of Penance: A Translation of the Principal Libri poeni-
tentiales and Selections from Related Documents. RCSS, 29.
New York: Columbia University Press, 1938; reprint ed.,
New York: Octagon Books, 1965.

ROBERT OF FLAMBOROUGH. The Liber poenitentialis: A Critical
Edition with Introduction and Notes. Edited by J. J. Francis
Firth. STex, 18. Toronto, Ont.: Pontifical Institute of
Medieval Studies, 1971.

2. Historical Studies

ANCIAUX, Paul. La théologie du sacrement de pénitence au XIIe
siècle. UCLD, 2/41. Louvain: Nauwelaerts, 1949.

GIGNAC, L. A. "Evoluzione delle forme liturgiche del sacramento
della penitenza." Sacra Doctrina, 46 (1967): 204-216.

HEYNCK, Valens. "Zur Busslehre des hl. Bonaventura." Franziskanische Studien, 36 (1954): 1-81.

IODICE, Antonio. "L'efficacia del Sacramento della Penitenza negli
Scolastici e in Gabriele Biel." Scuola Cattolica, 66 (1938):
141-160.

_____. "Due curiose opinioni teologiche di Gabriele Biel circa
la materia e la forma del sacramento della penitenza e il per-
cetto divino del confessione sacramentale." Divus Thomas, 44
(1941): 273-292.

JUNGMANN, Josef Andreas. Die lateinischen Bussriten in ihrer
geschichtlichen Entwicklung. FGIK, 3-4. Innsbruck: Rauch,
1932.

LEA, Henry Charles. History of Auricular Confession and Indul-
gences in the Latin Church. 3 vols. Philadelphia, PA: Lea
Brothers, 1896; reprint ed., New York: Greenwood Press,
1968.

LENTZEN-DEIS, Wolfgang. Busse als Bekenntnisvollzug: Versuch
einer Erhellung der sakramentalen Bekehrung anhand der
Bussliturgie des alten Pontificale Romanum. FTS, 86. Freiburg: Herder, 1969.

McSORLEY, Harry. "Luther and Trent on the Faith Needed for the
Sacrament of Penance." In The Sacramental Administration of
Reconciliation, pp. 89-98. Edited by Edward Schillebeeckx.
Concilium, 61 (1, 7). Edinburgh: T. & T. Clark, 1971.

MORTIMER, R. C. The Origins of Private Penance in the Western
Church. Oxford: Clarendon Press, 1939.

POSCHMANN, Bernhard. Die abendländische Kirchenbusse im frühen Mittelalter. BSHT, 16. Breslau: Müller & Seiffert, 1930.

POWER, David. "The Sacramentalization of Penance." The Heythrop Journal, 18 (1977): 5-22.

SCHMITZ, Herman Joseph. Die Bussbücher und das kanonische
Bussverfahren. Düsseldorf: L. Schwann, 1898.

_____. Die Bussbücher und die Bussdisciplin der Kirche.
Mainz: F. Kirchheim, 1883; reprint ed., Graz: Akademische
Druck- und Verlagsanstalt, 1958.

SPITZIG, Joseph Anthony. Sacramental Penance in the Twelfth and

Thirteenth Centuries.   SST, 2d ser., 6.   Washington, DC:
Catholic University of America Press, 1947.

TENTLER, Thomas N.   Sin and Confession on the Eve of the Reformation.   Princeton, NJ: Princeton University Press, 1977.

THOMAS AQUINAS.   Summa Theologiae, vol. 60:   Penance (3a.
84-90).   Edited and translated by Reginald Masterson and
T. C. O'Brien.   Cambridge: Blackfriars; New York: McGraw-
Hill; London: Eyre & Spottiswoode, 1966.

VOGEL, Cyrille.   Le pécheur et la pénitence au moyen âge.   CTT,
30.   Paris: Cerf, 1969.

3.   Contemporary Texts

National Liturgical Office (Canada).   Penance Celebrations.   Ottawa,
Ont.:   Canadian Conference of Catholic Bishops, 1981.

CRILLY, Oliver, ed.   Penitential Services.   Dublin: Columba
Press, 1986.

4.   Contemporary Studies

ANCIAUX, Paul.   Le sacrement de la pénitence.   2. éd.   ETS.
Louvain: Nauwelaerts, 1960; The Sacrament of Penance.
New York: Sheed & Ward, 1962.

AUBRY, A., BACIOCCHI, J. de, and ROZIER, C.   Célébrations
pénitentielles.   Lyon: Chalet, 1968.

BARTON, John M. T.   Penance and Absolution.   TCEC, 51.   New
York: Hawthorn Books, 1961.

BISHOPS' COMMITTEE ON THE LITURGY.   Rite of Penance.   Study
Texts, 4.   Washington, DC: United States Catholic Conference
Publications, 1975.

CATHOLIC THEOLOGICAL SOCIETY OF AMERICA.   The Renewal of
the Sacrament of Penance.   n.p.:   Catholic Theological Society
of America, 1975.

"Christian Reconciliation: Celebration and Pastoral Practice."
Lumen Vitae, 37, 2 (1982).

COMMUNITY OF SAINT-SEVERIN.   Confession: The Meaning and
Practice of the Sacrament of Penance.   Translated by A. V.
Littledale.   London: Chapman; Westminster, MD: Newman
Press, 1959; reprint ed., Notre Dame, IN: Fides, 1967.

CRICHTON, J. D. The Ministry of Reconciliation: A Commentary on the "Ordo paenitentiae" 1974. London: Geoffrey Chapman, 1974.

CURRAN, Charles E. "The Sacrament of Penance Today." Worship, 43 (1969): 510-531, 590-619; 44 (1970): 2-19.

DALLEN, J. "The Imposition of Hands in Penance: A Study in Liturgical Theology." Worship, 51 (1977): 224-247.

DELHAYE, Philippe, ed. Pastorale du péché. Tournai: Desclée, 1961; Pastoral Treatment of Sin. Translated by Charles Schaldenbrand, Firmin O'Sullivan, and Eugene Desmarchelier. New York: Desclée, 1968.

FEDERATION OF DIOCESAN LITURGICAL COMMISSIONS. General Absolution: Toward a Deeper Understanding. Chicago: FDLC, 1978.

FITZSIMONS, John, ed. Penance: Virtue and Sacrament. London: Burns & Oates, 1969.

GALLEN, John. "A Pastoral-Liturgical View of Penance Today." Worship, 45 (1971): 132-150.

GULA, Richard M. To Walk Together Again: The Sacrament of Reconciliation. New York: Paulist Press, 1984.

GUZIE, Tad, and McILHON, John. The Forgiveness of Sin. Chicago: Thomas More Press, 1979.

HAMELIN, Leonce. Reconciliation in the Church: A Theological and Pastoral Essay on the Sacrament of Penance. Collegeville, MN: Liturgical Press, 1980.

HEGGEN, Franz J. Boetviering en private biecht. 2. druck. Roermond: Romen, 1965; Confession and the Service of Penance. Translated by Peter Tomlinson. London: Sheed & Ward, 1967; Notre Dame, IN: University of Notre Dame Press, 1968.

HELLWIG, Monika. Sign of Reconciliation and Conversion: The Sacrament of Penance in Our Times. MS, 4. Wilmington, DE: Glazier, 1982, rev. ed., 1984.

KELLY, George A. The Sacrament of Penance and Reconciliation. Chicago: Franciscan Herald Press, 1975.

_____, ed. The Sacrament of Penance in Our Time. Boston, MA: St. Paul Editions, 1976.

Liturgie et rémission des péchés. Conférences Saint-Serge, XXe
    Semaine d'études liturgiques, Paris, 2-5 juillet 1973. BEL
    Subsidia, 3. Rome: Edizioni Liturgiche, 1975.

MARTINEZ, German. "Penance and the Lessons of History." The-
    ology Digest, 30, 1 (Spring 1982): 37-41.

ORSY, Ladislas. The Evolving Church and the Sacrament of Pen-
    ance. Denville, NJ: Dimension Books, 1978.

"Pénitence et réconciliation." La Maison-Dieu, 117 (1974). [Spe-
    cial issue]

POSCHMANN, Bernhard. Busse und letzte ölung. HD, 4/3.
    Freiburg: Herder, 1951; Penance and the Anointing of the
    Sick. HD. Translated and revised by Francis Courtney.
    New York: Herder & Herder, 1964.

PRICE, John, and SARAUSKAS, R. George. "Second Thoughts on
    the Rite of Reconciliation." Chicago Studies, 18 (1979): 223-
    232.

RAHNER, Karl. "Penance." Sacramentum Mundi, 4: 385-399.

_____. "Vergessene Wahrheiten über das Buss-Sakrament." In
    his Schriften zur Theologie, Bd. 2, pp. 143-183. Zürich:
    Benziger Verlag, 1958; "Forgotten Truths concerning Penance."
    In his Theological Investigations, vol. 2, pp. 135-174. Balti-
    more, MD: Helicon, 1963.

"Reconciliation and Forgiveness." National Bulletin on Liturgy
    (Canada), 52 (January-February 1976).

"Reconciliation in Our Life." National Bulletin on Liturgy (Canada),
    88 (March-April 1983).

The Rite of Penance: Commentaries. 3 vols. Washington, DC:
    Liturgical Conference, 1875-1979.
    1. Understanding the Document. By Ralph Keifer and Fred-
       erick R. McManus. 1975.
    2. Implementing the Rite. Edited by Elizabeth M. Jeep. 1979.
    3. Theological Background and Directions. Edited by Nathan
       Mitchell. 1977.

SAINT CYR, Carra D., et al. The Sacrament of Penance. Trans-
    lated by R. L. Sullivant, Agnes Cunningham, and M. Renelle.
    Glen Rock, NJ: Paulist Press, 1966.

SCHILLEBEECKX, Edward, ed. Sacramental Reconciliation. Con-
    cilium, 61. New York: Herder & Herder, 1971; also published
    as The Sacramental Administration of Reconciliation. Concilium,
    61 (1, 7). Edinburgh: T. & T. Clark, 1971.

SOTTOCORNOLA, R. A Look at the New Rite of Penance. Washington, DC: USCC Publication Office, 1975.

SPEYR, Adrienne von. Die Beichte. Herausgegeben von Hans Urs von Balthasar. Einsiedeln: Johannes Verlag, 1960; Confession: The Encounter with Christ in Penance. Translated by A. V. Littledale. New York: Herder & Herder, 1964.

TAYLOR, Michael, ed. The Mystery of Sin and Forgiveness. Staten Island, NY: Alba House, 1971.

TIERNEY, Clement. The Sacrament of Repentance and Reconciliation. Dublin: Dominican Publications; New York: Costello, 1983.

VORGRIMLER, Herbert. Busse und Krankensalbung. 2. Aufl. HD, 4/3. Freiburg: Herder, 1978.

E. PROTESTANT CHURCHES

ALLMEN, Jean-Jacques von. "The Forgiveness of Sins as a Sacrament in the Reformed Tradition." In The Sacramental Administration of Reconciliation, pp. 112-119. Edited by Edward Schillebeeckx. Concilium, 61 (1, 7). Edinburgh: T. & T. Clark, 1971.

BERTSCH, Ludwig, ed. Busse und Beichte: theologische und seelsorgliche überlegungen. Frankfurt: Knecht, 1967.

BOWMAN, George William, III. The Dynamics of Confession. Richmond, VA: John Knox Press, 1969.

DRURY, T. W. Confession and Absolution: The Teaching of the Church of England as Interpreted and Illustrated by the Writings of the Reformers of the Sixteenth Century. London: Hodder & Stoughton, 1903.

FISCHER, E. Zur Geschichte der evangelischen Beichte. 2 vols. SGTK, 8/2 & 9/4. Leipzig: Dieterich'sche Verlags-Buchhandlung, 1902-1903.
1. Die katholische Beichtpraxis bei Beginn der Reformation und Luthers Stellung dazu in den Anfängen seiner Wirksamkeit. SGTK, 8/2. 1902.
2. Niedergang und neubelebung des Beichtinstituts in Wittenberg in den Anfängen der Reformation. SGTK, 9/4. 1903.

GEISSER, Walther. Beichte und Absolution in evangelischer Sicht. Calwer Hefte, 81. Stuttgart: Calwer, 1966.

GUNSTONE, John. The Liturgy of Penance. SCW, 7. London:
Faith Press; New York: Morehouse-Barlow, 1966.

KOENEN, Josef. Die Busslehre Richard Hookers: Der Versuch
einer anglikanischen Bussdiziplin. FTS, 53. Freiburg:
Herder, 1940.

KONSTANT, David, ed. A Liturgy of Sorrow: Services of Penance for Communal Celebration. Great Wakering, Eng.:
Mayhew-McCrimmon, 1975.

MACKINTOSH, H. R. The Christian Experience of Forgiveness.
London: Nisbet; New York: Harper, 1927; reprinted, London:
Nisbet, 1954.

OBST, Helmut. Der Berliner Beichtstuhlstreit: Die Kritik der
Pietismus an der Beichtpraxis der lutherischen Orthodoxie.
AGP, 11. Witten: Luther Verlag, 1972.

[Prayer Book Studies.] The Penitential Office. PBS, 7. New
York: Church Pension Fund, 1957.

SCHWARZ, Reinhard. Vorgeschichte der reformatorischen Buss-
theologie. AK, 41. Berlin: De Gruyter, 1968.

XXXIII. MINISTRY TO THE SICK, THE AGING
AND THE DYING

A. GENERAL STUDIES

ARIES, Philippe. L'homme devant la mort. Paris: Editions du
Seuil, 1977; The Hour of Our Death. New York: Knopf,
1981.

BECKER, Ernest. The Denial of Death. New York: Free Press,
1973.

BENOIT, Pierre, and MURPHY, Roland, eds. Immortality and
Resurrection. Concilium, 60. New York: Herder & Herder,
1970.

BERG, Jan H. van den. The Psychology of the Sickbed. Pittsburgh, PA: Duquesne University Press, 1966.

BERRIGAN, Daniel. We Die Before We Live: Talking with the
Very Ill. New York: Seabury Press, 1980.

BOROS, Ladislaus. Mysterium mortis: der Mensch in der letzten
   Entscheidung. Olten: Walter-Verlag, 1962; The Moment of
   Truth: Mysterium Mortis. Translated by Geoffrey Bainbridge.
   London: Search Press, 1965; American ed. as The Mystery of
   Death. New York: Herder & Herder, 1965.

BORRELLI, Susan. With Care: Reflections of a Minister to the
   Sick. Chicago: Liturgy Training Publications, 1980.

BOWERS, M. K., et al. Counseling the Dying. New York: Thomas Nelson, 1964.

BOWMAN, Leonard. The Importance of Being Sick: A Christian
   Reflection. Wilmington, DE: Consortium, 1976.

CAMERON, J. M. "On Death and Human existence." Worship, 50
   (1976): 246-260.

CHORON, Jacques. Death and Western Thought. New York:
   Macmillan; New York: Collier Books, 1963.

CLEMENTS, William. Care and Counseling of the Aging. Philadelphia, PA: Fortress Press, 1979.

COLLOPY, Bartholomew J. "Theology and Death." Theological
   Studies, 39 (1978): 22-54.

"The Coming of Age." Liturgy, 21, 2 (February 1976). [Special
   issue]

COPE, Gilbert, ed. Dying, Death and Disposal. London: SPCK,
   1970.

DEEKEN, Alfons. Growing Old and How to Cope with It. New
   York: Paulist Press, 1972.

DOLAN, Joseph. Give Comfort to My People. New York: Paulist
   Press, 1977.

"En face de la mort." La Maison-Dieu, 144 (1980). [Special issue]

FOURNIER, William, and O'MALLEY, Sarah. Age and Grace: Handbook of Programs for the Ministry to the Aging. Collegeville,
   MN: Liturgical Press, 1980.

GREINACHER, Norbert, and MULLER, Alois, eds. The Experience
   of Dying. Concilium, 94. New York: Herder & Herder, 1974.

HAMILTON, Michael, and REID, Helen, eds. A Hospice Handbook:
   A New Way to Care for the Dying. Grand Rapids, MI: Eerdmans, 1980.

KASTENBAUM, Robert, and AISENBERG, Ruth. The Psychology
   of Death. New York: Springer, 1972.

KUBLER-ROSS, Elizabeth. Death, the Final Stage of Growth.
   Englewood Cliffs, NJ: Prentice Hall, 1975.

_____. Living with Death and Dying. New York: Macmillan,
   1981.

_____. On Death and Dying. New York: Macmillan, 1969.

_____. Questions and Answers on Death and Dying. New York:
   Macmillan, 1974.

MARTY, Martin E., and VAUX, Kenneth L., eds. Health/Medicine
   and the Faith Traditions: An Inquiry into Religion and Medicine. Philadelphia, PA: Fortress Press, 1982.

MEHL, Roger. Notre vie et notre mort. Paris: Société centrale
   d'évangélisation, 1953.

"Ministries to the Sick." Liturgy, 2, 2 (1982). [Special issue]

The Ministry of Healing: Readings in the Catholic Health Care
   Ministry. St. Louis, MO: The Catholic Health Care Association, 1981.

NIKLAS, Gerald, and STEFANICS, Charlotte. Ministry to the
   Hospitalized. New York: Paulist Press, 1975.

NOUWEN, Henri, and GAFFNEY, Walter. Aging: The Fulfillment
   of Life. New York: Doubleday, 1974.

Pastoral Care of the Sick: A Practical Guide for the Catholic Chap-
   lain in Health Care Facilities. Edited by the National Association of Catholic Chaplains. Washington, DC: USCC Publications Office, 1974.

RICHARDS, Larry, and JOHNSON, Paul. Death and the Caring
   Community: Ministering to the Terminally Ill. Critical Concern Books. Portland, OR: Multnomah Press, 1982.

SCHNEIDMAN, Edwin. Death: Current Perspectives. New York:
   Mayfield Publishing Co., 1976.

"The Sick and the Dying." Liturgy, 25, 2 (March-April 1980).
   [Special issue]

STEINFELS, Peter, and BEATCH, Robert, eds. Death Inside Out.
   Hastings Center Report. New York: Harper & Row, 1975.

TAYLOR, Michael. The Mystery of Suffering and Death. Staten
Island, NY: Alba House, 1973.

B. HEALING

CRAFER, T. W., ed. The Church and the Ministry of Healing.
London: SPCK, 1934.

DAWSON, George Gordon. Healing: Pagan and Christian. London:
SPCK, 1935.

DEARMER, Percy. Body and Soul: An Enquiry into the Effect of
Religion on Health, with a Description of Christian Works of
Healing from the New Testament to the Present Day. New
York: Dutton, 1909.

DiORIO, Ralph A., with GROPMAN, Donald. The Man beneath the
Gift. New York: William Morrow, 1980.

FARICY, Robert. Praying for Inner Healing. New York: Paulist
Press, 1979.

FROST, Evelyn. Christian Healing. 2d ed. Oxford: Mowbray,
1949.

KELSEY, Morton T. Healing and Christianity in Ancient Thought
and Modern Times. New York: Harper & Row; London: SCM
Press, 1973.

LAMBOURNE, R. A. Community, Church and Healing: A Study
of Some of the Corproate Aspects of the Church's Ministry to
the Sick. London: Darton, Longman & Todd, 1963.

LINN, Dennis, and LINN, Matthew. Healing of Memories: Prayer
and Confession--Steps to Inner Healing. New York: Paulist
Press, 1974.

LINN, Mary Jane, Matthew, and Dennis. Healing the Dying: Re-
leasing People to Die. New York: Paulist Press, 1979.

MacNUTT, Francis. Healing. Notre Dame, IN: Ave Maria Press,
1974.

_____. The Power to Heal. Notre Dame, IN: Ave Maria Press,
1977.

MARTIN, Bernard. The Healing Ministry in the Church. Richmond,
VA: John Knox Press; London: Lutterworth Press, 1960.

_____. Veux-tu guérir? Réflexions sur la cure d'âme des malades. Genève: Editions Labor et Fides; Paris: Librairie protestante, 1963; Healing for You. Translated by A. A. Jones. London: Lutterworth Press, 1965; Richmond, VA: John Knox Press, 1966.

SANFORD, John A. Healing and Wholeness. New York: Paulist Press, 1977.

SCHLEMON, Barbara. Healing Prayer. Notre Dame, IN: Ave Maria Press, 1976.

STANLEY, David. "Salvation and Healing." The Way, 10 (1970): 298-317.

TALLEY, Thomas. "Healing: Sacrament or Charism?" Worship, 46 (1972).

TYRRELL, Bernard. Christotherapy: Healing through Enlightenment. New York: Seabury Press, 1975.

C. RITES

1. General Studies

CONDON, Kevin. "The Sacrament of Healing (Jas 5:14-16)." In The Sacraments in Scripture, pp. 172-186. Edited by T. Worden. Springfield, IL: Templegate, 1966.

GLEN, M. Jennifer. "Sickness and Symbol: The Promise of the Future." Worship, 54 (1981): 397-411.

GUSMER, Charles. And You Visited Me: Sacramental Ministry to the Sick and Dying. New York: Pueblo, 1984.

_____. "Liturgical Traditions of Christian Illness: Rites of the Sick." Worship, 46 (1972): 528-543.

HOFMEISTER, Philipp. Die heiligen Öle in der morgen- und abendländischen Kirche: eine kirchenrechtlich-liturgische Abhandlung. OstC, n.F., 6-7. Würzburg: Augustinus Verlag, 1948.

ISAMBERT, François. Rite et efficacité symbolique. RS. Paris: Cerf, 1979.

PULLER, F. W. The Anointing of the Sick in Scripture and Tradition. 2d ed. CHS, 77. London: SPCK, 1910.

RENNER, H. P. V. "The Use of Ritual in Pastoral Care." Journal of Pastoral Care, 33 (1979): 164-174.

RUSH, Alfred. "The Eucharist, the Sacrament of the Dying in
    Christian Antiquity." The Jurist, 34 (1974): 10-35.

WOOLLEY, Reginald Maxwell. Exorcism and the Healing of the
    Sick. CHS, n.s., 8. London: SPCK, 1932.

2. Eastern Churches

a. Texts

CARTHEW, Alice Grace, ed. The Service of the Sacrament of Holy
    Unction. The Greek text with a rendering in English. Lon-
    don: Williams & Norgate, 1916.

b. Studies

SPACIL, Bohumil. Doctrina theologicae orientis separati de sacra
    infirmorum unctione. OC, 74. Rome: Pontificium Institutum
    Orientalium Studiorum, 1931.

3. Latin Churches

ALBERTON, Mario. Un sacrement pour les malâdes. Paris: Cen-
    turion, 1978.

ALSZEGHY, Zoltan. "L'effetto corporale dell'Extrema Unzione."
    Gregorianum, 38 (1957): 385-405; "The Bodily Effects of Ex-
    treme Unction." Theology Digest, 9 (1961): 105-110.

BARTSCH, Elmar. Die Sachbeschwörungen der römischen Liturgie:
    eine liturgiegeschichtliche und liturgietheologische Studie.
    LQF, 46. Münster: Aschendorff, 1967.

BERAUDY, Roger. "Le sacrement des malâdes: étude historique
    et théologique." Nouvelle revue théologique, 96 (1974): 600-
    634.

BISHOPS' COMMITTEE ON THE LITURGY. Anointing and the Pas-
    toral Care of the Sick. Study Text, 2. Washington, DC:
    USCC Publications, 1973.

BOTTE, Bernard. "L'onction des malâdes." La Maison-Dieu, 15
    (1948): 91-107.

BROWE, Peter. "Die letzte Olung in der abendländischen Kirche
    des Mittelalters." Zeitschrift für katholische Theologie, 55
    (1931): 515-561.

CHAVASSE, Antoine. Etude sur l'onction des infirmes dans l'église

latine du IIIe au XIe siècle. Lyon: Librairie du Sacré Coeur,
1942.

DAVIS, Charles. "The Sacrament of the Sick." In Theology for
Today. New York: Sheed & Ward, 1962.

DE CLERCQ, C. "Ordines unctionis infirmi des IXe et Xe siècles."
Ephemerides liturgicae, 44 (1930): 100-122.

DIEKMANN, Godfrey. "The Laying on of Hands in Healing." Liturgy, 25 (1980): 7-10, 36-38.

DUVAL, A. "L'Extreme Onction au Concile de Trente." La Maison-
Dieu, 101 (1970): 127-172.

EMPEREUR, James. Prophetic Anointing: God's Call to the Sick,
the Elderly, and the Dying. MS, 7. Wilmington, DE: Michael
Glazier, 1982.

GOUGAUD, L. "Etude sur les Ordines commendationis animae."
Ephemerides liturgicae, 49 (1935): 3-27.

GUSMER, Charles. "I Was Sick and You Visited Me: The Revised
Rites for the Sick." Worship, 48 (1974): 516-525.

KERN, Joseph. De sacramento extremae unctionis: tractatus dog-
maticus. Regensburg: Pustet, 1907.

KNAUBER, Adolf. Pastoral Theology of the Anointing of the Sick.
Collegeville, MN: Liturgical Press, 1975.

La maladie et la mort du chrétien dans la liturgie. Conférences
Saint-Serge, XXIe Semaine d'études liturgiques, Paris, 1-4
juillet 1974. BEL, subsidia, 1. Rome: Edizioni Liturgiche,
1975; Temple of the Holy Spirit: Sickness and Death of the
Christian in the Liturgy. 21st Liturgical Conference Saint-
Serge. Translated by Matthew O'Connell. New York: Pueblo,
1983.

MARSH, Thomas. "A Theology of Anointing the Sick." The Furrow, 29 (1978): 89-101.

McCORMICK, Richard A. Health and Medicine in the Catholic Tradition: Tradition in Transition. New York: Crossroad, 1984.

MURRAY, P. "The Liturgical History of Extreme Unction." The
Furrow, 11 (1960): 572-593; reprinted in Studies in Pastoral
Liturgy, vol. 2, pp. 18-38. Edited by Vincent Ryan. Dublin:
Gill, 1963.

"Le Nouveau rituel des malâdes." La Maison-Dieu, 113 (1973).
[Special issue]

ORTEMANN. Le sacrement des malâdes. CPT. Paris: Editions du Chalet, 1971.

PALMER, Paul. "The Purpose of Anointing the Sick: A Reappraisal." Theological Studies, 19 (1958): 309-344.

_____. Sacraments and Forgiveness. Sources of Christian Theology, vol. 2. Westminster, MD: Newman Press, 1961.

_____. "Who Can Anoint the Sick?" Worship, 48 (1974): 81-98.

PORTER, H. Boone. "The Origins of the Medieval Rite for Anointing the Sick or Dying." Journal of Theological Studies, n.s., 7 (1956): 211-225.

_____. "The Rites for the Dying in the Early Middle Ages." Journal of Theological Studies, n.s., 10 (1959): 43-62, 299-307.

POWER, David. "Let the Sick Man Call." Heythrop Journal, 19, 3 (July 1978): 256-270.

"Rites for the Sick and the Dying." National Bulletin on Liturgy (Canada), 57 (January-February 1977). [Special issue]

ROCCAPRIORE, Marie. Anointing of the Sick and the Elderly. Canfield, OH: Alba Books, 1980.

ROUILLARD, Philippe. "Le ministère du sacrement de l'onction des malâdes." Nouvelle revue théologique, 111 (1979): 395-402.

SESBOUE, Bernard. L'onction des malâdes. Lyons: Profac, 1972.

4. Protestant Churches

a. Texts

COMMUNAUTE DE TAIZE. Liturgie des malades. Macon: Combier, 1958?

MALANIA, Leo, ed. Ministry to the Sick according to the Use of the Episcopal Church as set forth in the Book of Common Prayer (Proposed). New York: Church Hymnal Corp., 1977.

"Ritual with the Dying." In Ritual in a New Day: An Invitation, pp. 53-72. Nashville, TN: Abingdon Press 1976. [United Methodist]

b.   Studies

BOTTING, Michael.   Pastoral and Liturgical Ministry to the Sick.
GBMW, 59.   Bramcote, Eng.:   Grove Books, 1978.

The Church's Ministry of Healing: Report of the Archbishops'
Commission.   London: Church Information Office, 1958.

GUSMER, Charles W.   "Anointing of the Sick in the Church of
England."   Worship, 45 (1971):   262-272.

_____.   The Ministry of Healing in the Church of England: An
Ecumenical-Liturgical Study.   ACC, 56.   Greak Wakering, Eng.:
Mayhew-McCrimmon, 1974.

MARTY, Martin E.   Health and Medicine in the Lutheran Tradition:
Being Well.   HMFT.   New York: Crossroad, 1983.

[Prayer Book Studies.]   The Order for the Ministration to the
Sick.   PBS, 3.   New York: Church Pension Fund, 1951.

TAYLOR, Jeremy.   The Rule and Exercise of Holy Dying.   Edited
by Thomas Kepler.   Cleveland, OH: World, 1952.

VAUX, Kenneth L.   Health and Medicine in the Reformed Tradition:
Promise, Providence and Care.   HMFT.   New York: Crossroad,
1984.

XXXIV.   DEATH AND BURIAL (INCLUDING PRAYERS FOR THE DEAD)

A.   GENERAL STUDIES

(See also material relating to death in Section XXXIII. A., p. 546)

BENDANN, Effie.   Death Customs: An Analytical Study of Burial
Rites.   New York: Knopf, 1930; reprint eds., Ann Arbor, MI:
Gryphon Books, 1971; Detroit, MI: Gale Research, 1974.

BENKO, Stephen.   The Meaning of Sanctorum Cummunio.   Translated by David L. Scheidt.   SHT, 3.   London: SCM Press;
Naperville, IL: Allenson, 1964.

BOWMAN, LeRoy Edward.   The American Funeral: A Study in
Guilt, Extravagance and Sublimity.   Washington, DC: Public
Affairs Press, 1959; reprint ed., Westport, CT: Greenwood
Press, 1973.

COPE, Gilbert, ed. Dying, Death and Disposal. London: SPCK, 1970.

"En face de la mort." La Maison-Dieu, 144 (1980). [Special issue]

GORER, Geoffrey. Death, Grief, and Mourning. Garden City, NY: Doubleday, 1965.

HABENSTEIN, Robert W., and LAMERS, William M. Funeral Customs the World Over. 2d ed. Milwaukee, WI: Bulfin Printers, 1974.

_____. The History of American Funeral Directing. Milwaukee, WI: Bulfin Printers, 1955.

ILUNGA, G. "Rites funéraires et christianisme en Afrique." Jeunes églises, 21 (October 1964): 1-11.

IRION, Paul E. The Funeral and the Mourners: Pastoral Care of the Bereaved. Nashville, TN: Abingdon Press, 1954; reprinted 1979.

_____. The Funeral: Vestige or Value? Nashville, TN: Abingdon Press, 1966; reprint ed., New York: Arno Press, 1977.

JACKSON, Edgar N. The Christian Funeral: Its Meaning, Its Purpose, and Its Modern Practice. New York: Channel Press, 1966.

KASTENBAUM, Robert, and AISENBERG, Ruth. The Psychology of Death. New York: Springer, 1972.

MITFORD, Jessica. The American Way of Death. New York: Simon & Schuster, 1963; Greenwich, CT: Fawcett, 1964, c1963.

PERHAM, Michael. The Communion of Saints: An Examination of the Place of the Christian Dead in the Belief, Worship, and Calendars of the Church. ACC, 62. London: SPCK, 1980.

POTEL, Julien. Les funérailles une fête? Que célèbrent aujourd'hui les vivants? RS. Paris: Cerf, 1973.

ROWELL, Geoffrey. The Liturgy of Christian Burial: An Introductory Survey of the Historical Development of Christian Burial Rites. ACC, 59. London: SPCK, 1977.

RULAND, Ludwig. Die Geschichte der kirchlichen Leichenfeier: Gekrönte Preissschrift. Regensburg: G. J. Manz, 1901.

B.　THE EARLY CHURCH

BAILEY, Lloyd R., Sr.　Biblical Perspectives on Death.　OBT.
Philadelphia, PA:　Fortress Press, 1979.

BROWN, Schuyler.　"Bereavement in New Testament Perspective."
Worship, 48 (1974):　93-98.

FREISTEDT, Emil.　Altchristliche Totengedächtnistage und ihr
Beziehung zum Jenseitsglauben und Totenkultus der Antike.
LQF, 24.　Münster:　Aschendorff, 1928; reprinted 1971.

KLAUSER, Theodor.　Die Cathedra im Totenkult der heidnischen
und christlichen Antike.　2. Aufl.　LQF, 21.　Münster:
Aschendorff, 1971.

NTEDIKA, Joseph.　L'evocation de l'au-delà dans la prière pour
les morts:　étude de patristique et de liturgie latines, IVe-
VIIIe siècle.　RAT, 2.　Louvain:　Nauwelaerts, 1971.

PELIKAN, Jaroslav.　The Shape of Death:　Life, Death, and Immortality in the Early Fathers.　New York:　Abingdon Press, 1961.

RUCH, A. C.　Death and Burial in Christian Antiquity.　SCA, 1.
Washington, DC:　Catholic University of America Press, 1941.

C.　EASTERN CHURCHES

1.　Texts

GRIGASSY, Julius, ed.　Holy Services for the Dead in the Catholic
Church of the Old-Slavonic Rite.　Pittsburgh, PA:　n.p.,
1943.　[Hagiasmatarion]

MALTZEW, Alexios von, ed.　Begräbniss-ritus und einige specielle
und alterthümliche Gottesdienste der orthodox-katholischen
Kirche des Morgenlandes.　Deutsch und slavisch unter Berücksichtigung des griechischen Urtextes.　Berlin:　Siegismund,
1898.

The Office of Christian Burial according to the Byzantine Rite.
Pittsburgh, PA:　Byzantine Seminary Press, 1975.

The Service for the Burial of the Dead according to the Use of
the Orthodox Greek Church in London.　Ditchling, Eng.:　Pepler, 1922.

2. Studies

LAZOR, Paul. "Burial. Orthodox." A Dictionary of Liturgy and
Worship, pp. 97-98.

D. LATIN CHURCHES

BURKI, Bruno. Im Herrn entschlafen: eine historisch pastoral-
theologische Studie zur Liturgie des Sterbens und des Begräb-
nisses. BPT, 6. Heidelberg: Quelle & Meyer, 1969.

Centre de pastorale liturgique, Strasbourg. Le mystère de la mort
et sa célébration. Vanves 27-29 avril 1949. LO, 12. Paris:
Cerf, 1951.

DIDIER, Jean-Charles. Le chrétien devant la maladie et la mort.
JSJC, 55. Paris: Fayard, 1960; Death and the Christian.
Translated by P. J. Hepburne-Scott. TCEC, 55. New York:
Hawthorn Books, 1961.

DOWDALL, J. "The Liturgy of the Dead." In Studies in Pastoral
Liturgy, vol. 1. Edited by P. Murray. Maynooth: The Furrow Trust, 1961.

GY, Pierre-Marie. "Le christianisme et l'homme devant la mort."
La Maison-Dieu, 144 (1980): 7-23.

MAERTENS, Thierry, and HEUSCHEN, Louis. Doctrine et pastorale
de la liturgie de la mort. PL, 28. Bruges: Apostolat liturgique, 1957.

La maladie et la mort du chrétien dans la liturgie. Conférences
Saint-Serge, XXIe Semaine d'études liturgiques, Paris, 1-4
juillet 1974. BEL, 1. Rome: Edizioni Liturgiche, 1975.

MEIER, John P. "Catholic Funerals in the Light of Scripture."
Worship, 48 (1974): 206-216.

MERK, Carl Josef. Die messliturgische Totenehrung in der römischen Kirche. Stuttgart: O. Scholz, 1926.

"Le nouveau rituel des funérailles." La Maison-Dieu, 101 (1970).
[Special issue]

PURSCH, Kurt, RUTHY, A. E., and TOL, C. "Burial. Old
Catholic." A Dictionary of Liturgy and Worship, pp. 105-106.

RAHNER, Karl. Zur Theologie des Todes. Freiburg: Herder,
1958; On the Theology of Death. 2d ed., rev. by W. J.

O'Hara.   Translated by Charles H. Henkey.   London: Burns
& Oates, 1965.

RUTHERFORD, Richard.   The Death of a Christian: The Rite of
Funerals.   SRR, 7.   New York: Pueblo, 1980.

SERPILLI, Bonifacio M.   L'offertorio della messa dei defunti.
Rome: Tipografia Agostiniana, 1946.

SICARD, Damien.   La liturgie de la mort dans l'église latine des
origines à la réforme carolingienne.   LQF, 63.   Münster:
Aschendorff, 1978.

WAGNER, Johannes, ed.   Reforming the Rites of Death.   Concilium,
32.   New York: Paulist Press, 1968.

E.   PROTESTANT CHURCHES

1.   Texts

BIDDLE, Perry H., Jr.   Abingdon Funeral Manual.   Nashville, TN:
Abingdon Press, 1976.

BLACKWOOD, Andrew W.   The Funeral: A Source Book for Ministers.   Philadelphia, PA: Westminster Press, 1942; reprint ed.,
Grand Rapids, MI: Baker, 1972.

CHRISTENSEN, James L.   Funeral Services.   Westwood, NJ: Revell, 1959.

_____.   Funeral Services for Today.   Old Tappan, NJ: Revell,
1977.

HARMON, Nolan B., ed.   The Pastor's Ideal Funeral Manual.   2d
ed.   New York: Abingdon-Cokesbury Press, 1966.

HUTTON, Samuel Ward.   Minister's Funeral Manual.   Grand Rapids,
MI: Baker, 1968.

INTER-LUTHERAN COMMISSION ON WORSHIP.   Burial of the Dead.
CW, 10.   Minneapolis, MN: Augsburg, 1976.

LEACH, William H., ed.   The Cokesbury Funeral Manual.   Nashville, TN: Cokesbury Press, 1932.

LOCKYER, Herbert.   The Funeral Sourcebook.   Grand Rapids, MI:
Zondervan, 1967.

MORRISON, James Dalton, ed.   Minister's Service Book.   Chicago:
Willett, Clark; New York: Harper, 1937.

REST, Friedrich. Funeral Handbook. Valley Forge, PA: Judson Press, 1982.

SMITH, W. Halsey, ed. A Service Book. Chicago: National Selected Morticians, 1925.

2. Studies

BARKLEY, John M. "Burial. Reformed." Dicitonary of Liturgy and Worship, pp. 106-109.

BEACH, B. B. "Burial. Seventh-day Adventist." Dictionary of Liturgy and Worship, p. 109.

BRUCE, F. F. "Burial. Plymouth Brethren." Dictionary of Liturgy and Worship, p. 106.

BUCHANAN, C. O. "Burial. Anglican." Dictionary of Liturgy and Worship, pp. 99-100.

Church of England. Archbishops' Commission on Christian Doctrine. Prayer and the Departed. London: SPCK, 1971.

_____. Liturgical Commission. The Burial of the Dead and Commemoration of the Faithful Departed. London: SPCK, 1967.

DAVIES, Horton. "Burial. Congregationalist." Dictionary of Liturgy and Worship, p. 101.

GEORGE, A. Raymond. "Burial. Methodist." Dictionary of Liturgy and Worship, p. 105.

HARDIN, H. Grady. "The Funeral." In Companion to the Book of Worship, pp. 90-102. Edited by William F. Dunckle and Joseph D. Quillian. Nashville, TN: Abingdon Press, 1970.

HOON, Paul Waitman. "Theology, Death, and the Funeral Liturgy." Union Seminary Quarterly Review, 31 (1976): 169-181.

JORDAHN, Bruno. Das kirchliche Begräbnis: Grundlegung und Gestaltung. VEGL, 3. Göttingen: Vandenhoeck & Ruprecht, 1949.

MASER, Hugo. Die Bestattung. Gütersloh: Mohn, 1964.

NIEBERGALL, Alfred. "Burial. Lutheran." Dictionary of Liturgy and Worship, pp. 102-105.

[Prayer Book Studies.] The Order for the Burial of the Dead and An Office of Institution of Rectors into Parishes. PBS, 13-14. New York: Church Pension Fund, 1959.

SCHULZ, F. "Die Begräbnisgebete des 16. und 17. Jahrhunderts."
   Jahrbuch für Liturgik und Hymnologie, 11 (1966): 1-44.

SKOGLUND, John E. "Burial. Baptist." Dictionary of Liturgy
   and Worship, pp. 100-101.

WINKLER, Eberhard. Die Leichenpredigt im deutschen Luthertum
   bis Spener. FGLP, 10/34. München: Kaiser, 1967.

XXXV. DEDICATIONS AND OTHER
OCCASIONAL RITES

A. TEXTS

Cérémonial de la consécration dúne église selon le rite byzantine.
   Introduction et notes par S. Salaville. Rome: Typografia
   Polyglottis Vaticana, 1937.

HORNER, G., ed. The Service for the Consecration of a Church
   and Altar according to the Coptic Rite. London: Harrison,
   1902.

HUTTON, Samuel Ward. Dedication Services. Grand Rapids, MI:
   Baker, 1964.

_____. Home Dedication Service. St. Louis, MO: Bethany
   Press, 1957.

LEACH, William H., ed. The Minister's Handbook of Dedications.
   New York: Abingdon Press, 1961.

LEGG, J. Wickham, ed. English Orders for Consecrating Churches
   in the Seventeenth Century, together with Forms for the Consecration of Churchyards, the First Stone of a Church, the
   Reconciliation of a Church and the Consecration of Altar Plate.
   HBS, 41. London: [Henry Bradshaw Society], 1911.

NATIONAL LITURGICAL OFFICE. A Book of Blessings. Ottawa,
   Ont.: Canadian Conference of Catholic Bishops, 1981.

B. STUDIES

ANDRIEU, Michel. "La Dédicace des églises à Rome et la déposition
   des reliques." In his Les Ordines Romani du haut moyen âge,
   vol. 4, pp. 359-384. Louvain: Spicilegium Sacrum Lovaniense,
   1956.

ARNOLD-FOSTER, Frances. Studies in Church Dedications; or,
England's Patron Saints. 3 vols. London: Skeffington, 1899.

BAUDOT, Jules. La Dédicace des églises. 2. éd. Paris: Bloud
& Cie, 1909.

BOND, Francis. Dedications and Patron Saints of English Churches.
London: Oxford University Press, 1914.

BUCHANAN, Colin O. Inaugural Services. GBMW, 32. Bramcote,
Eng.: Grove Books, 1974.

CRICHTON, J. D. The Dedication of a Church: A Commentary.
Dublin: Veritas Publications, 1980.

"La Dédicace des églises." La Maison-Dieu, 70 (1962).

EDMONDS, H., ed. Enkainia: gesammelte Arbeiten zum 800-
jährigen Weihegedächtnis der Abteikirche Maria Laach am 24.
August 1956. Düsseldorf: Patmos Verlag, 1956.

LOEW, J. "The New Rite of Consecration." Worship, 35 (1961):
527-536.

MUNCEY, R. W. A History of the Consecration of Churches and
Churchyards. Cambridge: W. Heffer, 1930.

SIMONS, Thomas G. Blessings: A Reappraisal of their Nature,
Purpose and Celebration. Saratoga, CA: Resource Publications, 1981.

STIEFENHOFER, Dionys. Die Geschichte der Kirchweihe vom 1.-7.
Jahrhundert. München: J. J. Lentnerschen Buchhandlung,
1909.

WORDSWORTH, John. On the Rite of Consecration of Churches,
especially in the Church of England ... together with the Form
of Prayer and Order of Ceremonies in Use in the Diocese of
Salisbury. London: SPCK; New York: E. & J. B. Young,
1899.

XXXVI. PUBLIC PRAYERS

A. COLLECTIONS

ADDISON, Charles Morris. Prayers for the Christian Year. New
York, London: Century, 1931.

_____, and SUTER, John Wallace. A Book of Offices and
Prayers for Priest and People. 2d revised [i.e. 13th] ed.
New York: Gorham, 1927.

BENSON, Edward White. Prayers, Public and Private. Edited by
Hugh Benson. London: Isbister; New York: Dutton, 1899.

A Book of Prayers for Students. 4th ed. London: SCM Press,
1923.

BRIGHT, William, ed. Ancient Collects and Other Prayers selected
for Devotional Use from Various Rituals. 8th ed. Oxford:
Parker, 1908.

BUCKLEY, Michael, ed. The Treasury of the Holy Spirit: An International Catholic Prayer Book. London: Hodder & Stoughton, 1984.

CARLOZZI, Carl G., ed. Prayers for Pastor and People. New
York: Church Hymnal Corp., 1984.

COLQUHOUN, Frank, ed. Contemporary Parish Prayers. London:
Hodder & Stoughton, 1975.

_____, ed. New Parish Prayers. Foreword by Donald Coggan.
London: Hodder & Stoughton, 1982.

_____, ed. Parish Prayers. London: Hodder & Stoughton,
1967.

COUGHLAN, Peter, JASPER, Ronald C. D., and RODRIGUES,
Teresa, eds. A Christian's Prayer Book: Poems, Psalms and
Prayers for the Church's Year. Chicago: Franciscan Herald
Press, 1972; London: Geoffrey Chapman, 1973.

CURRIE, David M. Come, Let Us Worship God: A Handbook of
Prayers for Leaders of Worship. Philadelphia, PA: Westminster Press, 1977.

DAVIES, Horton, and SLIFER, Morris. Prayers and Other Resources for Public Worship. Nashville, TN: Abingdon Press,
1976.

DEARMER, Percy, and BARRY, F. R. Westminster Prayers. London: Oxford University Press, 1936.

FALLA, Terry, ed. Be Our Freedom, Lord: Responsive Prayers
and Readings for Contemporary Worship. Adelaide: Lutheran
Publishing House, 1981; Grand Rapids, MI: Eerdmans, 1985.

FERGUSON, James. Prayers for Common Worship, Morning and

Evening, every Lords' Day throughout the Course of the Christian Year. London: Allenson, 1936.

_____. Prayers for Public Worship. American ed. Edited by Charles L. Wallis. New York: Harper, 1958.

FOSDICK, Harry Emerson. A Book of Public Prayers. New York: Harper, 1959.

FOX, Selina Fitzherbert. A Chain of Prayer Across the Ages: Forty Centuries of Prayer, from 2000 B.C. 6th ed. London: Murray, 1941; New York: Dutton, 1943.

GEFFEN, Roger. The Handbook of Public Prayer. New York: Macmillan, 1963.

GUSHE, Hermann Paul. A Book of Invocations. New York: Revell, 1928.

HIND, C. Lewis. One Hundred Best Prayers. London: Philpot, 1927.

McNUTT, Frederick Brodie. The Prayer Manual. 4th ed. London: Mowbray, 1968.

A Manual of Eastern Orthodox Prayers. London: SPCK for the Fellowship of SS. Alban and Sergius; New York: Macmillan, 1945; reprint ed., London: SPCK, 1977.

MARTIN, Hugh, ed. A Book of Prayers for Schools. London: SCM Press, 1936.

MICKLEM, Caryl, ed. Contemporary Prayers for Church and School. London: SCM Press, 1975; American ed., As Good As Your Word: A Third Book of Contemporary Prayers. Grand Rapids, MI: Eerdmans, 1975.

_____, ed. Contemporary Prayers for Public Worship. London: SCM Press; Grand Rapids, MI: Eerdmans, 1967.

_____, ed. More Contemporary Prayers: Prayers on Fifty-Two Themes. Grand Rapids, MI: Eerdmans, 1970.

MILLER, Colin F. Prayers for Parish Worship. London, New York: Oxford University Press, 1948.

MILLER, Samuel H. Prayers for Daily Use. New York: Harper, 1957.

MILNER-WHITE, Eric. After the Third Collect: Prayers and Thanksgivings for Use in Public Worship. 4th ed., rev. London: Mowbray, 1952.

_____. A Cambridge Bede Book. London: Longmans, Green,
1936.

_____. Memorials Upon Several Occasions: Prayers and Thanks-
givings for Use in Public Worship. London: Mowbray, 1933.

_____. A Procession of Passion Prayers. London: SPCK, 1950.

MILNER-WHITE, Eric, and BRIGGS, G. W. Daily Prayer. London:
Oxford University Press, 1941.

_____, and SMITH, B. T. D. Cambridge Offices and Orisons.
London: Mowbray, 1921.

MUSSER, Benjamin Francis. Kyrie Eleison: Two Hundred Litanies.
With Historico-Liturgical Introduction and Notes. Westminster,
MD: Newman Bookshop, 1944.

NOYES, Morgan Phelps, ed. Prayers for Services: A Manual for
Leaders of Worship. New York: Scribner, 1934; reprinted
several times to 1951.

OOSTERHUIS, Huub. Bid om vrede. Utrecht: Ambo, 1966; Your
Word is Near: Contemporary Christian Prayers. Translated by
N. D. Smith. Westminster, MD: Newman Press; New York:
Paulist Press, 1968.

_____. In het voorbijgaan. 3. druk. Utrecht: Ambo, 1968;
Prayers, Poems and Songs. Translated by David Smith. New
York: Herder & Herder, 1970.

PAINE, Howard, and THOMPSON, Bard. Book of Prayers for
Church and Home. Philadelphia, PA: Christian Education
Press, 1962.

PARKER, Joseph. Prayers for Worship Services. Grand Rapids,
MI: Baker, 1980.

PEARSON, Roy. Hear Our Prayer: Prayers for Public Worship.
New York: McGraw-Hill, 1961.

PHILLIPS, E. Lee. Prayers for Our Day. Atlanta, GA: John
Knox Press, 1982.

_____. Prayers for Worship. Waco, TX: Word Books, 1979.

PLUMMER, Charles. Devotions from Ancient and Medieval Sources
(Western). Oxford: Blackwell, 1916.

POTTS, J. Manning. Prayers of the Early Church. Nashville, TN:
The Upper Room, 1953.

ROBINSON, Arthur P. Prayers Old and New. London: SCM
   Press, 1932.

ROUILLARD, Philippe, ed. Le Livre de l'unité: prières oecu-
   méniques. Paris: Cerf, 1966; The Unity Book of Prayers.
   Foreword by David Paton. London: Geoffrey Chapman, 1969.

Society of St. John the Evangelist. A Book of Prayers for All
   Churchmen: "Father Field's Prayer Book." Morning, Evening,
   Confession, Communion. Cambridge, MA: Society of St. John
   the Evangelist, 1944.

STRODACH, Paul Zeller, ed. Oremus: Collects, Devotions, Litanies from Ancient and Modern Sources. Philadelphia, PA:
   United Lutheran Publication House, 1925; reprint ed., Minneapolis, MN: Augsburg, 1966?

THIRKIELD, Wilbur P., and HUCKEL, Oliver, eds. Book of Common Worship: for Use in the Several Communions of the Church
   of Christ, including the Psalter and Prayers for Use in Colleges,
   the Family, and for Personal Devotion. 2d ed. New York:
   Dutton, 1936.

TITTLE, Ernest Fremont. A Book of Pastoral Prayer: with an
   Essay on the Pastoral Prayer. New York: Abingdon-
   Cokesbury Press, 1951.

WALLWORK, C. N. R., ed. A Book of Vestry Prayers. London:
   Epworth Press, 1976.

WHITTLE, Donald, ed. Prayers and Services for Schools and Colleges. London: Epworth Press, 1962.

WILLIAMS, Dick, ed. Prayers for Today's Church. Minneapolis,
   MN: Augsburg, 1977.

WOTHERSPOON, H. J. Kyrie eleison ("Lord, Have Mercy"): A
   Manual of Private Prayers. Philadelphia, PA: Westminster
   Press, 1905.

B. GENERAL STUDIES

BLACKWOOD, Andrew W. Leading in Public Prayer. New York:
   Abingdon Press, 1958.

PUGLISI, Mario. Prayer. Translated by Bernard M. Allen. New
   York: Macmillan, 1929.

THURSTON, Herbert. Familiar Prayers: Their Origin and History.

Edited by Paul Grosjean. London: Burns & Oates; Westminster, MD: Newman Press, 1953.

C. EXTEMPORANEOUS AND SILENT PRAYER

DURHAM, John. Directed Silence. Foreword by E. R. Morgan.
SCW, 1. London: Faith Press, 1964.

HEPHER, Cyril, ed. The Fellowship of Silence: Being Experiences
in the Common Use of Prayer without Words. Narrated and
interpreted by Thomas Hodgkin, Percy Dearmer, L. V. Hodgkin, J. C. Fitzgerald. London: Macmillan, 1915.

HEPHER, Cyril. The Fruits of Silence: Being Further Studies
in the Common Use of Prayer without Words, together with
Kindred Essays in Worship. London: Macmillan, 1915.

SKOGLUND, John E. "Free Prayer." Studia Liturgica, 10 (1974):
151-166.

XXXVII. LITURGICAL PREACHING

A. HISTORICAL STUDIES

BOLGIANI, Franco, and DESIDERI, Paolo, eds. Testi greci e latini
relativi alla predicazione popolare e al cristianesimo del primo e
del second secolo d. C. Torino: Giappichelli, 1977.

BRILIOTH, Yngve Torgny. Predikans historia. 2. uppl. Lund:
Gleerup, 1962; A Brief History of Preaching. Translated by
Karl E. Mattson. Philadelphia, PA: Fortress Press, 1965.

CREW, Phyllis Mack. Calvinist Preaching and Iconoclasm in the
Netherlands, 1544-1569. CSEMH. New York: Cambridge
University Press, 1973.

DARGAN, Edwin Charles. A History of Preaching. 2 vols. New
York: Hodder & Stoughton, Doran, 1905-1912.

_____. _____. 3 vols. in 2. Introduction by J. B. Weather-
spoon. Vol. 3 by R. G. Turnbull. Grand Rapids, MI: Baker,
1954-1974.
1. From the Apostolic Fathers to the Great Reformers, A.D.
70-1572. 1954.
2. From the Close of the Reformation Period to the End of the

Nineteenth Century. 1954.
3. From the Close of the Nineteenth Century to the Middle of the Twentieth Century. By R. G. Turnbull. 1974.

DAVIES, Horton. Varieties of English Preaching, 1900-1960. London: SCM Press; Englewood Cliffs, NJ: Prentice-Hall, 1963.

DREHER, Bruno. Die Osterpredigt von der Reformation bis zur Gegenwart. Freiburg: Herder, 1951.

DUKE, Robert W. The Sermon as God's Word: Theologies for Preaching. Abingdon Preacher's Library. Nashville, TN: Abingdon Press, 1980.

ELLIOTT, Emory. Power and Pulpit in Puritan New England. Princeton, NJ: Princeton University Press, 1975.

GATCH, Milton McC. Preaching and Theology in Anglo-Saxon England: Aelfric and Wulfstan. Toronto, Ont.: University of Toronto Press, 1977.

GILMAN, Sander L. The Parodic Sermon in European Perspective: Aspects of Liturgical Parody from the Middle Ages to the Twentieth Century. Wiesbaden: Steiner, 1974.

HALTON, Thomas. "The Early Christian Homily." The Living Light, 17 (1980): 159-163.

MULHERN, P. F. "Preaching I (History of)." New Catholic Encyclopedia, 11:684-690.

OLIVAR, A. "Quelques remarques historiques sur la prédication comme action liturgique dans l'église ancienne." In Mélanges liturgiques offerts au R. P. Dom Bernard Botte, pp. 429-443. Louvain: Abbaye du Mont César, 1972.

SCHUTZ, Werner. Geschichte der christlichen Predigt. Berlin: De Gruyter, 1972.

SKUDLAREK, William F. "Assertion without Knowledge? The Lay Preaching Controversy of the High Middle Ages." Ph.D. dissertation, Princeton Theological Seminary, 1976.

SMYTH, Charles H. E. The Art of Preaching: A Practical Survey of Preaching in the Church of England, 747-1939. Revised ed. London: SPCK, 1953; reprinted 1964.

SZARMACH, Paul E., and HUPPE, Bernard F., eds. The Old English Homily and Its Backgrounds. Albany, NY: State University of New York Press, 1978.

ZINK, Michel. La prédication en langue romane: avant 1300.
NBMA, 4. Paris: Champion, 1976.

B. PRACTICAL AND THEOLOGICAL STUDIES

ACHTEMEIER, Elizabeth. "The Use of Hymnic Elements in Preaching." Interpretation, 39 (1985): 46-59.

ALLMEN, J.-J. von. "La prédication." Verbum Caro, 9 (1955):
110-157; Preaching and Congregation. Translated by B. L.
Nicholas. ESW, 10. London: Lutterworth Press; Richmond,
VA: John Knox Press, 1962.

BABIN, D. E. "Toward a Theology of Liturgical Preaching."
Anglican Theological Review, 52 (1970): 228-239.

BARTH, Karl. Homiletik: Wesen und Vorbereitung der Predigt.
Zürich: EVZ-Verlag, 1966.

_____. La proclamation de l'évangile. Neuchâtel: Delachaux &
Niestlé, 1961; The Preaching of the Gospel. Translated by
B. E. Hooke. Philadelphia, PA: Westminster Press, 1963.

BASS, George M. The Renewal of Liturgical Preaching. Minneapolis, MN: Augsburg, 1967.

BEST, Ernest. From Text to Sermon: Responsible Use of the New
Testament in Preaching. Atlanta, GA: John Knox Press, 1978.

BOHREN, Rudolf. Predigt und Gemeinde: Beiträge zur praktischen
Theologie. Zürich: Zwingli Verlag, 1963; Preaching and Com-
munity. Translated by David E. Green. Richmond, VA: John
Knox Press, 1965.

_____. Predigtlehre. 4. Aufl. EET, 4. München: Kaiser,
1980.

BOSCH, Paul. The Sermon as Part of the Liturgy. St. Louis, MO:
Concordia, 1977.

BROWNE, Robert E. C. The Ministry of the Word. SMW, 3. London: SCM Press; Philadelphia, PA: Fortress Press, 1976.

BUTTRICK, David G. "Preaching the Christian Faith." Liturgy,
2, 3 (Summer 1982): 51-55.

CONGAR, Yves. "Sacramental Worship and Preaching." In The
Renewal of Preaching: Theory and Practice, pp. 51-63.
Edited by Karl Rahner. Concilium, 33. New York: Paulist
Press, 1968.

COOKE, Bernard G. Ministry to Word and Sacraments. Philadelphia, PA: Fortress Press, 1976.

CRICHTON, J. D. "The Nature of the Liturgical Homily." In The Ministry of the Word, pp. 27-44. Edited by Paulinus Milner. London: Burns & Oates, 1967.

CRUM, Milton. "Preaching: What I Am About." Worship, 50 (1976): 194-206.

DAVIS, Charles. "The Theology of Preaching." The Clergy Review, 45 (1960): 524-545; condensed in Theology Digest, 9, 3 (Autumn 1961): 140-145.

DEISS, Lucien. "The Homily." In his God's Word and God's People, pp. 123-136. Collegeville, MN: Liturgical Press, 1976.

DELLING, Gerhard. Wort Gottes und Verkündigung im Neuen Testament. SB, 53. Stuttgart: KBW Verlag, 1971.

DREHER, Bruno. "Exegesis and Proclamation." In Theology, Exegesis and Proclamation, pp. 56-66. Edited by Roland Murphy. Concilium, 70. New York: Herder & Herder, 1971.

DULLES, Avery Robert. Protestant Churches and the Prophetic Office. Woodstock, MD: Woodstock College Press, 1961.

EASTON, Burton Scott, and ROBBINS, Howard Chandler. The Eternal Word in the Modern World: Expository Preaching on the Gospels and Epistles for the Church Year. New York, London: Scribner, 1937.

ESBJORNSON, Robert. "Preaching as Worship." Worship, 48 (1974): 164-170.

FANT, Clyde E. Preaching for Today. New York: Harper & Row, 1975.

FARMER, H. H. The Servant of the Word. London: Nisbet, 1941; New York: Scribner, 1942; reprint ed., Philadelphia, PA: Fortress Press, 1964.

FORSYTH, P. T. Positive Preaching and the Modern Mind. London: Hodder & Stoughton, 1907; reprint eds., London: Independent Press, 1960; Grand Rapids, MI: Eerdmans, 1964; Grand Rapids, MI: Baker, 1980.

FOSSION, André. "From the Bible Text to the Homily." Lumen Vitae, 35 (1980): 279-290.

FULLER, Reginald H. "Sermon." Dictionary of Liturgy and Worship, pp. 344-345.

_____. What is Liturgical Preaching? 2d ed. SMW, 1. London:
    SCM Press, 1960.

GALLEN, J. "The Sacrament of Liturgical Preaching." New Catho-
    lic World, 221 (1978): 100-104.

GRASSO, Domenico. Proclaiming God's Message: A Study in the
    Theology of Preaching. LS, 8. Notre Dame, IN: University
    of Notre Dame Press, 1965.

HAGEMAN, Howard G. "Conducting the Liturgy of the Word." In
    Celebrating the Word: The Third Symposium of the Canadian
    Liturgical Society, Worship '75: Ecumenical Insights, pp. 54-
    74. Edited by James Schmeiser. Toronto, Ont.: Anglican
    Book Centre, 1977.

_____. "The Need and Promise of Reformed Preaching." Re-
    formed Review, 28 (1974-1975): 75-84.

HALL, Thor. The Future Shape of Preaching. Philadelphia, PA:
    Fortress Press, 1971.

HEMPEL, Johannes. Die Vergegenwärtigung des Wortes: zur
    Frage der Konkretisierung christlicher Verkundigung. AT, 54.
    Stuttgart: Calwer, 1974.

HENDERSON, J. Frank. "The Minister of Liturgical Preaching."
    Worship, 56 (1982): 214-230.

KAHLEFELD, Heinrich. "The Pericope and Preaching." In The
    Human Reality of Sacred Scripture, pp. 39-51. Concilium, 10.
    New York: Paulist Press, 1965.

KECK, Leander E. The Bible in the Pulpit: The Renewal of Bib-
    lical Preaching. Nashville, TN: Abingdon Press, 1978.

KEIER, Thomas H. The Word in Worship: Preaching and Its Set-
    ting in Common Worship. London: Oxford University Press,
    1962.

KNOX, John. The Integrity of Preaching. London: Epworth
    Press; New York: Abingdon Press, 1957.

KOENKER, Ernest B. Worship in Word and Sacrament. St. Louis,
    MO: Concordia, 1959.

KRAUSE, Fred. "Homily." New Catholic Encyclopedia, 16:211.

LECLERCQ, Jean. "Le sermon, acte liturgique." La Maison-Dieu,
    8 (1946): 27-46.

"Liturgical Preaching" [Bibliography]. National Bulletin on Liturgy (Canada), 60 (1977): 201-220.

Liturgie als Verkündigung: Anton Hänggi zum 60. Geburtstag am 15. Januar 1977. Herausgegeber, Theologische Fakultät Luzern, Theologische Hochschule Chur. TB, 6. Zürich: Benziger, 1977.

MACLEOD, Donald. Word and Sacrament: A Preface to Preaching and Worship. Englewood Cliffs, NJ: Prentice-Hall, 1960.

MARSHALL, Paul V. "The Liturgy of Preaching: Proclaiming the Word of God." Liturgy, 1, 4 (1981): 44-50.

MARTY, Martin E. The Word: People Participating in Preaching. Philadelphia, PA: Fortress Press, 1984.

MEZGER, Manfred. Verkündigung heute: 11 Versuche in verständlicher Theologie. Studenbücher, 65. Hamburg: Furche-Verlag, 1966.

MILNER, A. Paulinus, ed. The Ministry of the Word. London: Burns & Oates; Collegeville, MN: Liturgical Press, 1967.

MULLER, Ulrich B. Prophetie und Predigt im Neuen Testament. SNT, 10. Gütersloh: Mohn, 1975.

MURPHY, Roland, ed. Theology, Exegesis and Proclamation. Concilium, 70. New York: Herder & Herder, 1971.

O'SHEA, William J. "Homily." New Catholic Encyclopedia, 7, 113-115.

OTT, Heinrich. Dogmatik und Verkündigung: ein Programm dogmatischer Arbeit, dargestellt im Anschluss an die Fragen I bis II des Heidelberger Katechismus. Zürich: EVZ-Verlag, 1961; Theology and Preaching: A Programme of Work in Dogmatics, arranged with reference to Questions I-II of the Heidelberg Catechism. Translated by Harold Knight. Philadelphia, PA: Westminster Press, 1965.

La Parole dans la liturgie. Semaine liturgique de l'Institut Saint-Serge. LO, 48. Paris: Cerf, 1970.

PITT-WATSON, Ian. A Kind of Folly: Toward a Practical Theology of Preaching. Edinburgh: St. Andrew Press, 1976.

RAHNER, Hugo. Eine Theologie der Verkündigung. 2. Aufl. Freiburg: Herder, 1939; reprint ed., Darmstadt: Wissenschaftliche Buchgesellschaft, 1970; A Theology of Proclamation. Translated by Richard Dimmler and others. Adapted by Joseph Halpin. New York: Herder, 1968.

RAHNER, Karl, ed. The Renewal of Preaching: Theory and Practice. Concilium, 33. New York: Paulist Press, 1968.

RITSCHL, Dietrich. A Theology of Proclamation. Richmond, VA:
John Knox Press, 1960.

RODGERS, John Bryden. Liturgy and Communication: An Uncer-
tain Sound? Slough, Eng.: St. Paul Publications, 1975.

ROUTLEY, Erik. Into a Far Country: Reflections upon the Tra-
jectory of the Divine Word, and upon the Communication in
Affairs, Human and Divine, of the Imperative and the Indica-
tive, incorporating material used in the Congregational Lectures, 1960. London: Independent Press, 1962.

ROVER, T. D. "Preaching III (Theology)." New Catholic Encyclopedia, 11:684-690.

SCHMAUS, Michael. Wahrheit als Heilsbegegnung. TFH, 1.
München: Hueber, 1964; Preaching as a Saving Encounter.
Staten Island, NY: Alba House, 1966.

SEARLE, Mark. "Below the Pulpit: The Lay Contribution to the
Homily." Assembly, 7, 2 (November 1980): 110.

SLEETH, Ronald. Proclaiming the Word. New York: Abingdon
Press, 1964.

SLOYAN, Gerard S. "An Instructional Cycle to Prop Up the Lectionary?" The Living Light, 17, 2 (Summer 1980): 182-186.

_____. "What Do You Say After You Say 'This is the Gospel of
the Lord?'" Liturgy, 19, 5 (May 1974): 8-11.

_____. Worshipful Preaching. Philadelphia, PA: Fortress
Press, 1984.

STECK, Wolfgang. Das homiletische Verfahren: zur modernen
Predigttheorie. AP, 13. Göttingen: Vandenhoeck & Ruprecht,
1974.

STEVENS, Clifford. "The Environment of Preaching." Liturgy, 19,
5 (May 1974): 14-15.

STOTT, John R. W. Between Two Worlds: The Art of Preaching
in the Twentieth Century. Grand Rapids, MI: Eerdmans,
1982.

STUEMPFLE, Herman G. Preaching Law and Gospel. Philadelphia,
PA: Fortress Press, 1978.

THUNUS, Jacques. "Pastoral Reflections on the Homily." Lumen Vitae, 35 (1980): 269-277.

TOOHEY, W. "Preaching and the Constitution of the Liturgy." Yearbook of Liturgical Studies, 5 (1964): 15-28.

TRILLHAAS, Wolfgang. Einführung in die Predigtlehre. Darmstadt: Wissenschaftliche Buchgesellschaft, 1974.

WILLIMON, William H. Preaching and Leading Worship. The Pastor's Handbooks, 1. Philadelphia, PA: Westminster Press, 1984.

WINGREN, Gustav. Predikan: en principeill studie. Lund: Gleerup, 1949; The Living Word: A Theological Study of Preaching and the Church. Philadelphia, PA: Muhlenberg Press, 1960.

XXXVIII. LITURGICAL PIETY

BEAUDUIN, Lambert. La piété de l'église: principes et faits. Louvain: Abbaye du Mont César, 1914; Liturgy: The Life of the Church. Translated by Virgil Michel. Collegeville, MN: Liturgical Press, 1926.

BOBRINSKOY, Boris. "Prayer and the Inner Life in Orthodox Tradition." Studia Liturgica, 3 (1964): 30-48.

BOUYER, Louis. Eucharistie: Théologie et spiritualité de la prière eucharistique. Paris: Desclée, 1966; Eucharist: Theology and Spirituality of the Eucharistic Prayer. Translated by Charles Underhill Quinn, Notre Dame, IN: University of Notre Dame Press, 1968.

_____. Liturgical Piety. LS, 1. Notre Dame, IN: University of Notre Dame Press, 1955; British ed. as Life and Liturgy. London: Sheed & Ward, 1956; abridged French translation, La vie de la liturgie. LO, 20. Paris: Cerf, 1956.

BRASO, Gabriel M. Liturgia y espiritualidad. Montserrat: Abadía de Montserrat, 1956; Liturgy and Spirituality. Translated by Leonard J. Doyle. 2d ed. Collegeville, MN: Liturgical Press, 1971.

BROWE, Peter. Die Verehrung der Eucharistie im Mittelalter. München: Hueber, 1933; reprint ed., Rome: Herder, 1967.

DIEKMANN, Godfrey. Personal Prayer and the Liturgy. London: Geoffrey Chapman, 1969.

DUMOUTET, Edouard. Le désir de voir l'hostie et les origines de
la dévotion au Saint-Sacrament. Paris: Beauchesne, 1926.

DURIG, Walter. Pietas liturgica: Studien zur Frömmigkeitsbegriff
und zur Gottesvorstellung der abendländischen Liturgie.
Regensburg: Pustet, 1958.

FISCHER, Balthasar, and WAGNER, Johannes, eds. Paschatis sollemnia: Studien zu Osterfeier und Osterfrömmigkeit. Freiburg:
Herder, 1959.

FLOROVSKY, George. "Worship and Every-Day Life: An Eastern
Orthodox View." Studia Liturgica, 2 (1963): 266-272.

GEORGE, A. Raymond. "Private Devotion in the Methodist Tradition." Studia Liturgica, 2 (1963): 223-236.

GRAMMONT, Paul. "Liturgy and Contemplation." In True Worship,
pp. 83-97. Edited by Lancelot Sheppard. London: Darton,
Longman & Todd; Baltimore, MD: Helicon Press, 1963.

HAMMAN, Adalbert. "Eucharistie I: Mystère eucharistique." Dictionnaire de spiritualité, ascétique et mystique, 4:1583-1586.

IRWIN, Kevin W. Liturgy, Prayer and Spirituality. New York:
Paulist Press, 1984.

JUNGMANN, Josef A. "Liturgie und Pia Exercitia." Liturgisches
Jahrbuch, 9 (1959): 79-86.

LONGPRE, E. "Eucharistie et expérience mystique." Dictionnaire
de spiritualité, ascétique et mystique, 4: 1586-1621.

MAGSAM, Charles M. The Inner Life of Worship. St. Meinrad,
IN: Grail Publications, 1958.

MARITAIN, Jacques and Raissa. Liturgie et contemplation. Bruges:
Desclée de Brouwer, 1959; Liturgy and Contemplation. Translated by Joseph W. Evans. New York: P. J. Kenedy, 1960.

OGGIONI, Constantino, and BIFFI, Giacomo. Introduzione alle vita
liturgica. Milano: Vita e Pensiero, 1959.

ORDONEZ MARQUEZ, Juan. Teologia y espiritualidad del año liturgico. BAC, 403. Madrid: EDICA, 1978.

Orthodox Spirituality: An Outline of the Ascetical and Mystical
Tradition. By a Monk of the Eastern Church. London: Pub-
lished for the Fellowship of SS. Alban and Sergius by SPCK;
New York: Macmillan, 1945.

PORTER, H. Boone. "The Eucharistic Piety of Justin Martyr."
Anglican Theological Review, 39 (1957): 24-33.

PREUSS, Hans. Die Geschichte der Abendmahlsfrömmigkeit in Zeug-
nissen und Berichten. Gütersloh: Bertelsmann, 1949.

REETZ, Benedikt. Liturgie und Streben nach Volkommenheit.
Salzburg: Verlag Rupertuswerk, 1951.

ROGUET, A. M. "L'adoration eucharistique dans la piété sacerdo-
tale." La Vie Spirituelle, 91 (1954): 5-12.

ROMANIDES, John S. "Man and His True Life according to the
Greek Orthodox Service Book." The Greek Orthodox Theological Review, 1 (1954): 63-83.

SALAVILLE, Séverien. Christus in orientalium pietate. BEL, 20.
Rome: Edizioni Liturgiche, 1935-1946?

SALIERS, Don E. Worship and Spirituality. Spirituality & the
Christian Life, 5. Philadelphia, PA: Westminster Press, 1984.

SHEPHERD, Massey H., Jr. "Implications of Liturgical Prayer for
Personal Meditation and Contemplation." Studia Liturgica, 9
(1973): 56-71.

THURIAN, Max. Joie du ciel sur la terre: introduction à la vie
liturgique. Neuchâtel: Delachaux & Nestlé, 1946.

To Worship in Spirit and Truth. Papers presented at the 1st Institute for Spirituality Conference, St. John's University, 2-3
March 1978. Collegeville, MN: St. John's University, 1978.

TOON, Peter. Knowing God through the Liturgy. GBMW, 33.
Bramcote, Eng.: Grove Books, 1975.

TYCIAK, Julius. Die Liturgie als Quelle österlicher Frömmigkeit.
EO, 20. Freiburg: Herder, 1937.

VAJTA, Vilmos. "Der Gottesdienst und das sakramentale Leben."
In Die evangelisch-lutherische Kirche, pp. 135-160. Heraus-
gegeben von Vilmos Vajta. Stuttgart: Evangelisches Verlags-
werk, 1977; "Worship and Sacramental Life." In The Lutheran
Church: Past and Present, pp. 121-145. Edited by Vilmos
Vajta. Minneapolis, MN: Augsburg, 1977.

VOLK, Hermann. "Eucharistische Frömmigkeit." In Geheimnis des
Glaubens, pp. 37-85. By Hermann Volk and Friedrich Wetter.
Mainz: Grünewald, 1968.

WAKEFIELD, Gordon S. Methodist Devotion: The Spiritual Life

in the Methodist Tradition, 1791-1945. London: Epworth Press,
1966.

ZIEGLER, A. W., ed. Eucharistische Frömmigkeit in Bayern. 2.
Aufl. BAK, 23/2. München: Seitz, 1963.

XXXIX. THE DAILY OFFICE

A. GENERAL AND COMPARATIVE STUDIES

BAUMSTARK, Anton. Liturgie comparée. 3. éd. revue par Ber-
nard Botte. Chevetogne: Editions de Chevetogne, 1953;
Comparative Liturgy. Translated by F. L. Cross. London:
Mowbray, 1958.

_____. Vom geschichtlichen Werden der Liturgie. EO, 10.
Freiburg: Herder, 1923; reprint ed., Darmstadt: Wissenschaftliche Buchgesellschaft, 1971.

GELINEAU, Joseph. "The Concrete Forms of Common Prayer."
Studia Liturgica, 10 (1974): 137-150.

GRISBROOKE, W. Jardine. "A Contemporary Liturgical Problem:
The Divine Office and Public Worship." Studia Liturgica, 8
(1971-1972): 129-168; 9 (1973): 3-18, 81-106.

NEALE, John Mason. Notes on the Divine Office: Historical and
Mystical. London: J. T. Hayes, 1877.

PARGOIRE, J. "Prime et complies." Revue d'histoire et de littérature religieuses, 3 (1898): 281-288.

B. THE EARLY CHURCH: ORIGINS OF
THE DAILY OFFICE

BAUMSTARK, Anton. Nocturna laus: Typen frühchristlicher
Vigilienfeier und ihr Fortleben vor allem in römischen und

monastischen Ritus. Aus dem Nachlass herausgegeben von
Odilo Heiming. LQF, 32. Münster: Aschendorff, 1957.

BRADSHAW, Paul F. Daily Prayer in the Early Church: A Study
of the Origin and Early Development of the Divine Office.
ACC, 63. London: Alcuin Club/SPCK, 1981.

_____. "Prayer Morning, Noon, Evening, and Midnight—an
Apostolic Custom?" Studia Liturgica, 13, 1 (1979): 57-62.

CHADWICK, O. "The Origins of Prime." Journal of Theological
Studies, 49 (1948): 178-182.

CULLMANN, Oscar. Urchristentum und Gottesdienst. Basel: H.
Majer, 1944; partial translation in Le Culte dans l'église primitive.
Translated by J.-J. von Allmen. 3e éd. CTAP, 8. Neuchâtel:
Delachaux & Niestlé, 1948.

_____. Urchristentum und Gottesdienst. 2. Aufl. Zürich:
Zwingli Verlag, 1950; and Les Sacrements dans l'évangile johan-
nique. Paris: Presses Universitaires de France, 1951; Early
Christian Worship. Translated by A. Stewart Todd and James
B. Torrance. SBT, 10. London: SCM Press; Chicago:
Regnery, 1953; reprint ed., Philadelphia, PA: Westminster
Press, 1978.

_____. Urchristentum und Gottesdienst. 4. Aufl. Zürich:
Zwingli Verlag, 1962.

DALMAIS, Irenée-Henri. "Origine et constitution de l'Office."
La Maison-Dieu, 21 (1950): 21-39.

DELLING, Gerhard. Gottesdienst im Neuen Testament. Göttingen:
Vandenhoeck & Ruprecht, 1952; Worship in the New Testament.
Translated by Percy Scott. Philadelphia, PA: Westminster
Press, 1962.

DUGMORE, Clifford W. The Influence of the Synagogue upon the
Divine Office. ACC, 45. London: Oxford University Press,
1944; reprint ed., Westminster, Eng.: Faith Press, 1964.

FROGER, Jacques. Les Origines de Prime. BEL, 19. Rome:
Edizioni Liturgiche, 1946.

HANSSENS, Jean Michel. Aux origines de la prière liturgique:
nature et genèse de l'office des matines. AG, 57. Rome:
Universitas Gregoriana, 1952.

JONSSON, Ritva. Historia: études sur la genèse des offices ver-
sifiés. AUS, Studia Latina Stockholmiensia, 15. Stockholm:
Almqvist & Wiksell, 1968.

MARCORA, Carlo. La Vigilia nella liturgia: ricerche sulle origini e sui primi sviluppi. AA, 6. Milan: Ambrosius, 1954.

MATEOS, Juan. "Office de minuit et office du matin chez Athanase." Orientalia Christiana Periodica, 28 (1962): 173-180.

_____. "The Origin of the Divine Office." Worship, 41 (1967): 477-485.

_____. "Quelques anciens documents sur l'office du soir." Orientialia Christiana Periodica, 35 (1969): 347-374.

MOULE, C. F. D. Worship in the New Testament. ESW, 9. Richmond, VA: John Knox Press, 1961.

WALKER, Joan Hazelden. "Terce, Sext and None: An Apostolic Custom?" In Studia Patristica, vol. 5, pp. 206-212. Edited by F. L. Cross. TUGAL, 80. Berlin: Akademie-Verlag, 1962.

WINKLER, Gabriele. "New Study of Early Development of the Divine Office." Worship, 56 (1982): 27-35.

_____. "Uber die Kathedralvesper in den verschiedenen Riten der Ostens und Westens." Archiv für Liturgiewissenschaft, 16 (1974): 53-102.

ZERFASS, Rolf. Die Schriftlesung im Kathedraloffizium Jerusalems. LQF, 48. Münster: Aschendorff, 1968.

C. EASTERN CHURCHES

1. Texts

The Agpeya: The Coptic Orthodox Book of Hours. Los Angeles, CA: Sts. Athanasius and Cyril of Alexandria Orthodox Publications, 1982.

ARMENIAN APOSTOLIC CHURCH IN AMERICA. The Book of Hours; or the Order of Common Prayers of the Armenian Apostolic Orthodox Church: Matins, Prime, Vespers and Occasional Offices. Evanston, IL: Ouzoonian House, 1964.

BLACK, Matthew, ed. A Christian Palestinian Syriac Horologion (Berlin MS. Or. Oct. 1019). TaS, n.s., 1. Cambridge: Cambridge University Press, 1954.

Breviarium armenium, sive dispositio communius Armeniacae Ecclesiae precum. A Sanctis Isaaco Patriarcha, Mesrobio doctore, Kiudio atque a Joanne Mantagunensi habita. Venetiis: In Insula S. Lazzari, 1908.

Breviarium iuxta ritum Syrorum orientalium, id est Chaldacorum.
4 vols.   Romae: S. Congregationem "Pro Ecclesia Orientali,"
1938.

Coptic Offices.   Translated by Reginald Maxwell Woolley.   TCL,
Ser. 3.   London: SPCK; New York: Macmillan, 1930.

MACLEAN, Arthur J.   East Syrian Daily Offices.   London: Rivington, Percival, 1894; reprint ed., Farnborough, Eng.:   Gregg,
1969.

MATEOS, Juan, ed.   Le Typicon de la grande église.   2 vols.
OCA, 165-166.   Rome: Pontificium Institutum, 1962-1963.

MOLITOR, Joseph, ed.   Chaldäisches Brevier: Ordinarium des
ostsyrischen Stundengebets.   Düsseldorf: Patmos, 1967.

The Office of Vespers in the Byzantine Rite.   London: Darton,
Longman & Todd, 1965.

RAYA, Joseph, and VINCK, José de.   Byzantine Daily Worship.
Allendale: Alleluia Press, 1969.

2. Studies

BORGIA, Nilo.   Horologion "Diurno" della chiese di rito bizantino.
OC, 16/2 [no. 56].   Rome: Pontificium Institutum Orientalium
Studiorum, 1929.

BREYDY, Michel.   L'Office divin dans l'église syro-maronite.
Beirut: Impr. catholique, 1960.

BURMESTER, O. H. E.   "The Canonical Hours in the Coptic
Church."   Orientalia Christiana Periodica, 2 (1936):   84-93.

CASPER, J.   "La Prière des heures canoniales dans les rites orientaux."   La Maison-Dieu, 21 (1950):   82-109.

MATEOS, Juan.   "Les Différentes espèces de vigiles dans le rite
chaldéen."   Orientalia Christiana Periodica, 27 (1961):   46-63.

_____.   "L'Invitatoire du nocturne chez les syriens et les maron-
ites."   L'Orient Syrien, 11 (1966):   353-366.

_____.   Lelya-Sapra: essai d'interpretation des matines chal-
déenes.   OCA, 156.   Rome: Pontificium Institutum Orientalium
Studiorum, 1959.

_____.   "Les Matines chaldéenes, maronites et syriennes."   Ori-
entalia Christiana Periodica, 26 91960):   51-73.

_____. "The Morning and Evening Office." Worship, 42 (1968): 31-47.

_____. "L'Office paroissial du matin et du soir dans le rite chaldéen." La Maison-Dieu, 64 (1960): 65-89.

_____. "Prières initiales fixes des offices syrien, maronite et byzantin." L'Orient Syrien, 11 (1966): 489-498.

_____. "Quelques problèmes de l'orthros byzantin." Proche-Orient Chrétien, 11 (1961): 17-35, 201-221.

_____. "La Vigile cathédrale chez Egérie." Orientalia Christiana Periodica, 27 (1961): 281-312.

MENSBRUGGHE, Alexis van der. "Prayer-time in Egyptian Monasticism (320-450)." In Studia Patristica, vol. 2, pp. 435-454. Edited by Kurt Aland and F. L. Cross. TUGAL, 64. Berlin: Akademie-Verlag, 1957.

MERCENIER, F., and PARIS, François, eds. La prière des églises de rite byzantin. 2. éd. Chevetogne: Monastère de Chevetogne, 1948- .

PUDICHERY, S. Ramša: An Analysis and Interpretation of the Chaldean Vespers. Dhamaram College Studies, 9. Dhamaram, India, 1972.

QUECKE, Hans. Untersuchungen zum koptischen Stundengebet. PIOL, 3. Louvain: Université catholique de Louvain, Institute Orientaliste, 1970.

RAES, Alphonse. Introductio in liturgiam orientalem. Rome: Pontificium Institutum Orientalium Studiorum, 1947.

SCHMEMANN, Alexander. Vvedenie v liturgiceskoe bogoslovie. Paris: YMCA-Press, 1961; Introduction to Liturgical Theology. London: Faith Press, 1966.

STRUNK, William Oliver. "The Byzantine Office at Hagia Sophia." In Dumbarton Oaks Papers, 9-10, pp. 175-202. Cambridge, MA: Harvard University Press, 1955-1956.

TABET, Jean. L'Office commun maronite: étude du Lilyō et du Safrō. Bibliothèque de l'université S.-Esprit, 5. Kaslik, Lebanon: L'Université Saint-Esprit, 1972.

TAFT, Robert. "Praise in the Desert: The Coptic Monastic Office Yesterday and Today." Worship, 56 (1982): 513-536.

VELAT, B. Etudes sur le Me'eraf, commun de l'office divin Ethiopien. PO, 33. Paris: Firmin-Didot, 1966.

WINKLER, Gabriele. "Stundengebet (Offizium)." Kleine Orientalisches Lexikon.

D. LATIN CHURCHES

1. Medieval Texts

BLEW, William, ed. Breviarium aberdonense. 2 vols. London:
Toovey, 1854.

Breviarium Bothanum sive portiforium secundum usum Ecclesiae
cujusdam in Scotia. London: Longmans, Green, 1900.

BROU, Louis, ed. The Psalter Collects from V-VIth Century
Sources. Edited, with introduction, apparatus criticus and
indexes by Louis Brou from the papers of André Wilmart.
HBS, 83. London: [Henry Bradshaw Society], 1949.

FRERE, Walter Howard, and BROWN, L. E. G., eds. The Hereford
Breviary. 3 vols. HBS, 26, 40, 46. London: Harrison,
1904-1915.

GAMBIER-PARRY, T. R., ed. The Colbertine Breviary. 2 vols.
HBS, 43-44. London: Harrison, 1912-1913.

LAWLEY, S. W., ed. Breviarium ad usum insignis ecclesiae eboracensis. 2 vols. SSP, 71, 75. Durham, Eng.: Andrews,
1880-1883.

LEGG, J. Wickham, ed. Breviarium Romanum a Francisco Cardinali
Quignonio. Cambridge: Typis atque impensis Academiae, 1888.

_____, ed. The Second Recension of the Quignon Breviary.
2 vols. HBS, 35, 42. London: Harrison, 1908-1912.

LIETZMANN, Hans, ed. Einführung in das römische Brevier. Liturgische Texte, X. KT, 141. Bonn: Marcus & Weber, 1917.

PROCTOR, Francis, and WORDSWORTH, Christopher, eds. Breviarium ad usum insignis ecclesiae Sarum. 3 vols. Cambridge:
Almae Matris Academiae Cantabrigiensis, 1879-1886.

TOLHURST, John B. L., ed. The Monastic Breviary of Hyde Abbey, Winchester. 6 vols. HBS, 69, 70, 71, 76, 78, 80. London: Harrison, 1932-1942.

TOMMASI, Giuseppe Maria. The Reformed Breviary of Cardinal
Tommasi. Edited, with an introduction, translation, notes and
appendices by J. Wickham Legg. London: SPCK, 1904.

2. Tridentine Texts

Breviarium Romanum ex decreta sacrosancti Concilii Tridentini re-
stitutum. (authorized 1568).

_____. Ratisbon: Pustet, 1885.

_____. Editio typica. Rome: Typis polyglottis vaticanis, 1914.

_____. Editio juxta typicam vaticanum. 4 vols. New York:
Benziger, 1941-1942.

The Roman Breviary. 4 vols. New York: Benziger, 1950-1951.

_____. Edited by Bede Babo. Translations of the prayers by
Christine Mohrmann. New York: Benziger, 1964.

The Hours of the Divine Office in English and Latin: A Bilingual
Edition of the Roman Breviary Text. 3 vols. Collegeville, MN:
Liturgical Press, 1963-1964.

3. Post-Vatican II Texts

Liturgia Horarum. Editio typica. 4 vols. Rome: Typis polyglottis
vaticanis, 1973.

The Liturgy of the Hours. 4 vols. New York: Catholic Book Publishing, 1975.

KEIFER, Ralph Allen, ed. Christian Prayer: The Liturgy of the
Hours: Morning Prayer, Evening Prayer, Night Prayer. English translation prepared by the International Commission on
English in the Liturgy. Collegeville, MN: Liturgical Press,
1976.

4. Studies

BAUMER, Suitbert. Geschichte des Breviers. Freiburg: Herder,
1895.

BATIFFOL, Pierre. Histoire de bréviaire romain. 3. éd. BhistR.
Paris: Picard, 1911; History of the Roman Breviary. Translated by Atwell M. Y. Baylay. London: Longmans, Green,
1912.

BAUDOT, Jules L. Le Bréviaire. Paris: Bloud & Gay, 1929; The
Breviary: Its History and Contents. Translated by the Benedictines of Stanbrook. CLRK, 4. London: Sands, 1929.

BISHOP, William C. The Mozarabic and Ambrosian Rites: Four Es-
    says in Comparative Liturgiology. Edited by Charles L. Feltoe.
    London: Mowbray, 1924.

BOHATTA, Hanns. Bibliographie der Breviere 1501-1850. 2. Aufl.
    Stuttgart: Anton Hiersemann, 1963.

BRINKTRINE, Johannes. Das römische Brevier. Paderborn:
    Schöningh, 1932.

CALLEWAERT, Camillus Aloysius. "De laudibus matutinis." Colla-
    tiones Brugenses, 27 (1927): 383-389, 448-451; 28 (1928):
    63-72, 152-166, 245-250, 328-338; reprinted in his Sacris Eru-
    diri, pp. 53-89. Steenbrugge: Abbatia S. Petri de Alden-
    burgo, 1940; reprinted 1960.

_____. Liturgicae institutiones. Vol. 2: De breviarii romani
    liturgia. Ed. 3 recognita et aucta. Brugis: C. Beyaert,
    1939.

CASSIEN, Mgr., and BOTTE, Bernard, eds. La Prière des heures.
    LO, 35. Paris: Cerf, 1963.

CRICHTON, James D. Christian Celebration: The Prayer of the
    Church. London: Geoffrey Chapman, 1976.

CUVA, A. La liturgia delle Ore: note teologiche e spirituali.
    BEL, 4. Rome: Edizioni Liturgiche, 1975.

GASTOUE, Amédée. Les Vigiles nocturnes. 2. éd. Paris: Bloud
    & Cie, 1908.

GIHR, Nikolaus. Prim und Komplet des römischen Breviers, litur-
    gisch und aszetisch erklärt. Freiburg: Herder, 1907.

HEIMING, Odilo. "Zum monastischen Offizium von Kassianus bis
    Kolumbanus." Archiv für Liturgiewissenschaft, 7 (1961): 89-
    156.

JUNGMANN, Josef Andreas. "Beiträge zur Geschichte der Gebets-
    liturgie." Zeitschrift für katholische Theologie, 72 (1950):
    66-79, 223-234, 360-366.

_____, ed. Brevierstudien. Trier: Paulinus-Verlag, 1958.

_____. Liturgisches Erbe und pastorale Gegenwart. Innsbruck:
    Tyrolia Verlag, 1960; Pastoral Liturgy. Translated by Ronald
    Walls. London: Challoner, 1962.

KASTNER, Karl. Praktischer Brevier-Kommentar. 2 Bde. Bres-
    lau: Goerlich, 1923-1924.

KROON, Sigurd. Breviarium Lincopense 1493: de förlorade partierna. LUA, n. f., avd. 1, 47/2. Lund: Gleerup, 1951.

LE CAROU, Arsène. L'Office divin chez les frères mineurs au
XIIIe siècle: son origine, sa destinée. Paris: Lethielleux,
1928.

"La Liturgie des heures: le renouveau de l'office divin." La
Maison-Dieu, 105 (1971).

MARTIMORT, A. G., ed. L'Eglise en prière. 3. éd. Paris:
Desclée, 1965; partial adaptation in The Church at Prayer:
Introduction to the Liturgy. Translated by Robert Fisher et al.
English ed. edited by Austin Flannery and Vincent Ryan.
New York: Desclée, 1968.

MORIN, G. "L'Uniformité dans les laudes du dimanche du IVe au
VIIe siècle." Le Messager des fidèles; Revue bénédictine, 6
(1889): 301-304.

PARSCH, Pius. Breviererklärung im Geiste der liturgischen Er-
neuerung. Klosterneuburg: Volksliturgischer Verlag, 1949;
The Breviary Explained. Translated by W. Nayden and C.
Hoegerl. St. Louis, MO: B. Herder, 1952.

PASCHER, Josef. Sinngerechtes Brevierbeten. München: Hueber,
1962.

_____. Das Stundengebet der römischen Kirche. München:
Zink, 1954.

PIAULT, Bernard. La Prière de l'église: le bréviaire romain.
Paris: Spes, 1958.

PORTER, A. W. S. "Cantica Mozarabici officii." Ephemerides Liturgicae, 49 (1935): 126-145.

_____. "Studies in the Mozarabic Office." Journal of Theological
Studies, 35 (1934): 266-286.

RAFFA, Vincenzo. La liturgica delle ore. Brescia: Morcelliana,
1959.

REYNAL, Daniel de. Théologie de la liturgie des heures. Paris:
Beauchesne, 1978.

"Richesses de la prière des heures." La Maison-Dieu, 143 (1980).

RIGHETTI, Mario. Manuale di storia liturgica. Vol. 2: L'Anno
liturgico, il breviario. 3. ed. Milan: Editrice Ancora, 1959-
1966.

SALMON, Pierre. "Aux origines du bréviaire romain." La Maison-
Dieu, 27 (1951): 114-136.

_____. L'Office divin: Histoire de la formation du bréviaire.
LO, 27. Paris: Cerf, 1959; The Breviary through the Cen-
turies. Translated by Sister David Mary. Collegeville, MN:
Liturgical Press, 1962.

_____. L'Office divin au moyen âge: histoire de la formation
du bréviaire du IXe au XVIe siècle. LO, 43. Paris: Cerf,
1967.

SANCHEZ ALISEDA, Casimiro. El breviario romano: estudio his-
tórico-litúrgico sobre el oficio divino. Madrid: Distribuciones
O.D.E.R., 1951.

TRIPP, David. "Ecumenical Notes on the New Breviary in Its English Form." One in Christ, 8 (1972): 384-392.

VAN DIJK, S. J. P., and WALKER, J. Hazelden. The Origins of
the Modern Roman Liturgy: The Liturgy of the Papal Court
and the Franciscan Order in the Thirteenth Century. Westminster, MD: Newman Press, 1960.

WILLI, Charles. Le Bréviaire expliqué. 2e éd. 2 vols. Paris:
Téqui, 1922.

E. LUTHERAN CHURCHES

Danske Folkekirke. Dansk Tidebog. Den Danske Tidegaerd. Til-
rettelagt af dag Monrad Møller, Finn Viderø og Harald Vilstrup
under medvirken af Ethan Rosenkilde Larsen. 2. udg. Copenhagen: Frimodt, 1971.

GREIFENSTEIN, Hermann, HARTOG, Hans, and SCHULZ, Frieder,
eds. Allgemeines evangelisches Gebetbuch: Anleitung und
Ordnung für das Beten des Einzelnen, der Familie und der
Gemeinde. Mit einer ökumenischen Gebetsammlung. 2. Aufl.
Hamburg: Furche-Verlag, 1965.

HEILER, Friedrich, ed. Evangelisch-katholisches Brevier. Münch-
en: Reinhardt, 1932.

HEROLD, Max, ed. Vesperale: Nachmittags- und Abendgottes-
dienste mit und ohne Chor. 2 vols. in 1. Gütersloh: Bertelsmann, 1893-1907.

INTER-LUTHERAN COMMISSION ON WORSHIP. Daily Prayer of the
Church. CW, 9. Minneapolis, MN: Augsburg, 1976.

MAUDER, Albert, ed. Evangelisches Tagzeitenbuch: Ordnungen
für das tägliche Gebet. Herausgegeben im Auftrag der Evangelischen Michaelsbruderschaft. Kassel: Stauda, 1967.

OTTO, Rudolf, and MENSCHING, Gustav. Chorgebete für Kirche,
Schule und Hausandacht. 2. Aufl. AWR, 3. Giessen: Töpelmann, 1928.

SCHUMANN, Horst, ed. Das Stundengebet: Als Entwurf herausgegeben vom Liturgischen Ausschluss der Evangelischen
Michaelsbruderschaft. 3. Aufl. Kassel: Stauda, 1953.

UNITED LUTHERAN CHURCH IN AMERICA. The Daily Office Book.
Philadelphia, PA: Board of Publication of the United Lutheran
Church in America, 1938.

Vereinigte Evangelisch-Lutherische Kirche Deutschlands. Agende
für evangelisch-lutherische Kirchen und Gemeinden. Bd. 2:
Gebetsgottesdienste. 2. Aufl. Berlin: Lutherisches Verlagshaus, 1963-1964.

F. REFORMED CHURCHES

1. Texts

COMMUNAUTE DE TAIZE. L'Office divin de chaque jour. Neuchâtel: Delachaux & Niestlé, 1949.

_____. _____. 3e éd. Neuchâtel: Delachaux & Niestlé,
1961.

CHURCH OF SCOTLAND. The Book of Common Order: Daily Offices for Morning and Evening Prayer throughout the Week.
Edinburgh: Blackwood, 1893.

MAXWELL, William D., ed. John Knox's Genevan Service Book,
1556. 2d ed. Edinburgh: Faith Press, 1965.

2. Studies

OLD, Hughes Oliphant. "Daily Prayer in the Reformed Church of
Strasbourg, 1525-1530." Worship, 52 (1978): 121-138.

G. ANGLICAN CHURCHES

1. Texts

GALLEY, Howard, ed. The Prayer Book Office. New York: Seabury Press, 1980.

JASPER, Ronald C. D., ed. The Daily Office. By the Joint Liturgical Group. London: SPCK and Epworth Press, 1968.

_____, ed. The Daily Office Revised. London: SPCK, 1978.

LEGG, J. Wickham, ed. Cranmer's Liturgical Projects. HBS, 50. London: Harrison, 1915.

PROTESTANT EPISCOPAL CHURCH IN THE U.S.A. Breviary Offices, from Lauds to Compline Inclusive. Translated and Arranged from the Sarum Book and Supplemented from Gallican and Monastic Uses. New York: Printed for the Society of S. Margaret by J. Pott, 1885.

_____. The Day Office of the Monastic Breviary. Peekskill, NY: Community of St. Mary, 1918.

_____. The Monastic Diurnal; or, Day Hours of the Monastic Breviary according to the Holy Rule of St. Benedict, with additional Rubrics and Devotions for its Recitation in accordance with the Book of Common Prayer. London; New York: Oxford University Press, 1932.

_____. Liturgical Commission. Morning and Evening Prayer. PBS, 6. New York: Church Pension Fund, 1957.

_____. The Daily Office. PBS, 22. New York: Church Hymnal Corporation, 1970.

_____. The Daily Office Revised. PBS, 27. New York: Church Hymnal Corporation, 1973.

2. Studies

BRIGHTMAN, Francis E., ed. The English Rite: Being a Synopsis of the Sources and Revisions of the Book of Common Prayer with an Introduction and an Appendix. 2d ed. 2 vols. London: Rivington, 1921.

CANDOLE, Henry de. The Church's Prayers. London: Mowbray, 1939.

CUMING, G. J. A History of Anglican Liturgy. 2d ed. London: Macmillan, 1982.

PORTER, Harry Boone, Jr. "What Does the Daily Office Do?" Anglican Theological Review, 56 (1974): 170-181.

PROCTOR, Francis, and FRERE, William H. A New History of the Book of Common Prayer. Revised ed. London: Macmillan, 1905.

ROGERS, Clement F. Matins and Evensong. London: Faith Press, 1924.

H. METHODIST CHURCHES

JASPER, Ronald C. D., ed. The Daily Office. By the Joint Liturgical Group. London: SPCK and Epworth Press, 1968.

_____, ed. The Daily Office Revised. London: SPCK, 1978.

METHODIST CHURCH (ENGLAND). Divine Worship, Approved by the Conference for Optional Use in Methodist Churches. London: Methodist Publishing House, 1935.

METHODIST SACRAMENTAL FELLOWSHIP. Forms for the Divine Office: Private and Communal Orders for Morning and Evening Prayer, for the Use of Methodists. Warrington, Eng.: Methodist Fellowship, 1975.

ORDER OF ST. LUKE. The Book of the Daily Office of the Order of St. Luke. Rockford, IL: Order of St. Luke, 1973.

I. FREE CHURCHES

1. Texts

MICKLEM, Nathaniel, ed. Prayers and Praises. 2d ed. London: Independent Press, 1954; reprint ed., Edinburgh: St. Andrew Press, 1977.

ORCHARD, William Edwin, ed. The Order of Divine Service for Public Worship, the Administration of the Sacraments and Other Rites and Ceremonies and a Selection from the Daily Offices compiled from Ancient and Modern Devotions together with an abridged and rev. Psalter and Canticles pointed for Chanting. London: Oxford University Press, 1919; 2d ed., London: Oxford University Press, 1926.

2. Studies

PEASTON, A. E. The Prayer Book Tradition in the Free Churches.
London: James Clarke, 1965, c1964.

XL. THE CHURCH YEAR AND CALENDAR

A. GENERAL STUDIES

ALEXANDER, Charles. The Church's Year. London: Oxford
University Press, 1950.

ARMITAGE, William J. Church Year Studies for the Sundays,
Sacred Seasons and Saints' Days of the Christian Year. New
York: Frowde, 1908.

BISHOP, John. Through the Christian Year. Foreword by Mald-
wyn L. Edwards. London: National Sunday School Union,
1962.

COWIE, Leonard W. The Christian Calendar. Springfield, IL:
G. & C. Merriam, 1974.

DENIS-BOULET, Noële Maurice. Le calendrier chrétien. JSJC,
112. Paris: Fayard, 1959; The Christian Calendar. Translated by P. Hepburne-Scott. TCEC, 113. New York: Hawthorn Books, 1960.

ELIADE, Mircea. Le mythe de l'éternel retour: archétypes et
répétition. Paris: Gallimard, 1949; The Myth of the Eternal
Return; or, Cosmos and History. Translated by Willard R.
Trask. Bollingen Series, 46. Princeton, NJ: Princeton
University Press, 1954; reprinted as Cosmos and History: The
Myth of the Eternal Return. New York: Harper Torchbooks,
1959.

GIBSON, George M. The Story of the Christian Year. New York:
Abingdon Press, 1945; reprint ed., Freeport, NY: Books for
Libraries Press, 1972.

GOUDOEVER, J. van. Biblical Calendars. 2d ed. Leiden: Brill,
1961.

GWYNNE, Walker. The Christian Year: Its Purpose and Its History. London, New York: Longmans, Green, 1915; reprint
ed., Detroit, MI: Grand River Books, 1971.

HENRY, P. The Liturgical Year: The Public Worship of God by the Church throughout the Year. Milwaukee, WI: Bruce, 1940.

JAMES, E. O. Seasonal Feasts and Festivals. London: Thames & Hudson; New York: Barnes & Noble, 1961.

KELLNER, Karl A. H. Heortologie, oder die geschichtliche Entwicklung des Kirchenjahres und der Heiligenfeste von den ältesten Zeiten bis zur Gegenwart. 2. Aufl. Freiburg: Herder, 1906; Heortology: A History of the Christian Festivals from their Origins to the Present Day. Translated by a Priest of the Diocese of Westminster. ICL, 14. London: Kegan Paul, Trench, Trübner & Co., 1908.

LECLERCQ, Henri. "Kalendaria." Dictionnaire d'archeologie chrétien et de liturgie, 8:624-667.

"Liturgical Time." Edited by Wiebe Vos and Geoffrey Wainwright. Studia Liturgica, 14/2-4 (1982).

McARTHUR, A. Allan. The Evolution of the Christian Year. London: SCM Press; Greenwich, CT: Seabury Press, 1953.

NILLES, Nicolaus. Kalendarium manuale utriusque ecclesiae orientalis et occidentalis. 3 vols. Ed. Altera. Innsbruck: Rauch, 1885-1897.

PIEPER, Joseph. In Tune with the World: A Theory of Festivity. Chicago: Franciscan Herald Press, 1965.

POWER, David, ed. The Times of Celebration. Concilium, 142. New York: Seabury Press, 1981.

RAHNER, Hugo. Griechische Mythen in christlicher Deutung. Zürich: Rheinverlag, 1945; Greek Myths and Christian Mystery. Foreword by E. O. James. Translated by Brian Battershaw. London: Burns & Oates; New York: Harper & Row, 1963; reprint ed., New York: Biblo & Tannen, 1971.

RICKABY, John. The Ecclesiastical Year. New York: J. F. Wagner, 1927.

TALLEY, Thomas J. The Origins of the Liturgical Year. New York: Pueblo, 1986.

WEISER, Francis X. Handbook of Christian Feasts and Customs. New York: Harcourt, Brace, Jovanovich, 1958.

WORDSWORTH, John. The Ministry of Grace. New York: Longmans, Green, 1901.

B. THE EARLY AND EASTERN CHURCHES

BAUMSTARK, Anton. Festbrevier und Kirchenjahr der syrischen
    Jakobiten: eine liturgiegeschichtliche Vorarbeit. SGKA, 3/5.
    Paderborn: Schöningh, 1910.

DEDDENS, K. Annus liturgicus?: een onderzoek naar de bete-
    kenis van Cyrillus van Jeruzalem voor de ontwikkeling van het
    kerkelijk jaar. Goes: Oosterbaan & Le Cointre, 1975.

KRETSCHMAR, Georg. "Festkalendar und Memorialstätten Jerusal-
    ems in altkirchlichen Zeit." Zeitschrift der deutschen Palästina-
    Vereins, 87 (1971): 167-205.

Un Moine de l'Eglise d'orient. L'an de grace du Seigneur: un com-
    mentaire de l'année liturgique byzantine. 2 vols. Beyrouth:
    Editions An-Nour, 1972- ; The Year of the Grace of the Lord:
    A Scriptural and Liturgical Commentary on the Calendar of the
    Orthodox Church. Translated by Deborah Cowen. London:
    Mowbray, 1980.

STOELEN, André. L'année liturgique byzantine. CI, 4/10. Amay-
    sur-Meuse: Prieuré, 1928.

TYCIAK, Julius. Das Herrenmysterium im byzantinischen Kirchen-
    jahr. 2. Aufl. Sophia, 1. Trier: Paulinus-Verlag, 1976.

VERGHESE, Pathikulangara. "The Liturgical Year of the Syro-
    Malabar Rite." Ephemerides Liturgicae, 90 (1976): 173-190.

C. LATIN CHURCHES

1. Texts

Calendarium Romanum. Rome: Typis Polyglottis Vaticanis, 1969.

The Roman Calendar: Text and Commentary. Washington, DC:
    United States Catholic Conference, 1976.

2. Studies

BAUR, Benedikt. Werde Licht! Liturgische Betrachtungen an den
    Sonn- und Wochentagen des Kirchenjahres. 3 vols. Freiburg:
    Herder, 1937; The Light of the World: Liturgical Meditations
    for the Weekdays and Sundays of the Ecclesiastical Year.
    Translated by Edward Malone. Revised ed. 3 vols. St.
    Louis, MO: Herder, 1958.

CABROL, Fernand. The Year's Liturgy. 2 vols. London: Burns, Oates & Washbourne, 1938-1940.

"The Calendar." Liturgy (Journal of the Liturgical Conference), 1/3 1981.

CASEL, Odo. Das christliche Festmysterium. Paderborn: Bonifacius-Druckerei, 1941.

The Church Year. 19th North American Liturgical Week. Elsberry, MO: Liturgical Conference, 1959.

DRUJON, P., and CAPPANERA, R., eds. Les Jours du Seigneur. 3 vols. Paris: Editions du témoignage chrétien, 1964; Days of the Lord. 3 vols. Edited by William G. Storey. New York: Herder & Herder, 1965-1966.

FRERE, Walter H. Studies in the Early Roman Liturgy. Vol. 1: The Kalendar. AC, 28. London: Oxford University Press, 1930.

GATTERER, Michael. Annus liturgicus cum introductione in disciplinam liturgicam. 5. ed. Innsbruck: Rauch, 1935.

GUERANGER, Prosper. L'Année liturgique. Edition nouvelle revue et mise à jour par les Moines de Solesmes. 5 vols. Paris: Desclée, 1948-1952; The Liturgical Year. 15 vols. Translated by Dom Lawrence Shepherd. Westminster, MD: Newman Press, 1949-1952.

LOHR, Emiliana. Jahr des Herrn: das Mysterium Christi im Jahreskreis der Kirche. Regensburg: Pustet, 1934; The Year of Our Lord: The Mystery of Christ in the Liturgical Year. Translated by a Monk of St. Benedict. New York: P. J. Kenedy, 1937.

_____. Das Herrenjahr: das Mysterium Christi im Jahreskreis der Kirche. 5. Aufl. Regensburg: Pustet, 1951; The Mass through the Year. 2 vols. Translated by I. T. Hale. London: Longmans, Green; Westminster, MD: Newman Press, 1958-1959.

MORIN, Germain. "La Part des papes du sixième siècle dans la développement de l'année liturgique." Revue bénédictine, 52 (1940): 1-14.

MULLER, Karl. Das Kirchenjahr: eine Erklärung der heiligen Zeiten, Feste und Feierlichkeiten der katholischen Kirche. Freiburg: Herder, 1911.

NOCENT, Adrien. Célébrer Jésus-Christ: l'année liturgique. 7 vols. Paris: Delarge, 1975-1977; The Liturgical Year. 4 vols.

Translated by Matthew J. O'Connell. Collegeville, MN: Liturgical Press, 1977.

ORDONEZ MARQUEZ, Juan. Teologia y espiritualidad del año liturgico. BAC, 403. Madrid: EDICA, 1978.

PARSCH, Pius. Das Jahr des Heiles. 3 Bde. 14. Aufl. Klosterneuburg: Volksliturgisches Apostolat, 1952-1953; The Church's
Year of Grace. 5 vols. Translated by W. C. Heidt. Collegeville, MN: Liturgical Press, 1957-1958.

PASCHER, Josef. Das liturgische Jahr. München: Hueber, 1963.

RIGHETTI, Mario. Manuale di storia liturgica. Vol. 2: L'Anno
liturgico. 3. ed. Milan: Editrice Ancora, 1959-1966.

ROGUET, A. M. La Vie sacramentelle dans l'année liturgique.
EsL, 19. Paris: Cerf, 1962.

STROMBERG, Bengt. Liturgiska termer i äldre svenska urkunder.
Lund: Gleerupska Universitets Bokhandeln, 1953.

THIERBACH, Alfred. Untersuchungen zur Benennung der Kirchen-
feste in den Romanischen Sprachen. VIRS, 6. Berlin:
Akademie-Verlag, 1951.

D. LUTHERAN CHURCHES

1. Texts

Inter-Lutheran Commission on Worship. The Church Year, Calendar
and Lectionary. CW, 6. Minneapolis, MN: Augsburg, 1973.

2. Studies

ASMUSSEN, Hans. Das Kirchenjahr. 2. Aufl. His Gottesdienstlehre, Bd. 2. München: Kaiser Verlag, 1937.

KLEINHANS, Theodore J. The Year of the Lord: The Church
Year, Its Customs, Growth, Ceremonies. St. Louis, MO:
Concordia, 1967.

PFATTEICHER, Philip H. Festivals and Commemorations: A Handbook to the Calendar in the Lutheran Book of Worship. Minneapolis, MN: Augsburg, 1980.

STRODACH, Paul Zeller. The Church Year: Studies in the In-
troits, Collects, Epistles and Gospels. Philadelphia, PA:
United Lutheran Publication House, 1924.

E. REFORMED CHURCHES

McARTHUR, A. Allan. The Christian Year and Lectionary Reform. London: SCM Press, 1958. [Church of Scotland]

NEVIN, John Williamson. "The Church Year." Mercersburg Review, 8 (January 1856): 456-478.

F. ANGLICAN CHURCHES (INCLUDING EARLY ENGLISH CALENDARS)

1. Texts

PROTESTANT EPISCOPAL CHURCH IN THE U.S.A. Liturgical Commission. The Calendar. PBS, 9. New York: Church Pension Fund, 1957.

_____. The Calendar and the Collects, Epistles, and Gospels for the Lesser Feasts and Fasts. PBS, 16. New York: Church Pension Fund, 1963.

_____. The Church Year: The Calendar and the Proper of the Sundays and Other Holy Days throughout the Church Year. PBS, 19. New York: Church Hymnal Corporation, 1970.

WORMALD, Francis, ed. English Kalendars before A.D. 1100. HBS, 72. London: Harrison, 1934.

2. Studies

DOWDEN, John. The Church Year and Kalendar. CHLS. Cambridge: Cambridge University Press, 1910.

HASSEL, Rudolph Chris. Renaissance Drama and the English Church Year. Lincoln, NE: University of Nebraska Press, 1979.

HOBART, John Henry. A Companion for the Festivals and Fasts of the Protestant Episcopal Church in the United States of America. New York: Swords, 1804.

_____. _____. 25th ed. New York: Dutton, 1877.

JASPER, R. C. D., ed. The Calendar and Lectionary: A Reconsideration. By the Joint Liturgical Group. London: Oxford University Press, 1967.

NELSON, Robert. Companion for the Festivals and Fasts of the
    Church of England. London, 1703.

_____. _____. 36th ed. London: Rivington, 1826.

_____. _____. [Last ed.] London: SPCK, 1850.

PORTER, Harry Boone. Keeping the Church Year. New York:
    Seabury Press, 1977.

STALEY, Vernon. The Liturgical Year: An Explanation of the
    Origin, History & Significance of the Festival Days & Fasting
    Days of the English Church. London: Mowbray, 1907.

G. ADVENT, CHRISTMAS, EPIPHANY

"Avent, Noël, Epiphanie." La Maison-Dieu, 59 (1959).

BOGOLEPOV, Alexander. Christmas in Orthodox Worship. OW, 2.
    Crestwood, NY: St. Vladimir's Seminary Press, n.d.

BOTTE, Bernard. Les Origines de la Noël et de l'Epiphanie. TEL,
    1. Louvain: Abbaye du Mont César, 1932.

CROCE, W. "Die Adventsliturgie." Zeitschrift für katholischen
    Theologie, 76 (1954): 257-296, 440-472.

_____. "Die Adventmessen des römischen Missale." Zeitschrift
    für katholischen Theologie, 74 (1952): 227-317.

CULLMANN, Oscar. Weihnachten in der alten Kirche. Basel: H.
    Majer, 1947.

ENGBERDING, Hieronymus. "Der 25. Dezember als Tag der Feier
    der Geburt des Herrn." Archiv für Liturgiewissenschaft, 2
    (1952): 25-43.

FRANK, H. "Frühgeschichte und Ursprung des römischen Weih-
    nachtsfestes." Archiv für Liturgiewissenschaft, 2 (1952): 1-24.

_____. "Zur Geschichte von Weihnachten und Epiphanie." Jahr-
    buch für Liturgiewissenschaft, 12 (1934): 145-155; 13 (1935):
    1-39.

GUNSTONE, John. Christmas and Epiphany. SCW, 9. London:
    Faith Press, 1967.

JUNGMANN, Josef Andreas. "Advent und Voradvent. Uberreste
    des gallischen Advents in der römischen Liturgie." In his
    Gewordene Liturgie, pp. 232-294. Innsbruck: Rauch, 1941.

_____. "The Extended Celebration of Epiphany in the Roman Missal." In his Pastoral Liturgy, pp. 214-223. New York: Herder, 1962.

LEMARIE, Joseph. La Manifestation du Seigneur: la liturgie de Noël et de l'Epiphanie. LO, 23. Paris: Cerf, 1957.

MOHRMANN, Christine. Epiphania. Nijmegen: Dekker & van de Vegt, 1953.

MOSSAY, Justin. Les Fêtes de Noël et d'Epiphanie d'après les sources littéraires cappadociennes du IVe siècle. TEL, 3. Louvain: Abbaye du Mont César, 1965.

NIKOLASCH, F. "Zum Ursprung des Epiphaniefestes." Ephemerides Liturgicae, 82 (1968): 393-429.

Noël-Epiphanie: retour du Christ. Semaine liturgique de l'Institut Saint-Serge. Par A.-M. Dubarle, B. Botte, K. Hruby, J. Daniélou, et al. LO, 40. Paris: Cerf, 1967.

ONASCH, Konrad. Das Weihnachtsfest im Orthodoxen Kirchenjahr: Liturgie und Ikonographie. QUKO, 2. Berlin: Evangelische Verlagsanstalt, 1958.

SELWYN, E. C. "The Feast of Tabernacles, Epiphany, and Baptism." Journal of Theological Studies, 13 (1911-1912): 225-249.

USENER, Hermann Karl. Das Weihnachtsfest. 2. Aufl. Bonn: F. Cohen, 1911; reprint ed., Bonn: Bouvier, 1969.

H. PRE-LENT TO EASTER

1. Texts

HAMMAN, Adalbert, and QUERE-JAULMES, F., eds. Le Mystère de Pâques: Textes choisis. Paris: B. Grasset, 1965; The Pascal Mystery: Ancient Liturgies and Patristic Texts. English editorial supervisor: Thomas Halton. Translated by Thomas Halton. APL, 3. Staten Island, NY: Alba House, 1969.

JOINT LITURGICAL GROUP. Holy Week Services. 2d ed. London: SPCK, 1983.

SCHMIDT, Herman A. P., ed. Hebdomada Sancta. 2 vols. in 3. Rome: Herder, 1956-1957.

United Methodist Church. Board of Discipleship. Section on Worship. From Ashes to Fire: Services of Worship for the Seasons

of Lent and Easter, with Introduction and Commentary. SWR,
8. Nashville, TN: Abingdon Press, 1979.

WALLIS, Charles L., ed. Lenten-Easter Sourcebook. Nashville,
TN: Abingdon Press, 1961.

2. Studies

AUSTERBERRY, David. Celebrating Holy Week: A Guide for
Priest and People. London: Mowbray, 1982.

BECKWITH, Roger T. "The Origin of the Festivals Easter and
Whitsun." Studia Liturgica, 13 (1979): 1-20.

BOTTE, Bernard. "La Question pascale." La Maison-Dieu, 41
(1955): 88-95.

BOUYER, Louis. La Mystère Pascal. 2e éd. LO, 4. Paris:
Cerf, 1947; The Paschal Mystery. Translated by Sister Mary
Benoit. Chicago: Regnery, 1950.

BROWE, Peter. "Die Kommunion an den drei letzten Kartagen."
Jahrbuch für Liturgiewissenschaft, 10 (1930): 56-76.

CALLEWAERT, Camillus Aloysius. La Durée et le charactère du
carême ancien dans l'église latine. Bruges: A. Maertens-
Matthijs, 1920.

_____. "L'Oeuvre liturgique de S. Grégoire: la septuagésime
et l'alleluia." Revue d'histoire ecclésiastique, 33 (1937): 306-
326.

"Carême, préparation à la nuit pascale." La Maison-Dieu, 31
(1962). [Special issue]

CASEL, Odo. "Art und Sinn der ältesten christlichen Osterfeier."
Jahrbuch für Liturgiewissenschaft, 14 (1938): 1-78.

CHAVASSE, Antoine. "La Structure du carême et les lectures des
messes quadragésimales dans la liturgie romaine." La Maison-
Dieu, 31 (1952): 76-119.

_____. "Temps de préparation à la Pâque d'après quelques livres
liturgiques romains." Recherches de science religieuses, 37
(1950): 125-145.

CLARKE, W. K. Lowther, ed. Good Friday: A Manual for the
Clergy. London: SPCK; New York: Macmillan, 1929; reprinted 1948.

_____, ed. Lent: A Manual for the Clergy. London: SPCK; New York: Macmillan, 1933.

DANIELOU, Jean. "Le Symbolisme des quarante jours." La Maison-Dieu, 31 (1952): 19-33.

DAVIES, John G. Holy Week: A Short History. ESW, 11. London: Lutterworth Press; Richmond, VA: John Knox Press, 1963.

FEASEY, Henry John. Ancient English Holy Week Ceremonial. London: Baker, 1897.

FISCHER, Balthasar, and WAGNER, Johannes, eds. Paschatis sollemnia: Studien zu Osterfeier und Osterfrömmigkeit. Freiburg: Herder, 1959.

FROGER, J. "Les Anticipations du jeûne quadragésimal." Mélanges de science religieuse, 3 (1946): 207-234.

GREENACRES, Roger. The Sacrament of Easter: An Introduction to the Liturgy of Holy Week. Foreword by E. L. Mascall. SCW, 4. London: Faith Press; New York: Morehouse-Barlow, 1965.

GRELOT, Pierre. La Nuit et les fêtes de Pâques. Paris: Ligne catholique de l'Evangile, 1959; The Paschal Feast in the Bible. Baltimore, MD: Helicon, 1966.

HUBER, Wolfgang. Passa und Ostern: Untersuchungen zur Osterfeier der alten Kirche. BZNW, 35. Berlin: Töpelmann, 1969.

JAUBERT, Annie. La Date de la Cène: calendrier biblique et liturgie chrétienne. EB. Paris: Gabalda, 1957; The Date of the Last Supper. Translated by Isaac Rafferty. Staten Island, NY: Alba House, 1965.

JONES, C. P. M., ed. A Manual for Holy Week. London: SPCK, 1967.

JUNGMANN, Josef Andreas. "Die Quadragesima in den Forschungen von Antoine Chavasse." Archiv für Liturgiewissenschaft, 5 (1957): 84-95.

KRETSCHMAR, Georg. "Zur Geschichte des Ostergottesdienstes, I." Jahrbuch für Liturgik und Hymnologie, 5 (1960): 75-79.

_____. "Neue Arbeiten zur Geschichte des Ostergottesdienstes II. Die Einführung des Sanktus in die lateinische Liturgie." Jahrbuch für Liturgik und Hymnologie, 7 (1962): 79-86.

"La Liturgie du mystère pascal." La Maison-Dieu, 67-68 (1961).

LOHR, Aemiliana. Die Heilige Woche. Rgensburg: Pustet, 1957;
    The Great Week: An Explanation of the Liturgy of Holy Week.
    Translated by D. T. H. Bridgehouse. London: Longmans,
    Green; Westminster, MD: Newman Press, 1958.

LOHSE, Bernard. Das Passafest der Quartadecimaner. BFCT, 2.
    Reihe, 54. Gütersloh: Bertelsmann, 1953.

McMANUS, Frederick R. The Rites of Holy Week: Ceremonies,
    Preparations, Music, Commentary. Paterson, NJ: Saint
    Anthony Guild Press, 1956.

MARTIN, John T. Christ Our Passover: The Liturgical Obser-
    vance of Holy Week. SMW, 4. London: SCM Press, 1958.

MARTINEZ SAIZ, Pablo. El tiempo pascual en la liturgia hispánica.
    Madrid: Instituto Superior de Pastoral, 1969.

MATEOS, Juan. "Les 'Semaines des mystères' du carême chaldéen."
    L'Orient Syrien, 4 (1959): 449-458.

MOHRMANN, Christine. "Pascha, Passio, Transitus." Ephemerides
    Liturgicae, 66 (1952): 37-52.

O'SHEA, William J. The Meaning of Holy Week. Collegeville, MN:
    Liturgical Press, 1958.

PEPLER, Conrad. Lent: A Liturgical Commentary on the Lessons
    and Gospels. St. Louis, MO: Herder, 1944.

PORTER, Harry Boone. "The Ash Wednesday Rites." Holy Cross
    Magazine, 65 (February, 1954): 35-37.

"Restauration de la semaine saint." La Maison-Dieu, 45 (1956).

SCHMEMANN, Alexander. Great Lent. OW, 1. Crestwood, NY:
    St. Vladimir's Seminary Press, 1969.

_____. Holy Week. OW, 3. Crestwood, NY: St. Vladimir's
    Seminary Press, n.d.

SCHURMANN, H. "Die Anfänge christlicher Osterfeier." Theo-
    logische Quartalschrift, 131 (1951): 415-425.

"La Semaine sainte." La Maison-Dieu, 41 (1955).

SHEPHERD, Massey H., Jr. The Paschal Liturgy and the Apocal-
    ypse. ESW, 6. London: Lutterworth Press; Richmond, VA:
    John Knox Press, 1960.

THIBAUT, Jean Baptiste. Ordre des offices de la semaine sainte
à Jérusalem du IVe au Xe siècle. Paris: Maison de la Bonne
Presse, 1926.

THURSTON, Herbert. Lent and Holy Week: Chapters on Catholic
Observance and Ritual. London, New York: Longmans, Green,
1904.

TYRER, John Walton. Historical Survey of Holy Week, Its Services
and Ceremonial. ACC, 29. London: Oxford University Press,
1932.

WINKLER, Gabriele. "Einige Randbemerkungen zum österlichen
Gottesdienst in Jerusalem vom 4. bis 8. Jahrhundert." Orientalia Christiana Periodica, 39 (1973): 481-490.

I. PENTECOST AND THEREAFTER

AKEHURST, Peter R. Liturgy and Creation: A Reappraisal of
Rogationtide and Harvest. GBMW, 30. Bramcote, Eng.:
Grove Books, 1974.

BRUYNE, D. de. "L'Origine des processions de la chandeleur et
des rogations à propos d'un sermon inédit." Revue bénédictine, 34 (1922): 14-26.

CABIE, Robert. La Penecôte: l'évolution de la cinquantaine pascale au cours des cinq premiers siècles. Tournai: Desclée,
1965.

DANIELOU, Jean. "Les Quartre-temps de Septembre et la Fête des
Tabernacles." La Maison-Dieu, 46 (1956): 114-136.

FISCHER, Ludwig. Die kirchlichen Quatember: Ihre Entstehung,
Entwicklung und Bedeutung in liturgischer rechtlicher und
kultiv-historischer hinsicht. München: J. J. Lentner, (E.
Stahl), 1914.

GUNSTONE, John. The Feast of Pentecost: The Great Fifty Days
in the Liturgy. SCW, 8. London: Faith Press, 1967.

JUNGMANN, Josef Andreas. "The Octave of Pentecost and Public
Penance in the Roman Liturgy." In his Pastoral Liturgy, pp.
238-256. New York: Herder, 1962.

MORIN, G. "L'Origine des Quatre-temps." Revue bénédictine, 14
(1897): 337-346.

RATTENBURY, John E. Festivals and Saints' Days: Trinity Sunday to Advent. London: Epworth Press, 1956.

TALLEY, Thomas Julian. "The Development of the Ember Days to
the Time of Gregory VII." Th.D. dissertation, General Theological Seminary, New York, 1969.

J. SAINTS' DAYS AND OTHER FEASTS AND
    FASTS INCLUDING MARTYROLOGIES

1. Texts

BASSET, R., ed. Le Synaxaire arabe jacobite (rédaction copte).
6 vols. PO, 1/3, 3/3, 11/5, 16/3, 17/3, 20/5. Paris:
Firmin-Didot, 1905-1929.

DELEHAYE, Hippolyte, ed. Synaxarium ecclesiae Constantinopoli-
tanae e codice Sirmondiano nunc Berolinensi adiectis synaxariis
selectis. Propylaeum ad Acta Sanctorum, Novembris. Bruxellis: Apud Socios Bollandianos, 1902.

DUCHESNE, L. Le Liber Pontificalis: Texte, introduction et commentaire. 2 vols. BEFAR, 2/3. Paris: Thorin, 1886-1892.

_____. _____. 2. éd. 3 vols. Paris: Boccard, 1955-1957.
--Vol. 3: Additions et corrections de L. Duchesne publiée
par Cyrille Vogel, avec l'histoire du Liber pontificalis depuis
l'édition de L. Duchesne, une bibliographie et des tables
générales. 1957.

FORBES, A. P. Kalendars of Scottish Saints. Edinburgh: Edmonston & Douglas, 1872.

FORGET, I., ed. Synaxarium Alexandrinum, I-II. 6 vols. in 4.
CSCO, 47-49, 67, 78, 90. Louvain: Durbecq, 1953-1954.

LIETZMANN, Hans, ed. Die drei ältesten Martyrologien. 2. Aufl.
KT, 2. Bonn: Marcus & Weber, 1911.

LOOMIS, Louise R., ed. The Book of the Popes: Liber Pontificalis. RC, 3. New York: Columbia University Press, 1916;
reprint ed., New York: Octagon Books, 1965.

MALTZEW, Alexios von, ed. Menologion der orthodox-katholischen
Kirche des Morgenlandes. Deutsch und slavisch unter Berücksichtigung des griechischen Urtextes. 2 vols. Berlin: Siegismund, 1900-1901.

Martyrologium Romanum. (authorized 1584).

_____. Editio typica. Rome: Typis Polyglottis Vaticanis, 1914.

_____. Prima post typicam editio. Rome: Typis Polyglottis
Vaticanis, 1922.

_____. Quarta post typicam editio. Rome: Typis Polyglottis
Vaticanis, 1956.

Martyrologium Romanum ad formam editionis typicae scholiis histori-
cis instructum. Propylaeum ad Acta Sanctorum, Decembris.
Bruxellis: Socios Bollandianos, 1940.

O'CONNELL, J. B., ed. The Roman Martyrology. An English
translation from the 4th ed. after the typical edition. London:
Burns & Oates, 1962.

PROTESTANT EPISCOPAL CHURCH IN THE U.S.A. Liturgical
Commission. The Calendar and the Collects, Epistles, and
Gospels for the Lesser Feasts and Fasts. PBS, 16. New York:
Church Pension Fund, 1963.

_____. The Proper for the Lesser Feasts and Fasts, together
with the Fixed Holy Days. 3d ed. New York: Church Hymnal
Corp., 1980.

_____. Liturgical Commission. The Propers for the Minor Holy
Days. PBS, 12. New York: Church Pension Fund, 1958.

ROSSI, J. B. de, and DUCHESNE, L., eds. Martyrologium Hieronymianum. Acta Sanctorum Novembris, tomi II, pars prima.
Brussels: Socios Bollandianos, 1894.

WAINWRIGHT, John Bannerman, ed. The Office for the Commemoration of the Holy, Glorious and All-Praiseworthy Apostles and
Chief Primates Peter and Paul on Sunday, the 29th of June, in
the Years of Grace 1880, 1959, 2054 and 2127, Old Style, according to the Byzantine Rite. London: Cope and Fenwick,
1909.

2. Studies

AIGRAIN, René. L'Hagiographie: ses sources, ses méthodes, son
histoire. Paris: Bloud & Gay, 1953.

BOTTE, Bernard. "La Première fête mariale de la liturgie romaine."
Ephermides Liturgicae, 47 (1933): 425-430.

COPPENS, C. Tabulae geographicae; seu, Atlas in Martyrologium
Romanum indice alphabetico instructus. Turnholti: Brepols,
1945.

DE GAIFFIER, B. "La Lecture des actes des martyrs dans la

prière liturgique en Occident: a propos du passionnaire hispanique." Analecta Bollandiana, 72 (1954): 134-166.

DELEHAYE, Hippolyte. Commentarium perpetuum in Martyrologium Hieronymianum ad recensionem H. Quentin. Acta Sanctorum Novembris, tomi II, pars posterior. Brussels: Socios Bollandianos, 1931.

_____. Les Origines du culte des martyrs. 2. éd. AB, 20. Brussels: Société des Bollandistes, 1933.

_____. Sanctus: Essai sur le culte des saints dans l'antiquité. AB, 17. Brussels: Société des Bollandistes, 1927.

_____. Synaxaires byzantins, ménologes, typica. London: Variorum Reprints, 1977.

DRAPER, Martin, ed. The Cloud of Witnesses: A Companion to the Lesser Festivals and Holy Days of the Alternative Service Book 1980. With collects by G. B. Timms. Alcuin Club Special Manual. London: Collins, 1982.

DURIG, Walter. Geburtstag und Namentag: eine liturgiegeschichtliche Studie. München: Zink, 1954.

FENOYL, Maurice de. Le Sanctoral copte. RILOB, 15. Beyrouth: Imprimerie catholique, 1960.

FLICOTEAUX, E. "Notre Dame dans l'année liturgique." La Maison-Dieu, 38 (1954): 95-121.

FRERE, Walter Howard. Black Letter Saints' Days: A Companion to "Collects, Epistles, and Gospels for the Lesser Feasts according to the Calendar set out in 1928." London: SPCK, 1961.

JOUNEL, P. "Le Sanctoral romain du 8e au 12e siècles." La Maison-Dieu, 52 (1957): 59-88.

LANSEMANN, Robert. Die Heiligentage, besonders die Marien-, Apostel- und Engeltage in der Reformationszeit. BMGKK, 1. Göttingen: Vandenhoeck & Ruprecht, 1939.

PEETERS, Paul. Le Tréfonds oriental de l'hagiographie byzantine. AB, 26. Bruxelles: Société des Bollandistes, 1950.

PFAFF, R. W. New Liturgical Feasts in Later Medieval England. Oxford: Clarendon Press, 1970.

QUENTIN, Henri. Les Martyrologes historiques du moyen âge: étude sur la formation du Martyrologe romain. 2. éd. Paris: Gabalda, 1908.

SALAVILLE, Sévérien. "La Fête du concile de Chalcédoine dans
le rite byzantin." In Das Konzil von Chalkedon: Geschichte
und Gegenwart, Bd. 2, pp. 677-695. Herausgegeben von Aloys
Grillmeier und Heinricht Bacht. Würzburg: Echter-Verlag,
1953.

SAUGET, Joseph-Marie. Premières recherches sur l'origines et les
charactéristiques des Synaxaires melkites (XIe-XVIIe siècles).
AB, 45. Bruxelles: Société des Bollandistes, 1969.

SEIDENSPINNER, Clarence. Great Protestant Festivals. New York:
H. Schuman, 1952.

SIMPSON, W. J. Sparrow. The Minor Festivals of the Anglican
Calendar. London: Rivington, 1901.

VAILHE, S. "La Fête de la présentation de Marie au temple."
Echos d'Orient, 5 (1901): 221-224.

XLI.   THE READINGS FOR THE YEAR

A. LECTIONARIES

1. General Studies

GODU, G. "Epîtres." Dictionnaire d'archéologie chrétien et de
liturgie, 5:245-344.

_____. "Evangiles." Dictionnaire d'archéologie chrétien et de
liturgie, 5:852-923.

REUMANN, Johi.. "A History of Lectionaries: From the Synagogue
of Nazareth to Post-Vatican II." Interpretation, 31 (1977):
116-130.

2. The Early Church

CARRINGTON, Philip. The Primitive Christian Calendar: A Study
in the Making of the Marcan Gospel. Cambridge: Cambridge
University Press, 1952.

DAVIES, W. D. "Reflections on Archbishop Carrington's The Primi-
tive Christian Calendar." In The Background of the New
Testament and Its Eschatology, pp. 124-152. Edited by W. D.
Davies and D. Daube. Cambridge: Cambridge University
Press, 1956.

GOULDER, Michael D. The Evangelists' Calendar: A Lectionary
    Explanation of the Development of Scripture. London: SPCK,
    1978.

_____. Midrash and Lection in Matthew. London: SPCK, 1974.

MORRIS, Leon. The New Testament and the Jewish Lectionaries.
    London: Tyndale Press, 1964.

WILLIS, Geoffrey G. St. Augustine's Lectionary. ACC, 44. Lon-
    don: SPCK, 1962.

                    3. Eastern Churches

        a. Texts

CONYBEARE, F. C., ed. Rituale Armenorum. Oxford: Clarendon
    Press, 1905.

GARITTE, Gérard, ed. Le Calendrier palestineo-georgien du
    Sinaiticus 34. AB, 30. Brussels: Société des Bollandistes,
    1958.

NOLI, Fan Stylian. Epistle Lectionary of the Eastern Orthodox
    Church. Boston, MA: Albanian Orthodox Church in America,
    1956.

_____. Gospel Lectionary of the Eastern Orthodox Church. Bos-
    ton: Albanian Orthodox Church in America, 1956.

RENOUX, Athanase. Le Codex arménien Jérusalem 121. 2 vols.
    PO, 35/1, 36/2. Turnholt: Brepols, 1969-1971.

TARCHNISCHVILI, Michael. Le Grand lectionnaire de l'église de
    Jérusalem (Ve-VIIIe siècle). 2 vols. CSCO, 204-205. Lou-
    vain: Secrétariat du Corpus SCO, 1959-1960.

        b. Studies

BAUMSTARK, Anton. Nichtevangelische syrische Perikopenordnun-
    gen des ersten Jahrtausends, im Sinne vergleichender Litur-
    giegeschichte. LF, 3. Münster: Aschendorff, 1921.

BURKITT, Francis Cornford. "The Early Syriac Lectionary Sys-
    tem." Proceedings of the British Academy, 11 (1923): 1-38.

GY, Pierre-Marie. "La Question du système des lectures de la
    liturgie byzantine." In Miscellanea liturgica in onore di Sua
    Eminenza Cardinale Giacomo Lercaro, vol. 2, pp. 251-261.
    Rome: Desclée, 1967.

RAHLFS, Alfred. Die alttestamentlichen Lektionen der griechischen Kirche. Berlin: Weidmannsche Buchhandlung, 1915.

4. Latin Churches

a. Historical Texts

DOLD, Alban, ed. Das älteste Liturgiebuch der lateinischen Kirche: ein altgallikanisches Lektionar des 5./6. Jahrhunderts aus dem Wolfenbütteler Palimpsest-Codex Weissenburgensis 76. TuA, 26-28. Beuron: Kunstverlag Beuron Hohenzollern, 1936.

PEREZ DE URBEL, Justo, and GONZALEZ RUIZ-ZORILLA, Atilano, eds. Liber Commicus. 2 vols. Madrid: Consejo Superior de Investigaciones Cientificas Escuela de Estudios Medievales, 1950-1955.

SALMON, Pierre, ed. Le Lectionnaire de Luxeuil. 2 vols. Rome: Abbaye Saint-Jérôme, 1944-1953.

b. Historical Studies

BAUDOT, Jules. Les évangéliaires. 2. éd. Paris: Bloud & Cie, 1908.

_____. Les lectionnaires. 2. éd. Paris: Bloud & Cie, 1908; The Lectionary: Its Sources and History. Translated by Ambrose Cator. London: Catholic Truth Society, 1910.

BEISSEL, Stephan. Entstehung der Perikopen des römischen Messbuches: zur Geschichte der Evangelienbücher in der ersten Hälfte des Mittelalters. ESML, 96. Freiburg: Herder, 1907; reprint ed., Rome: Herder, 1967.

CAPELLE, Bernard. "Note sur le lectionnaire romain de la messe avant Saint Grégoire." Revue d'histoire ecclésiastique, 34 (1938): 556-559; reprinted in his Travaux liturgiques, vol. 2, pp. 200-203. Louvain: Centre liturgique, Abbaye du Mont César, 1962.

CHAVASSE, Antoine. "Les plus anciens types du lectionnaire et de l'antiphonaire romaines de la messe, rapports et dates." Revue bénédictine, 62 (1952): 3-94.

FRERE, Walter Howard. Studies in the Early Roman Liturgy. Vol. 2: The Roman Gospel Lectionary. ACC, 30. London: Oxford University Press, 1934.

_____. Studies in the Early Roman Liturgy. Vol. 3: The Roman

Epistle Lectionary. ACC, 32. London: Oxford University
Press, 1935.

KLAUSER, Theodor. Das römische Capitulare Evangeliorum: Texte
und Untersuchungen zu seiner ältesten Geschichte. 2. Aufl.
LQF, 28. Münster: Aschendorff, 1972.

MORIN, G. "Le plus ancien 'Comes' ou lectionnaire de l'église
romaine." Revue bénédictine, 27 (1910): 41-74.

WILMART, André. Le lectionnaire d'Alcuin. Rome: Typis Polyglottis Vaticanis, 1937.

    c. Contemporary Texts

Ordo Lectionum Missae. Rome: Typis Polyglottis Vaticanis, 1969.

Lectionarium. Editio typica. 3 vols. Rome: Typis Polyglottis
Vaticanis, 1970-1972.

Lectionary for the Mass. English translation approved by the National Conference of Catholic Bishop and confirmed by the
Apostolic See. New York: Benziger, 1970.

    d. Contemporary Studies

BISHOPS' COMMITTEE ON THE LITURGY. Proclaim the Word: The
Lectionary for Mass. Study Texts, 8. Washington, DC:
United States Catholic Cofnerence Publications, 1982.

BUGNINI, Annibale. "Die Reform des Lesordnung für die Messe."
Gottesdienst, 3 (1969): 123-125.

CHARLIER, Jean Pierre. "Le nouveau lectionnaire dominical: reflexions d'un exégète prédicateur." Questions liturgiques et
paroissiales, 51 (1970): 115-128.

DIGAN, Parig. "The Lectionary--A Brand New Thing." America,
128, 11 (October 17, 1970): 291-292.

FITZSIMMONS, J. "Learning to Live with the Lectionary." The
Clergy Review, 57 (June 1972): 419-431.

FONTAINE, Gaston. "Commentarium ad ordinem lectionum Missae."
Notitiae, 47 (July-August 1969): 256-282.

GUILLAUMIN, Marie-Louise. "Problèmes pastoraux du nouveau
lectionnaire." La Maison-Dieu, 99 (1969): 77-87.

KEIFER, Ralph A. To Hear and Proclaim: Introduction, Lectionary
for Mass. Washington, DC: National Association of Pastoral
Musicians, 1983.

NEVE, Thomas. "The Shape of the New Lectionary." In The New
Liturgy, pp. 41-58. Edited by Lancelot Sheppard. London:
Darton, Longman & Todd, 1970.

NEWNS, Brian. "The New Lectionary: A Note of Instruction."
The Clergy Review, 54, 12 (December 1969): 981-989.

PURDUE, Peter. "The New Lectionary." Doctrine and Life, 19
(1969): 666-674.

REARDON, Patrick Henry. "Some Reflections on the New Lectionary." American Ecclesiastical Review, 163, 2 (August 1970):
125-131.

SAINT-ESPRIT, Soeur Marie du. "Le 'lectionnaire dominical' à
travers quelques revues." La Maison-Dieu, 126 (1976): 145-
154.

SECRETARIES OF NATIONAL LITURGICAL COMMISSIONS. "The
Lectionary and Catechesis." Bishops' Committee on the Liturgy
Newsletter, 13 (August 1977): 78-80.

SLOYAN, Gerard S. "The Lectionary as a Context for Interpretation." Liturgy, 2, 3 (Summer 1982): 43-49.

WIENER, Claude. "Présentation du nouveau lectionnaire." La
Maison-Dieu, 99 (1969): 28-49.

5. Lutheran and Reformed Churches

    a. Texts

INTER-LUTHERAN COMMISSION ON WORSHIP. The Lessons. 3
vols. Minneapolis: Augsburg, 1974.

VEREINIGTE EVANGELISCH-LUTHERISCHEN KIRCHE DEUTSCH-
LANDS. Letionar für evangelisch-lutherische Kirchen und
Gemeinden. Berlin: Lutherisches Verlagshaus, 1953.

    b. Studies

ALLEN, Horace T. A Handbook for the Lectionary. Philadelphia,
PA: Geneva Press, 1980.

KUNZE, Gerhard. Die gottesdienstliche Schriftlesung VEGL, 1.
Göttingen: Vandenhoeck & Ruprecht, 1947.

SCHENCK, W. "Exegetisch-theologische Uberlegungen zur Frage
eines neuen Lektionars." Verkündigung und Forschung, 20
(1975): 80-105.

6. Anglican Churches

a. Texts

CAMPLING, Christopher R., ed. The Fourth Lesson in the Daily
    Office: Readings from outside Scripture for the Weekdays and
    Holy Days of a year, designed for use with the three Lessons
    in the Daily Office of the Joint Liturgical Group ('Series II,
    Revised'). 2 vols. London: Darton, Longman & Todd, 1973-
    1974.

The Christian Year: The Prayer Book Collects, with Epistles and
    Gospels as translated by J. B. Phillips together with notes by
    H. W. Dobson. New York: Macmillan, 1963, c1961.

Protestant Episcopal Church in the U.S.A. Liturgical Commission.
    The Liturgical Lectionary. PBS, 2. New York: Church Pen-
    sion Fund, 1950.

b. Studies

BORSCH, Frederick Houk. Introducing the Lessons of the Church
    Year: A Guide for Lay Readers and Congregations. New York:
    Seabury Press, 1978.

BUSHONG, Ann Brooke. A Guide to the Lectionary. Rev. ed.
    New York: Seabury Press, 1978.

COLLINS, W. C. Introductions to the Alternative Service Book
    Readings: Year One, Year Two, Sundays, Festivals and Holy
    Days, for the Order of Holy Communion in the Alternative
    Service Book 1980. London: Mowbray, 1982.

CUMING, Geoffrey, ed. The Ministry of the Word: A Handbook
    to the 1978 Lectionary. London: Bible Reading Fellowship;
    New York: Oxford University Press, 1979.

GUNSTONE, John. Commentary on the New Lectionary: A Scrip-
    tural and Liturgical Guide to the Two-Year Cycle of Readings
    for Holy Communion on Sundays and Holy Days. 2 vols. Rev.
    ed. London: SPCK, 1979.

JONES, Bayard Hale. The American Lectionary. New York:
    Morehouse-Gorham, 1944.

LEWIS, William P. Lectionaries, English and Irish: with sugges-
    tions for the Reconstruction of the American. Philadelphia,
    PA: Claxton, Remsen, and Haffelfinger, 1878.

MAROT, H. "Note sur le nouveau lectionnaire anglican de 1956."
    Irénikon, 29 (1956): 406-410.

SHEPHERD, Massey H. "The Eucharistic Lectionary." Anglican
   Theological Review, 32 (1950): 8-22.

7. Methodist Churches

   a. Texts

Methodist Church (England). The Methodist Church Lectionary,
   with Explanatory Introductions. Authorized for use by the
   Conference of 1957. London: Methodist Publishing House,
   1963.

   b. Studies

Companion to the Lectionary. London: Epworth Press, 1982- .
   --vol. 1: Prefaces to the Lessons. By D. Calvert and J.
   Stacey. 1982.
   --vol. 2: Hymns and Anthems. By Alan Dunstan and Martin
   Ellis. 1983.
   --vol. 3: A New Collection of Prayers. Edited by N. Dixon.

DUNCKLE, William F. "The Lectionary." In Companion to the Book
   of Worship, pp. 134-178. Edited by William F. Dunckle and
   Joseph D. Quillian. Nashville, TN: Abingdon Press, 1970.

SWIFT, Wesley F. "John Wesley's Lectionary." London Quarterly
   and Holborn Review, 183 (1958): 298-304.

B. THE PSALTER

1. Texts

[Bibliography of English Psalters, see:] The New Cambridge Bibliography of English Literature, vol. 1, cols. 1895-1914. Cambridge: Cambridge University Press, 1974.

CANADIAN REFORMED CHURCHES. Book of Praise: Anglo-
   Genevan Psalter. Hamilton, Ont.: The Committee for the
   Publication of an Anglo-Genevan Psalter, 1972.

CHURCH OF ENGLAND. The Revised Psalter (1963). London:
   Cambridge University Press, Eyre & Spottiswoode, Oxford
   University Press, 1966.

FROST, David L., ed. The Psalms: A New Translation for Worship. London: Collins, 1977.

LIVINGSTON, Neil, ed. The Scottish Metrical Psalter of A.D. 1635

reprinted in full from the Original Work. Glasgow: Maclure
& Macdonald, 1864.

NORSKE KIRKE. Nynorsk Salmebok for kyrkja og heim og skule.
Sjette upplaget; kyrkjeutgaave. Oslo: Det Norske Samlaget,
1961.

PROTESTANT EPISCOPAL CHURCH IN THE U.S.A. The Prayer
Book Psalter Revised. New York: Church Hymnal Corp.,
1973.

_____. The Psalter: A New Version for Public Worship and
Private Devotion. Introduced by Charles Mortimer Guilbert.
New York: Seabury Press, 1978.

The Scottish Psalter, 1929. London: Oxford University Press,
1929.

SHEPHERD, Massey H., ed. A Liturgical Psalter for the Christian
Year. Prepared with the assistance of the Consultation on
Common Texts. Minneapolis, MN: Augsburg, 1976.

The VVhole Booke of Psalmes faithfully translated into English Metre.
Cambridge: Imprinted by S. Daye, 1640; The Bay Psalm Book:
A Facsimile Reprint of the First Edition of 1640. Chicago:
University of Chicago Press, 1956.

.   2. Studies

ALLGEIER, A. "Die erste Psalmenübersetzung des heiligen Hieronymus und das Psalterium Romanum." Biblica, 12 (1931):
447-482.

ARENS, Anton. Die Psalmen im Gottesdienst der alten Bundes:
eine Untersuchung zur Vorgeschichte des christlichen Psalmen-
gesanges. TTS, 11. Trier: Paulinus, 1961.

BLANCHARD, P. "Le correspondance apocryphe du pape S. Dam-
ase et de S. Jerome sur le psautier et le chant de l'alleluia."
Ephemerides Liturgicae, 63 (1949): 376-388.

BOVET, Félix. Histoire du psautier des églises réformées. Neuchâtel: J. Sandoz; Paris: Grassart, 1872.

BRUYNE, Donatien de. "Le Problème du psautier romain." Revue
bénédictine, 42 (1930): 101-126.

CAPELLE, Paul. Le Texte du psautier latin en Afrique. CBL, 4.
Rome: Pustet, 1913.

CODDAIRE, Louis, and WEIL, Louis. "The Use of the Psalter in Worship." Worship, 52 (1978): 342-348.

CROSS, Earle Bennett. Modern Worship and the Psalter. New York: Macmillan, 1932.

DRIJVERS, Pius. Over de Psalmen: een inleiding tot hun betekenis en geest. 5. druck. Utrecht: Spectrum, 1964; The Psalms: Their Structure and Meaning. New York: Herder & Herder, 1965.

FISCHER, Balthasar. "Le Christ dans les Psaumes." La Maison-Dieu, 27 (1951): 86-109.

FROST, David L. Making the Liturgical Psalter. GLS, 25. Bramcote, Eng.: Grove Books, 1981.

GILSON, Julius Darnell, ed. The Mozarabic Psalter (MS., British Museum, Add. 30851). HBS, 30. London: Harrison, 1905.

HARASZTI, Zoltán. The Enigma of the Bay Psalm Book. Chicago: University of Chicago Press, 1956.

LAMB, John A. "The Liturgical Use of the Psalter." Studia Liturgica, 3 (1964): 65-77.

_____. The Psalms in Christian Worship. London: Faith Press, 1962.

LANDSTAD, Magnus Brostrup. Kirkesalmebog, efter offentlig foranstaltning. Kristiania: J. Dybwad, 1871.

LANGHE, Robert de, ed. Le Psautier: ses origines, ses problèmes littéraires, son influence: études présentées au XIIe Journées bibliques (29-31 août 1960). OBL, 4. Louvain: Publications Universitaires, 1962.

MULLETT, John. One People, One Church, One Song. LPT. London: Hodder & Stoughton, 1969.

PATERSON, John. The Praises of Israel: Studies Literary and Religious in the Psalms. New York: Scribner, 1950.

PETERS, John P. The Psalms as Liturgies. New York: Macmillan, 1922.

PIERIK, Marie. The Psalter in the Temple and the Church. Washington, DC: Catholic Unviersity of America Press, 1957.

"Les Psaumes, prière de l'assemblée chrétienne." La Maison-Dieu, 33 (1953). [Special issue]

PUNIET, Pierre de. Le Psautier liturgique à la lumière de la tradi-
    tion chrétienne. 2 vols. Paris: Desclée de Brouwer, 1935.

SALMON, Pierre. Les 'Tituli Psalmorum' des manuscrits latins.
    CBL, 12. Città del Vaticano: Libreria Vaticana; Paris: Cerf,
    1959.

SHEPHERD, Massey H. The Psalms in Christian Worship: A Prac-
    tical Guide. Minneapolis, MN: Augsburg, 1976.

SMITH, J. M. Powis. The Religion of the Psalms. Chicago: Uni-
    versity of Chicago Press, 1922.

WEBER, Jean Julien. Le Psautier, texte et commentaires. Tournai:
    Desclée, 1968.

WEBER, Robert, ed. Le Psautier romain et les autres anciens psau-
    tiers latins. Rome: Abbaye Saint-Jérôme, 1953.

WORDEN, Thomas. The Psalms are Christian Prayer. London:
    Geoffrey Chapman, 1964, c1961.

XLII. THE LITURGICAL WEEK

ANDREASEN, Niels Erik A. The Old Testament Sabbath: A Tradi-
    tion-Historical Investigation. SBLD, 7. Missoula, MT: Society
    of Biblical Literature, 1972.

BACCHIOCCHI, Samuele. From Sabbath to Sunday: A Historical
    Investigation of the Rise of Sunday Observance in Early Chris-
    tianity. Rome: Pontifical Gregorian University Press, 1977.

BECKWITH, Roger T., and STOTT, Wilfrid. This is the Day: The
    Biblical Doctrine of the Christian Sunday in its Jewish and Early
    Christian Setting. London: Marshall, Morgan & Scott, 1978;
    The Christian Sunday: A Biblical and Historical Study. Grand
    Rapids, MI: Baker, 1980.

BOTTE, Bernard et al. Le Dimanche. LO, 39. Paris: Cerf,
    1965.

CHIRAT, H. "Le dimanche dans l'antiquité chrétienne." In Etudes
    de pastorale liturgique, pp. 127-148. Paris: Cerf, 1944.

COTTON, Paul. From Sabbath to Sunday: A Study in Early Chris-
    tianity. Bethlehem, PA: Times Publishing Co., 1933.

GRELOT, P. "Du sabbat juif au dimanche chrétien." La Maison-
    Dieu, 123 (1975): 79-107; 124 (1975): 14-54.

HILD, Jean. Dimanche et vie pascale: thèmes bibliques et liturgiques présentés dans l'esprit des Pères de l'Eglise. Turnhout: Brepols, 1949.

JENNI, Ernst. Die theologische Begründung des Sabbatgebots im Alten Testament. TS, 46. Zollikon-Zürich: Evangelischer-Verlag, 1956.

JEWETT, Paul K. The Lord's Day: A Theological Guide to the Christian Day of Worship. Grand Rapids, MI: Eerdmans, 1971.

JUNGMANN, Josef Andreas. [Sonntag und Sonntagsmesse.] The Meaning of Sunday. Translated by Clifford Howell. London: Challoner; Notre Dame, IN: Fides, 1961.

_____. "The Weekly Cycle in the Liturgy." In his Pastoral Liturgy, pp. 251-277. New York: Herder, 1962.

PORTER, Harry Boone. The Day of Light: The Biblical and Liturgical Meaning of Sunday. SMW, 16. London: SCM Press; Greenwich, CT: Seabury Press, 1960.

REGAN, F. A. Dies Dominica and Die Solis: The Beginnings of the Lord's Day in Christian Antiquity. SST, 2d Ser., 125-A. Washington, DC: Catholic University of America Press, 1961.

RORDORF, Willy, ed. Sabbat und Sonntag in der alten Kirche. TC, 2. Zürich: Theologischer Verlag, 1972.

_____. Der Sonntag: Geschichte des Ruhe- und Gottesdiensttages im ältesten Christentum. Zürich: Zwingli Verlag, 1962; Sunday: The History of the Day of Rest and Worship in the Earliest Centuries of the Christian Church. Translated by A. A. K. Graham. Philadelphia, PA: Westminster Press; London: SCM Press, 1968.

SCHREIBER, Georg. Die Wochentage im Erlebnis der Ostkirche und des christlichen Abendlandes. Köln: Westdeutscher Verlag, 1959.

SEARLE, Mark, ed. Sunday Morning: A Time for Worship. Papers from the tenth annual conference of the Notre Dame Center for Pastoral Liturgy, University of Notre Dame, 1981. Collegeville, MN: Liturgical Press, 1982.

TREVELYAN, W. B. Sunday. OLPT. London: Longmans, Green, 1903.

PART FIVE:

WORSHIP AND THE ARTS

XLIII. GENERAL WORKS ON ART AND THE CHURCH

A. SYMBOLISM AND ICONOGRAPHY

APPLETON, LeRoy H., and BRIDGES, Stephen. Symbolism in Liturgical Art. Introduction by Maurice Lavanoux. New York: Scribner, 1959.

DANIELOU, Jean. Les Symboles chrétiens primitifs. Paris: Editions du Seuil, 1961; Primitive Christian Symbols. Translated by Donald Attwater. London: Burns & Oates; Baltimore, MD: Helicon, 1964.

DITCHFIELD, P. H. Symbolism of the Saints. ACh, 7. London: Mowbray, 1910.

DORLING, E. E. Heraldry of the Church: A Handbook for Decorators. ACh, 10. London: Mowbray, 1911.

DURANTIS, Gulielmus. The Symbolism of Churches and Church Ornaments: A Translation of the First Book of the Rationale Divinorum Officiorum. With an introductory essay, notes, and illustrations, by John Mason Neale and Benjamin Webb. 3d ed. London: Gibbings & Co., 1906.

FERGUSON, George Wells. Signs and Symbols in Christian Art. 2d ed. New York: Oxford University Press, 1955.

GALAVARIS, George. Bread and the Liturgy: The Symbolism of Early Christian and Byzantine Bread Stamps. Madison, WI: University of Wisconsin Press, 1970.

GOLDAMMER, Kurt. Kultsymbolik des Protestantismus. SR, 7. Stuttgart: Hiersmann, 1960.

616

GRABAR, André. Christian Iconography: A Study of Its Origins. Translated from the French MS. by Terry Grabar. Bollingen Series, 35/10. Princeton, NJ: Princeton University Press, 1968.

GRONDIJS, L. H. L'Iconographie byzantine du Crucifié mort sur la croix. BBB, 1. Bruxelles: Editions de Byzantion, Institut de sociologie, 1941.

HAMMERSCHMIDT, Ernst, HAUPTMANN, Peter, KRUEGER, Paul, et al. Symbolik des orthodoxen und orientalischen Christentums. Stuttgart: Hiersmann, 1962; and Tafelband. Stuttgart: Hiersmann, 1966.

HEATH, Sidney. The Romance of Symbolism and Its Relation to Church Ornament and Architecture. London: F. Griffiths, 1909; reprint ed., Detroit, MI: Gale Research, 1976.

HULME, F. Edward. History, Principles, and Practice of Symbolism in Christian Art. New York: Macmillan, 1891; reprint ed., Detroit, MI: Gale Research, 1969.

JUNGMANN, Josef Andreas, and SAUSER, Ekkart. Symbolik der katholischen Kirche. Stuttgart: Hiersemann, 1960; and Symbolik der katholischen Kirche: Tafelband. Stuttgart: Hiersemann, 1966.

KUNSTLE, Karl. Ikonographie der christlichen Kunst. 2. Bde. Freiburg: Herdr, 1926-1928.

Lexikon der christlichen Ikonographie. Herausgegeben von Engelbert Kirschbaum und Wolfgang Braunfels. 8 vols. Rome: Herder, 1968-1976.

MARTINEZ-FAZIO, Luis M. "Eucaristia, Banquete y Sacrificio en la iconografia paleocristiana." Gregorianum, 57 (1976): 459-521.

MILBURN, R. L. P. Saints and Their Emblems in English Churches. London: Oxford University Press, 1949.

MILLER, Madeleine S. A Treasury of the Cross. New York: Harper, 1956.

POST, W. Elwood. Saints, Signs and Symbols. 2d ed. New York: Morehouse-Barlow, 1974.

REAU, Louis. Iconographie de l'art chrétien. 3 vols. in 6. Paris: Presses universitaires de France, 1955-1959; reprint ed., Nendeln, Liechtenstein: Kraus Reprint, 1957-1974.

REST, Friedrich. On Christian Symbols. Philadelphia, PA: Christian Education Press, 1954; New York: Pilgrim Press, 1980.

SCHILLER, Gertrud. Ikonographie der christlichen Kunst. 2 vols.
    Gütersloh: Mohn, 1966-1968; Iconography of Christian Art.
    2 vols. Translated by Janet Seligman. Greenwich, CT: New
    York Graphic Society, 1971-1972.

STAFFORD, Thomas Albert. Christian Symbolism in the Evangelical
    Churches. New York: Abingdon-Cokesbury Press, 1942.

STEVENSON, Kenneth W., ed. Symbolism and the Liturgy. GLS,
    26. Bramcote, Eng.: Grove Books, 1981.

TYACK, Geo. S. The Cross in Ritual, Architecture, and Art.
    London: William Andrews, 1896?

TYRWHITT, R. St. John. Christian Art and Symbolism. London:
    Smtih, Elder, 1872.

WEBBER, Frederick R. Church Symbolism: An Explanation of the
    More Important Symbols of the Old and New Testament, the
    Primitive, the Mediaeval and the Modern Church. 2d ed.
    Cleveland, OH: J. H. Jansen, 1938; reprint ed., Detroit,
    MI: Gale Research, 1971.

WHONE, Herbert. Church, Monastery, Cathedral: A Guide to the
    Symbolism of the Christian Tradition. Short Hills, NJ: En-
    slow, 1977.

WILDRIDGE, Thomas Tindall. The Grotesque in Church Art. Lon-
    don: William Andrews, 1899; reprint ed., Detroit, MI: Gale
    Research, 1969.

WINZEN, Damasus. Symbols of Christ: The Old Testament, The
    New Testament. New York: Kenedy, 1955.

B. HISTORICAL STUDIES

ADDLESHAW, George W. O. Four Hundred Years: Architects,
    Sculptors, Painters, Craftsmen 1560-1960 whose Work is to be
    seen in York Minster. York, Eng.: Friends of York Minster,
    1962.

BADAWY, Alexander. Coptic Art and Archeology: The Art of the
    Christian Egyptians from the Late Antique to the Middle Ages.
    Cambridge, MA: MIT Press, 1978.

BECKWITH, John. Early Christian and Byzantine Art. 2d ed.
    New York: Penguin Books, 1979.

BEISSEL, Stephan. Bilder aus der Geschichte der altchristlichen
    Kunst und Liturgie in Italien. Freiburg: Herder, 1899.

BREHIER, Louis. L'Art chrétien: son développement iconograph-
ique des origines à nos jours. 2. éd. Paris: H. Laurens,
1928.

CHRISTE, Yves, VELMANS, Tania, LOSOWSKA, Hanna, and RECHT,
Roland. Art of the Christian World A.D. 200-1500: A Handbook of Styles and Forms. New York: Rizzoli, 1982.

COPE, Gilbert F., ed. Christianity and the Visual Arts: Studies
in the Art and Architecture of the Church. London: Faith
Press, 1964.

CORMACK, Robin. "Arts during the Age of Iconoclasm." In
Iconoclasm: Papers given at the Ninth Spring Symposium of
Byzantine Studies, University of Birmingham, 1975, pp. 35-44.
Edited by Anthony Bryer and Judith Herrin. Birmingham,
Eng.: Centre for Byzantine Studies, University of Birming-
ham, 1977.

COULTON, George G. Art and the Reformation. New York:
Knopf, 1928; reprint ed., Hamden, CT: Archon Books, 1969.

_____. _____. 2d ed. Cambridge: Cambridge University
Press, 1953.

CROSSLEY, Frederick H. English Church Craftsmanship: An Introduction to the Work of the Mediaeval Period and Some Account of Later Developments. London: B. T. Batsford, 1941.

CUTLER, Anthony. Transfiguraitons: Studies in the Dynamics of
Byzantine Iconography. University Park, PA: Pennsylvania
State University Press, 1975.

DEBIDOUR, Victor Henry. Brève histoire de la sculpture chréti-
enne. JSJC, 126. Paris: Fayard, 1960; Christian Sculpture.
Translated by Robert J. Cunningham. Additional material by
Eleanor A. Anderson. TCEC, 122. New York: Hawthorn
Books, 1968.

DU BOURGUET, Pierre. La Peinture paléo-chrétienne. Paris:
Pont-Royal, 1965; Early Christian Painting. Translated by
Simon Watson Taylor. London: Weidenfeld & Nicolson; New
York: Viking Press, 1966.

DYRNESS, William A. Rouault: A Vision of Suffering and Salvation. Grand Rapids, MI: Eerdmans, 1971.

FRERE, W. H., EELES, F. C., and RILEY, A. Pontifical Services.
4 vols. ACC, 3, 4, 8, 12. London: Longmans, Green, 1901-
1908.
1-2. Illustrated from Miniatures of the XVth and XVIth

Centuries, with descriptive notes and a liturgical introduction. By W. H. Frere. ACC, 3-4. 1901.
3. Illustrated from Woodcuts of the XVIth Century, with descriptive notes. By F. C. Eeles. ACC, 8. 1907.
4. Illustrated from Woodcuts of the XVIth Century, with descriptive notes. By A. R. Riley. ACC, 12. 1908.

GARRUCCI, Raffaele. Storia dell' arte cristiana nei primi otto secoli della chiesa. 6 vols. Prato: G. Guasti, 1872-1881.
1. Teorica. Annali. 1881.
2. Pitture cimiteriali. 1873.
3. Pitture non cimiteriale. 1876.
4. Musaici cimiteriali e non cimiteriali. 1877.
5. Sarcofagi ossia sculture cimiteriali. 1879.
6. Sculture non cimiteriali. 1880.

GARSIDE, Charles. Zwingli and the Arts. New Haven, CT: Yale University Press, 1966.

GLEN, Thomas L. Rubens and the Counter-Reformation: Studies in his Religious Paintings between 1609 and 1620. New York: Garland Publishing Co., 1977.

GOUGH, Michael. The Origins of Christian Art. London: Thames & Hudson, 1973; New York: Praeger, 1974.

GRABAR, André. L'Age d'or de Justinien, de la mort de Théodose à l'Islam. L'Univers des formes, 10. Paris: Gallimard, 1966; The Golden Age of Justinian, from the Death of Theodosius to the Rise of Islam. Translated by Stuart Gilbert and James Emmons. New York: Odyssey Press, 1967.

_____. L'Art de la fin de l'antiquité et du moyen âge. 3 vols. Paris: Collège de France, 1968.

_____. Martyrium: Recherches sur le culte des reliques et l'art chrétien antique. 2 vols. Paris: Collège de France, 1943-1946; reprint ed., London: Variorum Reprints, 1972.

_____. Le premier art chrétien (200-395). L'Univers des formes, 9. Paris: Gallimard, 1966; The Beginnings of Christian Art, 200-395. Translated by Stuart Gilbert and James Emmons. London: Thames & Hudson, 1967; reprinted as Early Christian Art: From the Rise of Christianity to the Death of Theodosius. New York: Odyssey Press, 1969.

HAEBLER, Hans Carl von. Das Bild in der evangelischen Kirche. Berlin: Evangelische Verlagsanstalt, 1957.

HENZE, Anton. Moderne christliche Kunst. Aschaffenburg: P. Pattloch, 1961.

_____. Moderne christliche Plastik. Aschaffenburg: P. Patt-
loch, 1962.

_____. Neue kirchliche Kunst. Reclinghausen: Paulus Verlag,
1958.

_____, and FILTHAUT, Theodor. Kirchliche Kunst der Gegen-
wart. Recklinghausen: Paulus Verlag, 1954; Contemporary
Church Art. Translated by Cecily Hastings. Edited by
Maurice Lavanoux. New York: Sheed & Ward, 1956.

HESS, Robert. Moderne kirchliche Kunst in der Schweiz. Zürich:
NZN-Verlag, 1951; revised ed., Neue kirchliche Kunst in der
Schweiz. SK, 6. Zürich: NZN-Verlag, 1962.

HIERS, H. H. "The Bread and Fish Eucharist in the Gospels and
Early Christian Art." Perspectives in Religious Studies, 3
(1976): 20-47.

KLAUSER, Theodor. "Studien zur Entstehungs geschichte der
christlichen Kunst." Jahrbuch für Antike und Christentum,
1 (1958): 20-55; 2 (1959): 115-145; 3 (1960): 112-133; 4
(1961): 128-145; 5 (1962): 113-124; 6 (1963): 71-100; 7
(1964): 67-76; 8/9 (1965-1966): 126-170; 10 (1967): 82-120.

KRAMREITER, Robert, and PARSCH, Pius. Neue Kirchenkunst im
Geist der Liturgie. Vienna-Klosterneuburg: Volksliturgischer
Verlag, 1939.

KRAUTHEIMER, Richard. Studies in Early Christian, Medieval,
and Renaissance Art. Translated by Alfred Frazer et al. New
York: New York University Press, 1969.

KRETZMANN, Paul Edward. Christian Art in the Place and in the
Form of Lutheran Worship. St. Louis, MO: Concordia, 1921.

LOWRIE, Walter. Monuments of the Early Church. New York:
Macmillan, 1901; also published as Christian Art and Archeol-
ogy: Being a Handbook to the Monuments of the Early Church.
London: Macmillan, 1901.

_____. Art in the Early Church. 2d ed. New York: Harper
& Row, 1965.

LUBKE, Wilhelm. Vorschule zum Studium der kirchlichen Kunst des
deutschen Mittelalters. 5. Aufl. Leipzig: E. A. Seemann,
1866; Ecclesiastical Art in Germany during the Middle Ages.
Translated by L. A. Wheatley. 4th ed. Edinburgh: T. C.
Jack, 1877; reprint ed., Boston, MA: Longwood Press, 1978.

LUETZELER, Heinrich. Die christliche Kunst des Abendlandes.

Belehrende Schriftenreihe, 8. Bonn: Verlag der Buchgemeinde, 1932.

McKINNON, James W. "Representations of the Mass in Medieval
and Renaissance Art." Journal of the American Musicological
Society, 31 (1978): 21-52.

MALE, Emile. L'Art religieux de la fin du moyen âge en France:
étude sur l'iconographie du moyen âge et sur ses sources
d'inspiration. 6. éd. Paris: A. Colin, 1969.

_____ . L'Art religieux de la fin du XVIe siècle, du XVIIe siècle
et du XVIIIe siècle: étude sur l'iconographie après le Concile
de Trente, Italie-France-Espagne-Flandres. 2. éd. Paris:
A. Colin, 1951.

_____ . L'Art religieux du XIIe au XVIIIe siècle: extraits choisis
par l'auteur. 2. éd. Paris: A. Colin, 1946; Religious Art
from the Twelfth to the Eighteenth Century. New York:
Pantheon Books, 1949; reprint ed., New York: Farrar, Straus
& Giroux, 1970.

_____ . L'Art religieux du XIIe siècle en France: étude sur les
origines de l'iconographie du moyen âge. 7. éd. Paris: A.
Colin, 1966; Religious Art in France, the Twelfth Century: A
Study of the Origins of Medieval Iconography. Bollingen
Series, 90/1. Princeton, NJ: Princeton University Press,
1978.

_____ . L'Art religieux du XIIIe siècle en France: étude sur
l'iconographie du moyen âge et sur ses sources d'inspiration.
3. éd. Paris: A. Colin, 1910; Religious Art in France, XIII
Century: A Study in Medieval Iconography and Its Sources of
Inspiration. Translated by Don Nussey. London: Dent;
New York: Dutton, 1913; reprint ed., The Gothic Image:
Religious Art in France of the Thirteenth Century. New York:
Harper & Row, 1972.

_____ . L'Art religieux du XIIIe siècle en France. 9. éd.
Paris: A. Colin, 1958; Religious Art in France, XIIIth Century. Bollingen Series, 90. Princeton, NJ: Princeton University Press, 1983.

MATHEW, Gervase. Byzantine Aesthetics. London: Murray; New
York: Viking Press, 1963.

MAUS, Cynthia Pearl. Christ and the Fine Arts. Rev. ed. New
York: Harper, 1959.

_____ . The Church and the Fine Arts. New York: Harper,
1960.

MEER, Frederik van der. [Oudchristelijke kunst.] Altchristliche Kunst. Translated by Auguste Schorn. Köln: Bachem, 1960; Early Christian Art. Translated from the German edition by Peter Brown and Friedl Brown. Chicago: University of Chicago Press, 1967.

MOREY, Charles Rufus. Christian Art. London, New York: Longmans, Green, 1935; reprint ed., New York: W. W. Norton, 1958.

_____. Early Christian Art: An Outline of the Evolution of Style and Iconography in Sculpture and Painting from Antiquity to the Eighth Century. 2d ed. Princeton, NJ: Princeton University Press, 1953.

MURRAY, Charles. "Art and the Early Church." Journal of Theological Studies, 28 (1977): 303-345.

MVENG, Engelbert. L'Art d'Afrique noire: liturgie cosmique et langage religieux. Point omega, 1. Tours: Mame, 1964.

_____. Art nègre, art chrétien? Rome: Les Amis italiens de Présence africaine, 1969.

NEWTON, Eric, and NEIL, William. 2000 Years of Christian Art. New York: Harper & Row, 1966.

PANOFSKY, Erwin. The Life and Art of Albrecht Dürer. 4th ed. Princeton, NJ: Princeton University Press, 1965, 1955.

PHILLIPS, John. The Reformation of Images: The Destruction of Art in England, 1535-1660. Berkeley, CA: University of California Press, 1973.

PICHARD, Joseph. L'Art sacré moderne. Paris: B. Arthaud, 1953.

_____. Images de l'invisible: vingt siècles d'art chrétien. Tournai: Casterman, 1958.

REGAMEY, Raymond. Art sacré au XXe siècle? CAD, 2. Paris: Cerf, 1952; Religious Art in the Twentieth Century. New York: Herder & Herder, 1963.

_____. La Querelle de l'art sacré: Assy et Vence. Paris: Cerf, 1951.

RICE, David Talbot. The Beginnings of Christian Art. London: Hodder & Stoughton; Nashville, TN: Abingdon Press, 1957.

ROHAULT DE FLEURY, Charles. Archéologie chrétienne: les

saints de la messe et leurs monuments. 10 vols. Paris:
Librairies-imprimeries réunies, 1893-1900.

_____. La Messe: études archéologiques sur ses monuments.
8 vols. Paris: Morel, 1883-1889.

RUBIN, William S. Modern Sacred Art and the Church of Assy.
New York: Columbia University Press, 1961.

SCHNELL, Hugo. Zur Situation der christlichen Kunst der Gegenwart. München: Schnell & Steiner, 1962.

SCHREYER, Lothar. Christliche Kunst des XX. Jahrhunderts in
der katholischen und protestantischen Welt. Hamburg: Christian Wegner Verlag, 1959.

SIMSON, Otto von. Sacred Fortress: Byzantine Art and State-
craft in Ravenna. Chicago: University of Chicago Press,
1948; reprinted 1976.

STIRM, Margarete. Die Bilderfrage in der Reformation. QFR, 45.
Gütersloh: Mohn, 1977.

STODDARD, Whitney S. Monastery and Cathedral in France:
Medieval Architecture, Sculpture, Stained Glass, Manuscripts,
the Art of the Church Treasuries. Middletown, CT: Wesleyan
University Press, 1966; reprint ed., Art and Architecture in
Medieval France. New York: Harper & Row, 1972.

STRZYGOWSKI, Josef. Ursprung der christlichen Kirchenkunst:
neue Tatsachen und Grundsätze der Kunstforschung. Leipzig:
J. C. Hinrichs, 1920; Origin of Christian Church Art: New
Facts and Principles of Research. Translated by O. M. Dalton
and H. J. Braunholtz. Oxford: Clarendon Press, 1923; reprint ed., New York: Hacker Art Books, 1973.

SUGER. Abbot Suger on the Abbey Church of St.-Denis and Its
Art Treasures. Edited, translated and annotated by Erwin
Panofsky. Princeton, NJ: Princeton University Press, 1946.

_____. _____. 2d ed. by Gerda Panofsky-Soergel. Prince-
ton, NJ: Princeton University Press,, 1979.

SWARZENSKI, Hanns. Monuments of Romanesque Art: The Art of
Church Treasures in North-Western Europe. 2d ed. London:
Faber; Chicago: University of Chicago Press, 1967.

SWIFT, Emerson H. Roman Sources of Christian Art. New York:
Columbia University Press,, 1951; reprint ed., Westport, CT:
Greenwood Press, 1970.

TARALON, Jean. Les Trésors des églises de France. Paris:
Hachette, 1966; Treasures of the Churches of France. Translated by Mira Intrator. New York: Braziller, 1966.

TAYLOR, Richard W. Jesus in Indian Paintings. Madras: Christian Literature Society, 1975.

VISSER 'T HOOFT, Willem Adolph. Rembrandt et la Bible. Neuchâtel: Delachaux & Niestlé, 1947; Rembrandts Weg zum Evangelium. Vollig umgearbeitete und erweiterte deutschsprachige
Ausgabe des Werkes: Rembrandt et la Bible. Aus dem Französischen übersetzt von Hilde Laederach. Zürich: Zwingli
Verlag, 1955; Rembrandt and the Gospel. Translated by K.
Gregor Smith from the German. English ed. revised by the
author. Philadelphia, PA: Westminster Press, 1958?; reprint
ed., New York: Meridian Books, 1960.

WALTER, Christopher. Art and Ritual of the Byzantine Church.
Birmingham Byzantine Series, 1. London: Variorum, 1982.

WEIDLE, Wladimir. The Baptism of Art: Notes on the Religion of
the Catacomb Paintings. Westminster, Eng.: Dacre Press,
194-?

WEITZMANN, Kurt, ed. The Age of Spirituality: Late Antique
and Early Christian Art, Third to Seventh Century. New
York: The Metropolitan Museum of Art in Association with
Princeton University Press, 1979.

WILPERT, Joseph. Fractio panis: die älteste Darstellung des eucharistischen Opfers in der "Capella Graeca." Freiburg:
Herder, 1895.

C. THEOLOGICAL AND LITURGICAL STUDIES

ACKEN, Johannes van. Christozentrische Kirchenkunst: ein Entwurf zum liturgischen Gesamtkunstwerk. 2. Aufl. Gladbeck:
Theben, 1923.

BAHR, Hans-Eckehard. Poiesis: theologische Untersuchung des
Kunst. Stuttgart: Evangelisches Verlagswerk, 1961.

BEALE, M. "Axiology of Art." Andover Newton Quarterly, 13
(1973): 198-205.

BELLM, R. "Liturgie und Kunst." Archiv für Liturgiewissenschaft,
16 (1974): 531-541.

BEVAN, Edwyn. Holy Images: An Inquiry into Idolatry and

Image-Worship in Ancient Paganism and in Christianity. London: Allen & Unwin, 1940.

CABROL, Fernand. "Esthetique dans la liturgie." In his Les Origines liturgiques, pp. 1–20. Paris: Letouzey & Ané, 1906.

CASAGRANDE, Vincenzo. L'Arte a servizio della chiesa. 2 vols. Turin: Società editrice internazionale, 1931–1938.

CRAM, Ralph Adams. The Catholic Church and Art. New York: Macmillan, 1930.

DAVIES, Horton and Hugh. Sacred Art in a Secular Century. Collegeville, MN: Liturgical Press, 1978.

DIXON, John W. "Liturgy as an Art Form." Anglican Theological Review, Supplemental Series, 6 (1976): 55–68.

FATTINGER, Rudolf. Liturgisch-praktisch Requisitenkunde für den Seelsorgsklerus, für Theologen, Architekten, Künstler, Kunst- und Paramentenwerkstätten; im lexikaler Form. Freiburg: Herder, 1955.

FRANK, Karl Boromäus. Kernfragen kirchlicher Kunst: Grundsätzliches und Erläuterungen zur Unterweisung des Heiligen Offiziums vom 30. Juni 1952 über die kirchliche Kunst. Wien: Herder, 1953; Fundamental Questions on Ecclesiastical Art. Translated by M. Nathe. Collegeville, MN: Liturgical Press, 1962.

GLENDENNING, Frank, ed. The Church and the Arts. London: SCM Press, 1960.

GOLLWITZER, Gerhard. Die Kunst als Zeichen. München: Kaiser, 1958.

GREENE, Theodore Meyer. The Arts and the Art of Criticism. 2d ed. Princeton, NJ: Princeton University Press, 1947; reprint ed., New York: Gordian Press, 1973.

HEYER, George S. Signs of Our Times: Theological Essays on Art in the Twentieth Century. Grand Rapids, MI: Eerdmans, 1980.

HOCHE-MONG, Raymond. "The Artistic Dimension of Liturgy." Studia Liturgica, 11 (1976): 118–130.

JAKOB, Georg. Die Kunst im Dienste der Kirche: ein Handbuch für Freunde der kirchlichen Kunst. 5. Aufl. Landshut: Thomann, 1901.

JUNGMANN, Josef Andreas.   "Church Art."   Worship, 29 (1955):
68-82.

KOCH, Hugo.   Die altchristliche Bilderfrage nach den literarischen
Quellen.   FRLANT, 27 (n. F. 10).   Göttingen: Vandenhoeck
& Ruprecht, 1917.

LAEUCHLI, Samuel.   Religion and Art in Conflict: Introduction to
a Cross-Disciplinary Task.   Philadelphia, PA: Fortress Press,
1980.

LEEUW, Gerardus van der.   Wegen en grenzen: een studie over de
verhouding van religie en kunst.   3. druck, herzien door
E. L. Smelik.   Amsterdam: H. J. Paris, 1955; Sacred and
Profane Beauty: The Holy in Art.   Preface by Mircea Eliade.
Translated by David E. Green.   New York: Holt, Rinehart &
Winston, 1963; reprint ed., Nashville, TN: Abingdon Press,
[1963].

LESKO, David S.   "Art and Liturgy: The Fixing of a Thesis."
St. Vladimir's Theological Quarterly, 22 (1978):   127-140.

Lutheran Society for Worship, Music, and the Arts.   Worship and
the Arts for Modern Man.   St. Paul, MN: North Central Publishing Co., 1964.

MALDONADO, Luis, and POWER, David, eds.   Symbol and Art in
Worship.   Concilium, 132.   New York: Seabury Press, 1980.

MARITAIN, Jacques.   Art et scolastique.   Nouvelle éd.   Paris:
L. Rouart, 1927; Art and Scholasticism, with Other Essays.
Translated by J. F. Scanlan.   New York: Scribner, 1930;
reprint ed., Freeport, NY: Books for Libraries Press, 1971.

_____.   Art et scolastique.   3. éd.   Paris: L. Rouart, 1935;
and Frontières de la poésie et autre essais.   Paris: L. Rouart,
1935; Art and Scholasticism and The Frontiers of Poetry.
Translated by Joseph W. Evans.   New York: Scribner, 1962;
reprint ed., Notre Dame, IN: University of Notre Dame Press,
1974.

MUSCULUS, Paul Romane.   La Prière des mains: l'église réformée
et l'art.   Paris: Editions "Je sers", 1938.

National Conference of Catholic Bishops.   Environment and Art in
Catholic Worship.   Washington, DC: United States Catholic
Conference, 1978.

NICHOLS, Aidan.   The Art of God Incarnate: Theology and Image
in Christian Tradition.   New York: Paulist Press, 1980.

OCHSE, Madeleine. <u>Un Art sacré pour notre temps</u>. Paris: Fayard, 1959.

_____. <u>La Nouvelle querelle des images</u>. Paris: Centurion, 1953.

RAMSEYER, Jean-Philippe. <u>La Parole et l'image: liturgie, architecture et art sacré</u>. Neuchâtel: Delachaux & Niestlé, 1963.

REINHOLD, Hans Ansgar. <u>Liturgy and Art</u>. New York: Harper & Row, 1966.

RICHARDSON, Cyril C. "Some Reflections on Liturgical Art." <u>Union Seminary Quarterly Review</u>, 8, 3 (March 1953): 24-28.

ROOKMAAKER, H. R. <u>Art and the Public Today</u>. 2d ed. Huémoz, Switzerland: L'Abri Fellowship, 1969.

SALIERS, D. E. "Beauty and Holiness Revisited: Some Relations between Aesthetics and Theology." <u>Worship</u>, 48 (1974): 289-293.

STEFANESCU, J. D. <u>L'Illustration des liturgies dans l'art de Byzance et de l'orient</u>. Brussels: Institut de philologie et d'histoire orientales, 1936.

VOGT, Von Ogden. <u>Art and Religion</u>. New Haven, CT: Yale University Press, 1921; rev. ed., Boston, MA: Beacon Press, 1948.

WOLTERSTORFF, Nicholas. <u>Art in Action: Toward a Christian Aesthetic</u>. Grand Rapids, MI: Eerdmans, 1980.

XLIV. CHURCH ARCHITECTURE

A. GENERAL STUDIES

BOWYER, Jack. <u>The Evolution of Church Buildings</u>. New York: Whitney Library of Design, 1977.

BRAUN, Hugh. <u>Cathedral Architecture</u>. London: Faber, 1972.

BRAUNFELS, Wolfgang. <u>Abendländische Klosterbaukunst</u>. Köln: DuMont Schauberg, 1969; <u>Monasteries of Western Europe: The Architecture of the Orders</u>. 3d ed. Princeton, NJ: Princeton University Press, 1973, 1972.

DAVIES, John G. The Architectural Setting of Baptism. London: Barrie & Rockcliff, 1962.

_____. Temples, Churches and Mosques: A Guide to the Appreciation of Religious Architecture. Oxford: Blackwell; New York: Pilgrim Press, 1982.

DEHIO, Georg Gottfried, and BEZOLD, G. von. Die kirchliche Baukunst des Abendlandes. 7 vols. (2 vols. text, 5 vols. atlas). Stuttgart: J. G. Cotta, 1887-1901.

DRUMMOND, Andrew Landale. The Church Architecture of Protestantism: An Historical and Constructive Study. Edinburgh: T. & T. Clark, 1934.

EVANS, Edward Payson. Animal Symbolism in Ecclesiastical Architecture. London: W. Heinemann, 1896; reprint ed., Detroit, MI: Gale Research, 1969.

GAMBER, Klaus. Sancta Sanctorum: Studien zur liturgischen Ausstattung der Kirche, vor allem des Altarraums. SPL, 10. Regensburg: Pustet, 1981.

MAGUIRE, Robert, and MURRAY, Keith. Modern Churches of the World. London: Studio Vista; New York: Dutton, 1965.

MIRSKY, Jeanette. Houses of God. New York: Viking Press, 1965; reprint ed., Chicago: University of Chicago Press, 1976.

MUNIER, Albert. Construction, décoration, ameublement des Eglises. 3 vols. Bruges: Desclée de Brouwer, 1925-1926.
1. L'Eglise dans les siècles passés.
2. L'Eglise à notre époque: sa construction.
3. L'Eglise à notre époque: sa décoration, son ameublement.

PRENTICE, Sartell. The Heritage of the Cathedral: A Study of the Influence of History and Thought upon Cathedral Architecture. London: Methuen; New York: W. Morrow, 1936.

SHORT, Ernest H. A History of Religious Architecture. 3d ed. New York: W. W. Norton, 1951.

WATKIN, David. Morality and Architecture: The Development of a Theme in Architectural History and Theory from the Gothic Revival to the Modern Movement. Oxford: Clarendon Press, 1977.

WHITE, James F. Protestant Worship and Church Architecture: Theological and Historical Considerations. New York: Oxford University Press, 1964.

B.   EARLY AND EASTERN CHURCHES

BABIC, Gordana. Les Chapelles annexes des églises byzantines:
fonction liturgique et programmes iconographiques. BCA, 3.
Paris: Klincksieck, 1969.

BUTLER, Howard Crosby. Early Churches in Syria: Fourth to
Seventh Centuries. Edited by E. Baldwin Smith. Princeton,
NJ: Published for the Department of Art and Archaeology of
Princeton University, 1929.

COQUIN, R. G. "Le Bima des églises syriennes." Orient Syrien,
10 (1965): 443-474.

CROSS, Samuel H. Mediaeval Russian Churches. Edited by Ken-
neth-John Conant. MAAP, 53. Cambridge, MA: Mediaeval
Academy of America, 1949.

CROWFOOT, J. W. Early Churches in Palestine. London: Published for the British Academy by Oxford University Press,
1941.

DALTON, O. M. East Christian Art, a Survey of the Monuments.
Oxford: Clarendon Press, 1925.

DAVIES, John G. The Origin and Development of Early Christian
Architecture. London: SCM Press, 1952; New York: Philosophical Library, 1953.

GAMBER, Klaus. Domus ecclesiae: die ältesten Kirchenbauten
Aquilejas sowie im Alpen- und Donaugebiet bis zum Beginn des
5. Jahrhunderts liturgiegeschichtlich untersucht. SPL, 2.
Regensburg: Pustet, 1968.

_____. Liturgie und Kirchenbau: Studien zur Geschichte der
Messfeier und des Gotteshauses in der Frühzeit. SPL, 6.
Regensburg: Pustet, 1976.

GERSTER, Georg. Kirchen im Fels: Entdeckungen in Athiopien.
Stuttgart: Kohlhammer, 1968; Churches in Rock: Early Chris-
tian Art in Ethiopia. Translated by Richard Hosking. New
York: Phaidon, 1970.

HAMILTON, George Heard. The Art and Architecture of Russia.
Pelican History of Art. Baltimore, MD: Penguin Books, 1954.

HAMILTON, John Arnott. Byzantine Architecture and Decoration.
2d ed. London: Batsford, 1956.

HICKLEY, D. "The Ambo in Early Liturgical Planning: A Study

with Special Reference to the Syrian Bema." Heythrop Journal,
7 (1966): 407-427.

HIRAM, Asher. "Die Entwicklung der antiken Synagogen und altchristlichen Kirchenbauten im heiligen Lande." Wiener Jahrbuch
für Kunstgeschichte, 19 (1963): 7-63.

JAMES, E. O. From Cave to Cathedral: Temples and Shrines of
Prehistoric, Classical, and Early Christian Times. New York:
Praeger, 1965.

KAHLER, Heinz. Die frühe Kirche: Kult und Kultraum. Berlin:
Mann, 1972.

KRAELING, Carl Hermann. The Christian Building. Excavation
at Dura Europos Final Report 8, Part 2. New Haven, CT:
Dura-Europos Publications, 1967.

KRAUTHEIMER, Richard. "The Beginning of Early Christian Architecture." Review of Religion, 3 (1939): 127-148.

_____. Early Christian and Byzantine Architecture. Pelican
History of Art. Baltimore, MD: Penguin Books, 1965.

LASSUS, Jean. Sanctuaires chrétiens de Syrie. Paris: Geuthner,
1947.

_____, and TCHALENKO, Georges. "Ambons syriens." Cahiers
archéologiques, 5 (1951): 75-122.

LIESENBERG, Kurt. Der Einfluss der Liturgie auf die frühchristliche Basilika. Neustadt an der Haardt: Pfälzische Verlagsanstalt, 1928.

MacDONALD, William Lloyd. Early Christian and Byzantine Architecture. New York: Braziller, 1962.

MADER, Andreas Evaristus. Altchristliche Basiliken und Lokal-
traditionen in Südjudäa. Paderborn: Schöningh, 1918; reprint
ed., New York: Johnson Reprints, 1967.

MATHEWS, Thomas F. The Early Churches of Constantinople:
Architecture and Liturgy. University Park, PA: Pennsylvania
State University Press, 1971.

MILLET, Gabriel. L'Ecole grecque dans l'architecture byzantine.
Paris: Leroux, 1916.

OVADIAH, Asher. Corpus of the Byzantine Churches in the Holy
Land. Translated from the Hebrew by Rose Kirson. Bonn:
Hanstein, 1970.

PEETERS, C. J. A. C. De liturgische dispositie van het vroeg-
christelijk kerkgebouw. Assen: Van Gorcum, 1969.

RAES, Alphonse. "La Liturgie eucharistique en Orient: son cadre
architectural." La Maison-Dieu, 70 (1962): 49-66.

SCHNEIDER, Alfons Maria. Liturgie und Kirchenbau in Syrien.
Nachrichten der Akademie der Wissenschaften in Göttingen,
Philologisch-historische Klasse, Jahrg. 1949, nr. 3. Göttingen:
Vandenhoeck & Ruprecht, 1949.

SUSSENBACH, Uwe. Christuskult und kaiserliche Baupolitik bei
Konstantin. AKML, 241. Bonn: Bouvier, 1977.

TAFT, Robert F. "On the Use of the Bema in the East-Syrian
Liturgy." Eastern Churches Review, 3 (Spring 1970): 30-39.

_____. "Some Notes on the Bema in the East and West Syrian
Traditions." Orientalia Christiana Periodica, 34 (1968): 326-
359.

VAN MILLIGEN, Alexander. Byzantine Churches in Constantinople:
Their History and Architecture. London: Macmillan, 1912.

C. CONTINENTAL CHURCHES

ARMELLINI, Mariano. Le chiese di Roma dal secolo IV al XIX. 2
vols. Nuova ed. Edited by Carlo Cecchelli. Rome: Edizioni
R. O. R. E. di N. Raffolo, 1942.

BOURKE, John. Baroque Churches of Central Europe. 2d ed.
London: Faber & Faber, 1962.

BREHIER, L. "Les Origines de la basilique romaine." Bulletin
Monumental, 86 (1927): 221-249.

BROSSE, Jacques, ed. Eglises de France. 3 vols. Paris: Robert
Laffont, 1966- .
    1. Histoire générale des églises de France; Belgique, Luxem-
        bourg, Suisse.
    2. Dictionnaire des églises de France; centre et sud-est.
    3. Dictionnaire des églises de France; sud-ouest.

CLAPHAM, Alfred William. The Renaissance of Architecture and
Stone-Carving in Southern France in the Tenth and Eleventh
Centuries. London: H. Milford, 1933.

_____. Romanesque Architecture in Western Europe. Oxford:
Clarendon Press, 1936; reprinted 1967.

CONANT, Kenneth John. A Brief Commentary on Early Medieval
Church Architecture. Baltimore, MD: Johns Hopkins Press,
1942.

_____. Carolingian and Romanesque Architecture, 800 to 1200.
Pelican History of Art. Baltimore, MD: Penguin Books, 1966,
1959.

EVANS, Joan. Monastic Architecture in France, from the Renaissance to the Revolution. Cambridge: Cambridge University
Press, 1964.

FRANKL, Paul. Baukunst des Mittelalters: Die frühmittelalterliche
und romanische Baukunst. Potsdam: Akademische Verlagsgesellschaft, 1926.

_____. Gothic Architecture. Translated by Dieter Pevsner.
Pelican History of Art. Baltimore, MD: Penguin Books, 1963,
c1962.

HEGE, Walter, and BARTHEL, Gustav. Barockkirchen in Altbayern
und Schwaben. 3. Aufl. München: Deutscher Kunstverlag,
1953.

HEITZ, Carol. Recherches sur les rapports entre architecture et
liturgie à l'époque carolingienne. Paris: S. E. V. P. E. N.,
1963.

KRAUTHEIMER, Richard. Corpus basilicarum christianarum Romae.
The Early Christian Basilicas of Rome, IV-IX Centuries. MAC,
2. ser., 2. Città del Vaticano: Pontificio istituto di archeologia cristiana, 1937- .

LASTEYRIE DU SAILLANT, R. C. de. L'Architecture religieuse en
France à l'époque romane: ses origines, son développement.
2. éd., rev. et augm. d'une bibliographie critique par Marcel
Aubert. Paris: Picard, 1929.

LEMAIRE, R. "L'Origine de la basilique latine." Annales de la
Société d'archéologie de Bruxelles, 25 (1911): 5-130.

LESSER, George. Gothic Cathedrals and Sacred Geometry. 2 vols.
London: A. Tiranti, 1957.

LIEB, Norbert. Barockkirchen zwischen Donau und Alpen. Auf-
nahmen von Max Hirmer. München: Hirmer, 1953.

MALE, Emile. Rome et ses vieilles églises. Paris: Flammarion,
1942; reprinted 1965; The Early Churches of Rome. Translated by David Buxton. Chicago: Quadrangle Books, 1960.

NORTON, Charles Eliot. Historical Studies of Church-Building in
the Middle Ages: Venice, Siena, Florence. New York: Harper, 1880; reprint ed., Boston, MA: Longwood Press, 1978.

OZINGA, Mark D. De protestantische kerkenbouw in Nederland
van hervorming tot franschen tijd. Amsterdam: H. J. Paris,
1929.

PANOFSKY, Erwin. Gothic Architecture and Scholasticism. La-
trobe, PA: Archabbey Press, 1951; reprint ed., Cleveland,
OH: World, 1963.

PORTER, Arthur Kingsley. Medieval Architecture: Its Origins
and Development. New Haven, CT: Yale University Press,
1908.

SAUER, Joseph. Symbolik des Kirchengebäudes und seiner Ausstattung in der Auffassung des Mittelalters. 2. Aufl. Freiburg: Herder, 1924; reprint ed., Münster: Mehren & Hobbe-
ling, 1964.

SEDLMAYR, Hans. Die Entstehung der Kathedrale. Zürich: At-
lantis Verlag, 1950; reprint ed., Graz: Akademische Druck-
und Verlagsanstalt, 1976.

SIMSON, Otto G. von. The Gothic Cathedral: The Origins of
Gothic Architecture and the Medieval Concept of Order. 2d
ed. Bollingen Series, 48. New York: Pantheon Books, 1962;
reprint ed., New York: Harper & Row, 1964.

_____. _____. Revised ed., with additions. Princeton, NJ:
Princeton University Press, 1974.

SMITH, G. E. Kidder. The New Churches of Europe: Las nuevas
iglesias de Europa. New York: Holt, Rinehart & Winston,
1964.

STRZYGOWSKI, Josef. Early Church Art in Northern Europe, with
Special Reference to Timber Construction and Decoration. New
York, London: Harper, 1929.

WEINGARTNER, Josef. Römische Barockkirchen. München: J.
Kösel & F. Pustet, 1930.

WITTE, Robert B. Das katholische Gotteshaus: sein Bau, seine
Ausstattung, seine Pflege im Geiste der Liturgie, der Tradition
und der Vorschriften der Kirche. 2. Aufl. Mainz: Matthias-
Grünewald Verlag, 1951.

D. CHURCHES OF ENGLAND AND SCOTLAND

ADDLESHAW, George W. O., and ETCHELLS, Frederick. The
Architectural Setting of Anglican Worship. 2d ed. London:
Faber & Faber, 1950.

BOND, Francis. The Cathedrals of England and Wales, being a
fourth edition of English Cathedrals Illustrated. London:
B. T. Batsford; New York: Scribner, 1912.

_____. Gothic Architecture in England: An Analysis of the
Origin and Development of English Church Architecture from
the Norman Conquest to the Dissolution of the Monasteries.
London: B. T. Batsford, 1905; reprint ed., Freeport, NY:
Books for Libraries Press, 1972.

_____. An Introduction to English Church Architecture: From
the 11th to the 16th Century. 2 vols. London: H. Milford,
1913; reprint ed., Boston, MA: Longwood Press, 1979.

BRAUN, Hugh. Parish Churches: Their Architectural Development
in England. London: Faber, 1970.

CLAPHAM, Alfred William. English Romanesque Architecture. 2
vols. Oxford: Clarendon Press, 1930; reprinted 1964.

CLARKE, B. F. L. Anglican Cathedrals Outside the British Isles.
Foreword by John Betjeman. London: SPCK, 1958.

_____. Church Builders of the Nineteenth Century: A Study
of the Gothic Revival in England. London: SPCK; New York:
Macmillan, 1938.

CLARKE, Basil, and BETJEMAN, John. English Churches. London: Vista Books, 1964.

CLINCH, George. Old English Churches: Their Architecture,
Furniture, Decorations and Monuments. London: L. U. Gill,
1900; reprint ed., New York: Gordon Press, 1977.

COOK, George Henry. The English Mediaeval Parish Church.
London: Phoenix House, 1954.

COX, J. Charles. The English Parish Church. London: B. T.
Batsford, 1914; reprint ed., Wakefield, Eng.: E P Publishing,
1976.

CROSSLEY, Frederick H. English Church Design, 1040-1540 A.D.:
A Study. 2d ed. London: B. T. Batsford, 1948.

DAY, E. Hermitage. Renaissance Architecture in England. ACh,
    6. London: Mowbray, 1910.

FELTON, Herbert, and HARVEY, John. The English Cathedrals.
    London: B. T. Batsford, 1950.

GWYNN, Denis R. Lord Shrewsbury, Pugin and the Catholic Re-
    vival. London: Hollis & Carter, 1946.

HAY, G. The Architecture of Scottish Post-Reformation Churches
    1560-1843. Oxford: Clarendon Press, 1957.

LITTLE, Bryan. Catholic Churches since 1623: A Study of Roman
    Catholic Churches in England and Wales from Penal Times to
    the Present Decade. London: Robert Hale, 1966.

MacGIBBON, David, and ROSS, Thomas. The Ecclesiastical Archi-
    tecture of Scotland from the Earliest Christian Times to the
    Seventeenth Century. Edinburgh: D. Douglas, 1896-1897.

POWYS, A. R. The English Parish Church. London: Longmans,
    Green, 1930.

PUGIN, A. C., PUGIN, A. W., WILLSON, E. J., and WALKER,
    T. L. Examples of Gothic Architecture. 3 vols. 2d ed.
    London: H. G. Bohn, 1838-1840; reprint ed., London: n.p.,
    1930-1940.

PUGIN, A. Welby. An Apology for the Revival of Christian Archi-
    tecture in England. London: J. Weale, 1843.

_____. Contrasts: Or, a Parallel between the Noble Edifices of
    the Fourteenth and Fifteenth Centuries, and Similar Buildings
    of the Present Day, showing the Decay of Taste. London:
    Printed for the author, 1836; 2d ed., Edinburgh: J. Grant,
    1898.

_____. The True Principles of Pointed or Christian Architecture.
    London: J. Weale, 1841.

SCHNORRENBERG, J. M. "Early Anglican Architecture, 1558-1662:
    Its Theological Implications and Its Relation to the Continental
    Background." Ph.D. dissertation, Princeton University, 1964.

SMITH, Edwin, HUTTON, Graham, and COOK, Olive. English Par-
    ish Churches. London: Thames & Hudson, 1976.

SPENCE, Basil. Phoenix at Coventry: The Building of a Cathedral.
    New York: Harper & Row, 1962.

THOMPSON, A. Hamilton. The Ground Plan of the English Parish
    Church. Cambridge: Cambridge University Press, 1911.

_____. The Historical Growth of the English Parish Church.
Cambridge: Cambridge University Press, 1911.

WHIFFEN, Marcus. Stuart and Georgian Churches: The Architecture of the Church of England Outside London, 1603-1837.
London: B. T. Batsford, 1948.

WHITE, James F. The Cambridge Movement: The Ecclesiologists
and the Gothic Revival. New York: Cambridge University
Press, 1979.

WILLIS, Robert. The Architectural History of Canterbury Cathedral. London: Longman, 1845.

YOUNG, Elizabeth and Wayland. Old London Churches. London:
Faber & Faber, 1956.

E. ENGLISH NON-CONFORMIST CHURCHES

BETJEMAN, John. "Nonconformist Architecture." The Architectural Review, 88 (1940): 161-174.

BRIGGS, Martin S. Puritan Architecture and Its Future. London:
Lutterworth Press, 1946.

DOLBEY, George W. The Architectural Expression of Methodism:
The First Hundred Years. London: Epworth Press, 1964.

DRUMMOND, Andrew L. "The Architectural Interest of English
Meeting Houses." Journal of the Royal Institute of British
Architects, 45 (1937-1938): 909-917.

GARVAN, A. "The Protestant Plain Style before 1630." Journal
of the Society of Architectural Historians, 9, 3 (1950): 5-13.

JONES, Ronald P. Nonconformist Church Architecture. London:
Lindsey Press, 1914.

LIDBETTER, Hubert. The Friends Meeting House: An Historical
Survey of the Places of Worship of the Society of Friends
(Quakers), from the days of their founder George Fox, in the
17th Century, to the Present Day. York, Eng.: William Sessions, Ebor Press, 1961.

THOMAS, John. "Liturgy and Architecture, 1932-1960: Methodist
Influence and Ideas." Proceedings of the Wesley Historical
Society, 40, 4 (February 1976): 106-113.

WHITE, James F. "Early Methodist Liturgical Architecture." Motive,
18, 6 (March 1958): 12-13, 19-20.

F. AMERICAN CHURCHES

BAER, Kurt. Architecture of the California Missions. Berkeley,
CA: University of California Press, 1958.

BAIRD, Joseph Armstrong. The Churches of Mexico, 1530-1810.
Berkeley, CA: University of California Press, 1962.

BENES, Peter, ed. New England Meeting House and Church:
1630-1850. Dublin Seminar for New England Folklife, vol. 4.
Boston, MA: Boston University, 1980.

BRODERICK, Robert C. Historic Churches of the United States.
New York: W. Funk, 1958.

BRUGGINK, Donald J., and DROPPERS, Carl H. Christ and Architecture: Building Presbyterian/Reformed Churches. Grand
Rapids, MI: Eerdmans, 1965.

_____. When Faith Takes Form: Contemporary Churches of
Architectural Integrity in America. Grand Rapids, MI: Eerdmans, 1971.

CRAM, Ralph Adams, ed. American Church Building of Today.
New York: Architectural Book Publishing Co., 1929.

DONNELLY, Marian C. The New England Meeting Houses of the
Seventeenth Century. Middletown, CT: Wesleyan University
Press, 1968.

DORSEY, Stephen P. Early English Churches in America, 1607-
1807. New York: Oxford University Press, 1952.

EMBURY, Aymar. Early American Churches. Garden City, NY:
Doubleday, Page, 1914.

GOWANS, Alan. Church Architecture in New France. New Brunswick, NJ: Rutgers University Press, 1955.

JONES, Edgar DeWitt. "Architecture and Worship among the Disciples." Shane Quarterly, 2, 2-3 (1941): 173-184.

RAWLINGS, James Scott. Virginia's Colonial Churches: An Architectural Guide. Richmond, VA: Garrett & Massie, 1963.

ROSE, Harold Wickliffe. The Colonial Houses of Worship in America.
New York: Hastings House, 1963.

SHINN, George Wolfe. King's Handbook of Notable Episcopal
Churches in the United States. Boston, MA: Moses King, 1889.

SINNOTT, Edmund Ware. Meetinghouse & Church in Early New England. New York: McGraw Hill, 1963.

STANTON, Phoebe B. The Gothic Revival and American Church Architecture: An Episode in Taste, 1840-1856. Baltimore, MD: Johns Hopkins Press, 1968.

WHITE, James F. "Current Trends in American Church Building." Studia Liturgica, 4 (1965): 94-113.

G. CONTEMPORARY PRACTICAL, THEOLOGICAL, AND
   CRITICAL STUDIES

ACKING, Carl A. "Får kyrkorummet se ut hur som helst: Reflektioner kring der arkitektoniska problemens samband med liturgin." Svensk Theologisk Kvartalskrift, 55 (1979): 17-23.

ALLMEN, J.-J. von. "A Short Theology of the Place of Worship." Studia Liturgica, 3, 3 (1964): 155-171.

ANSON, Peter F. The Building of Churches. NLCK, 10. London: Burns & Oates; New York: Hawthorn Books, 1964.

"Bâtir et aménager les églises: le lieu de la célébration." La Maison-Dieu, 63 (1960).

BAUR, Hermann, et al. Kirchenbauten. Zürich: NZN Buchverlag, 1956.

BECHTOLD, Otto, and DURIG, Walter. Kirchenbau und Liturgiereform. Karlsruhe: Badenia-Verlag, 1966.

BETTS, Darby Wood, ed. Architecture and the Church. Foreword by G. Ashton Oldham. Greenwood, CT: Seabury Press, 1952.

BIELER, André. Liturgie et Architecture. Genève: Labor et Fides, 1961; Architecture in Worship. Philadelphia, PA: Westminster Press, 1965.

BOUYER, Louis. Liturgy and Architecture. Notre Dame, IN: University of Notre Dame Press, 1967.

CHRIST-JANER, Albert, and FOLEY, Mary Mix. Modern Church Architecture: A Guide to the Form and Spirit of 20th Century Religious Buildings. New York: McGraw-Hill, 1962.

CIAMPANI, Pina, ed. Architettura e liturgia. Assisi: Edizioni Pro Civitate Christiana, 1965.

Comité National d'Art Sacré. L'Eglise, maison du peuple de Dieu, liturgique et architecture. Nouvelle éd. LO, 53. Paris: Cerf, 1971.

COPE, Gilbert. Liturgical Reordering of Parish Churches. Birmingham, Eng.: University of Birmingham, Institute for the Study of Worship and Religious Architecture, 1979.

_____, ed. Making the Building Serve the Liturgy. London: Mowbray, 1962.

_____. "Trends in Modern European Church Architecture." Studia Liturgica, 2 (1963): 285-300.

CRAM, Ralph Adams. Church Building: A Study of the Principles of Architecture in their Relation to the Church. 3d ed. Boston, MA: Marshall Jones, 1924.

DAHINDEN, Justus. Bauen für die Kirche in der Welt. Würzburg: Echter; Zürich: NZN Buchverlag, 1966; New Trends in Church Architecture. London: Studio Vista, 1967.

DAVIES, J. G. "Influence of Architecture upon Liturgical Change." Studia Liturgica, 9 (1973): 230-240.

_____, ed. Looking to the Future: Papers Read at an International Symposium on Prospects for Worship, Religious Architecture and Socio-Religious Studies, 1976. Birmingham, Eng.: University of Birmingham, Institute for the Study of Worship and Religious Architecture, 1976.

_____. The Secular Use of Church Buildings. New York: Seabury Press, 1968.

DEBUYST, Frédéric. Modern Architecture and Christian Celebration. ESW, 18. Richmond, VA: John Knox Press, 1968.

"Des Lieux pour célébrer." La Maison-Dieu, 136 (1978).

Espace sacré et architecture moderne. LO, 49. Paris: Cerf, 1971.

FILTHAUT, Theodor. Kirchenbau und Liturgiereform. Mainz: Matthias-Grünewald-Verlag, 1965; Church Architecture and Liturgical Reform. Translated by Gregory Roettger. Baltimore, MD: Helicon Press, 1968.

FINGESTEN, P. "Topographical and Anatomical Aspects of the Gothic Cathedral." Journal of Aesthetics and Art Criticism, 20 (1961): 3-23.

GIESELMANN, R. Contemporary Church Architecture. London: Thames & Hudson, 1972.

GROSCHE, R. "Überlegungen zur Theorie des Kirchenbaues." Das Münster, 13 (1960): 344-349.

HAMMOND, Peter. Liturgy and Architecture. New York: Columbia University Press, 1961; London: Barsie & Rockliff, 1963.

_____, ed. Towards a Church Architecture. London: Architectural Press, 1962.

HAUTECOEUR, Louis. Mystique et architecture: symbolisme du cercle et de la coupole. Paris: Picard, 1954.

HICKMAN, Hoyt L. United Methodist Altars: A Guide for the Local Church. Nashville, TN: Abingdon Press, 1984.

JOHNSON, Stephen, and JOHNSON, Cuthbert. Planning for Liturgy: Liturgical and Practical Guidelines for the Re-ordering of Churches. Farnborough, Eng.: St. Michael's Abbey Press, 1983.

KLAUSER, Theodor, ed. Richtlinien für die Gestaltung des Gotteshauses aus dem Geiste der römischen Liturgie. Münster: Aschendorff, 1947.

LOCKETT, W., ed. The Modern Architectural Setting of the Liturgy. Foreword by F. W. Dillistone. London: SPCK, 1964.

MAGUIRE, Robert, and MURRAY, Keith. "Architecture and Christian Meanings." Studia Liturgica, 1 (1962): 115-127.

Methodist Church (U.S.). Department of Architecture. Sanctuary Planning. Philadelphia, PA: 1967.

MILLS, Edward David. The Modern Church. New York: Praeger, 1956.

NICHOLS, James H., and TRINTERUD, Leonard J. The Architectural Setting for Reformed Worship. Rev. ed. Chicago: Presbytery of Chicago, 1960.

O'CONNELL, J. B. Church Building and Furnishing: The Church's Way, A Study in Liturgical Law. London: Burns & Oates, 1955.

PICHARD, Joseph. Les Eglises nouvelles à travers le monde. Paris: Editions des Deux-Mondes, 1960; Modern Church Architecture. Translated by Ellen Callmann. New York: Orion Press, 1962.

REINHOLD, Hans Ansgar. Speaking of Liturgical Architecture. Notre Dame: Liturgical Programs, University of Notre Dame, 1952; reprint ed., Boston, MA: Daughters of St. Paul, 1961.

ROGUET, A. M. Construire et aménager les églises: programme
d'une église. EsL, 25. Paris: Cerf, 1965.

ROULIN, Eugène A. Nos Eglises: Liturgie, architecture moderne
et contemporaine, mobilier, peinture et sculpture. Paris: P.
Lethielleux, 1938; Modern Church Architecture. Translated by
C. Cornelia Craigie and John A. Southwell. St. Louis, MO:
Herder, 1947.

RYKWERT, Joseph. Church Building. TCEC, 120. New York:
Hawthorn Books, 1965; London: Burns & Oates, 1966.

SCHNELL, H. "Der neue Kirchenbau und die Konzilsberatungen."
Theologie und Glaube, 53 (1963): 292-299.

SCHUBERT, Guilherme. Arte para a fé: igrejas e capelas depois
do Concílio Vaticano II. Petrópolis, Brasil: Vozes, 1979.

SCHWARZ, Rudolf. Kirchenbau: Welt vor der Schwelle. Heidelberg: F. H. Kerle, 1960.

_____. Vom Bau der Kirche. 2. Aufl. Heidelberg: L. Schneid-
er, 1947; The Church Incarnate: The Sacred Function of Christian Architecture. Translated by Cynthia Harris. Chicago:
Henry Regnery, 1958.

SEASOLTZ, R. Kevin. The House of God: Sacred Art and Church
Architecture. New York: Herder & Herder, 1963.

SMITH, Peter F. Third Millenium Churches. London: Galliard,
1972.

SOVIK, Edward A. Architecture for Worship. Minneapolis, MN:
Augsburg, 1973.

SPINDLER, Marc. Pour une théologie de l'espace. CTAP, 59.
Neuchâtel: Delachaux & Niestlé, 1968, 1969.

TEGELS, Aelred. "The Church: House of God's People." Worship,
35 (1961): 494-501.

TURNER, Harold W. From Temple to Meeting House: The Phenom-
enology and Theology of Places of Worship. Religion & Society,
16. The Hague: Mouton, 1979.

VAN LOON, Ralph R. Space for Worship: Some Thoughts on Liturgy, Architecture, Art. Philadelphia, PA: Lutheran Church
in America, 1975.

WEYRES, Willy, and BARTNING, Otto, eds. Kirchen: Handbuch
für den Kirchenbau. München: Callwey, 1959.

XLV. CHURCH FURNISHINGS AND DECORATION

A. GENERAL AND MISCELLANEOUS STUDIES

ANSON, Peter F. Fashions in Church Furnishings, 1840-1940.
London: Faith Press, 1960.

BOND, Francis. Dedications and Patron Saints of English Churches.
London: Oxford University Press, 1914.

_____. Wood Carvings in English Churches. 2 vols. London,
New York: H. Frowde, 1910- .

COX, J. Charles. Bench Ends in English Churches. London: Oxford University Press, 1916.

_____. English Church Fittings, Furniture and Accessories.
London: B. T. Batsford, 1923.

_____. Pulpits, Lecterns and Organs in English Churches. Lon-
don: Oxford University Press, 1915.

DIRSZTAY, Patricia. Church Furnishings: A NADFAS Guide.
London: Routledge & Kegan Paul, 1978.

DURET, D. Mobilier, vases, objets et vêtements liturgiques.
Paris: Letouzey & Ané, 1932.

HENZE, Anton. Das Kunsthandwerk im Dienste der Kirche. Aschaffenburg: P. Pattloch, 1963.

HOWARD, Frank E., and CROSSLEY, F. H. English Church Wood-
work: A Study in Craftsmanship during the Medieval Period,
A.D. 1250-1550. 2d ed. New York: Scribner, 1927.

LEGG, J. Wickham. Church Ornaments and their Civil Antecedents.
CHLS. Cambridge: Cambridge University Press, 1917.

LESAGE, Robert. Objets et habits liturgiques. Paris: Fayard,
1958; Vestments and Church Furniture. Translated by Fergus
Murphy. New York: Hawthorn Books, 1960.

MacCOLL, Malcolm. The Royal Commission and the Ornaments Rubric. London: Longmans, Green, 1906.

MUNDELL, Marlia. "Monophysite Church Decoration." In Iconoclasm: Papers given at the Ninth Spring Symposium of Byzantine Studies, University of Birmingham, 1975, pp. 59-74.
Edited by Anthony Bryer and Judith Herrin. Birmingham,

Eng.: Centre for Byzantine Studies, University of Birmingham, 1977.

NEALE, John Mason. The History of Pues. 3d ed. Cambridge: Stevenson, 1843.

POCKNEE, Cyril E. Cross and Crucifix in Christian Worship and Devotion. London: Mowbray, 1962.

RANDALL, Gerald. Church Furnishing and Decoration in England and Wales. New York: Holmes & Meier; London: Batsford, 1980.

ROHAULT DE FLEURY, Charles. La Messe: études archéologiques sur ses monuments. 8 vols. Paris: Morel, 1883-1889.

SOWERS, Robert. Stained Glass: An Architectural Art. New York: Universe Books, 1965.

WALTERS, Henry Beauchamp. Church Bells. ACh. London: Mowbray, 1908.

_____. The Church Bells of England. London: Frowde, 1912.

Warham Guild. The Warham Guild Handbook: Historical and Descriptive Notes on "Ornaments of the Church and the Ministers Thereof." 2d ed. London: Mowbray, 1963.

B. ALTARS AND CHANCELS

BISHOP, Edmund. "On the History of the Christian Altar." In his Liturgica Historica, pp. 20-38. Oxford: Clarendon Press, 1918.

BOND, Francis. The Chancel of English Churches: The Altar, Reredos, Lenten Veil, Communion Table, Altar Rails, Houseling Cloth, Piscina, Credence, Sedilia, Aumbry, Sacrament House, Easter Sepulchre, Squint, etc. London: Oxford University Press, 1916.

BRAUN, Joseph. Der christliche Altar in seiner geschichtlichen Entwicklung. 2 vols. München: Alte Meister Guenther Koch, 1924.

_____. Das christliche Altargerät in seinem Sein und in seiner Entwicklung. München: M. Hueber, 1932; reprint ed., Hildesheim: Georg Olms, 1973.

COMPER, John Ninian. Of the Christian Altar and the Buildings which Contain It. London: SPCK, 1950.

HOPE, W. H. St. John, ed. English Altars from Illuminated Manuscripts. ACC, 1. London: Longmans, Green, 1899.

KING, Harold C. The Chancel and the Altar. ACh, 8. London:
Mowbray, 1911.

NUSSBAUM, Otto. Der Standort des Liturgen am christlichen Altar
vor dem Jahre 1000: eine archäologische und liturgiegeschichtliche Untersuchung. 2 vols. Bonn: Hanstein, 1965.

POCKNEE, Cyril E. The Christian Altar in History and Today.
London: Mowbray, 1963.

WEBB, Geoffrey. The Liturgical Altar. 2d ed. London: Burns,
Oates & Washbourne, 1939; reprint ed., Westminster, MD:
Newman Press, 1949.

C. BAPTISTERIES AND FONTS

BEDARD, Walter Maurice. The Symbolism of the Baptismal Font in
Early Christian Thought. SST, 2d Ser., 45. Washington, DC:
Catholic University of America Press, 1951.

BOND, Francis. Fonts and Font Covers. London: H. Frowde,
1908.

CORBLET, J. "Des lieux consacrés à l'administration du baptême."
Revue de l'art chrétien, 23 (1877): 276-281; 24 (1877): 112-
182, 300-310; 25 (1878): 26-49, 275-316.

DOLGER, Franz Joseph. "Zur Symbolik des altchristlichen Tauf-
hauses." In his Antike und Christentum, Bd. 4, pp. 153-187.
Münster: Aschendorff, 1934.

KHATCHATRIAN, Armen. Les Baptistères paléochrétiens: plans,
notices et bibliographie. Paris: n.p., 1962.

ROGERS, C. F. "Baptism and Christian Archaeology." Studia biblica et ecclesiastica, 5 (1903): 239-361.

TYRRELL-GREEN, Edmund. Baptismal Fonts, Classified and Illustrated. London: SPCK; New York: Macmillan, 1928.

D. SCREENS AND ICONOSTASES

BOND, Francis. Screens and Galleries in English Churches. London, New York: H. Frowde, 1908.

HALL, Marcia B. "The Italian Rood Screen: Some Implications for
    Liturgy and Function." In Essays Presented to Myron P. Gil-
    more, vol. 2, pp. 213-218. Edited by Sergio Bertelli and Gloria
    Ramakus. Florence: La Nuova Halia Editrice, 1978.

HOLL, Karl. "Die Entstehung der Bilderwand in der griechischen
    Kirche." Archiv für Religionswissenschaft, 9 (1906): 365-384.

OUSPENSKY, Leonide. "The Problem of the Iconostasis." St.
    Vladimir's Seminary Quarterly, 8 (1964): 186-218.

PACE, B. "Nuova ipotesi sull' origine dell' iconostasio." Byzantion,
    19 (1949): 195-205.

VALLANCE, Aymer. English Church Screens. New York: Scrib-
    ner; London: Batsford, 1936.

_____. Greater English Church Screens. London: Batsford,
    1947.

WALTER, Julian. "The Origin of the Iconostasis." Eastern
    Churches Review, 3 (1970-1971): 251-267.

E. ICONS

BREHIER, Louis. La Querelle des images: VIIIe-IXe siècles.
    Paris: Bloud & Cie, 1904.

DIRKS, Ildefonse. Les Saintes icones. 2. éd. Belgique: Prieuré
    d'Amay-sur-Meuse, 1939.

EVDOKIMOV, Paul. "Initiation à l'icone." In his L'Orthodoxie, pp.
    216-238. Neuchâtel: Delachaux & Niestlé, 1959.

FELICETTI-LIEBENFELS, Walter. Geschichte der byzantinischen
    Ikonenmalerei von ihren Anfängen bus zum Ausklänge, unter
    Berücksichtigung der maniera greca und der italo-byzantinischen
    Schule. Olten: Urs-Graf-Verlag, 1956.

FLOROVSKY, Georges. "Origen, Eusebius and the Iconoclastic
    Controversy." Church History, 19 (1950): 77-96.

GALAVARIS, George. The Icon in the Life of the Church: Doc-
    trine, Liturgy, Devotion. IR, 24/8. Leiden: Brill, 1981.

GRABAR, André. L'Iconoclasme byzantin: dossier archéologique.
    Paris: Collège de France, 1957.

_____. La Peinture byzantine: étude historique et critique.

Genève: Skira, 1953; Byzantine Painting: Historical and
Critical Study. Translated by Stuart Gilbert. Geneva: Skira,
1953.

JOHN OF DAMASCUS. On the Divine Images: Three Apologies
Against Those who Attack the Divine Images. Translated by
David Anderson. Crestwood, NY: St. Vladimir's Seminary
Press, 1980.

KITZINGER, Ernst. "The Cult of Images in the Age before Iconoclasm." In Dumbarton Oaks Papers, Number 8, pp. 83-150.
Washington, DC: Trustees for Harvard University, The Dumbarton Oaks Center for Byzantine Studies, 1954.

KONDAKOV, Nikodim Pavlovich. L'Icone russe. 4 vols. Prague:
Seminarium Kondakovianum, 1928-1933; The Russian Icon. 4
vols. in 3. Partially translated by Ellis H. Minns. Prague:
Seminarium Kondakovianum, 1928-1933.

_____. The Russian Icon. Translated by Ellis H. Minns.
Abridged from the Russian Original. Oxford: Clarendon
Press, 1927.

KOTTER, P. Bonifatius, ed. Die Schriften des Johannes von
Damaskos. Vol. 3: Contra imaginum calumniatores orationes
tres. PTS, 17. Berlin: De Gruyter, 1975.

LASAREFF [LAZAREV], Victor. Russian Icons from the Twelfth to
the Fifteenth Century. London: Collins; New York: New
American Library of World Literature, 1962.

MARTIN, Edward James. A History of the Iconoclastic Controversy.
CHS. London: SPCK; New York: Macmillan, 1930.

MURATOV, Pavel Pavlovich. Les Icones russes. Paris: J. Schif-
frin, Editions de la Pléiade, 1927.

ONASCH, Konrad. Ikonen. Gütersloh: Gütersloher Verlagshaus,
1961; Icons. Translated by Marianne von Herzfeld, rev. by
Talbot Rice. New York: Barnes; London: Faber & Faber,
1963.

OSTROGORSKY, Georg. Studien zur Geschichte des byzantinischen
Bilderstreites. Breslau: Marcus, 1929; reprint ed., HU, 5.
Amsterdam: Hakkert, 1964.

OUSPENSKY, Léonide. Essai sur la théologie de l'icone dans l'Eglise orthodoxe. Paris: Editions de l'Exarchat patriarcal russe
en Europe occidentale, 1960; Theology of the Icon. Translated
by Elizabeth Meyendorff. Crestwood, NY: St. Vladimir's
Seminary Press, 1978.

_____. La Théologie de l'icone dans l'Eglise orthodoxe. Paris:
Cerf, 1980.

_____, and LOSSKY, Vladimir. Der Sinn der Ikonen. Bern:
Urs Graf-Verlag, 1952; The Meaning of Icons. Translated by
G. E. H. Palmer and E. Kadloubovsky. Boston, MA: Book
and Art Shop, 1952, 1969.

RICE, D. Talbot. Russian Icons. London: Penguin Books, 1947.

ST. THEODORE THE STUDITE. On the Holy Icons. Translated by
Catharine P. Roth. Crestwood, NY: St. Vladimir's Seminary
Press, 1981.

SCHWARZLOSE, Karl. Der Bilderstreit: ein Kampf der griechischen
Kirche um ihre Eigenart und ihre Freiheit. Gotha: F. A.
Perthes, 1890.

STUART, John. Ikons. London: Faber, 1975.

THEUNISSEN, Wilhelmus Petrus. Ikonen: historisch, aesthetisch
en theologisch belicht. 's-Gravenhage: Servire, 1948.

THON, Nikolaus. Ikone und Liturgie. Trier: Paulinus-Verlag,
1979.

TRUBETSKOI, Eugene. Umozrenie v kraskakh. Moscow: Sytina,
1916; reprint ed., Tri ocherka o russkoi ikone. Paris: YMCA
Press, 1965; Icons: Theology in Color. New York: St. Vladimir's Seminary Press, 1973.

WEITZMANN, Kurt. The Icon: Holy Images--Sixth to Fourteenth
Century. New York: Braziller, 1978.

WEITZMANN, Kurt, ALIBEGASVILI, Gaiané, VOLSKAJA, Aneli,
CHATZIDAKIS, Manolis, BABIC, Gordana, ALPATOV, Mihail,
and VOINESCU, Teodora. Le Icone. Milan: Mondadori, 1981;
The Icon. New York: Knopf, 1982.

WEITZMANN, Kurt, et al. Ikone sa Balkana: Sinaj, Grčka, Bug-
arska, Jugoslavija. Beograd: Bugarski hudoznik, 1970; Icons
from South Eastern Europe and Sinai. Translated by R. E.
Wolf. London: Thames & Hudson, 1968.

WULFF, Oskar, and ALPATOFF, Michael. Denkmäler der Ikonen-
malerei in kunstgeschichtlicher Folge. Hellerau bei Dresden:
Avalun-Verlag; Leipzig: K. W. Hiersemann, 1925.

F.   CHURCH PLATE AND VESSELS

ELBERN, Victor Heinrich. Der eucharistische Kelch im frühen Mittelalter. Berlin: Deutscher Verein für Kunstwissenschaft,
1964.

Eucharistic Vessels of the Middle Ages. Cambridge, MA: Busch-
Reisinger Museum, 1975.

GILCHRIST, James. Anglican Church Plate. London: Connois-
seur; M. Joseph, 1967.

OMAN, Charles Chichele. English Church Plate, 597-1830. London, New York: Oxford University Press, 1957.

G.   LIGHTS

BISHOP, Edmund. "Of Six Candles on the Altar: An Enquiry."
In his Liturgica Historica, pp. 301-313. Oxford: Clarendon
Press, 1918; reprinted 1962.

DENDY, D. R. The Use of Lights in Christian Worship. London:
SPCK, 1959.

MUHLBAUER, Wolfgang. Geschichte und Bedeutung der (Wachs-)
Lichter bei den kirchlichen Funktionen. Augsburg: Kranz-
felder'schen Buchhandlung, 1874.

H.   INCENSE

ATCHLEY, Edward G. C. F. A History of the Use of Incense in
Divine Worship. ACC, 13. London: Longmans, 1909.

CONNOLLY, Peter. "The Use of Incense in the Roman Liturgy."
Ephemerides Liturgicae, 43 (1929): 171-176.

CROSS, F. L. "Incense." Oxford Dictionary of the Christian
Church, p. 685.

FEHRENBACH, E. "Encense." Dictionnaire d'archéologie chrétien
et de liturgie, 5:2-21.

FORCADELL, A. M. "El incenso en la liturgia cristiana." Liturgia,
10 (1955): 219-225.

FRERE, Walter H. "Notes on the Early History of the Use of

Incense." In The Case for Incense, pp. 43-86. Edited by
Henry Westall. London: Longmans, 1899.

GRISBROOKE, W. Jardine. "Incense." A Dictionary of Liturgy
and Worship, pp. 196-198.

McCANCE, M. "Incense." New Catholic Encyclopedia, 7:417-419.

McCARTHY, Scott. "Holy Smoke." Liturgy, 23, 1 (January 1978):
25-26.

MEYER, Mangan. "Incense: Cents and/or Sense." Priest, 29, 11
(1973): 31-34.

WESTALL, Henry. The Case for Incense submitted to His Grace
the Archbishop of Canterbury on behalf of the Rev. H. Westall
on Monday, May 8, 1899, together with a Legal Argument and
the Appendices of the Experts. London: Longmans, Green,
1899.

XLVI. VESTMENTS AND OTHER ECCLESIASTICAL CLOTHWORK

BAUDOT, Jules. Le Pallium. 3e éd. Paris: Bloud & Cie, 1909.

BISHOP, Edmund. "Origins of the Cope as a Church Vestment."
In his Liturgica Historica, pp. 260-275. Oxford: Clarendon
Press, 1918; reprinted 1962.

BOCK, Franz. Geschichte der liturgischen Gewänder des Mittelalters. 3 vols. Bonn: Henry & Cohen, 1859-1871; reprint ed.,
Graz: Akademische Druck- und Verlagsanstalt, 1970.

BRAUN, Joseph. Die liturgische Gewandung im Occident und Orient nach Ursprung und Entwicklung, Verwendung und Symbolik. Freiburg: Herder, 1907; reprint ed., Darmstadt:
Wissenschaftliche Buchgesellschaft, 1964.

_____. Die liturgischen Paramente in Gegenwart und Vergangen-
heit. 2. Aufl. Freiburg: Herder, 1924.

BURMESTER, O. H. E. "Vesting Prayers and Ceremonies of the
Coptic Church." Orientalia Christiana Periodica, 1 (1935):
305-314.

CHRYSOSTOMOS, Archimandrite. "Historiographical Problematics in
the Study of the Origin of Liturgical Vesture." Greek Orthodox
Theological Review, 26 (1981): 87-96.

CLAYTON, Henry J.   Cassock and Gown.   ACT, 18.   London: Oxford University Press, 1929.

Convocation of Canterbury.   The Ornaments of the Church and Its Ministers (Upper Hosue Report 416).   London: SPCK, 1908.

DEAN, Beryl.   Ecclesiastical Embroidery.   London   Batsford; Boston, MA: Charles T. Branford, 1958.

DEARMER, Percy.   "Church Vestments."   In Essays on Ceremonial, pp. 176-204.   London: De La More Press, 1904.

_____.   Linen Ornaments of the Church.   2d ed.   ACT, 17. London: Mowbray, 1950.

_____.   The Ornaments of the Ministers.   New ed.   ACh, 1. London: Mowbray; Milwaukee, WI: Morehouse, 1920.

DURANTIS, Gulielmus.   The Sacred Vestments: An English Rendering of the Third Book of the Rationale divinorum officiorum of Durandus, Bishop of Mende.   Translated, with notes, by T. H. Passmore.   London: Sampson, Low, Marston, 1899.

FLUELER, Maria Augustina.   Das sakrale Gewand.   SK, 8.   Würzburg: Echter Verlag, 1964.

FORTESCUE, Adrian.   The Vestments of the Roman Rite.   New York: Paulist Press, 1912.

GEE, Henry.   The Elizabethan Prayer Book and Ornaments.   London: Macmillan, 1902.

GONZALEZ, Arthur E. John.   "The Byzantine Imperial Paradigm and Eastern Liturgical Vesture."   The Greek Orthodox Theological Review, 17 (1972):   255-267.

_____.   "Further Commentary on the Byzantine Imperial Prototype and Eastern Liturgical Vesture."   The Greek Orthodox Theological Review, 21 (1976):   71-84.

HANDS, Hinda M.   Church Needlework: A Manual of Practical Instruction.   4th ed.   London: Faith Press; Milwaukee, WI: Morehouse, 1929.

HAULOTTE, Edgar.   La Symbolique du vêtement selon le Bible. Théologie, 65.   Paris: Aubier, 1966.

HENZE, Anton.   Das Kunsthandwerk im Dienste der Kirche.   Der Christ in der Welt, 15/8.   Aschaffenburg: P. pattloch, 1963.

IRELAND, Marion P.   Textile Art in the Church: Vestments,

Paraments, and Hangings in Contemporary Worship, Art, and
Architecture. Nashville, TN: Abingdon Press, 1971.

JAMES, Raymund. The Origin and Development of Roman Liturgical
Vestments. 2d ed. Exeter, Eng.: Catholic Records Press,
1934.

JOHNSTONE, Pauline. The Byzantine Tradition in Church Embroidery. Chicago: Argonaut, 1967.

LEGG, J. Wickham. Church Ornaments and their Civil Antecedents.
CHLS. Cambridge: Cambridge University Press, 1917.

LEMPIAINEN, Pentti. "The Ministrant's Garb in Divine Worship in
the Evangelical Lutheran Church of Finland." In Ecclesia,
Leiturgia, Ministerium: Studia in honorem Toivo Harjunpää,
pp. 57-67. Redactores Martti Parvio, Eric Segelberg, Jan L.
Womer. Editionem curavit Seppo Suokunnas. Helsinki: Loi-
mann Kirjapaino, 1977.

MACALISTER, R. A. S. Ecclesiastical Vestments: Their Development and History. London: Stock, 1896.

MAGISTRETTI, M. Delle vesti ecclesiastiche in Milano. 2. ed.
Milan: n.p., 1905.

MARRIOTT, Wharton Booth. Vestiarum Christianum: The Origin
and Gradual Development of the Dress of the Holy Ministry in
the Church. London: Rivington, 1868.

MAYER-THURMAN, Christa C. Raiment for the Lord's Service:
A Thousand Years of Western Vestments. Chicago: Art Institute of Chicago, 1975.

MICKLETHWAITE, J. T. The Ornaments of the Rubric. 3d ed.
ACT, 1. London: Longmans, Green, 1901.

MINCHIN, Basil. Outward and Visible. London: Darton, Longman
& Todd, 1961.

MUYLDERMANS, J. "Le Costume liturgique arménien: étude historique." Le Muséon, 39 (1926): 253-334; offprint ed., Louvain: J. B. Istas, 1926.

NEFF, Elizabeth Clifford. An Anglican Study in Christian Symbolism. Cleveland, OH: Helman-Taylor, 1898.

NORRIS, Herbert. Church Vestments, Their Origin and Development. London: Dent, 1949; New York: Dutton, 1950.

PAPAS, Tano. Studien zur Geschichte der Messgewänder im

byzantinischen Ritus. MBM, 3. München: Institut für Byzantinistik und neugriechische Philologie der Universität München,
1965.

PIEPKORN, Arthur Carl. The Survival of the Historic Vestments
in the Lutheran Church after 1555. St. Louis, MO: School
for Graduate Studies, Concordia Seminary, 1956.

POCKNEE, Cyril E. Liturgical Vesture: Its Origins and Development. Westminster, MD: Canterbury Press, 1961.

PRIMUS, John H. The Vestments Controversy: An Historical
Study of the Earliest Tensions within the Church in England
in the Reigns of Edward VI and Elizabeth. Kampen: Kok,
1960.

PUGIN, A. Welby. Glossary of Ecclesiastical Ornament and Costume. 3d ed. London: B. Quaritch, 1848.

RAMSEY, B. M. "The Chasuble: Its History and Development to
the Present Day." M.S. thesis, University of Tennessee,
1972.

ROBINSON, N. F. "Concerning Three Eucharistic Veils of Western
Use." Transactions of the St. Paul's Ecclesiological Society,
6 (1906-1910): 129-160.

ROULIN, Eugène A. Linges, insignes et vêtements liturgiques.
Paris: Lethielleux, 1930; Vestments and Vesture: A Manual
of Liturgical Art. Translated by Justin McCann. Westminster,
MD: Newman Press, 1950.

SALMON, Pierre. Etude sur les insignes du pontife dans le rite
romain: histoire et liturgie. Rome: Officium Libri Catholici,
1955.

TRENKLE, Elisabeth. Liturgische Geräte und Gewänder der Ostkirche. München: Slavisches Institut, 1962.

WARHAM GUILD. The Warham Guild Handbook: Historical and
Descriptive Notes on "Ornaments of the Church and the Ministers Thereof." 2d ed. London: Mowbray, 1963.

XLVII.   LITURGICAL COLORS

COPE, G. F. "Liturgical Colours." Studia Liturgica, 7 (1970):
40-49.

HOPE, William St. John, and ATCHLEY, E. G. Cuthbert F. English Liturgical Colours. London: SPCK; New York: Macmillan, 1918.

_____. An Introduction to English Liturgical Colours. London: SPCK; New York: Macmillan, 1920.

LEGG, J. Wickham. Notes on the History of the Liturgical Colours. London: J. S. Leslie, 1882.

XLVIII. LITURGICAL DANCE AND DRAMA

[Bibliography of Medieval liturgical drama, see:] The New Cambridge Bibliography of English Literature, vol. 1, cols. 721-726. Cambridge: Cambridge University Press, 1974.

ADAMS, Doug. Congregational Dancing in Christian Worship. Rev. ed. Austin: The Sharing Co., 1980.

ALEXANDER, Ryllis Clair, and GOSLIN, Omar Pancoast. Worship through Drama. New York: Harper, 1930.

BACKMAN, E. Louis. Den religiösa dansen inom kristen kyrka och folk-medicin. Stockholm: Norstedt, 1945; Religious Dances in the Christian Church and in Popular Medicine. Translated by E. Classen. London: Allen & Unwin, 1952.

CARGILL, Oscar. Drama and Liturgy. CUSECL. New York: Columbia University Press, 1930; reprint ed., New York: Octagon Books, 1969.

CHALLINGSWORTH, Nell. Liturgical Dance Movement: A Practical Guide. London: Mowbray, 1982.

DAVIES, John G., ed. Worship and Dance. Birmingham, Eng.: University of Birmingham, Institute for the Study of Worship and Religious Architecture, 1975.

DEISS, Lucien, and WEYMAN, Gloria Gabriel. Dancing for God. Cincinanti, OH: World Library of Sacred Music, 1969.

DE SOLA, Carla. The Spirit Moves: A Handbook of Dance and Prayer. Washington, DC: Liturgical Conference, 1977.

FOATELLI, Renée. Les Danses religieuses dans le christianisme. Paris: Spes, 1947.

HARDISON, O. B. Christian Rite and Christian Drama in the Middle Ages. Baltimore, MD: Johns Hopkins Press, 1965.

JOHNSON, Albert. Best Church Plays: A Bibliography of Religious
    Drama. Philadelphia, PA: Pilgrim Press, 1968.

LONG, Anne. Praise Him in the Dance. London: Hodder &
    Stoughton, 1976.

MEAD, G. R. S. The Sacred Dance in Christendom. Quest Re-
    print Series, 2. London: John M. Watkins, 1926.

MERCHANT, William Moelwyn. Creed and Drama: An essay in Re-
    ligious Drama. London: SPCK, 1965.

OESTERLEY, W. O. E. The Sacred Dance: A Study in Compara-
    tive Folklore. New York: Macmillan, 1923.

TAYLOR, Margaret Fisk. A Time To Dance: Symbolic Movement in
    Worship. Philadelphia, PA: United Church Press, 1967.

PART SIX:

CHURCH MUSIC AND HYMNOLOGY

XLIX. CHURCH MUSIC IN GENERAL

A. REFERENCE WORKS

BUSZIN, Walter E., FINNEY, Theodore M., and McCORKLE, Donald M. A Bibliography on Music and the Church. New York: National Council of the Churches of Christ, Department of Worship and the Arts, 1958.

CARROLL, Joseph Robert. Compendium of Liturgical Musical Terms. Toledo, OH: Gregorian Institute of America, 1964.

CUNNINGHAM, W. Patrick, ed. The Music Locator. Saratoga, CA: Resource Publications, 1976.

DAVIDSON, James Robert. A Dictionary of Protestant Church Music. Metuchen, NJ: Scarecrow Press, 1975.

FRERE, Walter Howard, ed. Bibliotheca Musico-Liturgica: A Descriptive Handlist of the Musical and Latin-liturgical MSS. of the Middle Ages Preserved in the Libraries of Great Britain and Ireland. For the Plainsong and Mediaeval Music Society. London: Quaritch, 1901-1932; reprint ed., Hildesheim: G. Olms, 1967.

GROVE, George, and BLOM, Eric, eds. Dictionary of Music and Musicians, 1450-1880. 10 vols. New York: St. Martin's Press, 1954-1961.

The New Grove Dictionary of Music and Musicians. Edited by Stanley Sadie. 20 vols. London: Macmillan, 1980.

HUGHES, Anselm. Liturgical Terms for Music Students: A

Dictionary. Boston: McLaughlin & Reilly, 1940; reprint ed.,
St. Claire Shores, MI: Scholarly Press, 1972.

JACKSON, Irene V. Afro-American Religious Music: A Bibliography and a Catalogue of Gospel Music. Westport, CT: Greenwood Press, 1979.

KORMULLER, Utto. Lexikon der kirchlichen Tonkunst. Regensburg: Coppenrath, 1891, 1895; reprint ed., Hildesheim: G.
Olms, 1975.

KUMMERLE, Salomon. Encycklopädie der evangelischen Kirchenmusik. 4 vols. Gütersloh: Bertelsmann, 1888-1895; reprint
ed., Hildesheim: G. Olms, 1974.

METCALF, Frank J., ed. American Psalmody; or, Titles of Books
containing Tunes Printed in America from 1721-1820. New
York: C. F. Heartman, 1917; reprint ed., New York: Da
Capo Press, 1968.

MEYER-BAER, Kathi. Liturgical Music Incunabula: A Descriptive
Catalogue. London: The Bibliographical Society, 1962.

ORTIQUE, Joseph Louis d'. Dictionnaire liturgique, historique et
theorique de plainchant et de musique d'église. Paris: J. P.
Migne, 1853; reprint ed., New York: Da Capo Press, 1971.

PORTE, Jacques, ed. Encyclopédie des musiques sacrées. 3 vols.
Paris: Editions Lagergerie, 1968- .

ROSSLER, Martin. Bibliographie der deutschen Liedpredigt. BHR,
19. Nieuwkoop: de Graaf, 1976.

SCHALK, Carl, ed. Key Words in Church Music. St. Louis, MO:
Concordia, 1978.

VON ENDE, Richard C. Church Music: An International Bibliography. Metuchen, NJ: Scarecrow Press, 1980.

WARRINGTON, James. Short Titles of Books Relating to or Illustrating the History and Practice of Psalmody in the U.S.,
1620-1820. Philadelphia, PA: privately printed, 1898; reprint
ed., New York: B. Franklin, 1971.

YEATS-EDWARDS, Paul. English Church Music: A Bibliography.
London: White Lion, 1975.

B. GENERAL HISTORIES AND TEXTBOOKS

DANIEL, R. B. Chapters on Church Music. London: Elliot Stock, 1894.

DAVISON, Archibald T. Church Music: Illusion & Reality. Cambridge, MA: Harvard University Press, 1952.

DICKINSON, Edward. Music in the History of the Western Church. New York: Scribner, 1903; reprint ed., New York: AMS Press, 1970.

DOUGLAS, Winfred. Church Music in History and Practice. Revised with additional material prepared by Leonard Ellinwood. New York: Scribner, 1962.

EKVALL, Bo. Från gregoriansk sang till Bach. Tio sammankomster kring några verk ur kyrkomusikens historia. Stockholm: Verbum, 1967.

GELINEAU, Joseph. Chant et musique dans le culte chrétien. Paris: Editions Fleurus, 1962; Voices and Instruments in Christian Worship. Translated by Clifford Howell. Collegeville, MN: Liturgical Press, 1964.

_____. "Music and Singing in the Liturgy." In The Study of Liturgy, pp. 440-454. Edited by Cheslyn Jones, Geoffrey Wainwright, Edward Yarnold. New York: Oxford University Press, 1978.

HUMPHREYS, Francis L. The Evolution of Church Music. New York: Scribner, 1896.

HUOT-PLEUROUX, Paul. Histoire de la musique religieuse des origines à nos jours. Préface de Norbert Dufourcq. Paris: Presses Universitaires, 1957.

HUTCHINGS, Arthur. Church Music in the Nineteenth Century. London: Jenkins, 1967; reprint ed., Westport, CT: Greenwood Press, 1977.

LEEUW, Gerardus van der. Beknopte geschiedenis van het kerklied. Met medewerking van K. Ph. Bernet Kempers. 2. druk. Groningen: J. B. Wolters, 1948.

MEARNS, James. The Canticles of the Christian Church, Eastern and Western, in Early and Medieval Times. Cambridge: Cambridge University Press, 1914.

MEHRTENS, Frits. Kerk & Muziek. 2. druk. 's-Gravenhage: Boekencentrum, 1961.

The New Oxford History of Music. London: Oxford University
Press, 1954- .

PHILLIPS, C. H. The Singing Church: An Outline History of the
Music Sung by Choir and People. New ed. prepared by Arthur
Hutchings. London: Faber, 1968.

PRATT, Waldo Selden. The History of Music. Revised ed. New
York: Schirmer, 1942.

REDLICH, Hans F. "Early Baroque Church Music." In The New
Oxford History of Music, vol. 4, pp. 520-549. New York:
Oxford University Press, 1954- .

RICE, William Carroll. A Concise History of Church Music. New
York: Abingdon Press, 1964.

ROBERTSON, Alec. Sacred Music. London: Max Parrish, 1950.

ROUTLEY, Erik. The Church and Music: An Enquiry into the
History, the Nature, and the Scope of Christian Judgment on
Music. Revised ed. London: Duckworth, 1967.

_____. Music, Sacred and Profane. London: Independent
Press, 1960.

_____. Twentieth Century Church Music. New York: Oxford
University Press, 1964.

SOHNGEN, Oskar. Musica sacra zwischen gestern und morgen.
2. Aufl. Göttingen: Vandenhoeck & Ruprecht, 1981.

SQUIRE, Russel Nelson. Church Music, Musical and Hymnological
Developments in Western Christianity. St. Louis, MO: Bethany
Press, 1962.

STEWART, G. Wauchope. Music in Church Worship. London:
Hodder & Stoughton, 1926.

C. PRACTICAL AND CRITICAL STUDIES

BECKER, Hansjakolo, and KACZYNSKI, Reiner, eds. Liturgie und
Dichtung: ein Interdisziplinäres Kompendium. 2 Bde. Pietas
liturgica, 1-2. Sankt Ottilien: EOS Verlag Erzabtei St. Ottilien, 1983.

BLANKENBURG, Walter, HOFMANN, Friedrich, and HUBNER, Erich,
eds. Kirchenmusik im Spannungsfeld der Gegenwart. Kassel:
Bärenreiter, 1968.

BLISSENBACH, Wolfgang. Musik in Bibel und Gemeinde. Erz-
hausen: Leuchter-Verlag, 1975.

DAKERS, Lionel. Church Music at the Crossroads: A Forward
Looking Guide for Today. Foreword by Gerald H. Knight.
London: Marshall Morgan and Scott, 1970.

ELLSWORTH, Donald Paul. Christian Music in Contemporary Wit-
ness: Historical Antecedents and Contemporary Practices.
Grand Rapids, MI: Baker, 1979.

HOOPER, William Lloyd. Church Music in Transition. Nashville,
TN: Broadman Press, 1963.

KAPPNER, Gerhard. "The Church Service and Music." Scottish
Journal of Theology, 12 (1959): 243-256.

LOVELACE, Austin C., and RICE, William C. Music and Worship
in the Church. Revised and enl. ed. Nashville, TN: Abingdon Press, 1976.

MARTIN, Emile. Une Muse en péril: essai sur la musique et le
sacré. Paris: Fayard, 1968.

MITCHELL, Robert H. Ministry and Music. Philadelphia, PA:
Westminster Press, 1978.

PRATT, Waldo Selden. Musical Ministries in the Church: Studies
in the History, Theory, and Administration of Sacred Music.
New York: Schirmer, 1923; reprint ed., New York: AMS
Press, 1976.

RIEDEL, Johannes. "The New and the Old in Church Music."
Studia Liturgica, 5 (1966): 104-120, 151-165.

ROHRING, Klaus. Neue Musik in der Welt des Christentums.
München: Kaiser, 1975.

ROUTLEY, Erik. Music Leadership in the Church. Nashville, TN:
Abingdon Press, 1966.

_____. Words, Music and the Church. Nashville, TN: Abing-
don Press, 1968.

SOHNGEN, Oskar. Die Erneuerungskräfte der Kirchenmusik unserer Tage. Berlin: Evangelische Verlagsanstalt, 1949.

STAPLETON, Peter. New Directions for a Musical Church. Atlanta,
GA: John Knox Press, 1975.

WILLS, Arthur. "Emotion in Music." The Franciscan, 10 (1968):
210-212.

D. THEOLOGICAL STUDIES

FELLERER, Karl Gustav. Soziologie der Kirchenmusik: Materialen
zur Musik- und Religionssoziologie. Köln: Westdeutscher Verlag, 1963.

HOON, Paul W. "The Relation of Theology and Music in Worship."
Union Seminary Quarterly Review, 11, 2 (January 1956): 33-43.

KRAHE, Maria-Judith. "Psalmen, Hymnen und Lieder, wie der
Geist sie eingibt: Doxologie als Ursprung und Ziel aller Theo-
logie." In Liturgie und Dichtung, 2. Bd., pp. 923-957. Her-
ausgegeben von Hansjakob Becker und Reiner Kaczynski.
Pietas liturgica, 2. Sankt Ottilien: EOS Verlag Ereabtei St.
Ottilien, 1983.

KURZSCHENKEL, Winfried. Die theologische Bestimmung der Musik:
neuere Beiträge zur Deutung und Wertung des Musizierens im
christlichen Leben. Trier: Paulinus-Verlag, 1971.

PIKE, Alfred J. A Theology of Music. Toledo, OH: Gregorian
Institute of America, 1953.

ROUTLEY, Erik. Church Music and the Christian Faith. Foreword
by Martin E. Marty. Carol Stream, IL: Agape, 1978.

_____. Church Music and Theology. SMW, 11. London: SCM
Press, 1959; Philadelphia, PA: Fortress Press, 1965, c1959.

_____. "Church Music and Theology: A Pastoral Footnote."
The Franciscan, 10 (1968): 191-197.

_____. "Theology for Church Musicians." Theology Today, 34
(1977): 20-28.

SOHNGEN, Oskar. Theologie der Musik. Kassel: Stauda Verlag,
1967. [Revised version of "Theologische Grundlagen der
Kirchenmusik," In Leiturgia, vol. 4, pp. 1-267. Herausgegeben von K. F. Müller. Kassel: Stauda, 1961.]

E. SPECIAL STUDIES

BOGLER, Theodor, ed. Sakrale Sprache und kultischer Gesang:
Gesammelte Aufsätze. LM, 37. Maria Laach: Ars Liturgica,
1965.

BLUME, Clemens. "Der Engelhymnus Gloria in excelsis Deo: sein
Ursprung und seine Entwicklung." Stimmen aus Maria Laach,
73 (1907): 43-62.

BURN, A. E. The Hymn "Te Deum" and Its Author. London: Faith Press, 1926.

CLEALL, Charles. Music and Holiness. London: Epworth Press, 1964.

FELDMANN, Fritz. Die schlesische Kirchenmusik im Wandel der Zeiten. Lübeck: Unser Weg, 1975.

FELLOWES, Edmund H. Memoirs of an Amateur Musician. London: Methuen, 1946.

FROGER, P. "Symbolisme de la musique liturgique." La Maison-Dieu, 22 (1950): 146-153.

LEWER, David. A Spiritual Song: The Story of the Temple Choir and a History of Divine Service in the Temple Church, London. London: The Templars' Union, 1961.

LYSONS, Daniel, AMOTT, John, WILLIAMS, C. Lee, and CHANCE, H. Godwin. Origin and Progress of the Meeting of the Three Choirs of Gloucester, Worcester and Hereford, and of the Charity connected with It. Gloucester, Eng.: Chance & Bland, 1895.

MONRO, Mary. "Music in African Worship." The Franciscan, 10 (1968): 206-210.

PALMER, Larry. Hugo Distler and his Church Music. St. Louis, MO: Concordia, 1967.

RIEDEL, Friedrich W. Kirchenmusik am Hofe Karls VI (1711-1740). München: Katzbichler, 1977.

ROUTLEY, Erik. "The Vocabulary of Church Music." Union Seminary Quarterly Review, 18 (1963): 135-147.

_____. Martin Shaw, a Centenary Appreciation. London: E. M. Campbell, 1975.

SCHISLER, Charles Harvey. "A History of Westminster Choir College, 1926-1973." Ph.D. dissertation, Indiana University, 1976.

SMITHER, Howard E. A History of the Oratorio. 2 vols. Chapel Hill, NC: University of North Carolina Press, 1977.

STAPELMANN, Wilhelm. Der Hymnus angelicus: Geschichte und Erklärung des Gloria. Heidelberg: F. H. Kerle, 1948.

TERRY, Richard Runciman. A Forgotten Psalter and Other Essays. London: Oxford University Press, 1929. [The Scottish Psalter, 1635]

WEMAN, Henry. African Music and the Church in Africa. Translated by Eric J. Sharpe. Uppsala: Svenska Institutet för
Missionsforskning, 1960.

WORDSWORTH, John. The "Te Deum": Its Structure and Meaning, and Its Musical Setting and Rendering. London: SPCK,
1903.

L. CHURCH MUSIC IN THE TRADITIONS

A. EARLY CHURCH MUSIC

BRIOSO SANCHEZ, Máximo. Aspectos y problemas del himno cristiano primitivo. Salamanca: Consejo Superior de Investigaciones Cientificas, 1972.

DEICHGRABER, Reinhard. Gotteshymnus und Christushymnus in
der frühen Christenheit. Göttingen: Vandenhoeck & Ruprecht, 1967.

DEISS, Lucien. Hymnes et prières des premiers siècles. Paris:
Editions Fleurus, 1963.

DOLGER, Franz Josef. Sol Salutis: Gebet und Gesang in christlichen Altertum, mit besonderer Rücksicht auf die Ostung in
Gebet und Liturgie. 3. Aufl. Münster: Aschendorff, 1972.

GEROLD, Théodore. Les Pères de l'église et la musique. EHPRC,
25. Paris: Alcan, 1931; reprint ed., Genève: Minkoff, 1973.

HOLLEMAN, A. W. J. "Early Christian Liturgical Music." Studia
Liturgica, 8 (1971-1972): 185-192.

KROLL, Josef. Die christliche Hymnodik bis zu Klemens von Alex-
andreia. Konigsberg: Hartungsche Buchdruckerei, 1921; reprint ed., Darmstadt: Wissenschaftliche Buchgesellschaft, 1968.

LEEB, Helmut. Die Psalmodie bei Ambrosius. WBT, 18. Wien:
Herder, 1967.

LEUPOLD, H. S. "Worship Music in Ancient Israel: Its Meaning
and Purpose." Canadian Journal of Theology, 15 (1969):
176-186.

McKINNON, James William. "The Church Fathers and Musical Instruments." Ph.D. dissertation, Columbia University, 1965.

MESSENGER, Ruth E. Christian Hymns of the First Three Centuries. New York: Hymn Society of America, 1942.

QUASTEN, Johannes. Musik und Gesang in den Kulten der heidnischen Antike und christlichen Frühzeit. LQF, 25. Münster:
Aschendorff, 1930; reprinted, 1973.

ROBINSON, J. M. "Die Hodajot-Formel in Gebet und Hymnus des
Frühchristentums." In Apophoreta: Festschrift für Ernst
Haenchen zu seinem siebzigsten Geburtstag am 10. 1964, pp.
194-236. Herausgegeben von W. Eltester und F. H. Kettler.
Berlin: Töpelmann, 1964.

SANDERS, Jack T. The New Testament Christological Hymns.
Cambridge: Cambridge University Press, 1971.

SCHILLE, Gottfried. Frühchristliche Hymnen. Berlin: Evangelische Verlagsanstalt, 1965.

SENDRY, Alfred. Music in Ancient Israel. New York: Philosophical Library; London: Vision Press, 1969.

SHIRMANN, Jefim. "Hebrew Liturgical Poetry and Christian Hymnology." Jewish Quarterly Review, N.. 44 (1953): 123-161.

SMITH, William Sheppard. Musical Aspects of the New Testament.
Amsterdam: [Vrije Universiteit te Amsterdam], W. ten Have,
1962.

SMOTHERS, E. R. "Phos Hilaron." Recherches de science religieuse, 19 (1929): 266-284.

STAINER, John. The Music of the Bible, with Some Account of the
Development of Modern Musical Instruments from Ancient Types.
New ed., with additional illustrations and supplementary notes
by F. W. Galpin. London: Novello, 1914.

STANLEY, David M. "Carmenque Christo quasi deo dicere...."
Catholic Biblical Quarterly, 20 (1958): 173-191.

THOMPSON, Leonard. "Hymns in Early Christian Worship." Anglican Theological Review, 55 (1973): 458-472.

WENGST, Klaus. Christologische Formeln und Lieder des Urchris-
tentums. Gütersloh: Mohn, 1972.

WERNER, Eric. "The Doxology in Synagogue and Church: A Liturgico-Musical Study." Hebrew Union College Annual, 19
(1945-1946): 275-351.

_____ . The Sacred Bridge: The Interdependence of Liturgy and

Music in the Synagogue and Church during the First Millenium.
New York: Columbia University Press, 1959; reprint ed., New
York: Da Capo Press, 1979; abridged ed., The Sacred Bridge:
Liturgical Parallels in Synagogue and Early Church. New York:
Schocken Books, 1970.

B. EASTERN CHURCH MUSIC

1. Byzantine and Slavic

a. Texts

AYOUTANTI, Aglaïa, and STOHR, Maria, eds. The Hymns of the
Hirmologium. Revised by carsten Höeg. MMB, Transcripta,
6 & 8. Copenhagen: Munksgaard, 1952-1956.

BUGGE, Arne, ed. Contacarium palaeoslavicum Mosquense. MMB,
Facsimilia, 6. Copenhagen: Munksgaard, 1960.

COUTOURIER, A. Liturgie de saint Jean Chrysostome, résponses
du choeur en polyphonie. Paris: Sacristie de l'Eglise Saint-
Julien-le-Pauvre, 1915.

_____. Sylliturgikon; ou, La sainte liturgie byzantine avec les
responses. Jerusalem: Impr. des RR. PP. Franciscains, 1925.

FOLLIERI, Enrica. Initia hymnorum ecclesiae graecae. 5 vols. in
6. ST, 211-215. Città del Vaticano: Biblioteca Apostolica
Vaticana, 1960-1966.

FOLLIERI, Enrica, and STRUNK, Oliver, eds. Triodium Athoum.
1 vol. in 2 pts. MMB, Facsimilia, 9. Copenhagen: Munksgaard, 1975.

HEIMING, Odilo, ed. Syrische 'eniâné' und griechische Kanones:
die Handschrift sach. 349 der Staatsbibliothek zu Berlin.
Münster: Aschendorff, 1932.

HOEG, Carsten, ed. Contacarium Ashburnhamense. MMB, Facsimilia, 4. Copenhagen: Munksgaard, 1956.

_____, ed. Hirmologium Athoum. MMB, Facsimilia, 2. Copen-
hagen: Levin & Munksgaard, 1938.

HOEG, Carsten, TILLYARD, H. J. W., and WELLESZ, Egon, eds.
Sticherarium. MMB, Facsimilia, 1. Copenhagen: Levin &
Munksgaard, 1935.

_____, ZUNTZ, Günther, and ENGBERG, Gudrun, eds.

Prophetologium. 2 vols. (8 fasc.) MMB, Lectionaria, 1.
Copenhagen Munksgaard, 1939-1981.

JAKOBSON, Roman, ed. Fragmenta Chiliandarica palaeoslavica.
2 vols. MMB, Facsimilia, 5. Copenhagen: Munksgaard, 1957.

KIRCHHOFF, Kilian, ed. Hymnen der Ostkirche: Dreifaltigkeits
Marien- und Totenhymnen. 2. Aufl. Überarbeitet und heraus-
gegeben von Chrysologus Schollmeyer. Münster: Verlag
Regensburg, 1960.

MAAS, Paul, ed. Frühbyzantinische Kirchenpoesie. KT, 52-53.
Bonn: Marcus & Weber, 1910- .

MALTZEW, Alexios von, ed. Oktoichos oder Parakletike der orthodox-katholischen Kirche des Morgenlandes. Deutsch und slavisch unter Berücksichtigung der griechischen Urtexte. 2 vols.
Berlin: Siegismund, 1903.

Musical Setting for the Liturgy of St. John Chrysostom. Allendale, PA: Alleluia Press, 1974.

NEALE, John Mason. Hymns of the Eastern Church. London:
J. T. Hayes, 1882; reprint ed., New York: AMS Press, 1971.

RAASTED, Jørgen, ed. Hirmologium Sabbaiticum. 2 vols. in 3.
MMB, Facsimilia, 8. Copenhagen: Munksgaard, 1969-1970.

ROMANUS MELODUS. Cantica. Edited by Paul Maas and C. A.
Trypanis. Oxford: Clarendon Press, 1963; Kontakia of
Romanos, Byzantine Melodist. 2 vols. Translated and anno-
tated by Marjorie Carpenter. Columbia, MO: University of
Missouri Press, 1970-1972.

SCHIRO, G., ed. Analecta hymnica Graeca. Rome: n.p., 1966- .

STRUNK, W. Oliver, ed. Specimina notationum antiquiorum. MMB,
Facsimilia, 7. Copenhagen: Munksgaard, 1966.

TARDO, Lorenzo, ed. Hirmologium Cryptense. MMB, Facsimilia,
3/2. Copenhagen: Munksgaard, 1950.

TILLYARD, H. J. W., ed. The Hymns of the Octoechus. 2 vols.
MMB, Transcripta, 3 & 5. Copenhagen: Levin & Munksgaard,
1940-1949.

_____, ed. The Hymns of the Pentecostarium. MMB, Trans-
cripta, 7. Copenhagen: Munksgaard, 1960.

_____, ed. The Hymns of the Sticherarium for November. MMB,
Transcripta, 2. Copenhagen: Levin & Munksgaard, 1938.

_____, ed. Twenty Canons from the Trinity Hirmologion. MMB,
Transcripta, 4. Copenhagen: Munksgaard, 1952.

TRIPANIS, C. A., ed. Fourteen Early Byzantine Cantica. Wien:
Böhlau, 1968.

WELLESZ, Egon, ed. The Akathistos Hymn. MMB, Transcripta, 9.
Copenhagen: Munksgaard, 1957.

_____, ed. Die Hymnen des Sticherarium für September. MMB,
Transcripta, 1. Copenhagen: Levin & Munksgaard, 1936.

_____, ed. The Music of the Byzantine Church. Anthology of
Music, 13. Köln: Arno Volk Verlag, 1959.

_____, ed. Trésor de musique byzantine. 2 vols. Paris: Edi-
tions de l'Oiseau lyre, chez L. B. M. Dyer, 1934- .

b. Studies

BOGOLEPOV, Alexander A. Orthodox Hymns of Christmas, Holy
Week and Easter. New York: Russian Orthodox Theological
Fund, 1965.

CAVARNOS, Constantine. Byzantine Sacred Music. Belmont, MA:
Institute for Byzantine and Modern Greek Studies, 1956.

CONOMOS, Dimitri E. Byzantine Trisagia and Cheroubika of the
Fourteenth and Fifteenth Centuries: A Study of Late Byzantine
Liturgical Chant. Thessaloniki: Patriarchal Institute for
Patristic Studies, 1974.

GARDNER, Johann von. System und Wesen des russischen Kirchen-
gesanges. Wiesbaden: Harrassowitz, 1976; Russian Church
Singing. Translated by Vladimir Morosan. Scarsdale, NY:
St. Vladimir's Seminary Press, 1980.

GROSDIDIER DE MATONS, José. Romanos le mélode et les origines
de la poésie religieuse à Byzance. Paris: Beauchesne, 1977.

HOEG, Carsten. "Ein Buch altrussischer Kirchengesänge." Zeitschrift für slavische Philologie, 25 (1956): 261-284.

_____. La Notation ekphonétique. MMB, Subsidia, 1/2. Copen-
hagen: Levin & Munksgaard, 1935.

_____. "The Oldest Slavonic Tradition of Byzantine Music."
Proceedings of the British Academy, 39 (1953): 37-66.

HUGLO, M. "Les Chants de la Missa Graeca de Saint Denis." In
Essays Presented to Egon Wellesz, pp. 74-83. Edited by J.
Westrup. London: Oxford University Press, 1966.

KOSCHMEIDER, Erwin. "Byzantinische Elemente in der frühen
slawischen Kirchenmusik." In Bericht über den Neunten In-
ternationalen Kongres Salzburg 1964, vol. 2, pp. 167-175.
Vorgelegt von Franz Giegling. Kassel: Bärenreiter, 1964.

LEVY, K. "The Byzantine Sanctus and Its Modal Tradition in East
and West." Annales musicologiques, 6 (1963):   7-67.

MAAS, Paul. "Das Kontakion." Byzantinische Zeitschrift, (1910):
285-306.

MEERSSEMAN, Gillis. Der Hymnos Akathistos im Abendland. 2
vols. Freiburg: Universitätsverlag, 1958-1960.

MIONI, Elpidis, ed. Romano il Melode: Saggio critico. Torino:
Paravia, 1937.

MITSAKIS, K. "The Hymnography of the Greek Church in the
Early Christian Centuries." Jahrbuch der österreichischen
Byzantinistik, 20 (1971):   31-49.

MOROSAN, Vladimir. "Penie and Musikiia: Aesthetic Changes in
Russian Liturgical Singing during the Seventeenth Century."
St. Vladimir's Theological Quarterly, 23 (1979):   149-179.

PALIKAROVA VERDEIL, R. La Musique byzantine chez les Bul-
gares et les Russes (du IXe au XIVe siècle). MMB, Subsidia,
3. Copenhagen: Munksgaard; Boston, MA: Byzantine Institute, 1953.

PITRA, J. B. Hymnographie de l'église grecque. Rome: Impr.
de la Civiltà cattolica, 1867.

PSARIANOS, D. "Die byzantinische Musik in der griechisch-
orthodoxen Kirche." In Die orthodoxen Kirche in griechischer
Sicht, Bd. 2, pp. 144-154. Herausgegeben von Panagiotis
Bratsiotis. Stuttgart: Evangelisches Verlagswerk, 1959-1960.

RIESMANN, Oskar von. Die Notationen des altrussischen Kirchen-
gesanges. Leipzig: Breitkopf & Härtel, 1909; reprint ed.,
Wiesbaden: B. M. Sändig, 1973.

SAKELLARIDES, Iōannēs Th. Chrēstomathia ekklēsiastikēs mousikes:
periechousa pan oti anagkaion tō ieropsaltē, kai egcheiridion
pros didaskalian. Athenais: Ek. Philadelpheos, 1880.

SAVAS, Savas J. Hymnology of the Eastern Orthodox Church.
Washington, DC: University Press of America, 1977.

SCHORK, R. J. "Dramatic Dimension in Byzantine Hymns." In
Studia Patristica, vol. 8, pp. 271-279. Edited by F. L. Cross.
TUGAL, 93. Berlin: Akademie-Verlag, 1966.

STRUNK, William Oliver. "The Antiphons of the Oktoechos."
Journal of the American Musicological Society, 13 (1960): 50-
67.

_____. Essays on Music in the Byzantine World. New York:
W. W. Norton, 1977.

SZOVERFFY, Josef. A Guide to Byzantine Hymnography: A Classified Bibliography of Texts and Studies. Brookline, MA:
Classical Folia Editions, 1978- .

TARDO, Lorenzo. L'antica melurgia bizantina nell' interpretazione
della Scuola monastica di Grottaferrata. Grottaferrata: Scuola
tip. italo orientale "S. Nilo," 1938.

THODBERG, C. Der byzantinische Allelouiarionzyklus. Copenhagen: Munksgaard, 1966.

TILLYARD, H. J. W. Byzantine Music and Hymnography. London: Faith Press, 1923; reprint ed., New York: AMS Press,
1976.

_____. Handbook of the Middle Byzantine Notation. MMB, Sub-
sidia, 1/1. Copenhagen: Levin & Munksgaard, 1935; reprinted,
1970.

TIMIADIS, Emilianos. "Byzantine Music." In The Orthodox Ethos:
Essays in honour of the Centenary of the Greek Orthodox
Archdiocese of North and South America, pp. 200-206. Edited
by A. J. Philippou. Oxford: Holywell Press, 1964.

VELIMIROVIC, Milos M. Byzantine Elements in Early Slavic Chant:
The Hirmologion. 2 vols. MMB, Subsidia, 4. Copenhagen:
Munksgaard, 1960.

_____. "Sta.:d der Forschungen über kirchenslavische Musik."
Zeitschrift für slavische Philologie, 31 (1963): 145-169.

WELLESZ, Egon. Eastern Elements in Western Chant: Studies in
the Early History of Ecclesiastical Music. MMB, Subsidia, 2.
Copenhagen: Munksgaard, 1967.

_____. A History of Byzantine Music and Hynography. 2d ed.
Oxford: Clarendon Press, 1961.

_____. Die Hymnen der Ostkirche. Basel: Bärenreiter, 1962.

_____. "Melito's Homily on the Passion: An Investigation into
the Sources of Byzantine Hymnography." Journal of Theological
Studies, 44 (1943): 41-52.

_____, and VELIMIROVIC, Milos, eds. Studies in Eastern Chant.
New York: Oxford University Press, 1966- .

2. Other Eastern Churches

a. Texts

BIANCHINI, Pietro, ed. Les chants liturgiques de l'Eglise arménienne. Armenian, with English, French & Italian translations.
Venice: St. Lazare, 1877.

Chants of the Divine Liturgy of the Armenian Apostolic Orthodox
Church. Notated and harmonized by Komitas Vardapet. New
York: Delphic Press, 1950.

HUSMANN, Heinrich, ed. Die Melodien des chaldäischen Breviers
Commune, nach den Traditionen vor der Asiens und der Mala-
barküste. OCA, 178. Rome: Pontificium Institutum Orientalium Studiorum, 1967.

JEANNIN, Jules, ed. Mélodies liturgiques syriennes et chaldéenes.
2 vols. Paris: Leroux, 1925-1928.

O'LEARY, DeLacy, ed. The Difnar (Antiphonarium) of the Coptic
Church. 3 vols. in 1. London: Luzac, 1926-1930.

b. Studies

BURMESTER, O. H. E. "The Greek Kirugmata, Versicles and Responses and Hymns in the Coptic Liturgy." Orientalia Christiana Periodica, 2 (1936):   363-394.

DALMAIS, Irenée-Henri. "L'hymnographie syrienne." La Maison-
Dieu, 92 (1967): 63-72.

JEANNIN, Jules. "Le chant liturgique syrien." Journal asiatique,
10, 20 (1912): 295-363, 389-448.

LEEB, Helmut. Die Gesänge im Gemeinde-Gottesdienst von Jerusalem (vom 5. bis 8. Jahrhundert). Wien: Herder, 1970.

TER-MIKAELIAN, Nerses. Das armenische Hymnarium: Studien zu
seiner geschichtlichen Entwicklung. Leipzig: J. C. Hinrichs,
1905.

C. LATIN CHURCH MUSIC

1. General Studies

AIGRAIN, René. La Musique religieuse. Paris: Bloud & Gay, 1929; Religious Music. Translated by C. Mulcahy, to which is added a further section by the translator on English and Irish religious music. London: Sands, 1931.

CORBIN, Solange. L'Eglise à la conquête de sa musique. Paris: Gallimard, 1960.

FELLERER, Karl G., ed. Geschichte der katholischen Kirchen-musik. 2. Aufl. Düsseldorf: Schwann, 1949; The History of Catholic Church Music. Translated by Francis A. Brunner. Baltimore, MD: Helicon Press, 1961; reprint ed., Westport, CT: Greenwood Press, 1979.

_____. Geschichte der katholischen Kirchenmusik. Kassel: Bärenreiter, 1972.

FLECKENSTEIN, Franz, ed. Gloria Deo pax hominibus: Festschrift zum 100-jährigen Bestehen der Kirchenmusikschule affiliiert der päpstlichen Hochschule für Kirchenmusik en Rom. Bonn: All-gemeiner Cäcilienverband, Sekretariat, 1974.

GARRIDO BONANO, Manuel. Curso de liturgia romana. La parte destinada a la liturgia eucharistica ha sido redactada integra-mente por Augusto Pascual Diez. Madrid: Editorial Catolica, 1961.

GASTOUE, Amédée. Variations sur la musique d'église. Paris: Bureau d'Edition de la schola, 1912.

_____. La Vie musicale de l'église. Paris: Bloud & Gay, 1929.

HUCKE, Helmut. "Das Verhältnis der katholischen Kirche zur Mu-sik." In Katholiken und ihre Kirche in der Bundesrepublik Deutschland, pp. 302-308. Herausgegeben von Günther Gor-schenek. München: Günther Olzog Verlag, 1976.

HUME, Paul. Catholic Church Music. New York: Dodd, Mead, 1956.

LEMACHER, Heinrich, ed. Handbuch der katholischen Kirchenmu-sik. Essen: Fredebeul & Koenen, 1949.

McKENNA, Edward J. "Liturgical Music in Ireland." Worship, 51 (1977): 420-433.

MILNER, Anthony. "Music and Liturgy." Month, 34 (1965): 363-
376; 35 (1966): 31-39, 147-153.

MUSCH, Hans, ed. Musik im Gottesdienst: ein Handbuch zur
Grundausbildung in der katholischen Kirchenmusik. Regensburg: Bosse, 1975.

NEMMERS, Erwin Esser. Twenty Centuries of Catholic Church Music. Milwaukee, WI: Bruce, 1949; reprint ed., Westport, CT:
Greenwood Press, 1978.

PIERIK, Marie. The Song of the Church. New York: Longmans,
Green, 1947.

PIKULIKA, Jerzego, ed. Muzyka religijna w Polsce. Warszawa:
Akademia Teologii Katolickiej, 1975- .

PREDMORE, George Vincent. Sacred Music and the Catholic
Church. Boston, MA: McLaughlin & Reilly, 1936.

ROBERTSON, Alec. Christian Music. TCEC, 125. New York:
Hawthorn Books, 1961.

_____. Music of the Catholic Church. London: Burns & Oates,
1961.

SABEL, Hans. Die liturgischen Gesänge der katholischen Kirche.
Wolfenbüttel: Möseler Verlag, 1965.

SAMSON, Joseph. Musique et chant sacrée. Paris: Gallimard,
1957.

TERRY, Richard Runciman. Catholic Church Music. London:
Greening, 1907.

_____. The Music of the Roman Rite. London: Burns, Oates
& Washbourne, 1931.

URSPRUNG, Otto. Die katholische Kirchenmusik. Potsdam: Akademische Verlagsgesellschaft Athenaion, 1931.

WAGNER, Peter. Einführung in die katholische Kirchenmusik.
Düsseldorf: Schwann, 1919.

WEINMANN, Karl. Geschichte der Kirchenmusik. Kempten: J.
Kösel, 1906; History of Church Music. Boston, MA: McLaughlin & Reilly, 1906.

2. Official Church Teaching

AKADEMIE FUR MUSIK UND DARSTELLEND KUNST, Graz. Die

Kirchenmusik und das II. Vatikanische Konzil. Referate der
Kirchenmusikwoche in Graz. Graz: Styria, 1965.

ALCINI, Ilario. Pio X e la musica. Rome: Associazione Italiana
di Santa Cecilia, 1956.

Associazione Italiana di Santa Cecilia. L'enciclia Musicae Sacrae
Disciplina di Sua Santità Pio XII. Testo e commento. Rome:
Associazione Italiana di Santa Cecilia per la Musica Sacra, 1957.

AUBRY, Pierre. Les Idées de S. S. Pie Xe sur le chant de l'église. Paris: L. de Soye, 1904.

BEILLIARD, Jean, and PICARD, François, eds. Le Musique sacrée
après la réforme liturgique, décisions, directives, orientations.
Dossier établi par l'Union fédérale française de Musique Sacré
et présenté par Jean Beilliard et François Picard. Paris:
Centurion, 1967.

BERTOLA, Arnaldo. La musica sacra nelle leggi della chiesa.
Torino: Società tipografico-editrice nazionale, 1930.

DUCLOS, A. Sa Sainteté Pie X et la musique religieuse. Rome:
Desclée, 1905.

FELLERER, Karl Gustav. "Church Music and the Council of Trent."
The Musical Quarterly, 39 (1953): 576-594.

FERLAND, David J. Plenary, Provincial, and Synodal Legislation
concerning Liturgical Music in the United States as Causative
and Resultant of the Enactments of the Third Plenary Council
of Baltimore. Washington, DC: n.p., 1955.

GOTTRON, Adam. Kirchenmusik und Liturgie: Die kirchlichen
Vorschriften für Gesang und Musik beim Gottesdienst. Regensburg: Pustet, 1937.

HANIN, Aloys. La Législation ecclésiastique en matière de musique
religieuse. Paris: Société de saint Jean l'évangiliste, Desclée,
1933.

HAYBURN, Robert F. Digest of Regulations and Rubrics of Catholic Church Music. Revised ed. Boston, MA: McLoughlin &
Reilly, 1961.

_____. Papal Legislation on Sacred Music 95 A.D. to 1977 A.D.
Collegeville, MN: Liturgical Press, 1979.

_____. "St. Pius X and the Vatican Edition of the Chant Books."
D.M.A. thesis, University of Southern California, 1964.

HETTEMA, J. Kerkmuziek en kerkelijke wetgeving: alfabetisch overzicht van de geldende kerkelijke normen op het gebied van de kerkmuziek. Hilversum: Gooi & Sticht, 1961.

Instruction on Music in the Sacred Liturgy. London: Catholic Truth Society, 1967.

INTERNATIONAL CONGRESS FOR CHURCH MUSIC. Atti del Congresso internazionale de musica sacra organizzato dal Pontificio Istituto di Musica Sacra e dalla Commissione di Musica Sacra per l'Anno Santo. Pubblicati a cura di Mons. Igino Anglis. Tournai: Desclée, 1952.

_____. Perspectives de la musique sacrée à la lumière de l'Encyclique Musicae Sacrae Disciplina: Actes. Paris, 1959.

_____. Sacred Music and Liturgy Reform after Vatican II. Proceedings of the Fifth International Church Music Congress, Chicago-Milwaukee, August 21-28, 1966. Edited by Johannes Overath. Rome: Consociatio Internationalis Musicae Sacrae, 1969.

_____. IV. Internationaler Kongress für Kirchenmusik. Herausgegeben vom Präsidium des Kongresses. Schriftleitung: Wilhelm Lueger. Köln, 1961?

_____. IV. Internationaler Kongress für Kirchenmusik: Documente und Berichte. Herausgegeben von Johannes Overath. Köln, 1962.

_____. Zweiter Internationaler Kongress für katholische Kirchenmusik. Bericht vorgelegt vom Exekutivkomitee. Wien, 1955.

KRONSTEINER, Hermann. Kirchenmusik heute. Texte und Aussagen der Kirche: Kommentar. Wien: Veritas, 1967.

LEONARD, William J., ed. The New Instruction for American Pastors (on Sacred Music and the Liturgy). Boston, MA: McLaughlin & Reilly, 1959.

MANZARRATA, Tómas de. La música sagrada a la luz de los documentos pontificos. Madrid: Editorial Coculsa, 1968.

La Musique dans la liturgie: documents officiels. Paris: Editions Musicales de la Schola Cantorum et de la Procure Générale de Musique. 1967.

MYTYCH, Joseph F. Digest of Church Law on Sacred Music. Toledo, OH: Gregorian Institute of America, 1959.

NATIONAL COMMISSION FOR CATHOLIC CHURCH MUSIC. Music

in the Mass. Foreword by the Bishop of Northampton. London: Catholic Truth Society, 1969.

O'CONNELL, J. B., ed.   Sacred Music and Liturgy: The Instruction of the Sacred Congregation of Rites concerning Sacred Music and Sacred Liturgy in accordance with the Encyclical Letters of Pope Pius XII: Musicae Sacrae Disciplina and Mediator Dei. Westminster, MD: Newman Press, 1959.

PONS, André. Droit ecclésiastique et musique sacrée. 4 vols. St. Maurice, Suisse: Editions de l'oeuvre St.-Augustin, 1958-1961.

Rinnovamento liturgico e musica sacra: commento alla istruzione Musicam Sacram. Rome: Edizioni Liturgiche, 1967.

SCHNELL, Johanna. Asthetische Probleme der Kirchenmusik im Lichte der Enzyklika Pius' XII Musicae Sacrae Disciplina. Berlin, 1961.

UDINA, Antonio. Participación en la misa y música sagrada: prontuario práctico de la instruccione de 3 de septiembre de 1958 de la Sagrada Congregación de Ritos. Barcelona: Centro de Pastoral Litúrgica, 1959.

WEINMANN, Karl. Die Konzil von Trient und die Kirchenmusik. Leipzig: Breitkopf & Härtel, 1919.

3. Historical Works

a. Texts

ABAILARD, Pierre. Peter Abelard's Hymnarius Paraclitensis. 2 vols. Annotated ed. with introduction by Joseph Szövérffy. Albany, NY: Classical Folia Editions, 1975.

ADAM DE SAINT VICTOR. Oeuvres poètiques d'Adam de S.-Victor, précédées d'un essai sur sa vie et ses ouvrages. 2 vols. Editée par L. Gautier. Paris: Julien, Lanier, Cosnard, 1858-1859; The Liturgical Poetry of Adam of St. Victor, from the Text of Gautier. 3 vols. By Digby S. Wrangham. London: Kegan Paul, Trench, 1881; reprinted, 1931.

BANNISTER, Henry Marriott. Monumenti Vaticani di paleografia musicale latina. 2 vols. Leipzig: O. Harrassowitz, 1913; reprint ed., Farnborough, Eng.: Gregg, 1969.

BULST, Walther, ed. Hymni Latini antiquissimi LXXV, Psalmi III. Heidelberg: F. H. Kerle, 1956.

DANIEL, Hermann Adalbert, ed. Thesaurus Hymnologicus. 5 vols. in 2. Halis: sumptibus E. Anton, 1841-1856; Lipsiae: J. T. Loeschke, 1855-1862.

DREVES, Guido M., and BLUME, Clemens, eds. Analecta hymnica medii aevi. 55 vols. Leipzig: O. R. Reisland, 1886-1922; reprint ed., New York: Johnson Reprint, 1961.

FRERE, Walter Howard, ed. Antiphonale Sarisburiense. 2 vols. London: Plainsong and Mediaeval Music Society, 1901-1925; reprint ed., 6 vols., Farnborough, Eng.: Gregg, 1966.

_____, ed. Graduale Sarisburiense. PMMS. London: Quaritch, 1894; reprint ed., Farnborough, Eng.: Gregg, 1956.

_____, ed. The Winchester Troper: from MSS. of the Xth and XIth Centuries. HBS, 8. London: Harrison, 1894; reprint ed., New York: AMS Press, 1973.

GOEDE, N. de, ed. The Utrecht Prosarium: Liber Sequentiarum ecclesiae capitularis sanctae Mariae Ultraiectensis saeculi XIII, Codex Ultraiectensis, Universitatis Bibliotheca 417. Amsterdam: Vereniging voor Nederlandse Muziekgeschiedenis, 1965.

HESBERT, René Jean, ed. Antiphonale Missarum Sextuplex. Bruxelles: Vromant, 1935.

_____, ed. Corpus antiphonalium officii. 5 vols. RED, 7-11. Rome: Herder, 1963-1975.
1. Manuscripti "Cursus romanus." RED, 7. 1963.
2. Manuscripti "Cursus monasticus." RED, 8. 1965.
3. Invitatoria et antiphonae. RED, 9. 1968.
4. Responsoria, Versus, Hymni et Varia. RED, 10. 1970.
5. Fontes earunque prima ordinatio. RED, 11. 1975.

_____, ed. Monumenta musica sacra. Macon: Protat Frères, 1952- .

JONSSON, Ritva, ed. Corpus Troporum I. SLS, 21. Stockholm: Almqvist & Wiksell, 1975.

LORIQUET, Henri, POTHIER, Joseph, and COLLETTE, Amand, eds. Le Graduel de l'église cathédrale de Rouen au XIIIe siècle. 2 vols. Rouen: J. Lecerf, 1907.

MARBACH, Carolus, ed. Carmina Scripturarum, scilicet antiphonas et responsoria ex Sacro Scripturae fonte in libros liturgicos sanctae ecclesiae romanae derivata. Strassburg: Le Roux, 1907; reprint ed., Hildesheim: G. Olms, 1963.

MARCUSSON, Olof, ed. Corpus Troporum II: prosules de la messe. SLS, 22. Stockholm: Almqvist & Wiksell, 1976.

MONE, Franz Joseph, ed. Lateinische Hymnen des Mittelalters.
3 vols. Freiburg: Herder, 1853-1855.

Monumenta musicae sacrae. Macon: Protat Frères, 1952- .

Monumenta polyphoniae liturgicae sanctae ecclesiae Romanae. Rome:
Societas Universalis Sanctae Ceciliae, 1948- .

OTT, Carolus, ed. Offertoriale sive versus offertoriorum. Paris:
Typis societatis S. Joannis Evangelistae, 1935.

SZOVERFFY, Josef. Hymns of the Holy Cross: An Annotated Edition with Introduction. Brookline, MA: Classical Folia Editions, 1976.

TACK, Franz, ed. Gregorian Chant. Translated by Everett Helm.
Anthology of Music, 18. Köln: Arno Volk Verlag, 1960.

WAGNER, Peter, ed. Die Gesänge der Jakobusliturgie zu Santiago
de Compostela aus dem sog. Codex Calixtinus. CF, 29. VUF,
n. F., 20. Freiburg (Schweiz): Universitäts-Buchhandlung,
1931.

_____, ed. Das Graduale der St. Thomaskirche zu Leipzig. 2
vols. PAM, 5, 7. Leipzig: Breitkopf & Härtel, 1930-1932;
reprint ed., Hildesheim: G. Olms, 1967.

WALPOLE, A. S., ed. Early Latin Hymns. Cambridge: Cambridge
University Press, 1922.

WARREN, F. E., ed. The Antiphonary of Bangor. 2 vols. HBS,
4, 10. London: Harrison, 1893-1895.

WIELAND, Gernot R., ed. The Canterbury Hymnal. Toronto
Medieval Latin Texts, 12. Toronto, Ont.: Pontifical Institute
of Medieval Studies, 1982.

    b. Studies

BARDOS, Kornél. Volksmusikartige Variierungstechnik in den ungarischen Passoinen, 15. bis 18. Jahrhundert. Budapest:
Akadémiai Kiadó, 1975.

BENHAM, Hugh. Latin Church Music in England, c. 1460-1575.
London: Barrie & Jenkins, 1977.

BLUME, Clemens. Repertorium repertorii: kritische Wegweiser
durch Ulysse Chevaliers Repertorium Hymnologicum. Leipzig:
O. R. Reisland, 1901; reprint ed., Hildesheim: G. Olms, 1971.

_____. Unsere liturgischen Lieder: das Hymnar der altchristlichen

Kirche. Aus dem Urtext ins Deutsche umgedichtet, psycho-
logisch und geschichtlich erklärt. Regensburg: Pustet, 1932.

BRIDGMAN, Nanie et al. "Latin Church Music on the Continent."
In The New Oxford History of Music, vol. 4, pp. 218-418.
New York: Oxford University Press, 1954- .

BROU, L. "Les Chants en langue grecque dans les liturgies latines." Sacris Erudiri, 1 (1948): 165-180.

CAVANAUGH, Philip. "Early Sixteenth Century Cycles of Polyphonic Mass Propers: An Evolutionary Process or the Result
of Liturgical Reforms." Acta Musicologica, 48 (1976): 151-
165.

CHEVALIER, Cyr Ulysse J. Repertorium hymnologicum: catalogue
des chants, hymnes, proses, séquences, tropes en usage dans
l'église latine depuis ses origines jusqu'à nos jours. 6 vols.
BL, 3, 4, 10, 15, ?, 20. Louvain, 1892-1912, Brussels, 1920-
1921; reprint ed., n.p., 1959.

CORBIN, Solange. Essai sur la musique religieuse portugaise au
moyen âge (1100-1385). Paris: Les Belles Lettres, 1952.

COUSSEMAKER, Edmond de, ed. Scriptorum de musica medii aevi
novam seriem a Gerbertina alteram collegit nuncque primum.
4 vols. Paris: A. Durand, 1864-1876; reprint ed., Hildesheim: G. Olms, 1963.

DOREN, Rombaut van. Etude sur l'influence musicale de l'Abbaye
de Saint-Gall, VIIIe au XIe siècle. Louvain: Librairie universitaire, Vystpruyst, 1925.

DREVES, Guido Maria. Ein Jahrtausend lateinischer Hymnendichtung. Eine Blütenlese aus den Analecta Hymnica mit literar-
historischen Erläuterungen. Nach des Vergassers ableben re-
vidiert von Clemens Blume. Leipzig: O. R. Reisland, 1909.

DUFFIELD, Samuel Willoughby. The Latin Hymn-writers and their
Hymns. Edited and completed by R. E. Thompson. New York,
London: Funk & Wagnalls, 1889; reprint ed., Boston, MA:
Longwood Press, 1980.

EVANS, Paul. The Early Trope Repertory of Saint Martial de
Limoges. Princeton, NJ: Princeton University Press, 1970.

FRANCA, Umberto. Le antifone bibliche dopo pentecoste: studio
codicologico storico testuale con appendice musicale. Analecta
liturgica, 4. SA, 73. Rome: Editrice Anselmiana, 1977.

GERBERT, Martin. De cantu et musica sacra a prima ecclesiae aetate usque ad praesens tempus. 2 vols. St. Blasien, 1774; reprint ed., Graz: Akademische Druck- und Verlagsanstalt, 1968.

_____. Scriptores ecclesiastici de musica sacra potissimum. 3 vols. St. Blasien, 1784.

_____. Vetvus liturgia Alemannica. 2 vols. St Blasien, 1776; reprint ed., Hildesheim: G. Olms, 1967.

GIESEL, Helmut. Studien zur Symbolik der Musikinstrumente im Schriftum der alten und mittelalterlichen Kirche. KBM, 94. Regensburg: G. Bosse, 1978.

GNEUSS, Helmut. Hymnar und Hymnen in englischen Mittelalter: Studien zur Uberlieferung, Glossierung und Ubersetzung lateinischer Hymnen in England. Tübingen: M. Niemeyer, 1968.

HACKER, Joseph. Die Messe in den deutschen Diözesan-Gesang- und Gebetbüchern von der Aufklärungszeit bis zur Gegenwart. MTS, 1. München: Zink, 1950.

HANDSCHIN, J. "Trope, Sequence, and Conductus." In The New Oxford History of Music, vol. 2, pp. 128-174. New York: Oxford University Press, 1954- .

HARRISON, Frank Llewellyn. Music in Medieval Britain. London: Routledge and Kegan Paul; New York: Praeger, 1958.

HEINE, Herbert. Die Melodien der Mainzer Gesangbücher in der ersten Hälfte des 17. Jahrhunderts. Mainz: Selbstverlag der Gesellschaft für Mittelrheinische Kirchengeschichte, 1975.

HESBERT, René Jean. "L'Antiphonale Missarum de l'ancien rit Bénéventain." Ephemerides Liturgicae, 52 (1938): 28-66.

HOFFMANN-BRANDT, Helma. Die Tropen zu den Responsorien des Officiums. n.p., 1971?

JANOTA, Johannes. Studien zu Funktion und Typus des deutschen geistlichen Liedes im Mittelalters. MTU, 23. München: Beck, 1968.

LIPPHARDT, Walther. Die Geschichte des mehrstimmigen Proprium Missae. Heidelberg: F. H. Kerle, 1950.

_____. "Die liturgischen Funktion deutscher Kirchenlieder in den Klöstern niedersächsischer Zisterzienserinnen des Mittelalters." Zeitschrift für Kirche und Theologie, 94 (1972): 158-198.

_____. "Zur Entwicklung des deutschen Messgesanges." Musik und Altar, 7 (1954): 129-136.

LOCKWOOD, Lewis.   The Counter-Reformation and the Masses of
Vincenzo Ruffo.   SMV, 2.   Venice: Universal Edition, 1970.

MEARNS, James.   Early Latin Hymnaries: An Index of Hymns in
Hymnaries before 1100.   Cambridge: Cambridge University
Press, 1913.

MESSENGER, Ruth Ellis.   The Medieval Latin Hymn.   Washington,
DC: Capital Press, 1953.

MICHEL, Alain.   In hymnis et canticus: culture et beauté dans
l'hymnique chrétienne latine.   PM, 20.   Louvain: Publications
Universitaires, 1976.

MOLITOR, Raphael.   Die nachtridentinische Choralreform zu Rom:
ein Beitrag zur Musikgeschichte des 16. und 17. Jahrhunderts.
2 vols.   Leipzig, 1901-1902; reprint ed., Hildesheim: G. Olms,
1967.

OVERATH, Johannes, ed.   Musicae sacrae ministerium: Beiträge
zur Geschichte der kirchenmusikalischen Erneuerung im XIX.
Jahrhundert.   Köln, 1962.

PLANCHART, Alejandro Enrique.   The Repertory of Tropes at Winchester.   2 vols.   Princeton, NJ: Princeton University Press,
1977.

RABY, Frederick J. E.   A History of Christian Latin Poetry from
the Beginnings to the Close of the Middle Ages.   2d ed.   Oxford: Clarendon Press, 1953.

RONNAU, Klaus.   Die Tropen zum Gloria in Excelsis Deo.   Wiesbaden: Breitkopf & Härtel, 1967.

SCHUBERTH, Dietrich.   Kaiserliche Liturgie: Die Einbeziehung von
Musikinstrumenten insbesondere der Orgel, in den frühmittel-
alterlichen Gottesdienst.   VEGL, 17.   Göttingen: Vandenhoeck
& Ruprecht, 1968.

STEFANI, Gino.   Musica e religione nell' Italia barocca.   Palermo:
S. F. Flaccovio, 1975.

STEIN, Edwin Eugene.   The Polyphonic Mass in France and the
Netherlands, c. 1525 to c. 1560.   Rochester, NY: University
of Rochester Press, 1954.

STEVENSON, Robert Murrell.   Spanish Cathedral Music in the Gold-
en Age.   Berkeley, CA: University of California Press, 1961;
reprint ed., Westport, CT: Greenwood Press, 1976.

SZOVERFFY, Josef.   Die Annalen der lateinischen Hymnendichtung:
ein Handbuch.   2 vols.   Berlin: E. Schmidt, 1964-1965.

_____. "A Conscious Artist in Medieval Hymnody: Introduction to Peter Abelard's Hymns." In Classica et Iberica, pp. 119-259. Edited by P. T. Brannan. Worcester, MA: Institute for Early Christian Iberian Studies, College of the Holy Cross, 1975.

_____. "Crux fidelis: Prolegomena to a History of the Holy Cross Hymns." Traditio, 22 (1966): 1-41.

_____. "Iberian Hymnody: A Preliminary Survey of Medieval Spanish and Portuguese Hymnody." Classical Folia, 24 (1970): 187-253.

_____. Iberian Hymnody: Survey and Problems. Albany, NY: Classical Folia Editions, 1971.

_____. "Klassische Anspielungen und antike Elemente im mittelalterlichen Hymnen." Archiv für Kulturgeschichte, 44 (1962): 148-192.

_____. "A Mirror of Medieval Culture: Saint Peter Hymns of the Middle Ages." Transactions of the Connecticut Academy of Arts and Sciences, 42 (1965): 100-403.

_____. Religious Lyrics of the Middle Ages: Hymnological Studies and Collected Essays: Psallat Chorus Caelestium. Mediaeval Classics, Texts and Studies, 15. Berlin: Classical Folia Editions, 1983.

4. Western Chant

AGUSTONI, Luigi. Gregorianischer Choral: Elemente und Vortragslehre mit besonderer Berücksichtigung der Neumenkunde. Freiburg: Herder, 1963.

ANGLES, H. "Gregorian Chant." In The New Oxford History of Music, vol. 2, pp. 92-127. New York: Oxford University Press, 1954- .

_____. "Latin Chant before St. Gregory." In The New Oxford History of Music, vol. 2, pp. 58-91. New York: Oxford University Press, 1954- .

APEL, Willi. Gregorian Chant. Bloomington, IN: Indiana University Press, 1958.

AUBRY, Pierre. Le Rôle du chant liturgique et sa place dans la civilisation générale du moyen âge. Paris: Aux Bureau de la Schola Cantorum, 1897?

_____. Le Rhythme tonique dans la poesie liturgique et dans le chant des églises chrétiennes au moyen âge. Paris: Welter, 1903.

BARON, Ludovic. L'Expression du chant grégorien, commentaire liturgique et musical des messes des dimanches et des principales fêtes de l'année. 3 vols. Plouharnel-Morbihan: Abbaye Sainte-Anne de Kergonan, 1947-1950.

CATTANEO, Enrico. Note storiche sul canto ambrosiano. Milan: [Scuola tip. S. Benedetto], 1950.

COMBE, Pierre. Histoire de la restauration du chant grégorien d'après des documents. Sablé-sur-Sathe: Abbaye de Solesmes, 1969.

FERRETTI, Paola Maria. Estetica gregoriana. Rome: Pontificio Istituto di Musica Sacra, 1934; reprint ed., New York: Da Capo Press, 1977.

FROGER, Jacques. Les Chants de la messe au VIIIe et IXe siècles. Paris: Société de Saint Jean l'Evangéliste, Desclée, 1950.

GASTOUE, Amédée. L'Art grégorien. 3. éd. Paris: F. Alcan, 1920; reprint ed., New York: AMS Press, 1975.

_____. "Le Chant gallican." Revue du chant grégorien, 41 (1937): 101-106, 131-133, 167-176; 42 (1938): 5-12, 57-62, 76-80, 107-112, 146-151; 43 (1939): 5-12, 44-46.

_____. Musique et liturgie: le graduel et l'antiphonaire romains: histoire et description. Lyon: J. Frères, 1913; reprint ed., New York: AMS Press, 1974.

_____. Les Origines du chant romain: l'antiphonaire grégorien. Paris: Picard, 1907; reprint ed., New York: AMS Press, 1975.

_____. "Le Sanctus et le Benedictus." Revue du chant grégorien, 38 (1934): 163-168; 39 (1935): 12-17, 35-39.

GEVAERT, François Auguste. Le Mélopée antique dans le chant de l'église latine. Gand: Hoste, 1895; reprint ed., Innsbruck: Zeller, 1967.

_____. Les Origines du chant liturgique de l'église latine. Gand: A. Hoste, 1890; reprint ed., HIldesheim: G. Olms, 1971.

HUCKE, Helmut. "Die Einführung des gregorianischen Gesanges in Frankreich." Römische Quartalschrift, 49 (1954): 172-184.

HUGLO, Michel. Fonti e paleografia del canto ambrosiano. AA, 7. Milan: [Scuola tip. San Benedetto], 1956.

JOHNER, Dominic. Neue Schule des gregorianischen Choralge-
sanges. 2. Aufl. Regensburg: Pustet, 1911; A New School
of Gregorian Chant. 3d English ed. based upon the 5th enlarged German ed. by Herman Erpf and Max Ferrars. New
York: Pustet, 1925.

_____. Die Sonn- und Festtagslieder des Vatikanischen Graduale.
2. Aufl. Regensburg: Pustet, 1933; The Chants of the Vatican
Gradual. Translated by Monks of St. John's Abbey. Collegeville, MN: St. John's Abbey, 1940.

LABAT, Paule Elisabeth. Louange à Dieu et chant grégorien.
Paris: Téqui, 1975.

MOCQUEREAU, André. Le Nombre musical grégorien, ou Rhythmique grégorienne, théorie et pratique. 2 vols. Tournai,
Paris: Société Saint Jean l'évangéliste, Desclée, 1908-1927.

NEISS, Benoît. Le Chant grégorien en France. Paris: Ministère
des Affaires Culturelles, 1975.

PIERIK, Marie. Dramatic and Symbolic Elements in Gregorian Chant.
New York: Desclée, 1963.

_____. Gregorian Chant Analyzed and Studied. St. Meinrad,
IN: Grail Publications, 1951.

_____. The Spirit of Gregorian Chant. Boston, MA: McLaugh-
lin & Reilly, 1939.

POTHIER, Joseph. Les Mélodies grégoriennes: d'après la tradition.
Tournai: Impr. liturgique de Saint Jean l'évangéliste, Desclée,
1881; reprint ed., Collection musique, 6. Paris: Stock musique, 1980.

REGINALD, Brother. "Plainsong: What Can We Salvage?" The
Franciscan, 10 (1968): 200-205.

SESINI, Ugo. Decadenza e restaurazione del canto liturgico. Milan:
Casa Editrice d'Arte e Liturgia B. Angelico, 1933.

SMITS VAN WAESBERGHE, Joseph. Gregoriaansche muziek en haar
in den katholieken eeredienst. Amsterdam: Becht, 194?;
Gregorian Chant and Its Place in the Catholic Liturgy. Translated by W. A. G. Doyle-Davidson. Stockholm: Continental
Book Co., 1947?

SUNOL, Gregorio M. Introducció a la paleografia musical gregoriana.
Montserrat: Abadia de Montserrat, 1925; Introduction à la
paléographie musicale grégorienne. Tournai, Paris: Société de
saint Jean l'évangéliste, Desclée, 1935.

VALOIS, Jean de. Le Chant grégorien. 2e éd. Paris: Presses
Universitaires de France, 1974.

VOLLAERTS, Jan W. A. Rhythmic Proportions in Early Medieval
Ecclesiastical Chant. Leiden: Brill, 1958.

WAGNER, Peter. Einführung in die gregorianischen Melodien: ein
Handbuch der Choralwissenschaft. 3 vols. Leipzig: Breitkopf
& Härtel, 1911-1921; reprint ed., Hildesheim: Olms, 1962.
 1. Ursprung und Entwicklung der liturgischen Gesangformen
     bis zum Ausgange des Mittelalters. 3. Aufl. 1911.
 2. Neumenkunde, Paläographie des liturgischen Gesanges.
     2. Aufl. 1912.
 3. Gregorianische Formenlehre; eine Choralische Stilkunde.
     1921.

_____. Introduction to the Gregorian Melodies, Part I: Origin
and Development of the Forms of the Liturgical Chant up to the
End of the Middle Ages. 2d. ed. Translated by Agnes Orme
and E. G. P. Wyatt. London: Plainsong and Mediaeval Music
Society, 1901; reprinted in Caecilia, 84 (1957)-86 (1959).

WELLESZ, Egon. Eastern Elements in Western Chant: Studies in
the Early History of Ecclesiastical Music. MMB, Subsidia, 2.
Copenhagen: Munksgaard, 1967.

_____. "Recent Studies in Western Chant." The Musical Quar-
terly, 41 (1955): 177-190.

5. Mozarabic Music

a. Texts

BROU, Louis, and VIVES, José, eds. Antifonario visigótico moz-
árabe de la Catedral de León. Barcelona & Madrid: Consejo
Superior de Investigaciones Científicas, Instituto P. Enrique
Flórez, 1959?

GILSON, J. P., ed. The Mozarabic Psalter. HBS, 30. London:
Harrison, 1905.

b. Studies

ALLINGER, Helen. "The Mozarabic Hymnal and Chant with Special
Emphasis upon the Hymns of Prudentius." Th.D. dissertation,
Union Theological Seminary in the City of New York, 1953.

BROCKETT, Clyde Waring. Antiphons, Responsories and Other
Chants of the Mozarabic Rite. Brooklyn, NY: Institute of
Medieval Music, 1968.

BROU, Louis. "L'Alleluia dans la liturgie mozarabe: étude liturgico-musicale d'après les manuscrits de chant." Annuario Musical, 6 (1951): 3-90.

_____. "L'Antiphonaire wisigothique et l'antiphonaire grégorien au début du VIIIe siècle: essai de musicologie comparée." Annuario Musical, 5 (1950): 3-10.

PRADO, G. "Mozarabic Melodies." Speculum, 3 (1928): 218-238.

ROJO, Casiano, and PRADO, Germán, eds. El canto mozárabe: estudio historico-critico de su antigüedad y estado actual. Barcelona: Diputación provincial, 1929.

THORSBERG, Birgitta. Etudes sur l'hymnologie mozarabe. SLS, 8. Stockholm: Almqvist & Wiksell, 1962.

6. Contemporary Works

a. Texts

AINSLIE, John, ed. The Simple Gradual for Sundays and Holy Days. London: Geoffrey Chapman, 1970.

CARROLL, Joseph Robert, ed. The Grail/Gelineau Psalter: 150 Psalms and 18 Canticles. Text: The Grail (England). Psalmody: Joseph Gelineau. Chicago: Gregorian Institute of America, 1972.

CONNOLLY, Joseph. Hymns of the Roman Liturgy. London: Longmans, Green; Westminster, MD: Newman Press, 1957.

Crkvena pesmarica. Beograd: Blagovest, 1956.

CUMMING, Hildelith, ed. Music for Evening Prayer. London: Collins, 1978.

GELINEAU, Joseph. The Gelineau Gradual: Responsorial Psalms from the Lectionary for Mass for the Sundays and Principal Feasts of the Liturgical Year. Antiphons from the Hymnal Worship II. Psalms from the Grail/Gelineau Psalter. Chicago: Gregorian Institute of America Publications, 1977.

GOLLNER, Theodor, ed. Die mehrstimmigen liturgischen Lesungen. 2 vols. Tutzing: H. Schneider, 1969.

Graduale Simplex. Editio typica altera. Rome: Typis Polyglottis Vaticanis, 1975.

Le Graduel romain. Edition critique par les Moines de Solesmes. Solesmes: Abbaye Saint-Pierre, 1957- .

Liber usualis missae et officii pro dominicis et festis.   Edited by
   the Monks of Solesmes.   Paris: Typis Societatis S. Joannis
   Evangelistae;   Tournai: Desclée, 1953.

La Liturgie.   Présentation et tables par les Moines de Solesmes.
   Tournai: Desclée, 1954;   The Liturgy.   Selected and arranged
   by the Benedictine Monks of Solesmes.   Translated by the
   Daughters of St. Paul.   Boston, MA: St. Paul Editions, 1962.

Livret des fidèles.   Nouvelle éd.   Aprouvée par la Commission
   épiscopale de liturgie du Canada et par l'Assemblée épiscopale
   de la Province civile de Quebec.   Montréal, PQ: Fides, 1966.

Music for the Rite of Funerals and Rite of Baptism for Children.
   Washington, DC: International Commission on English in the
   Liturgy, 1977.

Music for the Rites: Baptism, Eucharist, and Ordinations.   Washington, DC: International Commission on English in the Liturgy,
   1978.

Ordo Cantus Missae.   Editio typica.   Rome: Typis Polyglottis Vaticanis, 1973.

   b.   Practical and Critical Studies

BAUMAN, William A.   The Ministry of Music: A Guide for the Prac-
   ticing Church Musician.   Washington, DC: Liturgical Conference, 1975.

CATHOLIC CHURCH.   National Conference of Catholic Bishops.
   Bishops' Committee on the Liturgy.   Music in Catholic Worship.
   Washington, DC: U.S. Catholic Conference, 1972.

Crisis in Church Music?   Washington, DC: The Liturgical Conference, 1967.

DEISS, Lucien.   Concile et chant nouveau.   Paris: Levain, 1969;
   Spirit and Song of the New Liturgy.   Translated by Lyla L.
   Haggard and Michael L. Mazzarese.   Cincinnati, OH: World
   Library of Sacred Music, 1970.

DUCHESNEAU, Claude, BARDON, Paul, and LEBON, Jean.   L'Important, c'est la musique!:   essai sur la musique dans la liturgie.   Paris: Cerf, 1977.

FUNK, Virgil C., ed.   Music in Catholic Worship: The NPM Commentary.   Washington, DC: National Association of Pastoral
   Musicians, 1982.

HABERL, Ferdinand.   Das Kyriale Romanum.   Bonn: Sekretariat d.
   ACV, 1975.

HARNONCOURT, Philipp. Gesamtkirchliche und teilkirchliche Liturgie: Studien zum liturgischen Heiligenkalendar und zum Gesang im Gottesdienst unter besonderer Berücksichtigung des deutschen Sprachgebiets. UPT, 3. Freiburg: Herder, 1974.

HERRING, William. The Role of Music in the New Roman Liturgy: A Practical Approach. Oak Park, IL: American Catholic Press, 1971.

MILNER, Anthony. "Recent Hymnals and Service Books." Worship, 40 (1966): 544-558.

MURRAY, Gregory. "The Future of Catholic Church Music." Downside Review, 96 (1978): 192-198.

MURRETT, John C. The Message of the Mass Melodies. Collegeville, MN: Liturgical Press, 1960.

Musique sacrée et langues modernes. Paris: Fleurus, 1964.

NATIONAL LITURGICAL CONFERENCE. A Manual for Church Musicians. Preface by Paul J. Hallinan. Washington, DC: Liturgical Conference, 1964.

PACIK, Rudolf. Volksgesang im Gottesdienst. Klosterneuburg: Osterreich katholisches Bibelwerk, 1977.

PAPINUTTI, Emigdio. La musica sacra dal Concilio Vaticano II al nuovo Ordo Missae. Rome: Edizioni Francescane, 1971?

RATZINGER, Joseph. "Theologische Probleme der Kirchenmusik." Internationale katholische Zeitschrift, 9 (1980): 148-157.

ROUTLEY, Erik. "Contemporary Catholic Hymnody in its Wider Setting." Worship, 47 (1973): 194-211, 258-273, 322-337; and "Contemporary Catholic Hymnody: An Afterword." Worship, 47 (1973): 417-423.

_____. "Progress Report in Hymnody." Worship, 49 (1975): 393-399.

_____. "Things are Looking Better." Worship, 50 (1976): 43-49.

ROWLANDS, Leo. Guide Book for Catholic Church Choirmasters. Enlarged ed. Boston, MA: McLaughlin & Reilly, 1962.

SCHMITT, Francis P. Church Music Transgressed: Reflections on Reform. New York: Seabury Press, 1977.

SMITH, Michael. "Music in the Parish Eucharist." The Franciscan, 10 (1968): 188-191.

SOUZA, José Geraldo de. Folcmúsica e liturgia: subsídios para o
estudio do problema. Petrópolis: Editôra Vozes, 1966.

STEFANI, Gino. L'Expressione vocale e musicale nella liturgia:
Gesti, riti, repertori. Torino: Leumann, Elle Di Ci, 1967.

SZOVERFFY, Josef. "Some Aspects of Recent Hymnological Literature and Hymns of the New Breviary." Traditio, 25 (1969):
457-472.

VERRET, Mary Camille. A Preliminary Survey of Roman Catholic
Hymnals published in the United States. Washington, DC:
Catholic University of America Press, 1964.

D. PROTESTANT CHURCH MUSIC IN GENERAL

BLUME, Friedrich. Die evangelische Kirkenmusik. Potsdam: Aka-
demische Verlagsgesellschaft Athenaion, 1931-1934; new ed.,
Geschichte der evangelischen Kirkenmusik. 2. Aufl. Kassel:
Bärenreiter Verlag, 1965; Protestant Church Music: A History.
Translated by F. Ellsworth Peterson. Foreword by Paul Henry
Lang. New York: Norton, 1974.

BURKHARD, Willy. Evangelische Kirchenmusik: die Briefe von
Willy Burkhard an Walter Tappolet. Zürich: Awingli Verlag,
1964.

DAVISON, Archibald Thompson. Protestant Church Music in America. Boston, MA: Schirmer, 1948, c1933.

ETHERINGTON, Charles L. Protestant Worship Music: Its History
and Practice. New York: Holt, Rinehart and Winston, 1962;
reprint ed., Westport, CT: Greenwood Press, 1978.

GEROLD, Théodore. "Protestant Music on the Continent." In The
New Oxford History of Music, vol. 4, pp. 419-464. New York:
Oxford University Press, 1954- .

JENNY, Markus. Die Zunkunft des evangelischen Kirkengesangs.
SAEK, 4. Zürich: Theologischer Verlag, 1970.

STEVENSON, Robert M. Patterns of Protestant Church Music. Durham, NC: Duke University Press, 1953.

_____. Protestant Church Music in America: A Short Survey of
Men and Movements from 1564 to the Present. New York:
W. W. Norton, 1966.

WINTERFELD, Carl Georg August Vivigens von. Der evangelische

Kirchengesang und sein verhältnis zur Kunst des Tonsatzes.
3 vols. Leipzig: Breitkopf & Härtel, 1843-1847; reprint ed.,
HIldesheim: Georg Olms, 1966.

E. LUTHERAN CHURCH MUSIC

1. Texts

DANSKE FOLKEKIRKE. The Danish High Mass and a Selection of
Hymns from the Danish Hymn-Book. Copenhagen: Church of
Denmark Council on Inter-Church Relations, 1958.

_____. Den danske Psalmebog, met mange Christelige Psalmer.
Ordentlig tilsammenset, formeret oc forbedret aff Hans Thomis-
søn. Kiøbenhaffn: L. Benedicht, 1569; reprint ed., Copenhagen: Samfundet Dansk Kirkesang, i Kommission hos D. Fog
Musikforlag, 1968.

_____. Den danske Salmebog. Copenhagen: Vajsenhus' Verlag,
1954.

_____. Den danske Salmebog. 25. februar 1953 aut. af Hans
Majestaet Kong Frederik IX til brug ved gudstjenesterne i
landets kirker. Copenhagen: Det Kgl. Vajsenhus (Haase),
1969.

_____. Evangelisk luthersk Sangbog. København: Evangelisk
Luthersk Missionsforenings Forlag, 1965.

_____. Niels Jesperssøns Graduale. Udgivet af Dansk organistog
kantor samfund af 1905, under medvirken af Erik Abrahamsen.
Copenhagen: J. H. Schultz, 1905.

Evangelisches Kirchen-Gesangbuch. Mit Ordnung des Hauptgottes-
dienstes in der Evang.-Luth. Landeskirche Mecklenburgs und
Ordnung der Tageszeiten-Gottesdienste. Berlin: EVA, 1973.

FORSMAN, Vainö Ilmari, ed. Messusävelmistö: Suomen kirkon
messuävelmät. Porvoo: W. Söderström, 1951.

General Council of the Evangelical Lutheran Church in North Amer-
ica. The Choral Service Book: Containing the Authentic Plain
Song Intonations and Responses for the Order of Morning Serv-
ice, the Orders of Matins and Vespers, the Litany and the
Suffrages of the Common Service for the Use of the Evangelical
Lutheran Congregations. Edited by Harry G. Archer and
Luther D. Reed. Philadelphia, PA: General Council Publica-
tion Board, 1900.

_____. Church Book for the Use of Evangelical Lutheran Con-
gregations. With music. Philadelphia, PA: J. K. Schryock,
1893.

HEROLD, Max. Vesperale, oder, die Nachmittage unserer Feste und
ihre gottesdienstliche Bereicherung: Vorschläge und Formu-
larien auf altkirchlichen Grunde für das gegenwartige Bedürf-
niss. 2 vols. in 1. Nördlingen: Beck, 1875-1881.

LIETZMANN, Albert, ed. Martin Luthers Geistliche Lieder. 2 vols.
KT, 24-25. Bonn: Marcus & Weber, 1907.

LINDEMAN, Ludvig Matthias. Koralbog indeholdenede melodier til
salmebog for lutherske kristne i Amerika. Minneapolis, MN:
Augsburg, 1899.

Norske Kirke. Koralbok for den Norske Kirke. Oslo: Aschehoug,
1947.

_____. Utkast til felles salmebok for den Norske Kirke. Forslag
fra salmeboknemnda, 1954. Oslo: Kirke- og Undervisninge-
departementet, 1968.

SANDVIK, Ole Mørk, and STEENBERG, Per. Graduale: Messebok
for den Norske Kirke. Oslo: J. W. Cappelen, 1925.

Suomen Evankelisluterialinen Kirkko. Svensk koralpsalmbok för den
Evangelisk-Lutherska Kyrkan i Finland. Antagen av Sextonde
Allmänna Kyrkomötet 1948. 2. uppl. Helsingfors: Fürbundet
för Svenskt Församlingsarbete i Finland, 1962.

Svenska Kyrkan. Den Svenska psalmboken av Konungen Gillad och
stadfäst ar 1937. Stockholm: P. Herzog, 1966.

_____. Veckans completorier. Fjärde, revid. och utvidgade
uppl. Lund: Utgivna av Laurentius Petri sällskapet, 1973.

_____. Veckans laudes. Fjärde, revid. uppl. Lund: Utgivna
av Laurentius Petri sällskapet, 1975.

_____. Veckans middagsböner. Fjärde, revid. och utvidgade
uppl. Lund: Utgivna av Laurentius Petri sällskapet, 1974.

2. Studies

AHLBERG, Bo. Laurentius Petris nattvardsuppfattning: zusammen-
fassung Laurentius Petris Abendmahlsauffassung. STL, 26.
Lund: Gleerup, 1964.

ALBRECHT, Christoph. Einführung in die Hymnologie. Berlin:
Evangelische Berlagsanstalt, 1973.

AMELN, Konrad, ed. Handbuch der deutschen evangelischen Kirchenmusik. Göttingen: Vandenhoeck & Ruprecht, 1935- .

_____. The Roots of German Hymnody of the Reformation Era. St. Louis, MO: Concordia, 1964.

AULEN, Gustaf Emanuel Hildebrand. Högmässans förnyelse liturgiskt och kyrkomusikaliskt. Stockholm: Diakonistyrelsens Bokförlag, 1961.

BENNIKE, Holger. Salmeordbog eller konkordans til Den danske salmebog. Copenhagen: Schultz, 1970.

BLANKENBURG, Walter. "Gottesdienstreform in der Sicht geschichtlicher, insonderheit kirchenmusikgeschichtlicher Entwicklung." Musik und Kirche, 45 (1975): 183-290.

BOSTROM, Otto H. "The Status of Liturgical Music in the Churches of the National Lutheran Council." The Lutheran Quarterly, 2 (1950): 369-381.

BUNNERS, Christian. Kirchenmusik und Seelenmusik: Studien zu Frömmigkeit und Musik im Luthertum des 17. Jahrhunderts. VEGL, 14. Berlin: Evangelische Verlagsanstalt, 1966.

BUSZIN, Walter E. Luther on Music. St. Paul, MN: North Central Publishing Co., 1958.

DEHNHARD, Walther. Die deutsche Psalmmotette in der Reformationszeit. Wiesbaden: Breitkopf & Härtel, 1971.

GABRIEL, Paul. Das deutsche evangelische Kirchenlied von Martin Luther bis zur Gegenwart. 3. Aufl. Berlin: Evangelische Verlagsanstalt, 1956.

_____. Geschichte des Kirchenliedes. Göttingen: Vandenhoeck & Ruprecht, 1957.

GARSIDE, Charles. "Some Attitudes of the Major Reformers toward the Role of Music in Liturgy." McCormick Quarterly, 21, 1 (1967): 151-168.

GLAHN, Henrik. Melodistudier til den lutherske salmesangs historie, fra 1524 til ca. 1600. 2 vols. Copenhagen: Rosenkilde og Bagger, 1954.

A Guide to Music for the Church Year. 4th ed. Minneapolis, MN: Augsburg, 1974.

HALTER, Carl, and SCHALK, Carl, eds. A Handbook of Church Music. St. Louis, MO: Concordia, 1978.

HEIDTKE, Waldemar Martin. "The Influence of the Early and Medieval Church on the German Evangelical Hymnody from 1524 un-
til 1675." Ph.D. dissertation, Marquette University, 1978.

HOBERG, Martin. Die Gesangsbuchillustration des 16. Jahrhunderts: Ein Beitrag zum Problem Reformation und Kunst. 2.
Aufl. Baden-Baden: Koerner, 1973.

HOELTY-NICKEL, Theodore. "Luther and Music." In Luther and
Culture, pp. 145-211. Decorah, IA: Luther College Press,
1960.

_____, ed. The Musical Heritage of the Lutheran Church. St.
Louis, MO: Concordia, 1959.

HONEMEYER, Karl. Thomas Müntzer und Martin Luther: ihr Ring-
en um d. Musik d. Gottesdienstes. Untersuchungen z. 'Deutzsch
Kirchenampt' 1523. Berlin: Verlag Merseburger, 1974.

HORN, Henry. O Sing Unto the Lord: Music in the Lutheran
Church. Revised ed. Philadelphia, PA: Fortress Press, 1966.

JACOBSSON, Jacob. Mässans budskap: en studie i de fasta sång-
partierna i svenska mässan under reformationstiden. BTP, 7.
Lund: Gleerup, 1958.

JALKANEN, Kaarlo. Lukkarin-ja urkurinvirka Suomessa 1809-1870.
Helsinki: Suomen Kirkkohistoriallinen Seura, 1976.

JENNY, Markus. Geschichte des deutschen-schweizerischen evangelischen Gesangbuch im 16. Jahrhundert. Basel: Bärenreiter-
Verlag, 1962.

_____. "The Hymns of Zwingli and Luther: A Comparison."
In Cantors at the Crossroads: Essays on Church Music in
Honor of Walter E. Buszin, pp. 45-63. Edited by Johannes
Reidel. St. Louis, MO: Concordia, 1967.

_____. "Was war neu am Kirchenlied der Reformation?" Musik
und Gottesdienst, 25 (1971): 80-88.

KAPPNER, Gerhard. Sakrament und Musik: zur liturgischen und
musikalischen Gestaltung des Spendeaktes. Gütersloh: Bertelsmann, 1952.

KEMPFF, Georg. Die Kirchengesang im lutherischen Gottesdienst
und seine Erneuerung. Leipzig: M. heinsius, 1937.

KLEMETTI, Heikki, ed. Liturgisia sävelmiä sekakuorolle. Helsinki:
Savellettären Toimisto, 1913- .

KOCH, Eduard Emil. Geschichte des Kirchenlieds und Kirchengesangs der christlichen inbesondere der deutschen evangelischen
Kirche. 8 vols. 3. Aufl. Stuttgart: C. Belser, 1866-1867.

KRATZEL, Günter. Das Thorner Kantional von 1587 und seine
deutsche Vorlagen: ein Beitrag zur Erforschung der deutsch-
polnischen Liedbeziehungen im Zeitalter der polnischen Reformation. Symbolae Slavicae, 6. Bern: Lang, 1979.

KROON, Sigurd. Ordinarium missae: studier kring melodierna till
Kyrie, Gloria, Santus och Agnus dei t. o. m. 1697 års Koralpsalmbok. LUA, n.f., 49/6. Lund: Gleerup, 1953.

_____. Tibi laus: studier kring den svenska psalmen nr 199.
LUA, n.f., 50/1. Lund: Gleerup, 1953.

LAGERCRANTZ, Ingeborg. Lutherska kyrkovisor. 2 vols. Helsingfors: Förbundet för Svenskt Församlingsarbete i Finland,
1948-1952.

LEAVER, Robin A. The Liturgy and Music: A Study of the Use
of the Hymn in Two Liturgical Traditions. GLS, 6. Bramcote,
Eng.: Grove Books, 1976.

LEUPOLD, Ulrich S. Die liturgischen Gesänge der evangelischen
Kirche im Zeitalter der Aufklärung und der Romantik. Kassel:
Bärenreiter, 1933.

_____. "Luther's Conception of Music in Worship." The Lutheran
Church Quarterly, 13 (1940): 66-69.

_____. "Luther's Musical Education and Activities." The Luth-
eran Church Quarterly, 12 (1939): 423-428.

LIEMOHN, E. The Chorale through Four Hundred Years of Musical
Development as a Congregational Hymn. Philadelphia, PA:
Muhlenberg Press, 1953.

LILIENCRON, Rochus Wilhelm Traugott Heinrich Ferdinand von.
Liturgisch-musikalische Geschichte der evangelischen Gottesdienste von 1523 bis 1700. Schleswig: J. Bergas, 1893; reprint ed., Hildesheim: Georg Olms, 1970.

LINDERHOLM, Emanuel. Tankar och förslag rörande svenska kyrkans ritual. Uppsala: Almqvist & Wiksell, 1938.

LINDQUIST, David. Oversyn av förslag til alternativt aftonsångs-
ritual. Avgivet av inom Ecklesiastikdepartementet till-kallad
sakkunnig. Stockholm, 1965.

LOCKWOOD, Lewis. "Music and Religion in the High Renaissance and the Reformation." In The Pursuit of Holiness in Late Medieval and Renaissance Religion, pp. 496-502. Edited by Charles Trinkaus and Heiko A. Oberman. Leiden: Brill, 1974.

MAHRENHOLZ, Christhard. Musicologica et Liturgica. Herausgegeben von Karl Ferdinand Müller. Kassel: Bärenreiter, 1960.

_____, and SOHNGEN, Oskar, eds. Handbuch zum Evangelischen Kirchengesangbuch. 3. Aufl. Göttingen: Vandenhoeck & Ruprecht, 1970.

MOSER, Hans Joachim. Die evangelische Kirchenmusik in Deutschland. 12 vols. in 8. Berlin: Merseburger, 1953-1954.

_____. "Luther als Musiker." In Speculum Musicae Artis: Festgabe für Heinrich Husmann zum 60. Geburtstag am 16. Dezember 1968, pp. 229-244. Herausgegeben von Heinz Becker und Reinhard Gerlach. München: Fink, 1970.

_____. Die Melodien der Lutherlieder. Leipzig: G. Schlössmann, 1935.

_____. Die Musik im frühevangelischen Osterreich. Kassel: Hinnenthal, 1954.

MULLER, Karl F., ed. Leiturgia: Handbuch des evangelischen Gottesdienstes, vol. 4: Die Musik des evangelischen Gottesdienstes. Kassel: Stauda, 1961.

NELLE, Wilhelm. Geschichte des deutschen evangelischen Kirchenliedes. 3. Aufl. Leipzig: Schlössmann, 1928.

NETTL, Paul. Luther and Music. Philadelphia, PA: Muhlenberg Press, 1948.

NUOTIO, Tarmo. Jumalanpalveluksemme musiikki. Helsinki: Agricola-Seura, 1963.

PELTO, Pentti. Kirkomusiikin suuria mestarieta. Helsinki: Suomen Kirkon Sisälähetysseura, Kirkon Opintokeskus, 1966.

PREUSS, Hans. Martin Luther der Künstler. Gütersloh: Bertelsmann, 1931.

RAMBACH, August Jakob. Uber D. Martin Luthers Verdienst um den Kirchengesang. Hamburg: Bohnische Buchhandlung, 1813; reprint ed., Hildesheim: Georg Olms, 1972.

RAUTENSTRAUCH, Johannes. Luther und die Pflege der kirchlichen Musik in Sachsen (14.-19. Jahrhundert). Leipzig: Breitkopf & Härtel, 1907; reprint ed., Hildesheim: Georg Olms, 1970.

RIEDEL, Johannes, ed. Cantors at the Crossroads: Essays on Church Music in Honor of Walter E. Buszin. St. Louis, MO: Concordia, 1967.

_____. The Lutheran Chorale: Its Basic Traditions. Minneapolis, MN: Augsburg, 1967.

ROSSLER, Martin. Die Liedpredigt: Geschichte einer Predigtgattung. VEGL, 20. Göttingen: Vandenhoeck & Ruprecht, 1976.

SCHLISSKE, Otto. Handbuch der Lutherlieder. Göttingen: Vandenhoeck & Ruprecht, 1948.

SCHUHMACHER, Gerhard, ed. Traditionen und Reformen in der Kirchenmusik: Festschrift für Konrad Ameln z. 75. Geburtstag am 6. July 1974. Kassel: Bärenreiter, 1974.

SCHWEITZER, Albert. J. S. Bach. Vorrede von Charles Marie Widor. Leipzig: Breitkopf & Härtel, 1908; J. S. Bach. Translated by Ernest Newman. London: Black, 1947.

SMEND, Julius. Vorträge und Aufsätze zur Liturgik, Hymnologie und Kirchenmusik. Gütersloh: Bertelsmann, 1925.

SOHNGEN, Oskar. Erneuerte Kirchenmusik: eine Streitschrift. VEGL, 19. Göttingen: Vandenhoeck & Ruprecht, 1975.

_____. Die kirchenmusikalische Amt in der Evangelischen Kirche der altpreussischen Union: die wichtigsten geltenden Verordnungen und Erlasse auf dem Gebiete der Kirchenmusik. Berlin: Evangelische Verlagsanstalt, 1950.

_____. "Die Musikanschauung der Reformatoren und die Uberwindung der mittelalterlichen Musiktheologie." In Musa, Mens, Musici: im Gedenken an Walter Vetter, pp. 51-62. Herausgegeben vom Institut für Musikwissenschaft der Humboldt-Universität zu Berlin. Leipzig: Deutscher Verlag für Musik, 1969.

_____. Die Wiedergrebut der Kirchenmusik: Wandlungen und Entscheidungen. Kassel: Bärenreiter, 1953.

STILLER, Günther. Johann Sebastian Bach und das Leipziger gottesdienstliche Leben seiner Zeit. Kassel: Bärenreiter, 1970.

SUNDBERG, Ove Kr. Musikk og liturgi. Oslo: Lutherstiftelsen, 1971.

TELL, Werner. Kleine Geschichte der deutschen evangelischen Kirchenmusik. Liturgik und Hymnologie. Bearb. von Georg Eberhard Jahn. Berlin: Evangelische Verlagsanstalt, 1962.

THUST, Karl Christian. Das Kirchen-Lied der Gegenwart. VEGL,
   21. Göttingen: Vandenhoeck & Ruprecht, 1976.

TUCHER VON SIMMELSDORF, Gottlieb, ed. Schatz des evangelisch-
   en Kirchengesangs im ersten Jahrhundert der Reformation. 2
   vols. Leipzig: Breitkopf & Härtel, 1848; reprint ed., Hildesheim: Georg Olms, 1972.

WIDDING, Severin. Dansk Messe, Tide- og Psalmensang 1528-1573.
   2 vols. Copenhagen: Levin & Munksgaard, 1933.

WOLFEL, Dieter. Nürnberger Gesangbuchgeschichte (1524-1791).
   Nürnberg: Stadtarchiv, 1971.

WOLFRUM, Philipp. Die Entstehung und erste Entwicklung des
   deutschen evangelischen Kirchenliedes im musikalischer Beziehung. Leipzig: Breitkopf & Härtel, 1890; reprint ed., Walluf:
   Sändig, 1972.

F. REFORMED CHURCH MUSIC

1. Texts

BERTHIER, Jacques. Music from Taizé. Chicago: G. I. A. Publications, 1981.

Nederlandse Hervormde Kerk. De gemeente zingt. Handreiking
   voor de zang der gemeente aan gemeenteleden, predikanten,
   cantorganisten, koorleden, kerkeraden en kerkvoogden. 2.
   druk. 's-Gravenhage: Boekencentrum, 1968.

PIDOUX, Pierre, ed. La Forme des prières et chants ecclésiastiques
   Genève 1542. Kassel: Bärenreiter, 1959.

_____, ed. Le Psautier huguenot du XVIe siècle. Mélodies et
   documents. 2 vols. Bâle: Editions Baerenreiter, 1962.

Psaumes, cantiques et textes pour le culte à l'usage des Eglises
   réformées suisses de langue française. Edité par la Fondation
   d'édition des Eglises protestantes romandes. Lausanne: Fondation d'édition des Eglises protestantes romandes, 1976.

Psaumes Octantetrois de David, mis en rime Françoise par Clément
   Marot et Théodore de Bèze. Genève: Jean Crespin, 1551;
   facsimile ed., New Brunswick, NJ: Friends of the Rutgers
   University Libraries, 1973.

SCHAFF, Philip, ed. Deutsches Gesangbuch: eine Auswahl geist-
   licher Lieder aus allen Zeiten der christlichen Kirche. Philadelphia, PA: Lindsay & Blakiston, 1859.

TERRY, Richard Runciman, ed. Calvin's First Psalter (1539).
Edited with critical notes and modal harmonies to the melodies.
London: E. Benn, 1932.

2. Studies

BRUNNER, Adolf. Musik im Gottesdienst: Wesen, Funktion und
Ort der Musik im Gottesdienst. 2. Aufl. Zürich: Zwingli
Verlag, 1968.

CLIVE, H. P. "The Calvinist Attitude to Music, and Its Literary
Aspects and Sources." Bibliothèque d'humanisme et renaissance, 19 (1957): 80-102, 294-319; 20 (1958): 79-107.

DOUEN, Orenlin. Clement Marot et le Psautier huguenot. 2 vols.
Paris: L'Imprimerie Nationale, 1878-1879.

GEROLD, Théodore. Les Plus anciennes mélodies de l'église protestante de Strasbourg et leurs auteurs. Paris: Alcan, 1928.

GUTKNECHT, Dieter. Untersuchungen zur Melodik des Hugenotten-
psalters. KBM, 67. Regensburg: Bosse, 1972.

HAGEMAN, Howard G. "Can Church Music be Reformed?" Reformed
Review, 14, 2 (1960): 19-28.

HASPER, H. Calvijns beginsel voor de zang in de eredienst, verk-
laard uit de Heilige Schrift en uit de gescheidenis der kerk:
een kerkhistorisch en hymnologisch onderzoek. 2 vols.
's-Gravenhage: Stichting Geestelijke Liederen uit den Schat
van de Kerk der Eeuwen, 1955-1976.

HONDERS, A. C., ed. Klinkend Geloof: uit de geschiedenis van
het Nederlandse kerkelijk en geestlijk lied. Hague: Boekencentrum, 1978.

JENNY, Markus. Zwinglis Stellung zur Musik im Gottesdienst.
Zürich: Zwingli Verlag, 1966.

KLING, H. "Les Compositeurs de la musique du Psautier hugenot
genevois." Rivista musicale italiana, 6 (1899): 496-530.

MILLER, Ross James. "John Calvin and the Reformation of Church
Music in the Sixteenth Century." Ph.D. dissertation, Clare-
mont Graduate School, 1971.

NEVIN, John Williamson. Address on Sacred Music. Princeton, NJ:
D. A. Borrenstein, 1827.

PATRICK, Millar. Four Centuries of Scottish Psalmody. London:
Oxford University Press, 1949.

PRATT, Waldo S. The Music of the French Psalter of 1562.
CUSM, 3. New York: Columbia University Press, 1939; reprint ed., New York: AMS Press, 1966.

REID, Stanford W. "The Battle Hymns of the Lord: Calvinist
Psalmody of the Sixteenth Century." In Sixteenth Century Es-
says and Studies, vol. 2, pp. 36-54. Edited by Carl S. Meyer.
St. Louis, MO: Concordia, 1970.

REIMANN, Hannes. Die Einführung des Kirchengesangs in der
Zürcher Kirche nach der Reformation. Zürich: Zwingli Verlag, 1959.

ROKSETH, Yvonne. "Les Premiers chants de l'église calviniste."
Revue de musicologie, 36 (1954): 7-20.

ROPER, Cecil Mizelle. "The Strasbourg French Psalters, 1539-
1553." Ph.D. dissertation, University of Southern California,
1972.

SCHNEIDER, Charles. L'Evolution musicale de l'église réformée de
1900 à nos jours. Avec cinq oeuvres musicales de Luther et
Calvin. Neuchâtel: Delachaux & Niestlé, 1952.

SOHNGEN, Oskar. "Zwinglis Stellung zur Musik im Gottesdienst."
In Theologie in Geschichte und Kunst, pp. 176-192. Heraus-
gegeben von Siegfried Herrmann und Oskar Söhngen. Witten:
Luther, 1968.

WEBER, Edith. "The French Huguenot Psalter: Its Historical and
Musical Background Yesterday and Today." Proceedings of the
Huguenot Society of London, 22 (1974): 318-329.

WIEDER, Frederik Caspar. De schriftuurlijke liedekens: de liederen der Nederlandsche Hervormden tot ap het jaar 1556.
's-Gravenhage: Nijhoff, 1900; reprint ed., Utrecht: HES,
1977.

G. ANGLICAN CHURCH MUSIC

1. Texts

BUCK, P. C., ed. Tudor Church Music. 10 vols. London, New
York: Oxford University Press, 1922-1929; reprint ed., Tudor
English Church Music. New York: Kalmus, 1976.

CHURCH OF ENGLAND. The Office of Holy Communion as Set by
John Merbecke. Introduction by E. H. Fellowes. London, New
York: Oxford University Press, 1949.

DAKERS, Lionel and TAYLOR, Cyril, eds. The Alternative Service
Book Psalter and Canticles Set to Anglican Chants. London:
Collins, 1981.

DANIEL, Ralph T., and LE HURAY, Peter, eds. The Sources of
English Church Music, 1549-1660. 2 vols. EECM, 1. London:
Stainer & Bell for the British Academy, 1972.

FELLOWES, Edmund H., ed. Tudor Church Music: Appendix with
Supplementary Notes. London: Oxford University Press, 1948.

JEBB, John, ed. The Choral Responses and Litanies of the United
Church of England and Ireland. 2 vols. London: G. Bell,
1847-1857.

KNIGHT, Gerald Hocken, and REED, William L., eds. The Treasury
of English Church Music. London: Blandford Press, 1965.

MARTENS, Mason. Music for the Holy Eucharist and the Daily Office for Trial Services in Contemporary Language. New York:
Music for Liturgy, 1971.

STAINER, John, and RUSSELL, William, eds. The Cathedral Prayer
Book: Being the Book of Common Prayer with the Music neces-
sary for the Use of Choirs, together with the Canticles and
Psalter pointed for Chanting and set to appropriate Chants.
London: Novello, Ewer; New York: H. W. Gray, 1871.

2. Studies

ARNOLD, John Henry. The Music of the Holy Communion. London:
Oxford University Press, 1946.

BARRETT, William Alexander. English Church Composers. New
York: Scribner & Welford; London: S. Low, Marston, Searle,
& Rivington, 1882; reprint ed., Freeport, NY: Books for Li-
braries Press, 1969.

_____. English Church Composers: The Great Musicians. With
extra chapters by Gilbert H. Beard. London: S. Low, Marston, 1925.

BELL, Maurice F. Church Music. New ed. ACh, 4. London:
Mowbray; Milwaukee, WI: Morehouse, 1922.

BENSON, Louis F. The English Hymn: Its Development and Use
in Worship. New York: Hodder & Stoughton, George H.
Doran, 1915.

BUMPUS, John S. A History of English Cathedral Music, 1549-1889.
2 vols. New York: Pott, 1908.

CHAPPELL, Paul. Music and Worship in the Anglican Church, 597-1967. SCW, 10. London: Faith Press, 1968.

CHURCH OF ENGLAND. Archbishop's Committee on Music in Church. Music in Church: The Report of the Committee appointed in 1948 by the Archbishops of Canterbury and York. Revised ed. Westminster: Church Information Board, 1957.

DAKERS, Lionel. A Handbook of Parish Music: A Working Guide for Clergy and Organists. London: Mowbray, 1976.

_____. Making Church Music Work. London: Mowbray, 1978.

DAVIES, Walford, and GRACE, Harvey. Music & Worship. 3d ed. London: Eyre & Spottiswoode, 1948.

DEARNLEY, Christopher. English Church Music, 1650-1750: In Royal Chapel, Cathedral, and Parish Church. New York: Oxford University Press, 1970.

DUFFIELD, Samuel W. English Hymns: Their Authors and History. New York: Funk & Wagnalls, 1886.

DUNCAN-JONES, A. S. Church Music. Milwaukee, WI: Morehouse, 1920.

FELLOWES, Edmund H. English Cathedral Music from Edward VI to Edward VII. 4th ed. London: Methuen, 1948.

FERNANDEZ, Dominique. La Rose des Tudors. Paris: Juilliard, 1976.

FOSTER, Myles B. Anthems and Anthem Composers: An Essay upon the Development of the Anthem from the Time of the Reformation to the End of the Nineteenth Century. New York: Novello, Ewer, 1901; reprint ed., New York: Da Capo Press, 1970.

FROST, Maurice. English and Scottish Psalm and Hymn Tunes, c. 1543-1677. New York: Oxford University Press, 1953.

GABLE, M. D., Jr. "The Hymnody of the Church--1789-1832." Historical Magazine of the Protestant Episcopal Church, 36 (1967): 249-270.

GARDNER, George. Worship and Music: Suggestions for Clergy and Choirmasters. London: SPCK, 1919.

_____, and NICHOLSON, Sydney H., eds. A Manual of English Church Music. London: SPCK; New York: Macmillan, 1923.

GILLMAN, Frederick J. The Evolution of the English Hymn. New York: Macmillan, 1927.

HARRISON, Frank L. "Church Music in England." In The New Oxford History of Music, vol. 4, pp. 465-519. New York: Oxford University Press, 1954- .

HATCHETT, Marion J. A Manual for Clergy and Church Musicians. New York: Church Hymnal Corporation, 1980.

_____. Music for the Church Year: A Handbook for Clergymen, Organists, and Choir Directors. New York: Seabury Press, 1964.

LE HURAY, Peter. Music and the Reformation in England, 1549-1660. New York: Oxford University Press, 1967; reprint ed., with corrections, New York: Cambridge University Press, 1978.

LONG, Kenneth R. The Music of the English Church. London: Hodder & Stoughton, 1972.

LUTKIN, Peter Christian. Music in the Church. Milwaukee, WI: Young Churchman, 1910; reprint ed., New York: AMS Press, 1970.

MARKS, Harvey B. The Rise and Growth of English Hymnody. New York: Revell, 1937.

MARSHALL, Madeleine F., and TODD, Janet M. English Congregational Hymns in the Eighteenth Century. Lexington, KY: University Press of Kentucky, 1982.

NICHOLSON, Sydney H. Quires and Places Where They Sing. London: G. Bell, 1932; reprint ed., London: SPCK, 1950, 1958.

PARRY, W. H. Thirteen Centuries of English Church Music. London: Hinrichsen Edition, 1946; reprint ed., New York: Gordon Press, 1977.

RAINBOW, Bernarr. The Choral Revival in the Anglican Church (1839-1872). SECM. New York: Oxford University Press, 1970.

ROUTLEY, Erik. A Short History of English Church Music. London: Mowbray, 1977.

SPENCE, Horace. Praises with Understanding: A Practical Handbook for Ordinands and the Clergy. Croydon, Eng.: Royal School of Church Music, 1959, 1960.

STEVENS, Denis. Tudor Church Music. New York: Merlin Press,
1955; reprint ed., New York: Da Capo Press, 1973.

_____. _____. 2d ed. London: Faber; New York: Norton,
1966.

TEMPERLEY, Nicholas. The Music of the English Parish Church.
2 vols. New York: Cambridge University Press, 1979.

WIENANT, Elwyn A., and YOUNG, Robert H. The Anthem in England and America. New York: Free Press, 1970.

H. PURITAN MUSIC

COTTON, John. Singing of Psalms, a Gospel Ordinance. London,
1647, 1650.

HARASZTI, Zoltán. The Enigma of the Bay Psalm Book. Chicago:
University of Chicago Press, 1956.

HOOD, George. A History of Music in New England, with Biographical Sketches of Reformers and Psalmists. Boston, MA: Wilkins,
Carter, 1846; reprint ed., New York: Johnson Reprint, 1970.

MacDOUGALL, Hamilton C. Early New England Psalmody. Brattle-
boro, VT: Stephen Daye Press, 1940.

PRATT, Waldo Selden. The Music of the Puritans. Boston, MA:
Oliver Ditson, 1921.

SCHOLES, Percy. The Puritans and Music in England and New
England. New York: Russell & Russell, 1962.

The VVhole Booke of Psalmes faithfully translated into English Metre.
Cambridge: Imprinted by S. Daye, 1640; The Bay Psalm Book:
A Facsimile Reprint of the First Edition of 1640. Chicago:
University of Chicago Press, 1956.

I. METHODIST CHURCH MUSIC

BETT, Henry. The Hymns of Methodism. 3d ed. London: Epworth Press, 1945.

LIGHTWOOD, J. T. The Music of the Methodist Hymnbook. New
and rev. ed. London: Epworth Press, 1955.

RICE, William C. "A Century of Methodist Music, 1850-1950." Ph.D.
dissertation, State University of Iowa, 1953.

J. OTHER FREE CHURCH MUSIC

ANDREWS, J. S. "Brethren Hymnology." Evangelical Quarterly,
    28 (1956): 208-229.

CARLEY, James R. "The Theology of Music in Worship." Encounter,
    24, 3 (1963): 365-378. [Disciples]

HEATON, Charles H. A Guidebook to Worship Services of Sacred
    Music. St. Louis, MO: Bethany Press, 1962. [Disciples]

PAYNE, Ernest A. "The First Free Church Hymnal (1583)." Trans-
    actions of the Congregational Historical Society, 18 (1956):
    3-16.

K. AMERICAN CHURCH MUSIC IN GENERAL

ELLINWOOD, Leonard. The History of American Church Music.
    New York: Morehouse-Gorham, 1953.

GOULD, Nathaniel D. Church Music in America, Comprising Its
    History and Its Peculiarities at Different Periods. Boston, MA:
    A. N. Johnson, 1853; reprint ed., New York: AMS Press,
    1972.

METCALF, Frank. American Writers and Compilers of Sacred Music.
    New York: Abingdon Press, 1921.

LI. HYMNOLOGY

A. REFERENCE WORKS

CLARK, Keith C. A Selective Bibliography for the Study of Hymns
    1980. PHSA, 33. Springfield, OH: Hymn Society of America,
    1980.

DIEHL, Katharine Smith. Hymns and Tunes: An Index. New York:
    Scarecrow Press, 1966.

FROST, Maurice, ed. English and Scottish Psalm and Hymn Tunes,
    c. 1543-1677. London: SPCK; London, New York: Oxford
    University Press, 1953.

HAYDEN, Andrew J., and NEWTON, Robert F. British Hymn Writers

and Composers: A Check-List giving their Dates and Places of
Birth and Death.   Croydon, Eng.:   Hymn Society of Great
Britain and Ireland, 1977.

JULIAN, John, ed.   Dictionary of Hymnology.   London: John Murray, 1892.

_____.   _____.   Rev. ed. with new supplement.   London:
John Murray, 1907; reprint eds., 2 vols.   New York: Dover
Publications, 1957; 2 vols.   Grand Rapids, MI: Kregel Publi-
cations, 1985.

McDORMAND, Thomas Bruce.   Judson Concordance to Hymns.   Valley Forge, PA: Judson Press, 1965.

MESSENGER, Ruth E.   A Short Bibliography for the Study of Hymns.
New York: Hymn Society of America, 1964.

PERRY, David W.   Hymns and Tunes Indexed by First Lines, Tune
Names, and Metres.   Croydon, Eng.:   Hymn Society of Great
Britain and Ireland, and The Royal School of Church Music,
1980.

ROGAL, Samuel J.   Sisters of Sacred Song: A Selected List of
Women Hymnodists in Great Britain and America.   New York:
Garland, 1981.

ROUTLEY, Erik.   An English-Speaking Hymnal Guide.   Collegeville,
MN: Liturgical Press, 1979.

B.   HISTORIES AND TEXTBOOKS

BENSON, Louis F.   The English Hymn: Its Development and Use
in Worship.   London, New York: Hodder & Stoughton, 1915;
reprint ed., Richmond, VA: John Knox Press, 1962.

_____.   The Hymnody of the Christian Church.   Richmond, VA:
John Knox Press, 1956.

BREED, David R.   The History and Use of Hymns and Hymn Tunes.
New York: Revell, 1903; reprint ed., New York: AMS Press,
1975.

BURKITT, F. C.   "Christian Hymns."   Proceedings of the Oxford
Society of Historical Theology, (1908):   1-38.

DUNSTAN, Alan.   "Hymnody in Christian Worship."   In The Study
of Liturgy, pp. 454-465.   Edited by Cheslyn Jones, Geoffrey
Wainwright, Edward Yarnold.   New York: Oxford University
Press, 1978.

ESKEW, Harry, and McELRATH, Hugh T. Sing with Understanding: An Introduction to Christian Hymnology. Nashville, TN: Broadman Press, 1980.

FOOTE, Henry W. Three Centuries of American Hymnody. Cambridge, MA: Harvard University Press, 1940.

HORDER, W. Garrett. The Hymn Lover: An Account of the Rise and Growth of English Hymnody. 2d ed. London: Curwen, 1900.

JACKSON, George Pullen. White Spirituals in the Southern Uplands. Chapel Hill, NC: University of North Carolina Press, 1933; reprint ed., New York: Dover Publications, 1965.

JEFFERSON, Herbert Alfred Lewis. Hymns in Christian Worship. London: Rockliff, 1950.

KEITH, Edmond D. Christian Hymnody. Nashville, TN: Convention Press, 1956.

LIGHTWOOD, James T. Hymn Tunes and their Story. New ed. London: Epworth Press, 1923.

LOVELACE, Austin C. The Anatomy of Hymnody. New York: Abingdon Press, 1965.

NINDE, Edward S. The Story of the American Hymn. New York: Abingdon Press, 1921.

NORTHCOTT, [William] Cecil. Hymns in Christian Worship: The Use of Hymns in the Life of the Church. London: Lutterworth Press; Richmond, VA: John Knox Press, 1964.

PARRY, Kenneth L. Christian Hymns. London: SCM Press, 1956.

PATRICK, Millar. The Story of the Church's Song. Edinburgh: The Scottish Churches Joint Committee on Youth, 1927.

_____. New ed. Edited by J. R. Sydnor. Richmond, VA: John Knox Press, 1962.

PHILLIPS, Charles Stanley. Hymnody Past and Present. New York: Macmillan, 1937.

PRATT, Waldo Selden. The History of English Hymnody. Hartford, CT: Hartford Seminary Press, 1895.

REYNOLDS, William Jensen. A Joyful Sound: Christian Hymnody. 2d ed. Prepared by Milburn Price. New York: Holt, Rinehart & Winston, 1978.

ROUTLEY, Erik. Ecumenical Hymnody. London: Independent
Press, 1959.

_____. Eternal Light. New York: Fischer, 1971.

_____. Hymn Tunes: An Historical Outline. Croydon, Eng.:
Royal School of Church Music, 196?

_____. The Music of Christian Hymnody. London: Independent
Press, 1957.

_____. A Panorama of Christian Hymnody. Collegeville, MN:
Liturgical Press, 1979.

_____. Words of Hymns: A Short History. Croydon, Eng.:
Royal School of Church Music, 1963?

SALLEE, James. A History of Evangelistic Hymnody. Grand
Rapids, MI: Baker, 1978.

STEVENSON, Arthur Linwood. The Story of Southern Hymnology.
Salem: A. L. Stevenson, 1931; reprint ed., New York: AMS
Press, 1975.

C. HYMN BOOKS

1. American

a. Denominations and Organizations

(1). Adventists

ADVENT CHRISTIAN GENERAL CONFERENCE OF AMERICA. The
Advent Christian Hymnal. Concord, NH: Advent Christian
Publications, 1967.

(2). Baptists (American)

Christian Worship: A Hymnal. Philadelphia, PA: Judson Press,
1941.

Hymns and Songs of the Spirit. Valley Forge, PA: Judson Press,
1966.

(3). Baptists (Southern Convention)

Broadman Hymnal. Nashville, TN: Broadman Press, 1940.

Baptist Hymnal (1956). Edited by Walter Hines Sims. Nashville, TN:
Convention Press, 1956.

Baptist Hymnal (1975). Edited by W. J. Reynolds. Nashville, TN: Convention Press, 1975; also published as Broadman Hymnal.

(4). Christian Church (Disciples of Christ)

Hymns and Songs of the Spirit. St. Louis, MO: Bethany Press, 1966.

Hymnbook for Christian Worship. St. Louis, MO: Bethany Press, 1970.

(5). Christian Reformed Church

Psalter Hymnal, Doctrinal Standards and Liturgy. Centennial ed. Grand Rapids, MI: Publication Committee of the Christian Reformed Church, 1959.

Psalter Hymnal Supplement, with Liturgical Studies and Forms. Grand Rapids, MI: Board of Publications of the Christian Reformed Church, 1974.

(6). Congregational Church

The Pilgrim Hymnal. Revised ed. Boston, MA: Pilgrim Press, 1935.

The Pilgrim Hymnal. Boston, MA: Pilgrim Press, 1958.

(7). Episcopal Church

PROTESTANT EPISCOPAL CHURCH IN THE U.S.A. The Hymnal (1892). Oxford: Oxford University Press; New York: Henry Frowde, 1892.

_____. The Hymnal (1916). New York: Church Pension Fund, 1916.

_____. The Hymnal (1940). New York: Church Hymnal Corporation, 1943.

_____. More Hymns and Spiritual Songs. Edited by Lee H. Bristol. New York: Walton Music Corp., 1971; enlarged ed., 1977.

_____. Hymns III: Church Hymnal Series III. New York: Church Hymnal Corporation, 1979.

_____. Cantate Domino: Hymnal Supplement G-2264. Chicago: G. I. A. Publications, 1979.

_____. Songs for Celebration: Church Hymnal Series IV. New York: Church Hymnal Corporation, 1980.

_____. The Hymnal 1982. New York: Church Hymnal Corp.,
1985.

(8). Evangelical and Reformed Church

The Hymnal. St. Louis, MO: Published for the Church by Eden
Publishing House, 1941.

(9). Evangelical Covenant Church of America

The Covenant Hymnal. Chicago: Covenant Book Concern, 1931.

The Hymnal of the Evangelical Covenant Church of America. Chicago: Covenant Press, 1950.

The Covenant Hymnal. Chicago: Covenant Press, 1973.

(10). Evangelical United Brethren Church

The Hymnal. Dayton, OH: Board of Publication, Evangelical United
Brethren Church, 1957.

(11). Inter-Varsity Christian Fellowship

Hymns II. Edited by Paul Beckwith, Hughes Huffman, and Mark
Hunt. Downers Grove, IL: InterVarsity Press, 1976.

(12). Lutheran Churches

American Lutheran Hymnal. Music ed. Compiled and edited by an
Intersynodical Committee. Columbus, OH: Lutheran Book Concern, 1930.

AMERICAN LUTHERAN CHURCH AND LUTHERAN CHURCH IN
AMERICA. Service Book and Hymnal. Minneapolis, MN: Augsburg, 1958.

AUGUSTANA EVANGELICAL LUTHERAN CHURCH. The Hymnal and
Order of Service. Rock Island, IL: Augustana Book Concern,
1926.

EVANGELICAL LUTHERAN CHURCH. Book of Worship with Hymns.
Philadelphia, PA: Lutheran Publications Society, 1899.

_____. The Lutheran Hymnary, including the Symbols of the
Evangelical Lutheran Church. Revised ed. Minneapolis, MN:
Augsburg, 1935.

INTER-LUTHERAN COMMISSION ON WORSHIP. Lutheran Book of
Worship. Minneapolis, MN: Augsburg, 1978.

LUTHERAN CHURCH--MISSOURI SYNOD. The Lutheran Hymnal.
Authorized by the Synods constituting the Evangelical Lutheran
Synodical Conference of North America. St. Louis, MO: Con-
cordia, 1941.

_____. Commission on Worship. Sing unto the Lord. Revised
and enl. ed. St. Louis, MO: Lutheran Church--Missouri Synod, 1969.

_____. Worship Supplement. St. Louis, MO: Concordia, 1969.

(13). Mennonites

Ausbund, das ist: etliche, schöne, christliche Lieder, wie sie in
dem Gefängnis zu Bassau in dem Schloss von den Schweitzer-
Brüdern, und von anderen rechtgläubigen Christen hin und her
gedichtet worden. Germantown: Saur, 1742; reprint ed., Mennonite Songbooks, American Series, 1. Amsterdam: Knuf,
1972?

The Christian Hymnary. Edited by John J. Overholt. Uniontown,
OH: Christian Hymnary Publishers, 1972.

GENERAL CONFERENCE MENNONITE CHURCH. The Mennonite
Hymnary. Edited by Walter H. Hohmann and Lester Hostetler.
Berne, IN: Mennonite Book Concern; Newton, KS: Mennonite
Publication Office, 1940.

MENNONITE BRETHREN CHURCHES. Worship Hymnal. Winnepeg,
Mon.: Christian Press; Fresno, CA: General Conference of the
Mennonite Brethren Churches; distributed by Hillsboro, KS:
Mennonite Brethren Publishing House, 1971.

OLD MENNONITE CHURCH AND GENERAL CONFERENCE MENNONITE
CHURCH. The Mennonite Hymnal. Newton, KS: Faith and Life
Press; Scottdale, PA: Herald Press, 1969.

(14). Methodist Churches

METHODIST CHURCH. The Methodist Hymnal. Baltimore, MD:
Methodist Publishing House, 1932.

_____. _____. Nashville, TN: Methodist Publishing House,
1964.

UNITED METHODIST CHURCH (U.S.). Supplement to the Book of
Hymns. Edited by Carlton F. Young. SWR, 11. Nashville,
TN: United Methodist Publishing House, 1982.

WESLEYAN METHODIST CHURCH. Hymns of the Living Faith.
Marion, IN: Wesleyan Publishing House, 1951.

_____. Hymns of Faith and Life. Winona Lake, IN: Light and
Life Press; Marion, IN: Wesley Press, 1967, 1979.

(15). Moravian Church

Hymnal and Liturgies of the Moravian Church. Bethlehem, PA:
Moravian Church in America, Northern and Southern Provinces,
1969.

(16). Presbyterian Churches

PRESBYTERIAN CHURCH IN THE U.S.A. The Hymnal. Edited by
Clarence Dickinson and C. W. Laufer. Philadelphia, PA: Presbyterian Board of Christian Education, 1933.

PRESBYTERIAN CHURCH, U.S., PRESBYTERIAN CHURCH IN THE
U.S.A., UNITED PRESBYTERIAN CHURCH OF NORTH AMER-
ICA, AND REFORMED CHURCH IN AMERICA. The Hymnbook.
Edited by David Hugh Hones. Richmond, VA: n.p., 1955.

PRESBYTERIAN CHURCH, U.S., UNITED PRESBYTERIAN CHURCH,
AND CUMBERLAND PRESBYTERIAN CHURCH. The Worshipbook:
Services and Hymns. Philadelphia, PA: Westminster Press,
1972.

(17). Reformed Church in America

Psalms of David with Hymns and Spiritual Songs. Also the Catechism, Confession of Faith and Liturgy of the Reformed Church in
the Netherlands. For the Use of the Reformed Dutch Church
in North America. New York: Printed by Hodge & Campbell,
1792.

REFORMED CHURCH IN THE U.S. AND REFORMED CHURCH IN
AMERICA. The Reformed Church Hymnal. New York: Board
of Publication and Bible-School Work, 1920.

(18). Roman Catholic Church

Hymnal of Christian Unity. Edited by Clifford A. Bennett and Paul
Hume. Toledo, OH: Gregorian Institute of America, 1964.

The English Liturgy Hymnal. Edition for the Congregation. Chicago: Friends of the English Liturgy, 1965.

Our Parish Prays and Sings: A Service Book for Liturgical Worship, with Official Texts, Hymns, Psalms and Paraliturgies.
Collegeville, MN: Liturgical Press, 1965.

Book of Sacred Song: A Selection of Hymns, Songs, Chants from
Contemporary and Folk Sources and the Church's Heritage of

Sacred Music. 6th ed. Collegeville, MN: Liturgical Press,
1977.

The Book of Catholic Worship. Washington, DC: Liturgical Conference, 1966.

Catholic Hymnal and Service Book. Edited by Frank Campbell-
Watson. New York: Benziger Editions, 1966.

People's Mass Book. Compiled by the People's Mass Book Committee.
Liturgical Commentaries by Alfred C. Longley. Cincinnati, OH:
World Library of Sacred Music, 1966; 3d ed., 1971.

Worship: A Complete Hymnal and Mass Book for Parishes. Chicago,
IL: G. I. A. Publicaitons, 1966, 1971.

Worship II: A Hymnal for Roman Catholic Parishes. Chicago, IL:
G. I. A. Publications, 1975.

Johannine Hymnal. Edited by Michael Gilligan and Joseph Cirou.
Oak Park, IL: American Catholic Press, 1970.

Psalm Praise. Chicago, IL: G. I. A. Publications, 1973.

The Catholic Hymnal: Hymns for Liturgical Celebration with the Order of the Mass and Masses from the Kyriale. English ed.
Huntington, IN: Our Sunday Visitor, 1974.

Jubilate Deo. Washington, DC: United States Catholic Conference,
1974.

Jubilate Deo. Arranged in modern notation by John Lee. Collegeville, MN: Liturgical Press, 1975.

The Catholic Liturgy Book: The People's Complete Service Book.
Baltimore, MD: Helicon, 1975; full score ed., Baltimore, MD:
Helicon, 1980.

Vatican II Hymnal. Edited by Terry L. Haws. Seattle, WA: New
Catholic Press of Seattle, 1975.

We Celebrate with Song: Companion Hymnal to We Celebrate, Seasonal Missalette. Edited by Charles G. Frischmann. Chicago,
IL: J. S. Paluch, 1976; 2d ed., 1979.

Swayed Pines Song Book. By Henry Bryan Hays. Collegeville, MN:
Liturgical Press, 1981.

(19). United Church of Christ

The Hymnal of the United Church of Christ. Philadelphia, PA:
United Church Press, 1974.

(20).   U.S. Armed Forces

Armed Forces Hymnal.   Washington, DC: U.S. Government Printing Office, 1958.

_____.   Catholic Supplement.   Chicago, IL: F. E. L. Church
   Publications, 1967.

Book of Worship for United States Forces.   Washington, DC: U.S.
   Government Printing Office, 1974.

   b.   Non-denominational and Commercial

American Hymns Old and New.   Edited by Albert Christ-Janer,
   C. W. Hughes, and Carlton Sprague Smith.   New York: Columbia University Press, 1980.

At Worship: A Hymnal for Young Churchmen.   Edited by Roy A.
   Burkhardt, W. Richard Weagly, and Hazel R. Brownson.   New
   York: Harper, 1951.

Christian Hymns.   Edited by R. P. Wetzler.   Minneapolis, MN:
   Art Masters Studios, 1979.

The Cokesbury Worship Hymnal.   Nashville, TN: Cokesbury Press,
   1938.

Ecumenical Praise.   Edited by Carlton R. Young, Austin C. Lovelace, Erik Routley, and Alec Wyton.   Carol Stream, IL: Agape,
   1977.

Harvard University Hymn Book.   With biographies and source notes.
   Cambridge, MA: Harvard University Press, 1964.

Hymnal for Colleges and Schools.   Edited by Ezra Harold Geer.
   New Haven, CT: Yale University Press, 1956.

Hymns for the Living Church.   Edited by Donald P. Hustad.   Carol
   Stream, IL: Hope Publishing Co., 1974.

Hymns for the Family of God.   Edited by Fred Bock.   Nashville,
   TN: Paragon Associates, 1976.

Inter-Church Hymnal: A Treasury of Hymns and Worship Material
   for Public and Private Use.   Edited by Frank A. Morgan and
   Katharine Howard Ward.   Chicago, IL: Biglow-Main-Excell,
   1936.

The New Church Hymnal.   Edited by H. Augustine Smith.   New
   York: Revell, 1937.

New Songs for the Church. Edited by Reginald Barrett-Ayres and
    Erik Routley. Norfolk, VA: Galliard, 1969.

The Oxford American Hymnal for Schools and Colleges. Edited by
    Carl F. Pfatteicher. New York: Oxford University Press, 1930.

Rejoice in the Lord: A Hymn Companion to the Scriptures. Edited
    by Erik Routley. Grand Rapids, MI: Eerdmans, 1985.

Songs of Thanks and Praise. Edited by Russell Schulz-Widmar.
    Chapel Hill, NC: Hinshaw, 1980.

Tabernacle Hymns, No. Five. Chicago, IL: Tabernacle Publishing
    Co., 1953.

Wesley Hymnbook. Edited by Franz Hildebrandt. London: A.
    Weekes, 1958; reprint ed., Kansas City, MO: Lillenas Publish-
    ing Co., 1963.

Westminster Praise. Edited by Erik Routley. Chapel Hill, NC:
    Hinshaw, 1976.

Worship and Service Hymnal. Chicago, IL: Hope Publishing Co.,
    1957.

2. Canadian

a. Anglican Church in Canada

The Book of Common Praise. Oxford: Oxford University Press;
    Toronto, Ont.: Henry Frowde, 1910.

_____. Being the Hymn Book of the Anglican Church of Canada.
    Revised ed. Toronto, Ont.: Humphrey Milford; Oxford: Ox-
    ford University Press, 1938.

UNITED CHURCH OF CANADA AND ANGLICAN CHURCH OF CAN-
    ADA. The Hymn Book of the Anglican Church of Canada and
    the United Church of Canada. Toronto, Ont.: Anglican Church
    of Canada and the United Church of Canada, 1971; corrected
    ed., 1972.

b. Baptist Church in Canada

The Hymnary. Being the Hymnary of the United Church of Canada
    with alterations. Toronto, Ont.: Ryerson Press, 1936.

c. Presbyterian Church in Canada

The Book of Praise. Revised ed. Don Mills, Ont.: Presbyterian
    Church in Canada, 1972.

d. Roman Catholic Church in Canada

Catholic Book of Worship. Toronto, Ont.: Gordon V. Thompson
Ltd., 1972.

e. United Church of Canada

The Hymnary. Toronto, Ont.: United Church Publishing House,
1930.

3. British

a. Hymnals for the Church of England

The Anglican Hymn Book. London: Tyndale Press, 1965; reprint
eds., London: Church Book Room Press, 1970, c1965; London:
Vine Books, 1977, c1965; Worthing, Eng.: W. Thompson, 1980,
c1965.

Church and School Hymnal. London: SPCK, 1926.

Church Hymnal for the Christian Year. Edited by Victoria Lady
Carbery, musical editors, Hugh Blair and L. R. Peace. London: Novello, 1917.

The English Hymnal. First ed. Edited by Percy Dearmer and
Ralph Vaughan Williams. London: Oxford University Press,
1906.

_____. First ed. [with 6 hymns omitted in response to protests
from 2 bishops]. London: Oxford University Press, 1907.

_____. New ed. London: Oxford University Press, 1933.

English Hymnal Service Book. London: Oxford University Press,
1962.

English Praise: a Supplement to the English Hymnal. London:
Oxford University Press, 1976.

Hymns Ancient and Modern. Trial ed. London: Novello, 1860.

_____. First ed. London: Printed for the Proprietors by Wm.
Clowes, 1861.

_____. First ed., with Supplement. London: Wm. Clowes, 1868.

_____. First revision. London: Wm. Clowes, 1875.

_____. First revision with Supplement. London: Wm. Clowes,
1889.

_____. Second revision. London: Wm. Clowes, 1904.

_____. Second Supplement [to 1889 ed.]. London: Wm. Clowes,
1916.

_____. Standard ed. [e plus g]. London: Wm. Clowes, 1922.

_____. Shortened ed. London: Wm. Clowes, 1939.

Hymns Ancient and Modern Revised. [Third revision.] London:
Wm. Clowes, 1950.

100 Hymns for To-day: A Supplement to Hymns Ancient and Modern. London: Wm. Clowes, 1969.

More Hymns for To-day: A Second Supplement to Hymns Ancient
and Modern. London: Wm. Clowes, 1980.

The New Office Hymn Book. 2 vols. London: Novello, 1908.

The Oxford Hymn Book. Edited by B. Harwood, William Sanday,
and Thomas B. Strong. Oxford: Clarendon Press, 1908.

A Plainsong Hymnbook. Edited by Sydney H. Nicholson. London:
Wm. Clowes, 1932.

b. Protestant Denominations

(1). Baptist Church

Psalms and Hymns. London: Psalms and Hymns Trust, 1858.

Psalms and Hymns with Supplement. London: Psalms and Hymns
Trust, 1880.

Baptist Church Hymnal. London: Psalms and Hymns Trust, 1900.

_____. Revised ed. London: Psalms and Hymns Trust, 1933.

Baptist Hymn Book. London: Psalms and Hymns Trust, 1962.

(2). Brethren Church

Christian Worship. Edited by H. Mudditt. Exeter, Eng.: Paternoster Press, 1976.

(3). Church of Ireland

Church Hymnal. Dublin: APCK, 1897.

_____. Dublin: APCK, 1919.

_____. Dublin: APCK, 1960.

(4). Church of Scotland

The Church Hymnary. First ed. London: Oxford University
Press, 1898.

_____. Revised ed. London: Oxford University Press, 1927.

_____. 3d ed. London: Oxford University Press, 1973.

LIVINGSTON, Neil. The Scottish Metrical Psalter of A.D. 1635 Reprinted in Full from the Original Work, the Additional Matter
and Various Readings found in the Editions of 1565 &c. being
appended; and the Whole Illustrated by Dissertations, Notes
and Facsimiles. Glasgow: Maclure & Macdonald, 1864.

TERRY, Richard Runciman, ed. The Scottish Psalter of 1635 edited
with Modal Harmonies. Facsimiles added. London: Novello;
New York: H. W. Gray, 1935.

The Scottish Psalter: Metrical Version and Scripture Paraphrases.
Last musical ed. London: Oxford University Press, 1929.

MACLAGAN, Douglas J., ed. The Scottish Paraphrases: ... Collected ... [with] an Account of their History, Authors and
Sources. Edinburgh: Andrew Eliot, 1889.

BROWN, James Rossie. The Murrayfield Psalter: A New Metrical
Version and Notes. Edinburgh: Church of Scotland Committee
on Publications, 1954.

(5). Congregational Union of England and Wales

Congregational Hymn Book. Edited by J. Conder. London: Jackson & Walford for Congregational Union of England and Wales,
1836.

New Congregational Hymn Book. London: Hodder & Stoughton for
Congregational Union of England and Wales, 1855.

New Congregational Hymn Book, with Supplement. London: Hodder
& Stoughton for Congregational Union of England and Wales,
1874.

Congregational Church Hymnal. Edited by G. S. Barrett. London:
Congregational Union of England and Wales, 1887.

Congregational Hymnary. London: Congregational Union of England and Wales, [1916].

Congregational Praise. London: Independent Press for the Con-
    gregational Union of England and Wales, 1951.

(6). Society of Friends

The Fellowship Hymn Book. Fist ed. London: Headley Brothers;
    Allen & Unwin, 1909.

The Fellowship Hymn Book with Supplement. London: Brotherhood
    Publishing House, 1920.

The Fellowship Hymn Book. Revised ed. London: Novello; Allen
    & Unwin, 1933.

(7). Methodist Church

A Collection of Hymns for the Use of the People called Methodists.
    Edited by John Wesley. London: The Foundery, 1780.

A Collection of Hymns for the Use of the People called Methodists,
    with New Supplement. [First ed. with music.] London: Wes-
    leyan Conference Office, 1876.

The Methodist Hymn Book. London: Wesleyan Conference Office,
    1904.

_____. London: Methodist Conference Office, 1933.

Hymns and Songs: A Supplement to the Methodist Hymn Book.
    London: Methodist Publishing House, 1969.

BRALEY, Bernard, ed. One World Songs. London: Methodist
    World Development, 1978.

(8). Presbyterian Church of England and Wales

Church Praise. London: J. Nisbet, 1885.

_____. Revised ed. London: Nisbet, 1908.

(9). United Reformed Church in England and Wales

New Church Praise. Edinburgh: St. Andrews Press, 1975.

c. Roman Catholic

Westminster Hymnal. 2d ed. Edited by Richard R. Terry. London:
    Washbourne, 1913.

_____. New and rev. ed. Edited by W. S. Bambridge. London:
    Burns, Oates & Washbourne, 1940.

A Daily Hymn Book. London: Burns, Oates & Washbourne, 1930.

Praise the Lord. Edited by Wilfred Trotman. London: Geoffrey
     Chapman, 1966.

_____. Edited by John Ainslie, Stephen Dean, and Paul Inwood.
     London: Geoffrey Chapman, 1972.

The Parish Hymn Book. Edited by J. Rush. London: L. J. Cary,
     1968.

New Hymns for All Seasons. Edited by James J. Quinn. London:
     Geoffrey Chapman, 1970.

Sing a New Song to the Lord. Edited by Kevin Mayhew. South-
     end-on-Sea, Eng.: Mayhew-McCrimmon, 1970.

New Catholic Hymnal. Edited by Anthony Petti and Geoffrey Lay-
     cock. London: Faber Music, 1971; New York: St. Martin's
     Press, 1972, c1971.

The Veritas Hymnal. Edited by Jerry Threadgold. Commissioned
     by the National Commission for Sacred Music and approved by
     the Irish Church Music Association. 2d ed. Dublin: Veritas,
     1974.

Sing the Mass. London: Geoffrey Chapman, 1975.

A Song in Season. Edited by J. Walsh, C. Watson, L. Bevenot,
     and Sr. Cecilia Cavenaugh. London: Collins, 1976.

          d. Non-denominational

BRITISH BROADCASTING CORPORATION. The BBC Hymn Book.
     London: Oxford University Press, 1951.

_____. Broadcast Praise. London: Oxford University Press,
     1981.

Christian Hymns. Edited by Paul E. G. Cook and Graham Harrison.
     Bridgend, Wales: Evangelical Movement of Wales, 1977.

Christian Praise. London: Tyndale Press; Chicago: Inter-Varsity
     Press, 1957.

Grace Hymns. London: Grace Publications Trust, 1977.

Hymns for Celebration: A Supplement for Use at Holy Communion
     Today. Edited by Erik Routley and John Wilson. Croydon,
     Eng.: Royal School of Church Music, 1974.

Hymns of Western Europe. Edited by H. Walford Davies, W. H.
    Hadow, and R. R. Terry. London: Oxford University Press,
    1927.

Hymns for Today's Church. London: Hodder & Stoughton, 1982.

Sixteen Hymns of To-day for Use as Simple Anthems. Edited by
    John Wilson. Croydon, Eng.: Royal School of Church Music,
    1978.

Songs of Praise. Edited by Percy Dearmer, Ralph Vaughan Wil-
    liams, and Martin Shaw. London: Oxford University Press,
    1925.

_____. Enlarged ed. London: Oxford University Press, 1931.

Y.M.C.A. Hymnal. Revised ed. London: YMCA, 1928.

    e. Hymnals for Schools and Young People

    (1). Public Schools (i.e., English Private Schools)

Public School Hymn Book. London: Novello, 1903.

_____. Revised ed. London: Novello, 1919.

_____. Revised ed. London: Novello, 1949.

Hymns for Church and School, being the Fourth Edition of the
    Public School Hymn Book. London: Novello, 1964.

The Clarendon Hymn Book. London: Oxford University Press,
    1936.

Eton College Hymn Book. Oxford: Oxford University Press, 1937.

Hymns for the Chapel of Harrow School. 7th ed. London: Oxford
    University Press, 1927.

Hymns for Use at Merchant Taylors School. First music ed. Lon-
    don: Oxford University Press, 1974.

Wellington College Hymn Book. Edited by W. K. Stanton. London:
    Novello, 1937.

Winchester College Hymn Book. First ed. with music. London:
    Oxford University Press, 1928.

_____. Revised ed. London: Oxford University Press, 1962.

Worksop College Hymn Book. Edited by L. J. Blake. London:
    Novello, 1938.

(2). State Schools and General Hymn Books
for Children

The Cambridge Hymnal. Edited by David Holbrook and Elizabeth
Poston. Cambridge: Cambridge University Press, 1967.

The Daily Service: Prayers and Hymns for use in Schools. Edited
by George W. Briggs. London: Oxford University Press,
1936.

_____. Revised ed. London: Oxford University Press, 1947.

The English School Hymn Book. Edited by D. MacMahon. London:
University of London Press, 1939.

Golden Bells: Hymns for Young People. London: Children's
Special Service Mission, 1925.

Hosanna! A Book of Praise for Children. London: SPCK, n.d.
[c. 1928].

Hymns Ancient and Modern. School ed., with daily services. London: Wm. Clowes, 1958.

The Kingsway Hymn Book. Edited by L. Russell. London: Evans
Brothers, 1952.

Prayers and Hymns for Use in Schools. [Abridged ed. of Songs
of Praise.] London: Oxford University Press, 1927.

Psalm Praise. London: Falcon Press; Chicago: G. I. A. Publications, 1974.

The School Hymn Book. London: Evans Brothers, n.d. [c. 1926].

School Worship. London: Congregational Union of England and
Wales, 1926.

Songs of Praise for Boys and Girls. Edited by Percy Dearmer, R.
Vaughan Williams, and Martin Shaw. London: Oxford University Press, 1929.

A Students' Hymnal. Edited by H. Walford Davies. London: Oxford University Press, 1923; also published [without Welsh
hymns] as Hymns of the Kingdom: Being the English Section
of A Students' Hymnal. London: Oxford University Press,
1923.

Sunday School Hymnary. Edited by Carey Bonner. London: National Sunday School Union, [1905].

Sunday School Praise. London: National Sunday School Union, 1958.

Youth Praise. London: Falcon Books, 1966.

    f. Private and Miscellaneous Collections

Cantate Domino. Geneva: World's Student Christian Federation, 1924.

_____. [2d ed.] Geneva: World's Student Christian Federation, 1930.

_____. [3d ed.] Geneva: World's Student Christian Federation, 1950.

_____. New [4th] ed. Oxford: Oxford University Press; Geneva: World Council of Churches, 1980.

The Chorale Book for England. Edited by Catherine Winkworth, William Sterndale Bennett, and Otto Goldschmidt. London: Longman, Green, Longman, Roberts, & Green, 1863.

_____. London: Longman, Green, Longman, Roberts, & Green, 1865.

Collected Hymns, Sequences and Carols of John Mason Neale. By John Mason Neale. London: Hodder & Stoughton, 1914.

Hymns: The Yattendon Hymnal. Edited by Robert Bridges and H. E. Wooldridge. Oxford: Clarendon Press, 1899.

Lyra Germanica: Hymns for the Sundays and Chief Festivals of the Christian Year. Edited by Catherine Winkworth. London: Longman, Brown, Green & Longmans, 1855.

Lyra Germanica: Second Series: The Christian Life. Edited by Catherine Winkworth. London: Longman, Brown, Green, Longmans & Roberts, 1858.

Mainly Hymns. By Brian Wren. Leeds, Eng.: John Paul the Preacher's Press, 1980.

Piae Cantiones: A Colleciton of Church and School Song, chiefly Ancient Swedish, originally published in 1582 by Theodoric Petri of Nyland. Revised and re-edited, with preface and explanatory notes by the Rev. G. R. Woodward. London: Chiswick Press for the Plainsong and Medieval Music Society, 1910.

Pilgrim Praise: Hymns. By Frederic H. Kaan. London: Stainer & Bell; New York: Galaxy, 1971; Great Yarmouth, Eng.: Galliard, 1972.

Songs of Syon.   Edited by G. R. Woodward.   Tune book only.
London: Schott, 1904.

_____.   3d ed., rev. & enl. [with full texts].   London: Schott,
1910.

Twenty-Six Hymns (with Music).   By Frederick Pratt Green.   London: Methodist Publishing House, 1971.

Worship Song.   Edited by W. Garrett Horder.   London: Eliot Stock,
1896.

Treasury of Hymns.   [As above without chants & anthems.]   London: Eliot Stock, 1896.

Worship Song.   2d ed.   London: Novello, 1905.

g.   Other Hymn Books

The Australian Hymn Book.   Sydney: Collins, 1977; reprint ed.,
With One Voice: A Hymn Book for All the Churches.   London:
Collins, 1979.

CHURCH OF ENGLAND IN AUSTRALIA AND TASMANIA.   The Book
of Common Praise, with Supplement.   Melbourne: Oxford
University Press, 1947.

ERICKSON, J. Irving.   Twice Born Hymns.   Chicago, IL: Covenant Press, 1976.

D.   COMPANIONS AND HANDBOOKS TO HYMNALS
(arranged chronologically)

1.   American

CREAMER, David.   Methodist Hymnology: Comprehending Notices
of the Poetical Works of John and Charles Wesley, showing the
Origin of their Hymns in the Methodist Episcopal, Methodist
Episcopal South, and Wesleyan Collections; also, of such other
Hymns as are not Wesleyan, in the Methodist Episcopal Hymnbook, and some account of the Authors; with Critical and Historical Observations.   New York: Published for the Author,
1848.

HUTCHINS, Charles L.   Annotations of the Hymnal: Consisting
of Notes, Biographical Sketches of Authors, Originals and Ref-
erences.   Hartford, CT: Church Press, M. H. Mallory, 1872.
[Episcopal]

NUTTER, Charles S. Hymn Studies: An Illustrated and Annotated Edition of the Hymnal of the Methodist Episcopal Church [1878]. New York: Phillips & Hunt, 1884.

DUFFIELD, Samuel W. English Hymns: Their Authors and History. New York: Funk & Wagnalls, 1886; 3d ed., 1888. [Companion to Laudes Domini, 1884]

TILLETT, Wilbur F. Our Hymns and Their Authors: An Annotated Edition of the Hymn Book of the Methodist Episcopal Church South [1889]. Nashville, TN: Publishing House of the Methodist Episcopal Church, South, 1889.

ROBINSON, Charles Seymour. Annotations upon Popular Hymns. New York: Hunt & Eaton, 1893. [Laudes Domini, 1884, and New Laudes Domini, 1892]

NUTTER, Charles S., and TILLETT, Wilbur F. The Hymns and Hymn Writers of the Church: An Annotated Edition of the Methodist Hymnal [1905]. New York: Eaton & Mains, 1911.

BRITT, Matthew, ed. The Hymns of the Breviary and Missal. New York: Benziger, 1922.

_____. _____. Revised ed. New York: Benziger, 1955.

RODEHEAVER, Homer A. Hymnal Handbook for Standard Hymns and Gospel Songs. Chicago, IL: The Rodeheaver Company, 1931; reprint ed., New York: AMS Press, 1975.

COVERT, William Chalmers, and LAUFER, Calvin Weiss, eds. Handbook to the Hymnal. Philadelphia, PA: Presbyterian Board of Christian Education, 1935. [Presbyterian Hymnal, 1933]

McCUTCHAN, Robert Guy. Our Hymnody: A Manual of the Methodist Hymnal [1935]. New York: Methodist Book Concern, 1937.

_____. _____. 2d ed. New York: Abingdon Press, 1942.

POLACK, W. G. The Handbook to the Lutheran Hymnal [1941]. St. Louis, MO: Concordia, 1942.

_____. _____. 3d ed. St. Louis, MO: Concordia, 1958; reprint ed., Milwaukee, WI: Northwestern Publishing House, 1975.

HOSTETLER, Lester. Handbook to the Mennonite Hymnary [1940]. Newton, KS: General Conference of the Mennonite Church, Board of Publications, 1949.

The Hymnal 1940 Companion. New York: Church Pension Fund,
    1949. [Protestant Episcopal]

HAEUSSLER, Armin. The Story of Our Hymns: The Handbook to
    the Hymnal of the Evangelical and Reformed Church [1941].
    St. Louis, MO: Eden Publishing House, 1952.

CORNWALL, J. Spencer. Stories of Our Mormon Hymns. Salt
    Lake City, UT: Deseret Book Co., 1961; 2d ed., 1963. [Com-
    panion to Hymns: Church of Jesus Christ of Latter-Day Saints]

REYNOLDS, William Jensen. Hymns of Our Faith: A Handbook for
    the Baptist Hymnal [1956]. Nashville, TN: Broadman Press,
    1964.

RONANDER, Albert C., and PORTER, Ethel K. Guide to the Pil-
    grim Hymnal. Philadelphia, PA: United Church Press, 1966.

BUCKE, Emory Stevens, ed. Companion to the Hymnal: A Hand-
    book to the 1964 Methodist Hymnal. Nashville, TN: Abingdon
    Press, 1970.

WAKE, Arthur N. Companion to Hymn book for Christian Worship.
    St. Louis, MO: Bethany Press, 1970.

REYNOLDS, William Jensen. Companion to the Baptist Hymnal
    [1976]. Nashville, TN: Broadman Press, 1976.

HIGGINSON, J. Vincent. Handbook for American Catholic Hymnals.
    Springfield, OH: Hymn Society of America, 1976.

SEAMAN, William R. Companion to the Hymnal of the Service Book
    and Hymnal [1958]. Minneapolis, MN: Commission on the Lit-
    urgy and Hymnal, 1976. [Lutheran Church in America]

ROUTLEY, Erik. Companion to Westminster Praise. Chapel Hill,
    NC: Hinshaw Music, 1977.

HUSTAD, Donald P. Dictionary-Handbook to Hymns for the Living
    Church. Carol Stream, IL: Hope Publishing Co., 1978.

HUGHES, C. W. American Hymns Old and New: Notes on the
    Hymns and Biographies of the Authors and Composers. 2 vols.
    New York: Columbia University Press, 1980. [Companion to
    Christ-Janer, Hughes, and Smith, American Hymns Old and
    New]

2. Canadian

ANGLICAN CHURCH OF CANADA. The Book of Common Praise:

Being the Hymn Book of the Church of England in Canada
[1908]. Annotated ed., the notes written and compiled by
James Edmund Jones. Toronto, Ont.: Oxford University
Press, 1909.

MACMILLAN, Alexander. Hymns of the Church: A Companion to
the Hymnary of the United Church of Canada [1930]. Toronto,
Ont.: United Church Publishing House, 1935.

OSBORNE, Stanley L. If Such Holy Song: The Story of the Hymns
in the Hymn Book, 1971. Whitby, Ont.: Institute of Church
Music, 1976.

3. British

BURGESS, William Pennington. Wesleyan Hymnology; or, A Companion to the Wesleyan Hymn Book. London: Thomas Riley,
1845.

————. ————. 2d ed. London: John Snow, 1846.

GADSBY, John, ed. Memoirs of the Principal Hymn-Writers & Com-
pilers of the 17th, 18th, & 19th Centuries. London: Gadsby,
Groombridge & Sons, 1851; 5th ed., London: J. Gadsby, 1882.
[Companion to Gadsby's Selection of Hymns and its supplements]

KUBLER, Theodore. Historical Notes to the Lyra Germanica: Containing Brief Memoirs of the Authors therein translated, ...
with Notices of other German Hymnwriters represented in other
English Collections. London: Longman, Green, 1865. [with
notes to the Chorale-Book for England]

MILLER, Josiah. Our Hymns: Their Authors and Origin: ... A
Companion to the New Congregational Hymn Book [1855, 1859].
London: Jackson, Walford & Hodder, 1866.

BIGGS, Louis Coutier, ed. Hymns Ancient and Modern for Use in
the Services of the Church, with Annotations, Originals, Ref-
erences, Authors' and Translators' Names, and with some Metrical Translations of the Hymns in Latin and German. London:
Novello, 1867.

BICKERSTETH, Edward Henry, ed. The Annotated Hymnal Companion to the Book of Common Prayer. London: Sampson Low,
Marston, Searle & Rivington, 1873; 3d ed., 1890.

CRAWFORD, G. A., and EBERLE, J. A. Church Hymnal (Church
of Ireland) with Biographical Index. Dublin: APCK, 1873;
revised ed., 1878; musical ed., 1894.

SULLIVAN, Arthur, ed. Church Hymns with Tunes. With notes
and illustrations to the hymns by John Ellerton. London:
SPCK, 1881.

MOORSOM, Robert Maude, ed. A Historical Companion to Hymns
Ancient and Modern: Containing the Greek and Latin, the
German, Italian, French, Danish and Welsh Hymns; the First
Lines of the English Hymns; the Names of All Authors and
Translators; Notes and Dates. London: Parker, 1889.

_____. _____. 2d ed. London: Clay, 1903.

LOVE, James. Scottish Church Music: Its Composers and Sources.
Edinburgh: Blackwood, 1891.

STEVENSON, George John. The Methodist Hymn Book [1876]: Illustrated with Biography, History, Incident and Anecdote. 2d
ed. London: Charles H. Kelly, 1894.

COWAN, William, and LOVE, James. The Music of the Church
Hymnary [1898] and the Psalter in Metre, Its Sources and Composers. Edinburgh, London: Henry Frowde, 1901.

FURNEAUX, William M. A Companion to the Public School Hymn
Book [1903]. London: Novello, 1904.

TELFORD, John. The Methodist Hymn Book Illustrated. London:
Charles H. Kelly, 1906. [1904 ed.]

_____. The New [1933] Methodist Hymn Book Illustrated in His-
tory and Experience. London: Epworth Press, 1934.

_____. The Methodist Hymnbook Illustrated in History and Ex-
perience. 7th ed. London: Epworth Press, 1959.

LINDSAY, T. S. The Church's Song: A Companion to the Irish
Church Hymnal [1897]. Dublin: APCK, 1908.

FRERE, Walter Howard. Hymns Ancient and Modern for Use in the
Services of the Church, with Accompanying Tunes. Historical
Edition. London: Wm. Clowes, 1909.

BROWNLIE, John. The Hymns and Hymn Writers of the Church
Hymnary [1898]. London: Henry Frowde, 1911.

BROOKE, C. W. A., ed. Companion to Hymns Ancient and Modern
(Old Edition) [1889]. London: Pitman, 1914.

GILLMAN, Frederick John. The Story of Our Hymns: Being an
Historical Companion to "The Fellowship Hymn Book" [1920].
London: Swarthmore Press, 1921.

DEARMER, Percy. A Subject Index of Hymns in the English Hymnal and Songs of Praise. London: Oxford University Press, 1926.

KINLOCH, Tom Fleming. An Historical Account of the Church Hymnary, Revised Edition [1927]. Cambridge: Heffer, 1928.

DEARMER, Percy, and JACOB, Archibald, eds. Songs of Praise Discussed: A Handbook to the Best-known Hymns and to Others recently introduced. London: Oxford University Press, 1933; reprinted 1952.

BONNER, Carey, and WHITLEY, W. T., eds. A Handbook to the Baptist Church Hymnal Revised [1933]. London: Psalms and Hymns Trust, 1935.

LIGHTWOOD, James T. The Music of the Methodist Hymn Book: Being the Story of Each Tune with Biographical Notices of the Composers. London: Epworth Press, 1935.

_____. _____. New ed., edited and revised by Francis B. Westbrook. London: Epworth Press, 1955.

MOFFATT, James, and PATRICK, Millar, eds. Handbook to the Church Hymnary, with Supplement [1927]. London: Oxford University Press, 1935; reprinted 1951.

GREGORY, Arthur Stephen. Praises with Understanding. 2d ed. London: Epworth Press, 1949. [Methodist Hymn Book, 1933]

KELYNACK, William S. Companion to the School Hymn Book of the Methodist Church. London: Epworth Press, 1950.

MARTIN, Hugh, ed. A Companion to the Baptist Church Hymnal [1933]. London: Psalms and Hymns Trust, 1953.

PARRY, Kenneth Lloyd, and ROUTLEY, Erik, eds. Companion to Congregational Praise. London: Independent Press, 1953.

ROUTLEY, Erik. The Organist's Guide to Congregational Praise. London: Independent Press, 1957.

FROST, Maurice, ed. Historical Companion to Hymns Ancient and Modern. London: Clowes, 1962.

MARTIN, Hugh, ed. The Baptist Hymn Book Companion [1962]. London: Psalms and Hymns Trust, 1962.

WILSON, John. A Short Companion to Hymns and Songs [1969]: (A Supplement to the Methodist Hymn Book). Iron-Bridge, Eng.: Methodist Church Music Society, 1969.

BARKLEY, John M., ed. Handbook to the Church Hymnary [3d
ed., 1973]. London: Oxford University Press, 1979.

E.   HYMN BOOK CRITICISM

BUNN, Leslie H. "English Presbyterian Hymnody." Bulletin of the
Hymn Society of Great Britain, 3, 8 (1953): 129-134.

_____. "The Impact of Hymns Ancient and Modern upon Hymn-
ody." Bulletin of the Hymn Society of Great Britain, 5, 12
(1964): 198-204.

CLARKE, W. K. Lowther. A Hundred Years of Hymns Ancient and
Modern. London: Wm. Clowes, 1960.

GILLMAN, F. J. "Reality in Worship, with Some Reference to the
Society of Friends and their Relation to Hymn Singing." Bulletin of the Hymn Society of Great Britain, Occasional Papers,
no. 2 (October 1939).

GOLDHAWK, Norman. "Hymns for the Use of the People called
Methodists, 1980." Bulletin of the Hymn Society of Great Britain, 9, 9 (1980): 170-175.

HUTCHINGS, Arthur J. B. "The Literary Aspects of the English
Hymnal." Bulletin of the Hymn Society of Great Britain, 4, 3
(1956): 34-48.

MACMEEKEN, J. W. History of the Scottish Metrical Psalms, with
an Account of the Paraphrases and Hymns, and of the Music
of the Old Psalter. Glasgow: McCulloch, 1872.

MARTIN, Hugh. "The Making of the Baptist Hymn Book." Bulletin
of the Hymn Society of Great Britain, 5, 10 (1963): 147-154.

ROUTLEY, Erik. "Antiquissima, Novissima." Bulletin of the Hymn
Society of Great Britain, 4, 14 (1959): 213-219. [Hymns Ancient and Modern's antecedents]

_____. "The Chorale-Book for England, 1863." Bulletin of the
Hymn Society of Great Britain, 5, 11 (1963): 173-186.

_____. "The English Hymnal, 1906-1956." Bulletin of the Hymn
Society of Great Britain, 4, 2 (1956): 17-26.

_____. "Hymns Ancient and Modern: The 1868 Supplement."
Bulletin of the Hymn Society of Great Britain, 6, 10 (1968):
103-109.

_____ . "Hymns Ancient and Modern Revised: A Review." Bulletin of the Hymn Society of Great Britain, 2, 10 (1950): 145-159.

_____ . "That Dreadful Red Book." Bulletin of the Hymn Society of Great Britain, 8, 5 (1974): 80-85. [Hymns Ancient and Modern, 1904]

_____ . "Worship Song, 1905." Bulletin of the Hymn Society of Great Britain, 5, 13 (1964): 225-234.

WILSON, John. "The Public School Hymn Book, 1949, 1959." Bulletin of the Hymn Society of Great Britain, 5, 1 (1960): 1-10.

YOUNG, John. "Scottish Hymn Books Antecedent to the Church Hymnary (1927)." Bulletin of the Hymn Society of Great Britain, 3, 3 (1952): 58-66.

F. SACRED CAROLS AND FOLK SONGS

1. Collections (arranged chronologically)

SANDYS, William. Christmas Carols, Ancient and Modern; including the Most Popular in the West of England, and the Airs to which they are Sung. Also Specimens of French Provincial Carols. With Introduction and Notes. London: Richard Beckley, 1833.

BRAMLEY, Henry Ramsden, and STAINER, John, eds. Christmas Carols New and Old. London: Novello, [1871]; reprinted, 1947.

WOODWARD, George Ratcliffe, ed. Carols for Christmas-tide. London: Pickering & Chatto, 1892.

CHOPE, R. R., ed. Carols for Use in Church during Christmas and Epiphany. Music edited by Herbert Stephen Irons. Introduction by S. Baring-Gould. London: Wm. Clowes, 1894.

WOODWARD, George Ratcliffe, ed. Carols for Easter and Ascensiontide. London: Pickering & Chatto, 1894.

_____ , ed. The Cowley Carol Book, for Christmas, Easter, and Ascensiontide. Series 1-2. 2 vols. Vol. 2 edited by G. R. Woodward and Charles Wood. London: Mowbray, 1902-1919; reprint ed., 1 vol. London: Mowbray, 1948.

DEARMER, Percy, and SHAW, Martin, eds. The English Carol Book. Series 1 & 2. 2 vols. London: Mowbray, 1919.

RICKERT, Edith, ed. Ancient English Christmas Carols, 1400–1700.
New ed. London: Chatto & Windus, 1914.

WOOD, Charles, and WOODWARD, George Ratcliffe, eds. The Cambridge Carol-Book. London: SPCK, 1924.

DEARMER, Percy, VAUGHAN WILLIAMS, Ralph, and SHAW, Martin,
eds. The Oxford Book of Carols. London: Oxford University
Press, 1928; Music ed., 1961; reset and revised ed., 1964.

ROUTLEY, Erik, ed. The University Carol Book: A Collection of
Carols from Many Lands, for All Seasons. London: E. H. Free-
man, 1961; reprint ed., London: E. M. I. Music Publishing
Co., 1978.

POSTON, Elizabeth, ed. The Penguin Book of Christmas Carols.
Baltimore, MD: Penguin Books, 1965.

_____, ed. The Second Penguin Book of Christmas Carols.
Baltimore, MD: Penguin Books, 1970.

BRICE, Douglas. The Folk Carols of England. London: Herbert
Jenkins, 1967.

2. Histories

DUNCAN, Edmonstoune. The Story of the Carol. London: Walter
Scott; New York: Scribner, 1911.

GREENE, Richard Leighton, ed. The Early English Carols. Oxford:
Clarendon Press, 1935.

ROUTLEY, Erik. The English Carol. London: Herbert Jenkins,
1958; New York: Oxford University Press, 1959; reprint ed.,
Westport, CT: Greenwood Press, 1973.

G. STUDIES OF AUTHORS, COMPOSERS, AND HYMNOLOGISTS
(arranged alphabetically by subject)

1. General Studies

ENGLAND, Martha Winburn, and SPARROW, John. Hymns Unbidden:
Donne, Herbert, Blake, Emily Dickinson and the Hymnographers.
New York: New York Public Library, 1966.

GREGORY, Arthur Edwin. The Hymn-Book of the Modern Church:
Brief Studies of Hymns and Hymn-Writers. London: Charles
H. Kelly, 1904.

HATFIELD, Edwin F. The Poets of the Church: A Series of Bio-
graphical Sketches of Hymn-Writers with Notes on their Hymns.
New York: Randolph, 1884; reprint ed., Detroit, MI: Gale
Research, 1978.

MARTIN, George Currie. The Church and the Hymn Writers. London: Clarke, 1928.

MOORE, Sydney H. Sursum Corda: Being Studies of some German
Hymn-Writers. London: Independent Press, 1956.

ROUTLEY, Erik. I'll Praise My Maker: A Study of the Hymns of
Certain Authors Who Stand in or near the Tradition of English
Calvinism, 1700-1850. London: Independent Press, 1951.

_____. "Victorian Hymn Composers." Bulletin of the Hymn Soci-
ety of Great Britain, 1, 1 (1948): 2-5; 1, 2 (1948): 4-12; 1,
3 (1948): 1-8; 1, 5 (1948): 71-79; 1, 7 (1948): 103-110.

STEPHENSON, H. W. Unitarian Hymn Writers. London: Lindsey
Press, 1931.

2. Individual Studies

a. Henry Williams Baker

BAKER, Henry Williams. "Correspondence between the Reverend
Sir Henry Baker and the Reverend Dr. John Bacchus Dykes."
Bulletin of the Hymn Society of Great Britain, 6, 1 (1965): 1-
12.

TAYLOR, Cyril V. "Henry Williams Baker, 1821-77." Bulletin of
the Hymn Society of Great Britain, 9, 1 (1978): 7-14.

b. Richard Baxter

CAIRNS, W. T. "Richard Baxter, Hymn Writer." Bulletin of the
Hymn Society of Great Britain 1, [24] (July 1943): 1-6.

c. P. P. Bliss

WHITTLE, Major, and GUEST, W. P. P. Bliss: His Life and Work.
London: Morgan & Scott, 1877.

d. Henry Walford Davies

ROUTLEY, Erik. "Henry Walford Davies, 1869-1941." Bulletin of
the Hymn Society of Great Britain, 7, 3 (1969): 54-61.

e. Percy Dearmer

ROUTLEY, Erik. "Percy Dearmer, Hymnologist." Bulletin of the
Hymn Society of Great Britain, 6, 9 (1967): 169-185.

f. J. B. Dykes

HUTCHINGS, Arthur J. B. "J. B. Dykes: Amateur or Profes-
sional?" Bulletin of the Hymn Society of Great Britain, 8, 12
(1977): 209-215.

g. John Ellerton

HOUSMAN, Henry. John Ellerton: Being a Collection of His Writings on Hymnology, together with a Sketch of His Life and
Works. London: SPCK, 1896.

h. John Keble

FOX, Adam. "Keble and Neale, their Place in Church History."
Bulletin of the Hymn Society of Great Britain, 6, 5 (1966):
83-97.

i. Henry Francis Lyte

ROUTLEY, Erik. "Henry Francis Lyte 1793-1847." Bulletin of the
Hymn Society of Great Britain, 1, [40] (July 1947): 4-9.

j. John Mason Neale

LOUGH, A. G. The Influence of John Mason Neale. London:
SPCK, 1962.

PECK, A. L. "John Mason Neale as a Translator of Latin Hymnody." Bulletin of the Hymn Society of Great Britain, 7, 1
(1969): 14-24; 7, 2 (1969): 25-35.

k. John Newton

CAIRNS, W. T. "The Relations between John Newton and William
Cowper." Bulletin of the Hymn Society of Great Britain, 1,
[16] (July 1941): 1-5.

l. Charles Steggall

BLACKALL, A. K. "Charles Steggall, 1826-93." Bulletin of the
Hymn Society of Great Britain, 4, 14 (1959): 220-230.

m. Thomas Sternhold

WEIR, Richard Baird. "Thomas Sternhold and the Beginnings of

English Metrical Psalmody." Ph.D. dissertation, New York
University, 1974.

n. Isaac Watts

BISHOP, Selma L. [Isaac Watts'] Hymns and Spiritual Songs, 1707–
1748: A Study in Early Eighteenth Century Language Changes.
London: Faith Press, 1962.

_____. Isaac Watts's Hymns and Spiritual Songs, 1707: A Pub-
lishing History and a Bibliography. Ann Arbor, MI: Pierian
Press, 1974.

ESCOTT, Harry. Isaac Watts, Hymnographer: A Study of the Beginnings, Development, and Philosophy of the English Hymn.
London: Independent Press, 1962.

FOUNTAIN, David G. Isaac Watts Remembered. Worthing, Eng.:
Henry E. Walter, 1974.

PAYNE, Ernest A. "Isaac Watts's Theology in his Hymns." Bulletin of the Hymn Society of Great Britain, 2, 4 (October 1948):
49–58.

ROGERS, James A. "From Israel to England to America: The
Psalms of Isaac Watts." Bulletin of the Hymn Society of Great
Britain, 8, 4 (1974): 57–67.

ROTH, Herbert John. "A Literary Study of the Calvinistic and
Deistic Implications in the Hymns of Isaac Watts, Charles Wes-
ley, and William Cowper." Ph.D. dissertation, Texas Christian
University, 1978.

o. The Wesleys

BAKER, Frank. Charles Wesley's Verse: An Introduction. London: Epworth Press, 1964.

DURNFORD, F. H. "The Hymns of Charles Wesley included in Ancient and Modern." Theology, 39 (1939): 354–362.

FLEW, R. Newton. The Hymns of Charles Wesley: A Study of their
Structure. London: Epworth Press, 1953.

FOX, Adam. "Charles Wesley's Hymns and the Anglican Tradition."
Bulletin of the Hymn Society of Great Britain, 4, 8 (1958):
113–117.

FROST, Maurice. "The Tunes Associated with Hymn Singing in
the Lifetime of the Wesleys." Bulletin of the Hymn Society of
Great Britain, 4, 8 (1958): 118–126.

GREGORY, A. S.   "Moravian Associations of Charles Wesley's
Hymns." Bulletin of the Hymn Society of Great Britain, 4, 9
(1958):   135–141.

HOUGHTON, Edward.   "John Wesley or Charles Wesley?" Bulletin
of the Hymn Society of Great Britain, 9, 6 (1979): 93–99.

KER, R. E.   "The Sources of Methodist Hymnody." Bulletin of the
Hymn Society of Great Britain, 3, 7 (1953): 107–116; 3, 8
(1953):   134–137.

MANNING, Bernard Lord.   The Hymns of Wesley and Watts: Five
Informal Papers. London: Epworth Press, 1942; reprinted,
1960.

RATTENBURY, John E.   The Eucharistic Hymns of John and Charles
Wesley. London: Epworth Press, 1948.

_____. The Evangelical Doctrines of Charles Wesley's Hymns.
London: Epworth Press, 1941; 3d ed., 1954.

ROUTLEY, Erik.   "The Case Against Charles Wesley." Bulletin of
the Hymn Society of Great Britain, 4, 15 (1960): 252–259.

_____. "Charles Wesley and Matthew Henry." Bulletin of the
Hymn Society of Great Britain, 3, 12 (1954): 193–199.

_____. The Musical Wesleys. New York: Oxford University
Press, 1968; reprint ed., Westport, CT: Greenwood Press,
1976.

_____. "Samuel Sebastian Wesley and the European Psalmist
(1872)." Bulletin of the Hymn Society of Great Britain, 7, 12
(1972): 221–235.

WATERHOUSE, John Walters. The Bible in Charles Wesley's Hymns.
London: Epworth Press, 1954.

    p.   William Williams

HODGES, H. A.   "Williams Pantycelyn." Bulletin of the Hymn Society of Great Britain, 8, 9 (1976): 145–152; 8, 10 (1976):
161–166.

    q.   Catherine Winkworth

LEAVER, Robin A.   Catherine Winkworth: The Influence of her
Translations on English Hymnody. St. Louis, MO: Concordia,
1978.

_____. "The German Hymn in English: The Challenge of

Catherine Winkworth." Bulletin of the Hymn Society of Great
Britain, 9, 4 (1979): 61-65.

H. SPECIAL STUDIES

ADEY, Lionel. "The Secularization of the Victorian Hymn." Bulletin of the Hymn Society of Great Britain, 9, 7 (1980): 116-125.

BLAKE, Leonard. "The Public School Hymn Tune." Bulletin of the Hymn Society of Great Britain, 2, 12 (1950): 180-185.

BUTCHER, Vernon. "The Public Schools' Contribution to Hymnody." Bulletin of the Hymn Society of Great Britain, 3, 16 (1955): 354-360.

ESKEW, Harry. "American Folk Hymnody." Bulletin of the Hymn Society of Great Britain, 7, 8 (1971): 142-155.

FROST, Maurice. "Harmonia Sacra, by Thomas Butts." Bulletin of the Hymn Society of Great Britain, 3, 4 (1952): 66-71; 3, 5 (1953): 73-79.

_____. "On the Legality of Hymns in the Church of England." Bulletin of the Hymn Society of Great Britain, 4, 11 (1958): 168-171.

HUGHES, Donald. "Hymns in School Worship." Bulletin of the Hymn Society of Great Britain, 6, 2 (1965): 25-36.

LUFF, Alan. "Welsh Hymn Melodies." Bulletin of the Hymn Society of Great Britain, 7, 4 (1970): 70-79.

McCUTCHAN, Robert Guy. Hymn Tune Names: Their Sources and Significance. Nashville, TN: Abingdon Press, 1957; reprint ed., St. Clair Shores, MI: Scholarly Press, 1974.

MARSH, J. B. T. The Story of the Jubilee Singers, including their Songs. London: Hodder & Stoughton, 1875.

_____. _____. New ed., with supplementary material by F. J. Loudin. London: Hodder & Stoughton, 1899.

MOZLEY, Henry Williams. Sequences and Hymns, Chiefly Medieval. London, New York: Longmans, Green, 1914.

POCKNEE, Cyril E. The French Diocesan Hymns and their Melodies. London: Faith Press; New York: Morehouse-Gorham, 1954.

_____. "Hymnody since the Oxford Movement." Bulletin of the

Hymn Society of Great Britain, 3, 2 (1952): 21-26; 3, 3 (1952):
42-48.

_____. "Veni, Veni Immanuel." Bulletin of the Hymn Society of
Great Britain, 7, 4 (1970): 65-68.

PRATT GREEN, Frederick. "The Social Gospel in Modern Hymnody."
Bulletin of the Hymn Society of Great Britain, 9, 8 (1980):
137-140.

RESSLER, Martin E. "A History of Mennonite Hymnody." Journal
of Church Music, 18, 6 (June 1976): 2-5.

RILEY, Athelstan [i.e., John Athelstan Laurie]. Concerning Hymn
Tunes and Sequences. London: Mowbray; Milwaukee, WI:
Young Churchman, 1915.

ROSSLER, Martin. "Die Frühzeit hymnologischer Forschung." Jahrbuch für Liturgik und Hymnologie, 19 (1975): 123-186.

ROUTLEY, Erik. "Christian Hymnody and Christian Maturity."
Worship, 51 (1977): 505-523.

SAMPSON, George. "The Century of Divine Songs." In his Seven
Essays, pp. 199-232. Cambridge: Cambridge University Press,
1947; reprint ed., New York: AMS Press, 1969.

SCHILLING, S. Paul. "God and Suffering in Christian Hymnody."
Religion in Life, 48, 3 (Autumn 1979): 323-336.

SLATER, J. T. "What Shall They Sing?" Bulletin of the Hymn
Society of Great Britain, 5, 12 (1964): 205-209.

TAYLOR, Cyril V. The Way to Heaven's Door: Broadcast Talks
on Some Favourite Hymn-Tunes. London: Epworth Press,
1955.

TRIPP, David. "Hymns as Ecumenical Liturgy." One in Christ,
10 (1974): 267-275.

WILSON, John. "The Sources of the 'Old Hundredth' Paraphrase."
Bulletin of the Hymn Society of Great Britain, 5, 7 (1962):
96-104.

WRAYFORD, Geoffrey. "Hymns in School Worship." Bulletin of the
Hymn Society of Great Britain, 8, 14 (1977): 237-243.

YOUNG, William C. "Hymns and Psalms in the Punjab Church."
Bulletin of the Hymn Society of Great Britain, 3, 13 (1955):
205-213.

WILLIAMS, Henry L. "The Development of the Moravian Hymnal."
Transactions of the Moravian Historical Society, vol. 18, pt. 2
(1962).

I. PRACTICAL AND CRITICAL STUDIES

ANDREWS, John S. "Surveys of Popular Hymns." Bulletin of the
Hymn Society of Great Britain, 6, 10 (1968): 193-202.

BRIDGES, Robert. Collected Essays, Papers &c. of Robert Bridges,
vol. 9. Edited by M. M. Bridges. London: Oxford University
Press, 1935.

CAIRD, Viola Mary. "Blest Pair of Sirens." Bulletin of the Hymn
Society of Great Britain, 1, [41] (October 1947): 6-15.

_____. "The Hymn as a Literary Form." Bulletin of the Hymn
Society of Great Britain, 1, [38] (January 1947): 1-9.

CAIRNS, W. T. "The Constituents of a Good Hymn." Hymn Society of Great Britain, Occasional Papers, 1 (April 1939).

CURWEN, J. Spencer. Studies in Worship Music [First Series]:
Chiefly as Regards Congregational Singing. London: Curwen,
1880; 3d ed., 1901.

_____. Studies in Worship Music [Second Series]. London:
Curwen, 1885.

HALL, Raymond W. "Hymns for the Times." Bulletin of the Hymn
Society of Great Britain, 8, 6 (1975): 95-104.

MARTIN, Hugh. "Mending and Marring: The Doings of Hymn Book
Editors." Bulletin of the Hymn Society of Great Britain, 5, 4
(1961): 49-57.

NICOLSON, Norman. "Bad Poetry or Good Light Verse?" Bulletin
of the Hymn Society of Great Britain, 5, 13 (1964): 220-225.

PARKES, David. "Why Sing Hymns?" The Franciscan, 10, 4
(1968): 212-215.

PATRICK, Millar. "Music in Hymnody." Bulletin of the Hymn Society of Great Britain, Occasional Papers, 3 (July 1945).

PRATT GREEN, Frederick. "Hymn Writing To-day." Bulletin of
the Hymn Society of Great Britain, 7, 6 (1971): 122-124.

ROUTLEY, Erik. Hymns and Human Life. 2d ed. Grand Rapids,
MI: Eerdmans, 1959.

_____. "Hymns and Music in Church Worship." Union Seminary Quarterly Review, 18 (1963): 235-242.

_____. Hymns and the Faith. Grand Rapids, MI: Eerdmans, 1968.

_____. "Hymns and Youth." Bulletin of the Hymn Society of Great Britain, 3, 14 (1955): 222-227.

_____. Hymns To-day and To-morrow. New York: Abingdon Press, 1964; London: Darton, Longman & Todd, 1966.

_____. "On Congregational Singing: The New Chapter." Bulletin of the Hymn Society of Great Britain, 7, 5 (1971): 113-122.

_____. "Ought We to Sing Whittier?" Bulletin of the Hymn Society of Great Britain, 8, 13 (1977): 221-227.

_____. "What Makes a Good Hymn?" Bulletin of the Hymn Society of Great Britain, 3, 6 (1953): 90-96.

_____. "Whither Hymnody?" Bulletin of the Hymn Society of Great Britain, 5, 2 (1960): 24-30.

SAMPSON, George. "Hymns and No-Hymns." Bulletin of the Hymn Society of Great Britain, 1, [29] (October 1944): 1-6.

SANDILANDS, Arthur. "Making Hymns in Africa." Bulletin of the Hymn Society of Great Britain, 3, 9 (1954): 141-148.

STEWART, Malcolm. "Michael, Run the Boat Aground." The Franciscan, 10, 4 (1968): 197-199.

SYDNOR, James Rawlings. The Hymn and Congregational Singing. Richmond, VA: John Knox Press, 1960.

THIMAN, Eric Harding. "Recent Thought and Tendency in Congregational Singing." In Congregational Hymn Singing, ch. 15. By W. T. Whitley. London: Dent, 1933.

WHITE, Richard Grant. National Hymns: How They are Written and How They are Not Written. New York: Rudd & Carleton, 1861.

WHITLEY, W. T. Congregational Hymn Singing. With a survey of modern congregational musical worship by Eric H. Thiman. London: Dent, 1933.

WREN, Brian. "Genesis of a Hymn." Bulletin of the Hymn Society of Great Britain, 9, 3 (1978): 39-44.

_____. "Making Your Own Hymn." Bulletin of the Hymn Society of Great Britain, 9, 2 (1978): 21-24.

_____, WILSON, John, and LUFF, Alan. "The Hymn To-day." Bulletin of the Hymn Society of Great Britain, 8, 12 (1977): 197-209.

Barhebraeus, Gregorius 120
Barker, V. L. 430
Barkley, John M. 320, 340, 497,
528, 559, 728
Barnes, Arthur Stapylton 529
Barnes, Ralph 215
Barnett, James M. 516
Baron, Ludovic 682
Barratt, Thomas H. 418
Barre, Henri 175
Barrett, William Alexander 699
Barrois, Georges 27, 127, 249
Barrosse, Thomas 67
Barrow, Henry 404
Barry, F. R. 562
Barsoum, Severius Ephrem 121
Barth, Gerhard 485
Barth, Karl 472, 497, 568
Barth, Markus 473, 497
Barth, Peter 473
Barthel, Gustav 633
Bartlett, Gene E. 21
Bartning, Otto 642
Barton, J. Hamby 418
Barton, John M. T. 542
Bartsch, Elmar 551
Basdekis, A. 127
Bass, George M. 568
Basset, R. 602
Bassett, William 534
Bastiaensen, A. A. R. 106
Bate, Herbert Newell 382
Bates, W. H. 86, 104
Batiffol, Pierre 160, 169, 203,
238, 475, 538, 583
Batteaux, Jean 252
Baudot, Jules L. 158, 186, 203,
231, 561, 583, 607, 650
Bauer, Georg Lorenz 182
Bauer, Johannes 323
Bauer, Walter 63, 249
Baum, William W. 483
Bauman, William A. 686
Bäumer, Suitbert 213, 583
Baumstark, Anton 16, 17, 29,
67, 108, 112, 124, 172, 186,
187, 206, 212, 246, 264, 273,
276, 577, 592, 606
Baur, Benedikt 592
Baur, Ferdinand Christian 56
Baur, Hermann 639
Baus, Karl 56
Bausch, William J. 461
Baxter, Richard 403
Bayne, Peter 362
Bayne, Stephen F., Jr. 450
Beach, B. B. 447, 505, 530,

536, 559
Beachy, Alvin J. 350
Beale, M. 625
Beardslee, John W. 320
Beasley-Murray, G. R. 485, 503
Beatch, Robert 548
Beauduin, Lambert 47, 258, 573
Bebis, George S. 97, 127
Bechoffen, Johann 185
Bechtold, Otto 639
Beck, Edmund 92
Beck, Henry G. J. 210
Becker, Ernest 546
Becker, Hansjakolo 659
Beckmann, Joachim 21, 46, 308,
464, 496
Beckwith, John 618
Beckwith, Roger T. 318, 465, 598,
614
Becon, Thomas 367
Bedale, Stephen 517
Bedard, Walter Maurice 645
Bedell, Kenneth B. 424
Beebe, David Lewis 407
Beesley, Alan 362
Begheyn, Paul 244
Behm, Johannes 71
Beilliard, Jean 673
Beinert, Wolfgang 189
Beissel, Stephan 607, 618
Belcastro, Joseph 504
Bell, Maurice F. 699
Bellm, R. 625
Benckert, Heinrich 467
Bendann, Effie 554
Bender, Harold S. 350, 503, 508
Beneden, Pierre van 523
Benedict, F. W. 437
Benes, Peter 638
Benham, Hugh 677
Benko, Stephen 554
Bennike, Holger 691
Benoit, André 483, 486, 506
Benoit, Jean-Daniel 47, 279, 320,
451, 506
Benoit, Pierre 72, 546
Benson, Edward White 562
Benson, Louis F. 699, 704
Bentley, James 379
Benz, Suitbert 170
Beran, J. 98
Beraudy, Roger 278, 551
Berengar of Tours 179
Beresford-Cooke, Ernest 41, 242
Beresford-Hope, A. J. B. 379
Berg, Jan H. van den 546
Bergendorff, Conrad J. I. 312

CHURCH BODIES/CONFERENCES/ORGANIZATIONS INDEX

For larger denominational families, see Table of Contents